Covert Capital

The publisher gratefully acknowledges the generous support of the Fletcher Jones Foundation Humanities Endowment Fund of the University of California Press Foundation, which was established by a major gift from the Fletcher Jones Foundation.

Covert Capital

LANDSCAPES OF DENIAL AND THE MAKING OF
U.S. EMPIRE IN THE SUBURBS OF NORTHERN VIRGINIA

Andrew Friedman

UNIVERSITY OF CALIFORNIA PRESS

BERKELEY LOS ANGELES LONDON

University of California Press, one of the most distinguished university presses in the United States, enriches lives around the world by advancing scholarship in the humanities, social sciences, and natural sciences. Its activities are supported by the UC Press Foundation and by philanthropic contributions from individuals and institutions. For more information, visit http://www.ucpress.edu.

University of California Press
Berkeley and Los Angeles, California

University of California Press, Ltd.
London, England

Library of Congress Cataloging-in-Publication Data
Friedman, Andrew, 1974–
    Covert capital : landscapes of denial and the making of U.S. empire in the suburbs of Northern Virginia / Andrew Friedman.
        pages cm. — (American crossroads ; 37)
    Includes bibliographical references and index.
    ISBN 978-0-520-27464-8 (cloth : alk. paper) — ISBN 978-0-520-27465-5 (pbk. : alk. paper)
    1. Intelligence service—United States—History.   2. Federal areas within states—Virginia.   3. Virginia, Northern—Buildings, structures, etc.   I. Title.
    JK468.I6F76   2013
    327.1273009755'29—dc23   2013015305

Manufactured in the United States of America

22 21 20 19 18 17 16 15 14 13
10 9 8 7 6 5 4 3 2 1

In keeping with a commitment to support environmentally responsible and sustainable printing practices, UC Press has printed this book on Rolland Enviro100, a 100% post-consumer fiber paper that is FSC certified, deinked, processed chlorine-free, and manufactured with renewable biogas energy. It is acid-free and EcoLogo certified.

For Asali

AMERICAN CROSSROADS

Edited by Earl Lewis, George Lipsitz, George Sánchez, Dana Takagi, Laura Briggs, and Nikhil Pal Singh

CONTENTS

Introduction

THE SUBURBS OF NORTHERN VIRGINIA once formed part of the nation's capital. They weren't suburbs then. They were a mix of farms, parade grounds, colonial ports, and small incorporated towns and villages. Still, their lands joined with the topography of Maryland to create the District of Columbia's square political boundaries. Each state willed its acreage as a gift, as a testament to the project of the nation. Majestically linked by the Potomac River, the square is still visible on any map.

In 1846, in a racialized protest leading up to the Civil War, Virginia took its land back. Like many rural areas near cities, the land eventually filled with suburbs. But the severed part of the capital remained. Like a phantom limb, grafted onto DC, it waited to receive its secret geopolitical mandate.

Its covert capital destiny.[1]

With the suburbs, the landscape became known as the Dulles Corridor, a twenty-five-mile-long swath of land that stretches from the border of DC at the Pentagon and National Airport in a northwesterly angle all the way to Dulles International Airport in Virginia. The first major federal government development completed in the area—National Airport in 1941 and the Pentagon in 1943—went up as islands in the section of Virginia that had once been part of the District, located directly west of the DC line. In 1961, the direction of development changed. Rather than continuing apace to the west, building shot into the exurban north, with the opening of the CIA headquarters at Langley.

This book chronicles how the landscape that consolidated along this corridor served as the domestic front for a distinct epoch in American imperial policy. By studying the landscape's close interweaving of national security institutions, houses for covert agents, and sprawling suburbs, I reveal how the geography of empire established abroad by the United States reproduced itself at home in architecture and spatial relations, and how that home front, in turn, incubated the empire.

For years, scholars have explored how the United States' history of racial nationalism and exploitation, extreme violence and extermination, and the production of national space through territorial seizure and dispossession provided the content for the "empire of liberty" that Thomas Jefferson had already declared by the nation's founding. After World War II, in the face of a shaken European colonialism, the nation held a "preponderance of power" that allowed it to order and reorder a world, in historian Walter LaFeber's words, "safe and assessable for the American economic system," guided by a hunger for raw materials, export markets, and labor. In this new role, the United States shepherded the expansion of U.S.-shadowed multinational capitalism into a global "free market" that was inherently less than free and, in the name of order, incessantly sowed disorder. As the United States took up its role as both the "patron" of European empires and their self-appointed "heir," the "trade wars" of the new superpowers became, in some parts of the world, a war on life itself.[2]

America's redesigned approach to the globe after World War II arose with a new kind of capital city. It appeared in the Dulles Corridor and gave DC its contemporary metropolitan shape. Unlike those in many suburbs, the major highways—the Capital Beltway 495, opening in 1964, and I-66, which came even later—followed, rather than led, much of the development. Rather, the Dulles Corridor essentially tracked local roads along the north-south axis of Fairfax County, which since colonial times linked the slave port of Alexandria with the city of Leesburg.[3] Less developed and more isolated than the lands to the south, this canvas allowed covert agents to design their own spaces anew, to create a landscape where their proximity and secrecy coalesced in built form. Importantly, the corridor, as though remembering its old union with the capital, rarely dips below the southern limit of the District of Columbia.

Seen in this way, in its narrower iteration, the Dulles Corridor leaks out from its eastern border at the Pentagon and National Airport in a thin V, perhaps five miles across at its widest point. On the north, it is bordered by the Potomac River, as it snakes up from Washington. The southern border is Route 7, until it reaches the Dulles Access Road, where it banks harder to the west on the way to Dulles Airport. In the corridor's wider version, one could extend the southern boundary to Route 236 (Little River Turnpike) to include Vienna, Falls Church, Oakton, Reston, Bailey's Crossroads, and Fairfax. Even drawn this way, it is nowhere more than eighteen miles wide.

Together, these three designators give the Dulles Corridor the shape of a pitchfork's head, with its base below old Hell's Bottom, the swamp where the Pentagon was built. Although the long tines are distinctly apparent on maps, someone placed inside the Dulles Corridor would have a hard time knowing they were in a "covert capital," or a place connected to U.S. imperialism or U.S. governance at all. The suburban built environment's own power contributed to this. The fifties and sixties were a time when Northern Virginia residents were actively overthrowing democratic Guatemala and Iran in covert coups, attempting to overthrow the governments of Costa Rica and Syria, and directing the national fate of the Congo. They invaded Cuba at the Bay of Pigs, sent troops to occupy Lebanon and the Dominican Republic, supported coups and determined governments in Brazil and Guyana, and traveled from the Dulles Corridor to establish a lasting American presence in a Vietnam that was casting off the yoke of European colonial rule.[4]

Specific, apparently neutral suburban design features masked the political landscape as it formed, making it hard to map. The seemingly natural privacy afforded by the suburbs lent itself to the secrecy beneficial to both the U.S. government and suburban life. Suburban culture, contextualized by U.S. geopolitics, nurtured the strategies that shaped agents' actions in its home front and in its connected spaces abroad—while working, through the built environment, to cover and deny the existence of those very imperial relationships. For most observers, the global power of the United States emanates not from suburban Northern Virginia but from Washington. The common shorthand is that the CIA and the Pentagon are simply "in Washington." If Northern Virginia has an empire, it is an "education empire," home to some of the nation's finest schools.[5] Its large, diverse immigrant population is most noted for altering the political culture of the southern state of Virginia. Its subdivisions, traffic jams, fast-food restaurants, Edge Cities, McMansions, and luxury malls only make it one of the country's fastest-growing and desirable suburbs, home to the two wealthiest counties in the nation.[6]

But Northern Virginia has been the central management point and habitat for U.S. imperial planning and residence for more than half a century. Taking this fact into account, its pile of suburban amenities assumes a different character: as the condensation of imperial resources, as the means of planning imperial actions, and managing imperial debts and exclusions. This was an era when the economic relationships that the United States forged with its power abroad extracted wealth and resources from other places. These resources, domestically, were linked to the formation of post–World War II suburbs, which became a key residential space at the very core of American identity, a place where "abundance was freedom, and freedom was abundance." The activities of U.S. imperial agents in Northern Virginia arose alongside and inside perhaps the most dramatic postwar symbol of American prosperity, security, and the new abundant life environments that U.S. imperial extraction had reaped at home.[7] The repatriation of imperial intimates and subjects to this space was cast as a sign of welcome diversity but also a threat, a dual status that guided rights, benefits, and privileges within pre-existing relationships. Local residents and institutions, meanwhile, consistently used these same suburban spaces as the material stages for U.S. imperial planning, ones that arose in the first place to manage key shifts in U.S. imperial work.

For many, the White House and the Capitol dome represent the triumphant side of America and its foreign policy, its public idea of itself as a champion of freedom. DC's Northern Virginia landscape, inaugurated by its first modern institution, the CIA, housed America's covert foreign policy as it turned into a way of life. Other historians have explored how U.S. imperialism creates a way of life for its citizens through its addictive economic rewards, the selective wealth and unbounded markets it creates for certain classes within the bounded nation, and the secular theology of purpose with which it imbues national rhetoric.[8] In this book, I take the phrase more literally. The United States did not have just an empire. It had imperialists. They lived in the covert capital.

The covert capital nurtures a way of life. It produces particular subjects, people who, even while working in the geopolitical doubleness of the landscape around them, still find themselves beholden to and bearing complex emotional stakes in its visual and cultural identity as suburbia. This subjectivity and way of being, I believe, then circles back to enable and excuse the imperial policies formed in the landscape. Through a detailed exploration of local space in Northern Virginia, this book looks at how the global and transnational power relations of imperialism are rooted not only in the rational abstractions of so-called foreign policy but in the everyday habits, cultural tropes, and behavior expressed through the built environment. At the same time, through its entanglements abroad, U.S. global power forms those local American domestic spaces that seem most sealed off from international engagements. Scholars have detailed how U.S. imperialism has shaped the world, but they have been more reticent in addressing how it shaped places seen as core to the domestic nation, particularly after World War II.[9] This book illuminates imperialism as a system of scope, hierarchy, appropriation, and domination that works explicitly through this co-constituting of home and abroad. Retying this area to its deep relationship to the federal state and the forging of postwar American nationalism, I bring the foreign into the domestic, or more precisely, I reveal those categories to be false constructions in this place and in this period.

In these suburbs, two institutions charged with overseeing and implementing U.S. policy abroad in the second half of the twentieth century—the Defense Department and the CIA—occupied two of the largest office buildings built in the country during and after World War II. They also built a social world, a home front where U.S. imperialism became something that people lived through their relationships and organized their lives around. Empire was not just a vague idea but something that had to be done, a set of actions, an administrative problem. "Foreign policy" or "diplomatic history" perhaps still unfolded in the formal capital in Washington. But the physical and managerial tasks of empire at home often took place here, in Washington's shadow, in the suburbs of Northern Virginia.

AN IMPERIAL CORRIDOR IN THE NEW FRONTIER

The Dulles Corridor's prehistory begins in 1941 with the start of construction on the Pentagon on the Virginia shore of the Potomac River in Arlington County. A good portion of the land was owned by the U.S. government and tepidly militarized already as the site for an Army Quartermaster depot, complementing longtime nearby Army posts such as Fort Myer and Arlington National Cemetery.[10] But another reason that military leaders located the Pentagon in Virginia was to create a strategic break with DC and its grounding of the military as one function within a wider set of civic activities in American life. James Carroll, whose father was founding director of the Defense Intelligence Agency (DIA) in 1961, grew up in the garden-apartment neighborhoods in dusty swaths of Alexandria and Arlington created for those who worked there. As the Pentagon's moral biographer, Carroll depicts how its construction reshaped Washington's geography and psyche.[11]

It was the nation's largest building. It consumed thirty acres. It had seventeen and a half miles of corridors and eighteen dining rooms that served 60,000 meals a day. It had the technology to transmit and receive five million words a day in correspondence with global U.S. military forces. There were six hundred drinking fountains, twenty acres of lawns, thirty miles of approach roads, and three of the nation's first cloverleaf highway intersections. It had its own lagoon, created when the Army Corps of Engineers dredged 700,000 tons of sand from the Potomac riverbed to create its cement. Its 15,000 workers, many of them Northern Virginians stirred out of old patterns of labor by the new project, often didn't even wait for specs and improvised parts of the building themselves.[12] One of these laborers—in an early signal of the deep, structural links that would develop between American culture in this period and the cultures of this imperial corridor in Northern Virginia—was Jack Kerouac.[13] The Pentagon went up in a record sixteen months, and, with more than 25,000 occupants, held more people than appeared in Arlington County's full 1930 census population.[14]

For Carroll, the building marshaled energy on its Potomac outlook to turn America into Fortress America, a permanent garrison state. But another radical realignment was how it mapped the geopolitical stance of the country onto the spatial interrelationships of the Washington area. The Army pushed for the Pentagon just as its new headquarters on 21st and C streets in Foggy Bottom was completed. Although designed for the Army, by 1941, the building wasn't large enough for its wartime plans. The Army chose the Virginia site because it wanted a massive structure, and a Virginia footprint freed it from DC's stringent architectural supervision. The building intended as the headquarters, now too modest, went to the State Department, symbolizing its diminished role in the American state of the twentieth century.[15]

Beyond these logistical concerns, the Pentagon's settlement in Virginia had politically symbolic significance. Dislodging the War Department from a latticework of federal branches in the old Federal West Executive area, the "public city," where it had been embroidered into a mutual decision-making process responsive to the president, the move created what Carroll calls "a massive bureaucratic power center broken loose from the checks and balances of the government across the river."[16] Detached from the ostensibly democratic requirements of the overt capital, this break formed the footprint of the Dulles Corridor. It prefigured the legal consolidation four years after the Pentagon's opening of the Department of Defense, which called the Pentagon home, and carried with it in the same 1947 National Security Act two other crucial foreign policy tools of the period—the National Security Council and the CIA.[17]

Not only did the Pentagon (and National Airport, to the south) hatch a landscape on the edges of the colonial port city of Alexandria. The buildings also ushered in Northern Virginia's first major suburban encampments. The Shirley Highway and the just-add-water subdivisions were soon leaping out toward Springfield in a southwesterly line from the DC border.[18] Cold War threat managers, working at the dawn of the 1950s on nuclear dispersion maps for Washington with the National Security Resources Board, imagined their alternate, emergency capitals along this same axis, with easy road access in Springfield and Annandale.[19] Still, while forming the southern boundary of the Dulles Corridor, this militarized landscape stretching toward the military bases of southern Virginia did not create the Dulles Corridor. Although the military is certainly part of what one might call the imperialist pincer, to focus exclusively on the Pentagon and its satellites would be to ignore how U.S. imperialism tucked itself into the fabric of mainstream American life.

To tell this larger story, one must shift the direction of analysis away from the overt actions of the Pentagon and the traditional suburbanization of the immediate postwar period to the covert Central Intelligence Agency. Its headquarters opened quietly to the north two decades later, in rustic Langley, Virginia, in 1961. In the early twentieth century, the terrain served as the access route to the capital city's pleasure ground. Urbanites rode the electric trolley through its grasslands and past its orchards to the merry-go-rounds and dance pavilions of Great Falls. By the thirties, when the trolleys began to die, the area settled into sleepiness.[20]

This sleepiness made it useful. U.S. imperialism's home front depended on the tree-shaded terrain of northwestern Fairfax County, rather than the densely populated land to the south. The history of segregation and the Confederacy had equipped the landscape with a habit of division: large plantations from the colonial period, racial covenants, and zoning laws administered to maintain segregation had protected it from heavy settlement and primed its agents on their future encounters with the globe. Camp Russell A. Alger, a major encampment mustering troops fighting in the Spanish-American War, had spurred its first development boom and given it an imperial tradition. Later, the mansions already present around Langley endowed it with social capital, and its role as retreat for the power elite of Georgetown in the fifties gave it an authority that enabled geopolitical planners to exercise dominant control there.[21]

But it was in the early sixties that the Dulles Corridor and its empire came into full being through a more pronounced presence in the Northern Virginia landscape. Thomas McCormick describes this as a period when a "foreign policy elite" held the reins in U.S. international affairs.[22] Northern Virginia was their home and backyard. The early sixties was also the time when the CIA's civilian experiments in imperial work and warfare of the 1950s, often innovated by the same people, became institutionalized in American government and space. With the advancing pressure for decolonization after 1960, the United States' blithe sense of itself as postcolonial and thus "like" the new colonies looking for freedom rhetorically undergirded its interventions abroad. This assertion, of course, substituted for an admission of the United States as a colonial power or a nation whose very notions of freedom and democracy were formed through violent, racialized nation-building at home, a nation that constituted its promises of liberal safety by constantly identifying and producing enemies who fell outside its boundaries. New nations, meanwhile, taking form in this period under the United States' shadow and beholden to U.S. power in new ways, became the very vehicle for the assertion of U.S. power. Exerting power through such conditionally independent nations was cheaper for the United States. It also created the sense of a radical break from the global imperial past. At the very same time, as Mimi Thi Nguyen argues, the universalist claim of granting freedom to the world gave U.S. empire purchase on new dimensions of global life and subjectivity.[23] Through such techniques, U.S. imperialism in this era also made a series of innovations in imperial accountability, in no small part through Northern Virginia's new covert security state itself.

In 1961, many events marked the U.S. imperial presence in the Dulles Corridor. The exposure of the U.S. invasion of Cuba at the Bay of Pigs brought the brazen routine of covert action into the public eye. Robert McNamara's ascension to secretary of defense gave the Pentagon its first civilian strongman. Dwight Eisenhower warned the country of the "unwarranted influence" of the new "military-industrial complex." Kennedy drastically expanded the corridor's American "advisors" in Vietnam. The Alliance for Progress was born, and the "decade of development" advanced the United States into every corner of global life. Military brass at the Pentagon even doffed their uniforms and started wearing civilian clothes to work.[24] By 1961, the uniforms were redundant. The Dulles Corridor was making the entirety of Northern Virginia a home for American agents and military figures.

This is a crucial geographical shift from the purely military landscape of

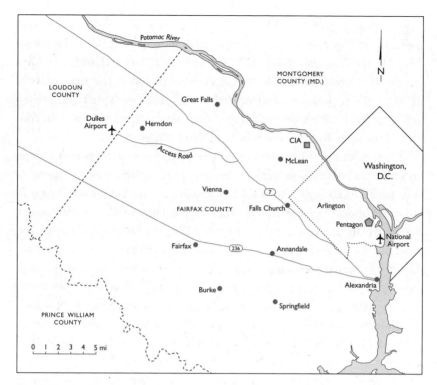

The Dulles Corridor.

the south to the northwest. CIA culture seeped from its headquarters to sculpt the green landscape in its immediate surroundings, as much as its agents developed its buildings. CIA covert wars populated the landscape with residents. But inside the frame of the Pentagon and the CIA, the military and the civilian, a place also developed, filled with people—agents and refugees, suburbanites and soldiers, citizens and foreigners, builders and cultural producers—who lived and experienced, at home and abroad, the empire wrought by these institutions. The incipient landscape of the north-south axis between the CIA and the Pentagon was then fulfilled in a western wave toward Dulles Airport, which formally opened in 1962. Dulles Airport's opening framed an endpoint to the corridor. It gave it a shape, as covert agents defined local residential space between the headquarters buildings where they worked and the airport where they left to meet the globe.

In concert with Dulles and National airports, the Pentagon and the CIA, separated by less than ten miles, were active makers of place. In this era, many forces converged to develop suburban America—federal policy, bank lend-ing practices, big real estate builders, transit corridors, a consumer economy, and a racist response to the long civil rights movement.[25] But in Northern Virginia, the Pentagon and the CIA dramatically inflected those forces. They developed Northern Virginia during a crucial period in the area's growth. In 1950, the population of its central county, Fairfax, hadn't yet reached 100,000. It tripled by 1960, when the population reached 275,002, and continued to climb. By 1970, it was nearly half a million.

Shantytowns of "filthy country shacks," equipped with pit privies, sprung up across the county to shelter the working laborers, often African American, who built Dulles Airport, the CIA headquarters, and the surrounding subdivisions, shocking planners and generating the first local code for housing standards. The extension of the George Washington Parkway to Langley, and other CIA road-widening projects, opened the northern sections of Fairfax County for development in 1960. Dulles Airport's sewer alone, the $28 million Potomac interceptor, made the surrounding suburban boom possible. Highway planners found their work plotting routes easier in Northern Virginia for the same reason CIA agents preferred it—for its minimal development. One engineer found it "remarkable that fewer than 100 houses had to be taken" to construct the Beltway in Virginia in 1961.

The broader security state preferred it for the same reason. In the mid-1950s, a program erected two Nike missile stations, set to protect DC in case of nuclear attack, in the western reaches of Fairfax County. Military planners most likely chose their northernmost site explicitly because the lack of "masking" trees on farms there allowed the radar to freely sweep the sky. Federal agencies crucial to the national suburban boom also admired the county's spaciousness. The Defense Homes Corporation built a series of experimental spray-form concrete "bubble houses" in Falls Church in the forties that would have been impossible to get past residents in more densely developed parts of the region, little half-globes later exported across the world as affordable housing and exemplars of American ingenuity. The Langley site was available for CIA because it was already federally owned, part of the larger property where the Bureau of Public Roads tested its road-building plans, securing the easy mobility that underwrote national suburbanization.

In 1955, amid this landscape's comparatively minimal building, 31,000 of 65,000 employed people in Fairfax County worked for the federal government. Soon, more than 11,000 worked for the CIA.[26] Surrounding counties and cities underwent similar shifts. "The most striking changes in the last fifteen years have occurred in northern Virginia," wrote geographer

Jean Gottman in 1969. "There urban and suburban sprawl has taken on an immense and intense character."[27]

For many ideologues of Kennedy's "New Frontier"—the rhetorical trope first delivered on his campaign trail that fused idealism with imperialism, hope with U.S. expansion and a global mandate at the dawn of the sixties— the suburbs of Northern Virginia *were* the New Frontier, placed in actual space. As they rose to political power in Kennedy's cabinet, academics and former intelligence agents, such as Walt Whitman Rostow, taught special night classes to policymakers at the Kennedy family's suburban mansion in McLean.[28] They theorized development as the signature concept through which the United States would extend its reach and authority over the decolonizing world as, outside local windows, the booming suburban development of the covert capital, marching out from the border of Washington, seemed to reflect the rightfulness of their own theory back to them and to stand in as a call to arms for the inevitability of U.S. development for a globe where the country's "sense of responsibility," as Kennedy secretary of state Dean Rusk put it in 1961, "has no geographical barriers."[29] In locating in Northern Virginia, the covert capital also opportunistically attached itself to the cocktail of cultural silences, compartmented living, and open secrets already being produced as indigenous suburban identity in the cultural landscape of *The Feminine Mystique*—in the context of what Betty Friedan described as "the year Castro led a revolution in Cuba" and "the African continent brought forth new nations."[30] But while Friedan frequently linked the personal to the political, the covert capital linked it to the geopolitical.

Zeroing in on the tightened scale of this bounded geopolitical space, far below the state but tied directly to its formation, this study brings U.S. imperialism to the doorstep of everyday middle-class American life in the contemporary era.[31] While drawing on the rich work on American empire that has emerged in the last two decades,[32] this book also raises questions for these studies, whose domestic analyses often stop at a higher or more metaphorical altitude, at responsible bodies above the level of the individual and his or her cognitive life, or at earlier periods in U.S. history. Empire was not just a system, concept, or abstraction. It was a set of actions pursued in and creating a material world, the effect of human agents chasing their most fervent ambitions through three-dimensional private lives intricately bound up with their global agendas. Rather than seeing the effects and costs of empire as taking form at home primarily through metaphoric traces, this book examines the Northern Virginia suburbs as both a critical geopolitical space *and* an ardent investment that its residents were fighting for, both staging ground and home. Imperialism did not just put nation-state containers into dialogue with one another. Imperial agency as reflected in and from Northern Virginia reveals important features of the empirical production of transnational space.

Northern Virginia wasn't like any other sprawling suburb. Yet studying its construction also complicates the new historiography of the U.S. suburbs, which, while transforming pat notions of suburbia as always wealthy, white, or filled with housewives lacking feminist autonomy or class differences, has often taken America at its word, failing to question the national frame, oddly rearticulating suburbs as ultra-domestic spaces in works explicitly designed to challenge that notion.[33] As I situate these suburbs—the obscured second pole of modernist mass construction in the second half of the twentieth century—in their international and geopolitical context, I also recontextualize many architects and builders well known in American modernism's overt first pole: high-end corporate and expressionistic late-modern architects, city planners, and developers who defined the era. Wallace K. Harrison, Max Abramovitz, Eero Saarinen, Philip Johnson, Gilmore D. Clarke, William Conklin, Charles M. Goodman—and their lesser-known colleagues—Frederic R. King, Nicholas Satterlee, Harbin S. Chandler, Mark Merrell, and Rudolph Seeley—all came to and lived in Northern Virginia as they raised these suburbs from the ground.

Some directly built U.S. imperial space and action abroad. In highlighting their designs and construction in the covert capital, this project returns aesthetic modernism in the New Frontier to its complicated intimacies with U.S. imperial effort, geopolitical building abroad in postcolonial contexts, and actual intelligence work, revising and specifying at times vacant conceits such as efficiency and flexible space, rationality and process, new materials and economies of scale, by relinking them with the geopolitical content and violent histories that helped give them coherence. By looking at the construction of a domestic suburb that was simultaneously an imperial, international capital and a global, managerial space, I suggest that the stylistic vocabulary that often defined the split ethical persona of the spaces of the New Frontier at home and abroad, giving the United States its global diplomatic profile and strategic stages for covert action, drew its split ethics and design practices not only from the grammar of architectural aesthetics but from the Dulles Corridor's stretched-out geopolitical landscapes and local habits of denial and double life.

In looking at these and other building projects, I also continually stress the power that research into material space brings to the study of imperialism as lived practice. Heretofore, the study of American empire's material spaces and cultural landscapes has remained dispersed. Scholars have investigated military bases and towns[34]; early U.S. imperial cities and displays at home and abroad[35]; embassies[36]; national security state headquarters[37]; the infrastructures of occupations[38]; reservations and camps[39]; corporate and capitalist spaces, such as Hilton hotels and manufacturing plantations[40]; islands engulfed in U.S. power[41]; the life worlds and death worlds of U.S. oil[42]; and the fields of development and destruction caused by U.S. counterinsurgency and modernization campaigns.[43] In doing so, they have forcefully described the varied and underappreciated ways that the United States most certainly *claimed* space at home and abroad—if not always directly ruled it—as a signature feature of its empire. But this line of inquiry has not tended to see itself as a field. The suburbs of Northern Virginia—with their stretched-out and sequential connections to many of these other spaces—stress the necessity of pursuing it as one: not only for the intimate and ingrained qualities of U.S. imperial relations revealed through its inhabited settings around the world, but for the ways material spaces testify to the nature and endurance of U.S. imperialism through time, a record of effects that tends to vanish within the single moment of imperial warfare, violence, or occupation that conventionally organizes so much of the study of U.S. intervention abroad.

THE CIA'S LANDSCAPES OF DENIAL

Northern Virginia was a suburb and a covert capital, a local space and a transnational space, a manager of global violence and itself a subjugated colony structured around the absent presence of that violence, what deposed Dominican Republic president Juan Bosch calls a "metropo-colony," where the suburban resident "placed his desire for well-being and personal security above his duties toward humanity."[44] While examining its flanking institutions—the Pentagon, the National Security Council, the defense contractors, and public-private shadow wings of the military-industrial complex—I tend to return to the CIA as a tonic. The CIA, because its political terrain was human secrets, compartmentation, intelligence, and the soul, foregrounds psychic life in Northern Virginia as an object of study. As much as it played an insinuating role globally, the CIA at home secreted the mechanisms of being and ways of knowing that handled the transfers between violence abroad and well-being at home, turning what sociologist Stanley Cohen calls a "state of denial"—a political body that strategically, collectively, and cognitively evades the ethical implications of its violent actions—into a state-sanctioned landscape of denial.[45] The CIA accomplished this ethical buffering not only through what Cohen describes as "professional ethics, traditions of loyalty and secrecy, mutual reciprocity, or codes of silence," but through its design and use of the most intimate spaces, relationships and everyday spatial pathways of its own suburban life.[46] In the covert capital, place structured denial. But these became the very same places where violent actions returned to haunt, shape, and inform on the landscape in their own right.

The CIA is further useful as an object of study in that the agency often took the lead in developing U.S. policy in the decolonizing world. Evan Thomas identifies this as Allen Dulles's contribution when he assumed the CIA directorship in 1953: "In the Dulles years, the CIA shifted its focus. The target for most covert action enthusiasts . . . was no longer liberating the East Bloc, but rather stopping the dominoes from falling in other parts of the world—the Middle East, Asia, Africa, Latin America."[47] Eleanor Dulles, State Department official and Allen Dulles's sister, followed this same logic in her 1968 book, *American Foreign Policy in the Making*, where she saw "the determination to support the small nations," the "limited war for political objectives," and the "security action" as defining principles of the period.[48] Stationed in specific countries and regions over the long term, charged with infiltrating the everyday life of those cultures as the basic feature of their work, CIA agents developed the abiding, ingrained and long-term intimate relationships with people abroad—as friends, lovers, allies, servants, agents, and sometimes combinations of those categories—that served as the basis for the tendriled ethical networks and migrations that returned to shape the space of Northern Virginia. One reason to examine the CIA and the United States as agents of imperialism is that the study of "foreign policy" simply has no name for these human relationships and intimacies forged in the crucible of U.S. power abroad, while they are quite common points of focus in the historiography of empire.

In studying Northern Virginia as the covert capital of U.S. imperialism in the long and unfinished era of global decolonization and colonial renewal, this book also helps retrieve the degree to which the projects of the United States and the Soviet Union in the Cold War were about adjudicating the economic, social, and political stakes of decolonization. In his book *The Global*

Cold War, Odd Arne Westad describes the Cold War as a kind of "civil war," in which Moscow and Washington "needed to change the world in order to prove the universal applicability of their ideologies," a war that while similar to imperialism was not fundamentally about "exploitation or subjection, but control and improvement."[49] It was true that the idea that the United States only exercised global stewardship as "the first postcolonial nation" permeated the period's discourse. Eisenhower's secretary of state, John Foster Dulles, himself advertised the "natural sympathy" that arose from being "the first colony in modern times to have won independence."[50] But even before these gestures shaped political rhetoric, U.S. officials understood the need for this stewardship as a racial one, informed by colonialism. As one of the period's crucial ideologues, Arthur Schlesinger Jr., explained in 1949, "the break-up of a colonial system leaves a vacuum." As "power abhors a vacuum," Schlesinger implied that the United States needed to fill in these "empty spaces," these "great gaping holes . . . in the international fabric," or the Soviets would.[51] This sense of the Third World as a void and a vacuum fundamentally underlay the logic of Cold War superpower competition, and as Westad chronicles, the effects of this global "civil war" in the "new nations" were much like the effects of empire—control and improvement, but also exploitation, subjugation, and extreme violence. Studying the lives of CIA and other imperial agents of this period and the material effects of their work over arcs of time, this book looks for empire not in intent—or what Paul Kramer calls "imperial self-consciousness"—but in ongoing sets of relations.[52]

The CIA was not only an agent of imperialism but a cultural product of its time. It exported the art of literary "close reading," developed by the new university establishment, into the practice of U.S. foreign policy.[53] Ivy League academics, modernists, and poets, such as counterintelligence guru James Jesus Angleton, educated by New Critics at Yale University, entered intelligence tradecraft not just to collect data. They interpreted and re-interpreted each gesture, each urge, as a surface puncture in an ocean of conscious and unconscious meaning. As the CIA's political actions were silenced as a matter of record, agents themselves wrote novels to express qualities of their practices and identities that couldn't be uttered aloud in conventional settings for public discourse. The CIA also paid agents to publish novels as propaganda and strategy.[54] The literary critical origins of the CIA persist today in the quite militant ways even the most diligent covert warriors and analysts monitoring the high geopolitical threat take time out to police the minute grammar of CIA vernacular. Those who work for the CIA are always *CIA officers*.

CIA agents are those who spy for the CIA abroad. The classified structure of CIA projects is never called *compartmentalization*, it must be *compartmentation*. And it's never, ever "the CIA." It's *CIA*. Always.

I bring literary sources and literary techniques to bear on CIA agents and Northern Virginia not only because such symbolic analyses were basic forms of expression and intellectual production for the CIA. The cultural production of Northern Virginia arises from a landscape immersed in and producing U.S. imperial action. As with any body of literature, its novels take on aspects of their embedded sociocultural world. But Northern Virginia's cultural texts express these urges at times despite themselves. Local fictions reflect U.S. power yet also silence it on behalf of the hallowed images the United States has of its own idealistic and individualistic domestic life.

CIA agents theorized that close reading as a technique could pry out secret knowledge, over and against overt messages individuals were trying to send. Through the study of literary works alongside many other archival sources, I follow that proposition, engaging in a rigorous gathering of the clues that reveal the covert capital's coded cultural mores. Truths that can't or won't be spoken directly reappear in Northern Virginia's cultural production as gestures, lies, secrets, and "cover stories," in Michael Denning's phrase, that surface in often surprising and unconventional ways.[55] But because these cultural expressions were coded, I don't look only at spy novels. In the imperial corridor, various genres and types of literature and history coded imperial culture—each in a particular way.

Common underlying features of the landscape emerge from the plots of Northern Virginia's stories about itself, but only when the landscape's cultural production is taken in sum. Interdisciplinarity is code-breaking. To force the genres to reveal their codes, I traverse many sources—literary realism, geopolitical spy novels, immigrant novels, science fiction, and domestic thrillers. But rather than reading them through the optics of their artificially discrete bodies of literature, my analysis sets them in the context of the covert capital's other indigenous forms of storytelling: declassified documents, tell-all memoirs (and memoirs that strategically refuse to tell all), scandal reportage, local phone books and maps, love letters, federal testimony, oral history, and the county zoning and building permits through which even the most covert agents have to meet the overt state. Over the course of this book, through these practices of reading and narrating, I form an archive that arises from a landscape rather than a discipline. These various "fictions," alongside the history books that usually rest segregated in their own micro-disciplines of "intelligence history" or "local history," layer in the cognitive and embodied life of the covert capital. By setting them next to one another in odd juxtapositions, deeper and more integral portraits of U.S. power emerge, ones lost by reading the coded genres in isolation or by simply reading the landscape's history alone, which would be as pointless as trying to read any map without its key, any coded message without its cipher.

Yet if covert capital agents were literary critics, they were also international businessmen. These agents, particularly at the CIA, carried the modernist efficiency promised by the rising corporate culture into the art of a new global management for the United States. The "Company," as it is often called, made a case for its authority by presenting this new, radical efficiency to policymakers.[56] It could change governments, reshape political life, secure markets, make friends, and dispose of enemies without recourse to formal wars that would have to be accountable to the public realm in terms of morality and cost. Instead, there would be what Eleanor Dulles described as "half known" and "half hidden" operations conducted with "speed of decision and swiftness of execution,"[57] and what formal U.S. policy called actions "so planned and executed . . . that if uncovered the US Government can plausibly disclaim any responsibility for them."[58] In a radical division of labor, the CIA could do the dirty work of the U.S. superpower behind the scenes from Northern Virginia and take the blame when things went awry. Politicians could make noble, idealistic speeches and hand out aid in front of the TV cameras from the White House. Foreign policy, thanks to the CIA's suburban home, could be as easy as fast food.

In theory, the idea that the negative urges, actions, and obsessions of U.S. power could be repressed from the public mind and denied public life, via an institution whose function would be devoted to results-oriented dispatch and the silence of the company man, was an attractive concept to overt capital policymakers. At least in the collective awareness, the program worked with such effectiveness that to this day it remains difficult to introduce detailed, proven, widely witnessed, and historically documented CIA actions into conversations about U.S. history without seeming to enter the realm of the phantasmal. This was the legacy of the CIA's efficiency promise. It extended in later years as the agency tracked corporate flexibility by contracting and semi-privatizing its projects, agents, and space to further mystify the U.S. role abroad. Taking form in the repetitious cubicles of Northern Virginia's Edge Cities of the 1980s, these efficiencies then continued on into our own times, as the covert capital spun itself off into ever-more inaccessible and unaccountable wings of War on Terror–era "national intelligence," leaping into the corridor's uncharted rural lands.[59]

NAMING A DISAVOWED LANDSCAPE

I generally use four terms to describe this landscape over the course of the book: Dulles Corridor, Northern Virginia, covert capital, and imperial corridor. At times, I use them interchangeably, but their distinctions highlight different features of this landscape.

Traditionally, one finds the term *Dulles Corridor* describing a much narrower area, commonly the land around the road that connects the Edge City at Tysons Corner and Dulles International Airport. But the label remains useful when studying the terrain's full scope. For one, the Dulles Corridor carries the family name of the triumvirate of geopolitical siblings who in some sense were its earliest organic intellectuals—Allen Dulles, the head of the Central Intelligence Agency until 1961; John Foster Dulles, the expansionist secretary of state under Eisenhower; and Eleanor Dulles, the State Department official whose house in McLean became one of the landscape's earliest conspiratorial gathering places. When the future Washington International Airport, twenty-five miles to the west of the city line, was named after John Foster Dulles in 1959, it sealed the family's presence and synchronicity with the landscape. Formally, the term *Dulles Corridor* appeared later. While bandied about in the mid-seventies, it received official sponsorship in 1978, when Fairfax County planners slated the land between Tysons and Dulles, "one of the last big relatively undeveloped areas in the county," for an "industrial corridor."[60] Twenty years later, the renaming of National Airport, below the Pentagon, after Ronald Reagan, another figure whose officials dramatically used the Dulles Corridor as a stage for covert action and U.S. imperial planning, seemed to fulfill the Dulles legacy and affirm the appropriateness of the corridor's longer boundaries. This local geopolitical and cultural space that unfolds between "Reagan National" and "Dulles International" came to encrypt a coded historical explanation for covert American empire after World War II into the space built to define it. The second reason the phrase *Dulles Corridor* is useful is that it is a vernacular term. By mapping the corridor's vernacular cultural landscape—its "three-dimensional, shared reality," in J.B. Jackson's words—alongside its buried imperial presence, the term rehearses the rhetorical moves of this project: its treatment of space, not just as rocks and earth, but as composed of political and human relationships.[61]

In different contexts, it is useful to employ other terms. *Northern Virginia* describes the Virginia lands around Washington, including Fairfax and Arlington counties, which play the major roles here, but also the wider local landscape. Although it is often defined as the terrain north of the Rappahannock River,[62] that line is flexible because the concept of Northern Virginia has been deeply connected to DC over time—from the landscape's early and still-resonant identity to Confederate nostalgists as "Occupied Virginia" to its more contemporary life as the Northern Virginia suburbs. As terms, the *Northern Virginia suburbs*, or the *Edge Cities of Northern Virginia*, which came in the eighties to describe the denser, city-like knots of sprawl that were arising locally, stress this point—the space takes the form it does because it developed near and is forever linked with Washington. Using Northern Virginia as a concept also allows one to fold in geopolitical sites located near the Dulles Corridor because of its magnetism and sprawl, but perhaps just outside the formal boundaries—both those to the southwest toward Fort Belvoir, and those, even more importantly, to the west, in Loudoun and Fauquier counties out past Dulles Airport, in the extensions of the corridor over time, the exurbs of the exurbs, and even past them, to key geopolitical sites after World War II such as the international training center for the American Institute for Free Labor Development in Front Royal.

The second two terms, *covert capital* and *imperial corridor*, are cognates for the first two, stressing that the Dulles Corridor bore not just a parade of physical developments but a unique culture and politics. The *covert capital* is shorthand for the covert capital of U.S. empire, as rooted in space from the Eisenhower administration forward. As a covert *capital*, the term links Northern Virginia with the imperial system that it manages abroad, a system of "interlaced forms of economic and cultural impositions and holdings," in Ann Laura Stoler's words.[63] This is why I use it over terms that arose with this landscape and also seem to describe it, most notably "Invisible Government" (coined by David Wise and Thomas Ross in their 1964 book of the same name) and "Pentagonism" (as defined by Juan Bosch in 1968).[64] But *covert* is also useful for my purposes in the etymological sense the word has of the "covered over." The covert is not merely a secret, being kept from wider knowledge. Rather, it is covered over, which carries with it the sense of the involvement of human agents and joins it with the psychological concept of denial and the open secret, which is closer to how these actors experienced and defined its life, space, and politics.

But *imperial corridor* is useful here too. A corridor is always itself a connection between at least two points. Thus, imperial corridor can refer to this local, geographically bounded site in Northern Virginia, the Dulles Corridor, while simultaneously describing this corridor's stretched-out spatial relations with and exertions of power upon non-contiguous landscapes abroad. Corridor residents drew a sense of their own being and selfhood—their masculinity; their idealism; their security; their cultural values of home, freedom, family, and the good life—by scripting narratives onto the landscapes, bodies, and biographies of people in the decolonizing world. But many of those who had worked and conspired with these agents abroad also then returned to the home front alongside them to settle and build the landscape. These circuits and travels of empire—these back-and-forth movements and relations that always focused on place and its creation—made it so that, as the Dulles Corridor developed locally, it also took form intertwined with places far from it. Bonded by imperial relationships and physical developments, these landscapes, although not contiguous to Northern Virginia, can and should be considered as co-constituted with it as they meet in the vortex of the U.S. imperial project, a physical instance of the way that, through the movements of imperialism, "the domestic and the foreign mutually constitute one another," in Amy Kaplan's words.[65] The Dulles Corridor was a bounded space. But it was also part of places that stretched from the CIA and the Pentagon to National and Dulles airports to nations all over the world and back to the Northern Virginia suburbs—true imperial corridors.

These terms oscillate and fold in and out of one another in probing a space that simultaneously bears local geographical and geopolitical relationships, a specific history in time and space, intimate geographical and imperial ties with other countries and spaces, and a built environment often determined by the covering over of these connections. I use them all throughout—and other variations such as *imperial home front, metropo-colony,* and *global managerial space*—not simply to proliferate the neologisms that often spring forth when writers confront the curious paradoxes of Northern Virginia. I intentionally want them to have an estranging effect on the disciplinary certainties as to what it means to study a Washington suburb such as Northern Virginia *or* a central place in the management of a global U.S. empire. Northern Virginia wasn't merely a covert capital that handed out dictates on high to a foreign field segregated from it. It was an imperial corridor that breached geographic borders and could be traversed in multiple directions. Northern Virginia was not only the topmost part of the southern state of Virginia or the suburban bedroom accoutrement to the busy overt capital at DC, wrestling over its regional identity on the eastern seaboard. It was a place whose shape and culture was often directly drawn from distant spaces that were visually inaccessible from it. The Dulles Corridor was not only an important national node in the condensation of defense contracting dollars that reshaped and developed places throughout the Sunbelt after World War II, but also a node in a U.S. imperial Sunbelt of actions directed at the decolonizing world.[66] The terms proliferate because their contradictions, to my mind, have theoretical implications. I move between them because I believe that the study of the staccato spatial relationships suggested by these terms and their intersections can, finally, reveal important features about the workings and mutable territorializations of a U.S. empire that, as many scholars agree, continually shifted in form: sometimes informal, sometimes quite formal; sometimes liberal, sometimes directed at the extinction of entire peoples; sometimes based in culture, aid, and development, sometimes in military invasion, experiment, and assassination; sometimes officially marking space, sometimes inhabiting and claiming it in more dialectical ways; sometimes forged through formal policies and elite social relationships, sometimes through covert actions and casual intimacies; sometimes excluding, sometimes welcoming; sometimes clearly stated, sometimes disavowed.

To this end, here in the introduction, I'll add one more term: Northern Virginia was the CIA's *safe house*—an inherently doubled domestic environment. A safe house is a space of transnational work that also hides the transnational, blending with the indigenous domestic landscape. It doesn't stand out, it doesn't look special, it doesn't draw attention. Yet in objectifying the everyday and the mundane, it casts the everyday under suspicion. If there can be one safe house, any house could be one. Pairing "safe" with "house" insinuates a lack of safety. Every safe house is also an unsafe house, with an interior, intimate, and domestic life instantly penetrable by the international and the geopolitical. The safe house is not just a house, but a liminal space, a conjunction between two states of geopolitical work, between acts of spying. At the same time, a safe house *is* domestic space. It promises shelter, privacy, and comfort, socially reproducing the inhabitant for more spying. But the safe house also creates "an imaginary space," in Michael Denning's words, "where the contradictions are suspended, and the public and private temporarily united."[67] In the safe house, with its promise of guarded safety and the protected relaxation of cover, the estranged features of the spy's everyday life can, albeit briefly, unite. In the exposure of the politicized private space, alongside those who share his or her paradoxes, the spy paradoxically rests. The safe house is a site of debriefings for this reason. It is a space of admission, of unloading burning secrets, and in this function, it doubles as a psychiatrist's office.

In evoking the safe house here, I aim to create a narrative space where political and intimate relationships, estranged and hidden in everyday space in Northern Virginia, can unite. But Northern Virginia was also literally a safe house for covert capital agents. It served all these functions—as a place for disguise, nurturing rest, the disruption of domesticity, social reproduction, shelter, threat, and confession. The safe house finally also provides one example of (and motivating metaphor for) why I turn to the built environment as an object of study. A space records and stages experience for the individuals who inhabit it—specific spaces do so for individuals with particular strategies and necessities. In this definition, the space of Northern Virginia bears a useful relationship to the "habitus," Pierre Bourdieu's formulation for how a bounded set of actors—"agents" for Bourdieu, with obvious provocations here—produce and are produced by a shared system of meaning.[68] The built environment of Northern Virginia provides the physical architecture, or a kind of physicalization of the architecture, of the habitus of the CIA and the other covert geopolitical agents who implemented U.S. policy abroad.

Bourdieu argued that by carefully observing and recording the details, even seemingly inconsequential, of a complete social world of a set of agents in space—their tics, precepts, sayings, dress, bearing, manners, families, choices, actions, houses, ways of thinking, ways of perceiving, love affairs, sexuality, secrets—one could interpret how that social world molded and regulated behavior at a collective scale without actual, conspiratorial intent. It wasn't that there was no free will. It was just that individual actions, because of the habitus, were always "regulated improvisations."[69] Agents played the game of their lives, yet did so by the rules of the game, the group "common sense." In its etymological relationship to habitation, the habitus had a distinctive spatial component. It transpired in and included "inhabited space," where "above all the house . . . is the principal locus for the objectification of the generative schemes."[70]

Seeing the Northern Virginia landscape, or the stretched-out safe house that is the landscape, as a habitus for the agents of the covert capital offers a powerful model with which to study the repetitions of behavior, explanatory mechanisms, thought processes, intimate relationships, and spatial choices of these agents alongside the built environments they produced in Northern Virginia. The CIA, as the prime entity in this respect, fits models of collective secret psychiatric action because it modeled such action institutionally. But to see the covert capital as habitus for the CIA and its adjacent acronyms extends that institutional kinship deep into private, public, political, and intimate life and space.

The shape of space and behavior were not random in the Dulles Corridor but group practice born from necessity. Covert agents shaped and passed through built space in Northern Virginia, which worked as both record and armature of a habitus. And the group at hand extended beyond the agents themselves to those without the appropriate security clearances—the architects, builders, novelists, migrants, and even non-aligned suburban residents who frequented this space. This is another useful conceptual quality of the habitus—by looking beyond conscious choice and rational calculation, it provides a means of explaining how people could behave and signify as practitioners in a specific local culture without always actively and overtly conspiring to plan covert capital policy.[71] This sense of the covert capital's extended habitus perhaps also explains why so many covert agents who created the United States' empire abroad and engaged in its day-to-day management, returned from developmental and destructive international engagements to become the real estate agents, developers, interior decorators, public planners, and open-space advocates whose efforts defined the corridor's physical space. The Dulles Corridor as habitus educated all those who passed through and existed in its landscape—teaching the art of the covert to the architects, and the art of the living room to the covert agent.

Agents' biographies, passions, personal lives, and social networks carried their internalization and production of the habitus, but agents also designed monuments to these cultural mores in the houses they built and occupied in Northern Virginia. Edward Lansdale, the inventor of U.S. counterinsurgency in the Philippines and Vietnam; the head of CIA counterintelligence, James Jesus Angleton; high-level analyst Huntington Sheldon; early counterinsurgency program officer Rufus Phillips; Lucien Conein, who oversaw the coup against Ngo Dinh Diem in Vietnam; Kim Roosevelt, who led the coup against Mohammad Mossadegh in Iran; and Miles Copeland, the CIA agent who plotted coups as station chief in Damascus—these were only a few who secured their private spaces in Northern Virginia in the era of the CIA's arrival.[72]

In time, whole CIA families spread across the landscape, such as that of Larry Devlin, the station chief in the Congo who supported Joseph Mobutu as he launched a coup in the country, marginalized Prime Minister Patrice Lumumba leading up to his assassination, and later returned to the Congo as a representative for Western diamond merchants. Devlin's parents lived in Arlington; his daughter, also a CIA agent, lived in Great Falls; and he moved to a town south of Alexandria.[73] In a range of grand and modest houses, some modernist dwellings of flat roofs and transparent glass walls, some historic and pseudo-historic brick, they formed covert U.S. policy. They used strip mall pay phones to arrange secret meetings, bucolic split rail fences and park trails for dead drops, and placid suburban homes for safe houses. They had their own classified psychiatrists and their own cleared real estate agents.[74] Over gin and tonics and tennis matches, "Bankruptcy Balls" and serious flirtations, they and their wives developed U.S. policy against peoples of color abroad.[75] New generations of covert activists settled the neighborhoods they built and built their own new neighborhoods. They extended the life patterns and wars of their predecessors as the covert capital moved on through time—Oliver North, who fomented the contra war in Central America; Richard Secord, practitioner of U.S. imperial management and militarization in Iran; Gust Avrakotos, who ran the covert war in Afghanistan; and the new generation of activists who run the War on Terror from the covert capital in the present day.

Imperial intimates from abroad who settled and passed through Northern Virginia included South Vietnamese general Nguyen Cao Ky, police chief Nguyen Ngoc Loan, shah-in-exile Reza Pahlavi, Kurdish guerrilla fighter Mustafa Barzani, Bay of Pigs veterans Manuel Artime and Nestor Pino, contra leaders Edén Pastora and Arturo Cruz, Grenadan prime minister Sir Eric Gairy, and many others. For them, arriving in this landscape could serve as a geo-specific testimony about U.S. power and its associated social debts. They came to the covert capital knowing more about the reality of the international activities of the United States than many of their new neighbors did. In following the lives of these repatriates of empire, who arrived in the Dulles Corridor testing the complex promises of U.S. imperial inclusion, I consider the broad, if troubled, human communities formed by imperialism as they unfolded in the home front. Often debarking simultaneously, in overlapping communities, their migration stories stress the degree to which race, class, and status in the covert capital were not just the product of well-worn domestic narratives. They were always and ever bound up with racial formations and hierarchies that followed them from the U.S. imperial context abroad and then continued on into, clashed with, or reorganized themselves in the racialized domestic context of the Northern Virginia suburbs.

IMPERIAL STRUCTURE

There are five chapters in this book. In the first two, I narrate the physical and cultural development of the imperial suburbs of Northern Virginia after 1950. The first tells the story of the creation of the CIA headquarters building in Langley's rural environs. Arguing that its overt planning process was secondary to CIA social networks already defining the exurbs to the northwest of Georgetown, most notably at the personally designed house of Eleanor Dulles, I trace the CIA headquarters project from its design by the New York architects Harrison and Abramovitz through its opening and inhabitation after 1961. A year later, Eero Saarinen's International Airport, a progressive, modern architectural island in the countryside, opened at the other end of the corridor. But, named for John Foster Dulles, I argue, it was not so different. In treating these buildings that bracket the ends of the Dulles Corridor as in dialogue, this chapter shows how the built environment of the covert capital spatialized and processed the paradoxes of imperialism, idealism, and disavowal in the CIA's domestic landscape, using two buildings designed by famous American modernists with biographies based in intelligence work to explore intimate relations between aesthetic modernism and U.S. imperialism writ large.

The second chapter tracks Langley and Dulles beyond their walls to show how the CIA and U.S. imperialism shaped the suburban cultural landscape. Agents returned from early covert wars and operations in Asia and elsewhere to design Northern Virginia's early suburban houses, bars, restaurants, public culture, and social world. But they also shaped domestic lives that, I argue, were crucial spaces for the reproduction of U.S. imperial culture and work. Here, I examine several CIA families but zoom in on one CIA couple in depth: Huntington and Alice Sheldon, who lived in a modern house across Dolley Madison Boulevard from Langley. Their personally designed transparent glass house opened itself to painful gender divisions and life-threatening emotional blowback from covert capital policy that rehearsed, in microcosm, the difficulties that arose in the covert capital when CIA families tried to manage a geopoliticized intimate life. The result for Alice Sheldon was unique. She developed her own cover story. Disguising herself as a man and changing her name, she claimed a second identity as science fiction writer

James Tiptree Jr. Through Tiptree's voice, I argue, Sheldon inverted the concept of CIA "cover" to create a safe house from CIA gender roles and family life, while drafting inquiries into the uneasy state of CIA women in the covert capital—inquiries that ended in a return-of-the-repressed act of physical violence.

The third and fourth chapters delve deeply into a case study, depicting how an incident of U.S. imperial effort molded space in the covert capital—through the way it co-constituted Northern Virginia's suburbs with the site of U.S. imperial endeavor in Vietnam. In the third chapter, I trace the geopolitical projects of CIA and other agents who used Northern Virginia, and particularly the domestic social spaces of McLean, as a staging ground to subvert the political order of the newly independent country of Vietnam. Beginning with a small street called Saigon Road in one of McLean's first subdivisions, one whose history carries the story of U.S. imperialism in Vietnam back to 1950, I then follow the projects wrought by the well-known CIA operative Edward Lansdale and members of his team over the next two and a half decades, which brought Northern Virginia into a deep transnational intimacy, to use a conceptual field explored by Ann Laura Stoler,[76] with Vietnam. Through sex, love, friendship, and longtime working partnerships developed by covert capital agents stationed in Vietnam for nearly two decades, agents and Vietnamese intimates created a mobile U.S. shadowed transnationalism, underwritten by empire, that literally took place locally between South Vietnam and Northern Virginia in houses, offices, leisure landscapes, and other social spaces.

Intimacies—often complex, racialized, and exploitative—were the strategy by which the covert capital extended its power, yet in their wake they served as a basis for difficult but enduring U.S. imperial communities. My fourth chapter turns to these intimacies. When the North Vietnamese entered Saigon in 1975 and drove out the last of the U.S. presence, Vietnamese agents, officials, family members, and employees of the stretched-out U.S. imperial state measured that state's rhetorical promises as they fled, migrating to the covert capital. To meet the returnees, the covert capital insisted on presenting its friends, equals, and intimates as pastless immigrants and refugees in an attempt to recreate history. In contrast, I examine the forms of daily life and expression that agents and intimates used to experience and publicize these intimacies in a landscape fixed on erasing them, focusing on two cultural products. One was the Eden Center, a converted strip mall that became the most important center of Vietnamese goods and services on the East Coast. The second is the novel *Monkey Bridge*, by the writer Lan Cao, a participant and family intimate of the covert capital state in Vietnam who settled in Falls Church. In a novel that nested Northern Virginia and Vietnam inside one another, Cao details the complex, split senses of belonging between places that arose for subjects of the covert capital's transnational spaces of uneven power relations. She also, hesitantly, invites an independent, autonomous Vietnam back into the story of the covert capital along a new reparational axis of intimacy.

My final chapter gauges how the physical and cultural habitus of the covert capital that was formed in the sixties fostered U.S. imperial policy over time. In 1987, observers noticed two new formations in the covert capital. The first was the Edge City, a popular urban studies term born in Northern Virginia to describe the mass of offices, malls, and hotels that, at Tysons Corner, gave the covert capital its first recognizable skyline. The second was the Iran-Contra Affair, the public-private campaign to sell arms to Iran and funnel the profits to the contra war in Central America. Iran-Contra and Edge City, the chapter argues, grew up alongside one another—as a new semi-public system for managing covert action work, one expressed in Edge City architecture and one that rearticulated the social networking that had always undergirded U.S. imperial labor in the suburbs.

But this chapter goes beyond Iran-Contra as scandal and male insurgent fantasy to examine the ways the phrase *Iran-Contra,* nonsensical as domestic political scandal, operated as a cipher that revealed a set of multi-sited U.S. imperial relations vectored through the suburbs of Northern Virginia. Long imperial histories had chained Northern Virginia, Iran, and Central America together since the covert capital's founding. The U.S. imperial economy of the 1970s and 1980s had further tied the three sites of Northern Virginia, Tehran, and El Salvador in a set of uneven spatial developments and destructive economies that at times took quite similar built forms, at times were strategically different, but physically shaped all three places.

Even as U.S. officials tried to disavow the country's long connections with U.S. imperial Tehran by denying the ailing Shah residence in the United States after the Iranian revolution, Iranian exiles and Pahlavi royalists with close ties to agents from Northern Virginia fulfilled these histories with their own migration to the covert capital. They designed and settled some of Edge City's most vital modern and postmodern spaces. As the secret U.S. war in Central America dragged on, those cast outside the covert capital's boundaries of security also refused to obey its architectures of exclusion. Salvadoran migrants, driven off their land in San Miguel, La Unión, Usulután, and Morazán as a result of the imperial corridor's policies, migrated to the covert capital as laborers—landscaping, cleaning, polishing, and serving the new consumer spaces of Edge City. These migrants also became cultural workers. This chapter uses the work of the Salvadoran writer Mario Bencastro and others to explore what I argue was an architecture of counter-exposure and acknowledgment from below, which responded to the built environment of Northern Virginia with a literary method that reversed the erasure of Edge City's inaccessible and opaque bands of glass with the spaces of embodied lives perpetually denied by the local landscape in which these subjects settled.

Reagan's reinvigoration of covert action with the invasions of Grenada and Central America and his promotion of the Star Wars missile defense system in 1983 led to the first notice of Edge City in 1987. A decade and a half later, George W. Bush's wars on Iraq and Afghanistan and his promotion of a new War on Terror/Homeland Security state led to another rash of building, which sent the covert capital sprawling toward and past Dulles International Airport into the countryside. In my conclusion, I set the coexistence of this new infrastructure of the War on Terror alongside the unresolved memorials, presences, and uses left over from the Cold War to stress a continuity of U.S. imperialism as a set of lived relationships in the home front that transcends the epochs that organize so much of American foreign policy scholarship and public culture. I finally consider how creative acts of mapping and their ensuing ironies, proximities, and irreconcilable spatial arguments about the nature of the U.S. state mark out a restless set of ethical questions about U.S. imperial culture and society as they trickle down to the present day.

In these stories, similar characters emerge repeatedly. The tragedy of Edward Lansdale returned three decades later as the farce of Oliver North. Wallace K. Harrison and Max Abramovitz, the designers of the CIA, returned as Gerald Halpin and Rudolph Seeley, the developers of Tysons Corner's Edge City. Other characters frequenting the following pages have similar matches: Lan Cao reappears as Saideh Pakravan, Eero Saarinen as Kamran Diba, Nguyen Ngoc Loan as Edén Pastora. In some sense, similar figures appeared so regularly for the very reason that these people, despite their crucial role in building and expressing the culture of the imperial corridor, and despite their individuality, were not merely important as one-of-a-kind actors. They and their intimacies were important because they were productions of this landscape—scenes in the life of this book's true, enduring protagonist: the covert capital itself.

ONE

The Covert Intimacies of Langley and Dulles

MANY OBSERVERS SEEM UNSURE as to whether "Langley" is a place or an idea. Just as "Washington" is a synonym for the executive branch and Congress, Langley is often the CIA writ large: Langley thinks, Langley acts, Langley feels. But the CIA complex is a three-dimensional place. Its placement and proximities in local and distant space, its architectural form and everyday use were the result of strategic choices made by some of U.S. imperialism's major theorists and activists, who saw Langley as the space necessary to manage a newly sprawling empire in the days of the Cold War.

Eight miles from the White House, Langley achieved two things for the agency, according to conventional wisdom. The building's fixed physical footprint ensured the CIA a lasting place in the federal bureaucracy, ushering the agency from seat-of-the-pants agent handling and improvisational coups around the world to a humdrum round of paper shuffling, technological eavesdropping, and oversight. Tucked in the woods, it gave the CIA security not possible in its many offices scattered around busy 1950s Washington.[1]

At the same time, the CIA complex wasn't merely an architectural site. The goal of a permanent headquarters drove Director Allen Dulles throughout his career in intelligence.[2] When the dream finally took physical form at Langley, it was the spatial articulation of how Dulles's philosophies of intimacy, secrecy, security, and efficiency could provide a civilian foundation for U.S. global management and authority, philosophies that mobilized American political forces within the triumvirate that ran between John Foster Dulles at the State Department, Allen Dulles at the CIA, and Dwight Eisenhower in the White House.

Set at one end of what became the Dulles Corridor, the Langley complex was also part of an unrecognized spatial sequence of Dulles family buildings that played crucial roles in postwar U.S. foreign policy, a sequence including the modernist Eleanor Dulles house on Spring Hill Road in McLean, and the modernist airport named after John Foster Dulles at the endpoint of the corridor. These structures provided a set of instructions and blueprints for the performance and ethics of imperial management as a way of life domestically. They linked the transformation of modern American architecture and landscape after World War II to the transformation of modern American empire in the same period, magnifying missing relays between key cultural histories of the 1950s.

Both a machine for generating covert action globally and a stark invisibility, the CIA headquarters holds all these histories. The secret heart of a covert capital, it trapped its social and political agendas in the very grain of its concrete, in the serial length of its corridors.

THE MOVE TO VIRGINIA

In 1954, the CIA was dispersed across the nation's capital in more than thirty-nine government buildings and temporary structures huddled around the Washington Mall. The spread was the shambling result of the hectic and disorganized expansion of the federal bureaucracy during World War II. The agency's headquarters was located in a columned brick building at 2430 E Street, near the State Department. But the "Tempos," as they came to be known, were more famous—perhaps the most legendary federal eyesores of the period. Named blandly for letters of the alphabet, testament to the government's inability to accommodate its staff, the "ghostly white" wooden Tempos froze in winter and grew so sweltering during humid DC summers that secretaries had to dash out at lunch, roll up their skirts and pant legs, and douse themselves in the Reflecting Pool to cool off. Agents peeled classified documents off their sweaty forearms. Lunches hung suspended on strings from ceilings to guard them from ant columns, mice, and insects. The ramshackle, stinking structures leaked in the rain and saw safes holding classified documents plummeting through rickety upper floors to crash into the offices below. Some had been there since the First World War, while others started as barracks for newly recruited navy women during the Second World War. The agency paid $3 million a year for secure maintenance and shuttles to connect the offices to E Street. Allen

The "Tempos," or temporary structures, on the National Mall were the result of the hectic expansion of the federal bureaucracy during World War II. CIA Director Allen Dulles called the buildings, which housed early CIA offices, "a damned pig sty." The CIA headquarters at Langley was meant to be their opposite in every way—more secure, isolated, modern, efficient, and monumental. National Capital Planning Commission.

Dulles dubbed the Tempos, with their warped floors and clapboard walls, "a damned pig sty."[3]

Two events in 1954 dislodged a new headquarters from the realm of ideas into reality. Approaches for the new Roosevelt Bridge across the Potomac promised to pave over some Tempos. Others were to be knocked down by a Department of Interior project to clear obstructions from the Mall. On November 16, Dulles wrote to the director of the Office of Defense

Mobilization, Arthur S. Flemming, and stated the CIA's case: "Security problems, inefficiency and excessive costs . . . have long indicated the high desirability of providing space for the Central Intelligence Agency in Washington in one permanent building."

That Flemming, the man charged with shielding DC from nuclear attack, was one of the first officials Dulles addressed is important. Dulles needed Flemming's approval to break the dispersion standards drafted to cope with an imagined nuclear threat to the city. Federal regulations mandated that new government buildings be located ten or more miles from the perimeter of an "urban target," that is, DC. But Dulles needed permission to locate his new complex *within* the allowable security boundary. "It is essential that the Director be immediately available to the President and the National Security Council," he said.[4]

Some historians claim the suburbanization of the CIA was a Cold War nuclear security move. It was not. At a more conceptual level, the Dulles-Flemming letter contests the still-implicit idea that the nuclear Cold War and armed Soviet Union were the motive forces guiding Dulles's project for the agency. Even as the Dulles brothers used nuclear threat to frighten the nation—and Dulles stressed this in public, claiming before capital planners that Langley could better resist fallout from a hydrogen bomb than other sites—Dulles chose to design a home for his agency that, rather than a model of how to spatially reorganize a nation under a nuclear shadow, reorganized space in metropolitan DC in a subtler, more covert fashion, one suited to the agency tasked with mediating between the high-flying rhetoric of the Cold War and the realities of U.S. imperial management on the ground.

As early as 1947, Dulles had expressed his view that postwar U.S. power and intelligence would need to be equipped to deal not only with ideological conflicts "between Soviet Russia and the countries of the west," but also "in the internal political conflicts within the countries of Europe, Asia, and South America." Some scholars suggest that the CIA was formed in the first place as a response to the creation of the United Nations in order "to explain international events in a manner that would defend American interests." In the newly aggressive foreign policy blessed by the Eisenhower administration—driven by a feeling that "containment" of communism and leftist national struggles had been too passive—U.S. agents abroad took on a wider mandate, one that could and did reach beyond conventional Cold War and Soviet perimeter defense concerns per se.

In the words of one CIA officer, a Soviet expert who lived in Northern

Virginia, the United States would only succeed if the country took into account "the powerful nationalist, racial, religious, and economic forces at work in the world that have little to do with the Soviet-American confrontation."[5] As another local officer who specialized in Soviet analysis put it, the CIA was soon becoming an agency that "seeks largely to advance America's self-appointed role as the dominant arbiter of social, economic, and political change in the awakening regions of Asia, Africa, and Latin America."

Dulles—the son of a Presbyterian pastor and the grandson of the secretary of state who approved the taking of the Hawaiian Islands—reoriented the CIA toward the Third World. According to a history prepared for Congress, this shift occurred at the same time that "the Agency emerged as an integral element in high-level United States policymaking" because of "the ways covert operations could advance U.S. policy." By November 1954, Dulles and his staff had generated a number of models for the role he saw for the United States in the world as a "hands-on nation," none that had to do with all-out nuclear war—the harassment of the democratically elected president of Costa Rica in March 1954; the secret CIA coup against the democratically elected president of Guatemala on June 27; the CIA agents who arrived in Hanoi and Haiphong in North Vietnam to train paramilitary units in July after the French colonial defeat at Dien Bien Phu; the trial of American agent Hugh Redmond for spying against China in September. To execute the secret wars and "preventative" ventures in the Third World overseen by Dulles, an immediate, informal intimacy with those in power was the central priority; a bunkered nuclear defense was only marginal.[6]

The Dulles-Flemming letter also illustrates the degree to which Dulles had committed to the Langley site, eight miles from the White House, as early as 1954. Through the extensive site search and hearings of 1955, many rural and urban locations for the new CIA headquarters were supposedly considered. The CIA received lavish proposals, and most made more obvious sense—cheaper sites in Prince George's County, Maryland; sites more secure from nuclear fallout in Charles County, Maryland; sites more convenient to commuters off Shirley Highway near the new subdivisions of Springfield, Virginia, southwest of the city; sites in Southwest DC, then being redeveloped; sites in Montgomery County, near the National Institutes of Health and the Naval Hospital; sites in Alexandria, once part of the District, with easy access to defense development at National Airport and the Pentagon, in a county where a greater percentage of CIA agents already lived. A staff committee of the National Capital Planning Commission, chaired by Harland

Bartholomew, America's most famous city planner, submitted an exhaustive report to the wider commission in May that analyzed twenty-nine possible locations.[7] Beloved by Eisenhower and then in the dignified twilight of his career, Bartholomew favored a different site, likely a tract in Alexandria.[8]

Yet by February 1955, CIA officials were already meeting Northern Virginia planning officials. By March, they were in talks with water and utility companies about connecting the Langley site to the grid, and CIA officials were making chart and map presentations to planners about Langley, two months *before* the Capital Planning Commission—which technically had to approve any choice—even delivered an initial report on the preliminary options, and three months before mandatory appropriations meetings before Congress. By summer, stories leaked to the press headlined "Allen Dulles Favors Langley," and Dulles's friend Gilmore D. Clarke, former chairman of DC's Fine Arts Commission and frequent Robert Moses collaborator in New York, became the CIA's New York consultant on the headquarters project. On October 25, 1955, Clarke's landscape architecture firm, Clarke and Rapuano, delivered not so much a study as a reverential paean to the wonders of Langley, and the utter insufficiency of all other proposed sites.[9]

It was common knowledge in those days that the CIA director was a minor celebrity, overseeing matters so important that democratic process was a formality at best. Dulles eased these relationships with a legendary social life centered around dinners at his house in Georgetown and after-hours chats over highballs with the power elite of fifties Washington.[10] These networks and Allen Dulles's vision of the headquarters, its intended function and strategic possibilities, accounted for the persistence with which Langley rose to the top of CIA wish lists.[11]

Allen Dulles favored Langley. But the question remains as to why this woody land crossed by a creek lodged itself so deeply in his imagination. A former Robert E. Lee family plantation on the Potomac with no major roads or utilities—only "horse and buggy streets"—the place was surrounded by a centenarian Episcopal church, lonely dairy farms, a shuttered trolley line, and a foxhunting forest. Not even a real village, Langley was "simply the name for a fork in the road." By 1911, it had merged into McLean—itself a mere trolley stop—and only retains its discrete identity (and that, only for people who have never been there and seen how little of it exists) because of the headquarters.[12]

The answer to this question lies in the particular geographic and social features offered by the Langley ecology. From bucolic and rural roots, the area had undergone a distinct gentrification of country homes since the early part of the century. By the 1950s, Langley was seen as an alluring terrain that had "the beauty and charm of the countryside," but could "reflect in modern living the graciousness of the past." Chicago real estate heir Joseph Leiter had bought 700 acres, built a seventy-two-room mansion called the Glass Palace on a portion of the future CIA site by 1912, and hard-surfaced the area's first major road. Dulles's uncle, Woodrow Wilson's secretary of state, Robert Lansing, was a guest with his wife at the Leiter estate, "the scene of brilliant social functions and . . . a favorite gathering place for those members of society who liked to ride and hunt," and a place where Lansing might have expressed his concerns about Wilson's idea of national "self-determination," which he considered "simply loaded with dynamite." Dulles, who was close to his uncle, had first seen the area while attending parties there with his wife, Clover, in Coolidge's Washington, when many ambassadors began settling its environs.

By the fifties, Langley residents included Trevor Gardner, the Pentagon's top ballistic missile advocate; Supreme Court Justice Byron White; the wealthy magnate Hugh Auchincloss, who had been married to, in turn, the mothers of Gore Vidal and Jackie Bouvier; and the "young Sen. John Kennedy" himself, who had moved into the country mansion of late Supreme Court Justice Robert Jackson, American prosecutor at the Nuremberg Trials. Dulles didn't simply cultivate an elite, informal social life in Washington to get the headquarters built—elite, informal social connections were the grounds for his politics. This area provided a crucial setting for them.[13]

Most critically, by the fifties, McLean was home to the striking and revered bungalow of Allen Dulles's sister Eleanor, whose gleaming swimming pool became a kind of Round Table for Cold War Washington, a watering hole and serene meeting place for the Dulles brothers to make policy—the early site for their presidentially empowered conversations over dry martinis and Overholt rye whisky. The brothers met there at least once every few weeks, frequently on Sunday afternoons, and swam there individually more often. Eleanor herself was an official at the State Department and joined in the conversations, but her role in the family seemed to fall in the realm of consummate politicized suburban hostess.[14]

The distinct leisure of her estate pool, like the parties of Coolidge's Washington or the air of entitlement and status surrounding the residential landscape of estate-laden McLean, was the constitutive setting for the presumptive derring-do that characterized early CIA interventions across

Eleanor Dulles's modernist bungalow preceded the CIA in McLean. The gleaming swimming pool was completed first. At its geopolitical pool parties, State Department, military, CIA, and international figures mixed in unpredictable combinations. Such domestic spaces provided the constitutive setting for CIA interventions across the globe. Eleanor Lansing Dulles Papers, Special Collections Research Center, The George Washington University. Courtesy of David Dulles.

the globe. In her autobiography, written thirty years later, Eleanor Dulles recalled with nostalgic whimsy the almost uncanny power her personally designed domestic space in Virginia had to influence world affairs in the actual capital of DC, like an invisible magnet that could somehow change the stuffy, formal city's inherent polarity.

"I think back to the evening when the new German Army was planned in my swimming pool in McLean, Virginia," she wrote in *Chances of a Lifetime*, her memoir, with an only somewhat acknowledged sense of the absurd. "Jimmy Riddleberger [an official at the State Department] came to me with a request. He said the German generals, in Washington to discuss their military contribution to Europe's defense, were stiff and uncommunicative. Jimmy suggested it might ease matters if I would invite them for supper and a swim in the pool. They came . . . I pressed them to have a swim before supper. They started to refuse, but I gave each a pair of swimming trunks and before long they were bobbing about in the pool, along with five Americans I had invited. The formality was gone . . . "[15] Understated, and serious about her career, Eleanor was open to the ways in which her gendered access to the category of "hostess" could have a curveball effect on the stiff and masculine regimes of capital foreign policy.

By 1950 she had bought the land, then an acre and a half of cornfield on a former plantation, from a Labor Department official and friend, Clara Beyer. She moved out from her house on Chain Bridge Road opposite Kemble Park in DC into the new bungalow on Spring Hill Road in McLean on Washington's Birthday, 1951. Almost immediately, political DC followed her. As if to lure them, the swimming pool was completed and used first. Eleanor hired young modernist architect Nicholas Satterlee for the house because she "expected to have a lot to say about the design," and had balked at the expertise of Jackson Place architect Gertrude Sawyer, who had designed her house in the city. Undoubtedly influenced by Frank Lloyd Wright and modernist American architecture interpenetrated by nature, she wanted the house "embracing" the pool, creating a social flow between the two spaces. When she signed the contract, anticipating wartime shortages owing to the Korean War, she immediately directed Satterlee to buy all the materials, down to the kitchen fixtures, which she then stored in Beyer's barn. She regularly drove out dusty Chain Bridge Road to check the progress. From start to finish, the work was hers. "It was the house I designed," she marveled as it came along, "one floor, open to the sun, a simple structure . . . There was space for a garden and some three hundred small trees and bushes, many of which I dug up in the woods and replanted myself."[16]

Over the next two decades, more than a dozen ambassadors from France, Germany, Switzerland, Austria, Italy, and elsewhere dined there, their motorcycle escorts rattling the quiet suburb. "A principal pleasure in these years came from entertaining," she wrote. She would later claim that John Foster and Republican senator Jim Duff engineered Eisenhower's presidential campaign poolside in early 1952. Richard Nixon, future CIA clandestine service chief Richard Bissell, Barbara and Covey Oliver (the future ambassador to Colombia), and Assistant Secretary of State Bob Bowie appeared at the parties, and the Dulles family celebrated Thanksgiving at the house—while managing the fate of Berlin in 1958—waited on by her "adoring" Austrian servants, Trudy and Relly Rotter, in a dining room divided from the garden by sliding glass panels. The Rotters lived in a detached bedroom on the property and prepared the Mai Bowle cocktail of white wine and strawberries the ambassadors loved.[17]

Powerful guests would drift in the swimming pool, mirth fueled by the

The early McLean landscape as seen from the edge of Eleanor Dulles's pool. For powerful guests, the pastoral view became the symbol of a precarious good life that needed defending. It was also a metonym for world building. It represented all the underdeveloped landscapes, taking form at home as developable property, that only they could guide and supervise. Eleanor Lansing Dulles Papers, Special Collections Research Center, The George Washington University. Courtesy of David Dulles.

scotch, bourbon, and gin Eleanor bought by the gallon, and take in the rolling pastoral view, still uninterrupted by settlement. The secluded house didn't even have an address until 1965, which added a discreet portion of its power—this sense that the Langley-McLean area, unlike almost any other section of Virginia (or Maryland) that close to Washington, remained unlocatable by the fixed grids and circles of DC. But while the inspiring backdrop, elevated by Eleanor's good graces, could lubricate the intimacies of power and the tasks of decision making and mutual affirmation, the content of conversations could be quite dark. Eleanor recalled one early visit just after the Korean War began, before the house had been raised. Covey Oliver was just leaving a job with the State Department when Eleanor invited him and his wife Barbara to the pool. They undressed in the car, took a dip, and picnicked on a beautiful day. Then the talk turned apocalyptic. Sitting at the pool's edge, they asked, "Is this World War III? Is this going to be the great catastrophe to civilization?" "Everything was so bright," Eleanor recalled later. "And there was a sharp contrast between this dramatic danger hanging over us and the beauty of the countryside."[18]

The exurban land beyond the edge of the pool worked as a symbol of a precarious good life that needed defending and could slip away at any moment. It was also a metonym for world building, for all the underdeveloped landscapes, taking form at home as developable property, that could only be protected and cajoled along under their own wise supervision. The American modernist house alone in the countryside was the nascent first step in a process at times optimistic, at times fearfully possessive, which spread out from its own backyard. At the same time, the isolated social authority of the landscape, like an expanded, outdoor version of what had only formerly been possible in one of Georgetown's elite drawing rooms (and poised in the northeast section of Fairfax County that directly bordered Georgetown and Allen Dulles's house at 2723 Q Street), provided the context for the making of world policy—the pleasant distance from the traditional power centers of DC mirroring an ethical distance from the democratic presumptions of American government.

In this regard, the Eleanor Dulles house was representative of the wider pattern. At elite CIA homes and dinner parties, "social life and politics were inextricable and indistinguishable." Agents coaxed tipsy political elites to reveal useful information. Their wives did the same at gender-segregated gatherings after dinner. For this reason, the CIA even financed some parties, at $100 a guest, and, at times, staffed them with a "stud detail" charged with "making sure no one was left unattached or was bored or in need of a drink." McLean in the fifties added something new to the equation: a break with the proximities and accountability of the capital. The strategic move dovetailed with an invigorating social one. The Georgetown parties were migrating to McLean for a greater novelty and rustic chic, one that, usefully, kept the parties well attended. CIA "fun couples," such as Tom and Joan Braden, rented houses in the rural surroundings to tantalize day-trippers with the riches of the countryside, drawing guests like CIA covert action enthusiast Frank Wisner and his wife, Polly, and one of the Cold War's founding ideologues, State Department official and Pentagon liaison Paul Nitze, and his wife, Phyllis.[19]

Many attendees arrived from their own Northern Virginia retreats. Desmond FitzGerald, the CIA's millionaire Far East chief—who ran guerrilla operations against communist China, steered attempted coups against

Sukarno in Indonesia and later directed the CIA's sabotage missions against Cuba and attempted assassinations of Fidel Castro—had a farmhouse in Virginia at this time. Lyman Kirkpatrick Jr., CIA inspector general—who had in 1956 trained Fulgencio Batista's political police, the Bureau for the Repression of Communist Activities, and helped Batista evaluate the political and military state of the country in 1958—lived in a "delightful pink house" in Fairfax, near the OSS training center, Station S, that had first brought many of these people to Northern Virginia in the 1940s.[20]

Chief of the brainwashing research done by the CIA's Technical Services Staff, Sidney Gottlieb—who devised the biotoxins meant to assassinate many postcolonial leaders, including Fidel Castro, Patrice Lumumba in the Congo, and Abdel Karim Qasim in Iraq—lived in a cabin on a Vienna farm, where he kept goats, sold Christmas trees at the holidays, and rose to prominence in local folk-dancing circles, hollering into the microphone as a square dance caller. J.C. King, the clandestine officer who directed the agency's Western Hemisphere division and ran many CIA anti-government operations in Guatemala leading up to the 1954 coup, hunted game and socialized with Latin American ambassadors, State Department officials, and William D. Pawley (former ambassador to Peru and Brazil, fellow coup plotter, and Allen Dulles's friend) on Pawley's 800-acre estate, Belvoir, a regular stop on local garden tours.[21]

James Jesus Angleton, soon to be the CIA's chief of counterintelligence, lived in a white house that he built in 1949 in North Arlington, near the Langley site. His dinner parties drew Allen Dulles and other CIA neighbors, such as Alexandria resident Win Scott, Mexico City station chief, and his wife, Paula; and McLean resident Cord Meyer, who ran operations infiltrating student groups and the labor movement in Brazil and the Dominican Republic, and his wife, Mary.[22] Kim Roosevelt, the grandson of Teddy Roosevelt, who directed the coup against Iranian Prime Minister Mohammad Mossadegh in 1953, had a house in the McLean area with his wife, Polly, and helped found the local ski club. Roosevelt boasted longtime family connections to the county. His grandparents on his mother's side, the Willards, owned Layton Hall, one of the most famous estates in Fairfax, which they had loaned to the OSS for its Virginia training site. Before serving as Wilson's ambassador to Spain, his mother's father, Colonel Joseph E. Willard, the son of a Confederate intelligence agent, fought in the Spanish-American War, commanding a company of Fairfax troops. These elders highlight the imperial family connections that, for some individual actors in the

CIA such as Roosevelt, intimately linked the period of U.S. empire at the turn of the twentieth century to the one after World War II as a single, sentimental project, one with deep connections to Northern Virginia. "Easily the most influential political figure in Fairfax County," in the words of one local history, Willard then played a crucial role in developing the built landscape, financing its roads and first trolleys, and extending the trolley line to Fairfax, which generated the foundations of the suburbs CIA officers then came to inhabit.[23]

President Eisenhower, who encouraged the CIA's move outside DC, also knew the area in the earlier period, when he stayed in his brother Milton's Colonial Revival house in Falls Church during World War II, when Milton was designing the national program for Japanese internment.[24] This was the social history that hovered behind CIA officials' banal pronouncement that Langley was·"more accessible to most Agency employees" than other possible sites.[25]

Like these soirees, but elevated in stature by the family connection to the Dulleses, parties at Spring Hill stirred foreign officials, State Department, military, CIA, and international figures in unpredictable combinations, flouting capital protocol. For at least one party, Eleanor pre-circulated typed sheets so the guests could prepare in order to draw the most from their social engagements. A list annotated with capsule biographies of each guest explained breezily, "this information is to make your afternoon more pleasant—Hope you come early and park on the grass."[26] Why knowing that Clare Timberlake had been U.S. ambassador to the Congo or that Seymour Bolton worked for the CIA would make an afternoon more pleasant was not self-evident, until one recognized that the ensembles were the entertainment. Slipping into borrowed swimming trunks, undressing in a car, parking on the grass, meeting strangers—these titillating promises that the color-within-the lines norms of the overt capital could be gently violated in an accessible and slightly wild McLean with erotic overtones increased the excitement. But the American officials and "determined interventionists" joining the parade were the most powerful in U.S. government. Leisure and work intertwined at events meant to be both leisure and work, and shared sensory experiences at home provided the setting for sharing and reaffirming geopolitical experiences abroad—from tours of duty just ended or those about to begin.

Brief, alluring violations of social rules in exurban McLean acted both as rehearsals and reflections of the brief, alluring violations of political rules that defined the work of the attendees bolstering covert action as a tool of U.S. foreign policy in this same period. Their biographies testify to the degree to which their efforts concentrated against the decolonizing world, rather than the Soviet Union per se. Allen Dulles himself affirmed this view of their work as not relating to proxy wars and communist subversion alone, writing: "Sometimes, I am inclined to believe that a century from now historians will view the Soviet revolution as merely another episode in European history, and find in the emergence of these new states the truly significant development of our age." The Spring Hill house was one powerful space where the Dulleses formulated their attempts to control the fate of those new states, amid what one historian describes as the mood of "lighthearted, romantic activism" that became the clandestine service's "trademark."[27]

It is no small thing to say that Dulles liked Langley as home for his headquarters because it, through his sister's powerful intervention, made him feel socially comfortable and allowed him a broad, unmowed field to explore his social seeding of policy, intelligence, and political change. In moving the CIA there, close to DC but not in the capital, he was able to spur a redesign of the landscape of power of the capital along a countrified suburban axis. This is in notable contrast with the traditional understanding of the capital city as a stable house of government, a container elected officials pass through but which outlasts them as individuals and the policies they bring with them—a framework of government, like the Constitution, sealed in monumental architecture. Dulles, an unelected official, made himself a physical capital loosed from the bounds of the old one, immersed in a social and architectural network that echoed his own values and worldview, in the form of his sister's house quite literally—a place where the everyday imbrication of social life with activist geopolitics and often violent international action was the norm, rather than the exception.

That the apparently undeveloped locale of Langley, and particularly the CIA site, once neighbored a free black community called Lincolnsville and that the apparently empty locale of Spring Hill, and particularly the Eleanor Dulles house, once neighbored a slave plantation and then free black community called Odrick's Corner suggests a further impulse. By leading the CIA into a Northern Virginia still laced with Confederate nostalgia and Jim Crow modernism, where whites worked for half a century to erase both the history of the local black communities and the intense civil rights struggles over the implantation of segregation on the border of DC after Virginia's 1902 Jim Crow constitution took effect, Dulles and the agency explicitly benefited from the atomized democratic polity and human estrangement fostered by racial apartheid.[28]

While McLean's white founding citizens recalled slavery in Fairfax County as a paternalistic and friendly affair, disrupted only by "carpet baggers" in the "Tragic Era," who turned "the colored man against his best friends, the white race," slave patrols had roamed Langley in the early 1860s, policing rumors of insurrection at the DC border. Northern Virginians recalled the use of particular trees as gibbets on the central road, Route 7, for decades. Upon emancipation, many freedmen resettled their former plantations or bought property from northern arrivals, and the black community in Fairfax County grew throughout Reconstruction—land and work on new trolley and railroad lines opening a route to security. Prominent members of the Falls Church chapter of the NAACP, considered the first rural branch in the United States when it started in 1915, arrived to the organization through success in early real estate and property ownership. Blacksmiths, farmers, stonemasons, and sawmill and stone quarry laborers also settled the area's black communities, as did early federal workers, lawyers, and military veterans.[29]

As a key transfer point between south and north, Northern Virginia also always served as a flashpoint of racist organizing and civil rights struggle. The fact that the Virginia end of the Key Bridge in Arlington was the place where train and bus riders had to reorganize themselves into Jim Crow seating after leaving DC made it a frequent battleground, as did the prominent presence of the local Ku Klux Klan, with its day of featured activities at the annual Fairfax County fair. Virginia was one of the last five states in the country with a poll tax, which lasted until 1966. It was one of the last with a miscegenation law, and black men in Fairfax and surrounding counties were harassed and jailed for false accusations of rape through and after World War II. Punitive local curfews went into effect and new laws made buying property more difficult. School desegregation was only ordered in Fairfax County in 1960 and did not fully proceed until 1965. Local residents battled the state in these years, as they had for decades. Jessie Butler, the first black woman to challenge the poll tax in court, brought her case in Arlington in 1950. Also in Arlington, black parents sued over school segregation. Northern Virginia localities responded with even more Confederate organizing. Arlington was home to an aggressive unit of "pro-segregation extremists," the Defenders of State Sovereignty and Individual Liberties. The year Eleanor broke ground on her former plantation, the Virginia General Assembly commissioned a new history textbook, which lauded slavery as providing, among other things, "comprehensive social security" for enslaved black people. The next year, Alexandria passed an ordinance to name all north-south streets in that town—with its slave-laid cobblestones—after Confederate generals, just as local highways bear Confederate names to this day.[30]

At the same time, Northern Virginia congressmen who encouraged and eased the CIA's move to Virginia helped lead the long, bitter fight to keep the federal colony of DC from ruling itself or gaining democratic rights, particularly after 1960—the year seventeen African nations won independence—when Washington became nationally recognized as America's first black majority city. Just as the housing squeeze created by the Pentagon and its disruption of black communities in Arlington in the 1940s soon reshuffled black residents into segregated trailer camps designed by the Farm Security Administration, the pace of suburbanization in Northern Virginia in the fifties and sixties eroded the habitable space and fabric of local black neighborhoods stable since Reconstruction, as white developers lowballed black owners for their property and encroached on their land. The black population in Fairfax County dropped from 16 to 4 percent from 1940 to 1970. Visiting foreign emissaries not invited to Eleanor's parties—such as the poet Kaluta Amri Abedi, the first African mayor of Dar Es Salaam and a close advisor to Tanzanian president Julius Nyerere—were denied service at local segregated cafeterias, triggering rearguard public relations apologies from the State Department. Traces of the "racially closed housing market" remained in Northern Virginia until the 1970s, even as black residents found themselves doing local construction work, gathering at Arlington's "Hard Corner" for roundups that to one participant felt "like the old notion of the slave market," selling manual labor for two-dollar-an-hour jobs clearing land, grading roads, and building the new suburban infrastructure across the region. White Langley residents, meanwhile, continued to see local black and white relationships as merely based on "mutual respect and admiration, each benefiting from the other," despite the arrival of the civil rights movement, which they saw as "present-day attempts to destroy" that presumed closeness.[31]

These links to the Confederacy and Southern racism, on the one hand, and the colonial nature of Virginia's relationship to black DC, on the other, are not coincidences in the history of the land Allen Dulles chose but its constitutive features. The very availability and emptiness of the CIA site on the river, eight miles from the White House and owned by that time by the Bureau of Public Roads, was the result of a racist spatiality. Shaped by a plantation economy that reserved river sites in large tracts, even rocky up-river ones like Langley, for white ownership, Virginia's political representatives then blocked the powerless city that they (along with other Southerners) dominated and kept it from making the annexations that had expanded the size and resources of most American metropolises, hemming it in and squeezing its tax base. These efforts led directly to the wealth, power, and controlled development of northeastern Northern Virginia, most notably expanded with the CIA's arrival.[32]

To get a feel for the distance between downtown DC and Langley, one need only recognize that if you stood on the Upper West Side of Manhattan, the Langley site would be closer than Wall Street. In downtown Los Angeles, Langley would be the Miracle Mile. But in Fairfax County, it was free and clear in the place where CIA friends at McLean High School in the fifties and sixties would recall "the Dixie-playing, Confederate flag-waving types at the football games." This culture would go on to shape the domesticity of the headquarters once it was built. It underwrote its violent behaviors toward black and brown people abroad by rehearsing them in its own strategic environment, where, until the agency began to target postcolonial nations in Africa in the 1960s and finally hired its first few black officers, its only African American employees drove buses and cleaned out wastebaskets on the night office cleaning crew.[33]

This landscape provided the context for social life at Eleanor Dulles's house on Spring Hill. To seal it, Eleanor financed the development of the house on the McLean cornfield with the displacement of black residents in Washington. To pay for the house, she engaged in a series of speculative housing ventures, "rebuilding the inner city," as she called it, on the alley of Green's Court in the "new" Foggy Bottom. The gentrification of that neighborhood followed the opening of the State Department in the old War Department digs in 1947. In her memoir, she describes the houses there as "rat-infested, with bad flooring and rotten staircases," before she renovated them for "young professional people and government workers" with "imagination." But she had gone to Green's Court in the first place in 1940 to visit a genteel African American man called Madison, who had served her grandfather and uncle as a butler in the State Department and who kept in his "little old house" mementos of his contact with international figures, like a photograph of the Duke of Windsor. A black neighborhood's dispossession in the visible capital helped fund the pool in the suburbs where policies were hatched to dispossess people of color abroad.[34]

Even the reasons Allen Dulles often mentioned when selling the idea to local Northern Virginia businessmen—the convenience, privacy, and good parking that would appeal to any suburban dreamer—were invoked in his speeches through a concept of family that, in this period of American urban and political struggle, always had a veneer of racial protection. At times, he reached out to his audience by casting the CIA as just another concerned white-flight suburbanite leaving the "congested conditions in a metropolitan area" that "do not constitute nowadays an ideal environment for an enterprise that employs office workers any more than they do for one's own family."[35]

The social and familial favors of the area that Dulles called "that charming locality" and "this fine community in this historic section of Virginia" thus point to more than just a tangle of nepotism and elitism.[36] The social echo chamber that defined the all-white parties at Eleanor's and their self-evident guest lists affirmed ideas about who could rule themselves and who could not, who could be invited and who could not, what was beautiful and what was not. These affirmations, and the cultural landscape of Washington and Northern Virginia that surrounded them, influenced the policies and actions that emerged from that landscape. Exaggerating the gendered pivot of homemaker, Eleanor—whom historians cast as more of an intellectual heavyweight than her younger brother—had designed a house that explored her vision of a geopolitical social sphere that served as an anchor for a series of transnational power relationships that stretched far beyond it. So too would Allen for the house he built for the CIA less than five miles away.

But Langley's spatiality and the social and racial buffers offered by these histories gave Dulles one further, strategic, and more practical benefit. The openness and perceived fresh start of Langley—the ability to carve out spatial relationships on high, open ground within a wider landscape lacking dense development—allowed Dulles to create a building that would, at last, embody his unique vision of the covert. The headquarters expressed in physical space the shifting ideas in which Dulles was shrouding the agency by the mid-fifties, a veil of open secrecy that served its murky, strategic interventions for the rest of the century and set the course for shaping the covert capital's everyday life.

DULLES'S OPEN SECRETS

Many would agree the United States has and has had an empire. Few Americans would claim or even be able to describe their own lived imperial citizenship. In Northern Virginia at mid-century, Allen Dulles innovated a relationship between empire and secrecy that helps account for why we have such trouble imagining the lived dimensions of empire. His ideas about this open secret took form at the CIA. By modeling physical space—the medium through which the everyday is lived—the Langley complex prefabricated a powerful model for the disavowal of U.S. imperialism, as practiced through the motions of everyday life. That this landscape of denial operated in the home front where the stretched-out political power of U.S. empire was managed—that disavowal was, in a sense, part of the work of managing it—testified to its effectiveness. In sum, the way Allen Dulles hid the CIA headquarters in plain sight mattered.

To get the headquarters built, Dulles appeared in public and gave testimony in open sessions, a divorce from habit as the agency commonly met Congress in private. His arguments for Langley closely tracked two popular cultural discourses—security and efficiency—making the CIA's case in the era's own vernacular. In public, security took on a conventional sense suited to the 1950s—a bureaucratic, systemic notion of protection for its own sake. Efficiency was the same. Without a central building, the CIA was losing "20 percent efficiency and a great deal of money." With it, the agency could trim guards from $1,173,000 to $320,000, and reception staff from $110,000 to $30,000. The agency even quantified its "loss of time" under the current arrangement, valued at $607,000 and counted as one of the new building's economies. Langley would shave time-wasting commutes for CIA employees from Northwest Washington and Montgomery County compared to sites farther south. The building itself was to be utilitarian with "no frills" and at the same time a streamlined corporate or academic campus visually representing the scholarly professionalism, civilian coordination, and departmental streamlining that were the CIA's core traits as a "service agency." "Reminds me of Princeton," Dulles would quip to visitors at his E Street office as he showed off early architectural models.[37]

But the CIA was not only "secure," it was a security organization, extending its authority internationally. Men who created the headquarters had direct knowledge of CIA actions across the globe and defined priorities among the trees of Langley based on this knowledge and its discrepancies. This was true for Dulles, and it held for administrators he appointed to the project. Overseeing it was Colonel Lawrence K. "Red" White, a former clandestine officer who wore a West Point ring on his finger and joined the CIA after losing the use of one leg in combat in the Philippines during World

War II. While White was connected to the Langley project, he also appeared elsewhere: meeting about China operations, designing U-2 plans, in Lyndon Johnson's office during the Vietnam escalations.[38] The idea of security could lean toward the offensive violence of covert action and "national security" as a code for secret war. It could also signify disguise, mystification, and the covert as a means of politics. The CIA's public arguments for the headquarters doubled as stand-ins for the silent content of its work.

As director, Allen Dulles cloaked the CIA in a particular kind of secrecy, a technique that created space for the transitions between the analytical and operational sides of the agency. Dulles had his own notion of keeping a secret, best articulated in his 1963 book, *The Craft of Intelligence*. Written in restless forced retirement in the two years after Kennedy dismissed him for the CIA's botched invasion of Cuba at the Bay of Pigs, the book is refined propaganda. In it, Dulles saves face for the newly shamed agency he built. He courts the American public in the way he best knew how: by charming them, by opening up to them, by explaining, by welcoming, by revealing. But since his subject is the CIA, the book bursts with contradictions. He writes: "CIA is not an underground operation. . . . It has, of course, a secret side . . . These functions are not disclosed." It is through these contradictions that a vision of Dulles's complex notion of the covert emerges.[39]

In the "Personal Note" opening the narrative, he lays out the terrain with characteristic convolution: "One of my own guiding principles in intelligence work when I was Director of Central Intelligence was to use every human means to preserve the secrecy and security of those activities, but only those where this was essential, and not to make a mystery of what is a matter of common knowledge or obvious to friend and foe alike." He rails against what he calls "futile secrecy." He claims Eisenhower couldn't even find the CIA director's office. He mocks the pretentious "Government Printing Office" sign that labeled the E Street headquarters, when tour bus guides would park outside and "harangue the occupants of the bus with information to the effect that behind the barbed wire they saw was the most secret, the most concealed place in Washington." As Dulles notes, every cab driver knew the location. "As soon as I put up a proper sign at the door, the glamour and mystery disappeared. We were no longer either sinister or mysterious to visitors to the Capital; we became just another government office." The CIA, in this view, is the most normal of entities, engaged in the plain bureaucratic work promised by its charter. But on the very next page, Dulles writes, again contradictorily, "Americans are inclined to talk too much about matters which should be classified."[40]

Dulles never resolves these paradoxes. At best, he leaves the impression that the downside of excessive secrecy is silliness, or an administrative dissipation of effort for an endeavor thriving on efficiency. Unspoken is the implicit flipside, that the truly covert, one to "maintain the security of operations where secrecy is essential," comes with a tactic of strategic openness. Strategic openness is the theme and point of *The Craft of Intelligence*, but the fullest expression of this idea—that openness has a vital, dialectical relationship to secrecy—appears in the headquarters itself, finished and overseen by Dulles two years earlier.

The first level at which strategic openness operates is relatively transparent. One major problem with the Tempos had been that their clandestine purpose allowed enemy agents to watch people coming and going, marking down license plates. As far back as the 1948 Dulles-Jackson-Correa report that critiqued the early CIA, Dulles suggested the benefits instead of "a building having so many services and visitors that the identification of a secret staff and their visitors would be rendered difficult. Further, the staff could more easily cover the explanation of its work by giving a well-known and relatively innocuous address." So many cars going in and out would inhibit specific identifications. This was certainly Dulles's approach in other areas, such as his appearances before committees. Social by nature, instead of being reticent or protective before Congress, Dulles was known for inundating representatives with information, with his glamorous "*tour d'horizon* that tended to blur agency activity and foreign policy," where "members would ask few questions which dealt with internal agency matters or with specific operations." Dulles took a similar approach with Eisenhower, preferring "to present vast amounts of raw intelligence material" that "was usually contradictory, and always terribly bulky." "The President simply did not have the time to read it and evaluate it," according to one historian, providing Dulles with discretion "while he directed his agents in their paramilitary activities." In each of these examples, the stream of openness about secrecy, ironically, sweeps the secret into its flow and dilutes it into invisibility. Within the flow of information, it also created rare autonomy for CIA. The publicity surrounding the headquarters, cast in the era's familiar tropes, should be seen as part of the same technique.[41]

But Dulles's method of establishing the covert was based on more than publicity and openness. While managing the headquarters project, Dulles kept up a busy schedule lecturing powerful groups of businessmen, think tanks, and social clubs about the place of U.S. power in the world. On the surface, the speeches track the conventional ideas of the period's foreign policy establishment. Through the fifties, one sees Dulles's dismissal of the communist world as a "no-man's-land of knowledge" shift to a more liberal stance. As American elites across the spectrum tried to answer the question of "what are we for?" on the world stage, vying for the hearts and minds of Third World observers who took a dim view of U.S. racism and its closeness to European colonial powers, Dulles, like many, argued that the American Revolution and the Declaration of Independence bestowed upon the United States a natural leadership role among all revolutionary, freedom-loving peoples, who deserved respect for their own "valid claims and aspirations."[42]

In this regard, he was in sync with what Christina Klein calls the period's "global imaginary of integration," which cast the United States and the Third World as natural bedfellows in the cultural sphere in order to ease the argument for observers in the "new nations" for a globe integrated by a reoriented world system, anchored to U.S. political, military, and global market power and banded by strategic pacts.[43] But the extraordinary thing about Dulles's speeches is the way he adopts this rhetoric, despite the fact that his own CIA was the gray space that mediated between the United States as liberal beacon and the United States as violent imperial power on the ground. Dulles frequently marshals results achieved by his own CIA officers with his direct participation and support as accomplishments for the Free World chosen and put into effect by its oppressed peoples.

"More than a quarter of a million in these recent days have opted to leave Ho Chi Minh's Communist paradise in northern Viet Nam . . ." Dulles told the Herald Tribune Forum in October 1954. But those people had left only after a relentless propaganda campaign by CIA agents reporting to Colonel Edward G. Lansdale, Dulles's personal representative in Vietnam. "There have been successes in Iran and in Guatemala, for example, but over the last decade more people have been lost to freedom than have regained it," Dulles said. The "successes" in Iran and Guatemala were CIA coups Dulles had overseen and planned. Less than a year after he approved and unleashed a coup attempt against Sukarno in Indonesia, Dulles triumphantly informed DC's Women's Forum on National Security that "the doctrines of Jefferson are household words with Asiatic revolutionary leaders such as Sukarno of Indonesia." Days after he returned from a classified "consultation" with Ramón Magsaysay, the chief of state Lansdale had installed in the Philippines after a U.S.-directed counterinsurgency campaign, Dulles lauded Magsaysay to the Carabao, a military camaraderie association formed in 1900 during the U.S. colonization of the Philippines that lasted for nearly half a century, as "a real democratic leader in that fine, up-and-coming nation." He trumpeted the jailing and scattering of nationalist Huk rebels, the dedicated result of his own orders, as having occurred "not by any actions of ours but through the determination of the Filipinos' own very young government."[44]

Publicizing CIA actions by relabeling them as autonomous events abroad simultaneously reclassified them and dared audiences to think differently. In a sense, this was propaganda directed against U.S. citizens. But since Dulles's audiences, packed with federal retirees and personal friends, would have boasted wide knowledge of CIA involvement in these events, the lies are better read as Dulles's open secrets, a kind of ritual performance of group unity. Dulles would advertise these events as one truth, while by their very mention drawing back the curtain on the secret history, affirming the intrapersonal solidarity of those in the know. The open secret, itself a form of covert action, could thus encompass fraternity and thrill, the thrill and the pleasure of fleeting revelation blunting any ethical call of the events. Out in the open, with the *facts* of an action kept at arm's length, laundered or erased, the *results* of a secret event could become something new. The monument of the endpoint could blur the means of its achievement. The Langley complex concretized this set of ideas.

If Dulles had believed in a *mere* efficient openness, the CIA could have remained tucked into the web of governmental activities around Foggy Bottom or flung open its doors to the Mall, to the human trace of democracy congregating in front of the Lincoln Memorial that symbolized it. A *mere* secrecy, on the other hand, as colleagues like OSS veteran Frank Wisner defended, with agents "lurking in scrubby old hideouts, with peeling plaster and toilets stopped up," on what they considered a British model, would have limited the agency and drawn shackling suspicion.[45] Dulles's innovation in his seemingly paradoxical celebrations and disavowals of both secrecy and openness was to erase the line: to hide things in plain sight. He knocked the covert off its binary secret/not-secret axis and reconfigured the CIA (much like U.S. empire itself) as America's open secret.

The Langley complex's security thus depended both on the site's own secure features and the openness of its surroundings as well, transforming that very openness into a kind of security. Langley bonded overt and covert CIA employees into one site, but by no means were there "so many services" there that would forbid identifying employees, particularly when the building opened. Visitors were highly regulated. But on the barren farm roads of 1960s McLean, enemy agents themselves couldn't have remained secret. Any stray car was obvious. At the same time, the four entrances to the complex did make it difficult to track individuals across entries and exits, again dissembling the complex's apparent openness to its surroundings.[46]

The move to Langley was thus itself a kind of paradox, in that it necessitated a series of extreme withdrawals: from the city, from proximity to the State Department, from the grid of accessible roads, and, once at Langley, from the main road. Even inside the complex, the agency continued to withdraw, from its own vast parking lots and into the corridors of the structure itself. In this vision of inaccessibility and withdrawal, within a seemingly more easily identifiable consolidation in form at Langley, Dulles geographically and publicly placed the CIA for decades, while inventing a tiered secrecy, a proliferation of secrets and openness, the open secret of the covert capital's signature suburban institution.[47]

The document that translated this idea into bricks and mortar was the Clarke and Rapuano report, written by Gilmore Clarke at Dulles's request with information from CIA staff. It offered the first and only detailed public account of how the CIA imagined secrecy as a design feature. Essentially, the Langley complex was to model the organizational secrecy of the CIA in stone, encapsulated by the guiding practice of "Compartmentation," which defined the CIA's core structure. As one officer explained, "compartmentation is the process of strictly limiting the number of people who are aware of a given intelligence operation. . . . Only personnel with an absolute 'need to know' should be admitted into the compartment. Simply having the requisite clearances is not enough." By the time the Langley project was launched, the CIA's clandestine service had become, according to a history, "a highly compartmented structure in which information was limited to small groups of individuals," particularly for "highly sensitive political action and paramilitary operations" but even in "routine practice." But the point of compartmentation was not rigidity. It was, according to a former high-ranking CIA official, "flexibility." It allowed the agency to retarget its agendas, expand, and contract its work abroad on the immediate call of the director, his staff, or field agents, unhampered by the restrictions of group, public, or congressional knowledge.

Architecturally, Langley's compartments would operate on a continuum with design features that promoted strategic coordination and flow. The landscape architects incorporated this idea into their report: "Elaborate com-

CIA headquarters at Langley, as seen from Dolley Madison Boulevard. The trees were a crucial part of the program, making the building invisible from the road. "Not one tree will be cut down that possibly can be spared," Allen Dulles said. The design of the road itself made it extremely difficult to stop a car anywhere near the CIA's entrance. Photo by author.

partmentation is necessary both for functions and for individuals to a degree far greater than in any other activity, public or private, and yet this compartmentation must not interfere with the free and rapid flow of information to those who have a need for it." Documents could never be unattended and required escort in transit as they moved through corridors joining together officers working on the relevant compartmented project. "Unusual amounts of vault and safe space," meanwhile, locked secrets literally into the walls and foundation of the building. The building needed secrecy vis-à-vis the outside, but also in the relationships between and within its parts, which at the same time, often had to be connected. Originally the agency considered an "invisible" or windowless building, perhaps buried underground. Langley's 140-acre site was the next best thing. Its borders were not only secure but, thanks to geography, rather invisible themselves—the "wooded banks of the Potomac" and National Park Service forest to the north and east, Turkey Run river to the west, and private lands to the south. Sunk within 582 acres of federally owned Bureau of Public Roads property, it enjoyed "a tight screen of security" forever after. This was a major reason Dulles always preferred

Langley and its "isolation, topography and heavy forestation." As he told Congress: "I want security. I want this building to be away from the road. . . . I get a measure of security and protection by being on the Potomac River here. I want to guard this area pretty carefully."[48]

Langley's native forestland and trees were thus a critical part of the program. In the early days of the acquisition, Dulles and his wife, Clover, strolled across the hillsides on weekends choosing which old trees would remain. Dulles spoke about the secretive function of the trees in public, stressing that "not one tree will be cut down that possibly can be spared. . . . In the summer you won't be able to see the building from the road."[49] But the secrecy these trees provided would not position the complex in a mere inside-out relationship with the surrounding world but be only one feature in its internal, layered secrecy, according to the dictates of compartmentation. "Physical security of the entire site and of each component within the site must provide assurance against unauthorized entry," Clarke wrote. Yet the headquarters couldn't be a bunker. The architects were to shape the picturesque slopes and hills of Langley into "a dignified setting high above the Potomac," in keeping with Dulles's concerns about "openness" and its uses.[50] The challenge for the makers of Langley was to create a physical headquarters both monumental and secret at a variety of scales, appealing to the CIA's full range of functional contradictions. Most observers agree that Dulles micromanaged the project, but, arguably, he maintained control for this reason: he wanted Langley to serve the CIA in its broadest range of actions and functions, ones only half-spoken and always incompletely known, and not meant to be known, in their totality by anyone, perhaps even him.

The open secret of Langley bore a similarly complex relationship to the nearby village of McLean. From the building's opening, pilots flying into National Airport used the CIA as beacon and checkpoint. Signs identified it, until Robert Kennedy, who lived nearby after he took ownership of his brother's house at Hickory Hill, forced their removal. Later, the signs returned. Yet those in the surrounding suburbs agreed to deny the complex's existence at the same time, allowing the tree cover to erase its ramifications for the local landscape and the world at large.[51]

This agreement was visible from the beginning of the complex's life, most starkly in one document: the McLean Central Development Plan, prepared by Fairfax County planners in 1963. Planners drafted the report just after the CIA opened its doors, as it filled with 11,000 employees whose only nearby shopping was in McLean. The planners' task was to "report on the economic future of the McLean commercial district," based on its population, use, landscape, and industries. Yet while they found space to acknowledge twelve different gas stations in McLean, they didn't even mention the mammoth CIA. As on maps at the time, the CIA "appeared" in the report as a great void, a known absence contributing to the supposedly pastoral nature of the area. The "dignified" 2.3 million-square-foot building merged into the topography and vanished: "To the north, the Potomac River is bordered by the George Washington Memorial Parkway. Not only is this federally owned land, safe from development, but also the steep terrain, wooded areas, and scenic river lend a truly suburban character to the community."[52]

It wasn't safe from development. It was the most developed parcel in the suburb. But of course, Fairfax County planners and businessmen knew that. The Chamber of Commerce had been the CIA's major advocate before the local Board of Supervisors in securing the agency's place in the county. Dulles repaid them by visiting a well-attended chamber dinner in 1957, where he explained the need for the consolidated headquarters and offered an early account of the global vision the CIA would install in the local landscape—where "any one of a number of possible missteps anywhere in the world could mean sudden and overwhelming disaster." The chamber's executive director expressed its immediate interest in the CIA's arrival slightly differently, noting that "the payroll is exceptionally high."[53]

Local elites also appreciated that the CIA, as an elite institution with a "quiet" business and well-heeled staff, could take over a large river site once slated to become a national park. It would now, as Dulles asserted, "help in preserving [the] character of the community," essentially providing CIA cover for the exclusionary large-lot zoning that made Langley such a desirable security location in the first place. Yet, after an initial burst of interest from a bank, a confectioner, a bookstore, and retail stores who lobbied for concessionary space in the building that was then denied, when it came time to publicly plan for the county's space and life, the CIA headquarters again went invisible, as Dulles had always promised, once explaining, "You'll hardly know it is there."[54]

THE MAKERS OF LANGLEY

This dialectic of secrecy and openness also informed Dulles's choice of architects for the complex. Wallace K. Harrison had led the international team that designed the United Nations buildings, which redefined the cityscape of New York after World War II. His firm, Harrison and Abramovitz, was one of two outfits "that dominated architectural practice after World War II." The second was Skidmore, Owings and Merrill (SOM); Eero Saarinen was perhaps a close third. For the public image the CIA wanted to craft, Harrison and Abramovitz was the perfect choice, as the firm had been working in those years to reform and adjust a softer, more expressionistic modernism to appeal to American businessmen, while still crafting fresh iconographic symbols that preserved a sense of its functional clarity and dynamic forms. The firm's style fell in line with the agency's stated desires for security, efficiency, and making a memorable visual statement to official Washington.[55]

For the architects, the CIA project also had serious appeal. Another child of the 1947 National Security Act, the Air Force, had also made plans for a new home for its academy in Colorado Springs the year before. "There were hardly any examples of major built work for government bodies or public institutions in America at the time the Academy competition was announced," explains architectural historian Robert Bruegmann.[56] The CIA was the next project in the pipeline for modernist architects and, in a sense, one with even greater prestige since it was closer to the federal seat and monumental Washington and meant to house the agency most involved in vital, secret work close to the president, an agency led by the brother of the secretary of state.

Furthermore, the CIA headquarters would be a prime early entry into a "brand new typology" of mid-century architecture—the suburban corporate campus or "estate," which garnered significant attention in these years. By 1955, Saarinen and SOM had completed buildings that were inventing the modernist campus for the corporations who were these architects' key clients—Saarinen at the General Motors Technical Center outside Detroit, SOM at the Connecticut General Life Insurance Company outside Hartford. Harrison, known for his metropolitan skyscrapers, had not yet built a campus. The Langley headquarters was his first—and now completely overlooked by historians—contribution to the canon of that mid-century form that was just taking root.[57]

But the overt choice of Harrison for Langley also had a secret side. As with any major federal building, a larger government entity, the Public Buildings Service, had to compile a long list of possible architects for the project. Allen Dulles handpicked Harrison and Abramovitz from the list of fifty-seven firms in August 1955. But why a man named Frederic Rhinelander King rose to the position of associate architect is unclear, not explained or even noted by the CIA's detailed, mostly declassified history.[58]

Characteristically absent from the record are King's ties to intelligence work. Dulles met King in Europe just after World War I. The genteel New Yorker was an army lieutenant serving as a U.S. intelligence agent in Czechoslovakia, reporting on its internal affairs during the Versailles Conference. He filed reports directly to the young Dulles, then an intelligence officer for the State Department, who sat on the Versailles committee redrawing Czech borders. After the war, the pair cemented a friendship. Both were devout members of New York's Council on Foreign Relations (CFR), the gentlemen's club of cigar-smoking, port-drinking bankers, lawyers, academics, and architects, whose research and government sway began as a liberal internationalism in an isolationist era and grew through the forties into an anticommunist center of secretive, moneyed influence. Dulles and King frequently socialized (Dulles called him "Freddie"), and as they stood at the threshold of the CIA project, Dulles wrote to King warmly, "I am delighted that we are going to be working together again."[59]

King, a colleague of Harrison's from when they worked at the architectural firm of McKim, Mead, and White, brought the idea for the CIA building to Harrison in the first place, according to Victoria Newhouse, Harrison's biographer. Although Harrison and Abramovitz led the design, it stands to reason that the commission began with King. The council bond was strong, and if King had not been there from the start, it is hard to imagine why a studied but traditional architect—most noted for the First National Bank in Greenwich, Connecticut, a chapel at Smith College, mansions on Long Island, and a renovation of the CFR headquarters itself—would be involved at all. Harrison and King had become close after the war, so it makes sense that King would go to Harrison and Abramovitz when searching for a big firm to take the reins. But Dulles knew Harrison as well. Their summer houses practically neighbored each other on Long Island. When Dulles rented office space for early American intelligence with its founder, William Donovan, he did it in the Rockefeller Center towers on Fifth Avenue that Harrison designed and where Harrison's office was then based.[60]

Thus, not only had Dulles inhabited a Harrison office building, but Harrison had already designed a building used extensively for covert intelligence (the UN headquarters would be a second). Former CIA officers link the intelligence presence at Rockefeller Center after the war to Nelson Rockefeller's use of his chairmanship of the State Department's Office of the

Coordinator of Inter-American Affairs during World War II to run "a vast intelligence-gathering network for Latin America" that "controlled intelligence units in Latin America from offices in the center," with FBI backing. That Harrison himself had directed that office's cultural department—charged with undercutting German and Italian activities, using what one scholar calls the first U.S. money booked for a propaganda program—raises further questions about Harrison's relationship to intelligence work in these years. But at the very least, he knew Dulles, and Dulles paid close attention to Harrison's work in Latin America, praising the architect's "original and inventive mind" and calling him a "life-long friend."[61]

Even if Dulles didn't first approach Harrison, he felt more than comfortable with the choice, explaining to the General Services Administration: "I have personally known Mr. Wallace K. Harrison for many years and believe that he, as well as his partner, are particularly qualified to deal with certain of the specialized problems involved in a building for CIA." The reference to Max Abramovitz referred to his career as, in the words of one scholar, a veritable "denizen of the military-industrial complex." As a lieutenant colonel in the Army and full colonel in the Air Force, Abramovitz built airfields in southern China used for the bombing of Japan, redesigned the Air Force's internal construction bureaucracy, and worked in a Pentagon office to design buildings to "resist" the H-bomb blast. "I enjoyed this new experience because I was learning something that nobody else of the public could know," he mused later, expressing the covert, and its moral blinders, as a motive force. For the job, the architects received $1,975,150.[62]

This was one level on which Dulles's reliance on social foundations for politics blended with security at the CIA complex. Social intimacies provided a framework for security. Familiarity limited unpredictable outcomes. Ironically, Public Buildings Service commissioner Peter Strobel's financial ties to architects on the list for the CIA headquarters sparked a scandal in 1955 that led to his resignation. Dulles had just as immediate personal ties to the architects commissioned, pointing to the degree to which the cloud of emergency hovering around the CIA's work exempted Dulles from the procedural expectations of the overt capital. But intimacy for Dulles had a strategic function, the ingraining of "particular qualifications."[63]

For the modernists and their romance with mid-century American power, Langley fell within a broader series of projects where architects experimented with and developed a grammar that could speak for not just the American corporation but the expansionist postwar American state. The sleek, transparent dynamism, progress, and abundance seen as adhering to modern architecture outfitted U.S. authority with a scenic rhetorical argument for its claims to the future. But it also adapted its form to the functional necessities of U.S. imperial rule at home and abroad and was shaped by men like Harrison and Abramovitz, who themselves emerged from the social and professional circles of intelligence and military work.[64]

Critics interested in the New York modernist architect tend to study Harrison's superblocks that transformed Manhattan—Rockefeller Center, the United Nations, Lincoln Center. Right before the Langley job, Harrison and Abramovitz designed two buildings more like the CIA: the U.S. embassies in Rio and Havana for the State Department's Office of Foreign Buildings Operations. The buildings bore many formal similarities to Langley, but most importantly, the Havana embassy was perhaps the firm's first attempt to model secrecy in one of its buildings, through its design solutions for what historian Jane Loeffler calls "the functional division of the embassy." Consular offices, visa desks, and public information outlets occupied a one-story building facing the street; a difficult-to-access tower held "diplomatic offices and others that required security." These "others that required security" included the offices of CIA officers with embassy cover who Loeffler and practically every historian of the agency say "swelled many embassy staffs at the time." The secrecy that the architectural firm promoted in these target cities of the CIA informed the home-front designs they drafted for CIA three years later.[65]

This masking function accomplished by the divorce of symbolic surface and private interior in modern architecture after the war can be seen as one crucial purpose for the separation. As American architects allied themselves with state and corporate patrons intent on dominating nationalist independence movements and economies in the Third World, modern architecture came to articulate the sequences of shapes, facades, and interiors that made transposable U.S. authority between domestic and foreign spheres, turning them, in a sense, into one continuous landscape, where American power could be exerted, received, and disguised. Architects provided the cover and the setting for American agents across national borders, sequencing identical spaces for new forms of U.S. corporate and state power that needed to be expressed yet linked non-contiguously. At the very least, thanks to the architects, U.S. agents could travel hundreds of miles and still work in familiar rooms, ones meant to remind them of their home and home office, as well as their greater sense of American progress and mission.

Understandably, Harrison and Abramovitz found the covert contradictions of Dulles's project rather daunting. The CIA posted officers in the firm's New York offices to "safeguard the Agency material," and every scrap of working drawings, models, and papers had to be returned to the agency after completion. Even the most basic uses planned for building sections were difficult to come by, as Harrison was only given vague details, organizational charts, and a "coded Space Directive." But soon, five or six architects gained top-secret clearance, and began to design, in some concert with King. Their earliest efforts show a seven-story building, generally rectangular. As with the Havana and Rio embassies, the architects clustered the CIA's more public activities—map division, cafeteria, shops, printing room, training, security office, medical center, and library—on the lower three floors in relatively open, large spaces. As the building rose, the large adaptable spaces narrowed, divided, and specialized, turning the structure into an apparatus to hold corridors. The corridors were the architects' physical response to the covert requirements. "The new building will consist of block-type wings," the CIA told Congress, "readily compartmented from one another, so that specially restricted areas can be established and special security controls maintained in each section."[66]

The tension between these block-type wings and the need for monumentality guided the design. One 1956 model was based on the "campus" plan. Lower buildings, expressing the architects' vision of a corporate campus, climbed along the topography, carrying the structure into the natural environment. While each building interconnected with at least two others, allowing different compartmented pathways within the complex, the design followed its suburban corporate cousins too closely. The campus plan, with its dynamic, devolved authority, relaxed efficiency, and functional transparency, countered the Langley complex's simultaneous need for the monumental and did not take into account the fact that the CIA did not really want its functions to be transparent. More expensive, the campus also repeated the problem with the Tempos—accessibility at ground level.[67]

By early 1958, the architects changed the design. Sited on nine acres overlooking the Potomac, the modular components gathered back into a "large compact" eight-story structure in white reinforced concrete with 1.4 million square feet of usable space. While the long horizontal front and textured fenestration blended the mass into the wooded landscape, the repetitive serial windows in precast concrete frames echoed the architecture of monumental Washington. Monumentality also returned at the first two

Photographs of Langley emphasized the efficiency and expressionism in Harrison and Abramovitz's design. The long facade with repetitive windows spoke for efficiency. The "Bubble" auditorium to the left of the entrance and the bird-like cafeteria in back (one "wing" just visible here behind the complex) suggested dynamism. The squat towers rising from the base met the CIA's covert requirements. Avery Architectural and Fine Arts Library, Columbia University.

floors, now a wide oblong pedestal base with curved walls and an undulating, amoeba-shaped roofline, which softened the massive geometries. Glass walls and balconies at setbacks in the third and top floors opened views of the landscape. The architects extended sculptural touches to two structures away from the main body—the white-tiled globe of the auditorium to the left of the entrance known as "the Bubble" (a junior cousin to Harrison's Perisphere from the 1939 World's Fair) and the white, bird-in-flight cafeteria in back with its triple-arched, wing-like roof. These three features—the long facade with its uplifting portico, the globe auditorium, and the swooping cafeteria—were Langley's seductive and expressionistic first impression, visible from its access road and in many photographs of the complex.[68] But the modular components now stacked on top of the oblong base to form a long rectangular facade with two T-shaped legs, in keeping with the pressure toward compartmentation, resegregated the ensemble into five discrete six-story towers. The squat towers, each maintaining an individual presence, reprised the architectural "cutouts" the agency had wanted from the beginning and stressed the functional relationships and discrepancies between the complex's surface and interior.

This tension between surface and interior goes to the heart of modernist questions over form and function, and the pathways modern architecture took in the United States. Architectural theorist Reinhold Martin's *The Organizational Complex* provides a provocative account. Purist, form-follows-function European modernism translated into the corporate architecture of the United States in this period. Two design features catalyzed the shift. Both found their full expression in the hands of Wallace Harrison. The first was the development of flexible, pre-built adaptable office space—and the revelation of rentable, air-conditioned, electronically lit "deep space" thanks to technological innovation. This came into being in Rockefeller Center in the thirties. The second was the curtain wall, which freed the wall from its roof-supporting function. The first full-height curtain wall on a major postwar office building appeared at the United Nations in 1950.

These weren't neutral developments. By hollowing out internal space and turning architectural practice toward the manipulation of the skin of institutional buildings, and then marketing raw internal space and its switchability back to people as "choice," "the organizational complex" welded individuals into the mass "system" of postwar society through their very individuality. People joined the system through personal expression. They acted out their national belonging, sense of community and everyday work and life in ever more mass-produced, modular, blank, and mutable office buildings and the decorated boxes of suburban homes like those of Northern Virginia. These places were meant to represent their freedom but, for many observers, they were places that structurally least lent themselves toward free will or individuality, always connecting individuals back to the large corporate and economic forces that were organizing postwar American society.[69]

The dialectical relationship between choice and system that Martin describes—the movement "from system, to freedom, and back" as Abramovitz himself put it—was an important part of how the CIA processed individuals into agents of empire in Northern Virginia's suburbs.[70] The headquarters' organic, expressive surfaces symbolized its absorptive capacities, ushering people into the building. Extending the idea of a curtain wall by recreating it in the form of the mutable tree line—the complex's most visible "wall"—Langley created and erased itself, defined its presence by its absence. The interior withdrew even further. A capitol for the covert capital that was also a headquarters, it was the architecture of plausible deniability writ large. Yet as Harrison and Abramovitz's hidden entry into the canon of corporate campuses, Langley also opens up effects of that form crucial to understanding the CIA's role in the organizational complex of American power at mid-century.

The corporate campus in an isolated suburban location signed up workers in new ways. Like its contemporaries, Langley stepped into the trees, stood at the end of a landscaped drive, and shuffled its parking behind and to the side of the building. It "warmed up" modernism with curves. It explored reinforced concrete for dramatic sculptural tendencies toward the monumental, representing its authority to the world and its own employees. Langley also "laterally integrated" the CIA's dispersed operations through space. It was the reparative and restorative home office for the CIA's global chain, and it was, like the Connecticut General campus, the image of protective security itself, which observers had come to associate with the "long free span" of a spacious building swaddled in a green landscape. It made the CIA seem like a kind of geopolitical insurance company. At the same time, like those corporations, the CIA at Langley conceived of its organization through a softer, integrative, and familial language of home, drawing in the exaggerated domesticity of its surrounding suburb as an organizational feature of the agency and means of fostering attachment.[71]

The Langley complex did all these things not merely because it was built in a style applicable across businesses, institutions, and contexts in the 1950s but for two more important reasons. Adopting the common stylistic vocabulary and cultural forms of the period made the CIA appear to be *like* every other business and institution, which is exactly what Allen Dulles had always wanted, an optimum cover. Even more importantly, Langley so adeptly summarizes broader features of the organizational or military-industrial complex's corporate estate because the CIA was a crucial switching point between the civilian and corporate world and the government and military world, institutionally making the connections that were defining the conjunctions of American power in the period. It was the agency of U.S. imperialism whose work entailed the "human relations" and "applied knowledge" that were catchphrases across such a broad array of fields. It is no accident that one of the most concise phrases summarizing the CIA's philosophy of its work comes not in an Allen Dulles speech but from William Whyte, describing a General Electric training program in his book *The Organization Man*: "They see the manipulative skills as something that in the long run will make other people *happy*."[72]

Modernist geometric blocks expressing compartmented, flexible functions in suburban locales were not only useful for bureaucratic management, information flow, and the display of executive hierarchy. Whether it was Harrison and Abramovitz at Langley, Rio, and Havana; SOM at Oak Ridge and the Air Force Academy; or Saarinen at his embassies and Dulles International Airport, the work of the three big modernists at mid-century as they skipped back and forth between projects for large corporations, educational institutions, and the U.S. government cemented the visual, spatial conjunctions between corporate and government power. They provided the setting and formal structure for the militarizing of corporate and campus research as well as the civilianizing of war making and its extension into everyday life—a major CIA function.

These themes coalesced in Dulles's efficiency arguments about the need for the headquarters. Dulles's appeal to Congress for getting more with less was rooted in the need for efficiency: using the modernist headquarters and its controlled site innovations to produce better analysis more quickly for less money, coating the complex in a civilian, quasi-corporate veneer of expertise. As Dulles explained to local businessmen, "No bank would be likely to house each of its departments and some of its money in each of several separate buildings with separate guards for each. The maintenance problem alone would be enough to horrify a good businessman."[73] But efficiency, like security, was multivalent. The CIA complex worked on the line between two cultural fantasies of efficiency united in the CIA after 1947—efficiency as bureaucratic management and the orderly processing of information and efficiency as obtaining *results*, sometimes deadly, in direct and silent fashion, without the intervention or unwieldiness of democratic debate or the conventional armies that commonly had to answer to democracy.

Scholars in the insular discipline of intelligence history cast the tension between the elephantine bureaucracy of the home office and the lithe, renegade independence of the field agent as the pivot in understanding the CIA. The scholarship is divided up between administrative histories on one side and coup autopsies on the other. But the key to the CIA as an instrument of global U.S. power is in comprehending how Dulles fused images of the CIA as both a secure, efficient arm of the conventional civil service and as an organization that could exert unconventional forms of power and fill in gaps between public moral rhetoric and the covert demands of U.S. power abroad. Langley institutionalized the CIA within the federal government but with its different faces playing to different audiences. The duality was not a paradox. Powerful U.S. political figures wanted and needed both agencies.

Efficiency summarized them both. Dulles told Congress:

> When this agency was organized, I think we had a little different outlook as to what was happening in the world. Since that time we have been assigned to other functions.... I am convinced we can increase our own efficiency and our ability to meet the needs of this country 10 or 20 percent if we have adequate facilities in the form of a building so that we can be together, and I can give the proper direction to an enterprise that is not easy to run, but which I can assure you is improving in efficiency year by year.

The "other functions" were the CIA's covert action activities, a direct reference to the innocuous phrase "such other functions and duties" in its charter, which soon gave the agency its paramilitary mandate. But Dulles's wish for his agency to "be together" was just as important—a central task of the CIA complex. It wasn't just an office. It was a home.[74]

As a home, it defined intimacy and solidarity, conscripted emotional allegiance, and organized its own domestic labor. Dulles stressed these features at the ceremony where Eisenhower laid the building's cornerstone on November 3, 1959. The cornerstone laying debuted the newly institutionalized CIA to an audience of powerful observers and the CIA's own officers. Elaborate, "time-consuming and tedious" planning went into the event. Agency elites saw it as an opportunity. Executive Director Lyman Kirkpatrick advised Dulles to assert in his welcoming speech that the building symbolized "that Intelligence has achieved a permanent role in the United States Government." The guest list affirmed the event as a family affair, attended by Wallace Harrison's wife, Ellen, Frederic King, and Eleanor Dulles. Invitations went to the families of Eisenhower intimates and security state developers Charles Hook Tompkins and Edwin Lee Jones, whose construction companies built the CIA. Also in attendance were General Lyman Lemnitzer and his wife, Katherine, Guatemala coup planner William Pawley, and Edward Lansdale, now back from Vietnam and devising counterinsurgency programs from a Pentagon office.

The gathering emphasized the way Langley could serve as a space for domestic reception and reunion. It affirmed at home, to "Ruffles and Flourishes" and "Hail to the Chief," actions conducted by these men abroad without

In November 1959, the CIA held its cornerstone-laying ceremony. President Eisenhower and Allen Dulles climbed the bandstand to debut the newly institutionalized agency to a powerful audience and to the CIA's own officers. The laborers who dug the building's foundation, mostly African Americans with a few white workers, stood on a hill and watched. Princeton University Library.

anthems. Packages and audiotapes recounting the event's details were "sent to each overseas station and base" to intentionally link the two spheres. Top brass arrived from the Defense Department, the National Security Agency, the FBI, the State Department, the National Security Council, the Atomic Energy Commission, and the United States Information Agency, as though to formally welcome the CIA into the wider family of U.S. governance. Five thousand guests arrived by bus from DC.[75]

The crew of laborers that dug and poured the foundation and raised parts of the first two floors, mostly African Americans with a few white workers, stood in rough clothes and hats on a hill of dirt outside the perimeter of the event and watched the formal proceedings of suits, overcoats, and military regalia on the bandstand. In an indication of the consistent strategizing of gender that went along with its new home, the agency ordered some women employees, at Dulles's behest, to occupy prominent seats by the bandstand "to highlight the vital role which women play in the Agency." At the same time, the CIA deployed "some of the Agency's most attractive young ladies" to usher important guests and leaven the event with a flirtatious air.[76]

After an invocation by the U.S. Senate chaplain, whose length, one agent joked, "far exceeded any staff study CIA had ever prepared," Dulles spoke. He called the headquarters "a home." But this was a particular kind of home, which would have the capacity to draw toward it accurate "information from the four corners of the earth" based on the knowledge that "our vital interests are at stake in places as distant as Korea, and Laos, in Central Africa and in the islands of the Pacific as well as in this Hemisphere and in Europe." This imagined geography of an imperial globalism situated the headquarters as local domestic space and simultaneously as an open cipher, where a set of spatial relations stretching far beyond it could enter the domestic sphere. But, like any domestic space, the building would only be animated by the CIA's people, who took over when mere structure and law were not enough. "Laws can create agencies of government; they cannot make them function," Dulles explained. To him, the line testified to his staff's dedication. It doubled as a trace of the extrajudicial interpretive space outside the law in which the CIA often labored.

Eisenhower took the microphone after Dulles. He lauded the "beautiful and useful structure" that would rise from and "endure" on the site. Then, ceremonially claiming the spot, Eisenhower and Dulles spread mortar on the cornerstone box, and it was lowered into the ground. The event was pure pageantry. For one, the cornerstone laying did not even take place. The mortar was "damp sand and sugar." The cornerstone was removed after the ceremony and locked away. But Dulles used the event on the newly cleared plain, occupied by the beginnings of a stately complex that still called for the hard, hands-on work of building, to instill a message in the audience through the drama of raising collective shelter. The event and its speeches conveyed a feeling of the perilous global tension between stability and flux. The "new edifice to house, to concentrate and coordinate" the CIA's work would stand as an exception on a planet "where change is the rule." Dulles painted a picture of a fragile yet vital world that demanded intervention and the CIA's expertise—as both a secure, comforting, efficient, permanent civil service branch and a dynamic, risk-taking, molder of events—at intervening in that world. The idea of the CIA having a home to build and defend attached the sentiment of domesticity to the civilian agency charged with fighting the country's secret wars.[77]

The program, which Harrison kept, narrated Dulles's vision of the head-quarters' monumental functions. A wistful painting showed rough grounds behind the complex blending into the plashing, distant Potomac and a gleaming flat horizon line. The overt capital was nowhere in sight. Trees in full flower not only erased evidence of the hectic construction process and graded land; they also framed a complex alone in a robust green silence opposite the river from the city, a watchful bulwark on its defensive perimeter facing its challenges alone. The rendering seemed to hitch an invisible Washington's future to the covert agency. But while the exterior had the sweep and symbolic ability to take up such space, the hard work of making a functional home for the CIA's geopolitical labor still lay ahead. This was accomplished by the building's interiors, where the CIA took over the design with its "own draftsmen and personnel with other skills."[78]

Dulles took an active role in the interiors, ordering around contractors and movers, and, "fearing communist penetration," banning union laborers while internal communications were being installed.[79] The lobby introduced his vision—the frequency with which it appears in CIA memoirs speaks not only to its life as one of Langley's more public and overt spaces but also to its key role in guiding officers through the headquarters' carefully staged domestic sequences.

CIA staff architects such as Harbin S. Chandler, who served as a major in the army, helped create National Airport and renovated the White House for Harry Truman, designed the space, a massive gray and white Georgia marble cocoon with columns. Its entryway was decorated in what one architecture critic called the "old Federal Dignified style" with gold stars representing officers who died in the field, and the CIA's eagle seal embedded in the floor. The design and material nodded toward the CIA's life within the wider U.S. government. But agents also understood the lobby's solidity and enclosure as the place where they could experience the security originally promised by Dulles to Congress within the architecture of the building itself. "The white marble walls and columns of the gigantic foyer meant the beginnings of security, exclusivity," remembered one officer. "It reminded me that . . . while I was here I was safe from a hostile world." Another described the lobby's "stillness" as "cathedral-like, holy, mysterious." It was the building's space of felt security.[80]

Inscribed on a foyer wall, agents could see Dulles's favorite biblical quote: "And ye shall know the truth and the truth shall make you free." Some thought it in "bad taste to cloak the covert operations of the Agency behind the words of Jesus," but the quote was another crucial design feature. It instructed individuals on the interior's use, incorporating the promise of truth into the lobby and suggesting that going deeper into the complex would fulfill that promise. But because of compartmentation, truth at Langley became a constantly receding horizon in a place where truth perhaps existed but could never be completely accessed by any one agent. The quote and the lobby instilled a longing to access that truth—and the individual freedom that was its gift—while making that access individually impossible. The biblical line engendered a kind of obsession within the CIA family, the favored epigraph of books about the agency, a key emotional marker for officers arriving for the first time and leaving for the last, even the motto of a CIA front organization. Its simultaneous promise and withholding of revelation granted the CIA a crucial part of its authority and mystique with the public and its own agents. Through its daily intervention, the lobby staged an individual reason to go to work and a collective, sacral argument for that work's necessity. "It was always the last thing you saw as you headed off into the world to do the Agency's bidding," recalled one officer, "and often the last thing you remembered once you got there."[81]

An escalator served the ground and first floor. As in the early designs, more public functions clustered there—travel, medical, credit union, insurance claims, and library, including a library of spy fiction "employees were encouraged to peruse for ideas." After a checkpoint, where guards examined entrants' plastic laminated badges, four color-coded elevator banks rose onto authorized floors in the intersecting sub-rectangles seen from outside and cut out access to other floors. They opened into corridors named blandly for letters of the alphabet with varying levels of security. The corridors were arranged along the lines of the globe. The Soviet Union was on the fifth floor; Angola and China on the third; Iran, India, Afghanistan, and the Congo on the sixth; Cuba in the basement.[82]

These geographic divisions provided a critical component of the complex's flexibility, organizing it as a structure "geared to adjust to the world's endless crises." Depending on the CIA's geopolitical targets, "overnight a sleepy little desk ... becomes a bustling hub of activity for two dozen people." Spatial similarities across the corridors created a framework for the loose flexibility and swift reorientations of the CIA's charge as country projects needed to expand and contract personnel from month to month—with what the clan-

On the inside, corridors defined the CIA headquarters. Used as cutouts, they could divide the building into compartments secret from one another. They also made the interior a dreamlike meditation on sameness. Modernist paintings lent by DC's Corcoran Gallery emphasized the fungible qualities. James Reber. Avery Architectural and Fine Arts Library, Columbia University.

destine service called "optimum flexibility for moving units within the space assigned"—while providing no obvious, enduring traces in the corridors' setting as to what was occurring where and no permanent architectural obstructions to these shifts. As the CIA increased its presence in countries and began to alter their built and human spaces, its interior would be able to provide for that work functionally, while bearing no trace of its magnitude and place specificity domestically.[83]

To make this functionality possible, the interior offered a dreamlike meditation on sameness and repetition—making it, according to one agent, "extremely complicated to orient oneself on the inside." The agency commissioned photography books, with photographs taken by the officer who chose the CIA's U-2 spy plane targets, to visually emphasize the interiors' serial patterns, what one officer called their "unremitting purity." At one time, the interior was monochrome. Officers worked in small offices in bare off-white corridors with gray vinyl tile without knowing where other officers worked, at times without even knowing each other's names. Snack bars and vending machines kept them working without trips to the cafeteria for coffee. Soon after the opening, a CIA psychiatrist fought to paint the doors primary colors "for the sake of the staff's emotional stability," following a "psychology of color" for the design. The addition of modernist color-field paintings lent by DC's Corcoran Gallery also softened the interior, while further aestheticizing and emphasizing the corridors' fungible qualities with the paintings' interchangeable abstract forms.[84]

But at every turn compartmentation also tasked the identical interiors with minute systems of division and blocked access. Doors had black combination locks or keypad entries. Some bore small cryptic signs denoting functions; others were signless or marked by number—the institutional preference. Visitors only graduated through the complex with escorts, and colored badges permitted different degrees of access. Inside the rooms, alarms, safes, burn bags, and classified trash destined for churning shredders in the basement helped determine the decor. Some entire offices were "vaulted," that is, the offices themselves became the safe, locked down every night. Officers worked inside the safe.[85]

Even the exterior's most expressive elements housed interiors stressing strategic fragmentation. The cafeteria, that organic swoop on the outside, divided into a secret and open section. To enter the larger, secret side, agents flashed badges to guards; they ate with their families or visitors on the other "small, dismal" side. The globe auditorium's external connection to the main building via tunnel allowed it to be used as another cutout, a site of more public events over the years where visitors would not see members of the clandestine service and had no access to the main building while on the grounds.[86]

The office established for Dulles on the seventh floor, a legendary suite given older cultural authority with wood paneling and a mahogany desk, somewhat relieved the serial modern environment. Arrived at by a private key-operated elevator located up a small staircase at the left of the lobby, the office summarized his theories about secrecy and access. Max Abramovitz, in the many interviews he later gave on the building, suggested Dulles designed it himself. A flight of glass opened the room to the east, but only onto a view of the trees. Open doors and easy entrances belied that the multiple doors were originally designed so different visitors would not have to see one another as they entered and exited. A telephone buzzer system allowed CIA officers to reach Dulles directly without the intervention of a secretary. A small room, eventually known as the "French Room" and decorated with French Empire furniture, adjoined the office. Dulles designed it as a holding area, so he could have mutually secret visitors awaiting him in both rooms. This mirrored the arrangement of his own home on Q Street, where visitors reported waiting "in a little sitting room" while they would hear, beyond closed doors, Dulles and other men speak in a foreign language and never see the men leave.[87]

Even the flight of windows overlooking the woods had an operational purpose, impressing visitors with exclusivity and bucolic delight. Those guests included members of many foreign intelligence services whose friendships defined CIA policy abroad, including General Hendrik van den Bergh, head of South Africa's secret police; Manuel Contreras, head of Augusto Pinochet's secret police in Chile; Nematollah Nassiri, head of SAVAK, the Shah's secret police in Iran; Panamanian dictator Manuel Noriega; and Hmong general Vang Pao. The view imported the idea explored by Eleanor Dulles a decade earlier—that the isolated landscape of Northern Virginia could relax guarded guests into a nonchalance that fostered intelligence gathering and political maneuvering—into Langley itself. Marveling at the "top-floor dining room overlooking a beautiful pastoral scene in northern Virginia," one SAVAK agent recalled fondly feeling that seeing this sight "was a great privilege . . . as very few foreign citizens were allowed to enter CIA headquarters."[88]

While the Dulles suite was Langley's most personalized, outfitted with the dining room with a gold and silver table service and "a large and luxurious conference room," it cued the wider complex on how to imagine interior spaces as both operationally useful and moderately expressive of personal work, affiliation, and independence. Higher officials took offices at setbacks in the facade, the glass window walls and private balconies granting better access to the natural views, although the facade had other uses as well. In at least one case, a division leader took an office with a view through his windows into his staff's office, set in a corridor at a right angle to his own, allowing him to monitor his workers, while organizing his own workspace like a fortress, so no one could stand behind him.[89]

More importantly, the spies who occupied the complex's eight-by-twelve-foot cubicles with standardized desks and movable partitions personalized them by decorating them as microcosms of the countries they worked on penetrating. In such interiors, the complex directly connected itself to spaces abroad, its ostensibly bland cubicles acting as, in a sense, safely reenacted bits of foreign soil, reminding officers of the places absorbing them. Offices devoted to covert actions directed against specific countries and regions took on mementos, posters, flags, maps, trophies, and visual images of those places. The Soviet-Eastern Europe division was decorated with color photographs of wolves. The Iran office had a Persian rug. The Indonesia office had Indonesian masks. The Afghanistan office had the uniform of a dead Soviet soldier pierced by a bullet-hole. Topographic maps reenacted those countries in all the minutiae of their landscapes along the cubicle walls, albeit stripped of their human presence.[90]

Compartmentation thus constructed Langley as a transnational imperial space that could separate itself off from itself and its own internal continuities. It could then reconnect it with distant parts of the globe with an intimacy that outstripped connections with even the next corridor around the bend. It could do all this while transforming those global projects into the minutiae of everyday suburban work. As an Army captain recruited for the agency's covert attacks on Cuba observed, "The daily decisions of these people caused governments to be overthrown; yet, with bureaucratic anonymity, they ate their lunches out of paper bags and promptly at 5:00 PM stopped the war. The incongruity grated on my military sense of immediacy and commitment."[91]

Langley's bland interiors were frames for its estranged and violated areas elsewhere. They literally contained those places' politics and landscapes, rehearsing unequal power relationships through diminutive dioramas of interior design. The times of other places defined time at Langley, where, according to one officer, "it is always noon somewhere in the world." Into twenty-four-hour watch centers buried in the complex, the voices and languages of agents and people from those places flowed, streaming across dedicated phone lines. Intimate parts of their bodies entered the complex, the hair, fecal matter, and bodily fluids of foreign political figures studied in the CIA's labs for signs of weakness, detaching and dispossessing them from their lived reality. Officers processed inhabitants of those countries and their political futures on a massive electronic "brain" designed for the CIA by IBM. The cartography office reassembled their homes, offices, and intimate spaces on its maps, blueprints, and globes—some constructed from family photos taken by agents on their holiday trips abroad. The in-house printing plant produced new citizens of those places, issuing their passports, birth certificates, and identification documents to the CIA's own officers. Through this interior machinery, Langley ceaselessly worked to reproduce its target countries and cultures, according to its own angle of vision.[92]

The headquarters was partially completed by September 1960, the north half ready for occupancy a year later, when the first branches moved in. Immediately the clandestine service despised it. "Many senior operators objected strongly to being housed in such a public place ... " recalled one operative. Some wanted to sever ties with the agency and go underground. In their waning days skulking in their decrepit Tempos, they overflowed with nostalgia for "their very shabbiness and informality" that "gave little room for pomposity or self-promotion, fakery, or bureaucratic intrigue." The memos in Tempo hallways on blue tinted paper from Langley were dimly viewed. One prankster fabricated a fake memo, "Toilet Arrangements for the New Building," to mock the whole process: "During the transition period there will be insufficient toilet facilities.... In case of necessity, personnel are authorized to make use of the shrubbery ... to satisfy urgent personal requirements."[93]

Once the move was complete, agents prolonged their resistance to the very mass of the massive intelligence institution they themselves had created through their global field work and unlimited budgets. They rejected the conveyer belt and pneumatic tube message delivery system built into Langley's walls, seeing it as a security risk. One bought a plate of saucy spaghetti at the cafeteria and shot it through the system, triggering a nightmarish cleanup. Concluding that the belts would make it too easy to deliver bombs through the building, CIA security eventually shut the system down, and it was thereafter used mostly to store batteries.[94]

Officers also frequently turned their training as spies and infiltrators against the CIA building itself. As had the brand new air-conditioning system at Harrison's Havana embassy, the CIA's air conditioning promptly failed in the humid DC climate. Secrecy-obsessed CIA planners had refused to tell a subcontractor how many officers would inhabit the building. The subcontractor guessed wrong (it would eventually be some fifteen thousand), and the air conditioning began to fail. The subcontractor installed thermostats, but as agents constantly adjusted them, the problem grew worse. Lawrence White's office sealed the thermostats. Agents used their lock-picking skills to bust them back open. The CIA sued the subcontractor in court and lost, and the heat remained.[95]

Rejecting the instant traffic jams and forty-five-minute reverse commutes on exurban roads that made reaching the headquarters "an impossibility" without staggered work hours, some spies took to paddling across the Potomac from Georgetown and Montgomery County, Maryland, then hiking to the office through the trees. To prove the building lacked security, others climbed a nearby hill and snapped photographs of the first director to occupy Dulles's suite, John McCone, which, when blown up, clearly identified him, forcing administrators to acquire neighboring parcels of land for half a million dollars from private owners to secure the site. Clandestine officers reveled in recounting how easy it was for Soviet agents to loiter at Langley entrances, how at one point the cast of the movie *Scorpio* breached the complex by flashing American Express credit cards to somnolent guards, and how, supposedly, KGB officers could be seen dining in the open side of the cafeteria.[96]

Further galling was the fact that the DC bus stopped at a modernist concrete stop within the grounds, disgorging dowdy passengers in gray flannel suits with mundane brown paper lunch bags, summing up the new home office's opposition to the messy "reality" of the "field stations" where case officers and spies could express what they saw as a radical individuality and autonomy. Inside the complex, covert warriors flouted regulations to irritate CIA police—leaving doors ajar, squirreling bottles of cognac and gin in desks and safes, cracking open boxes of contraband Cuban cigars. Once, an employee—who needed to add a name to the book in the lobby memorializing officers who died in the field—grew tired of waiting for the key to the display box and simply broke in and stole the book to complete his work. The headquarters' similarities to a corporate office, its name recognition, and overt modernity were at odds with the anonymity, closed social networks, and unsupervised freedom abroad through which clandestine operators had come to understand their work. It also revealed the systemic national and managerial functions of their work that they preferred to keep out of sight.[97]

A significant proportion believed that, as one put it, "Maybe the agency should abandon the Langley headquarters and start all over in a *bordello* in Pittsburgh," again linking gender to the core of the agency's project and the male freedoms of the field. The failure of the complex in their eyes seemed to be summarized by the Bay of Pigs scandal itself, when in the wake of the attack's failure and Kennedy's wavering public support, elected politicians and observers cast a new public eye on the agency, briefly constricting its independence as never before. This led to Allen Dulles's abrupt dismissal and a perfunctory goodbye ceremony for him at Langley in November 1961, during which Kennedy was visibly bored. To add further insult, the end of the building occupied by the clandestine service was exposed for several months to open air as workmen completed construction. Field mice infested it—the headquarters' first "moles," or illicit spies, chewing through the telephone wires, and, as the cafeteria did not open until February 1962, brazenly eating the bagged lunches of the covert agents.[98]

But as Dulles suggested during his cornerstone speech, the building only acquired its deeper meaning through habitation. And even some critics came to express an abiding emotional attachment to it, and in doing so, affirmed Dulles's vision of its incorporative powers. They returned from the field soothed to find that "many of the same people were still around—the Headquarters cadre," and used those reunions to collect and compare operational experiences. They choked back tears at seventh floor retirement parties that recollected dispersed lives in the field and redeemed actions through the emotional solidarity of passing time and the touchstone of familiar headquarters spaces, even as the names of close friends in attendance remained classified because of their controversial work. As one officer recalled, "'Wally,' with whom I had worked in Chile, Mexico, and the Dominican Republic was there as well as 'Hector' from Guatemala days. And 'John,' who had chortled so when we heard the Communist flatulence in Mexico City."[99] They jogged Langley's trails, strolled at lunch, relaxed on benches, read and napped in the grass, and used Dulles's "campus" to reproduce and restore their energy for their work abroad—the suburban "home" nourishing them before and after their long-distance commutes.[100]

This incorporative effect was the complex's final central significance, which Dulles saw, and some in the clandestine service missed. At each point in Langley's sequence, individual and system met. CIA people encountered the lobby and its atmosphere of the sacral collective as individuals in awe. When they arrived at their desks in personalized offices and worked on projects dependent on their individual labor, they did so for the good and propagation of the system. This feature of the complex takes the CIA to the heart of the organizational impulses of American power at mid-century. It highlights the switching between wider global awareness and absorptive minute everyday labor that explains how people ethically managed the violent work of imperialism in the American suburban domestic context—Langley becoming both an "agency" without agents and a series of individual tasks that coalesced in covert action but never individually amounted to imperialism. It also further illuminates the way that the idea of the organization at mid-century, and the CIA itself, renovated the idea of the romantic individual—and sent that newly endowed and inspired individual off to serve the systemic forces of an expansionist American power to a degree not seen since the turn of the twentieth century.

This incorporative effect depended on a scale, design, and horizontal staging of the material landscape only available to the agency in this newly developing section of Northern Virginia. Some fretted that the move across the Potomac would isolate the CIA from the "corridors of power." "The physical isolation of the Agency from the policymakers it was created to serve" did occur, in the words of one historian, but produced quite the opposite effect, perhaps one unimaginable from their historical viewpoint: they created their *own* corridor of power.[101] As the CIA ratcheted up its webs and laces of control, Langley also extended the corridor with an ever-increasing need for more physical, horizontal space. The CIA was like a highway—the more space you gave it, the more it wanted. Over the next decade, the agency that secured appropriations from Congress with Allen Dulles and Lawrence White's efficiency-oriented promises that pricey bus drivers and couriers would be rendered obsolete by the consolidation of functions into one building had more buses than ever. They ferried agents to offices all across Northern Virginia.

The CIA soon had half a dozen components in Tysons Corner, forming a "mini-intelligence community for technical work." It took "considerable" office space in Rosslyn. It occupied the Broyhill Building at 1000 North Glebe Road, the Chamber of Commerce Building at 4600 North Fairfax Drive, and the Ames Building at 1820 Fort Myer Drive in Arlington. It took offices in Reston. It inhabited rooms at 1016 Sixteenth Street, 1717 H Street, and 1750 Pennsylvania Avenue in Northwest Washington. It bought safe houses all over Vienna, McLean, Falls Church, and Great Falls. It moved into the cryptic "Building 213" in Southeast Washington. "This multiplicity of buildings . . . reflected the growth of the CIA's operations within the United States."[102]

But Northern Virginia's suburban corridor of power waited another year for fulfillment, a year after Allen Dulles's exit at the November ceremony at Langley. On November 17, 1962, the soaring, white, modernist terminal at Dulles International Airport held its opening ceremonies in Chantilly, Virginia, twenty-five miles from Washington. A daring sculptural icon on

Named for Secretary of State John Foster Dulles, Eero Saarinen's Dulles International Airport opened in 1962. One of Saarinen's partners described it as "in the Virginia fields that stretch west from the Capitol." This was quite a field: it lasted twenty-five miles. Thanks to the apparent emptiness of the surroundings, the American capital seemed to have more, inspiring room to grow. FAA. Fairfax County Public Library Photographic Archive.

a sweeping open landscape, it had been a massive project, drawing 4,000 laborers to create its sixteen sixty-five-foot columns, one-and-a-half acres of glass windows, and 11,500-foot runways, all on fifteen square miles of land. The Dulles family had lobbied long and hard to get the airport—which had been known through early planning as Washington International Airport— named after John Foster Dulles, who, in the words of the opening day program kept by Allen, "flew more than half a million miles in 60 trips abroad," more than any secretary of state to that point, testifying to the era of U.S. expansion that the airport itself seemed to symbolize. John Foster's wife paid personally for the bronze bust of him that would adorn the airport's interior, and the Dulleses attended the ceremony at which Eisenhower and Kennedy gave speeches celebrating their family.[103]

Dulles Airport completed and defined the covert capital's skeletal form at a crucial early moment, providing the western pole of the axis convention- ally known as the Dulles Corridor. But few pause on the historical basis for the name of this corridor, which was formed by the buildings of three siblings—Allen Dulles's modernist building at Langley, Eleanor Dulles's modernist house near the foot of what became the Dulles Access Road, and the modernist John Foster Dulles airport. Through these architectural monuments, the international policies the three helped establish for the United States were ingrained in ritual spatial sequence along the covert capital built to house the shadow side of their work.

Dulles Airport bore direct formal connections to Langley. Like Wallace Harrison, its architect, Eero Saarinen, came directly out of U.S. intelligence circles. From 1942 to 1945, working from a Northern Virginia office near the Pentagon, Saarinen was chief of the Special Exhibits Division of the OSS's Visual Presentation branch, an early "multidisciplinary, multimedia hothouse" of the organizational complex. For the CIA's predecessor, he created propagandistic dramas to recruit Americans to the war effort and configured secrecy into federal buildings as a design element. He also innovated the panoramas of "concentrated information" that became the basis for how U.S. global planners understood and explained war, the world, and their own work. These dynamic, three-dimensional displays of terrain maps, illuminated globes, sliding panels, revolving platforms, lights, and graphics technologically enacted an American administrative domain on the world stages arising after World War II. They were used everywhere from the UN meetings in San Francisco and the Nuremberg courtroom to the war rooms of the CIA, State Department, and Joint Chiefs of Staff.[104]

With its long facade lifting skyward like a jet or a bird in a "massive gesture of sculptural freedom," the airport is conventionally seen as an exemplar of the expressionistic turn in modernism at mid-century. It followed Langley's own swooping cafeteria in this regard. The airport's dramatic expressionist exterior and front lobby contrast with the bland interiors that then disappear altogether in the form of the mobile lounges carrying passengers to their flights, echoing Langley's similar division between outside and inside, between surface symbol and functional, back-office labor. The airport's modular horizontality and design for lateral extension also mirrors Langley's horizontality and further points to the way the drama of taking up land for midcentury modernists arose as a cultural expression of the United States in a dramatic period of its own expansion.

But for the covert capital, Dulles Airport accomplished three more important effects. The first was bound to the idea, propagated by its architects and planners, that Dulles was "a formal entrance to the American republic," a "gateway to the nation's capital." Saarinen considered it "part of the whole complex of buildings that create the image of our nation's capital," and one of his partners dramatized the idea, describing the airport as "in the Virginia fields that stretch west from the Capitol." This was quite a field: it stretched twenty-five miles. But the elision was the point. Announcing itself with a dramatic sculptural gesture on a cleared, flat plain, the airport, if thought of as in Washington, DC, skillfully and rhetorically erased the twenty-five miles between it and the federal city, fusing them into one. In doing so, John Foster Dulles International Airport erased Allen Dulles's "temple of intelligence" at Langley. One vision of internationalism, by its very stridency, could dissolve the other in space. Meanwhile, thanks to Dulles's location and its surroundings' appearance of emptiness, the U.S. capital it was supposedly attached to seemed to have more, inspiring room to grow.[105]

This first effect directly connected to the second. Langley's expressionistic gestures did serious metaphorical labor for its denizens, but it largely pitched its address to a closed audience within the CIA, the federal establishment, or other cleared observers. Its public face was faceless, a line of trees. Dulles Airport was just the opposite—it was the elevated, idealistic gesture of American power and authority at its most visible and optimistic, making its pitch for U.S. global authority through an outward-reaching likeness and inspiration, rather than assertion and violence, one according with John Foster Dulles's view that, as he once said, "Our foreign policy is not just a United States foreign policy; it becomes the foreign policy of many nations and many peoples." By putting Dulles Airport in direct interplay with Langley, the covert capital emphasizes in space how the free sculptural leaps of Dulles emerged from the same hands, in the same space, at the same moment as those of its sibling Langley nearby. They were two faces of the same power. Their dialectical relationship between symbol and political content would go on to shape U.S. power in the world, a relationship mediated by the CIA and the covert capital itself—the paradoxes creating a perpetual unease captured on camera soon after the airport's opening, when, in John Frankenheimer's 1964 film, *Seven Days in May*, a patriotic colonel is flown in to protect the White House from a right-wing Pentagon coup. At one instant, he is standing before the airport's open glass windows filled with light, and in the next, he has vanished altogether, the oddly placed windows and swooping ceiling instantly transformed to convey not the soaring promise of humanity and freedom but the disorienting vertigo of the covert plotters' looking-glass world of bent axes and unfamiliar geometries.[106]

But perhaps most significantly, Dulles Airport was the space where the

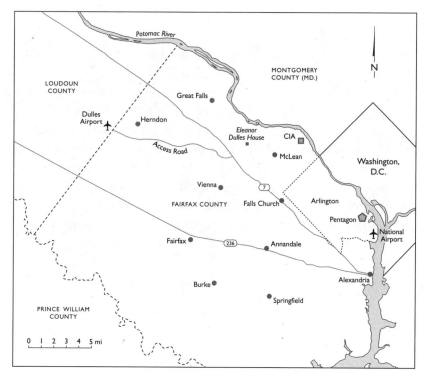

It is little recognized that the Dulles Corridor took its name from three siblings—Allen Dulles, the director of the CIA with its new headquarters at Langley; Eleanor Dulles, whose modernist house was situated near the foot of the Dulles Access Road; and John Foster Dulles, for whom the modernist airport was named.

transnational imperial relationships of Langley went through their literal changes between the domestic and the foreign. The airport launched spies on their covert missions. Hidden behind the curved modernist walls and a changing public art exhibition of the best objects "made in America" were private offices and interview rooms used by the CIA. The terminal held stages for the arrest of double agents, springboards for agents running clandestine operations in Okinawa and turning back the tide of nationalism in the Congo, and eateries indulged in by touring CIA counterinsurgents and their suburban romantic interests. From Dulles's tarmacs, proprietary CIA companies flew arms to its informants and agents in the Third World, flew paramilitary groups home from their covert missions, and landed defectors and agents at two and four in the morning after their own engagements abroad. "At 1:00 PM a secretary drove me to Dulles in her Nova," remembered one CIA officer on his way to Angola. "On the way she handed me my

worn black diplomatic passport, my tickets, and fifteen hundred dollars. . . .
She also handed me a slender notebook which looked at first like an ordinary
checkbook. Inside was a pad of edible, water-soluble rice paper, which, supposedly, I could gobble down if I were captured."[107]

Buildings in this period were both symbol and function. The two Dulleses,
Allen's covert and invisible headquarters for the CIA and John Foster's overt
and aggressively visible international airport, mark a landscape portrait of
global U.S. geopolitics in the postwar period. Between this visibility and
invisibility, idealistic democracy and covert threat, the human histories of
U.S. empire after World War II grew into three-dimensional space. Between
the ensembles of Dulles Airport and the Langley headquarters—and their
domestic point of mediation, the Eleanor Dulles house—emerged a home
front for U.S. empire in the second half of the twentieth century.

At Home with the CIA

IN RANGOON, BURMA, in 1952 and 1953, in the wake of the Chinese revolution, Donald and Jane Wilhelm enjoyed "an unusually good family life" in a five-bedroom house with two bathrooms. Large ceiling fans stirred the air over their teak furniture. "Due to a semi-caste system of labor," nine servants waited on them, including two gardeners. Fresh flowers and polished floors graced the atmosphere every morning. In the country to make "converts to democracy," they had left their modest home on North Harrison Street in Arlington so Donald could take an official position as U.S. advisor on a Point IV project in Rangoon, working as an industrial economist drafting an economic survey and then a study of Burma's timber resources with five Burmese assistants.[1] It was a politically charged time for the United States in Burma. CIA agents trained Chinese soldiers in the northeast to attack the People's Republic of China, just across the border, actions which destabilized the Burmese state. From Rangoon, the army responded to a leftist revolt in the countryside with a violent counterinsurgency program, which elevated Burma's military to a primary place in the nation's governance. The country's timber industry was often the central site of these endeavors, as the government fought to reclaim its teak forests from the rebels.[2]

Despite these politics unfolding around them, the Wilhelms lived quite luxuriously as part of a U.S. imperial life in Burma settling over the recently abandoned infrastructure of British colonialism. What's more, going abroad, these agents of the United States had already found a version of Northern Virginia. Their boys learned to swim in the whites-only swimming pool—resisted at first by their liberal mother—and they became Cub Scouts in a troop led by a Burmese Eagle Scout and a Louis de Rochemont film executive from Manassas as den father, perhaps one of those who worked on de Rochemont's CIA-commissioned 1954 production of George Orwell's *Animal Farm*. They socialized with several families they knew from Arlington. When Adlai Stevenson made a stop in Burma, Donald shook his hand, proudly wearing his 1952 Virginia State Democratic ribbon. Jane wrote Northern Virginia friends by State Department pouch and volunteered at the church next to the Methodist English school that her children attended. In an era when U.S. aid programs and embassies frequently offered CIA covers—although there is no public record that this was the case with him—Donald also disappeared into the countryside on side trips by military escort to visit factories in "areas infested by Communist and other insurgents" and to tour a U.S. Information Service outpost in Mandalay.[3]

Property in the booming Northern Virginia suburbs was often on the Wilhelms' minds. In addition to their house on Harrison Street, the couple monitored from afar a parcel off Little Falls Road, which they, like many operatives abroad who had similar properties, wished to develop. But eventually they sold it to fund their move back home.[4] The family departed Rangoon with regret. A surge in "anti-American feeling" among Burmese nationalists had ended their stay. Jane described it as "the somehow natural and inevitable growth of resentment of the contributor by the receiver." While perhaps "natural," the fact that the Americans were "accused of being imperialists" particularly stung, and Jane sighed to a friend, "of course, any person does care."[5]

After they debarked, Donald Wilhelm went on to Cambridge, England, "to do some independent study" on technical development. By 1961, he was in Iran, where he had become a "personal friend" to the Shah, holding the title of "visiting professor of political science" at the University of Tehran, yet known to Americans in Tehran as "sort of an historian" who wrote the Shah's memoir in English. Jane Wilhelm returned to Northern Virginia with her children, at least one of whom had acquired "an Anglo-Burmese accent."[6] A committed liberal, she planned to continue the socially oriented work she had done abroad, to start a day care for working mothers, using her many friends in Northern Virginia as a base for the new venture, friends who were themselves returning from Burma and other posts in Asia. Some were buying land and building houses in the new subdivisions stretching up from Arlington and over the border into Fairfax County toward Langley.[7] The Wilhelms took a new house on North Dinwiddie Street in North Arlington, and Jane began teaching at Fairfax County's new McLean High School, where, alongside other newly arriving CIA wives, she helped to define the village's high school as a worldly institution, even if, then, still an all-white, segregated one.[8]

In the late forties and early fifties, renting a little starter apartment or shabby but respectable house in Arlington or Alexandria had been de rigueur for the CIA's new covert action warriors. Some had moved into neo-colonial red-brick garden apartments and townhouses built to the south-west of the DC line, such as Met Life's Parkfairfax and the Defense Homes Corporation's Fairlington, large complexes that offered a quick shot over the bridges and the Shirley Highway to the CIA's Tempo offices on the National Mall. Other agents scrimped for rented rooms in genteel Victorian houses along trolley routes or in the denser neighborhoods of North Arlington and Cherrydale, between the Pentagon and Langley.[9]

But by the mid-fifties, and particularly after the CIA headquarters' decisive public announcement in 1955, CIA officers and other U.S. geopolitical figures returned from abroad to Langley's surroundings and began building their own houses en masse, often in "a rural part of Fairfax County."[10] Like the Wilhelms, many were liberals. As activist types, they imagined the suburban landscape not as a retreat from a public city but as an extension of participatory development work in the thrumming social milieus of the expatriate spaces of U.S. empire. Many repatriated migratory experiences of the "good life" abroad as core tenets of what covert capital places could be like. Having gone into the world as liberals who fundamentally believed in change, progress, and participation, they returned to Fairfax County with the same values, which translated easily into an active shaping of the local landscape. Dream houses sprouted in the secluded new subdivisions and large-lot parcels in the streets around the CIA or in lanes winding off downtown McLean, the homes becoming branch offices of the complex.

George Carroll, the social scientist who ran military operations for the 1953 coup in Iran, and his wife, Anne Ickes Carroll, a niece of FDR brain-truster Harold Ickes, moved to a little home on Waggaman Circle. On Basil Road, next to the complex, John Richardson, a covert operative in Korea and the Philippines, built a white house on a hill with his wife, Eleanore. Carleton Ames, an agent returning from Burma and a close friend of the Wilhelms, moved his family to a Cape Cod–style cottage on Davidson Road across from McLean High School, where his wife, Rachel, became a respected English teacher, and where she and Jane Wilhelm helped start the school's first American Studies program, which aimed, in the words of one participant, to take "a long look at that which is American." Carleton Ames became a prominent figure in the local repertory culture. He gave a notable turn as Peter Stockmann, the mayor in Ibsen's political corruption play *An Enemy of the People*, to rave reviews in the newly renovated Fairfax City Hall courtroom. In the summers, Ames's son, Aldrich, and other CIA kids labored at and painted the Langley headquarters as it went up—the perfect construction staff because of their secure clearance.[11]

These agents did not see themselves as homogenous organization people. They were adventurers, taking on the world on the twinned fringes of the metropolis and the globe. They developed these suburbs not as passive pattern-book consumers or as corporate developers coolly observing abstract squares on a map, but as residents with an intense, personal, and emotional investment in this particular landscape's strategic future. CIA officer and China expert Richard Crowe, and his wife, the novelist Cecily Crowe, skied with their neighbors down the suburb's snow-laden hills, flew planes through its skies, and became known for throwing parties at their Crest Lane house on the edge of the Potomac, parties that defined the area's lively and daring social scene, amplifying the covert capital's own politics of risk and speculation.[12]

Ambitious developers and real estate agents—including Crowe himself, who developed one of McLean's first important subdivisions—also began using the prospect of the CIA headquarters to sell local land, advertising sites "6 minutes to proposed CIA headquarters." They warned buyers to act fast: "We have new and old homes for sale and rent near new CIA area in Va. These properties are priced right today, but may increase at any time. Why wait and pay more?" As speculator houses and subdivision build-outs joined early CIA self-designed dream houses filling in the farmland in a place where all comprehensive planning fell to the whim of the thousands of regular, developer-led rezonings, the land market tightened. By 1960, the CIA had become indigenous, in what realtors simply summarized as the fused entity of "CIA-McLean."[13]

Local Virginians were pulled into CIA support work and real estate by the agency's presence. Among them was the Mutersbaugh family—one brother became a CIA machinist and the other, a developer of local subdivisions populated by CIA agents. Intelligence agents of all sorts turned to real estate. One of the first Pentagon covert intelligence operatives, James J. Kelleher Jr., went into the McLean restaurant business, opening the Pikestaff on Cedar Lane, known for its art exhibits and good food. Another, David C. Jolly, became a "top lister" for the popular realtor Long & Foster in Fairfax.

Sometimes agents enjoyed taking foreign posts so they could more dramatically view progress in the real estate market when they returned. "I think it is going to be rather fun to go away for a couple of years and see what happened when we come back," one wife wrote to her husband in his post in Southeast Asia. "But I do want our beautiful land to become more beautiful as we are gone."[14]

Thanks to branch sewers, water trunk lines, and road improvements connected to the CIA, including the northern extension of the GW Parkway, which opened in 1960, the headquarters soon spurred what one journalist called "the greatest concentration of construction activity in county history."[15] In the December 1959 issue of *Home Builders Monthly*, the magazine of the metropolitan real estate industry, a writer explained that while to the south "most of the 'good' land has been occupied," observers expected that "all of the area north of Vienna . . . is going to be hit by one of the greatest population explosions yet to be experienced in the Washington Metropolitan area." Counting on three service workers for each new employee, the writer explained the anticipated boom this way: "There will be at least 15,000 basic employees at C.I.A., 10,000 at Chantilly, 5,000 at the approved industrial park at Tysons Corner, 10,000 at a possible 'little Pentagon' in this area, and another 6,000 to 8,000 by 1970."[16] McLean as a whole was growing more slowly than the rest of the county due to its single-family housing stock and large tracts, which ranged from lots close to the area average of 12,700 square feet all the way up to "residential estates built upon many acres." But much of that development had arrived since the announcement of the CIA headquarters in 1955. From 1950 to 1960, Fairfax County's population grew from 98,557 to 275,002. In the next five years, 75,000 more arrived. In McLean itself, housing units jumped from 300 in 1950 to some 4,800 in 1970, about half of them built after the headquarters' opening. A full 71 percent of McLean's resident households in 1970 had arrived in the previous ten years.[17]

Often friends from field stations returned home and "became neighbors in suburban Virginia." "Everyone seems to have moved out that way," commented one agent in early 1964.[18] There were different ways to express a sense of adventure through habitation in the early covert capital suburbs. Some gravitated to modern architecture, which featured their preference for the "hands-on" action, the flexible dynamism and the feeling of a dramatic intervention into history that they cherished abroad. The interchangeable glass and wood panels of their walls provided a welcome domestic reminder that, as *House Beautiful* put it, "a house you can't change freezes your pattern of

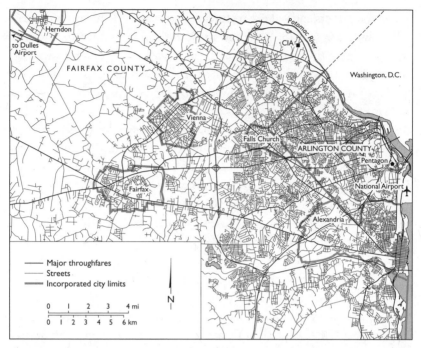

Northern Virginia development, 1964. In the less than built-out landscape north and west of Falls Church, everything felt closer together.

living." Glass walls, paradoxically, were also a brazen testament to the self-evident security of the surrounding landscape, in which owners could "afford to dispense with the safety" of solid walls, as a Danish reporter pointed out about large picture windows more generally, while inviting nature into domestic architecture as a patriotic celebration of America's "spaciousness" and "bigness." These modern homes could be their own self-built visions, commissioned by local modern architects. They could also be addresses in the modernist subdivisions sweeping the suburbs since the forties, such as Hollin Hills and Holmes Run Acres, designed by the well-known architects with geopolitical connections who frequently shaped the corridor—such as Chloethiel Smith (wife of a key State Department official and NSC advisor); Charles M. Goodman (head architect of the Air Transport Command, who had designed National Airport with CIA house architect Harbin S. Chandler); and Nicholas Satterlee (who designed Eleanor Dulles's house in McLean). Other small, more traditionalist developments filled in the land around the self-built houses, as the CIA pumped new life into subdivisions and ailing trolley resort communities stalled since the thirties.

Individual officers also bought plots and contracted with local builders, such as Annandale's popular Commonwealth Custom and Henry de Longfief, an active Falls Church builder known for shaving prices for those "agreeing to do some of the work, such as painting," themselves.[19]

Whatever their preferred style, an extraordinary number of families took advantage of early Fairfax County's potential for "outdoor living." Wives attended political parties at the manses of McLean with a double eye, popular and worldly conversationalists, but also appraisers and collectors of design ideas. Some casually asked to peruse each other's floor plans. Just as they and their husbands' experiences abroad were defined by a life that often took place outside, overlooking harbors, ensconced in a passing show of rivers and rice fields, their attentions at home gravitated to architecture that stepped into the elements, to houses that turned away from roads, faced toward ridges and natural features, or used siting techniques to obscure entrances and windows. Facades that promoted outdoor living caught their eye—decks over carports, outside power outlets for cooking, double-decker front porches, glass window back walls. So did living rooms and kitchens opening onto flagstone terraces, sidewall fireplaces, cellars filled with built-in bookshelves, and "amazing closet space."[20] Many decorated their pine-paneled living rooms and additions with the gifts and booty acquired in their foreign posts—Korean dolls, extensive collections of Canton porcelain, African sculptures.[21]

Some craved a rustic privacy and living "closely with nature" so ardently that they moved farther into the rural reaches of Fairfax County. In Great Falls, northwest of McLean on Georgetown Pike, agents could still find five-acre sites into the sixties. Some had not yet been electrified, so they took their hot showers at the Langley headquarters, while their families enjoyed "elegant camping." One of the CIA's most legendary clandestine operatives, Duane "Dewey" Clarridge, went this route when, returning from planning election interventions during a two-year stint in Nepal, "after considerable searching," he and his wife, Maggie, found a "charming house" far out in Leesburg, "a two-story log cabin about a century old with additions on either side—the guest cottage of an estate that had been broken up." Some CIA liberals venturing into the less suburbanized parts of the county were often surprised to find themselves facing its stalwart Jim Crow infrastructure. Analyst Sam Adams, who moved to Sterling in 1964, recalled trying to register to vote at the local Southern States agricultural store. In a room with a billy club propped against the wall, he and his wife failed the literacy test, only to be walked back through it by a white storeowner who offered to explain to them, as whites, a trick question about the Constitution that "relied on reverse logic."[22]

Businesses formed, sensitive to their peculiar needs. A local industry arose for CIA families to ship beloved pieces of furniture and decor from covert capital abroad and back again, sorting items between sea, air, and storage. In time, Northern Virginia landlords and real estate agents—often themselves with CIA connections—marketed properties to their domestic arrangements, such as subletting houses for long periods, obtaining provisional month-to-month leases, and swapping domiciles with other families when each was in and out of the country. Fairfax County planners added rentable townhouses to McLean's master plan to accommodate just these uses. Resident agents put up friends at McLean houses for the night when they arrived from overseas looking for housing or awaiting new assignments. Wives created feminine solidarities and cohabitation arrangements when their husbands were away. The ephemeral newness and just-add-water domesticities frequently associated with the post–World War II suburbs, for transnational CIA families, became functional necessities, just as the neocolonial architecture seen as indigenous to these suburbs often played the double role of importing the comfort and style of colonial bungalows they inhabited abroad into their home environment.[23]

The open secret of Langley blended into the local suburban public culture. Cartoons of the headquarters building hung on the walls of McLean pizza joints on Chain Bridge Road. The Northern Virginia landscape also developed many spaces for literal, functional politics. CIA safe houses, masquerading under the rules of family privacy, slipped into the fabric of new, under-construction places where people knew not to ask too many questions. Before long, CIA watering holes like O'Toole's on Old Dominion Drive in McLean and the Vienna Inn on Maple Avenue in Vienna became internationally known sites of male sociability and imperial organizing. Run by an army veteran who claimed to have worked for the Kennedy brothers as a handyman at Hickory Hill (their house in McLean), O'Toole's was a one-story brick building attached to a hardware store with a faded "seafood" sign over the door, along the route of the old trolley line in central McLean. Inside the bar, a tapestry depicting Kennedy with the White House in the background hung on the wall as did a poster from John Wayne and Anthony Quinn's 1945 guerrilla warfare vehicle, *Back to Bataan*. Later, a sign that said "Tipping Is Not a City in China" embellished the décor, as did a KGB T-shirt, a French Foreign Legion recruiting poster, and an

Imperial Iranian air force plaque bearing the image of an F-14. There was no name on the door, and there were no bills; the bar ran confidently on the male "honor system."

The place was a covert mail drop rumored to be the "most efficient" of "any world capital," where an unmarked letter could find its way to a distant destination and where "you could tell all the CIA people by the chains around their necks leading to their shirt pockets," where they hid their identification badges. The bar's owner, who claimed fans had established O'Toole's bars in Africa and Australia, an "O'Toole's East" in Thailand, and others "all over the globe," sometimes called it the McLean Inn, as if to mirror the Vienna Inn, which served a similar function. Opened in 1960 in a 1925 ice cream parlor, the Vienna Inn had an always-busy pay phone, beer paid for with checks that just read "government" on the back, autographed pictures of CIA officers on the walls, and decent chili. When asked, patrons at O'Toole's would inevitably claim their profession as Northern Virginia's other booming career at the time: real estate. Covert intelligence work and the generic work of real estate provided cover for one another, and men and women transferred back and forth between them.[24]

But Northern Virginia's domestic spaces were not removed from formal politics either. Major decisions happened in them—in none more centrally than Hickory Hill itself, perhaps the consummate single-family house as political space in the area. John F. Kennedy transferred the Georgian house on six acres to his brother Robert and his wife Ethel in 1956. At the time of the headquarters' opening, Hickory Hill was becoming an informal White House for the Kennedy cabinet. Kennedy wise men who lived in Northern Virginia, including Stewart Udall, Pierre Salinger, John Macy, and Ted Sorenson, stopped in on short notice. They participated in, and often defined, the area's lively social scene and loose, wild envisioning of the possibilities of suburban life. In the days immediately after Kennedy's election, even the sedate economist John Kenneth Galbraith donned a kilt for a boisterous all-night McLean costume party near Hickory Hill. "All the liberal establishment was present without exception," he recalled. By 1962, local writers were grousing to their friends: "I wanted to send you my revised story . . . but the typist still has it. The New Frontier Braintrusters all live in McLean and keep her occupied with their manuscripts."

The Kennedys' pageantry of masculine sociability defined life at Hickory Hill and the "offbeat spontaneity" of its pool parties, which echoed those at the Eleanor Dulles house. Robert Kennedy regularly challenged guests to push-up and arm-wrestling contests. "Ferociously competitive" games of touch football were common. Soon, two prominent former OSS agents in Kennedy's inner circle, Walt Whitman Rostow and Arthur M. Schlesinger Jr., began conducting weekly seminars for an "unusual 'night school'" at Hickory Hill. "Robert and Ethel asked me whether I would organize a series of evening meetings . . ." remembered Schlesinger, "at which heavy thinkers might remind leading members of the administration that a world of ideas existed beyond government."[25]

Robert Kennedy was "dean." Rostow and Schlesinger dubbed themselves "assistant deans." Attendees included Secretary of Defense Robert McNamara, Deputy Secretary of Defense Roswell Gilpatric, Agency for International Development (AID) director David Bell, Treasury Secretary Douglas Dillon, State Department Soviet expert Charles Bohlen, Peace Corps director Sargent Shriver, and economist Walter Heller, who lived in Arlington. Many women, political wives and not, including Eunice Kennedy, Elspeth Rostow, and Teddy Roosevelt's oldest daughter, Alice Roosevelt Longworth, also were regulars. The aura of the family affair settled around the seminars, particularly with Robert and Ethel Kennedy's many children frolicking over the grounds with a large, rude Newfoundland called Brumus. But the seminars' purpose was to showcase speakers who could translate the abstract or academic idea into the "applied" utilitarian forms so popular with both the CIA and the Kennedys. Topics included "why distinctions made by philosophers matter in practical life," "the uses of poetry," and "Is preventative psychiatry possible?" Schlesinger and Rostow led sessions, which also migrated to the city, as did Cold War ideologue George Kennan of the State Department, the philosopher and former MI6 agent A.J. Ayer, the political cartoonist Al Capp, and a CIA cybernetics expert—all to the mixed interest of the guests.[26]

But as an avowed "symbol of the New Frontier," Hickory Hill was defined by more than just talk. Men like Rostow, who attended many McLean parties in these years, theorized development as the signature category by which the United States should encounter the decolonizing world. The booming alterations of the landscape outside the windows of McLean parties served as their literal New Frontier, an immediate context, backdrop, and inspiration for their theorizing. McLean's exceptionalist perception of its own genre of suburbia, meanwhile, progressing and developed, yet wild, free, and hands-on, helps explain how Kennedy elites continued to see the suburbs as the end stage of history—what Rostow in his most influential book had called "the

As the CIA moved to Langley, the Hickory Hill mansion nearby was becoming an informal White House for the Kennedy cabinet. It was also a locus of covert action planning. A rude Newfoundland called Brumus helped give the estate its casual air. The dog stands to the right of the table as Robert Kennedy, Ted Kennedy, Ted Sorenson, and others talk at Hickory Hill in 1968. George Silk/Getty Images.

diversion of the fully mature economy to the provision of durable consumers' goods and services" that would produce wealth and leisure "for its increasingly urban—and then suburban—population"—despite the fact that other Hickory Hill speakers, not to mention the Fairfax County government itself, were cautioning against the perils of unchecked suburban development at the very same time. In his seminar, Galbraith had warned of "cities spreading at random in countryside," and the "blight of highways," but to men in the CIA's suburbs around Langley, the suburban landscape as the end of imperial history made perfect, everyday common sense. It was the rustic, sunny place the advisors, CIA agents, experts, and functionaries from the covert capital who went abroad in this period returned and wanted to return to.[27]

Hickory Hill's white rising form and historic pedigree suggested an alternative White House, but it was just as frequently an alternate Langley, a locus of covert action planning at a time when, in the words of one historian, the CIA "was the institution which best reflected the New Frontier's self-image: fast-acting, adventuresome, impatient with conventions, gutsy, and subversive." It was a space for important transitions between formal and informal politics, where the executive branch blurred into the CIA and O'Toole's came to Camelot. Roger Hilsman laid out his counterinsurgency theories to Robert Kennedy in a two-hour session at Hickory Hill, after which "there was a personal intimacy" between them. Hickory Hill fostered this kind of decisive contact, a space where a political operator who had "failed to get his point across through normal channels" could get someone "off in a corner and do it casually and informally." When Bay of Pigs veterans Manuel Artime, Erneido Oliva, and Rafael Quintero came to the DC area to plan their next attacks on Cuba in 1962, they didn't go to the White House but to the same estate for informal meetings with Robert Kennedy. When their commander, Pepe San Román, arrived in the United States after his release from a Cuban prison, Kennedy found him a small furnished CIA safe house near Hickory Hill, and soon the two men were riding horses together down the median strip of Dolley Madison Boulevard, the street that passes in front of the CIA headquarters. As early as May 1961, just days after escaping the island, San Román's brother Roberto, another Bay of Pigs veteran, was a Hickory Hill regular, drinking Cuba Libres at pool parties and becoming "part of Kennedy's extended family." He and Kennedy conferred in the living room about getting a "second shot" at Castro, including assassinating him, and San Román observed Kennedy's display of sensitive male parenting, which impressed the "typical Latin father, too proud to be that way" with his own children, a style of sensitivity that for Robert included hugging his boys if they were crying, and murmuring, "Hush now. A Kennedy never cries."[28]

Covert capital inhabitants also sought out communicative landscapes that accorded with their view of the world as an incipient America, buildings and spaces that would have an inherent pedagogical role for what they imagined as a dedicated audience of global observers gazing from the decolonizing countries toward the United States as their rational and inevitable future. This had been a central function of Dulles Airport when it opened in 1962, with its swooping white expressionistic terminal on its plot of land where it had such promising room to grow. Eero Saarinen had even once imagined creating an installation at Dulles that would have narrated American power for foreign visitors stepping off their flights, an elaborate three-dimensional display that would stress "the various presidential philosophies that link our history and have led us to successive frontiers." The exhibit, never fully installed, would have visually and rhetorically joined the "discovery of the new world," "westward expansion," the Spanish-American War, and "space frontier" in a permanent, technologically advanced sensory environment.[29] Other covert activists dreamed of establishing "an instrument for continuing the American Revolution today, abroad, through enlightenment" called "Liberty Hall" in the area, one that would have included a center with offices and a school to teach "practical American political action, for export abroad."[30]

In the domestic sphere, the most advanced of these experiments was the modernist new town at Reston, whose planning got underway in 1961 on a swath of forestland between the CIA and the airport. In the era's most celebrated vision for metropolitan Washington, *A Policies Plan for the Year 2000*—issued in 1961 and soon endorsed by Kennedy—planners had called for concentrating suburban development in "satellite towns" along a series of corridors stretching out from the DC border. When a New York developer and tireless promoter named Robert Simon bought 6,800 acres near one of those corridors, he was quick to declare his town a part of the plan's fulfillment, giving it the feel of a national space and garnering international attention.

Simon wanted to create on his plot a modernist architectural creation of major scope, the "physical framework for the Great Society." It would include seven different villages, each with a distinct natural feature. It would have arresting designs by covert capital architects, including Chloethiel Smith and Charles Goodman, alongside those of well-known Americans who'd spent the fifties building crucial new designs in the Third World, architects and planners such as William Conklin and his colleagues James Rossant and Edward Echeverria. Reston would also create a community and an argument about community. Quasi-socialist, liberal, and ecological experiments in global cooperative living would combine with a private American suburban development that would turn a profit and promote individualism and privacy.[31]

The core of Reston's early form was the village center at Lake Anne, where a pinwheel of modernist concrete townhouses cupped a brick plaza decorated with abstract modernist sculptures designed to reflect an iconographic "Esperanto of human culture," near an artificial lake and a fifteen-story skyscraper with jutting balconies that gave Fairfax County its tallest building in 1965. Pathways transported walkers through cast-concrete, sculpted tunnels to at times quite aggressively modernist designs that stepped dramatically out of the forest along a rising and falling topography. Populated by liberals and often seen as freakish by the neighboring southern small towns, this vision appealed to many early geopolitical settlers in Northern Virginia.

Some were drawn to its utopian tenets. Others saw it as providing some of the only suitable new pre-built housing in the developing suburban landscape for migrants with urbane expectations but covert capital priorities.[32]

Reston was also viewed to a surprising degree by its earliest occupants and managers as an argument for U.S. global power in dialogue with U.S. empire both functionally and conceptually, although a kind of power that preferred not to name itself as such. Robert Simon was explicit in his desire to use Reston as a national test case to display the propagandistic fruits of American abundance and its potential to claim a hold over imaginations in the decolonizing world. This was a period when U.S. intellectuals were obsessed with renarrating for the 1960s, in Walt Rostow's words, the "transcendent quality which has long suffused American life . . . the conviction that the adventure of America has a meaning and relevance for the world as a whole." Simon and his wife, the world-traveling journalist and TV critic for *The Nation* Anne Simon, constantly reiterated, through the early days of Reston's construction, a vision of the town as a physical materialization of what the open market, liberal freedom-speak, and a Rostowian "world structured for order" could achieve for a revolutionary period they redefined, to restate America's centrality to it, as an era of "global, national, and personal choice." "People around the world are watching to see what becomes of Reston because the project has become a real test of the capabilities of our private enterprise system," wrote one of the town's PR directors.[33]

Simon repeatedly approached Kennedy-and-Johnson-era policymakers to formalize this relationship between Northern Virginia's domestic architecture and the nation's foreign affairs. Many Kennedy and Johnson elites visited the town, including Stewart Udall, Lady Bird Johnson, Averell Harriman, Sargent Shriver, Arthur Schlesinger, and McGeorge Bundy. The U.S. Information Agency displayed cartoons of Reston at the U.S. pavilion at the 1964 World's Fair and staged displays of its houses in the windows of the U.S. Information Library on Knesa Milosa Street in Belgrade. The international office of the Housing and Home Finance Agency even brought in United Nations housing officials for an "American picnic" on the shores of Reston's artificial Lake Anne.

For Reston's dedication in May 1966, the most significant of these theatrical events, the town's promoters invited more than thirty ambassadors for a daylong program that stressed the role of suburban new towns in establishing new global ties. Representatives from Indonesia, the United Arab Republic, Algeria, Brazil, Ghana, Pakistan, Libya, Venezuela, Sudan, and India gath-

Developers wanted the modernist town at Reston to display the fruits of American abundance and to rivet imaginations in the decolonizing world. At Reston's dedication in May 1966, more than thirty ambassadors assembled on the plaza for a daylong celebration, surrounded by their national flags, and exhibits and booths about their countries. Jane G. Wilhelm Papers, Albert and Shirley Small Special Collections Library, University of Virginia.

ered at the modernist Lake Anne Plaza for an all-day celebration, surrounded by their national flags and exhibits and booths about their countries. "Our hopes for Reston," read the invitation, "are our hopes for all men." Simon gave the ambassadors dogwoods that had been uprooted to form Reston's artificial lake and urged that they plant the trees on their "national soil" as landscape-based symbols of a transnational new-towns culture that would "form a new bond of friendship among the peoples of the world." "This is a time when the barriers between people—economic, racial and social barriers—are under assault," Simon announced. "This is a time when laissez-faire is an echo of the past, and communal responsibility is reaching toward the goal of helping every individual who wants a rewarding life to achieve it."[34] More than 270 groups from around the world toured the town in its early years, often brought by American propagandists hoping to win hearts and minds. Reston and Dulles Airport were the centerpieces of these tours, but they would stop at even mundane suburban housing developments in far Fairfax County, irritating Soviet officials—their trumpeting anticommunist political content growing so repetitive and hectoring that they seemed to want to leave these visitors with the "impression that the United States' houses are not built for the benefit of the citizens of the country, but rather in order to fight communism."[35]

Reston itself generated and received architectural propaganda that defined U.S. imperialism's efforts in the global housing field. Architects William Conklin and Edward Echeverria came to the project after innovating suburban-style, poured-concrete, and modernist housing for the International Basic Economy Corporation, the Ford Foundation, and American corporations in Guatemala, El Salvador, Colombia, and India. Other architects tested designs at Reston, including Wallace Neff's "bubble house," igloo-like hemispheres "built of reinforced concrete sprayed from a gun onto a balloon form," which the United States was also exporting around the world—to Senegal, Pakistan, South Africa, Brazil, and Egypt.[36] Some Reston architects expressed views of their craft that sounded like literal allegories for the U.S. project in the world as conceived by the leaders and advisors who moved into the suburbs they designed. As Charles M. Goodman put it in a key 1964 essay: "Our cause and our struggle are to elevate the standards of the entire social body, not because the people have shown they want it, not because they will ever know or recognize it . . . but simply because man himself is a noble idea and we must endeavor to maintain standards if there is to be any meaning to his life." Written around the time he designed Reston's Hickory

Cluster, such words captured perfectly what might be called a particularly American (or Rostowian) vision of global progress by fiat or humanism without people.[37]

Even Reston's social planning bore the stamp and human traces of the U.S. imperial engagements of this period. To develop the cultural and social life of the town, Robert Simon established Reston's Foundation for Community Programs, a kind of domestic technical assistance project and Point IV mission for the covert capital suburbs. It was charged with the "direction of cultural, educational, health and welfare programs for the people of Reston," and "establishing sound institutions in Reston during the first year of settlement." As its first director, he hired someone with Point IV experience in Burma: Jane Wilhelm, who left her job as a teacher and assistant principal at McLean High to serve as executive director of the foundation and director of Reston's community relations.

It would be hard to overstate Wilhelm's centrality to the new town planned for 75,000 people. Just as designers working as U.S. advisors had carried the vexed dreams of New Deal spatial planning abroad in the forties and fifties to roll out in the United States' new sites of imperial endeavor projects that seemed politically impossible at home, the vexed dreams of liberal technical assistance returned home in the sixties as idealistic suburban planning. Covert capital projects of control abroad could be cleansed and tested at home as uplift and progress, even in the hands of genuine liberals like Wilhelm, and then cycled back as liberal imperial uplift around the world. In Reston's early days, Wilhelm worked to populate the community. She led tours for those first visiting the town. She escorted visitors in a rickety chicken-wire construction elevator to the top of Reston's skyscraper, Heron House. On the night before the town's press opening in October 1964, she ran a team installing furnishings in Lake Anne display townhouses. She helped organize some of the new town's basic institutions, such as its cooperative nursery and gallery. As residents inhabited the town, she prepared the "community information kits" that grounded and oriented their domestic lives and included groceries to see them through a first dinner and breakfast.[38]

Many of the first residents, meanwhile, were CIA agents and U.S. geopolitical figures, drawn to the modernist visage and activist liberal spirit. CIA officer Karl Ingebritsen, who moved into one of the houses Wilhelm had furnished before the press opening, later organized the town's cooperative bus system, one of its most celebrated examples of resident activism.[39] Another early arrival was Harry Mustakos, one of the CIA's major counterinsurgents and guerrilla warriors in the 1950s. At Da Chen, an islet off the coast of Taiwan, he monitored and disrupted shipping to and from China. By 1957, Mustakos was continuing his anti-China work, teaching hand-to-hand combat, swordplay, and the finer points of artillery drops to a group of Tibetan guerrillas for an invasion mission that October. Returning to the covert capital, he and his wife, Diana, toured Reston in 1962. An intervening post training another group of Tibetan guerillas in Chakrata, India, to invade Tibet and trigger a "long-range resistance movement" delayed their move, but soon the Mustakoses built one of Reston's first single-family detached houses, a 1,500-square-foot brick four bedroom near the golf course just beyond Lake Anne Village Center on a small cul-de-sac.

Still making frequent counterinsurgency trips to Southeast Asia, Mustakos also became one of Reston's most visible public figures, president of the Reston Community Association, a local citizens' group. He boasted about keeping up with Reston's doings on his trips abroad by reading the local weekly, the *Reston Times*. Reston was filled with many such stories of transnational use and experience—including one foreign service family who even on domestic leaves dwelled in a tent on the lake to be near Reston when long-term tenants were in the family home. The Mustakoses raised three children in Reston "because of neighborhood schools and also because it is like being in a resort year-round—you don't need to leave home for a vacation," and, like so many of his colleagues, Mustakos later became a successful local real estate agent, further developing the landscape and compiling a half-million-dollar portfolio at Panorama Real Estate.[40]

All across the Dulles Corridor, Northern Virginia's "niceness," quality of life, and engaged, participatory public culture took shape as the negative space around its covert political action abroad and counterinsurgency and paramilitary work abroad found its twin at home in real estate. Around the Pentagon, observers soon noticed the "extremely active participation by retired military personnel as leaders of parent-teachers associations, community associations, and political pressure groups," work encouraged by the Defense Department, which saw "valuable public relations potential in their activities." Before long, local politicians could often be found on the stump backed by their requisite group of "military friends." Hunter's Woods, the "horse village" of detached traditional single-family houses that Robert Simon built as his hedge against Lake Anne's modernist townhouse clusters, was particularly appealing to CIA clandestine officers, who could drive down Route 7 to work and arrive at Langley in a couple of turns. The pattern was repeated elsewhere. In Great Falls, CIA officers with broad experience in Southeast Asia, the Middle East, and South America helped found the River Bend Golf and Country Club the same year the Langley headquarters opened. There they worked on their golf game, which they used to recruit agents and collect intelligence abroad, as many developed the broad range of interests that were useful to CIA agents because they could "be parlayed into allowing them to meet a large and varied community of people."

Others joined Westwood Country Club in Vienna, shopped at the Safeway and Giant supermarkets, and dined at local Italian and American restaurants like the Mosby in Fairfax, the McLean Family Restaurant, the Evans Farm Inn, and the ever-popular restaurant at the Tysons Corner Holiday Inn, all miraculously filled at lunchtime, some of them constructed from materials salvaged from local mills and inns demolished to build the surrounding suburban landscape. At the same time, agents began to bring to Northern Virginia the "different foods" they had grown accustomed to in their foreign posts. Some shared "exotic recipes" in regular features in local newspapers, such as what one U.S. AID woman called "Pulkoggi (Korean for 'Fire Meat')." One of the suburbs' most acclaimed restaurants, the Imperial Garden Chinese restaurant at the Tysons Corner Mall, was bankrolled by CIA agents and staffed with Chinese friends and allies from abroad, who, after the Chinese revolution, worked in Hong Kong and Africa before settling together in a McLean split-level they called "the barracks" and drawing up their menu. With its "pagoda" ceiling and dragons hand carved in Hong Kong, Imperial Gardens became another popular lunch spot for CIA officers who wanted to eat traditional Northern Peking-style cooking, rather than Americanized Chinese food.[41]

In time, the ties between the covert capital's imperial and local security functions also became tight. The CIA began to train and equip Fairfax County police officers as adjuncts to its own security force. The police department, in turn, provided CIA officers with badges and county police credentials as cover for "national security reasons." On one occasion, Fairfax City police even accompanied CIA Office of Security personnel while they broke into a business in Fairfax without a warrant to photograph some papers. These practical blendings of security state at home and imperial security abroad took place in more quotidian ways as well. In one example, a U.S. military–educated South Korean colonel from a political family in South Korea, Seung Joon Kim, who taught martial arts to American troops in Korea and Vietnam, became manager of a celebrated karate school in Falls

Church oriented to local teens and twenty-somethings with its motto "might for right."[42] The high number of Soviet agents in the area was soon leading to bizarre encounters between Russian spies in FBI witness protection programs, who would bump into each other at barbershops on Maple Avenue in Vienna and make plans to meet up again in local chain hotels.[43]

Many allies from abroad found their way in the local residential landscape. Lake Barcroft was a development near Falls Church built in the fifties as an "international community" for diplomatic officials, with demonstration houses personally designed by Bauhaus founder Walter Gropius. Immediately after the Cuban revolution, anticommunist Cuban exiles arrived in the large subdivision up Columbia Pike from the Pentagon and began to buy and build houses on the waterfront there. One housing group at Lake Barcroft was briefly known as "Little Havana," and had its own Cuban grocery. Other arrivals formed one of the first Cuban social clubs in the DC area. The community included former Cuban government officials, businessmen, and at least one modernist architect, Max Borges, whose Tropicana nightclub had defined the elite culture of U.S. imperial Havana in the fifties, and who went on to design some of the first major apartment and commercial buildings with modernist touches that brought density to the Arlington landscape.[44] Some U.S. imperial migrants arrived under the special CIA 100 Persons Act, which played a role in shaping the transnational ethnic community of the Northern Virginia suburbs, as it permitted the agency to bring in one hundred people a year from anywhere without regard for other U.S. immigration laws, restrictions or quotas.[45]

But U.S. imperial activists and their friends did not merely settle the landscape. They consistently designed and inhabited it in dialogue with their stations abroad, lacing it with the transnational experiences of empire. Overseas, agents reported chatting idly about Herndon at counterinsurgency cocktail parties in Southeast Asia or navigated madcap misunderstandings in the Philippines about which *Vienna* they meant when they said they knew people who lived there. At home, one agent jogged along isolated rock formations in Great Falls Park while he planned the CIA's war in Angola. Another swore he bought a house in a Northern Virginia with "trees everywhere" to heal his senses after months in a remote, treeless mountain spy station on the Iranian border, where he scrapped for food and urinated into a slit-trench latrine.[46]

Agents imagined the Northern Virginia suburbs as retreats, places to plan and rest from U.S. imperial endeavor, their domestic reward. But imagining such woody suburban domesticities also worked as its own kind of weapon. The idea of the Dulles Corridor as natural and inherently connected to life— as opposed to the landscapes they cast as barren and inherently stripped of it—worked to establish which kinds of lands were able to be violated, which had a stake in a recognizable everyday life and which did not. "In the middle of winter in snowy Virginia where we had just purchased coats, leggings, mittens, boots, and skates, we headed to the equator where every day was guaranteed to provide a private sauna," recounted the wife of a CIA agent moving to Mogadishu. Rather than self-evident recollections about geography, resonant experiences of salubrious landscapes in Northern Virginia stood as a strategic sign of the difference and distance that preceded and informed imperial trips abroad, allowing varied impositions into foreign landscapes innately defined as less valuable and nurturing of life. Such reflections also suggested their opposite: the very continuity for CIA agents between the local space of agent houses and the foreign space of their imperial offices. At times, such transnational, spatial connections could lead to frustrations for the many CIA agents and geopolitical figures who went into local politics—which at one time included even the chairman of the county planning commission. After losing a local election, one CIA officer complained bitterly that his colleagues were "completely oriented to Uganda, not Reston."[47]

As they had from the beginning, these narratives also took form in a triangulated relationship with colonial DC. From the "vantage point on the bluffs" of "a house across the Potomac River in Virginia," one China hand watched the DC riots after Martin Luther King's assassination and mused "that the United States was coming apart at the seams," just as agents often concluded about the decolonizing landscapes they ventured into abroad. Others worried that black people would soon be "coming up from Washington" to harass local white residents. Covert capital friends migrating to the suburbs from other countries picked up these same ideas, avoiding DC because they did not "like the people."[48] Racialized points of view, fostered in domestic and foreign landscapes by particular, geographically induced ways of seeing, influenced one another. Through these seemingly off-handed transitions and commonsense associations, Northern Virginia became the terrain of the CIA's plotting, the place it was fighting for, and its plausible deniability all in one.

The difficulties experienced by the many covert agents who fell out with the CIA over the years but who had trouble leaving the Dulles Corridor, or who, after leaving it, were still strangely haunted by it, testified to its role as a total environment for U.S. imperial actors. For those staring down uncertain futures in the agency, a move back to a Fairfax temporary apartment bare of furniture and belongings could be a grim one, "not a good time." In 1965, when Lyndon Johnson sent the Marines to invade the Dominican Republic to keep the democratically elected president Juan Bosch from taking his seat, CIA officer Philip Agee lost faith in the agency he served, eventually exposing its covert agents and escaping to Europe rather than face what he saw as a corrupt U.S. justice system. The CIA sent an agent from the covert capital to talk sense into him, and Agee bitterly recalled gritting his teeth through a chat about Nicholas Satterlee and Chloethiel Smith's development of Holmes Run Acres, where Agee's wife lived and worked on a community history. The discussion about the modernist subdivision served as his narrative flashpoint for the surreal break between his life at home in conflicted Northern Virginia and his life abroad. "I offered him a drink while I finished mine," Agee wrote. "He accepted, and we began an inane conversation about Holmes Run Acres, Falls Church, Virginia, the schools, his kids, and the soccer team." Victor Marchetti, another CIA whistleblower, stayed in the area for much of his life, attached to the habitus he had broken with, teaching his kids to face down the local "CIA brats" who were terrorizing them with lines like "Your old man's a traitor!" with their own jibe, "No, *yours* is a dirty killer!"[49]

They settled the landscape so densely that they soon found their first satirist—the spy novelist Ross Thomas, a curious figure who moved into one of the pastel modernist townhouses overlooking Lake Anne in 1966, after a series of international jobs that included two years as a civilian correspondent in Bonn for the American Forces Network and several months as a "campaign organizer" in Nigeria. In his Reston townhouse in Waterview Cluster, where he enjoyed two fireplaces, two bedrooms, large windows, and a gently pitched metal roof, Thomas drafted his first novels detailing the sleazy ironies of the Cold War at street-level that mocked its grand geopolitical narratives and his neighbors who spun them. Thomas delighted in revealing and ribbing the mores of "the boys who work in the new building out in Virginia just past the sign that says Bureau of Public Roads," in marking their physical presence in the landscape, and in knocking the gaps between his neighbors' cozy middle-class domesticity—their small dream of having "sent in a Form 57 to the CIA or State" so one "could be an FO 2 or 3 with a house in Fairfax County"—and its covert international implications. Arriving in 1966, these reflections also marked the first time the Langley headquarters and Fairfax County appeared together in a work of fiction.[50]

Thomas spent his career sending his global fixers and secret agents back to this seedbed of the "home-grown imperialism of the U.S." In doing so, he recovered the early imperial suburbs' absurdist qualities, with the airport "a little lonely sitting out there all by itself on the edge of the Virginia hunt country" and the back roads "lined by the usual Stuckey candy stands, billboards, gas stations, motels, and quiet, closed-mouthed houses stuck off by themselves as if their owners didn't mind living by the side of the road, but to hell with that friend-to-man nonsense." But he did so to mine the transnational hypocrisies of empire in space. In one novel, a liberal veteran of an American "police action" adjudicates between different claimants of a stolen shield, the icon of power in an imaginary postcolonial African country, Jandola. But the American becomes depressed after he nobly grants the shield to an emissary from greater Jandola, who has invoked his pity by trotting out graphic descriptions of starving children. The emissary, instead of bravely flying home, triggers the "Virginia contingency plan" instead, airlifting out the shield from Dulles Airport for sale on the global art market, violating the terms of African victimhood on which the deal depended and questioning why the American was at the center of the drama in the first place.[51] In another novel, Reston's "new town that was no longer new" sets a scene where a CIA Burma expert—who lives essentially in Thomas's own townhouse—is murdered by an assassin. The assassin is trying to keep secret the fact that the CIA basically murdered a liberal American couple in Vientiane around the time Reston was being built and then covered up the murders with the help of "the CIA's pet Laotian general." The Lake Anne shoreline's hopeful rhetorical liberalism thus came to finally backdrop a homecoming for the event the space provided actual cover for in Reston's history: political assassination in Southeast Asia[52]—one of the many specters of postcolonial returns, violent and otherwise, that came to haunt covert capital fictions.[53]

The Northern Virginia suburbs had a particular culture, the kind of fingerprint that writers about cities identify as their starting point, but that many assume is absent, by design, from the suburbs. A study of the CIA and the Pentagon stresses the ways that a place's indigenous institutions specify the general, and the need for suburban historians to attend to transnational spatial power relations more broadly. But Langley's transformation of Northern Virginia did not stop at the access road to the subdivision or the door of the suburban house.

In the progressive rhetorical frame that U.S. imperial actors carried abroad in this period, "development" would not just modernize a country's infrastructure—it would revolutionize lives. Development was such a useful category to U.S. imperial thinking and expansion specifically because of the ways it assumed that physical changes to a place generated broader social and individual transformations. The CIA did the same thing in Northern Virginia for its own employees and those in its orbit. It created a complex political ecology in Northern Virginia, where built structures and a way of life arose in a tight embrace.

The nature of the CIA exaggerated Northern Virginia's breach between the physical and cultural landscape. The CIA intentionally blurred geopolitics and everyday life as part of its political work. To Allen Dulles, the CIA from the beginning was intensely gendered "life work," "directed by a relatively small but elite corps of men with a passion for anonymity and a willingness to stick at that particular job." An "open congeniality" defined good spies for Tom Braden, who ran the CIA's covert cultural activities and settled early McLean with his wife, Joan, and their children—the family that provided the basis for the TV sitcom *Eight Is Enough*. Braden called this congeniality a "gregariousness" that never slipped into a "garrulousness." To another officer, spying focused on the male "human element." It was "two men . . . meeting in private to transact their business."[54] "Once you establish a good personal relationship, people begin to forget who you are and you begin to get into the circle and be accepted as a friend," explained one covert practitioner.[55]

The CIA's move toward the social, the civilian, and the emotional attachment as the foundation for U.S. geopolitics in a peacetime that was also a perpetual war had a coordinate move in politicizing the CIA's domestic life in Northern Virginia. At home, the CIA was not only a job or a spur to physical construction but an imperial way of life. It traversed public habits, errands, and sociability. Its gender roles, sex habits, marriages, and intimate lives were cut from the cloth of its geopolitics. Intimacies between men and women became central spaces for propagating and continuing US imperialism at home and abroad, and these intimacies were restored in Northern Virginia's home landscape. This landscape's culture also recorded the discursive anxieties through which agents came to understand life stories in the grip of imperial labor.

As far as early CIA officers went, Huntington Sheldon was typical. He was one of the elite New Englanders whose work in intelligence during World War II led to the founding of the agency. Born in Greenwich to an investment banking family, educated at Eton College and Yale (where he roomed with Dr. Benjamin Spock his freshman year), he left banking in 1942 and joined military intelligence, and then went on to the CIA in 1952. He was director of current intelligence, a high-level analyst. He knew of the coup against Mossadegh in Iran, he talked orchids with counterintelligence spyhunter James Jesus Angleton, and he worked under Allen Dulles, with whom Sheldon clashed due to his independent-mindedness.[56]

In 1961, Sheldon moved into the new Langley headquarters, part of its first generation of dwellers, breathing life into its gray corridors. That year, at Kennedy's request, he led the design of the President's Intelligence Check List, which became a "no-holds-barred publication" that culled secret operational field reports and sensitive information every morning for the president to act on—the main wire from Langley to the executive branch. To do so, he often arrived at Langley at 5:30 AM. He oversaw a group that sorted field reports from dozens of countries that flashed into the office overnight, shuffling time zones every morning, all to prepare and deliver the report to the White House by 8:30. Dulles used the reports to brief the president personally, but Sheldon sat in on National Security Council meetings, and Kennedy directly engaged him over points.[57]

The move to Langley would have been a welcome switch for Sheldon's commute, as he and his wife, Alice, had already relocated to McLean from their apartment in the District by then. In 1956, they bought five wooded acres across the street from the headquarters site on a parcel subdivided by a Pentagon general a few years before. On the land, working with the DC architectural firm Brown and Wright Associates, they designed an "idiosyncratic" seven-room house at the end of an unpaved driveway. The architects were an appropriate choice for the CIA couple, as the firm had international scope, renovating the U.S. chanceries in Oslo, Strasbourg, and Leningrad in the same era that they built the Sheldon house.

Integrated with nature but modern, the Sheldon house's big glass-paneled window-walls looked onto the trees. Huntington—or Ting, as his wife called him—had a greenhouse for his orchids in the middle of the living room. There was a fireplace, a porch, polished concrete floors they could wash with a hose, and a pond filled with fish. Alice described the house, which cost $36,258, as "a large transparent shell full of space and healthy plants and food and water and fire." With her first husband she had commissioned a house in California by the architect Richard Neutra. The house in McLean obviously took inspiration from his therapeutic "bio-realistic" style. Alice deco-

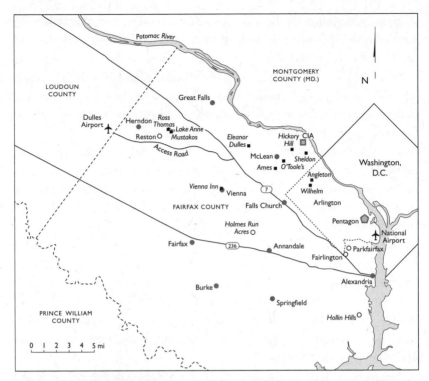

Early CIA settlement. Dream houses sprouted in secluded new subdivisions and large-lot parcels in the streets around the CIA or in lanes winding off downtown McLean. The homes became branch offices of the complex.

rated it herself with sleek Danish furniture, a chaise lounge, and a John Sloan nude over the fireplace. Ting had been flying to Thailand in those years for the agency, but in the spring of 1959, the house completed, they moved into 6037 Ramshorn Place.[58] The house was theirs, designed from scratch, yet its interplay of glass exposure and private tree-shrouded lot also encapsulated the open secrecy that defined Sheldon's covert work life, its combination of secret surveillance and the threat of being seen. Standing in a neighborhood that was outlandishly hard to navigate, filled with dead-ends, perilous one-car cutbacks over steep drop-offs, private drives, and no access turns, it forbid entry under the guise of the pastoral and the private. Yet its wider secrecy of surroundings, where neighbors simply worked "for the government," also reaffirmed the allowable openness of the house's modern interiors, the tenuously safe space of the security-cleared family. The house's cellular makeup, modular shapes, and open plan, meanwhile, exaggerated its continuities with Langley's own cubicles.

In such domestic spaces, the CIA complex became a family affair. As CIA politics crept into domestic spaces, everything was public. Thanks to the CIA's confidential culture, everything was private. As the agency eroded these conventional distinctions, it also overemphasized them as intense points of focus and obsession, instrumentalizing gender and concepts like privacy as useful categories that could be marshaled to get the agency's functional work done. Because of the rigorous screening and secrecy enacted by the complex and the CIA's covert mandates, it was often easier for the agency to use the legal act of marriage, where confidences were already privileged, as a baseline contract for its secret-privileged hiring. Heterosexual marriage comforted a CIA staff that correlated homosexuality with treason and exploitability. Being gay, or even having a single same-sex sexual experience, was a quick way to fail the security and polygraph tests required for entrance, ostensibly because that would open one up to blackmail. Doubly certifying heterosexual marriage by hiring spouses, the agency turned the private suburban homes around itself into even more severe extensions of its own security-cleared, confidential domestic environment.[59] In this compulsory context, many CIA couples were created. Sheldon's wife, Alice, had already gone through this processing. She herself had been a CIA agent from 1952 to 1955.[60]

Despite these domestic arrangements, inside the complex, Langley remained an overwhelmingly male world. The Old Boys of the complex were the CIA's first family, and Sheldon, although reserved, was one of their own. The complex came to represent and contextualize their bonding, which reaffirmed the rightness of their project. Bottles of booze stood on desks. Barbers in the unisex barbershop provided *Penthouse* and *Playboy* magazines to customers waiting for trims. Few women were hired. Those who were, often found jobs as office workers and secretaries. Many of them were young high school graduates from the "mostly white small towns and cities of Virginia," steered to the CIA by their guidance counselors as the agency began to shape the rural horizons and early suburban life of Northern Virginia outside its own immediate social group.

These secretaries provided another level on which the secret "family" of Langley operated. The CIA bundled these young women, in a gendered, surveilled version of a company town, into agency-selected and -monitored apartment buildings in McLean, Vienna, and Falls Church, where many of the other tenants were CIA employees. In this manner, these young women's home and work life were combined under the agency's watchful and protective eye. Divisions paternalistically adopted secretaries for life. Their hiring was an economic decision: small-town women were cheaper, their pasts easier to investigate. It was also a racial one. Young white women's supposed "all-American image" figured race as national loyalty—CIA hirers, according to one officer, perceived them as less "'corrupted' or 'politicized' than their urbanized sisters." DC and Northern Virginia's black communities provided few of the CIA's early secretaries. However, most of the complex's guards and cleaning staff were black, as were the white-coated waiters who served the director in his private dining room on the seventh floor, again recycling the surrounding landscape's Confederate patterns.[61]

Women advanced through the ranks slowly. Some who did "theorized that the intrigue and excitement were worth the occasional discrimination." Others, in the words of one woman who worked in covert operations early on, learned to use the gendered options offered by Langley as outline for their covers, playing "tour director . . . someone's girlfriend, a photographer, an art collector, even a young teenage boy." Alice Sheldon had become disillusioned with the gendered culture of the agency even before the move to the suburbs. She had attended Army Air Force intelligence school and worked in photo interpretation in a Pentagon basement during the war, recommending bombing targets. The CIA approached her to start up its photo intelligence division based on this experience. Rare in being personally sought out independent of Ting, she began at the agency in the summer of 1952, analyzing photos of the Soviet Union.[62]

As independence and decolonization movements spread through Africa, Alice received operations field training for clandestine work. Then she went into counterintelligence, monitoring and tracking African nationalist movements. She was uniquely qualified for CIA work. Born into a wealthy Chicago family, she was the daughter of the famous writer and adventurer Mary Hastings Bradley. As a child she had gone with her parents on a series of native-African-guided colonial adventures, safaris, and hunting trips through the Congo and Uganda. At the head of these trips was Carl Akeley, the inventor of modern taxidermy. Alice's father, Herbert, shot the gorilla that Akeley embalmed and made to beat its chest at the Museum of Natural History in New York, which symbolized Africa and, according to one scholar, helped embody the hierarchies of race for early twentieth century America.[63]

Alice deployed the knowledge gained of Africa on these trips—where her elders used her whiteness, innocence, and childhood as a device to measure the humanity of Africans they met and as a melodramatic hook to sell books about their travels to the U.S. market—in her CIA work. The cauldron of colonialism repetitively produced the international experts of the CIA era. "Working in the Far East were children of missionaries to China and former servicemen who had been stationed in the Orient," recalled one prominent CIA officer. "The Middle East attracted children of the oil industry executives." Alice's reports at this time bore titles such as "The Pattern of Soviet/Communist Activities and Interest in Africa," with topics on "Travel of Africans to the Bloc for Conferences or Tours." "I was supposed to keep records on these Africans because countries were being taken over by these people . . . and all of a sudden these guys we'd never even heard of would be in charge of the place," she said later in an interview.[64]

At the CIA, Alice operated at a low level, confined there by her gender as her husband advanced. An intent performer of the showmanship of gender, she flirted and had an emotional and perhaps physical affair with a married colleague, infidelity being another major vehicle for intimacy in the agency, the sanctimonious emphasis on loyalty reproducing its seductive opposite in the complex's intimate life. At the same time, Alice wore flat heels and boyish clothes to tailor her appearance to fit in with the men she worked with, deemphasizing her gender. In the end, according to her biographer Julie Phillips, the overextensions of the job taxed her. Both she and her husband worked at the CIA, but at home in their apartment in Northwest DC, Alice was shackled by the labor-intensive social category of wife. The agency didn't free her from the second shift, the "second job of entertaining him every night." She made lists of her feelings: "Intense desire for never-experienced personal freedom; husband as jailer" and "resent having to mother grown man who dominates me." Spying on the world didn't negate serving in the home; one instrumentalized the other. In the summer of 1955, depressed, bored, and increasingly critical of the covert action side of the agency, Alice quit the CIA.[65]

She left Ting and took an apartment at 2619 Green's Court, where Eleanor Dulles was her landlord. Alice was one of the "young professional people" with "imagination" whose rents funded the Dulles summer home, and one wonders if the apartment in the city, the land in McLean, or both, came from Alice and Ting's connections with the Dulleses. But by the spring of 1959, they were together again and living in McLean. And in this way Alice came to inhabit another gendered identity available to women in the CIA's covert landscape of politicized suburban intimacies: housewife. She had her own study built in the house, where she was working on a PhD in psychology at George Washington University (a program she entered at 43), but she constantly mocked and attacked the perceived self she had become in Langley's shadow—the person she called "a chatty, if erratic McLean matron." The "idiosyncratic" house she and Ting had designed came with its own idiosyncratic problems: the living room had to be not only cleaned but weeded; bugs, lizards, and snakes crept in through the greenhouse drainpipes; concrete floors and windows put a chill on the house in winter; condensation from the greenhouse once brought the roof in on her desk. She oversaw the maintenance. To do so, she managed the work of other men and women. She let in the roofers, found wax for the cleaning lady. She tended the lettuce and shopped for dresses at Lord & Taylor at the mall.[66]

But this somewhat familiar litany of the housewife's labor was made more complicated by the ecology of Langley. Langley's gendered intimacies were its arsenal—the home as the space of planning for and retreat from violence, the street that kept secrets, the estranged public sphere. While Alice was becoming housewife and entertainer, Ting became busier. When Dulles was fired after the Bay of Pigs debacle, he came to Ting for advice. In 1962, then an assistant deputy director for intelligence, Ting designed the "rigid," "compartmented" PSALM control and security system, a complex administrative order for dispensing and regulating intelligence on Cuba. He collected missile intelligence and managed aerial reconnaissance and surveillance missions over South China and North Korea. He became, according to a CIA colleague, a "terribly cautious guy, terribly security-minded." During the Cuban Missile Crisis, he was intelligence support officer during "critical discussions with the Russians relative to the removal of the missiles and Il-28 bombers from Cuba," reporting directly from Wallace Harrison's CIA building to Wallace Harrison's UN building. Emergency calls came in and woke the couple at two in the morning. He rushed out to the complex. He came home and stocked the basement with canned food, fearing a nuclear attack.[67]

For dwellers in the domestic environment of the CIA, the real and anticipated violence of work shaped the sense of time and emotional calm of the space of the house. The Sheldons were so close to Langley it is almost impossible to describe dramatically enough. Their house was like an extension of the headquarters, a wired-in, satellite office. The complex's calls reached inside their walls and drew Ting out at a moment's notice. He could be at the CIA and back within minutes. The two places created a continuous spatial flow.[68]

So while she went through her days, in Phillips's words, as "a Virginia housewife," attending parties, fixing sandwiches when her husband's friends came over to play bridge or watch Redskins games on TV, Alice's experiences of common suburban gender roles were always shaded by the CIA with the global and geopolitical. CIA officers boasted about their work, and she worried about these men she knew and the policies they made based on "greed and fear." Male power, routinized in the habits and roles of suburban life, effected world destiny. Eventually, Phillips reports, Ting didn't stop with canned foods. Late in life, going blind, he stockpiled gasoline in the garage, opened offshore bank accounts, and tucked gold coins into the walls of their light-filled modern house.[69]

McLean's hard-to-find houses were the home front incubator where U.S. imperial policy was made. This domestic sphere and its habits tended to normalize Langley's international sphere and policy, and vice versa. The domestic sphere also recorded and reflected the half-spoken desires of U.S. imperialism abroad, and its offstage harms. The CIA responded to its proliferation of international agendas with a proliferation of gendered identities in the landscape around its headquarters. Some divisions became known as "sex pits," the heterosexual fidelity of the agency's surface family and the sexual undercurrent to its international acts of violence reshuffling at home to reincarnate as fervent, illicit sex. As time went on, the "man without qualities" of the early CIA also began to leave the trace history of his global labor in the local cultural landscape in the form of the CIA "widows" who soon proliferated around the headquarters: women made famous by the loss of their husbands to unknown aggressions.[70]

Some widows were confused as to whether they should even be grieving, unsure about their husbands' allegiances. One, Maryann Paisley, herself formerly with the CIA, had lived in McLean for years with her husband John Paisley, a Soviet specialist who may or may not have been found floating in the Chesapeake Bay in 1978, may or may not have been a double agent, and may or may not have sent the family postcards from whatever country he may or may not have ended up in. Maryann lived out her days in their house in McLean, in a bugged home, with a tapped phone, never knowing what had happened to him. CIA widows began to look upon the complex as an institution that had both produced their family life and then brought a veil across it, keeping their own intimate history a secret from them.[71] Some spent lifetimes challenging the CIA for information about their husbands. The complex cast a shadow over knowledge in the Dulles Corridor, creating a landscape of the known and the not known even at fundamental levels of family and self.

But the widows, in this sense, were extensions of Langley's most enduring and basic gendered category—articulated by some as a new entity altogether, the "CIA wife," the often invisible but mandatory figure who provided the domestic, emotional, and covert labor that allowed the CIA's international and covert actions at home and abroad to function. It was no incidental connection for these women that wives, under the eighteenth-century British law that once ruled Virginia, had been legally designated "feme coverts," "existing under their husband's 'cover,'" and "unable to control their own earnings or property or to independently sign contracts or initiate lawsuits." In an era when U.S. imperial expansion secured an abundant domestic economy and where federal programs channeled mortgages and other resources to suburban white male homeowners, attaching ideas about security to the single-family home and the nuclear family, the work of CIA wives in the Dulles Corridor was similarly hamstrung, but in a way always locally inflected by the CIA. The CIA wife's invisible labor buffeted and parried the daily, extended life challenges and experiences of empire into the perceived normalcy of suburban work and life, as she supported and nurtured men who saw their "other life" as entitling "them to do things that no one else felt entitled to do, either morally or legally."[72]

For CIA wives, patriotic loyalty wrapped domestic labor into national responsibility.[73] At one level, the work of CIA wives was functional. They divided houses into gendered zones where political truths could be spoken or silenced as needed, pretended not to hear or have opinions on leaked tidbits of covert knowledge, ran geopolitical carpools, and planned babies to not interrupt the schedules of global and personal politics.[74] They also provided vital cover for clandestine trips abroad, giving imperial business the imprimatur of family business, and hosted the dinners where their husbands recruited agents, developing a "sixth sense" for "potential assets."[75]

At another level, the work of the CIA wife was emotional. It included managing strange hours, long absences, and intra-family deceptions as a matter of child upbringing, guarding personal and national secrets, and maintaining a sense of domestic continuity for husbands and children in houses that had to break camp and be rebuilt abroad, and then just as quickly be struck and rebuilt in Northern Virginia, while contending with extreme personal isolation. At times, CIA kids found benefits to their association with the agency—as CIA "master" craftsmen built their Boy Scout Pine Wood

Derby cars and CIA duty officers on emergency hotlines got their cameras working for graduation photographs. Just as often they found themselves taking long, silent walks by the side of the suburban highway, going on family picnics that turned out to be cover for secret agent meetings in remote settings, and dealing with fathers who saw even parents of their friends, school board colleagues, exchange students on home stays, and classmates as fair game for recruitment. Eventually, these family challenges produced their own nonfiction genre, which might be termed "Shit Dad Did," where history is "a family romance written in headlines." Or in the bleaker versions, where CIA children realized that "a family is like a cover, it's just window dressing."[76]

CIA wives took unpaid leaves from work to travel abroad, putting their careers inside and outside the agency on hold. Others took jobs as CIA secretaries or "contract wives" to make ends meet, filling out stations with "cheap labor," even as some already did CIA work in their personal lives, making dead drops in butcher shops and markets, disposing of packages, posing as cooks or restocking pantries in safe houses. In the era of *The Feminine Mystique*, the CIA used the gap between conventional representations of femininity and feminine fulfillment, and the reality of politically aware women with varied background in education and literal operational training, to double and triple staff abroad, without acknowledging them as staff.

At times, CIA wives turned to this intimacy with specific covert actions and national secrets as their own political power, "a lever" and threat of revelation that they used to force the agency and its congressional allies to "adopt benefit packages that address their special needs" and to create a special office at Langley to deal with their concerns—just as they and their CIA husbands used secrets and their potential revelation to force political and governmental change abroad. But one might caution against reading this as a liberating form of feminist politics. The CIA's feminine mystique routed their self-expression and participation into imperial work, politics, and policies. And just as frequently, CIA wives censored women who violated collective norms, reproducing their culture and stabilizing U.S. empire as a system by, for example, disciplining pregnant women who tried to contact husbands who were engaged in deep cover work or who fled warlike situations abroad with their children, "abandoning their husbands," in the words of one CIA wife.[77]

But on the whole CIA wives appear in their archives of reminiscences less as unambiguously powerful than as mediating figures of empire—required not only to do its work, but to manage the fact that the post–World War II

U.S. foreign policy they were implementing did not even acknowledge it as work.[78] The silence and secrecy of the CIA, the very repression of the geopolitical as overt politics, cut deeply into the private lives of spy families in the covert capital. These cuts were sutured by CIA wives, as they joined the secrets of U.S. power and imperial governance to the perfunctory domestic, emotional, and family life that occurred in visible, local space. "We CIA wives were all exhausted women, worn to the bone," Cicely Angleton, wife of counterintelligence chief James Angleton, told an interviewer. "The men were decent enough, but their nerves were shot. . . . It was so much more than a career."[79]

As they moved outward against the world, interiors became a point of focus. On a lot adjoining his house in North Arlington on Thirty-Third Road, Angleton built a hothouse for his orchids and painstakingly tended them. He made dry flies to catch trout in the Potomac River and collected and stored precious stones in his basement, diligently polishing them through long insomniac nights. In the basement, he also kept a workbench and a milling machine that he used to design leather items and gold jewelry.[80] But these at-times minute passions—orchids, stones, fish—didn't just serve as metaphors for patient intelligence work. They reflected the trappings of a hermetic inner life—"innerism," Stanley Cohen calls it in the context of 1970s Brazil—that absorbed the space where a wider ethical or affective accounting with either an intimate family circle or a wider public life might have lived.[81] In a home infiltrated by work and the political sphere at any time, Angleton pulled the phone cord, doused the lights, drew the blinds, and ordered his children from the room when agents came to meet with him. Alongside these urgent practices, private, hobbyish pursuits somehow *replaced* a private life of intimacy, confession, and care with the busywork of a sealed mental life. That technique echoed through the lives of many agents in Northern Virginia. For some, it was orchids; for most, it was alcohol.

Angleton and his wife separated three times, yet he once spent twelve years breeding a hybrid white cattleya orchid that he named after her, which could not be publicized because Angleton didn't want his name in any of the professional horticultural journals. As her husband tended orchids, Cicely Angleton arguably developed her own brand of innerism, studying to become a poet and a PhD in medieval history. Many well-known CIA wives developed arcane and magnificent specialties in pursuits such as abstract painting, translating folktales, gardening, and Jungian psychoanalysis. These private pursuits provided traces of these women's dynamic pasts and lives, but they were also emotional necessities when living with tight-lipped husbands. As they were abroad, they were often enabled by the labor of women of color, repatriated from the colonial setting or just as frequently the nameless "black live-in maid who did housework and some cooking" and came to McLean from the colony of DC or the segregated spaces nearby that wrote conditional U.S. citizenship into the landscape.[82]

But while obsessed with the idea of dying alone on the modernist concrete floor of her house, Alice Sheldon wasn't waiting for the intimate deaths of Langley to infiltrate her life. For her, this culture elicited a different response. Using the materials with which the CIA had furnished the landscape of Langley, and herself in her operations training, she created a new identity, a newly gendered persona, outside the regimes of truth and reality forged by the complex whose shadow she lived in. In the late 1960s, in the middle of the Vietnam War she hated and just before Ting retired, she rented P.O. Box 315, her dead drop at the McLean post office. She opened a bank account, picked up her pen in the study she built for herself, and became the science fiction writer James Tiptree Jr. He wasn't a pen name. He was a man, known for a writing style that science fiction luminary Robert Silverberg called "ineluctably masculine." Silverberg described his imagined image of Tiptree, "a man of 50 or 55, I guess, possibly unmarried, fond of outdoor life, restless in his everyday existence, a man who has seen much of the world and understands it well." Tiptree spoke out in a voice, Sheldon said, from behind her pancreas. She lived as him for a decade. He wrote stories and novels and won awards. He had his own typewriter, his own handwriting, and he had a nickname, "Tip." He made dozens of friends by mail, all of whom thought he existed.[83]

This "cover" allowed her to produce some of the most profound accounts of the lengths and limits, the spatial and psychic effects of the stretched-out cartography of the lands wrought in Northern Virginia by the Langley complex. This cover was also a cover in a second way in that, as her biographers explain and as she explained in letters to friends, despite her marriages and her bitter and restless adoptions of the feminine identities allowed by Langley, Alice Sheldon loved women.[84] The man she became, James Tiptree, allowed her to express this love under the nose of the agency that declared it illegal and created a place that outlawed it. At the same time, he gave her a route to authorship, to "writing like myself," using the male voice certified by the complex.

Of all the forms of doubleness offered by Langley, Sheldon then—a woman, a science fiction writer, a man, an agent, a housewife, a person of many names, a person who said that "My Lai—etc. etc. etc. did not *surprise* [her] one bit" and who wrote about batting "around jungly parts of the globe when young and worse jungles with desks when old"—was the true double agent in this double agent landscape. "At last I have what every child wants, a real secret life," she wrote early on. "Not an official secret, not a Q-clearance polygraph-enforced bite-the-capsule-when-they-get-you secret, nobody else's damn secret but MINE." By personalizing the complex's secrecy in the form of new authorial and bodily identity, Sheldon retrieved interior authorial space for the covert capital's colonized female self. But, to do it, she had to wipe that self out. Through this violent act of freedom, her cover, Tiptree, became the grim bard of the Dulles Corridor.[85]

In one of Tiptree's first stories, "Mama Come Home," published in 1968, three eight-foot women land on earth. The drama strikes deepest at a CIA outpost in Georgetown. "Our office is a little hard to explain," explains the narrator, a male agent named Max. "Everybody knows C.I.A. is out in that big building at Langley, but the fact is that even when they built it there it fit about as well as a beagle-house fits a Great Dane. They got most of the Dane in somehow, but we're one of the paws and tails that got left out." The landing affects the office so intensely, says Max, because events in all places do. The CIA had already "decided that outer space fell under the category of foreign territory in its job description." This is an agency with great reach.[86]

But in "Mama Come Home," the imperial scenario flips. The eight-foot women want batches of fifty men delivered to them. They rape them and turn them into slaves. The ethics of the story center on a female CIA agent named Tillie. Raped herself by a street gang as a girl, "intelligence had found her, as they often do, a ready-made weapon," and had her use sex to gather secrets for the Company. She is a model of the corrupted intimacies of the Dulles Corridor, where violence abroad can reappear in the hollow space of the soul and because of this, for her, "it was permanent guerilla war inside."

The alien women take to Tillie and she to them as they are "immune from rape" and "conception is a voluntary function with them."[87] But when Max manipulates her into siding with the humans by raising the plight of the raped men, she agrees to repeat her own violation and stage a brutal, horrific rape scenario with a seven-foot-tall CIA man that the CIA broadcasts into the alien ship, sending the women fleeing. Earth is saved. So is Tillie's heterosexuality. In the next scene, she is Max's girlfriend. They shop at a local grocery and then go to his place for a steak dinner.

As with many Tiptree stories and crucial covert capital texts, this one reverses colonialism's polarity. The colonization of earth recasts the drama of imperialism, in this case depicting its white, male aggressors as victims. Within this reversal, by further describing this colonial violation as a sexual one—in the rape of the men—she suggests that men's "normal" behavior toward women, or at least the CIA's normal behavior toward Tillie, is itself an oppressive, colonial microproject, triangulating the women of the Dulles Corridor, in a sense, as colonized. This raises interesting possibilities for alternate global solidarities—domestic women and colonial subjects, for instance. But in this case, with the giant "alien" women configured as both a sex and a race, it produces a dilemma. Tillie must decide between gender and racial loyalty—the race, in this case, being "human." She chooses race.

This plot repeats itself throughout Tiptree's work.[88] Oppressed people, often women, meet a racialized, often female, alien with whom they can identify. These aliens of color are like the oppressed protagonists with one difference: they have cruel power. They must, usually biologically, express this power through violence. Because she fears terrible violence and has past experiences with bodily invasion, the oppressed person can't side with the aliens, in the end, despite her intense identifications, or she would sacrifice her own life. So she returns, grimly, to the colonized fold of her everyday life, or she chooses to die.

The anguish inside Tiptree's stories is that Sheldon seems to have considered herself both. She was the object of the Dulles Corridor, the "internally colonized" as one scholar would have it, who proliferates oppressed and abused others of color and shape in her fiction as metaphors for this colonized self and its potential liberation.[89] And she was the author of the Dulles Corridor, the agent with a colonial past. Through these years of decolonization her affiliates developed the very imperialist scope of intervention and happiness controlling other places and supposedly disorderly and reckless people that, logically, would lead them to decide "that outer space fell under the category of foreign territory" in their job description. Sheldon expressed this in fiction in the form of racialized, irresponsible, unethical aliens run amok with their newfound power.

The universal, colonial, and planetary scale of the stories is the very thing that shuts down Sheldon's own longings and strivings for alternate global visions. It is no wonder that the Alice Sheldon who was trying to control African national destinies only a decade before, as Tiptree, held out bleak prospects for liberation. While Alice Sheldon might have wished Ting and his friends were wrong in their grim assessment, James Tiptree had "weapon"

Using techniques learned in her CIA operational training, Alice Sheldon created a newly gendered persona for herself as the science fiction writer James Tiptree Jr. Under this cover, she drafted inquiries into the uneasy state of women in the covert capital. Just after her true identity was exposed, in 1977, she sat for her first author photo. James Reber. Courtesy of Terry Flood.

in hand, so, in case they were right, he wouldn't get caught on the terrifying, wrong side of the barrel. This "split sort of life" and self-colonization is a product of the Dulles Corridor and a central means by which it created complicity in the community of mutually oppressed suburbanites around its complex.[90] There's no way out for Tiptree. When one with a colonial background lives in the covert capital near Langley, there are only new colonialisms. In almost all of Tiptree's work, any shift in power must come with a riotous act of violence. The appearance of this violence, its repetition and necessity, emerged as a direct product of the work done by the people Alice lived with in the corridor.

In 1977, after Tiptree's true identity was revealed, her biographer says, Sheldon couldn't write as powerfully anymore. As if to symbolize her exposure and the end of her flight toward reinvention, her first widely circulated author photo was taken by the CIA's in-house photographer, who chose the agency's U-2 spy plane targets two decades before. Part of the problem for her readers might have been that without the cover of irony and the coded joys of male, potentially CIA, authorship, the agony of the aggressor-victim, of the guilty subject inflicting a pain that was also intensely felt, was laid too bare in the later books—like the torture-filled *Brightness Falls from the Air.*

At the same time, without Tiptree's gun in hand, Sheldon herself seemed to fear that the only other option was to be on the other side of it, nothing but a vulnerable "old lady in Virginia." Stuck in the CIA's world and landscape, she ended her story like the ones she wrote. On a night in 1987, she shot her elderly and sleeping husband, Ting, twice in the head and then shot herself in their house in McLean. Or perhaps it was Tiptree who held the gun.[91]

"Mama Come Home" does have a sequel. In that story, "Help," written the same year, two sets of religiously fervent aliens descend to earth, decide humans are heathens, and in their war over the planet's soul begin to destroy its life. As the CIA clan wonders what will happen to them, Max bleakly explains how colonial wars end. When he is finished, one of his colleagues murmurs "Viet Nam." The overt war's most intense years almost perfectly tracked the prime period of Sheldon's writing career. She hated Nixon and wrote letters demanding his impeachment. She participated in the Quaker Vigil, an antiwar protest in front of the White House.[92]

Perhaps the war recalled to her memories of her experiences as a colonial visitor in Saigon in the 1920s. Her family went to the city after they left Africa. Her mother killed a tiger in the interior. French development displeased them. They weren't "explorers" in Vietnam, more like tourists. Yet during the Vietnam War, Tiptree recalled the trip nostalgically, how he "rode a pony in peaceful woodlands in a place now called Vietnam." The phrasing, like Sheldon's writing about Africa, suggests a melancholy, a sense that the nationalization of Saigon in the form of Vietnam is regrettable, even as she actively denounced the war. This liberal melancholy carried through in the impossibly split ethical identifications in her stories, where all would-be transnational contacts somehow ineluctably reverted to violent exterminations.[93]

But it is the final irony of the struggles within Sheldon's writing that Vietnam could only appear as a supposedly transparent simile for alien, apocalyptic horror, as a colonial Saigon half a century old, or as a brief touchstone for liberal moral protest but not as an actual political entity or series of actors making direct political claims on her own landscape. This is odder than usual in the stories the CIA and its families told about themselves in this era in the orbit of Langley. For a mere five minutes away, just after Tiptree's second short story collection was published, thousands of Vietnamese refugees were moving into the suburbs of the Dulles Corridor, changing and inhabiting the architecture, landscape, and culture of the next town over from McLean—Falls Church—and many Dulles Corridor villages, perhaps pointing to some of the alternate political solidarities and proximities she longed for and providing important insights into how the CIA's violent universals swallowed the real geopolitical intimacies of the local in their frustrated, far-reaching haze.

A little suburban street three miles down the road from her house might also have seemed inconsequential to Sheldon. It was called Saigon Road. In one immediate sense Saigon Road was a shady, tree-lined suburban lane. It was no more than a half mile long. But "immediate space" in Northern Virginia was itself mystifying, for the built environment in the covert capital had a leaping power equivalent to its most fantastically imagined science fiction, and Saigon Road was its own stretched-out geographical frame—a short road but also an imperial corridor that could intimately collapse the 9,000 miles that separate Northern Virginia and Vietnam with a power at least as enduring as Tiptree's own imaginings of like relations.

THREE

Saigon Road

THE CO-CONSTITUTED LANDSCAPE
OF NORTHERN VIRGINIA AND SOUTH VIETNAM

IMPERIAL SPACE IS OFTEN IMAGINED through a binary relationship between metropole and colony, in which power trickles from center to periphery, and both retain their location. As an American suburb, Northern Virginia would appear to be sealed off from these relationships by design, as a domestic, residential space inherently defined by the gap between the foreign and the domestic. In the U.S. context, the assertion that this nation has a non-territorial empire also tends to sideline spatial analysis or to draw it away from civilian places to the harder military manifestations of American imperial space—bases and coaling stations, for instance—inadvertently helping to obscure the fact that U.S. empire took territory in manifold, strategic, and dialectical ways, even if it didn't always formally incorporate it.

Verbs like *repatriate* at times bridge the gap, tracking U.S. empire into domestic life, and one could easily use the term here to describe the imperial spatial relations between Northern Virginia and Vietnam. Northern Virginia sent agents to Vietnam who developed crucial imperial intimacies that brought some refugees back to Northern Virginia after the fall of Saigon on April 30, 1975—"repatriating" them. But this suggests that both places involved begin the story as separate, and as Stuart Hall writes, colonization was always "inscribed deeply" in the "societies of the imperial metropolis" just as "it became indelibly inscribed in the cultures of the colonised."[1] The next two chapters build on this space-imprinting idea of inscription to make a wider claim: through the workings of empire, suburban Northern Virginia and South Vietnam were a co-constituted landscape. At the start of their chronology as U.S. imperial spaces, they were the product of an imbricated relationship between Vietnam and Northern Virginia.

Fredric Jameson once offered, via Kevin Lynch, the term *cognitive map-*

ping to describe the way people try to build a sense of a transnational local in a world where "structural coordinates are no longer accessible to immediate lived experience" or even "conceptualizable for most people."[2] The geographer Doreen Massey offers, instead, the "story" as the raw building material of space. She uses the story not as a plot with beginning, middle, and end but as "simply the history, change, movement, of things themselves." She leaves it open to further change by qualifying it: these are "stories-so-far," not complete ones. Space is not just a flat surface or an empty container, but the "meeting-up" place of these simultaneous stories-so-far, the dynamic point where the widest networks of interrelations and heterogeneity coexist.[3] Stories-so-far have a living history and future *and* a material presence, both time and space. Connections don't happen because all places are always connected. These meetings, these stories-so-far, happen because people have a complex agency, they initiate stories, which set off social processes that further make and change the places and the people inside them.

The next two chapters narrate stories-so-far between Vietnam and Virginia as a route toward describing the Dulles Corridor as imperial corridor. In doing so, they put forward a means of imagining the broadest ways the United States claimed and marked imperial space in the post–World War II period. The stories in these chapters focus on those projects initiated by the U.S. imperial state as it was located in the Dulles Corridor, but obviously, and importantly, Vietnam has its own stories-so-far, and this is only one of them, just as Vietnam is only one of the stories-so-far of the Dulles Corridor. Yet through these recitations, the depth of the mutually constituted nature of South Vietnam and Northern Virginia—its ghostly connections along the stories-so-far wrought and received by the home front of U.S. empire and its covert capital—will begin to emerge. It will *begin* to emerge only because it will forever be emerging.

MARK MERRELL'S SAIGON ROAD— MCLEAN'S SAIGON 1950

Saigon Road, off Georgetown Pike in McLean, is the main street in a winding, woody subdivision. It branches off what is essentially the same main road that passes the CIA headquarters. Saigon appears at first to be a kind of Vietnam War reference, the whim of a developer in the late seventies, when subdivisions were sweeping across Fairfax County. It is not. The history of

Saigon Road goes back to the time before almost any subdivisions had come to McLean, before the CIA had even decided to move to McLean. It reaches back into the world of the nouveau gentry and literary set connected to the massive federal expansion of Washington in the thirties who first hoped to experience that largesse from the tree-shaded reaches of the upper Potomac on the Virginia side.

Charles Marquis Merrell was born in St. Louis, where he worked for his family's pharmaceutical business. He moved to the East Coast, and in New York City in 1929, he married a woman from Evansville, Wisconsin, named Marion Clinch Calkins. They came to DC in 1933 when Merrell, at the age of 32, took a job with the National Recovery Administration, the New Deal's industrial arm. He made a name for himself as head of the NRA's drug section. In 1935, the Merrells moved to their first house in McLean and before long settled down in the village of Langley on the Rokeby Farms estate, next to the future CIA site.[4]

Marion Merrell was the more famous of the two. In college, she won the *Nation*'s annual poetry contest but was demoted to third place because her poem was so "advanced in its thinking," telling of the tragedy that occurred when a young maiden was barred from having sex with her fiancé before marriage. The poem launched her on a career as a writer under the name Clinch Calkins. In New York City, the settlement house movement drew her into activist work. The couple could well have decided to move to DC because of Calkins's career. In 1933, Harry Hopkins, the chief FDR advisor who supervised the New Deal's work relief programs, asked her to be his speechwriter. She served as researcher for Wisconsin senator Robert La Follette's committee investigating corporate assaults on the rights of labor and held a position as assistant chief in the housing development division of the Resettlement Administration. All the while, she wrote poetry for the *New Yorker, Good Housekeeping,* and the *New Republic.*[5]

In those early days, the Merrells easily mingled in the social world, often composed of large landowners such as the Mackalls and the Smoots, who enjoyed fox hunts, thoroughbred horses, and country gatherings that the Dulles family and the Kennedys took advantage of slightly later in the century. As "Mrs. Mark Merrell," Calkins was a regular face helping out at the tea table for local debutantes at well-heeled social functions, at least one at Hickory Hill. In 1941, the Merrells started a "community auto plan" with four other federal government couples, including a lieutenant commander in the navy. Rather than each of the wives independently driving the men into the city, the men gathered in the driveway of a McLean estate and one wife made the trek. They called the ride, which went to the old District Building in DC, the "Defense Special." Calkins wrote plays and novels, including a satire of her new neighbors, *Lady on the Hunt*, which mocked the local "horsey set."[6] She and her husband came to Northern Virginia as migrants. They settled a landscape with few suburbs and many wide-open spaces, one undergoing its first significant blushes of development as a federal and geopolitical place.

A large international influence exerted itself on the couple through Merrell's brother George, a State Department official who worked on Latin American issues and then held posts across China, India, Ethiopia, and Afghanistan.[7] In 1950, Mark Merrell himself went abroad. In what was arguably McLean's first geopolitical contact with Vietnam, he became director of drug allocation for the Economic Cooperation Administration (ECA), administrator of the Marshall Plan. His station was Saigon, one of only three capitals in Asia included in the Plan. As a "supply officer" with the Special Technical and Economic Mission (STEM), he spread American medical infrastructure, supplies, and improvements to Vietnamese farms, towns, and cities damaged during World War II, as Calkins stayed home in McLean to write.[8]

Merrell reached Saigon in August and soon moved into the brand-new Majestic Hotel. He was one of the first guests to inhabit the quarters that would define American experience in the country for the next two and a half decades. A corner room on the fourth floor became his home in Saigon, the view from the balcony his most diurnal, panoramic understanding of the country and its politics. Hoisted over the treetops, out of the busy city streets, he raised a spyglass to sharpen a vista where Vietnamese life and French imperialism appeared seamlessly blended. At sunrise, rowboats circuited the busy harbor, peacefully sharing the water with "French Warships lined up right out your window."[9]

Merrell met the members of STEM, his social world in the country. They included director Robert Blum, deputy and PR man Leo Hochstetter, and the agricultural officer Harold E. Schwartz, a Northern Virginian who lived in the Jefferson Village Apartments just below Falls Church.[10] On Sundays, they played baseball or drank beer at sidewalk bars. Many evenings they staked piaster gin rummy bets on Merrell's balcony and once went to a swanky Chinese restaurant in Cholon, where Merrell drank cognac and danced with a "Chinese taxi-dance girl." Merrell tried to get used to

Vietnamese food, which he called "very strange indeed. Not Chinese." Just as often, he retreated to the Mill, a nearby restaurant run by a French chef. At sunset, he sipped Old Crow and Old Smuggler whiskey and listened to the swinging tides and muted score of mortars and machine guns that picked up after 9 PM, the sound of the French colonial war and the Vietnamese national resistance—which launched an offensive at the time of his arrival—always offstage, always cast as a threat.[11]

Soon after he arrived in Saigon, the first members of the U.S. military assistance group landed. Merrell met them at a cocktail party at U.S. minister Donald Heath's house, where he became a frequent guest at the consular functions at which Americans socialized with STEM's Vietnamese staff, who organized a party that New Year's featuring a "native orchestra."[12] Thereafter, Merrell's distribution work was often intertwined with the advisory work of the military. Finding a Filipino interpreter, he rode to Hanoi in bucket seats in a C-57 beside General Francis Brink. Combined units of French soldiers and navy officers guided him through Haiphong's Red River Valley, and he flanked military representatives to tour a gun factory. His travels to review battalions of Cao Dai soldiers reflected the search, even at this early point, for a "third force" between the nationalist Viet Minh and the French, who could put into effect American interests in Vietnam. Merrell found the lavish village dinners and waving of American flags at these reviews distasteful. He viewed them as openly cynical bids to get more U.S. aid, not genuine displays of affection. Other receptions could be even more discomfiting. In at least one village, STEM was met with a banner that read "Mr. Roosevelt said that Colonialism was the cause of all war." Across his travels, Merrell faced down the earliest complexities of the on-the-ground transition to the U.S. presence and occupation in the country.[13] All along, he sent reams of letters to Marion and his daughter, Julie, processing his understanding of Vietnam through travel, political reflections, landscape impressions, and generally pleasant social engagements with Frenchmen. Traversing the terrain in a Ford Suburban station wagon, Merrell donned his fanciful uniform of bush jacket and long white pants and trolled the shops looking for a bit of "Saigon art works" that he might bring home to his family, even as they awaited news in Northern Virginia of their own departure to join him in the distant city.[14]

But through many of Merrell's impressions, Saigon was not so distant. Under his narrative eye, the family home in Northern Virginia was already present in Vietnam. He often ventured into the rural landscape to see Vietnam's version of the countryside, which he measured against home. His comparisons expressed his nostalgia for Virginia, but they also suggested the commonsense necessity of Virginia in Vietnam. "Shooting started across the River . . . ," he would write, setting the scene, "then it stopped and it's like McLean Va."[15] One Cao Dai temple in Tay Ninh was most distinguished by the fact that "it was twice as long as the McLean firehouse."[16] Rather than the ostensibly neutral impressions of the tourist, Merrell's incorporative vision of Northern Virginia and Vietnam's relative likeness was a critical mode of understanding and insinuating the U.S. political presence in the country for one of its earliest agents.

On the surface, much of Merrell's work in Saigon appears to be numbingly mundane. He read memos with titles such as "Procurement of Paper Bags."[17] He wrote letters with lines like, "It is also suggested that considerable thought be given to the type of wooden container to be used in this program."[18] He made suggestions on the size of labels. He ordered ether, first aid kits, vitamins B and K.[19] But to fully understand his work, it is crucial to grasp the function of the Marshall Plan as a Cold War weapon, cover for the early CIA and its covert action arm, the Office of Policy Coordination. The point of the Marshall Plan, approved in 1948, was, according to one observer, to "help rebuild civilization, with an American blueprint." But it also inaugurated, along with the CIA itself, "organized political warfare." Allen Dulles consulted on the Marshall Plan's drafting. Under its auspices, $685 million in foreign currency "was made available to the CIA" overseas, providing untraceable funds for covert political action.[20]

Marshall Plan money went to Vietnam alongside the return of French colonial administration. STEM and Merrell came with it, charged with a broad mission as the crucial and often overlooked U.S. outfit in Vietnam during the late French colonial period that mediated the transition from French to American power. Supporting French-certified emperor Bao Dai in the face of Vietnamese nationalism and "modernizing the infrastructure of the rural-based economy," STEM's technical assistance traversed the medical, social, cultural, and agricultural, with the broader goal of the "recapture of prewar export markets." It was the only American entity that could work directly with Vietnamese without passing through French officials. It was the first to send Americans out for significant contact with Vietnamese administrators "at the regional and even village level."[21] Merrell was one of the first Americans to do this work.

These efforts proved a constant irritant to the French and prefigured U.S. imperial technique in Vietnam. Like so many early figures working under the cover of the technical assistance missions, STEM director Robert Blum was what one U.S. Congressional history calls a CIA officer, a man who intentionally emphasized direct assistance to the Vietnamese as a concerted "political program" that "would appeal to the masses of the population."[22] Deputy Leo Hochstetter—Merrell's "poker, gin-rummy, chess, roulette and other companion"[23]—shared a room with Graham Greene on Greene's 1951 visit to the French command in Ben Tre province, and through this contact, Hochstetter likely became an important model for Greene's *The Quiet American*, one of the plucky, hands-on Americans, in the British author's reminiscences, "attached to an economic aid mission" whose "members were assumed by the French, probably correctly, to belong to the CIA."[24]

There is nothing that ties Merrell directly to the CIA in Vietnam in 1950. But some of his supplies extended beyond the strictly medical. He ordered movie projectors, sewing machines, canned milk, station wagons, Land Rovers, hand pumps, metal corrugated roofing, tons of asphalt, and earthmoving and road-making machines.[25] These materials wrought daily changes in the landscape of Vietnam. Much of his work had an explicitly political bent. The paper bags he procured, for example, were used to repackage commercial fertilizers. He shipped the fertilizers to facilities that distributed them at provincial and village centers in the Vietnamese countryside. One of his greatest concerns was for the beneficiaries to know the fertilizer came from the United States: "Each bag should carry the imprint of the American Aid Symbol to Vietnam in color," Merrell wrote.[26] Many of his duties concerned getting this symbol—a quilt composed of American, French, Vietnamese, Cambodian, and Laotian flags—onto different goods, down to syringes and bottles of penicillin. He wove the symbol into blankets to cover shivering refugees in the northern mountains. He printed it on armbands worn by DDT spray teams. He even insisted upon the symbol's presence "on notebooks, pencils etc. for schoolchildren."[27] Merrell thus helped train the generation of South Vietnamese that came of age during the Vietnam-American War to recognize American beneficence from their earliest schooling.

Merrell was also one of the first Americans to set up training programs for Vietnamese nurses and village first aid workers.[28] At their medical education program, he and his colleagues screened films on American surgical techniques to Vietnamese public officials. Their weekly radio broadcasts demonstrated American technical expertise in what Merrell called a "general propaganda show," and he helped stock Saigon's U.S. Information Service

Library, coaxing his wife to send an autographed copy of *Lady on the Hunt* for its shelves—perhaps the first novel of Northern Virginia's land and life to be read in Saigon.[29] By December, Merrell began to set up his distribution systems, which took him far into the countryside. As part of these efforts, he organized two of the earliest, perhaps the first, quasi-covert flying missions in Vietnam of CIA proprietary Civil Air Transport (CAT), with its commander, Claire Chennault. Merrell and Chennault arranged for CAT to fly a delivery of blankets, cloth, and needles from Tokyo to Hanoi and then to move five tons of hospital equipment from Paris to Saigon, before lifting "evacuees out of the Hanoi area," in an operation conducted long before most historians date the serious presence of the airline in Vietnam.[30]

Merrell lived in Vietnam for less than a year. But through his work, particularly as it extended to road-building machines and the activities of small rice farmers, he was a forefather of the "pacification" other McLean residents brought more violently to Vietnam soon afterward. Coming just as the United States was bolstering the French colonial position in Vietnam, his work established a beachhead of American enterprise in the country, an American domain, which later became one way U.S. agents secured control over Vietnam. More profoundly, years before Americans are seen as having significant spatial impact on the country, this Northern Virginia agent's work—with its focus on material, on building, on housing, and on changing everyday practices of caring for the body—entered, altered, and established crucial aspects of the built environment and material life of Vietnam that became incorporated into its physical expression as a place, that defined how it was experienced by local residents and later observers. Some of the last STEM projects to go up using Merrell's supplies as he left Saigon were major American land developments.[31] One was Cite Nguyen Tri Phuong, a massive demonstration housing project in Cholon that included more than a thousand housing units, forty-four commercial buildings, a school, a dispensary, and a police station.[32] Another was an early model of what became known as a strategic hamlet, a village at Dong Quan in the Mekong Delta that included new buildings, a fortified perimeter, and artillery supplies.[33] In Virginia, Merrell also lived in the social world that surrounded Langley. He could have been one of the ECA men who knew of the earliest CIA activities in Vietnam as well.

Calkins never visited Merrell in Saigon, despite making many plans and preparations for such a trip. Instead, Merrell finished his work in March 1951 and returned home, reporting cheerfully to the society columns that "he was no closer to the Chinese Communists when he was in French Indo-China than New York is to Chicago."[34] The comment, printed during the Vietnamese struggle for independence, suggested the U.S. position he represented, insinuating that the French in "French Indo-China" were what kept the communists at bay but also that Vietnam, in a sense, was already a convenient part of the United States. But this was Merrell's last political trip. He came back to McLean and became a developer, or to put it more precisely, continued his land development work.[35]

This transition from global to local is tightly chronicled in the novel Calkins wrote while Merrell was in Vietnam, *Calendar of Love*, which she dedicated to him as "Mark Merrell, generous provider of my leisure." The book tells the story of two couples, the Fleets and the Porters, who, like the Merrells, uproot their lives in Philadelphia industry to enter the alluring vortex of New Deal Washington. Cast in the geography of World War II's "Pacific Islands," there are traces of the correspondence Calkins and Merrell enjoyed while he was stationed in Vietnam: "She knew the Pacific Islands as she knew the District of Columbia. . . . She knew about volcanic ash, rice-paddies, jungles, rest-camps, tunnels, and air-strips."[36] But the core plot concerns social status and land use in the Northern Virginia area.

When a moral stand knocks young Adam Porter off course in Washington politics, he and his wife must migrate in shame across the river to live in a tiny apartment on Glebe Road in Arlington.[37] But it is their friends, the Fleets, who get trapped by the magnetism of undeveloped land on DC's edge. Miranda Fleet falls in love with a pastoral parcel in Northern Virginia that describes the place where the Merrells came to live and develop one of their subdivisions: " . . . down below them the Potomac River glittering far away through wilderness a hand's throw from the city."[38] But when Miranda buys the land on a whim, without a responsible, clear-sighted plan for its development and future, the Fleets become so hamstrung by debt and difficulties obtaining credit for the unimproved land that they can't enjoy the lovely scene. The answer in the novel is a violent intervention from Asia. The Fleets are only able to keep the property when a grenade kills the Porters' son in Okinawa the day before the atomic bomb is dropped on Hiroshima. Adam gives the couple his son's insurance check as testament to their friendship. Only a death in Asia can secure the pastoral idyll in McLean.

In one sense, the novel is an allegory of smart development, the need for friendly aid, and the hazards of soft-minded, sentimental attachments to places that ignore the cruel realities of the world. But the book's sense of the connection between life in the sphere of American influence in Southeast Asia and the land of the Virginia suburbs of Washington comes from the personal connection between Merrell and Calkins. It is directly underwritten by Merrell's station in Vietnam. The original title, *The Costly Woods*, a phrase quoted toward the novel's end, signifies the double sense of "cost"— both financial and in the costs of violent death—and the novel binds the two together in the McLean landscape, linking the violence and necessity of war and the perils of development at home and abroad.[39]

In real life, Merrell himself acted out a version of this intervention when he returned home from Vietnam to clear the trees of these costly woods and plat them for a new subdivision named after the Vietnamese city he had just left: Saigon.[40] It is worth pausing on the decision. Merrell was only in Saigon for six or seven months. Yet in his first land development he forewent the gestures common to developers, who often name properties after loved ones or banal features of the local landscape. Instead, he chose to name this piece of McLean Saigon. He could have made this choice for many reasons: a name that would make the property seem stylish for travelers who knew Saigon as the colonial "Paris of the Orient"; a name for federal hands who knew the city as one of America's geopolitical hopefuls abroad; or simply a distinctive name that would set the subdivision apart. But all these possibilities depend on a relationship in which a genre of dominance in Vietnam produces a recollection of comfort in the Virginia landscape for people who participated in that relationship enough to recognize the name at home. If they didn't recognize the name, they might experience its distant allure, a vague feeling which derives from a similar kind of geographical privilege—of *not* knowing the place with which Northern Virginia was already becoming so intimately involved.

But perhaps more than this even, the name suggests the kind of love that could cause someone to forever imprint the name of a foreign place where they only spent mere months in their fifties, into the land they bought at home for their own retirement. It suggests that, through Merrell as a vessel, Saigon and McLean had established a spatial concert, a complex mutuality that would feed back through violence and love over the next five decades, albeit a genre of love scored by its grimmer notes—possessive obsession, continuing violation. The connection seeped into Calkins's poetry. Even her verses steeped in the quiet hours of Virginia's landscape contain details clearly drawn from Vietnam, such as the line that opens the domestic "December Morning at Home": "I have placed the ruby amber Buddha."[41]

These connections continued on as Saigon grew up to become a neighborhood. The Merrells had bought the core of the property in May 1946. While Merrell was away, Calkins prepared tracts for possible sale, clearing undergrowth, establishing rights of way, tending the landscaping for the future. They subdivided the land upon Merrell's return from Vietnam into wedge-shaped lots ranging from 30,000 to 98,000 square feet, although many were later further divided. Merrell formalized blueprints for the first phase in August 1954. After the CIA's announcement, he appeared before the Fairfax County Planning Commission in 1956 with other developers looking to rezone their properties from "rural residential" to "suburban residential," to shrink the allowable average lot sizes to a minimum of 10,000 square feet.[42] That summer, when the state announced a new program that would bisect Georgetown Pike near Merrell's property with the highway that eventually became the Beltway and that would further disrupt it by expanding the GW Parkway and Route 123 to provide access to the future CIA headquarters, the Merrells hosted a party to protest the incursion. On their bucolic property, mourners gathered for a potluck and a poetry reading. "Fie, upon you, CIA, to spoil our lane with a new highway," contributed one melancholy local bard.[43] But behind the scenes, the Merrells bought more land, adding acreage through 1955, 1956, and 1957.

They were committed to the area. In 1956, they cast down stones for their own new shelter on Swinks Mill Road, a five-bedroom wood-framed house on a hill overlooking the subdivided lots below.[44] The same year, houses began going up in Saigon. The results were a suburban mix of mostly one-story, fifteen-foot-high brick and wood-frame houses with five to eight rooms and pitched roofs, raised mostly by local builders contracting with individual buyers for anywhere from $16,000 to $25,000. But there was some variety. Styles ranged from "rural residence" and "brick rambler" to Williamsburg colonial. Several owners sought out modern plans by architects such as Carl Koch, who had a house in the New York Museum of Modern Art's 1945 Tomorrow's Small House exhibit, and the well-known Virginia modernist-populist Charles M. Goodman, who both shaped the prefabricated designs provided to Saigon residents through companies such as Techbuilt and National Homes.[45]

In 1959, Merrell began marketing his subdivided lots to CIA agents, using the coming of the headquarters as a sales tool for the area. His first ad read "2 miles from CIA on Saigon Road, protected sites." It promised lots sized at two-thirds of an acre and larger and listed security as one of the property's fundamental amenities. Merrell was often the contact for interested parties.[46]

Before too long, Washingtonians phoned up, thinking they were inquiring about property in Vietnam. In 1967, the *Washington Post* mistakenly listed an $85,000 house with a pool in their "International Real Estate" section. A call to the realtor revealed the correct location. "Well, the Saigon is in McLean on Saigon Road," wrote the *Post*, "hardly international. But then Washington has been called a world capital."[47]

The subdivision Merrell named while working in 1950 for an internationally expanding American state could factor into Virginia's domestic landscape as a feature of that internationalized state a decade and a half later. And when Saigon subdivision found its occupants, among them were numerous emissaries from the Dulles Corridor military, intelligence, and defense establishment, just as Merrell had hoped, some with intimate ties to the corridor's geopolitical work in Asia.[48] The intersecting histories of Vietnam and Virginia thus preceded the development of much of Virginia's suburban landscape—Vietnam was an integral influence and inspiration for the landscape of the Dulles Corridor at the moment of its inception, not simply an addition tolerated in the form of its refugees twenty-five years later.

But another crucial link between Merrell's work in Vietnam and his work in Northern Virginia was what one might call the politics of speculation through which covert capital elites experienced the shaping of land at home and abroad in this period. Despite the family squabbles that could arise between the French and the Americans,[49] Merrell's letters from Vietnam display the abiding sense of common heritage, interests, and racial solidarity that existed between them as they faced the Viet Minh. Merrell associated Vietnam's security with the French. But his time in Vietnam also took on an intriguing relationship to time itself, opening an imaginative space for the U.S. presence in the country. He was sure the Viet Minh were "about to be wiped out if the French can shoot straight." After seeing Thailand, he imagined that "if Vietnam had peace and were independent their people would develop over a few generations like the Thais." He mused on a free Vietnam but only after "a lot of doing—ECA, Point 4, or what have you." This sense of futurism pervaded his own work, as he focused on "long pull things," such as his road building, and "short pull things," such as his malaria treatments, hoping all the while that "maybe China won't come into the fight up North and this American Aid will help."[50] America in Vietnam and Vietnam itself were projects never complete, eternally in formation—about to be, over a few generations, coming after a lot of doing. Whatever happened with the French, America couldn't leave any time soon, and Vietnamese independence was always deferred.[51] Merrell was there laying the very first stones in an edifice of modernism, progress, and an American-framed local and world economy that would, along the linear logic of development itself, mature for human and national benefit and autonomy in some distant future, over the next horizon, with an offstage violence and a fear of loss always as its secret partner.

This same sense of U.S. imperial time defined the American project in Vietnam for the next twenty-five years. But it also underlay the emotional experience of development in the covert capital. At home, preparing parcels of their land, crossing fingers for successful ventures, targeting the exact moment to sell a strategic plot, worrying that the pastoral atmosphere could slip away at any moment or be destroyed by less-wise stewards, wondering if she would join her husband in Vietnam, Calkins expressed in her letters prospects with a sense of time closely matched to that of her husband, one that continually drew its urgency and melodrama from the political and historical moment to which her husband's interventions were central. "We are all in this together, loneliness and danger," she wrote in one letter. "Our love can support us across the world as well as the love of other people has to support those who have no hope of being united."[52] The symbol of their commitment and the sign of its power was the same in both places: a visible intervention on the land. The politics of speculation demanded not only a rhetorical hope and optimism but a constant, vigilant intervention to pry quite personal dreams into real space. To the Merrell family, in Vietnam and in Virginia, building was a bulwark, fending off a loss. Speculation was their trope, as they bet on the future. Land itself, alternately, was their major site of hope and security.[53] Development and empire saw existing places through a utilitarian language of current imperfection and endless, anxious evolution that irrevocably changed the landscape in both Vietnam and Virginia. Eyes on the idealistic distance and their personal relationships, U.S. agents in Northern Virginia did not often acknowledge that their own work was an important reason why people elsewhere had "no hope of being united."

McLEAN'S VIETNAM, 1944–1989

The CIA agents who created the very shape of South and North Vietnam, who laid the groundwork for the U.S. empire in Vietnam, either came from Northern Virginia or returned to settle in McLean. Over a twenty-five year period, these agents went to and from Vietnam and Virginia so many times it would be hard to call one or the other place their home. Their home became some place across the two countries, jointly present in the domestic spaces of both. But before taking them into their domesticity in the Dulles Corridor, it is worth spending some time exploring who these men were, how they were central to the earliest U.S. imperial projects after World War II and helped to define those projects through their work and lives in Vietnam.

Lucien Conein claimed to be the first U.S. intelligence agent in Vietnam.[54] The Paris-born American established himself using his French language skills on the jump teams that parachuted into occupied France to help resistance fighters in 1944.[55] In 1945, the CIA's predecessor, the Office of Strategic Services, sent the demolition and guerrilla expert from his post in Kunming, China on to Hanoi to run raids against the Japanese.[56] There, he met Ho Chi Minh and other anti-colonial fighters in the League for the Independence of Vietnam, the Viet Minh. He relied on them for intelligence and help in rescuing downed American pilots during the last months of the war. In turn, he and other U.S. agents gave Ho Chi Minh, whose "sincerity and personal commitment" Conein found "mesmerizing," arms and supplies to help him make his own raids on the imperial Japanese.[57]

But by 1950, the OSS had given way to the CIA, and American policy had changed. Stabilizing a rebuilt capitalist Japan as a world trading partner, bolstering France as a market for American products and a military ally, and securing Vietnam's valuable tin, tungsten, and rubber mines as a resource for Western business trumped supporting anti-colonial struggles.[58] By the time the Viet Minh routed the French at Dien Bien Phu in 1954, the United States was paying 78 percent of France's Indochina war bills.[59] Even as the parties were signing the Geneva Accords to promote the independence and reunification of Vietnam, the CIA sent in a team called the Saigon Military Mission to make sure it never happened, or that if it did, the country formed part of "a healthy postwar order" organized through "an economic and military world system dominated by the United States."[60] Eisenhower put it only slightly differently the same year the Mission went to Vietnam, saying the United States was "the central key" to world order, "the core of democracy, economically, militarily and spiritually," inherently conflating the political system of democracy at home with a new global economic and military mandate abroad, inflicted on a system of countries welded to the core of the United States.[61] The Mission went in to do the welding.

American intelligence tapped Conein in March 1954 because of contacts he had gained in Hanoi in 1945. The group's leader was Edward Lansdale. Lansdale was a Dulles Corridor veteran, even in its prehistory. He called Northern Virginia "an area that has been home to his family for the past three hundred years." The son of a DC-born businessman, the former ad man made his name as an international intelligence agent in the Philippines. When not on leave at his apartment in the bachelor quarters of Fort Myer in Arlington or in the house he was constantly refurbishing in Georgetown, where his wife and two sons lived, or at his office in wood Tempo building M on the Washington Mall, Lansdale worked in the Philippines for U.S. intelligence and what became the covert action arm of the CIA almost continuously from 1945 to 1954.[62] He occupied a similar historical position to Conein. They were the figures in the field who executed the transition as America's postwar obsession with prying open and locking up the world's markets converted it from potential supporter of freedom to panicked anticommunist hammer.

With much fanfare, the United States granted its colony in the Philippines independence on July 4, 1946—forever branding it with the U.S.'s own independence day—but not before installing the new country's president. With his help, essentially as a condition of independence, the United States forced through three laws: the first tied the Philippines economy to a few agricultural export crops grown for the U.S. market and gave American businesses control over the country's utilities and natural resources; the second limited postwar reparations to the Philippines and war damage assistance to $500, unless the country agreed to these conditions; the third established permanent U.S. military bases at Clark Field and Subic Bay on Philippine soil. The only snag in these measures was the People's Anti-Japanese Army. Known as the Huks because of their acronym in Tagalog, the resistance organization united multiple labor and peasant groups, including the urban political left of the communist party, to fight business elites and landlords who sided with the Japanese during the war. When those elites switched their allegiances to the United States upon liberation, the Huks continued to fight. The covert action arm of the CIA sent Lansdale in to fight the Huks.[63]

In his time in the islands with Ramón Magsaysay, the protégé he would steer into the Philippine presidency, Lansdale laid what historians mark as the U.S. foundations for the doctrines and practices known as "counterinsurgency." This doctrine—essentially all those programs designed to woo, kill, move, indoctrinate, interrogate, reform, bribe, develop, and imprison (rather than simply bomb) people into loyalty toward America and its appointed gov-

ernments—ravaged the Vietnamese countryside from the Kennedy administration on.[64] Lansdale brought it to Vietnam himself. Although some historians date his entry into Vietnam from 1954, Lansdale first traveled there on a
six-week inspection trip in summer 1953, making him one of the first formal
CIA advisors in the country.[65]

Allen Dulles suggested ordering Lansdale to form the Saigon Military
Mission in January 1954, just before Dulles began scouting sites for the CIA
in Virginia.[66] The Mission was to engineer "the birth of a southern government that could successfully compete with and oppose Ho's Democratic
Republic of Vietnam," and to "undertake paramilitary operations against the
enemy and to wage political-psychological warfare" against the Viet Minh.
Both missions were in violation of the Geneva Accords.[67] Saigon looked like
"a beautiful garden" to Lansdale, passive, tendable, and ready to be weeded,
perhaps, but he noted it "wasn't ready at all for independence."[68] The guiding strategy he brought with him was simple: "Our psychological warfare
must turn this war from a 'colonial' war in Communist terms to a civil war
in our terms."[69]

The activities of Conein and Lansdale in Hanoi and Saigon are legendary.
They draw a detailed picture of what securing another country for a "world
system dominated by the United States" meant in practice. In June 1954,
Lansdale moved to Saigon. He soon settled into a bungalow on rue Miche.
Before long, Conein arrived, along with other key team members—a young
Harvard journalism major named Arthur "Nick" Arundel; a CIA-trained,
Virginia–bred figure named Rufus Phillips, a football player from Yale just
into his twenties and armed with college French; Joe Redick, an energetic
interpreter who could speak French, Japanese, Spanish, and German; and
Joe Baker, a number cruncher who had majored in economics at Michigan
State. All had military cover—Lansdale with the air force, Arundel with the
marines, Conein, Phillips and Baker with the army, Redick with the navy.
As the team grew, Lansdale rented a three-story walk-up apartment over a
shoemaker's shop; a compound with a large two-story house, a five-car driveway, and a smaller building for servants' quarters at 51 rue Duy Tan; and a
second large, walled house with a pool on rue Tabard.[70] The houses staged
a set of politics that needed to transpire outside formal U.S. political channels at the embassy and a "regular" CIA station also in Vietnam at the time.
Both were compounds the team could retreat to from Saigon's streets at will.
Both echoed the architecture and historic presence of France. One journalist recalled visiting the "dreary little compound on a Saigon side street . . .

Members of Edward Lansdale's Saigon Military Mission, such as Joseph Baker and Lucien Conein (pictured here), traveled to and from Vietnam and Virginia so often it would be hard to call one or the other place their home. Their home became some place amid the two countries, present in the domestic spaces of both. Their tight social network irrevocably changed both places. Courtesy of Vicki J. Baker.

A score or so of beardless young Americans . . . streamed in and out of the house or simply lounged cheerfully in the various rooms and discussed the events of the day." The team, accompanied at times by Filipino agents flown into Saigon by Lansdale, brainstormed in the "family" living room in sessions known as "Lansdale's coffee klatches," where the scotch flowed and a mutt named Pierre romped through their legs. A Saigon tailor made the Americans matching outfits of khaki shorts and long socks, only a slight variation on the French colonial uniform.[71] It was either the tailor's joke or their own—the group would assume many duties of French colonial management.

They operated under a sort of geographic division of labor, overseen by Lansdale from Saigon. In the first phase, they worked directly to subvert the Geneva agreement as it temporarily divided the country en route to national elections. Conein went north to conduct paramilitary work, using the chaotic French withdrawal as cover to disrupt and attack the Viet Minh government as it tried to establish itself according to the negotiated agreement. Putting into effect what he called "a general sabotage," his team incapacitated his former allies' bus, tram, and rail system with acid-laced oil and tried to blow up a printing plant. They smuggled eight and a half tons of supplies to two guerilla groups they trained to stay behind and harass the North after partition. Conein always called this work "playing cowboy and Indian."[72]

Lansdale ran central operations from Saigon. One of his strengths was political manipulation conducted through close friendship. After a group of powerful U.S. citizens steered in Ngo Dinh Diem, the scion of an elite family during the French colonial period, as premier for South Vietnam in July 1954, Lansdale immediately became his confidant, spending nearly every day with him, including many "family meals." Lansdale secretly cycled these intimacies into marketable knowledge back in the Pentagon and the CIA, where he provided U.S. militarists with microscopic details of Diem's life that transcended traditional ideas of useful diplomatic data, such as the fact that Diem "enjoys eating," "has a good appetite," and "doesn't parade his feelings for everyone to see." Lansdale and his men trained and recruited Diem's bodyguards; wrote Diem's speeches in the diction of American patriotism; hand-edited the South Vietnamese constitution that a friend from the Philippines flew in to draft; and manipulated a referendum to confirm Diem's position, bringing in 605,025 votes for Diem (when there were only 450,000 registered voters), which finally subverted the true elections that were to reunite Vietnam.[73] A North Vietnamese history put it succinctly: "The U.S. 'advisers' were the real masters of the country."[74]

In "informal" sessions at his house, Lansdale set about meeting with various Vietnamese to put into place the physical and administrative presence of Diem's government in the cities, countryside, and villages of South Vietnam, then being vacated by the French and the Viet Minh. Mission member Arthur Arundel formed propaganda squads that blanketed the countryside to spread the new government's messages, which they also often wrote.[75] Helpful in these endeavors was Vietnamese journalist and author Bui Anh Tuan, who became the Mission's point person for circulating articles into Saigon newspapers, including a "Thomas Paine type series of essays on Vietnamese patriotism" that were based on a copy of *Common Sense* Lansdale had given him.[76] The Vietnamese singer Pham Duy also joined the team, using his musical talents to bolster enthusiasm for Diem.[77] For their participants, the friendships formed within these endeavors could be transformative. As Dr. Emmanuel Ho Quan Phuoc, a dentist, longtime confidant, and sponsor of Lansdale's Operation Brotherhood medical relief and propaganda program, said to Lansdale, "You were the only one chief I knew who tried and did the same thing to your friends and collaborators. One appreciates more those casual meals at your houses in Saigon than parties at the Independence Palace or the Embassy."[78]

Such friendships traversed boundaries of closeness where manipulation and emotions blended in order to create a leadership cadre of recognized collaborators with the U.S. imperial effort. Participants reaped both monetary and affective rewards. When Diem needed the powerful Cao Dai sect to join his army and support his government, Lansdale wrangled American dollars to directly pay Cao Dai general Trinh Minh Thé to declare his allegiance.[79] But Lansdale instantly translated the source of their contact and American influence in political purchase into the hallowed rubric of robust friendship and freely chosen kinship relation. His houses in central Saigon, only blocks from the palace, continually fostered this process. During one folk dance where Lansdale and other Mission members launched into a whirl around a bamboo pole, Lansdale forced Trinh to take off his shoes and join in, after which the general, known for starting his campaigns against enemy units by immediately assassinating their leaders, gave Lansdale "a great big hug," the sign of their new bond. Soon, Lansdale, South Vietnamese general Cao Van Vien, and Trinh were spending pleasant afternoons drinking tea and Vietnamese coffee at Lansdale's house, and Trinh brought Lansdale two pet mongooses.[80]

As part of the Geneva Accords, anyone could cross the 17th parallel to the "country" of their choice before the border solidified. Diem, the Red Cross, and the U.S. Agency for International Development all expected the number coming south to be no more than 10,000. Lansdale didn't think it had to be that low. Looking to build popular support for Diem where none existed, he embarked on an aggressive campaign to terrify residents of the North. He directed Rufus Phillips to publish an almanac that foretold certain disaster for the North's government and "people in Communist areas." Conein, whose cover was to engage in "refugee work," oversaw a vast rumor campaign through Hanoi and Haiphong that told Catholics that Christ and the Virgin Mary had gone south, scared the affluent and small shopkeepers with concocted versions of the Viet Minh's economic and monetary regulations (which ended up devaluing the North's currency by half in two days), told peasants that Chinese troops were crossing the border to rape and rob them with Viet Minh permission, and informed everyone else that the United States would be dropping nuclear bombs on those who stayed.[81] Under the hectic cover of the evacuation, meanwhile, Lucien Conein looted North Vietnam, using ten airplanes to ship out people, equipment, and arms.[82]

In all these senses, the Saigon Military Mission played more than a disruptive advisory role in Vietnam. Their actions established the literal form of the two "countries," which twenty years later observers experienced as spatial reality. But the agents most thoroughly shaped Vietnam by bringing counterinsurgency to its countryside. That was Rufus Phillips's job—literal physical development projects. As the Viet Minh ceded southern posts to abide by the Geneva Accords, Lansdale saw a need to repoliticize peasants in support of the American-installed government of South Vietnam. Phillips went in with teams of Vietnamese to convince the rice farmers that this was a good idea.[83] "The Vietnamese loved this hulking big paratrooper," Lansdale recalled, "and he returned the affection."[84]

"Phillips believed that their support might be won by providing them with mosquito nets, blankets, and food, and by improving roads and bridges, almost nonexistent in many areas, so that the farmers could get their crops to market," writes one observer.[85] He dug wells. He brought fertilizer. He handed out medical kits. He rebuilt markets, roofs, roads, and bridges. Like Mark Merrell before him, he sculpted American aid, American material, and American building techniques into the physical landscape of Vietnam—in Long My, in Ca Mau, in Quang Ngai, in Giai Phong, in Binh Dinh, in Qui Nhon.[86] The team stressed medical relief work in their projects because Lansdale saw it as a gateway to other forms of access—as "the first instinct of any person is survival"—and because it could, over the long term, open Vietnam as a market, offering a "golden opportunity" for U.S. companies "demonstrating their products in areas of the world that are hungry for technological improvement," which, as nations, would then request "the brands they were most familiar with."[87] Phillips reveled in the racially transformative intimacies of the work. His Vietnamese counterparts would cap projects by telling him, "Maybe you were born Vietnamese in a previous incarnation."[88] But it is crucial to understand that the point of this work, which Phillips called "pacification," the term the French had used, was not goodwill. It was to win political fealty in order to increase "security."[89] If Vietnamese peasants who received American development refused to support American policies in return, pacification's fist waited around the next corner, and the men around the Mission implicitly accepted, in the words of a CIA historian, "that a judicious level of repression would not compromise the nation-building program," even one that included "non-judicial police action."[90]

In his communications to Allen Dulles, Lansdale could be blunt. One month after his arrival in Saigon, he asserted to Dulles that his "political base" in Vietnam could "give CIA control [of the] government and change [the] whole atmosphere."[91] At the same time, the Mission's focus on pacification gave its members a curious relationship to the Vietnamese people. Although terrible violence waited in the shadows of its doctrine, its primary discourse was love. Lansdale prided himself on understanding not only the politics but the cultures of places he entered. Like most of his staff, he often didn't even speak the languages. He claimed to communicate on good humor alone. And he almost always acquired his cultural knowledge through one-on-one experiences of extreme intimacy with people he knew for political reasons. His relationships with Magsaysay and Diem were nearly romantic, at least familial. He and Magsaysay shared a bedroom in Manila, vacationed and skinny-dipped together, and in a famous photograph, Lansdale plays harmonica while Magsaysay sleeps with his head essentially in his lap.[92] In Vietnam, Lansdale forged a similar intimacy with Diem, vacationing and picnicking with his family on isolated beaches near Saigon that eventually became training camps for counterinsurgency warriors.[93]

Diem, himself well versed in the high-wire politics of colonial affiliation and independence, "eagerly exploited CIA's readiness to help establish the new government's authority." But even when Diem resisted Lansdale's advice—with a politics of delay and miscomprehension in the face of U.S. directives that Americans often caricatured as a racial trait rather than seeing it as a strategy of imperial collaboration and autonomy—family metaphors held strong. After a difficulty with Diem, Lansdale once reported to CIA headquarters: "Well, [I] am also unsuccessful getting my sons [to] wash behind [the] ears." Even when Diem distanced himself from Lansdale, he acknowledged the abiding "sentiment" between them and called Lansdale a friend, who, if Diem died, "will grieve for me a long, long time."[94]

Personal intimacy was the terrain on which Lansdale expressed his, and through him, America's right to be in the country and right to belong, as well as its apparent softness as an imperial power. Lansdale was a "friend," never a colonialist. Vietnam was Lansdale's "home," never a battlefield. To his local agents, he was "Uncle Ed." As a feature of this, if shrewd Americans like Lansdale *belong* in Vietnam, then the Vietnamese, at least those who consent to America's vision for them, implicitly belong in America, or, through Lansdale's entry into their country, are already in a version of America. Lansdale renarrated their history to make this so: "I like the Vietnamese people, hard working, full of poetry, music, and earthy good humor, they seemed to recognize this liking in me and responded," he explained. "I believe that the Americans at Concord Bridge or Valley Forge would have recognized them as kindred souls."[95]

U.S. imperialists like Lansdale did not merely pine to control a country administratively, even when they were doing just that. They wanted to colonize desire. Shedding light on the body-snatcher undertones that harrowed the spirited liberal phrase "winning hearts and minds," Lansdale and the Mission insisted upon their Vietnamese friends and intimates wanting exactly what they wanted, on being them, in a sense. As Lansdale put it, "The strongest control is one that is self-imposed; it is based upon mutual trust and the awakening of unselfish patriotism on ideals or principles we ourselves cherish . . . the foreign person or groups serve our own best national interests by serving their own highest national interests, which coincide with ours."[96] This invented family relationship between the countries, underwritten by power politics and sold by Lansdale in 1954, was the birth point for an intimacy that became a crisis for those who believed it in 1975.

Members of the Mission legalized this intimacy in their personal lives. As Lansdale gradually became estranged from his white American wife at home in Georgetown, he fell in love with Patrocinio Yapcinco Kelly, the ethnically Chinese Filipina journalist who had taken her last name from the Filipino-Irish man she was briefly married to during World War II and who guided Lansdale into mountains north of Manila, showing him what he described as "things in the Zambales Mountains that I would never have known otherwise."[97] Kelly then came on to Vietnam, vacationing with Lansdale and the Diem family, where she and Madame Nhu would swim together in the ocean.[98] Later, she became Lansdale's wife. Conein met his wife in Hanoi while devising ways to destroy its transportation system. The granddaughter of a white French coffee plantation owner and his Vietnamese mistress, and the stepdaughter of the French official who ran the Hanoi transportation system, Elyette Bruchot was part of Hanoi's colonial elite. She and Conein met at one of the cocktail parties her stepfather attended as president of Le Cercle Sportif, the French colonial sports club. She worked as a ground flight attendant for Air France in Hanoi and then Pan Am in Saigon. Her Vietnamese citizenship legitimized Conein's place in the country as he infiltrated the Saigon government to monitor its coup plots. She facilitated his intelligence gathering as a trilingual hostess for Vietnamese generals at their villa.[99]

It is thus important to remember that these sexual relationships, literally only made possible by an often-violent American political presence in Asia, existed alongside the agents' political infiltration into the high echelons of

Vietnamese society. As they established an American domain in Southeast Asia, the realm of the most personal was, arguably, another of its staging grounds. An embittered French colonialist emphasized this point to Rufus Phillips with a metaphor that suggests the degree to which sex also shaped understandings of French and American imperial competition in Vietnam, linking racial and gendered ideas about the country to the everyday experiences of the imperialists and subjects who inhabited it: "To understand how we feel, how would you feel if you had a mistress, and you were very, very close to her. Finally, after this long relationship, you broke it off because really you couldn't afford to support her anymore. You're sitting in a sidewalk café, and the very next day she comes roaring by in this Cadillac with this American. How would you feel?"[100]

By 1957, the Mission was over. Vietnam divided. The team disbanded. Rufus Phillips went on to Laos to continue his pacification work.[101] Then he moved to his house in the Dulles Corridor, on Ridge Road in McLean in the patrician Langley Farms subdivision a half mile down Georgetown Pike from the CIA, where he lived with his Chilean wife, Barbara, and took over his father's airport engineering business.[102] Conein traveled to Tehran to, as he put it, "play cowboy and Indian in Iran," training SAVAK, the brutal secret police that kept the Shah in power after the CIA coup run by McLean residents kept him there in 1953.[103]

Arthur Arundel returned to his house in McLean on Waverly Way, also in Langley Farms. Once Rufus Phillips made it home, they were practically next-door neighbors. Arundel started one of Northern Virginia's largest and most successful newspaper chains, narrating the development of the suburbs back to its builders and residents using propaganda techniques he had perfected abroad, celebrating his success by putting an $8,000 two-story addition on his house.[104] And Lansdale also went to the Dulles Corridor, exiled from the fieldwork he loved at an office at the Pentagon, yet spreading his covert action and counterinsurgency technique to Cuba, Colombia, Bolivia, and Indonesia.[105]

But in a sense, none of them truly left Vietnam. One reason for this was emotional. The practice of American empire had carved them and those intimate with them in Vietnam a new space in the world, not Vietnam exactly, yet not quite at home in the United States either—even as those mélanges of Vietnam and America, those interpenetrations, defined nationalism in both countries. "I don't know whether I am homesick for Vietnam or merely want to see if you ever tried on those red Hawaiian swim trunks," Lansdale wrote ardently to Diem in 1959 from the belly of the Pentagon, expressing this transposable sense of home, "but anyhow I am thinking of you at this moment." Still married to his wife, Helen, he exchanged long, longing letters with Pat Kelly for years.[106]

But the other reason the agents never truly left Vietnam is that they were constantly going back there, constantly burrowing deeper into its politics and landscape. In fact, as these agents shuttled to and from Vietnam and Virginia over the ensuing decades, one could almost see the moving, multidirectional trajectories of their flights, each of their stories-so-far in action, lacing the Dulles Corridor and the places of Vietnam ever more tightly together. With each trip their pacification work adopted a new name—civic action, strategic hamlets, political action, rural construction, revolutionary development, provincial reconnaissance, and eventually the Phoenix program. And with each name, the pastoral idea ramped up both the intensity of the physical development—eventually forcing the Vietnamese into new towns surrounded by barbed wire—and the violence, which eventually led to torture and murder for those suspected of not enjoying the gifts. As the agents' domestic lives in the corridor became more established—and they all ended up there eventually—their work turned rural Vietnam into complete havoc, chronicled in detail by historians and those who personally endured the programs. "Two thirds of my village disappeared this way: in smoke and prison trucks," recalls one of them, the memoirist Le Ly Hayslip. Around the city of Hué in central Vietnam, people simply called their programs "Rural Destruction." In their inverted ethical world, "the detention and interrogation of an entire community" came to be known by U.S. agents as the "county fair," and removing "infrastructure" became the banal code word for killing. And if the intimacy the agents formed with some Vietnamese created an extra-national dream space that they shared and converted those Vietnamese into honorary Americans—be it under the auspices of big-hearted rural aid programs or the bed sheets of personal life—then those intimacies and racial passes granted to America's family in Vietnam must be seen as the constitutive racial technology and conditional zone of safety that allowed the rest of the Vietnamese people to be turned into those who could be disposed of by the unspoken terror of the other side of pacification: the gun, the knife, the bulldozer, the electrode shock.[107]

The agents' trips between Vietnam and Virginia were legion, so dizzying that to track them recreates some of the vertigo involved in so deeply intervening and living in two places at once. But the exact places in which they lived on these trips were important too. Houses, in both geographies, were the continuous spaces, the key physical and territorial manifestations, that allowed them to experience at times identical social lives across these physically distant landscapes—even as their work outside their houses physically and permanently reshaped both Virginia and Vietnam.

Conein was the first one back for an extended tour. In late 1961, he and Elyette rented a "beautiful villa" in Saigon. She sold a mink coat to pay a French decorator to furnish an entertaining room for Conein's events at the house, complete with a bamboo bar.[108] Conein worked on counterinsurgency in conjunction with Diem's younger brother and co-ruler, Ngo Dinh Nhu, who was setting up what was then called the "strategic hamlet" program. It bulldozed ancestral villages and moved the residents into new shanty-towns severed from their farmland and subject to random violent searches. Dwellers in these strategic hamlets even had to pay for the barbed wire that caged them.[109] In mid-1962, Rufus Phillips left McLean and joined Conein in Saigon. Diem greeted him, he said, almost as if he were "a lost son." Elyette Conein helped him and his family settle into a two-story, colonial, white stucco villa with a servants' quarters surrounded by eight-foot walls on the old rue Charles de Gaulle, staffed by a Vietnamese houseboy, maid, nursemaid, and a "succession of cooks," also hired by Elyette. He "streamlined" the "aid side" of the hamlet program. Circumventing the "sovereignty issue" thanks to his personal relationships with Vietnamese people and his friendship with Lansdale, Phillips brought a "complete change to the Vietnamese centuries-old system of raising pigs" by importing a "much faster growing breed of pig . . . of American origin," introduced new varieties of rice and seeds, and distributed guns to peasants. Appointed the first head of "rural aid," he became "the father of a bureaucracy that underwent numerous name changes and grew into CORDS—Civil Operations and Revolutionary Development Support," whose invention was later credited to Northern Virginia's Robert Komer. CORDS oversaw the Phoenix program, where small cadres tracked down presumed enemy suspects for interrogation and often execution.[110] The team was joined in Saigon by the new CIA station chief, John Richardson. Elyette found the Richardson family a home on the old rue Miche, a house where French colonial intelligence once tortured its Vietnamese prisoners. While living there, Richardson flew to hamlets and paramilitary training camps with Phillips and Conein, oversaw U.S. advisors training paramilitary groups, and developed South Vietnam's new national interrogation center.[111]

In 1963, U.S. policy turned on Diem and Nhu. They saw how easily one could fall from being a Vietnamese intimate who could rule South Vietnam to becoming a Vietnamese enemy who could be dispensed with. Diem had supporters, such as Richardson and U.S. ambassador Frederick Nolting, the longtime resident of a plantation house near Dulles Airport who backed Diem for his "efficiency" no matter his (often American-supported) authoritarian technique. But both were removed. In September, Phillips again left Saigon for Virginia to see his father, who was dying of cancer, and he briefed Kennedy, arguing that Nhu should be forced out. That same month, the CIA sent deputy director Huntington Sheldon, Alice Sheldon's husband, from McLean on a flight to Saigon to investigate the possibility of overthrowing the brothers. U.S. officials decided the coup should go forward.[112]

Conein became the Dulles Corridor's point man for changing Vietnam's government. Throughout 1963, he met with the plotters, who included one of the Vietnamese Conein had known running raids against the Japanese in 1945, who referred to him as "an old friend."[113] Conein became the man a CIA history called "the exclusive channel of communication between the US Government and the rebellious generals, who made it clear that he was their interlocutor of choice." During some of their meetings, generals, according to Conein, would halt their conversations just to praise Elyette and call her at the Coneins' villa, and once, immediately had a bouquet of flowers rushed to her, suggesting her prominence in their social contacts.[114]

Conein hand-delivered the plotters a CIA satchel with $70,000 to pay for the coup. While Phillips and other guards watched Elyette and his kids, Conein spent the day of the attack riding around in his jeep, monitoring its progress and radioing in blow-by-blow reports to the CIA. Just before the assassination of Diem and Nhu, he sat with the coup generals who were preparing to interrogate Diem, smoked cigarette butts, and drank bottles of Bireley's orange soda. When they devised a story about Diem and Nhu's supposed suicide that was scarcely believable, Conein prompted them to concoct a more credible scenario. When the coup was over, he chauffeured the generals who had ordered the murder of Diem and Nhu to the U.S. embassy to meet the new U.S. ambassador, Henry Cabot Lodge.[115] After the next coup, Conein served as General Nguyen Khanh's personal security advisor, training his bodyguards and armoring Khanh's passenger vehicles by simply ripping plates off of Diem's own Cadillac.[116]

Then the agents flew from Saigon back to Virginia. Huntington Sheldon went to the house he and Alice Sheldon had built in McLean. John Richardson designed a big white house on a hill for his family next to the

CIA headquarters on Basil Road. The family moved to another nearby house while it was being built, and Richardson enrolled his kids in the local schools, while embarking on a long reading list of books about Vietnam, books he fervently underlined. Phillips celebrated his return home by spending $20,000 to refurbish his house, adding two new bedrooms, a bath, and a living room, as many did after returning from their stations abroad. Lucien and Elyette Conein also moved to McLean, to a red brick Georgian house on Ingleside Avenue. It was one of the oldest houses near the village center, built in 1939 with a cedar roof.[117] When he left Saigon that year, even John Paul Vann, the famous general who captivated the U.S. press corps with his on-the-ground, "sensitive" way of war-making similar to Lansdale's, moved his family to McLean, where they stayed with a Methodist minister who had befriended him as a youth.[118] Friends and Mission colleagues Joe Baker and Joe Redick soon also moved with their wives to subdivisions in McLean, Redick to a two-story house built in 1963 in the first addition to the Bryn Mawr subdivision near the village center,[119] and Baker into a "posh" four-bedroom townhouse "designed to look more a part of the 18th century than the 20th" in the King's Manor subdivision.[120]

Then, in 1965, they left Virginia and went back to Saigon. Lansdale received an appointment as Ambassador Lodge's "special assistant"[121] to organize and carry out what was now called a "rural construction" program. He moved into an old white stucco French villa with six bedrooms and chessboard floors at 194 Cong Ly Street, near a French girls' school on the road from Saigon to Tan Son Nhut airport.[122] The names in his crew—eventually known as the Senior Liaison Office (SLO)—were familiar. Lucien Conein ran counterinsurgency programs. Joe Baker handled office business and economic warfare against the North Vietnamese state. Joe Redick was Lansdale's personal assistant. Other old faces included Lansdale's Filipino comrade Napoleon Valeriano, former Smithsonian folklorist and counterinsurgent Charles "Bo" Bohannan, Shanghai-born guerrilla warfare expert Bernard Yoh, and Hank Miller, another intelligence operative whom Lansdale had known since the fifties, when Miller's wife, Anne, worked for the U.S. Information Service in Saigon during the Military Mission's first tour.[123] Their social and political life at Cong Ly also depended on a variety of working women and men to function, ones who appeared in the laboring background of their lives and are frequently edited out of more heroic accounts of their work: the maid they called Thoa, or "the upstairs girl"; the cook, Nham; their so-called girl Fridays from the Foreign Service, who typed their memos and did other tasks; and a cook who moved into their safe house full of guerrilla operatives at 35 Nguyen Thong with two children "of unclear ownership," as did a later Cong Ly cook with her "young daughter and another young girl."[124]

The head of rural construction at this time was the air force general who now ran the government, Nguyen Cao Ky. Lansdale became one of Ky's main supporters in the U.S. mission, and they spent long days together in "marathon five-hour conversations."[125] Lansdale slipped Lyndon Johnson quotations into Ky's speeches to impress the U.S. president when the two met in Hawaii.[126] At times, he advised Ky while the general was in bed in his pajamas, once while Ky's wife, in a bathrobe, nursed their child nearby.[127] Working with Ky and Brigadier General John Fritz Freund, one of the new military bureaucrats running pacification, on an operation designed "to encourage members of the Viet Cong to desert and join the other side," Lansdale helped organize Tet New Year's dinners at rural centers, preparing the food "their mama used to make" in order to lure hungry and lonely liberation fighters in to surrender to the South.[128]

In 1966, Phillips left McLean for Saigon. Now his job was to set up an electoral system for South Vietnam, so the supposedly independent country could create a constituent assembly and then hold presidential and parliamentary elections that would legitimize the generals' military rule. Phillips had to find people "who would consent" to run for office in South Vietnam, and then he and Lansdale "began conducting classes for candidates at Lansdale's house." The point, according to Conein, who also participated, was "to make the Vietnamese think they came up with the idea of holding elections."[129]

When Ky appointed the Hanoi-born General Nguyen Duc Thang, his chief of pacification, to run the election, Thang soon became a popular presence at Cong Ly, lighting up the house with his "forceful good humor" and "exuberant" personality. Thang began to hold his official staff meetings at Cong Ly, and Lansdale claimed members of Thang's staff began calling each other Batman and Robin, after watching the show on Lansdale's TV.[130] By then, the spatial connection between Northern Virginia and Saigon took on another physical presence when the infantry brigade that usually garrisoned at Fort Myer above the Pentagon in Arlington, where Lansdale once lived, and provided the honor guard at Arlington National Cemetery, painted a large sign saying "Fort Myer" across the shacks of their post on the periphery of Saigon.[131]

But this time, Lansdale's house in Saigon became the space where he truly expressed his vision of an American domain in Vietnam by means of a series

One of U.S. agent Edward Lansdale's specialties was political manipulation conducted through close friendship. Nguyen Duc Thang, South Vietnam's pacification chief, became a frequent guest at Lansdale's house on Cong Ly Street in the mid-sixties. Here, they share a meal together. Edward Geary Lansdale Papers, Hoover Institution Archives, Stanford University.

of raucous "hootenannies" that intertwined his political mission with a personal one. "Almost nightly," through 1966, 1967, and 1968, military men, bureaucrats, Army soldiers, CORDS officials, ministers of "rural rehabilitation," and labor leaders from both the United States and South Vietnam would drop in for drinks, discuss the "urgent needs of the nation," and then, over guitars and harmonicas, sing Vietnamese and American folk songs deep into the night. Some attendees were members of the Cosmos Tabernacle Choir of CIA agents who met at the Cosmos Bar near the U.S. embassy to sing ditties like "I Feel Like a Coup Is Coming On." Even Ky, who held his post-election party at Cong Ly in 1966, came to raise his voice in song, enjoying what he called the "wonderful hospitality" and "very relaxed atmosphere," and Lansdale recorded hundreds of hours of the songs on tape.[132] Henry Cabot Lodge, who once did a solo vocal part, loved the "grand evenings," which included watermelons, candied fruit, and ginseng wine. In spring 1967, he affirmed Lansdale's strategic design of the gatherings by telling him, "You knew exactly what it was that would give me the greatest pleasure—the music; the quality of the company (and neither too many nor too few); and the delicious food and drink. . . . It explains why you have done us so much good here."[133] Lansdale's "mingling with Vietnamese of all kind" and "many friendships" provided Lodge "with valuable information on which to base important judgments."[134] Other guests included Henry Kissinger, John Steinbeck, and Richard Nixon, who appreciated the "opportunity to meet and learn from the officials working on Revolutionary Development in such relaxed and gracious surroundings." "They didn't even think you were an American or something," Lansdale recalled Nixon telling him. "You were just a friend sitting there. I think that's great."[135]

These hootenannies, of course, had familiar counterparts in the social sphere of suburban Northern Virginia, from the Eleanor Dulles house to Hickory Hill. They served an intelligence function, easing talk about state matters over drinks, male camaraderie, and good cheer. The songs themselves, many of them "occupational" anthems of different wings of the military, contained intelligence. Lansdale had even commissioned the writing of some of them as a psychological warfare tactic, "to help raise the morale of the Vietnamese people." Songs he commissioned and patronized, written by South Vietnamese agents like the singer Pham Duy, who attended the gatherings, were then disseminated through the countryside, sung by school-children in the rural villages and by the Phoenix cadre that were killing its peasants.[136] In 1966, after a State Department–sponsored trip to the United States, Pham Duy added a new song to his repertoire, one that "touched him deeply, with its statement of human purpose in a time of struggle": "We Shall Overcome." Of course, in Duy and Lansdale's translation, the chorus was altered to "We Shall Win the War," as it was taught to the assassination cadre at Vung Tau.[137]

Yet the hootenannies also operated at a more conceptual level. In collecting hundreds of hours of tapes of the "folk" of Vietnam at his house, Lansdale performed his vision of the intersection of the United States with the countries in its domain. Appreciative Vietnamese men willingly donate their folk culture to American men for a cultural harvest that can be taken back to the United States (and Lansdale sent tapes of the songs to U.S. policymakers), or they simply open their folk culture so Americans can create it, and pay people to create it, for them. Good-willed Americans, in turn, bless the Vietnamese for their cooperation with the inspirational tunes of America's own folk melodies. Through these exchanges, Vietnam and America, through the travels of empire, could bond and be rewritten into a single cultural space, at least virtually, that would underwrite and legitimize American political goals in the country. The songs were the fictions that narrated this cultural space into being, and Lansdale reveled in the new name a Vietnamese CIA agent had given him, Lan Dien, which he translated roughly as "orchid field."[138] Lansdale's house could contain, in this way, both America and Vietnam. It could sanctify culturally the blood that ran militarily.

The Lansdale team's focus on domesticity and the home as a political space also related closely to innovations in counterinsurgency and pacification that Lansdale and Rufus Phillips had overseen since they first arrived in Vietnam in the early 1950s. Their French counterpart, psychological warfare theorist Roger Trinquier, identified these ideas alongside the American team and perhaps even discussed them with Lansdale when the two met on Lansdale's 1953 trip to Vietnam. The basic idea, formed in a comparative milieu where mid-century European and American empires shared knowledge, was that colonial warfare and imperial spatial management in its iteration as counterinsurgency created a war of what Kristin Ross calls "altered spatial dimensions." On a poorly "delineated battlefield," the target of this new war shifted from a terrain to a subject: "the inhabitant." "The inhabitant in his home," Trinquier explained, "is the center of the conflict."[139] Lansdale's work depended on this notion of the inhabitant in his home, where, in his words, "the people of the country actually constitute the true battleground of the war." This inhabitant was the Vietnamese peasant. This peasant had no politics. He would cast his lot with whoever could secure his house.[140]

But the shift of the battlefield to this inhabitant and his home had to contend with the obvious fact that "simple peasants" both resisted American efforts to dictate the shape of their houses and villages and chose to actively support the National Liberation Front against the wishes of their American supervisors, their homes linking them directly to the nationalist struggle. Lansdale's programs thus came to target, regulate, and destroy Vietnamese domestic spaces in the very name of producing an idealistic, sustaining domesticity that stretched beyond politics. Counterinsurgency's house as a space of life and security was steadily linked with the house as a space of death and fragility. The Cong Ly house consolidated these resonances for his team in the mid-1960s, selectively dealing out both life and death.[141]

By late 1966, though, the SLO had begun to unravel. Conein left after six months, taking a position as the CIA's regional officer in charge of III Corps, in central Vietnam, stationed in Bien Hoa, while remaining "close enough to Saigon in case they were going to play cowboy and Indian again."[142] Some colleagues resented Lansdale's closeness with pacification general Nguyen

Duc Thang. They warned Lansdale that, in order to impress him, Thang was lying "about winning over the people rather than just control with police, about holding hamlet elections, then village ones . . . about getting a whole new spirit in the military, about protecting the people," but Lansdale found him sincere.[143] In general, family as political horizon and strategy started to look more like family as many people know it: a tedious knot of long-nursed gripes, petty grudges, and unshakeable annoyances tangled together by blood. More and more, Lansdale spent his time fielding visits from old Vietnamese friends complaining about the politics of Saigon. In one case, General Cao Van Vien came to express his feeling that Thieu and his supporters were intentionally seeking to destroy Vien's image "as a highly respected soldier . . . by disseminating malicious rumors concerning corruption on the part of Mrs. Vien." Vien's wife was a prominent Saigon capitalist. For good measure, she too conveyed to Lansdale her own hatred of Thieu and Thieu's wife.[144] Saigon was also becoming less of a playground for Lansdale and his team, more of a war zone, and the archives convey a melancholic sense that, to put it frankly, Vietnam wasn't as fun for Lansdale this time around, stressing the degree to which political access and dominance could translate for covert capital agents into invigorating personal experiences. In dangerous periods, they now holed up and lived on C rations and food scrounged from the Hotel Rex kitchen, making "whopping big" stews. But at times, to Lansdale, Saigon sounded "like the battle of Little Big Horn (and there's not a Custer on the team.)"[145]

In Lansdale's twilight days in Vietnam, the folk song project possessed him more and more. One historian observes that his "passion for cultural knowledge grew in intensity until at the end of his government career it seemed to subsume his political efforts and ambition."[146] But his cultural knowledge wasn't what subsumed Lansdale's political ambitions by 1968. It was the American war in Vietnam. The quiet, subversive intimacy of empire in its early phase was drowned in the thunder of Defense Secretary Robert McNamara's bombs, the thuggish domain of American soldiers swarming the streets and hamlets of the country, the mass death in between. And as Lansdale recorded the folk songs of Vietnam up until and through the North Vietnamese and National Liberation Front Tet Offensive, it is also worth noting what else his total library of Vietnam's folk music could not contain: not only the actual folk songs of the North (and there was only one tape of "Viet Cong" songs in nearly one hundred unedited field tapes), but any of the many old Vietnamese songs that contain an affront to power or a vision of a world turned upside-down. Lansdale preferred to hear and fund songs that "reminded participants of national heritage and patriotic themes" and "that yearned for peace and an end to the war."[147] Even this diorama of America in Vietnam, as represented by Lansdale's villa, couldn't contain a vision of an independent nation that didn't need any American folk songs, or any Americans, and that, through armed resistance, had rejected the softness of American intimacy and forced it to show its explosive side.

By that time moonlighting military men had come onto the scene of pacification. General Fritz Freund, son of a German father and a French mother and "an unusual and effective officer," also sang and played folk songs on the accordion. CORDS official Jean André Sauvageot, a "Vietnamese linguist" "who loved the exoticism of the villages," immersed himself in his idea of Vietnamese culture just as Lansdale had, sleeping on hardwood beds with his Vietnamese students and wearing "Ho Chi Minh sandals," as he trained them at the counterterror camps that now ruled the beaches that Lansdale once enjoyed with Diem.[148] Gradually nudged out of pacification work by new factions in the intelligence bureaucracy they created, the Lansdale team finally exited Vietnam in 1968.

Lansdale stayed longer than any of his friends. In his last days in Saigon, his can-do tone faded into its blue period. "Although the rains come with the afternoons now, some of the flowering trees and shrubs still hold their blossoms," he wrote in one of his letters to "The Old Team." He reported sadly that South Vietnamese nationalist attacks had forced General Thang and his family to move into the garage of their house. Even worse, he suspected that the lawyer who owned the apartment house next door to 194 Cong Ly was a National Liberation Front agent and had been using their American neighbors' rents to fund nationalist offensives. He quietly prepared for his farewell party. More than 300 people, mainly Vietnamese, according to Rufus Phillips, who serially flew to Vietnam in these last years, attended in the summer of 1968, to say "goodbye to an American who they knew genuinely cared for them." Before he left, he took up a final collection to support the Vietnamese who had staffed the SLO, but he also stressed that the Vietnamese had "made it plain" to him that they drew courage from the team members and the "principles [they] taught and lived by." He went on to add, "Maybe we've been an American conscience at work in Viet-Nam." But as one of his last expressions of that conscience, Lansdale taught General Creighton Abrams how to use psychological warfare to manipulate commander Cao Van Vien, Lansdale's friend, for information about the South Vietnamese military.[149]

Phillips returned from Saigon to his house in McLean and to his father's business. One of his first consoling acts was to extend his house's entrance hall and add a bath, studio, and garage just after New Year's Day 1969. When South Vietnamese official and ambassador Bui Diem and his wife came to visit, Phillips took them to the Super Giant in McLean to show off the consumer promises of suburban life.[150] Lucien and Elyette Conein returned to their house in McLean, where Elyette spent many years steering its renovation, adding a kitchen, a new two-car garage with a brick veneer and a breezeway to join the garage to the house.[151] Lansdale returned to his wife, Helen, and his sons in Georgetown. After a stint at an apartment in the West Building of Hunting Towers, in Alexandria, where Lansdale had lived as a young man and where they looked for a new house in the suburbs, the Lansdale family moved to 1917 Wakefield Street in Alexandria, where Vietnamese friends like Cao Van Vien and Tran Van Don came to visit him.[152] Even Jean André Sauvageot moved in with his Vietnamese family to one of the rustic and nautical Mediterranean townhouses in the brand-new Villas de Espana subdivision in the Tall Oaks Village at Reston. Fritz Freund soon arrived as well, to a little brick house in Vienna where his family had lived since 1960 near a large tract that became the Westwood Country Club.[153]

Back in McLean, Phillips wanted to try his hand at political action again. In 1971, he ran as the Democratic candidate for the Dranesville district seat on the Fairfax County Board of Supervisors, the county's governing body. Elyette Conein threw fundraising receptions for the Phillips campaign at the Coneins' stately brick house in McLean. Phillips won. As soon as he settled into the new Government Center on Balls Hill Road in McLean, the man who had assaulted rural Vietnam with development for nearly two decades became one of the strongest advocates for controlling development in the wealthy American suburb.[154]

Lamenting Fairfax County sprawl, McLean's "gasoline station-populated crossroads," and "disconnected sub-divisions," as supervisor, Phillips pushed for comprehensive master planning, citizen control, timed development to cluster buildings near available public services, public transportation, landscaping and tree planting, a new system of trails, broader public zoning powers, and even radical zoning and building "pauses," which would allow the supervisors to focus on long-range planning instead of simply succumbing to the will of developers. As he put it nobly in the *Fairfax Herald* in 1972, "The basic issue is: are we going to continue treating land primarily as a commodity or are we going to start treating it first and foremost as an irreplaceable resource?" His goal was the latter, to enhance in the "environment that condition called the quality of life which is so closely related to the use of land."[155]

But Phillips had spent his life working on projects that gave control over the land of Vietnam not to Vietnamese developers or to Vietnamese people, but to Dulles Corridor Americans exported into the country to use that land as a weapon to force the Vietnamese into acquiescence with American political goals. A committee of Vietnamese agents of the state sitting in judgment of and developing land in Fairfax County would have been an absurd image to Phillips and his friends, a nightmare drawn from U.S. Cold War films. To suggest it in the context of Phillips's litany of slow growth and environmentalist tenets still celebrated by American planners and land stewards seems somehow trivial. But it is not trivial. It is exactly what Phillips did in Vietnam. Growth control and people's planning in McLean was, in fact, a luxury created in an interdependent relationship with the lack of people's control in Vietnam. Dulles Corridor agents like Phillips working for America's empire in Vietnam inflicted land-use decisions (not to mention actual violence) on its Vietnamese subjects. Those encroachments provided the underpinnings of meaning that made the freedom from such encroachments a sign of the "quality of life" in Fairfax County, where developers themselves are cast as semi-imperial agents working against local autonomy. Phillips could demonize developers as a genre of imperial encroacher because he had so recently been one.

In numerous ways, agents of the Dulles Corridor turned its domestic life into a series of lived exceptions such as this one that proved the rule of U.S. empire in its subjected lands abroad. One biographer was somewhat shocked to visit Conein at his McLean house and find its interior a palace where Vietnam was both respected and racially menaced: "I was greeted at the door by his part-Vietnamese and part-French wife, Elyette, and taken into a living room filled with stunning Asian artifacts. I then proceeded to interview a man who in the course of an hour used such racist epithets as 'goddamn slopes' innumerable times as I asked for his thoughts and recollections about his time in Vietnam."[156] But racial violence lay at the foundation of the racial intimacies that comprised the Dulles Corridor's project in Vietnam. Both were forms of racial objectification that proved a lasting implement of imperial inspiration and technique. The spaces of intimacy and love they carved into both Vietnam and McLean were like rural aid and land-use planning both—hesitant, narrow safe spaces that existed between the fields of death and disposability.

These dialectics continued to play out in the Dulles Corridor as agents extended and encrypted lives developed in Vietnam into the suburban spaces of Northern Virginia. Just before Lansdale's wife died in 1972, Patrocinio Kelly and Lansdale renewed their correspondence. She was working in the U.S. embassy in Manila as special assistant under their mutual friend, SLO propagandist Hank Miller. Lansdale was home getting used to retirement. The letters they wrote one another are extraordinary documents, passionate missives that blend Kelly's enthusiastic accounts of Philippine martial law, updates about mutual CIA friends known across continents, and their dreamy speculative reveries on the future they might enjoy together in suburban Northern Virginia.[157]

For Kelly, Lansdale was omnipresent in the Philippine landscape where they had conducted covert work together. When she saw mountain sunsets, she thought of their beach trips. Her jaunts to forests in Laguna in Luzon only reminded her of their travels to Atimonan and Baler years before.[158] For both of them, Kelly was also already beside him in the suburbs. Lansdale sent her alluring photos of his Alexandria house to prompt this mutual imagining. He even drew a picture for her at one point, coloring his barn-end front-facing gable in crayon. "Why you even bother to live inside a house when you have all that wooded surrounding mystifies me," she wrote. "All you need is a stream running through the place to make it Edenlike."[159]

Northern Virginia housing, sunk into nature, was both resource and reward, but these exchanges also produced their sense of a twinned, transnational domesticity, forged through U.S. empire. They also staged their Philippines of love and covert action in the past—even as she still inhabited it—as a prehistory to the reward of the Northern Virginia suburbs, setting up an inherent and poignant spatial progress narrative within their intimate life. Their writing moved easily from house to landscape, and then on into domestic details, at times entering a particularly perilous, almost contractual, negotiation of their inevitable future domestic life together. While sharing her *bibing ka* recipe, for instance, emphasizing her useful domestic knowledge, she also lobbed brief warnings that she was "not going to uproot" her life so she could "cook adobo in Washington." Their fantasies about pristine suburban land also took form in contradistinction to a racialized urban geography of a black DC, of which Kelly had heard, even in Manila, through embassy stories chronicling "how unsafe it is in certain areas to be out at night," where one friend had told her how "one noon time just before he came over, he was accosted by several young blacks who demanded some money to buy records."[160]

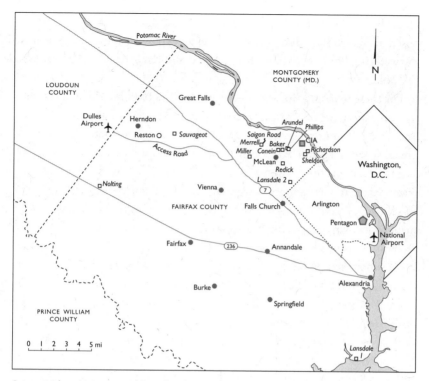

Saigon Military Mission and friends at home. Edward Lansdale moved from his house at the southern end of the corridor to his house in McLean in the seventies to be closer to his "pals."

But soon she had initiated a visa request to join him. After Lansdale's wife died, Patrocinio Kelly came to the United States in February 1973, and she and Lansdale married on the fourth of July at Alexandria's Good Shepherd Catholic Church.[161] To Lansdale, it was the apotheosis of his political intimacies, as he clearly thought of her as both a romantic soul mate and a colleague from the trenches of empire, "an old comrade who shared dangers in the Huk country—in the unwritten chapter" left out of his book.[162] In 1975, the couple moved to McLean, to winding Lorraine Avenue in the Franklin Forest subdivision up the street from CIA headquarters along Kirby Road, then ringed by wooded hills. The house was a white rambler with a long driveway, black shutters, and a carport, built just after World War II.[163] They chose the place, in Lansdale's words, "because a lot of my pals were in close here."[164] Inside the house, Lansdale quickly recreated the life of Cong Ly Street. He held gatherings where all available intimates from Vietnam convened again "to perform songs from the Saigon days," which he recorded. In 1975, the CIA's Cosmos

Choir held a reunion to reenact their old songs, and their choir patch, composed of crossed Bau Muoi Ba bottles over an explosion, hung on the walls at the watering hole where they also gathered and reminisced in McLean: the O'Toole's bar.[165]

For these men and women, oceans were only a brief interlude in the contiguous experience of physical and social space between Saigon and McLean. The Lansdale house was one of its central mediators. It stood in Saigon as a dream space of a gentle American empire that did not exist, and in McLean as the carved-out site of the extra-national where those conscious of the intimacy between Vietnam and Virginia could experience their knowledge of this intimacy amid the aggressive forgetting built into the landscape around them by its own officials like Rufus Phillips.

Phillips spent many years running for office in Virginia. In 1974, while still a supervisor, he ran for Congress in the covert capital's Tenth District, where he would have faced longtime Southern power broker Joel Broyhill in the general election. Pat and Ed Lansdale held fundraising receptions for Phillips on Lorraine Avenue, and the attendees were essentially the Vietnam teams, now airlifted and relocated wholesale to Northern Virginia: Peggy and Nick Arundel; Elyette and Lou Conein; Fran and singer Dolf Droge; Marion and Sam Karrick (an Arlington resident, who had been with Lansdale since the fifties and then run the SLO's Nguyen Thong safe house); Margaret and Joe Redick; Emma and Val Valeriano; Joan and Bernie Yoh; and Anne and Hank Miller (recently settled into their new house in the nearby "McLean Hamlet" subdivision). Lansdale billed the events in that very way, as the invitation queried: "How about joining us for a holiday gathering of 'old Saigon hands' to help Rufe Phillips start his campaign for Congress?"[166] It was the 1966 South Vietnam election all over again.

From the beginning of his career in local politics, Phillips had carried Lansdale's flair for political spectacle into his campaigns and work. He planted trees by hand on highly visible McLean median strips and marched through stream valley neighborhoods in the rain with idealistic students advocating for hiking and biking trails. He gave tours to French transportation officials using his own "fluent French," and once, he even dressed up in full colonial garb with a powdered wig and rode on horseback to the opening of a restored historic mill.[167] For the congressional run, Lansdale revised some of Phillips's speeches wholesale, and one night had the brainstorm that Phillips should build his entire campaign through a series of neighborhood meetings, in which the Virginia election blurred for them into a strategic hamlet and civic action program. Phillips could use his current post as supervisor to get his "adherents organized." Attracting "partisans" to local schools with coffee and cookies, he would engage their deepest individual dreams by leading participatory discussions about "What your future holds in Fairfax County." It was a particularly appropriate strategy for Phillips, as Lansdale explained: for it was "the sort of thing you were always advising politicos to do in Asia . . . and thus is right within your own character and familiar abilities."[168] Campaign materials showed Phillips in shirtsleeves, as had photos of him working in the provinces of Vietnam.[169] His "regional growth policy" bore the stamp of seventies environmentalist suburban politics—with their own anti-apartment, anti-urban and anti-density exclusions—but it also accorded with the discourse of planning and directed resources that had always defined his civic action work in Vietnam, from strategic hamlets to rural development. Phillips's whole life, in this light, had merely been dedicated to planning: "careful planning—planning led by the government to ensure that the needs of all regions of this country are met."[170]

Phillips as growth control advocate with a passionate interest in the land finally pointed to the numerous ways, in the single, co-created landscape of both imperial Northern Virginia and South Vietnam, that the production of postwar American space took form through the shaping of farmland for geopolitical ends. In landscapes being remade anew by bursts of development, floods of capital, and the imprimatur of the U.S. state, these men's central claim was that managed land produced new populations and subjectivities, ways of living that would produce arguments, subjects, and conscripts for American power. In two conjoined places marked and claimed by the covert capital, they worked to produce habitable American space: land knit into a comprehensive, traversable, and manageable fabric; land meant to be nurturing, modern, and conducive to robust, participatory life; but also land that through various barricades and strictures—large-lot zoning, rigorous notions of single-family life, apartment freezes, rigid notions of property value, and security often defined by race, political agreement, policing and violence—produced visions of secure, healthy imperial American space forever defined by their exclusions.

"Newcomers have asked me," wrote Phillips when he became supervisor, in the only election he ever won, "'where is McLean, the center, I mean, the main street where the public buildings are?' Any visions they might have of some shaded town square instead of a gasoline station-populated crossroads soon fade."[171] But McLean had no centers not only because of the generalities of developer-guided sprawl, but because the business of McLean—global management for U.S. interest—was a secret. Its true centers lay in its covert interiors: in the gigantic tree-shrouded CIA up the street, in the bars only the initiated knew existed, in domestic interiors like Lansdale's. Fairfax County was more unplanned than other Washington suburbs not only because its officials weren't minding the store but because the focus of its planning work lay both outside the country and in designing a built environment that tactically downplayed the public sphere and obscured its relationship to local space.

But the final say on the mutually composited nature of physical space in McLean and Vietnam probably went to Elyette Conein. In the 1980s, she became a successful Northern Virginia real estate agent. Working for the dominant local agency, Long & Foster, she used her CIA and Vietnamese contacts to sell and rent houses, just as she had in Saigon. "Immaculate executive residence," ran one of her ads for a four-bedroom in McLean in April 1986. "Lovely 4 year old home with charm shows like new. Neutral carpet, nice kitchen with island. Deck," promised another in June 1989 for an Alexandria home selling for $195,000. "If you want charm, quaint, craftsmanship, privacy and a lovely neighborhood, look no further!" exclaimed a third, for a modified five-bedroom Cape Cod in McLean with two garages and an "in-law suite." In 1985, she even made it into Long & Foster's "Director's Club," for those with $2 to $3 million in settled sales volume.[172]

In this work as one of the true "agents" of the development-wild Dulles Corridor, Elyette Conein perhaps had learned and brought to her new home in McLean the lesson of the Saigon Military Mission's exploits in Vietnam in a way that Phillips, who initiated so many of them, had not. When it came to land, and "the quality of life which is so closely related to the use of land," exploitation paid more than utopian planning. But as a group, their work also calls attention to the complex relationship between post–World War II American suburbia and the U.S. national state writ large—as well as the degree to which suburban actors executed the global policies that generated the postwar abundance that enabled their own built forms.

FOUR

The Fall of South Vietnam and the Transnational Intimacies of Falls Church, Arlington, and McLean

FRANK SNEPP'S HOMECOMING: ARLINGTON'S SAIGON 1972

Recently returned from the fall of Saigon, CIA analyst Frank Snepp sat in a brand-new apartment complex on Columbia Pike in Arlington, Virginia. The complex stood at the metropolitanized DC edge of the Dulles Corridor. It was September 1977. Just up the street from the Pentagon, he was finishing his memoirs.

Snepp's apartment was one of 218 in a complex built by the Richmarr Development Company, one of the area's largest builders. Since the mid-1950s, the company had helped turn Arlington's smattering of World War II–era garden apartments, duplexes, and military housing units built to serve the house of war into a bustling and dense residential environment. The late modernist huddle of connected towers, done in beige concrete with cantilevered balconies and small courtyards, was typical of the new construction. Out the window, Snepp could see the other high-rises and townhouses now coming to dominate the county once known for its chummy rows of garden apartments. The nearby Pentagon City and Rosslyn Metro stations had opened in July. Arlington was changing.[1] But the complex still stood on one of the major roads that had defined Arlington's shape for a hundred years.[2] And some other things in Arlington would never change again. It was now part of the country's capital—if an unacknowledged part. By 1968, more than a third of its population worked for the federal government. The federal government held more than nine million square feet of office space in Arlington.

Most recently, 12,000 employees of the U.S. Navy were relocating there. A study by a local planning firm acknowledged that, because of this federal presence, a large portion of the county's landscape was a wild card, governed less by "the area's economic viability" and more by "the national and international decision-making function and political factors."[3]

Snepp had moved into the "modest bachelor pad in an Arlington high-rise" in August 1975, right after his evacuation from Saigon by helicopter and naval ship to the Philippines and a stint debriefing Vietnamese refugees in Thailand.[4] Four months later, he was summoned by CIA Director William Colby to a ceremony at the Langley headquarters' bubble-shaped auditorium, where Colby gave him a classified medal honoring his work. But when Snepp decided to write the memoir about what he had witnessed in Vietnam, his relationships with his superiors quickly soured. He resigned from the agency. By January 1976, 2200 Columbia Pike was his home and writing studio where he would soon be defending himself from an agency confidentiality lawsuit.[5]

In some ways, the apartment by the Pentagon must have felt a welcome buffer during those months of writing. It was separated from Langley by a network of densely developing space, only easily navigable by several major north-south connectors, such as Route 7 and the George Washington Parkway. The buffer symbolized his own distance from the lifeworld of the agency he once served. In other ways, the apartment wasn't far away enough. Snepp took meetings on his cantilevered balcony to avoid the eavesdropping he feared inside. He bolted his doors and acquired a .38, worrying that "some overzealous patriot" might use the balcony to climb into his apartment and steal his manuscript. He stashed copies of his book, Dulles Corridor–style, "all over town."[6]

Yet when Snepp sat down to write *Decent Interval: An Insider's Account of Saigon's Indecent End Told by the CIA's Chief Strategy Analyst in Vietnam*, his surroundings did not seriously enter his work. He called the first chapter "Homecoming." The phrase "Chapter One" does not even appear. This word *Homecoming* emblazons the page alone. But this homecoming is not about his return to the apartment complex in Arlington, to the Dulles Corridor, to Washington. In fact, in a later book he explains, "The city seemed as far from home as anyplace I'd known in the past five years."[7] Arlington only appears in *Decent Interval* on the last pages of the foreword, which he signs "Arlington, Va., September 1977," and is separated from "Homecoming" by a wall of paper. With the Pentagon's "long corridors . . . that had served as the burial ground for so many Vietnam truths in the past" only blocks away, and the Langley headquarters with its "prefab niches and cubbyholes" a short drive, one might expect both complexes to loom large in Snepp's book, but they barely linger under his narrative eye.[8]

Instead, at the beginning of "Homecoming," Snepp is flying into Saigon. It is October 1972. And over the next 580-plus pages, he devotes his book to the landscape of Saigon, the Vietnamese people who trusted the United States in Vietnam, and the Dulles Corridor officials who betrayed them. *Decent Interval* has gone on to become one of the major documents of the 1975 fall of both the city and the South Vietnamese government. It is used by any historian chronicling the evacuation's play-by-play moments. But it is of course rarely noted that the book's source and the setting for its writing was Arlington, Virginia, amid the very real Dulles Corridor that produced its contents. Sequestered in the apartment in Arlington, Snepp conjured Saigon into space.

Snepp's intention in *Decent Interval* is to assert that the officials of the American governmental establishment owe a moral debt to their Vietnamese employees, collaborators, and their families and to show how this debt was honored and disavowed during their last moments together in Saigon, after more than twenty years of a complex mutuality. But it is that wall of pages between Arlington and Saigon that stands in for the geographic distance of the left behind. Bridging that wall—like the bridging of the wall that surrounds the U.S. embassy in Saigon and provides the setting for its final, distraught evacuation scenes—is the book's unexpressed moral challenge. Snepp cordons the Vietnamese narratively in Saigon. But by September 1977, due to the very same "international decision-making function and political factors," many Vietnamese had already crossed the barrier and were making a new community for themselves only blocks from Snepp's apartment, positioned, as he was, between the Pentagon and the CIA that defined their lives for so long.

The story of this movement, the way U.S. imperialism and the desire of some Vietnamese made these two places not only intimate but contiguous, is the continuing story of this chapter. Erasing the confidentiality agreement that holds the Vietnamese as "victims of war" in Saigon and "immigrants" in Northern Virginia, this chapter breaks through another layer of the Dulles Corridor's secrecy about itself and helps bring its covert map into the light. But first, it is important to see the problem of this intimacy as it became real for people in Saigon in the spring of 1975. For that, Snepp's account is invaluable.[9]

Snepp flies into Tan Son Nhut airport. From his jet's window, Vietnam materializes slowly, green and brown. Patchwork terrain unfurls into the distance, but the landscape is cramped by the corrugated tin shanties of the new refugees to Saigon—farmers driven from the countryside by U.S. bombing and pacification campaigns.[10] A chauffeur escorts Snepp by Chevrolet from the disorderly airport to the Hotel Duc, the CIA's residential complex. In his time away, Langley has modernized the building. A sleek new restaurant has opened upstairs, equipped with bar, swimming pool, and sun deck, replacing the rough and rangy atmosphere of his last visit, which he typifies as the city's natural state.

Snepp's Saigon is distinctly spatial; it is as detailed in his opening pages as Dickens's London or the Paris of the turn-of-the-century feuilletons, and it emulates those genres. Snepp borrows the agency's standard Ford Pinto and weaves through the traffic into the city's streetscape. The clock on the Post, Telephone and Telegraph Building, the shadowy Catholic cathedral, the shabby apartments of Lam Son Square, the urchins gamboling up Nguyen Hue Boulevard—all are in place. Yet a melancholy has descended upon Snepp's city since its late sixties incarnation, when the massage parlors thrilled Tu Do Street, and the nightclubs played "American Woman" on the waterfront. That earlier version of Saigon was the one that had shamed and soiled France's tree-lined and well-heeled "Paris of the Orient" into America's "frontier Dodge City," yet it was, Snepp implies, for all its faults, America's city then, if not an American city. Soon after it would be an American city without Americans.

The melancholy that hangs over Saigon on this 1972 trip is the visual swan song of the declining American presence, a shadow visible in a disquieting urban silence (although 9,000 Americans are still in Vietnam).[11] The city's elites, meanwhile, revel in their illusions. At the French colonial sports club, Le Cercle Sportif, "lean, bronzed mixed-bloods" and "quiet men gone to flab" record a century of colonialism with their skin. Rich, American-imitating Vietnamese youth drink ink-black coffee in tie-dyes at Givral's café and flaunt their own corruption. French-obsessed Vietnamese ladies wander amid the Eden Arcade's elegant shops and ignore Snepp. The grotesque, "florid, bull-necked" American contractor holds his obscene court at Mimi's Flamboyant, the "incomparable" brothel and club on Nguyen Hue. "Master to a cringing Vietnamese wife or mistress, keeper of the American superiority complex, the last of us they will see when the Americans go home," writes Snepp of this contractor. He is a postmortem on Saigon's elites—the foreshadowing of many other clueless Americans to come, from Ambassador Graham Martin to the politicized report manipulators at Langley who deny and thereby fail to plan for South Vietnam's end.

The level of spatial detail in Snepp's opening pages is itself a sign of the Dulles Corridor's—or the Pentagon's and Langley's—spatial and visual domain over Saigon. The *object* of this sexual (the American-fueled sex trade), military (the American-armed soldiers), and developmental (the many American hotels and building projects) attention is mapped in geographic detail. Snepp has returned to analyze and narrate this place, but its residents' voices do not enter his narrative of arrival. His apartment on Columbia Pike, through this narration, can contain all of Saigon, yet all of Saigon can't contain the apartment. Its location at the center of power removes it from the stage of narrative, along with the Dulles Corridor's and Snepp's own domesticity.

This asymmetrical spatial relationship is codified by Snepp's final stop, the U.S. embassy on Thong Nhut Street. In 1967, the United States erected the embassy, designed by the architect Frank J. Martin, in response to the 1965 bombing of the former embassy that half-blinded a CIA station director. Ushering in a new era in State Department architecture, the building's stern form registered the U.S. shift away from its radical modernist program earlier in the decade to an epoch in which security and defensibility reigned supreme.[12]

"A self-sustaining fortress," Snepp dubs it. Locals called it "the bunker." Constructed in reinforced concrete, the building loomed bluntly amid a neighborhood of French colonial architecture, creating continuity between the two regimes. Sixty marines guarded a ten-foot-high wall at the perimeter. A helicopter pad stood poised on the rooftop. Even more severe, the building itself was wrapped in a terra cotta artillery shield with shatterproof plastic windows behind it.[13] The CIA occupied the top three floors; the embassy, the bottom three. "Looking out from inside, you could not see much of the surrounding grounds," Snepp writes, "for the portholes transformed the vista into a series of disjointed triptychs that seemed to bear little relation to each other. But perhaps that was a fitting metaphor for the way Americans had seen Vietnam all along—disconnected images, never the whole."

With its sheathing and its portholes, the embassy is the counterpart to the incoming plane—the bomber's and the tourist's view—that opens his account: His moves through the city as a member of the Dulles Corridor's intelligence establishment are ones of entry and withdrawal, strategic analytical journeys—into its torture chambers and bordellos—followed by bouts of defensive protection and reflective distance. These moves, he suggests in the above quote, had moral connotations, defining America's relations to Vietnam writ large. Snepp is surely not alone in casting Saigon as a corrupt, mixed-race (and corrupt because it is mixed-race) Paris filled with Orientalist stereotypes or a gonzo American frontier town rife with sin. But he is unique among political observers in describing in detail how America *makes* the city of Saigon by 1972, and how this place making goes hand in hand with an intently organized spatial buffering, where Americans, but only Americans, retreat at will to fortified spaces like the embassy bunker or the Hotel Duc.

This buffering is the on-the-ground geography of imperialism, which one scholar describes as "the exercise of power either through direct conquest or (latterly) through political and economic influence that effectively amounts to a similar form of domination."[14] It writes imperial intimacy and its blockages, its access and restraints, into the plan of the city. While this domination goes beyond what Snepp can see on the street, that it can be seen on the street testifies to its ingrained character. The U.S. presence dominates Saigon economically—in the form of the American patronage that fuels its street trades, the American funding that redesigns its hotels, the American dollars its beggars depend on. The United States dominates the city administratively—even the street-sweeping machines are American. The United States dominates the city culturally—in crisp waitress uniforms and water buffalo hamburgers at the hotels. The United States dominates the city architecturally—not only with the embassy itself but with eight other houses for the U.S. state scattered from Le Qui Don Street to the Tan Son Nhut air base. The United States dominates the city militarily—with its machine guns and Quonset huts. And the United States shadows the city sexually—in the American-centered sex trades, through the prostitutes who speak "Americanese" and the male American contractors who express their power through sexual relationships with local women.

But the American can, and does, end up behind the artillery shield of the embassy, where the passports and the citizenship lie. As Snepp himself hunkers behind this wall and ends his descriptive tour, the Vietnamese characters with whom he regales the reader vanish beyond the triptych windows. But the true spatial removal that haunts Snepp in these pages is the apartment in Arlington where he pens the scene—the literal experience of his and his fellow Dulles Corridor denizens' retreat to the booming comfort of seventies Northern Virginia, to the cool halls of Langley and the severe geometries of the Pentagon. In the book, the embassy of the analyst stands in for the apartment of the author. At home, meanwhile, the Dulles Corridor's directors work overtime to obscure this final retreat, to blank out the Dulles Corridor's existence in Saigon by trying to stop Snepp from writing his book, and to erase its existence as an integral landscape at home by using its suburban locales as a cover for its greater untraceability. Even the above definition of imperialism, from a highly credible, exhaustive, and useful book, goes on to comment, "Typically, it is the deliberate product of a political machine that rules from the centre, and extends its control to the furthest reaches of the peripheries: think of the Pentagon and the CIA in Washington." As Snepp and his antagonists well know, neither the Pentagon nor the CIA is located in Washington.

Snepp is in Saigon during what he calls the "decent interval." This he sees as the grim sliver of time between the American troop withdrawal in 1973 and the fall of the abandoned South Vietnam on April 30, 1975. Back in DC, America willfully forgets Vietnam. Snepp alone wrestles with the responsibilities of the *here* of the book's writing to the *here* of the book's story— the already-lost Saigon where thousands of South Vietnamese believed the United States would hold up their government forever. These people helped the United States rule and manage their fellow Vietnamese. They believed the promises made to them by the United States constituted a tacit agreement that they would be safe within an American sphere, that South Vietnam itself was an implicit part of America, even that Saigon was an American city. The idea is that of Americanness by imperial collusion, or Americanness by extreme geopolitical intimacy. It is so at odds with the twenty-year mantra of a U.S. policy that declared itself bent on helping a supposedly independently functioning democracy, not to mention American practices deriving citizenship by birth on American soil and even white racial membership as a ticket to full citizenship, that the negotiation of the gap induces a crisis. Snepp powerfully depicts the last days of Saigon as ones where harried agents and workers in the field negotiate the results of this crisis on the spot.

Inevitably, when the forces of the south's nationalist Provisional Revolutionary Government (PRG) and the North Vietnamese sweep the city and evacuation takes place, this too becomes a spatial morality, a decision of who will get to go to America and who will have to stay in Saigon, who will be pulled over the carefully constructed embassy wall and who will not. If Snepp can narrate Saigon from Arlington (as the CIA and the Pentagon do), does it mean that Saigon and Arlington are the same place, morally, politically, and geographically—contiguous rather than splintered? This is the question at the center of the smoke that April, which the Dulles Corridor, through Snepp, must ask itself.

By the end of the first week in January 1975, the North Vietnamese and the south's PRG had decided upon the basics of their final offensive. It quickly swept across the country, confirming what observers had said all along: that without the United States, there was no South Vietnam. If the United States had allowed countrywide democratic elections to occur in July 1956, as Vietnam's peace with the French at Geneva mandated, or allowed real elections at any other time during the twenty years since, the South Vietnamese government would have promptly tumbled for lack of popular support. The Paris peace agreement that began to send American troops home in January 1973 again called for automatic recognition of the PRG in South Vietnam, as well as a "National Council of Concord and Reconciliation," in which the South Vietnamese government, the PRG, and a third group would repair a unified country and plan for elections. Instead, the country got the "cease-fire war." By January 1975, no one in Hanoi believed the Paris agreements "would ever be seriously implemented." The North Vietnamese and their southern allies took their cause back to the battlefield.[15]

On March 10th they were in Ban Me Thuot. By March 25th, they had taken back the imperial city of Hué. By the 30th, Danang toppled; by April 1st, Nha Trang; by April 4th, Dalat.[16] As Marilyn Young writes in *The Vietnam Wars*, "American troops could clear territory, evacuate populations, drop napalm, defoliate crops, transform the landscape with bomb craters, take Vietnamese mistresses, vaccinate Vietnamese children, train troops, supervise interrogations and the administration of prisons . . . But they could not make the South Vietnamese love the government the United States had brought to power in Saigon, nor could they govern the country themselves."[17]

The wrinkle in this scenario was the many Vietnamese who had comprised that government and its military establishment, who had conducted those interrogations and administered those prisons alongside Americans. Around them were their families, and beyond those families were more who, because of their deep association with the American imperial presence or elite capitalism in Saigon in general, feared returning to the fold of a Vietnam now unified under their anti-colonial and communist adversaries. As Dulles Corridor officials held out the image of these people's imminent massacre to the U.S. Congress to convince legislators to allow a major evacuation, and those horror stories circled back through newspapers in Vietnam, the panic increased. All the while, U.S. embassy personnel in Saigon refused to do serious evacuation planning or even to evacuate their own families for fear of shaking the resolve of their already-shaken Vietnamese counterparts. Instead, they often used their time to unsuccessfully wrangle Congress for more massive aid packages to uphold the clearly terminal South Vietnamese state. As cities began to fall, the combination of these factors produced—at least around the American compounds, airports, and ports that defined so many of those cities—an apocalyptic level of fear.[18]

The situation also raised the vital question of who these Vietnamese people were. During the later seventies, the eighties, and beyond, the departees from Vietnam had more seemingly legible identities—the poverty-stricken boat people, the politically at odds of the multi-country Orderly Departure Program, the children of American fathers and Vietnamese mothers of the Amerasian Homecoming Act, the reeducation and labor camp prisoners of the Humanitarian Operation. But while all those exoduses also included a majority of "people closely associated with the U.S. presence in Vietnam," it was this first group, of April 1975, that originally demanded an answer to the question of what the Vietnamese had earned by working with America.[19] Unfortunately, the answer didn't come until North Vietnamese rockets were raining on the cities of the south.

With a mixture of guilt, responsibility, and shock, Snepp watches all this transpire from his barricaded office at the U.S. embassy on Thong Nhut Street. As American self-preservation kicks in, the codes of paternalistic intimacy promptly disintegrate. Too-little, too-late efforts to make rash lists of "key" or "politically sensitive" Vietnamese to evacuate quickly fall to personal friendships and eventually simple last-minute bribes, where if someone holds off the hordes at gunpoint, they earn their families a golden ticket onto the helicopters. Many agents and officers fight to evacuate Vietnamese employees.[20] But as the last instants tick away, many do not. They tell their Vietnamese friends to go one way, and they head toward the evacuation point. They slip up to rooftops while women who "prostituted themselves to this or that CIA officer...to reinforce their chances of getting out" wait downstairs.[21] As the helicopters take off, some smash their Vietnamese allies in the face with their boots.[22]

This betrayal comes into high relief in the last days of the evacuation before April 30, when a crowd assembles outside the ten-foot U.S. embassy wall. As waves of escapees from other cities converge on Saigon, the embassy becomes a paralyzed Marine-guarded fortress, radioing in airlifts, as they all await the end.

A *Chicago Daily News* reporter describes the feeling of being on the Vietnam side of the wall in those last hours. His passage raises the naked specter of the fragile, racially divided intimacies that underwrote the perceived solidarity of the American project in the country: "Once we moved into that seething mass we ceased to be correspondents. We were only men fighting for our lives, scratching, clawing, pushing ever closer to that wall. . . . We were like animals. Now, I thought, I know what it's like to be a Vietnamese. I am one of them. But if I could get over that wall, I would be an American again."[23]

Less explicit but obvious in Snepp's description is that many of the Vietnamese who had worked with America over its decades-long inhabitance felt similarly to this American. They felt American, or that they had rights to America. In the final hours, Thomas Polgar, himself a Hungarian immigrant and the CIA station head in Vietnam at the time, stands pressed against the front gate, surrounded by other agents and embassy officials equipped with revolvers and billy clubs, pointing to Vietnamese in the crowd he wishes to save, while the Marines lift them up. "Try to get a Vietnamese through the gates or over the wall and it was a free-for-all," one official relates. "The rest probably figured they had entry rights too, and in fact many did."[24] But if an "unwanted Vietnamese" tries to grasp a hand and heft himself up, he is booted back by the Marines or CIA. One woman in an *ao dai* tries to climb over anyway and is speared on the fence. Jade Ngoc Quang Huynh describes the alienation of being one of the Vietnamese not favored by American connections. "Since we didn't know anybody at the embassy, we didn't have much of a chance," he writes. "We gave up and went home."[25]

But eventually, once the "state of emergency" of evacuation reaches a fever pitch, race replaces political intimacy as an American sorting device. Even at the start of Saigon's evacuation, a white U.S. Marine arrives to assist at another site, gestures at the Vietnamese evacuees, and says, "Who're these gooks?" and must be assured they're indeed going to America.[26] Soon, assurances run out. An embassy administrative counselor decides the evacuation is ready to end when he looks out into the crowd and doesn't "see any white faces out there."[27] Grant Ichikawa, a CIA officer in Vietnam and one of the first Japanese Americans in U.S. intelligence, who joined as a linguist after seeing a poster at the Gila River camp in Arizona where he was interned during World War II, almost misses his own chance to get back into the embassy when he returns from a meeting with a local agent. Only when a group of white American friends spot him is he forcefully spirited inside the gate.[28] Even making it over the sacred wall isn't enough. Snepp boards his helicopter by 10 PM the night of April 29. The helicopter lifts him to the *USS Denver* in the South China Sea. Yet despite the moderate and relatively easy-to-evacuate group of Vietnamese left in the compound by 7:30 AM on the 30th, the Marine commander and his men just slam the embassy's huge oak doors, gas the elevator shafts, bar the landings, and dash up to the helipads, pulling away even as the Vietnamese, the chosen ones who did make it over the wall, break down the doors behind them. "The evacuation degenerated quickly into an improvised experiment in racism," Snepp writes in a later memoir. "Only those with white skin were assured a way out."[29]

In the end, 5,595 Vietnamese were evacuated during those last eighteen hours, in "the largest evacuation operation by helicopter in U.S. history." In April, the United States evacuated 45,125 Vietnamese, plus others on select "black flights," and many more found their own way out. The U.S. Congress and immigration agencies had expanded various parole categories and caps that April to facilitate the evacuation. Still, "while there was no debate over the President's right to protect American lives abroad, the legality of his using ships, warplanes, and fighting men to evacuate foreigners remained very much in dispute."[30]

Snepp clearly believes it was right. For him, South Vietnam was a country that was ending. These Vietnamese to whom America had "incurred an obligation" would be homeless in the mere geography where their country used to stand.[31] This idea of severing geography from political or ideological nationhood was a useful one for America to define its own right to Vietnam in the first place—the inverse and extension of a logic that defended the American presence in Vietnam all along by casting the North Vietnamese, in their "own country," as more "outsiders" to South Vietnam than the Americans, who were invited guests.[32] He doesn't say the next part, but it's obvious: if politically, Vietnam is no longer "their country," then of course, ethically, America should be. The failure of the evacuation is only that so many more of these Vietnamese were left behind. On the other hand, at times during his account, the staggering implications of evacuating one entire "country" to another become clearer.

In late March, a State Department official considers the problem: "Counting the 17,000 local employees of the various agencies in the Embassy, and their dependents (ten per household) plus some 93,000 others who had worked for the United States sometime in the past . . . the total came to well over a million." In Nha Trang numbers of "potential evacuees" "seemed to stretch toward infinity." As a Foreign Service officer in Danang put it, "I would have moved out everybody in the city if I'd been able to."[33] But what does it mean to move a whole city across the world?

Snepp sees the number of "key Vietnamese personnel" whom America got out as shamelessly low—one-third of those on lists for various U.S. departments.[34] But many did get out. More than 200 people from the Caravelle Hotel, the troops and family members of "former 'provincial reconnaissance' cadres" that "had been responsible for mounting terrorist operations against the Communists," were rescued.[35] General Cao Van Vien, the chairman of the South Vietnamese Joint General Staff, President Nguyen Van Thieu's "chief military advisor," and former Edward Lansdale confidant, strode into the embassy two days before the fall of the city, saluted the Marines, and stepped into an elevator his State Department escort held for him. "He was one happy fellow," an American general remarked condescendingly. "You would have thought we had a little kid on our hands." They airlifted him out by helicopter from a tennis court.[36]

Over 900 Vietnamese State Department employees left Vietnam that April. More than 1,000 Vietnamese employees of CORDS, which administered the Phoenix program, escaped. The Defense Attaché Office evacuated 1,500 of its employees; the CIA, more than 500.[37] With families, the numbers stretched into the thousands. Because of their deep intimacy and ties with the U.S. military and intelligence establishment and because without American family members or independent income, they needed individual sponsorships to leave the refugee camps established for them on American soil, many ended up in the Dulles Corridor. Identification by empire may have voided the landscape of South Vietnam as their homeland, but it allowed them to settle and claim the CIA's and the Pentagon's suburban landscape as their own. By Snepp's own logic of identification by politics rather than birth or race, they had as much right to it as he did. By the time he wrote the above tale, they were his neighbors in Northern Virginia.

The people whom Snepp calls "spies, collaborators, and employees" rode Navy cruisers to Subic Bay in the Philippines, to Guam, or to Wake Island.[38] The United States then airlifted them in stages to four refugee camps, all of them on land controlled by the Pentagon: Camp Pendleton in California, Fort Chaffee in Arkansas, Eglin Air Force Base in Florida, and Fort Indiantown Gap in Pennsylvania. A dozen designated voluntary agencies, including the DC-based U.S. Catholic Conference, found them sponsors, at which point they could leave the camps.[39] By that time the "spies, collaborators, and employees" who earned their passage to the United States by their deep connection with the American state in Vietnam were refugees on their way to becoming immigrants.

The camps were the territorial device that accomplished this transformation. White American military men, CIA agents, government workers, translators, torturers, and corporate contractors of the Dulles Corridor could transition to a domesticity relieved of ethical responsibility for their activities abroad as a matter of course. Their "offices" were commonly separated by oceans from their suburban bedroom communities. The Vietnamese partners in this particular project had no such luxury. Forced since the evacuation (and before) to experience their collaboration through the contingencies of racial hierarchy, they did not enter the camps so they could become new again but so America could. Just as they once could only enter the American-run Vietnamese power structure in Saigon as authentic yet friendly Vietnamese nationalists (not as so-called puppets who worked with America against the will of Vietnamese democracy), now they could only enter America's neighborhoods as authentic and enthusiastic Vietnamese immigrants (not as American intimates whose very presence would testify to both the content and failure of American foreign policy and state building in Vietnam).[40]

Generals, bankers, and presidents whom the United States wanted to control a mere month earlier now became wards the U.S. state wanted to heal, needing jobs, needing language, needing sponsor-parents to free them from the bases. In the process, as the United States reneged on $3.25 billion in actual reparations promised to the North Vietnamese in Paris,[41] the people who left Vietnam as equals and intimates would enter the United States as a form of substitute reparations and as a propaganda tool against communist Vietnam. Their very presence testified to the hazards awaiting citizens of countries that soldiered on without the influence of the United States (even as Vietnam and its refugee population were being shaped by a bitter U.S. embargo).[42] The warnings the Vietnamese received in the camps, meanwhile, about "prejudice" they might face on the outside only signaled the fruits that white Americans reaped from this strategy.[43] Accepting immigrants was an embraced or disavowed act of generosity, not an unavoidable, contractual moral duty. And even still, a majority of Americans, 54 percent, preferred not to be generous—they wished the Vietnamese hadn't come.[44]

To encourage the transformation from intimate to immigrant, the camps—their boundaries defined by white ropes—were run as patriotic American civics classes, often by the same men who ran pacification and village restructuring programs in South Vietnam. Members of the Saigon Military Mission had trained at the same bases. Despite what the Vietnamese might have witnessed of American behavior in their home country, they were now drilled on the bedtime stories America told itself at night. They learned "God Bless America" in English and Vietnamese. They learned American history and government, American customs, home economics, and cooking. They read about the specialties of America's different regions. They learned what officials called "English for children" in the YMCA tent. They learned about America's supposed gender norms, traditional sex roles, and the nuclear family. In lessons about work, when a woman made the motion of casting a fishing net, the teacher would correct, "I am a housewife." When a man made a gun with his hands and said, "I rat-a-tat-tat," the teacher would recommend, "I work with my hands." Advice in the camp newspaper—run in at least one case by an army psychological operations unit—taught them "how to give a firm handshake." They even got their own psychiatric condition, "Gapitis," whose "symptoms are a growing reluctance to think of life outside the camp."[45]

The director of a camp encapsulated the paternalistic and amnesiac tone in his farewell speech to his charges in August 1975:

> You have worked as hard as we Americans in getting yourselves resettled.... You have been honest and obedient to the law and you have shown great self-discipline.... If you do all these things in your new homes in America, just as you have done them here in Eglin: if you work hard, study hard, practice patience, be honest and obey the law, you will be happy and productive new members of our American society.[46]

Thus, the camps and the U.S. government worked to reproduce former Vietnamese friends and family members as hat-in-hand supplicants.

Yet when the Vietnamese left the camps, almost instantly, and as if in testimony against this reproduction, the Dulles Corridor was a major destination. Even as a single state, Virginia quickly had a high number of refugees—1,614 by June 19, 1975; 3,733 by December 31, 1975; 3,807 by January 1, 1976; 6,056 by September 1977; 6,791 by December 13, 1978; 9,541 by 1980.[47] While other states that took high numbers after the evacuation—California, Texas, Pennsylvania, and Florida—were near camps, providing a natural first destination and a local base of sponsors and still others, such as Washington, New York, and Minnesota, had well-established Asian American communities, Virginia fit neither category. If one adds in the Vietnamese who went to DC and Maryland, as refugee task force administrators did, then the DC area continuously had the third largest Vietnamese refugee population in the United States.[48]

They came to the Dulles Corridor because of contacts and personal connections implicitly denied by the rhetoric of the camps, for the same reason that a small South Vietnamese community of diplomats, translators, and other government officials had settled in Arlington since the sixties.[49] Administrators of the refugee task forces were aware of this connection. "The Washington area is presumably popular because of contacts and friendships that refugees may have had with U.S. Government employees, civilian and military," wrote the task force's newspaper, *Dong Song Moi*.[50] "Pentagon connections are today highly significant for first-wave refugees," explained a geographer who studied the community in Northern Virginia later.[51] "Those who came to the DC metropolitan area settled mainly in Arlington County in northern Virginia, due to their placement in this area by U.S. sponsor services," writes the ethnographer of the community, which is to say that the high number of military and governmental residents in the area provided the bulk of the sponsors, some of them "United States governmental organizations" themselves.[52]

The Pentagon even put out releases titled "If You Want to Help a Refugee Family" to convince people to sponsor the Vietnamese. The tone played to the paternalistic feelings pivotal to the intimacies between the Americans occupying Vietnam and the Vietnamese working in their offices, battalions, and cities. One release, in July, described life in the camp: "Here, they undergo their security checks, fill out endless forms, try to trace their missing children and relatives, and wait for that mystic entity known as a 'Sponsor.'"

Yet, perhaps remembering the sometimes-corrupted intimacies of Vietnam, the release went on to remind readers that "household chores are divided by mutual agreement (but do not expect this arrangement to provide a 'built-in' cook or servant)."[53] The Defense Attaché Office placed ads in camp newspapers asking its former Vietnamese employees to write to an address in Alexandria. All through the early days of May, the CIA, the Department of Defense, and other Dulles Corridor entities went even further. They scoured the camps for "their" people, conducting security checks to "verify claimed employees," and rushed them on from the camps as soon as possible. At one camp, the numbers of CIA "claims" mentioned—1,116—far exceeds the number Snepp says left Saigon.[54]

Military and government people in the Dulles Corridor promptly responded to the call. They directly contacted the Washington, DC, offices of the refugee task force, volunteering and requesting specific characteristics for their "adoptees." "Farm family preferred," wrote a retired Air Force colonel from McLean on June 17. "Single woman with or without a small child," wrote a civil servant from Alexandria on June 26. In July, an Army Ranger on duty at Fort Benning asked to sponsor a "single Vietnamese woman" and wished to have her contact his mother in Northern Virginia.[55] By December, South Vietnam's last chief of naval operations, Chung Cang, and his family had moved in with a retired U.S. admiral in Arlington. Cang was working as a $3-an-hour trainee at a Mexican food store.[56]

CIA officer Grant Ichikawa, who had been involved in high-level intelligence work in Vietnam up to the point of the evacuation, sponsored a Vietnamese family at his house in Vienna, collecting furniture for their apartment and helping others resettle in the area.[57] Another key figure in the resettlement was Jackie Bong-Wright. Born Le Thi Thu Van, Jackie Bong had entered U.S. friendship networks through her husband, Nguyen Van Bong, director of South Vietnam's National Institute of Public Administration, who was assassinated when a bomb blew up his car in 1971, just as he was about to be appointed Nguyen Van Thieu's prime minister. After his death, Jackie Bong had risen to become cultural director of the Vietnamese-American Association funded by the United States Information Agency (USIA). A week before the fall of Saigon, U.S. Ambassador Graham Martin lent her his car so she could catch a secret flight out of the country, posing as the wife of an American pilot. U.S. AID friends then sponsored her and her children in their move to a new townhouse in Old Town Alexandria, where former U.S. ambassador to Vietnam Ellsworth Bunker paid for her car insurance and first full tank of gas. Bunker's wife, Ambassador Carol Laise, gave Bong her first job in the Dulles Corridor, caring for Laise's mother in an Alexandria senior citizens home. Soon Bong reunited with a Saigon acquaintance, Lacy Wright, the State Department's political officer in Saigon and Can Tho, and they married and moved to Falls Church, where she interpreted and rented apartments for other arriving refugees, even greeting them as they stepped off flights at Dulles Airport.[58]

Edward Lansdale was also one of the Dulles Corridor military figures who wrote letters to liberate his friends and intimates from the camps. One was the singer Pham Duy, who had written many of the propaganda songs performed at Lansdale's houses in Saigon and McLean. Even in the camps, Duy continued his work—he was the man who led patriotic songs at the camp in Pennsylvania and translated "God Bless America" for the camp in Florida.[59] By June 7, only a little more than a month after the airlift, so many Lansdale friends from South Vietnam had reached Northern Virginia that he hosted a gathering at his house "where newly arrived refugees could organize some self-help programs."[60]

Many Vietnamese whom historians cite as crucial innovators and implementers of U.S. counterinsurgency programs in Vietnam ended up in Northern Virginia and reached out to Lansdale for support, including onetime director of the national psywar program, Nguyen Van Chau[61]; Phan Quang Dan, minister for land clearance and hamlet establishment[62]; ARVN colonel Nguyen Be, the former Viet Minh often credited with inventing counterinsurgency inside the South Vietnamese power structure[63]; General Nguyen Duc Thang, Ky's director of pacification and Lansdale's close friend and daily comrade on his return to Saigon with the Senior Liaison Office[64]; and Lieutenant General Nguyen Bao Tri, the minister of rural development.[65] At the Fairfax County Board of Supervisors, their old colleague Rufus Phillips put out "the first resolution welcoming them" to the area, and Phillips also helped in relocating the refugees.[66]

Often the last setting for their political association in Saigon, Lansdale's house became, for many, a first stop as they formally entered the suburbs of Northern Virginia. Some Vietnamese Lansdale sponsored had struck up close relationships with him in the first place through work in the domestic sphere, such as his assistant at the Cong Ly house, US AID telephone exchange operator Tran Sam Thong. Thong lived with Lansdale in McLean in 1975. For him, the CIA officer's private domestic consulate on Lorraine Avenue, way station between camp and suburb, had the power to transform identity. Thong took a new name there, S.T. Chen, pointing to the transitory and racialized status of the people who passed through that space—their ability to enter American space not according to their original identities but with a difference. "Please call him 'Chen' if you call me," Lansdale advised one potential employer. "It will help me identify him from the other Vietnamese whom I am trying to help."[67]

As more Vietnamese began settling the area, they too joined in the chorus as they searched for their own family members. In direct contacts to the task force in Washington and in the popular "Locator Service" feature that ran in the newspaper *Dong Song Moi* through April 1976, the new residents of the Dulles Corridor testified to their connections with America in Vietnam and the military and administrative wings of the South Vietnam government.[68] By May 1975, a woman who worked for U.S. AID in Saigon had moved to Annandale and was looking for her father in the camps.[69] By September, a former employee of the U.S. embassy in Saigon lived in Vienna. A South Vietnamese first lieutenant had arrived in Arlington by November, and so had a colonel. They searched for their friends and family members: the lieutenant colonel who commanded a military school at Vung Tao, the first lieutenant at the Phu Lam radar station, the deputy chief of the Hoa Lac district, an employee of the U.S. Military Assistance Command Vietnam in Saigon, the members of Nha Trang's Fifth Logistics Command. Each had Vietnamese family or friends living in the Dulles Corridor who wanted to bring them to their new homes.[70]

These homes consisted at first of a selection of Arlington and Falls Church garden apartment complexes and bigger apartment buildings, some originally built for the first Pentagon workers, now out of favor with the boom in townhouses, new high-rises, and single-family houses. This was the point of entry for many Vietnamese. They settled Arlington and Falls Church, on the land that separates the CIA from the Pentagon. As more came, they continued out along major county roads: Wilson Boulevard and Columbia Pike (where Snepp lived), deeper into the corridor, along what geographer Joseph Wood calls "a wedge-shaped sector" toward Annandale and Vienna.[71] But crucially, they also scattered from the start, according to the residences of their sponsors. Of ninety-two Vietnamese who wrote in to the Locator Service in 1975 from Northern Virginia, thirty-six lived in Arlington, eighteen in Falls Church, thirteen in Alexandria, and one in McLean, while farther into the corridor, four lived in Annandale, four in Vienna, four in Reston, five in Sterling, three in Fairfax, two in Springfield, one in Leesburg, and one in Woodbridge.[72] As Wood explained, most "dispersed within heterogeneous neighborhoods that are not visibly Vietnamese."[73] They claimed rights to a wide swath of the Dulles Corridor's landscape, not just an immigrant ghetto.

The president of a Saigon department store, the president of a paper company, and the president of a Saigon bank started a joint investment company on Old Chain Bridge Road in McLean, farming out small business loans to Vietnamese at a somewhat exorbitant 15 percent rate.[74] A young woman and her sister who had "worked for several American companies in Vietnam" became clerks at the Quality Inn in Fairfax, and another Navy commander became a "bag boy" at a Giant supermarket on Leesburg Pike.[75] Some chose to live near where services were available—one strong early cluster was around South Twenty-Eighth Road and Walter Reed Drive in Arlington. At 816 S. Walter Reed, the Arlington public schools hosted a career center where bilingual Vietnamese teachers taught nursing, cooking, typing, and English. From an office on Kent Street above the Pentagon and Arlington National Cemetery, Vietnamese staffers at the Center for Applied Linguistics published "a collection of Vietnamese textbooks for use in American schools" and "tips for housewives," such as "Make a shopping list before going to the supermarket so you will not be tempted by the beautiful display of goods."[76] In 1975, Rev. Nhi Tran opened Arlington's first Vietnamese Catholic church—the distinctly politicized "Holy Martyrs of Vietnam."[77] And new Arlington resident Truong Anh Thuy even went on to publish a bilingual children's book with Canh Nam, one of several Vietnamese-language publishers to spring up on Military Road. "April 30 should not go out of your mind," the illustrated book warned in verse, "revenge it you must."[78]

But the center of Vietnamese life in the Dulles Corridor was business, and the center of business was Clarendon, which soon had its own Little Saigon. Clarendon hugged Wilson Boulevard, along a 1920s streetcar strip. Once Arlington's main downtown, situated near the county's geographical center, it had lost its magnetism when more auto-oriented developments opened farther into the county during the fifties. In the sixties, Arlington planners fought to reroute the new DC Metro along Wilson. With this success behind them, by 1975 they embarked on an ambitious plan for a dense collection of apartments, offices, and stores around the future stop. The Vietnamese came in the pause just before the station arrived and the development plan went into effect.[79]

The first Vietnamese restaurant opened in Clarendon in 1972, marking a Vietnamese presence in the county even before the evacuation. A secretary from the South Vietnamese embassy opened a grocery store, soon followed by a second food market, run by the wife of a CIA agent. One of the early restaurants, the Queen Bee, took its name from a Saigon nightclub frequented by American soldiers.[80] A former colonel in the South Vietnamese air force managed another major destination, the Pacific Department Store, part of a string of Northern Virginia businesses that soon included a frozen food processing plant in southwest Alexandria.[81] A general opened a jewelry store, and a translator for U.S. military advisors and CIA officers opened the popular restaurants My-An and Nam Viet, holding annual Tet dinners for freed American POWs.[82] "Its low rents and available space—and the disarray that was part and parcel of Washington's Metrorail subway construction—were perfect for Vietnamese refugees in search of inexpensive retail space for dry goods, tailoring, bridal shops, jewelry shops, and beauty salons," writes Wood.[83]

Nearby, Nguyen Ngoc Bich, diplomat and director general of information for Nguyen Van Thieu in Washington and Saigon, opened what he called the first Vietnamese community center in the United States in a church basement in 1976, and then, by 1977, in the shuttered Page Elementary School at 1501 North Lincoln Street just above Clarendon.[84] Clarendon's Little Saigon also stretched to a major apartment complex the Vietnamese settled in Arlington, the Buckingham,[85] one of the country's first large, FHA-insured demonstration projects, designed by the well-known American garden city modernist Henry Wright, with a pair of longtime colleagues who had gone into businesses as Northern Virginia architects, Albert D. Lueders and Allan Kamstra. In the 1950s, the Buckingham provided crucial early housing for CIA secretaries, clerks, and stenographers.[86] It had a second claim to fame as one of the most vicious local bastions of segregated, whites-only housing, drawing pickets from the Congress of Racial Equality and, as late as 1968, a Federal Trade Commission investigation.[87] The Vietnamese moved in not long after the complex began to desegregate, facing lingering white racism. One longtime white tenant, as if to add grit to her insult of her new South Vietnamese neighbors, took to calling the Buckingham "Little Hanoi."[88]

Little Saigon in Clarendon became their footprint in the county. When Metro finally did open and rents shot up in 1979 (bringing in offices for the State Department and the Marine Corps that some Vietnamese had recently worked for), the Vietnamese restaurants and silk stores merely migrated farther out major corridors like Wilson, eventually to strip malls with parking lots in Bailey's Crossroads and Seven Corners in the Falls Church area. Businesses there that once competed with Clarendon were now themselves being emptied by larger malls on Beltway interchanges like Tysons Corner.[89]

This is the landscape chronicled by Lan Cao's 1997 novel *Monkey Bridge*, the first novel of the Dulles Corridor's Vietnamese community, hailed upon its release as the first major novel by a Vietnamese in America.[90] The novel animates the built environment the Vietnamese shaped in Falls Church through the story of Mai Nguyen and her mother, Thanh Nguyen, who works at a food store on Wilson Boulevard called the Mekong Grocery. The drama pivots on Mai's hunt for information about her mother's father, Baba Quan. Thanh had planned to meet Baba Quan in front of the national assembly building in Saigon on April 30 to leave by American plane along their pre-certified evacuation route. He never showed up. She came alone. The trauma that ensues within this basic human triangle—the teenager, Mai, who came to the United States a few months before the evacuation with a family friend, an American colonel; the mother, Thanh, who spent four months at Fort Chaffee in Arkansas before being sponsored by a Catholic church to reunite with her daughter in Falls Church; and the grandfather, lost in the landscape of a disappeared Saigon, and beyond that, in the terraces of the Mekong rice fields from which the family hails—cradles the narrative.

LAN CAO'S LIGHT BRIDGES

Cao's imagination is relentlessly rooted in space, both in specific spaces and in spatial means of organizing the world. In this way, her novel is not divorced from reality and history but can and should be read as a crucial account of the life of Northern Virginia, a cognitive map that overlays the actual landscape of the Dulles Corridor. The Vietnamese Northern Virginia she imbues with life is creative in its own right. In its forgetful suburban lanes, Saigon bar girls remember themselves as Confucian teachers, and lowly foot soldiers can become decorated battlefield heroes. It is also an amputation of the lost Saigon—"the still-tender, broken-off part of the old, old world."[91] It is incubator and memorial. In the novel, Cao posits two indigenous spaces as containers for the displaced political geography of South Vietnam: the food store and the apartment.

The relationship is most visible, as it is in the streets of Northern Virginia itself, in the food store. The Mekong Grocery is where Thanh works with her friend, Mrs. Bay. The store is located "in a small shopping complex,"[92] tucked into one of the many tiny strip malls that line Wilson Boulevard. Amid durians and dried arnica, Dulles Corridor GIs, also alienated from their American suburban environs, wander, looking for a connection with their emotional experiences of travel and war in Vietnam. In the outgoing Mrs. Bay, they find one. Stocked with the trappings of the country—including its women—yet embedded and accessible in the American landscape, the grocery is less a piece of Vietnam in Virginia than a "transfigured space," a "pool of common space."[93] It is one of the lens-like spaces where Vietnamese *and* Americans can still access the ghostly, exiled geography of the South Vietnam they both recently left.

The Nguyen women's apartment, only a "stretch of road" away, boasts similar power. The TV spirits detailed geographic imprints of Saigon's April 30 downfall into the railroad flat in the walk-up building, painting the bare walls with the flickering architecture of Saigon. Inside this political camera obscura, Thanh and Mai hover in "impermanence."[94] They sleep on a lump of plywood from Hechinger, a DC-area hardware store, and live from the blue china cups and chest of drawers donated by their Catholic church sponsors, yet fish sauce smells hang over their landings, and exiles parade across their threshold for weekly Vietnamese feasts. Despite this bicultural input, the remote Thanh still muses, "You can lose a house, a piece of land, even a country," even as they inhabit all three in Virginia.[95] The architecture of the Dulles Corridor provides both a home and a metonym for its rupture.

With these depictions, Cao shows how Vietnamese émigrés unsteadily inscribed themselves and their sense of geographic loss in the habitation of Northern Virginia. She narrates the existences that altered the built environment of Falls Church. But truly, tales of immigrant place claiming and the two-ness of the space of exiles are familiar themes in both literature and sociology. The spatial imagination that distinguishes Cao's novel, and through which it uniquely deepens a sense of the geographical imperatives of the Dulles Corridor—not merely its landmarks, streets, and town names—lies elsewhere. This elsewhere can best be called, employing her words, "an eerie topography of misshapen memories and warped psychological space."[96] The cold proof of seeable places—generalized containers like the "ethnic store"—reifies stable categories like "immigrant" and "suburb" over and above the stretched-out geopolitical relations that the imperial corridor depends on for its coherency and power. Separateness itself—between countries, between races, between concrete walls and the outside air, between home and work—

is an explicit geographic strategy, or at least a fact of geography that can be exploited by people with a stake in certain connections remaining invisible. Under such a regime, Cao's novel shows, mapping *experience* onto physical place is a mandate, modeling what migration anthropologist Roger Rouse calls a "new cartography . . . discoverable in the details of people's daily lives."[97]

Cao reimagines Vietnam and Virginia as pieces of larger acts of narrative and thereby breaks them out of the fetish of physical contiguity. In doing so, she answers questions about how distant political intimacy effects local physical experience and shape in the covert capital. A reading of Cao suggests that this means of mapping space is a duty for humans trapped under the politicized concept of "development." Development assaults both Cao's Vietnam and Cao's Northern Virginia—Vietnam in the form of strategic hamlets that turned the rice fields into the barbed-wire pens of American security and Virginia in the runaway suburbanization that posits the meaning of the lands outside the nation's capital as forever resting in the progress of raw building itself. Instead, she turns our attention to the political latticework of affective relationships that underwrite and imbue those buildings with sense, spatial structure, and historical function. Perhaps oddly, the result of rejecting "development"—and the progressive development of narrative—as a model is a narrative map that can depict and account for a more profound *physical* and geographically specific relationship between the offices, government buildings, and suburban houses of Northern Virginia than could one million statistical rehearsals of progress and the spread of arid "spatial uses" in the landscape.

When she is finished, the Dulles Corridor and Saigon are not so much imbricated but frankly liquefied together. Vietnam does not inhabit Virginia. This is more than a here-to-there, Euclidean account of binary geographic displacement and orientation. Rather, Vietnam *is* Virginia, just as politicized South Vietnamese refugees arguing their way onto American planes in Saigon's final hours implicitly maintained. The monsoons of Ba Xuyen beat against the windowpanes of the apartment near Wilson Boulevard. The neat Arlington Hospital is the Saigon military hospital where Mai once worked, and saw an explosion as "a fury of whiteness rushing" toward her. A music store in the "great brand-new" of the Tysons Corner mall can turn her American friend's index finger into the "blanched, pulpy stump of gauze" of a Saigon neighbor boy whose family hurts him so he can avoid the draft. Even as Mai's plane leaves Saigon, the city was already "an afterimage of a city suddenly no longer where it had always been." Yet later, in Falls Church with her mother, Saigon appears again as a row of cards on their coffee table that "shimmered like a lost city at night."

The novel spills over with these meshed descriptions, looking-glass shifts catalyzed by radical acts of light—breath as "soft fog," a "shadow slipping," a "current of grace . . . like golden light," air itself—yet these are just internal metaphors for the main one: the "luminous motion" that her grandfather Baba Quan lives his life by. This luminous motion is represented most intensely by her grandfather's canal-crossing "monkey bridge" of the title, "a thin, unsteady shimmer of bamboo," yet one, in Cao's hands, that blends the filament that links Saigon and Virginia into the elements of instantaneous everyday spatial experience.[98] Using these tools, Cao hurls her narrator against the bounds of her physical surroundings, trying to reach a human and spatial oneness between the two countries.[99] As the novel progresses, the quest for unity ushers her deep into a space scholars often have no access to, yet for a place like the Dulles Corridor might be the most important of all: interiors. Many of Mai's most horrific liquefactions transpire in the apartment she shares with her mother: "The bare, whitewashed walls rumbled and closed in on me, the sky would shift, an invisible hand would pull the earth from my feet as my mother cowered in a corner, banging her head into a mass of ruptured blood vessels as she searched desperately, desperately for her father." As the story spirals Mai closer to Thanh's secrets and the true story of Baba Quan, these interiors tighten to even more personal and bodily ones— curtained rooms, drawers, her own ribcage—yet these contracted interiors are, for Cao, only the accompaniment, the other side of the circle from the "'open-air world' out there," metaphors of light and filament-like connection that Mai gives us elsewhere.[100]

The coexistence of these seemingly contradictory metaphors is actually the point. The novel will go in every direction, along "the six dimensions of space—upward, downward, forward, backward, left, and right," and beyond those dimensions too—to reach the cohabitation, contiguity, and mutual insertion of Saigon and Falls Church. Mai will employ any and all tactics against the tyranny of frozen places to map such oneness. But she makes clear that the Dulles corridor itself is a co-author in this mapping. Just as the "unreal village" of a strategic hamlet in Vietnam allows Thanh's own mother to reveal secrets to Thanh at an earlier point, the South Vietnamese strategic hamlet in the "unreal village" of Falls Church allows Thanh to do the same for Mai.[101] It is important to linger over Cao's novel for this reason: to depict the fervent, unpredictable, but sustained work involved in mapping the experiential and confidential connections that breathe life, form, and political content into the resistant and often bland vernacular geography of a space like the Dulles Corridor, whose far-flung political mandates and open secrets are often largely inaccessible and illegible to traditional tools of spatial analysis.[102]

Yet the relationship of Cao's own life to the life of the characters in *Monkey Bridge* is opaque, despite the fact that the novel appeared with a blurb from one of the Vietnam-American War's most celebrated historians, Stanley Karnow, who called it "a memoir in the form of a novel." While Cao is exhaustive in her spelunking of the enmeshed political geographies of Saigon and Falls Church, and the various forms of immigrant place making within Northern Virginia, the direct connection posited here does not appear. There are no characters who actually worked in the American-infused political world of Saigon and came home to the Dulles Corridor that shaped them.

There are, of course, strong connections with the United States for her characters. Her protagonist, Mai, volunteers in an American military hospital where she meets the American colonel Michael MacMahon, who spirits her away from Saigon. Cao thanks a similarly named American general in her acknowledgments. Mai's mother, Thanh, marries into a family that runs a large department store. This explains her desire to flee to America, her belonging to a successful capitalist family, but it's a more general one. Mai's father is an absence. The philosophy professor and "member of the Third Force, the opposition movement that presented itself as the middle ground, the alternative to both the Vietcong and the government" is dead. He dies suddenly and strangely in the middle of the night, still in Saigon.[103] No reason for his death is given. Yet while the novel is dedicated to Cao's mother, who died in 1992, on the acknowledgments page her father receives the book's heartfelt, even martial, second dedication, "To my father, for his love, wisdom, and most humbling example of unconditional devotion and moral courage." In sporadic interviews, Cao's father's actual position as, not a Third Force member but a high-ranking South Vietnamese army officer, or even a general, did appear as background, but this was not central to how a novel by a refugee from Vietnam navigating a new America was packaged or received during its significant media acclaim.[104]

But that father was important: he was Cao Van Vien—the very same four-star general, chief of the South Vietnam Joint General Staff, chief military advisor to President Nguyen Van Thieu, and Edward Lansdale confidant whom Frank Snepp witnessed marching with his own State Department escort into the U.S. embassy two days before the fall of Saigon, saluting the Marines, smiling upon his imminent evacuation by private helicopter to the Dulles Corridor.

It would be almost impossible to overstate the power and centrality Cao Van Vien held in the American-shadowed South Vietnamese military effort. He commanded the Army for eleven years. He defended Saigon during the Tet Offensive. He stood on "countless" reviewing stands with the highest American military brass. He conferred "constantly" with America's senior commanders in Vietnam, Creighton Abrams and William Westmoreland. Vien's wife, Cao's mother, Tao Thi Tran, was from a large land-owning family in the Mekong Delta. One of the richest women in South Vietnam, she oversaw the family's finances and, according to American officials, "profited in real-estate and restaurant investments, aided by her husband's position." As a close contact of Edward Lansdale, Vien had been a key conduit between the covert capital and the South Vietnamese government. Vien came to socialize with Lansdale at the Cong Ly house and even visited Lansdale in his house in Alexandria in 1969. When Ambassador Graham Martin wanted to get messages to the South Vietnamese power structure, he contacted Cao Van Vien. When people wanted to stage coups in the final days, they met with Vien. When South Vietnam decided to rein in its troops to defend a "truncated" version of the country, Vien was a chief person responsible.[105]

After his evacuation, Vien moved to Falls Church to be close to his new job. The Pentagon hired him, along with "every expatriate Vietnamese general of any consequence to help write a highly classified, tightly controlled study of the war's final days." As a result, Vien spent nominal time, if any, in the refugee camps. For the studies, some of which became public, he was paid up to $1,500 a month from the private McLean defense contractor Flow General, Inc. (later General Research Corp.), which had received a $1 million, three-year contract for the work, and which also brought to the corridor and employed lieutenant generals like fighting I Corps commander Ngo Quang Truong and ARVN chief of staff and senior logistician Dong Van Khuyen, although Vien had the highest profile of the group. Vien wrote at least four reports for the project from 1980 to 1983, supervised by retired American generals he knew. Some Vietnamese were angered by his good fortune. One U.S. agent recalled a woman standing up at a local refugee meeting and saying that three people were to blame for the fall of Saigon. Of the three, Vien was the only one in America or Virginia full time.[106]

Yet the Cao Van Vien family's move to Falls Church also spoke to an even deeper political and intimate relationship they had formed in Saigon with the military man in Cao's acknowledgments and novel—John Fritz Freund. The U.S. Army colonel had gone from his family house on Oakmont Court in Vienna to Vietnam as a military advisor in 1964, advocating "the need for a more personal relationship with the South Vietnamese Army."[107] Soon drawn into pacification work, Freund at one point even bonded the landscape of Northern Virginia into counterinsurgency in South Vietnam with an operation he called FAIRFAX, where U.S. and South Vietnamese military squads launched "hundreds of small night ambushes," measuring their success in bodies: "more than a thousand VC killed."[108] An honorary member of Lansdale's staff,[109] the accordion player raised his voice at Cong Ly hootenannies. His friendship with the Caos was well known in Saigon, a model for U.S. political operations through the intimate sphere. After Freund was wounded during a helicopter raid, a military advisor approvingly reported having seen him at the hospital outside Tan Son Nhut airport "sitting up in bed getting a back rub from the wife of the chairman of the Vietnamese Chiefs of Staff, General Cao Van Vien, who immediately on hearing that he had been wounded had gone to the hospital to see him."[110] Westmoreland depended on the relationship between Freund and Vien to make policy. "Sometimes," Westmoreland recalled, "I capitalized on Fritz Freund's friendship with General Vien to have him plant an idea with Vien, whereupon Vien would suggest it to me and I would endorse it."[111] Freund sponsored the Cao family to settle in Falls Church, and Lan Cao thanked him in her acknowledgments as an "unwavering presence" in her life since they met when she was only six years old. Such a friendship could reach up to the most formal, violent levels of U.S. politics in Vietnam and down into long-held filial ties and chambers of the heart, all while cutting a physical pathway from Saigon to Falls Church.

The Cao family moved to Falls Church soon after the evacuation, by December 1975, to a quaint split-level house on Eppard Street off Sleepy Hollow Road, the street Lan Cao's character Mai walks "the full length of" with her American friend to see her first American movie. The brick house, built in 1955, stood in a development called Sleepy Hollow Manor. It had a neatly landscaped lawn, shutters, and a picture window.[112] A geographer who studied the Vietnamese community not long after the fall of Saigon found that 60 percent of Vietnamese lived within three miles of the Seven Corners area, where Arlington, Fairfax, and Falls Church meet. The Caos fit that definition in their new house.[113] Yet on the ground, in this place where they lived, the depth of their personal connections to the landscape remains only barely fathomable, as does the politicized presence of the Vietnamese community in Northern Virginia in general. This interpretability is probably most notable in Seven Corners, near the end of Cao's Sleepy Hollow Road and Wilson Boulevard, as well as other streets that converge to form an intersection that was once "the point of greatest accessibility in Northern Virginia."[114] The intersection is now home to the Eden Center, long the most visible central place of Vietnamese Northern Virginia. Because of this visibility, it is the setting for most existing scholarship on the community.

In 1982, four years after Cao's novel is set, Vietnamese were leaving Clarendon and searching for new places to settle. That same year, two Vietnamese stores moved in to what was then known as the Plaza Seven Shopping Center at Seven Corners. By 1984, a group of Vietnamese managers had converted a closed-down supermarket into the twenty-thousand-square-foot arcade that soon became the basis of the Eden Center, dubbed by Joseph Wood "the most important central place for Vietnamese goods and services on the East Coast."[115] The shopping center boasted centrality, accessibility, and affordable rents, less than four miles down Wilson Boulevard from Clarendon. It also stood near two major housing complexes settled by Vietnamese in the Dulles Corridor. Jefferson Village, just down the road, was a 500-unit red-brick complex of some seventy buildings, which had housed many U.S. imperial agents and military men, including Harold Schwartz, the agricultural officer who had gone with Mark Merrell on the STEM mission to Vietnam in 1950.[116] The Willston garden apartment complex, next door to the Eden, was built in 1948 and often credited with triggering the suburbanization of Seven Corners. Soon it had its own refugee community center and condominium agreements written in Vietnamese.[117] Also nearby, at the Knox Presbyterian Church, Jackie Bong-Wright had recently started a support group for refugees, who began calling a third nearby complex Knox Village, or "Noc Village," substituting a Vietnamese word for roof, and referring to Bong-Wright as "Madame Village Chief."[118]

The Eden Center came to mark Seven Corners with the displaced geography of U.S. imperial Saigon. It shares its name with the same Eden Arcade where elite Vietnamese women shoppers ignored Frank Snepp on his tour of the city in 1972. In Vietnam, the Eden Arcade sat across the street from the Rex Hotel, and soon another part of the Plaza Seven Shopping Center came to be known as the "Rex Mini-Mall."[119] As more Vietnamese stores appeared, the center's white landlord, Norman Ebenstein, collaborated with Falls Church architect David Van Duzer and some community members to extend a representation of the Vietnamese life of the shop interiors into the aging center itself. They created a clock tower to reflect one that stands over a market near the original Eden. They built an arched front gate and a creative 32,400-square-foot infill project in the middle of the old parking lot called Saigon West, densifying the original car-oriented space to approximate what one geographer compares to the stalls of an old Vietnamese market town.[120] A step beyond the space of the Mekong Grocery one reads about in *Monkey Bridge*, the Eden Center is one place that literally carves the displaced political geography of an old Saigon—then being made over into Ho Chi Minh City—into the land of the Dulles Corridor.

Names of Saigon stores sprang up again at the Eden Center. Rows between cars in the lot adopted names of Saigon streets—then being erased by the Vietnamese government—and honored ARVN fighters who died defending South Vietnam. Anti-Vietnam lobbying groups gathered in restaurants run by U.S. embassy and military intimates and converged annually to celebrate holidays to commemorate the fall of Saigon on April 30 and the devotion of South Vietnam army veterans on June 21. Some came to think of their altars memorializing South Vietnamese soldiers in the Eden parking lot as South Vietnam's equivalent of Arlington Cemetery. Store owners encrypted this politically intimate relationship into their leases, ensuring that the yellow and red flag of the Republic of South Vietnam forever flies next to the red, white, and blue of the United States on two dramatic flag poles in the center of the parking lot. What looks like a standard tribute to the absorptive capacity of American democracy actually provides, in this manner, the only physical witness in the center of the Dulles Corridor to the contractual moral duties created by U.S. imperialism in Vietnam.

For Vietnamese people who "worked with the United States government" in Vietnam, the location inside the power matrix of the Dulles Corridor matters. It imbues the created geography of the Eden Center—as that community's obvious central visual location—with its own world capital function. Claiming space as an immigrant in the Dulles Corridor is not like claiming space anywhere. It comes with a prefabricated authority. "All Vietnamese communities around the world look up to this one as the crown of the anti-Communist government and its sense of duty," says one interviewee in the ethnography of the center. Another former South Vietnamese government employee "considers Eden Center the nationalist seat for the broader

A veterans event at Eden Center, a shopping plaza in Falls Church long considered the most visible central place of Vietnamese Northern Virginia. Claiming space as an immigrant in the covert capital carries a prefabricated authority. "All Vietnamese communities around the world look up to this one as the crown of the anti-Communist government and its sense of duty," one denizen tells an ethnographer. Alan B. Frank.

Vietnamese community."[121] The Eden Center, a Northern Virginia mall, can be a political space, a capital within a capital. Cao's characters are also aware of the Dulles Corridor's ability to bestow political power, safety, and centrality on its occupants. Early on, Mai relates that "Virginia beckoned because it was a mere thirty minutes away from Washington, DC, capital of the United States and of the Free World." And Thanh whispers on their first night in Falls Church, "This is now the safest place in the world," because of that political centrality. Ethnographers have also found that for Vietnamese "from Saigon, the former capital of Vietnam, living near the capital of the United States seemed like a fitting choice."[122]

Lan Cao herself must have heard similar comments. Growing up down the street from the Eden Center, she surely spent time there. Yet while expanding some of Cao's connections into seeable space, the Eden is still just a suburban shopping center, one ultimately unable to bear and signal the depth of political connections in the surrounding landscape. The resonant geography

Leases ensure the American and South Vietnamese flags fly next to each other in the Eden Center parking lot. What looks like a tribute to absorptive American democracy became the only physical witness in Northern Virginia to the contractual moral duty created by U.S. imperialism in Vietnam. It was also the sign of something thought not to exist—a double capital, formed by empire. Joseph S. Wood.

of the old South Vietnamese state lived on in the memos and reports locked within the CIA and the Pentagon walls only a few miles away, yet one can't see those places from the Eden Center. Even right on top of them, thanks to screens and barriers, some of which are provided by the trees and highways of these generic American suburbs themselves, the Langley headquarters looks like nothing, and the Pentagon is only visible at the last moment of approach. After generals like Cao Van Vien detailed obsessive reports for the Pentagon of Saigon's fall, they went on to gather in everyday life at the Eden Center. Even for the most intimately connected, the two spaces remained divided.

The two flags in the parking lot—American and South Vietnamese— are one answer back to these enforced separations. With them, and to an extent, the center itself, Vietnamese intimates of U.S. empire in Vietnam crafted in the controlled space of the strip mall a testament to the intimacy and lost geography of Saigon right on the front lawn of their former collaborators. But Lan Cao's story offers a more nuanced spatial answer. Rather than weakening *Monkey Bridge*, the revelation of Van Vien Cao's centrality to America's state in Vietnam and his payback with one of the smoothest evacuations and best jobs granted any of the refugees—with a position in the heart of the Pentagon and a residence in the heart of the Dulles Corridor—completes the novel. The very secrecy of this geopolitical, familial intimacy between Lan Cao and Van Vien Cao, between Falls Church and Saigon, in a book obsessed with the intimacy between the two places, is part of what makes the book such an indelible map of the Dulles Corridor. Just as the Pentagon and CIA inhabit the suburban landscape of the corridor as invisible entities, so too does this drastic invisibility haunt and define the map of *Monkey Bridge*.

This background to the family's presence in Falls Church also confirms what is implicit in the preceding analysis. Cao's ability to write through this radical spatial intertwining, or physical coexistence, between Falls Church and Saigon, depends on the Dulles Corridor for its knowledge. It arises from the intimacies of the Dulles Corridor to which Cao is uniquely privy. The American military hospital where Mai volunteers in Saigon, the high-ranking American colonel "uncle" and family friend winning hearts and minds in the Mekong countryside, the aggressively political South Vietnamese community in the apartments and groceries of Falls Church: these are central places of knowledge in the novel that Cao uses to bridge distances. But her access to them—in the novel cast merely as Mai's access to the usual consumerist trappings of Vietnamese refugee life—is not usual at all. It arises from the spaces of American-Vietnamese political intimacy she inhabited in Saigon and those she came to inhabit in Northern Virginia.

But this heightened state of spatial knowledge provided by the Dulles Corridor depends on Cao's novel to become readable. It also produces in her hands an even greater and more radical act of spatial ethics than the political nostalgia of the two flags in the parking lot. This is what distinguishes the book. Once exposed politically to the oneness between this Northern Virginia and this Saigon along her own experiential geography, she uses her spatial access to reincorporate the space of Vietnam itself as a country that still exists—not just as a narcissistic fantasy of the exile community but as both geography and political space. Her father's eventually published

Pentagon accounts of Saigon are an incessant, nostalgic recitation of failures and blame, a "sad story" combing through the irrevocably lost geography of Saigon in its final days—months and years before. Their titles speak to their content—*The Final Collapse, The U.S. Adviser, Reflections on the Vietnam War*.[123] The secret at the heart of Cao's novel takes us in the opposite direction: Mai's grandfather, Baba Quan, was a "Viet Cong." The spatial crisis in the novel comes because her mother can't fit this fact into the constructed geography of Vietnamese Falls Church as it stands—this "world inclined toward the passion and fury of anti-Vietcong sentiments."[124]

Through this second secret, Cao invites, hesitantly, North Vietnam, current Vietnam, and the history of Vietnamese nationalism back into the space of South Vietnam and the Dulles Corridor in Northern Virginia. It is perhaps no accident that one of its voices in the novel is that of her fantasy father, the "intellectual whose radical ideas would lead Vietnam into the modern age." "The irreversible 'one wrong move' my father lamented was the American decision to side with a postwar colonially minded France against a vehemently anticolonial Vietnam," Mai tells us.[125] Thus the familial secret of the Pentagonized general father and the geographical disavowal of the current independent Vietnamese state—two facts that the Dulles Corridor has trouble allowing into its own space of imperial edicts and domestic blindness—reappear in a state of transformation in the voice of the fantasy father. If the VC grandfather is perhaps not even her "real" grandfather and is quickly revealed as ethically compromised—like the newly independent Vietnam itself—it is only to say that the Dulles Corridor and its longtime colonial associations are not free from responsibility for that fact either. It underscores that the corrupted landscapes of geopolitics in both places, intertwined or not, are often tended, suffered, mended, inflicted upon, and truly witnessed by the labor and voices of women. At the same time, the near elision of the Asian father in the mother-daughter story also testifies to what Americans expected of their immigrants, what one needed to be and hide in order to be accepted in this signifying culture, and points to one of Cao's final truths: that Vietnamese refugees might not be in the covert capital only because capitals are safe but because they were part of the extended, if vexed, U.S. imperial family in Vietnam. Just as those trying to fight their way onto the planes in Saigon's last hours had thrown into relief, this history of trust and relation was quickly edited out as these intimates arrived and were reproduced in the allowable refugee narratives of these imperial suburbs.

Nguyen Ngoc Loan was one of the refugees who fled Saigon after the fall of South Vietnam in April 1975 and moved to the Dulles Corridor. He flew out with his family in the cargo hold of a South Vietnamese Air Force C-130. He found a job as a maitre d' at a restaurant in Alexandria. By 1976, he had started his own place in a newly developing section of Fairfax County, the village of Burke. He was forty-seven. His place, "Les Trois Continents," opened in a bankrupt pizza parlor in the Rolling Valley Mall. He kept the pizza oven fired up and complemented an array of hamburgers, hot dogs, and hoagies with crispy spring rolls and ground pork meatballs in fish sauce. A jukebox played Dolly Parton and Freddy Fender.[126]

Burke was farther south than many of the villages discussed here as part of the Dulles Corridor. It lay closer to the original axis along which suburban development crept outward from DC to the west and southwest in the forties, albeit standing much farther along the route. Although only twenty minutes from Arlington, Falls Church, and McLean, it maintained its rural character. Often people simply called it Springfield, the name of the bigger town nearby. Loan's neighbors included a Woolco, a hairdresser, an A&P, a Harrison Music store, a Crown Books, and a short-order place called Giovanni's Italian Specialties.[127]

Loan would have appreciated the comparative remoteness. He wanted to start over. When he first arrived in Northern Virginia, he split restaurant time with work as a secretary at a private company in Washington. He wanted his restaurant to succeed. He ran after customers who didn't finish their food and asked them what he could fix. He liked when his children's friends studied there. His wife, his mother, a niece, and his four younger kids, when not in school, worked there. His oldest daughter, a college sophomore, helped during her vacations. They lived near the restaurant in a little house shared by eleven people. Loan woke up at 4:30 AM, read, put on his cardigan, prepared his children for school, and then worked, with an afternoon break to nurse his artificial leg, until 10 PM.[128]

Then the reporters found him. As a result, in November 1978, the Immigration and Naturalization Service began proceedings to rescind Loan's permanent resident status, leading to his potential deportation, or if no country would have him, his presence in the United States as a "stateless person." The grounds were "moral turpitude." The INS said Loan was a war criminal, who should leave Northern Virginia for Vietnam to be tried. Their major evi-

Nguyen Ngoc Loan, chief of South Vietnam's police and Central Intelligence Organization, executing a man in Saigon during the Tet Offensive, February 1968. Over three decades, observers would "identify" the victim with names ranging from Nguyen Tan Dat and Han Son to Bay Lap and Nguyen Van Lam, calling him everything from a "Viet Cong lieutenant" to a "civilian who robbed and killed." Associated Press/Eddie Adams.

dence: a photograph. Loan was the flak jacket–clad soldier depicted in AP photographer Eddie Adams's Pulitzer Prize–winning 1968 news photo. He had executed a man in a plaid shirt with a pistol to the head at point-blank range on a Saigon street during the Tet offensive.[129]

The photograph is the war's most famous. One journalist called the coverage of the shooting "the turning point, the moment when the American public turned against the war." Historians of the media and the war echo the photograph's—and through it the execution's—centrality: "No single event did more to undermine support in the United States for the war." "The picture outlasted the event, becoming a key memory and a potent symbol," writes Vicki Goldberg in *The Power of Photography*. "Not every day do newspapers get a close-up picture of one man shooting another at 'the instant the bullet slammed into the victim's head, his features in a grimace,'" explains a leading media analysis. The image reappeared as a haunting specter in *Miami Vice* episodes, Woody Allen movies, the War Museum in Ho Chi Minh City, and the collage art of Dinh Q. Le. In one of the deepest theoretical treatments, Sylvia Shin Huey Chong makes a convincing Freudian case that the photo is one of the "primal scenes" of violence in the Vietnam War.[130]

Because of the photograph, Loan couldn't simply start anew in the Northern Virginia suburbs. Congressional critics pushed him to account for the act ethically and juridically. His race as a Vietnamese person—and an embodied reminder of Vietnam in America—and his tenuous legal status in the United States were what made him vulnerable to the accounting. An army of defenders rose to protect Loan from serving as a lens for American guilt. Most of their defense pinned itself to one idea: those who would force Loan to answer for the execution did not understand his action's "context." This context was an explicitly spatial matter. Furiously, they entered spatial contexts into the record to counter the photograph: killings by Loan's and America's enemies elsewhere in Saigon in 1968, versions of the three-dimensional Saigon scenario that led to and followed the frozen moment in the photograph, Loan's inhabitance of and allegiance to America's country in South Vietnam.

But the greatest spatial context that made an ethical accounting for Loan impossible was the "pizza parlor" in Burke itself.[131] The setting in the sleepy reaches of the Dulles Corridor, and Loan's life in it, were the tools through which the case resisted justice and complicity vis-à-vis actions from the distant country of Vietnam, even though this very same Dulles Corridor geography was the cauldron for, initiator of, and partner in many compromised acts such as Loan's that demanded calls for justice and the placement of guilt in the first place. The immigration to the Dulles Corridor of former U.S. partners such as Loan was a testimony to the intimacy between the two places. Both his prosecutors and his defenders worked to erase traces of that intimacy. His judges made him into a racially guilty tool of Vietnamese violence that could be expunged. "We've got enough guys like that around here without importing them," commented a Republican congressman from Michigan.[132] Loan's defenders diluted the specifics of his case and his humanity in a pool of the supposedly sourceless brutality that saturated the Vietnam War (and by association, distant Vietnam), dissolving all notions of justice, while arguing for his inherent right as an immigrant and resident—but only as that—to "start over" in the newness of the Virginia suburbs. The correctives his story underwent to allow him to remain in a suburban shopping mall twenty miles from the White House, finally leading to an official intervention and rescue by Jimmy Carter, were part of the spatial tactics through which Americans, inspired by visits to the suburban landscape of the Dulles

Corridor, repaired the corridor's, and through it, America's, aura after it absorbed sometimes violent intimates and practitioners back into its apparently neutral built environment.[133]

But the corrective contexts offered by Loan's defenders are plagued by discrepancies. These disparate "facts" are meant to impart different moral meanings to the killing; but rather than exonerate, they dramatize the sheer work that people—often people who knew Loan in Virginia, Vietnam, or both—put into their narration. By the time they are through explaining, we don't know who the victim was, how Loan got involved, what his mood was, what Loan said afterward, or what the point of the adjacent battle was. These multiple contexts make the Tet Offensive, and through it, Saigon, into a conflicted mystery in order to uphold Northern Virginia's suburbs as the instantly readable land of fresh starts.

To rehearse the gaps and discrepancies would consume countless pages. But it is worth at least briefly going through one of the most chilling factual nether regions—the identity of the victim—to balance the narrative transformations that Loan himself underwent in Northern Virginia. The confusion starts instantly, in February 1968. In the AP log following the moment of execution, the victim is "a Vietcong officer"; on ABC, he is a "Vietcong terrorist."[134] In an April 1972 profile in *Harper's* by reporter Tom Buckley, who meets Loan in Saigon, the story acquires new details. Loan tells Buckley: "We knew who this man was. His name was Nguyen Tan Dat, alias Han Son. He was the commander of a sapper unit. He killed a policeman."[135] Then, in April 1976, Loan gives a completely new account to a *Washington Post* reporter who meets him at the Rolling Valley Mall. This time, startlingly, "This was no fighting man. He was a civilian who robbed and killed."[136] In a June 1979 profile of Loan in *Esquire*, also by Tom Buckley, who goes to the Burke mall to see him, Loan tempers the detail he gave Buckley in Saigon. This time, Loan is not part of the "we" who knew this man, and the man did not "kill" a policeman. Instead, the detail about the man comes from Loan's men: "They tell me that he had a revolver, that he *wounded* one of my policemen ... *They* say that they know this man. He is not a nameless civilian, as the press says. He is Nguyen Tan Dat, alias Han Son. [emphasis added]"

In 1979, in the documentary *Front Line*, Australian journalist Neil Davis reports that Loan told him "the VC had swept over a police compound in Saigon and that his best friend, who was a police colonel, and the colonel's wife and six children, had all been killed." When Loan's men reported that the man in the photo had been captured near this police compound, Loan shot him. Davis is not saying that *this* man actually killed anyone, just that Loan shot him at the time of these other alleged killings.[137] This new theme also curiously picks up information the AP cycled out with the original Loan photo for what they called "'atrocities-on-both-sides' balance," including in their package a photo of an unnamed South Vietnamese officer holding an unnamed child, as journalists described "one South Vietnamese major" who "wept as he carried one of his dead children out of the area." But beyond pairing the photographs, no one at that time posited any direct connection between the child's death and the man's execution.[138]

When Eddie Adams gets involved in the eighties, by this time feeling "very very very guilty" about having taken the photograph, the truth becomes even more obscure. Adams visits Loan in Northern Virginia and invites him to his own house in Jeffersonville, New York. By 1985, the victim suddenly has a rank, as Adams tells *Newsweek* that he had "recently found out that the Viet Cong lieutenant who was killed in the picture had just murdered a South Vietnamese police major—one of Loan's best friends—his whole family, wife, kids," a detail which Vicki Goldberg says came to Adams in "letters from U.S. military officers," possibly those from the corridor itself.[139]

In 1991, Goldberg reports that "rumors surfaced to the effect that the man wasn't a terrorist at all but someone the general had a grudge against."[140] Upon Loan's death in 1998, his *New York Times* obituary adds that Nguyen Cao Ky, South Vietnam's vice president at the time and Loan's political godfather, had stated a few days after the killing that the victim "had not been in the Viet Cong military but was 'a very high ranking' political official."[141] And Adams continues his charge, now asserting outright that the man "had been seen killing others and that General Nguyen was justified in executing him."[142] Subsequent accounts claim to finally "reveal" the victim's identity (despite the fact that other names for him had already circulated in the press) as, alternately, Nguyen Van Lam, Bay Lap, or Bay Lop.[143]

After reading these various descriptions, one would not be unjustified in saying, "Huh?" The facts designed to mitigate the guilt of Loan and his American allies only highlight that the victim never had a trial and the suspicion that someone's lying: killer of a policeman, wounder of a policeman, civilian who robbed and killed, someone the general had a grudge against, high-ranking political official, Nguyen Tan Dat, Han Son, Nguyen Van Lam, Bay Lop—the man seen in the photo clad in a plaid shirt cannot be all of them. And these identifiers, of course, are further complicated by the fact that "Viet Cong" was a term made up in the first place by the South

Vietnamese government under Diem to refer generally to any civilian work-ing with the independence-minded National Liberation Front. As one his-torian explains, it was "the Vietnamese equivalent of 'Commie.'"[144] The more detailed narratives designed to breathe spatial dimension and deeper veri-similitude into the events on that street in Saigon are similarly contradic-tory.[145] But one feature that almost universally slips out of the narration is the presence at the killing of a South Vietnamese cameraman from ABC. This cameraman, unlike the others, lowered his film at the moment of execution, taping only before and afterward. "Asked about that he said, 'I'm afraid of General Loan,'" ABC reported in its initial coverage.[146]

The idea that one could be "afraid of General Loan" is made implicitly ridiculous by the coverage of him in his suburban shopping center in Burke ten years later. Even when stories mention his violent acts, without any sensi-ble connections, or habitual cognitive ways to read the connections, between the image of him in Saigon and the image of him in the shopping center in Virginia, he seems brand new. The first reporter, from the *Post*, makes the pilgrimage in April 1976. In his "Burke café," Loan smiles, chats with teenagers buying hamburgers and pizza. He tells customers to "have a good day." He moves around slowly on a cane or crutches. He says his children are "doing well at school." "We don't have much. We have a simple life," he says, although he admits, "When you start a new life at my age and are handi-capped as I am, it is more difficult."[147]

When the INS files the case against Loan in November 1978, at the urg-ing of two U.S. Representatives, another *Post* reporter makes the journey to the mall. "To the customers crowded into his little shopping center res-taurant—Virginia housewives, shopkeepers from elsewhere in the Rolling Valley Mall—Nguyen Ngoc Loan's is a familiar and friendly face," declares the reporter. The story quotes an angry friend from the hairdresser's across the hall who takes her lunch break at Les Trois Continents every day: "A man's trying to rebuild his life and people are not giving him a chance." "You just earn a living, that's all," says Loan, limping on his artificial leg.[148]

In 1979, Tom Buckley goes to Burke to see Loan, waiting for him in a booth in the restaurant. "I remember you," Loan says and smiles, just as he did in Buckley's first profile of him for *Harper's* in 1972. But this time, "Loan looked frail." *Esquire* runs a picture of him in a slender sweater in the lonely mall in front of his "Pizza" sign. His food is "worth a detour," Buckley reports, and Loan wants his place "to be a kind of family restaurant. A place people can come and relax."[149] Eddie Adams also visits Loan and "consid-

Nguyen Ngoc Loan at the Rolling Valley Mall in Burke, late seventies, near his pizza place, Les Trois Continents. Supporters argued for Loan's right to "start over" in the newness of the Northern Virginia suburbs. Loan contended with how ethical debts could traverse borders between Saigon and Burke, and haunt them equally. Courtesy of Jim Moore.

ered him a friend" by then. "I was visiting his house in Virginia, after he was wounded, and he was teaching his little girl French," Adams says. "He wasn't a bad person."[150] The Vietnamese wife of an American State Department official affirms the distance between what happened in Saigon and what Loan is doing in the Virginia suburbs with a geographic insight: "Everybody did it, it's not only him . . . The past in Vietnam is not in the United States."[151]

This is the central idea: "The past in Vietnam is not in the United States," and especially not in the familiar-looking shopping center shown in photos accompanying the stories. Even when writers relate details of Loan's activities in Vietnam or reprint the photo of him executing the man on that sunstruck street in a foreign country, the physical setting of him in his Mr. Rogers sweater at the Virginia mall drains those distant acts from the present reality of the landscape.[152] Violence rests in the past, and the past is geographic, distant in every sense, relegated to the lost Vietnam that can't penetrate the resilient visual immediacy of Virginia's suburbs. But if this Virginia and this Vietnam are indeed unified, codependent spaces of interlaced "stories-so-far," a co-constituted landscape, as these chapters argue, then exactly the opposite should be true: The past in Vietnam *is* in the United States. It is in Virginia; it is in Loan; it is in his restaurant. A route toward this realization opens through another not very radical notion, yet one not always apparent to Loan's defenders: that he was not a photographic symbol but a person. His context was not merely the moments leading up to the shooting on a single street in Saigon in February 1968 but a career in the South Vietnamese power structure that is well chronicled. Through a renewed emphasis on this history, Loan's own relationship to the killing in the photograph, his immersion within the intimacies of the Dulles Corridor, and the Dulles Corridor's own textured ethical relationship to the murder in Vietnam become clearer.

Born middle class in Hué in 1930, Loan took a military commission when the French opened their army to Vietnamese soldiers—albeit in segregated units overseen by French officers—in 1952. He went to flight school with Ky at the École de l'Air in Provence, studied at Saint-Cyr (the West Point of France), trained in flying in French Morocco, and qualified as a jet pilot. He became a lieutenant in the Vietnamese air force.[153] After the coup against Diem in 1963, Loan was made the air force's deputy commander under Ky and Ky's chief of staff. When Ky became prime minister in 1965 following a string of coups, he appointed Loan director of the Military Security Service, an ARVN counterintelligence service. This made Loan responsible for anticorruption investigations inside the military, which, as one historian relates, put him "in an excellent position to protect members of Ky's faction." Several months later, Ky appointed Loan head of the Central Intelligence Organization, South Vietnam's CIA. In April 1966, he gained a further title, director-general of the National Police. He commanded the police, paramilitary battalions in the Police Field Force, and a regiment of spies and informers. He frequently met with Ky and Van Vien Cao about strategy and often worked alongside Cao in the field. "As long as Ky remains in power I will remain in power, and as long as I remain in power Ky will remain in power," Loan bragged to U.S. journalists in the summer of 1967. He kept his offices in a garrison once used by the French colonial cavalry, surrounded by concrete walls and barbed wire similar to those at the U.S. embassy.[154]

Loan was soon given the job of eliminating Ky's political enemies in Danang, where "he systematically combed Danang street by street, slaying hundreds of rebel troops and more than a hundred civilians, most of whom had taken refuge in Buddhist temples." He was accompanied in Danang by American police advisors. His mission to the city was only one occasion on record in which one of his men held a gun to someone's head as a threat, in this case to force reluctant South Vietnamese general Huynh Van Cao—who also later moved to Northern Virginia—to attack a pagoda. Because of this "successful" work in Danang, Ky assigned Loan to "clean up" his own hometown of Hué, where he jailed hundreds of students and adversaries.[155] At the same time, "the whole three-tiered US advisory structure at the district, province and national level was placed at his disposal," and Loan began to work on pacification with the members of the Military Mission, when they returned to Saigon under the patronage of Henry Cabot Lodge. Lucien Conein, Edward Lansdale, and Rufus Phillips all knew him personally. They called him "Laughing Larry," supposedly for his frequent guffaws.[156] But "at his command tens of thousands of persons were imprisoned in the tiger cages of Conson Island and elsewhere; tortured in the dreaded provincial interrogation centers; were assassinated, executed, or simply not heard from again." When Buddhists immolated themselves in the streets, Loan would mock them with fire extinguishers.[157]

Rather than purging corrupt factions in Saigon police and intelligence, Loan "systematized the corruption," in the words of one observer. In order to contain nationalist attacks against the American-backed government, Loan created door-to-door surveillance networks. To finance cash rewards paid to informers, he and police intelligence began "regulating how much each particular agency would collect, how much each officer would skim off for his personal use, and what percentage would be turned over to Ky's political machine," generating capital by selling government jobs and running protection for thousands of dens trafficking in opium, according to Alfred McCoy's book *The Politics of Heroin in Southeast Asia*. "Loan merely supervised all of the various forms of corruption at a general administrative level," McCoy writes, leaving "the mundane problems of organization and management of individual rackets to the trusted assistants."[158] By 1967, the U.S. embassy reported that, in addition to his police and enforcement duties, he "had connections" to the running of Maxim's, the most expensive nightclub in Saigon.[159]

Loan frequently expressed his power with public displays of menace. He had a bar in the back of his jeep that his U.S. advisors stocked with cases of beer. He would whisper, laugh, and drink Hennessy through police cadet induction ceremonies, many of whose positions were bought by parents who wanted their kids to avoid military service. When a member of the Constituent Assembly proposed a law in 1967 that would have banned Ky from upcoming elections, the man was murdered, and his widow publicly accused Loan of ordering the hit. When the assembly balked at approving the Thieu-Ky slate unless the pair complied with election law, Loan marched into a balcony in the chambers with two armed guards and opposition dissolved. Afterward, when the assembly voted on whether to invalidate Thieu and Ky's victory because of widespread fraud, Loan sat in the balcony drinking beer with more guards and spinning the chambers of his .38 until the assembly again complied. When security agents snatched people off the streets of Saigon to take them to the torture chambers, as National Liberation Front founder Truong Nhu Tang recalled, the only explanation was that one had been "invited" by General Loan "to come in for a talk."[160]

The Tet Offensive disrupted the security apparatus Loan had built for nearly two years to defend Saigon, and the day of the killing he "on his own authority . . . ordered a state of alert" and roamed "the capital in an attempt to stiffen its defenses," albeit "in liaison with U.S. Army Military Police authorities."[161] The .38 Smith & Wesson Airweight with which he shot the man in the plaid shirt was a gift from Air Force intelligence, which had always been Lansdale's cover.[162] The pistol could easily have come from a member of Lansdale's team. After the killing, reporters witnessed Loan repeating the gesture, in a way that further suggests that a gun to the temple, if not a regular means of assassination, was at least a regular form of torture under his command.

A mere ten days after the killing, NBC reported on Loan in another fight in Cholon. He approached two prisoners, asking how many weapons they were carrying. They answered. He drew his pistol, placed it to a prisoner's head, and said, "If you are lying, I will kill you." A month after the killing, another reporter rode with Loan on night patrol. They came upon a guarded group of civilians by the Saigon port. Loan called a man over, cursorily examined his identification, and then pointed a small automatic to his head. He pulled the trigger—only a small flame came out. He and his soldiers laughed at the joke cigarette lighter as the man stood silent.[163] A Vietnamese reporter for *Time*, on the scene at the time of the shooting of the man in the Eddie Adams photograph, returned to his office and didn't even report it. When asked about it by his deputy bureau chief, he replied, "General Loan does that all the time. That's not news."[164]

Returning Loan to the context of his actual work in Vietnam makes it easier to see why the Vietnamese cameraman might say, "I am afraid of General Loan," before he is largely expunged from the record of the event. It is also easy to see why Loan ended up in the Dulles Corridor, after a CIA "counterpart" financed his trip to the continental United States from Guam, and "American Army friends" loaned him $8,000 to open his restaurant (although Loan did not leave anything to chance; during the evacuation of Saigon, he warned his CIA contacts that "unless 'high-risk' Vietnamese were evacuated as promised, American hostages would be taken"). Loan had lived in the corridor before. When machine gun bullets tore apart his right leg in May 1968, only a few months after the killing in the photograph, he was flown to Walter Reed Army Medical Center in DC for surgery. He and his family stayed on and lived in a house in Alexandria, "closely watched by the Central Intelligence Agency," before returning to Saigon.[165]

Directly north of Burke, at a similarly comfortable distance from the more populated refugee and agent towns closer to DC, Ky himself had settled into a house rented by "friends" in Fairfax by late 1975, with the status of a "stateless person." It cost $450 a month, and he shared it with his wife and thirteen relatives, although he also bought a television, a Cadillac, and a Pacer on credit. They celebrated Christmas 1975 in that house. Ky had an office in DC at an organization called the National Center for Vietnamese Resettlement, run in part by CIA agent Drew Sawin, a Vietnam and Cambodia hand in the later sixties who went on to escort Ky on a college speaking tour in 1975. As Loan was renting his own place, the proximity to Ky, for a man who was "Ky's most trusted confidant and, according to many observers, second only to him in power" in Saigon ten years earlier, must have created a comfortable continuity, just as the proximity of Fairfax to Lansdale's and other U.S. agents' homes in McLean—agents whom Ky had known socially in Saigon—must have comforted the former military leader. Ky and Loan dined together in Northern Virginia. Ky himself was aware of the political connection between the two places. "We were fighting not only for Vietnam but for you as well," he told a reporter in Loan's defense.[166]

But Ky was also aware of how the Dulles Corridor's suburban environment had the power to transform that old political intimacy into a new emotional belonging. In his autobiography, he relates his trip to a Fairfax Cadillac dealership. Suburban salesmen recognize him cheerfully. Even though he's barefoot and wearing shorts, they let him test-drive a red convertible Coupe de Ville without a license. When a Fairfax County motorcycle cop pulls him over "on that spring day in suburban Virginia," and hears his name, the officer eagerly casts aside his suspicion and asks for Ky's autograph. In the following line, the one that essentially ends Ky's book, he writes, "The next day I bought the Cadillac, no money down, on the strength of my own good name." In Ky's suburban pastoral, political capital in America's state in South Vietnam easily morphs into social capital—emotional and financial "credit"—in the Dulles Corridor at home. A prototypical suburban experience—purchasing a car on credit after an invigorating test-drive—affirms Ky's sense of owner-ship of the Northern Virginia landscape, but it also proves to him that land-scape's capacity for newness and reinvention, just as Loan and his defenders wanted his pizza parlor to do for him.[167]

Saigon Military Mission members and Loan, meanwhile, extended their own emotional relationships into the new surroundings in Virginia. Loan accepted the interview with Buckley on one condition: that "an old friend from Saigon" could also be present. That friend was the CIA's Joe Baker, Lansdale's team member from 1954, the "unit administrator" who was known for being "always ready to do whatever was necessary" for many Mission activities and who returned to Saigon with Lansdale in 1965. That was when he met Loan, when Loan and Ky were consolidating power, and the Lansdale team was extending ties into their inner circle. Baker, his wife, Lillian, "and some other old friends," were the ones who helped Loan and his family when they first arrived in Northern Virginia after the evacuation and perhaps funded his migration there. Baker's townhouse in McLean was close enough to Les Trois Continents to meet there for the day. Only when he arrives does Loan seem calm enough to speak.[168] Lansdale himself also rose to defend his close friend. "I knew General Loan's character to be good," he wrote in an affidavit for the INS Immigration Court. "In my opinion it would have been out of keeping with his character for him to commit a crime of moral turpitude."[169]

At this level of human relationship and geographic experience, a more embedded vision of Loan in the Virginia landscape emerges. But a revelation of this intimacy does not necessarily lead to the bankrupt morality offered in a *Washington Post* editorial on his case in 1978. The newspaper argued, right-fully, that those calling for Loan to be deported wanted to evade "responsi-bility for the United States's own part in the Vietnam war." But rather than this initiating a wider national accounting of the ethical responsibilities of

U.S. involvement, the *Post* made it an issue of loyalty alone. Loan was "not like those Nazis who fought against the United States . . . He fought with the Americans."[170] In a word, former intimates—or more precisely, those who served "wider" American nationalism abroad—had a right to enjoy the same ethical force field of the U.S. border that Americans enjoyed when they came home from their own, at times, criminal work on behalf of U.S. foreign policy. Washington officials could fulfill their own ethical commitment to Vietnam by granting Loan succor in the capital's home suburbs. Corridor intelligence operatives could gain the same benefit for their consciences, making things right, not with Vietnam, but with an old friend through private economic support, job placement, sponsorship, or company keeping at the restaurant with the name that bound together three continents. This type of ethics was chosen with reason. A different scale of ethics, one that moved outward to a wider community accounting, could extend the list of those shipped to Hanoi for war crimes trials to many Northern Virginia residents, not just a single Vietnamese one.

But there is one person who seems to steadily contend with how ethical debts can traverse borders between Saigon and Burke and haunt their supposedly separate spaces equally. And that person is Loan. In a series of fugitive quotes over the years, he seems unable to shed moral anguish about this killing, even as his defenders reshape stories about the man he killed:

In 1976: "What can I do about it? You tell me what I can do about it."

In 1976: "We were under martial law. What could I do?"

In 1979: "If you hesitate, if you don't do your duty, the men won't follow you . . ."

In 1985: "I could have [seized] the film, I could have shot the photographers. I'll tell you another thing—I was following orders. But never mind about that. It was war. And there's a guy upstairs—I don't care what you call him—and when I die he will judge me. But you cannot judge me. No one can judge me."[171]

Most intense are the few more private words Loan conveys to historian David Culbert at Loan's house in Burke in 1979. The comments suggest the depth to which guilt over the killing had wound itself into his everyday domestic life. First he offers a summary of a probing question from his wife, which seems to follow a thought from him—a defense of what he did, perhaps based on notions of duty. "'You have your responsibility of course'— my wife asked—'but why do it?'" Loan goes on to, in a way, answer: "I did what I shouldn't do. For me I accept the consequences of my act." But Loan's acceptance was not enough. "How about my daughter, day and night, day and night—my daughter getting married in the near future—how will husband's family respond?"[172]

The "day and night, day and night" in this statement is the crucial part of its syntax. It can be read in one of two ways. Either his daughter asks him "day and night, day and night" why he shot the man on the street, presenting a terrifying image of their home life. Or, Loan himself thinks "day and night, day and night" about how the execution will affect his daughter's life and marriage, and through her, the rest of his children, offering a new anguished image of his own interior life, as someone we know only sleeps a few hours a night before he dies of cancer at the relatively young age of 67.

Either way, Loan's deeper, or at least more immediate, encounter with the act as he lives it domestically, in what others only interpret as the mundane, even restorative, built environment of the suburban mall and suburban house in Virginia, provides a different take on the legacy distant aggressions harbor in the covert spaces of the Dulles Corridor. In this view, they linger. They continue seamlessly through both spaces. They become permanent. Loan's quotes suggest that the space in which this violence most resonantly resides is the human interior, the same space Lan Cao posits as the most intimate yet furthest reaching in its geographic sensibilities. The literal distance between Vietnam and Virginia, then, is not defined by the ethical laundering device of the border or the whitewashed newness of the suburbs. Rather, it is defined by the tragedy of the physical gap between these two places, Vietnam and Virginia, a chasm across which the violent act can never be put right even as it continues to rear up in the human skull. In this alternate view, CIA agent Joe Baker's silent presence by Loan's side could itself be seen as a kind of testament—if not to the ethical crisis of the event, then at least to the agony of re-narrating it and the CIA's implication in its narration. The men's presence together at the mall is as much a reaction to the visual denials of the suburban landscape around them as are the presence of French colonial military anthems (identified only as "French Record") next to Dolly Parton records on Loan's restaurant jukebox.[173]

The dislocated communities created by American empire in Northern Virginia's home front suburbs need not only be block parties where "old friends" converge domestically to celebrate triumphs. They are also landscapes of silent, wrenching atonement, even if the atonement never occurs publicly. Like the Viet Cong at the roots of the family tree in *Monkey Bridge*, Loan's private encounter with violence he wrought in Saigon is a point at which the haunted landscape of the Dulles Corridor invites the postcolonial nation of Vietnam and its dead back in to continue the story-so-far between the two places along a different axis—an axis of truth, guilt, and mourning.

Guilt is always a connection. And it is this connection through guilt that Loan represents, so uncomfortably, for his neighbors, both those who defended him and those who objected to the racialized reminder of American violence he brought to their suburban shopping mall. Menacing him with similar tactics to those he used in Vietnam, one of those neighbors once scrawled, "We know who you are," on the wall in his restaurant's bathroom in Burke.[174] The suburbanites of Northern Virginia knew who Loan was. But did they know who they were?

LANSDALE'S FREEDOM HOUSE— McLEAN'S SAIGON, 1975

The migration of imperial intimates of the United States back to the covert capital home front could accomplish a variety of concrete tasks for U.S. empire. Their arrival could salve the consciences of U.S. imperial agents, making their jobs easier. It could symbolically follow through on implicit imperial promises about home and nation. It could accomplish rhetorical and political work on behalf of the covert capital as it cast itself as a restorative, habitable American space of democratic promise, inclusion, and ethnic succession, helping to produce the covert capital's landscape of denial. But it could also serve to extend for Lansdale, the Pentagon, and the CIA a set of more activist politics into the covert capital domestic sphere designed to destabilize and extend the counterinsurgent struggle and active war against nationalist Vietnam.

These projects started immediately upon these migrants' arrival in Northern Virginia. Soon after the evacuation, Dai Viet party chairman Ha Thuc Ky, government official and Saigon intriguer in the days after Diem's assassination, moved to the area and began organizing "former Dai Viet cadres" and ARVN personnel into the Free Vietnam Front to spread "facts about the present situation in Vietnam" and to warn people "against the futility and danger of an accommodating attitude in dealing with Communism." In touch with underground military and paramilitary men in Vietnam, the Free Vietnam Front also corresponded with Lansdale through a covert capital migrant, Le Chi Thao, a South Vietnamese diplomat who settled into a modernist little townhouse in Vienna after the fall of Saigon. Lansdale reviewed the group's "initial talking points."[175] Later, Le Chi Thao became the first Asian American representative on the Fairfax County School Board, a Republican appointee.[176]

Many whom Lansdale sponsored did vital, and often unrecognized, political and propagandistic work in and on behalf of the United States and the covert capital itself even as and explicitly because they inhabited the category of the refugee. Lansdale and Phan Quang Dan stayed in touch until 1985, at which point Dan planned to return to Vietnam to "continue the struggle for freedom."[177] Also continuing the struggle was Colonel Pham Van Lieu, Dan's colleague in a 1960 coup attempt against Diem and later part of Ky's "brain trust," whom Lansdale had supported in his entry into the United States, calling him a man "whom a George Mason or Tom Jefferson would have cottoned to immediately."[178] The colonel was a leader of the National United Front for the Liberation of Vietnam, which, in cooperation with U.S. Army intelligence veterans, raised money and organized actively to support anti-communist "freedom fighters" to retake Vietnam in a bicoastal campaign stretching from the street in front of the White House to the auditorium of a San Jose high school.[179]

Lansdale joined Vietnamese friends at unity meetings for Vietnamese anticommunists at the House Office Building.[180] In the wider suburban landscape, a refugee committee set up in Fairfax City began lobbying to "affect an appropriate American posture in Southeast Asia," and, in one of its first acts, selected a group of "boat people" to occupy a historic house once owned by R. Walton Moore, Franklin Roosevelt's assistant secretary of state, on Fairfax's main drag in 1979.[181] Little Saigon's Wilson Boulevard restaurants hosted benefit dinners where other boat people who had worked for the South Vietnamese government narrated their bitter ordeals in reeducation camps to mobilize supportive locals, such as former CIA director and pacification supervisor in Vietnam, Bill Colby.[182]

Lucien Conein's constant contact in the Diem coup, General Tran Van Don, also hosted political dinners in Northern Virginia.[183] On the edge of Falls Church, Khuc Minh Tho, a former South Vietnam official, founded the Families of Vietnamese Political Prisoners Association to lobby for the release of her husband, an ARVN colonel, and other reeducation camp prisoners in Vietnam under the Orderly Departure Program. Meeting in Tho's new split-level five-bedroom at night, the group worked with the U.S. State Department in support of those prisoners who had defended "democracy in South Vietnam with the collaboration of and assistance from the United States," and who "staked their lives and liberties with the American presence."[184]

Despite this labor, figures from South Vietnam whose intimacies with Lansdale and other U.S. imperial figures ensured their passage to the covert capital did not enter the suburbs with a full set of rights. Many did struggle, even when they continued to do political and rhetorical work on behalf of Lansdale, Northern Virginia, and the United States. No one better lays out this fact than Bui Anh Tuan. Without his propaganda work, the Saigon Military Mission would not have succeeded. Few had deeper relationships with Lansdale and his team.

Lansdale agreed to sponsor Tuan from the camp at Fort Chaffee, soon after the evacuation.[185] By the time Tuan prepared for the trip to Northern Virginia, prospects looked bright. The Mission would stride out again to receive their good friend "Pete." Lansdale contacted their colleague Nick Arundel, now the successful Northern Virginia publisher, to help Tuan seek work. And Arundel already had "prospects for him in literary and journal-istic fields."[186] Tuan, his wife, and twenty-one-year-old son would stay with Arundel in case, in Lansdale's words, "some of the other Viets I'm sponsoring fill up my house to the brim," and Arundel would help them seek housing. Tuan only asked that Lansdale come meet his family at the airport and allow them to stay briefly, regardless of the crowd. He wanted his family to "see the face of this legendary Colonel Landslide," Lansdale's nickname after bring-ing in elections for U.S.-approved candidates in the Philippines years before. It was as if seeing the Military Mission's leader first and renewing that bond would cast the entire move in a more reliable atmosphere of safety, security, and familiarity. Lansdale's house stood in as a first knowable, affective point of debarkation. Tuan promised only to talk a bit and "evoke the sour and sweet souvenirs." Then the family would adjourn to Arundel's.[187]

Yet, before much time passed, the job with Arundel had not materialized. Tuan began writing articles for *Soldier of Fortune* and, through similar con-tacts, began editing newsletters for die-hard anticommunist and new right think tanks staffed with CIA and Pentagon retirees, such as the American Council for World Freedom and the Committee for a Free China, becom-ing an editor at their DC publication, *China Report*. But *China Report* went broke and stopped publishing. A job at the Library of Congress did not pan out. New York publishers rejected his translated spy novels, which had been popular in South Vietnam. Before much time passed, Arundel stopped

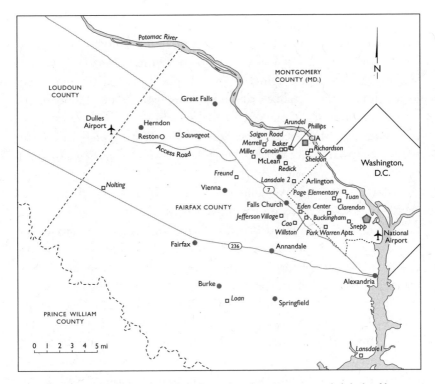

Saigon's Northern Virginia. U.S. imperial intimates from Vietnam settled the land between the Pentagon and the CIA that had defined their lives for so long.

responding to Tuan's letters. Tuan's family had moved to two different small apartments in North Alexandria and Arlington. He contacted Lansdale again for help applying for a job at the Rand Corporation. Lansdale arranged an interview, but their "Asian budget" was too small for more writers. Tuan tried other DC think tanks and many other jobs to no avail.[188] Lansdale mostly had words of encouragement at this point. "Hang onto that old fighting spirit, tiger," he wrote, using the sign-off he reserved for close intimates. "Love to you and the family."[189]

The initial pass out of the camps, the sponsorship, and reception at CIA houses in McLean and elsewhere could only go so far. These passes could not equalize a relationship stratified from the start. Tuan and his colleagues had been equally central to a project that had helped secure all their futures and that of U.S. empire abroad. But while Tuan's former comrades inhabited stable suburban domiciles and positions in Northern Virginia without significant adversity, Tuan could not. This might seem an obvious point—that refugees have a harder time than Americans—but it is worth stressing how the appearance and critical political function of mutuality in the imperial context and U.S. state in Vietnam could not transfer to the U.S. imperial landscape of Northern Virginia, despite rhetorical goodwill. In some sense, Tuan's story might seem like a conventional refugee tale, but it is not one of mere generic racism and indifference. Rather, it was a violation of an earlier trust, one that perhaps needs to be theorized as a further expression of imperial aggression, this time directed against those who had made U.S. empire possible in the first place.

Lansdale expressed an abiding interest in the Tuan family that his CIA colleagues did not share, displaying an almost microscopic commitment to keeping up their correspondence, perhaps more attuned to the ways the armature of U.S. empire in Vietnam had rested on such foundations, ones that lasted far into the future. He wrote depositions and recommendations for their green card and permanent resident application in 1976,[190] again when they became naturalized citizens in 1981,[191] and even for Tuan's son to apply for academic scholarships and to medical school.[192] But structurally, the U.S. imperial landscape in the suburbs of Northern Virginia, by design, had no mechanism to incorporate an equal partner in its work abroad, even as Tuan continued to do crucial U.S. imperial propaganda work in the domestic sphere. He even won the George Washington Honor Medal by the Freedoms Foundation at Valley Forge for an essay in which he frowned upon the fact that America's "constructive diversity" had "since Vietnam . . . degenerated into a heresy of attacks on the nation's defense and security interests." He defended U.S. political allies and right-wing dictators abroad from the critiques of those he considered irresponsible liberal Americans, those who "refused to settle for anything less than instant democracy when looking into the records of Park's South Korea, Pinochet's Chile, Marcos' Philippines and Smith's Rhodesia." In turn, the Freedoms Foundation lauded the fact that Tuan had "come to love America more than some . . . who were born here."[193]

Such sentiments had always been the price of the ticket into U.S. imperial networks of friendship and benefit. They were now the price charged for the ticket out of the camps and into the secure and national security space of Northern Virginia and the United States.[194] But for the United States, the price of the ticket, now individualized, was cheap, particularly next to the more substantive notion that Vietnamese expertise, status, and intimacies with U.S. goals over a long period of time might have led to calls for a more expansive set of rights and claims on the U.S. nation.

But neither ardent affiliation with U.S. politics or immediate immigrant incorporation according to U.S. domestic consumer dictates won the day as the dominant script of the Vietnamese arrival in the covert capital. As the first 3,000 Vietnamese refugees began to move into the Northern Virginia suburbs of Arlington, Alexandria, and Falls Church, reporters, officials, and residents instead framed their arrival as an obvious challenge to the mores of the white suburban landscape, a "Strange Land" to them, "Worlds Apart,"[195] where what was "once a virtually all-white middle-class suburb full of upwardly mobile federal bureaucrats" now had to contend with immigrants struggling to "abandon Oriental customs" while "learning to tolerate a much colder climate."[196] At best, the Vietnamese needed to move quickly from refugee to immigrant, to embrace what one newspaper called "the American Dream, Nguyen-style."[197] For some local racists, the Vietnamese needed to move out altogether, or "soon there won't be any 'real' Americans left in Arlington."[198] Encounters with white and black locals read as test cases for their difficult prospects of incorporation. For some whites, their arrival carried with it the threatening, racialized tropes of the war itself, leading to what some framed as a kind of domino theory of apartments where housing for refugees could have "a domino effect that could never be reversed" and collecting rent was "a war."[199]

These articulations of an essentially insurmountable divide between "middle-class white suburbia" and new "immigrants of color" provide important insight into the utility of race as an imperial category. The rhetorical theatrics that met the Vietnamese upon their arrival deployed the trope of race to downplay a whole series of relationships defined by a preexisting closeness. Just as it had during the evacuation, race arose in the covert capital and its imperial intimacies as a sudden, difficult-to-navigate border. Whereas the national borders of countries could be turned porous by an evacuation, and the intimate borders of human relationships could be traversed by narratives of likeness, camaraderie, and friendship, race could arise as an instant resource to biologize, essentialize, and give an aura of solidity to imperial logics of difference that could not be maintained under other modes of human sorting and relation. If emotional intimacy was a discourse as evanescent as a human relationship or as not feeling like answering a letter, racial emotives— active expressive claims relying on notions of race for their emotional content—held public power as a seeming foundation that could not be argued.[200]

The fact that the deployment of race had no stability—ascribing specific behaviors and tendencies sometimes, vanishing at others, rearing up again at useful points, then softening yet again—only pointed to the ways that race had always maintained the defining background of U.S. imperial intimacy, the "not quite" inside a friendship, which could guide rights, settlement, power, and claims of payment on emotional, professional, and quasi-legal imperial debts, not to mention the basic safety and chances for a good life possible for different actors engaging in imperial work, or those cast on the other side of it, as the objects of its violence.[201] The capaciousness and mutability of the concept of race—its ability to claim immediate viewing publics and their "common sense" and its determining limits and strictures, which, in Northern Virginia, routed into already pre-patterned, spatial means of habitation and division stretching back to Jim Crow and before—made it empire's trump card, at home as abroad, or in the continuous, co-constituted cultural landscape that crossed both spaces. Despite exceptions at the intimate scale, in the form of the strategic and useful friendship, or at the public scale, in the form of the suburban progress narrative's breezy triumphs, race remained a resilient armature channeling benefits, safety, and the easy right of return to Northern Virginia toward white Americans at work on U.S. imperial projects, and determining always only partial access to similar benefits for Vietnamese people at work on the same imperial projects. Vietnamese imperial repatriates' white covert capital allies never had to explain their returns from the U.S. imperial context or their reasons for being in the American suburbs. Their acts of extreme and random violence never appeared in photographs that fascinated the American public or appeared in photographs at all. Just as the skin and surface of Langley hid its compartmented imperial interiors, so the skin of whiteness provided a cover for some American imperial agents that allowed them to operate with ease in the broader suburban landscape.[202]

Vietnamese interactions with the United States in Vietnam had always been based on conditional, racially stratified intimacies, which could evaporate or turn violent at any moment. Rather than seeing the racialized public greeting Vietnamese received in Northern Virginia as an aberration from an uncomplicated intimacy, it is more useful to think of the public script as itself a kind of warning that the welcome to Northern Virginia was offered on the premise of a similar conditionality. Before entering the suburbs, Vietnamese had to undergo a racial "rehabilitation," to use a term from Jodi Kim, which transformed them from geopolitical intimate to American Dream immigrant.[203] It came with a demotion in class, power, and authority, and the threat of violence, exclusion, and revoked status that had defined the U.S. project in Vietnam. But the threat of violence—and the actual violence engaged in by Northern Virginia residents and Vietnamese friends to establish American power in this period—was not an exception to suburban Northern Virginia. It was the very foundation for these suburbs.

Because my focus is on the effects American imperial goals have on this local space—and the way this local space in America makes its empire—the stories in the last two chapters inevitably concentrated on those projects initiated by the U.S. imperial state as it was located in the Dulles Corridor after 1950, when both U.S. empire and the landscape of Northern Virginia moved toward consolidation. But obviously, and importantly, Vietnam has its own stories-so-far, and this is only one of them, just as Vietnam is only one of the stories-so-far of the Dulles Corridor (and at that, in itself, not just a single story-so-far). One need only consider other stories that could be told in Northern Virginia at this time to highlight this. For instance, CIA agent and Pinochet intelligence chief Manuel Contreras met in Virginia with CIA officials in 1975 "at a time when the agency reported that he was personally responsible for thousands of cases of murder and torture in Chile." At this same moment, many Cambodian and Laotian intimates also arrived in Arlington and Falls Church. Other stories of long duration transpired further out along the skeins of empire and geography, such as those skating along the 39th parallel, the latitude Northern Virginia shares with Pyongyang, North Korea.[204]

But as they twist down to the present, the stories-so-far between Northern Virginia and Vietnam themselves endure, change, and tangle. In the 1980s, the South Vietnamese flag first rose next to the American flag in the Eden Center parking lot. It was a physical witness in the center of the Dulles Corridor to the contractual moral duty created by the former imperial interest of the United States in Vietnam—the material sign of something often thought not to exist: a double capital, formed by empire. By the 2000s, denizens of the covert capital were publicly fulfilling this material promise in a way often disavowed thirty years earlier. In 2003, the local Board of Supervisors recognized South Vietnam's flag as the "heritage flag" of Vietnamese-American Northern Virginia, a measure fought for by residents asserting that Fairfax County "is not the United Nations" and "doesn't have to observe the international protocol" by recognizing Vietnam's actual flag.[205]

The pattern and cultural forms of Vietnamese settlement in Northern

Virginia testified back against an erasure, staking a claim to political identities with long durations and, in the process, taking on a range of resonances—honoring, witnessing, and critiquing U.S. empire, creating complex memorials to power relationships. The built environment designed to guide U.S. imperial intimates into a circumscription of rights in bounded spaces in certain sections of the suburban landscape simultaneously came to contain and bear witness to relationships that often cannot be named in traditional scripts of either U.S. foreign policy or the American suburb—to reveal relationships that the very same spaces set out to mask and deny.

The double representational effect of these spaces is exactly why the built environment in the Dulles Corridor offers a powerful way to reread and reveal connections left unsaid discursively and historically. Imprinting the geography of McLean with the referenced geography of Vietnam, McLean's Saigon Road subdivision takes the stories-so-far between these two places back to the Northern Virginia suburbs' earliest moments of being and publicizes them forward onto its most contemporary maps. It finds its twin in the suburbs now built in Ho Chi Minh City by the Dulles Corridor's Vietnamese intimates, who returned to Vietnam in the nineties, not as conquering South Vietnamese Republicans but as American capitalist emissaries looking to develop its land.

One Dulles Corridor denizen, Vietnamese American developer Tien Hoang, who was twenty in 1975, returned to Ho Chi Minh City in 2003 at age forty-eight. He hired a crew of contractors and began to build a subdivision called Green City that included 500 houses and duplexes. A sales office in Falls Church sold the homes. Later Hoang planned to add a strip mall. He thought about calling the mall in Vietnam "Little Fairfax." "It's like Reston was back then," Hoang told the *Post*, sweeping his arm across his property in Vietnam. "It's a new area ready for development."[206] In this final, for our purposes, story-so-far, the decades of the Dulles Corridor's interest in, damage to, intimacy with, and abandonment of Vietnam in conjunction with the decades of Vietnam's resistance to, populating of, intimacy with, and inspiration for the Dulles Corridor had merely cleared the country of Vietnam for the suburban development of the Dulles Corridor—which, at least in the case of Saigon Road, Vietnam had inspired to begin with.

In a 1996 book, Lan Cao cautioned against stereotypes that suggest that Asian American "communities are crawling with . . . hidden lives."[207] In one sense, there is a danger in recounting these stories of merely reinscribing Vietnamese in Northern Virginia as shadowy foreign interlopers. But there is also the greater prospect of the opposite: that illuminating the family trees of transnational violence and imperial pasts of *all* geopolitical actors in Northern Virginia has the power to tell profound stories about the ethics and debts of U.S. imperial policy and suburban life. Imperial violence and networks were the foundation and purpose of the suburbs of Northern Virginia. Turning toward rather than away from these complexities can narrate anti-racist social histories of suburban and imperial migration and movement that do not merely recast suburbia as the implicit and natural ground for an apolitical, everyday middle-class life, and do not merely recast empire as something that always happens somewhere else, inflicted by system onto no one, and, as such, having no insistent and tortured echoes in the cul-de-sacs of everyday spatial and domestic American life at the lived scale.

FIVE

Iran-Contra as Built Space

U.S. IMPERIAL TEHRAN IN EXILE
AND EDGE CITY'S CENTRAL AMERICAN PRESENCE

GROWING UP IN EDGE CITY[1]

In 1987, observers noticed a new skyline in the suburbs of the covert capital. The seventeen-story Tycon Towers I, designed by the architects John Burgee and Philip Johnson and the whimsical developer James T. Lewis, surged over the trees. At the height of his fame as the inventor of the postmodern skyscraper and designer of the corporate towers that visually marked the Reagan years, Johnson chose Tycon Towers as a new challenge, his only skyscraper in the 1980s built in the suburbs. Its gargantuan, faux classical detailing, its superscale freestanding columns done in Virginia brick and said to be the world's tallest, its arches resembling the handles on a shopping bag—all of these features defined the tower placed on what the architects called a green "front yard." It seemed to herald the end of dense, modernist urbanism. Around it, an entire city seemed to molt. Modular office buildings and skyscrapers marched over lawns and parking lots, ever swelling in size. They orbited around a mall called Tysons Corner, built two decades before.

To observers, the buildings announced an era: "strange, sprawling, towering shapes" had landed in the low-lying suburbs, defined by their repetitious bands of opaque glass. But unlike the style of building elsewhere, Tysons Corner still looked green amid the remnants of Virginia's countryside. Dark glass window rows reflected the green hills and curving cloverleaves, imbuing all with a slightly futuristic quality. Northern Virginia journalist Joel Garreau, who passed these places commuting to his job at the *Washington Post*, gave them a name: Edge City. Thanks in no small part to his work, Tysons Corner's slightly futuristic quality grew into a boom industry in nineties urban studies. Garreau defined Edge City by its mass: "high-rised, semi-autonomous, job-laden, road-clogged communities of enormous size, springing up on the edges." It was a conceptual product of the covert capital. But it soon came to stand for everything about America except its empire: its love of individualism and free enterprise, its love of opportunity and choice, its love of privacy and security, its love of nature and technology in a "constantly reinvented land." The fact that Edge City sounded an epitaph for the capital at DC had nothing to do with politics for Garreau. Northern Virginia was simply where it was *at*.[2]

The same year, a second phenomenon also rocked the Dulles Corridor: the Iran-Contra Affair. Next to Edge City's heady visibility, Iran-Contra was the epitome of murk. A convoluted network of federal officials, contractor CEOs, and quasi-official shadow agencies had, in violation of two federal orders, sold arms to Ayatollah Khomeini's revolutionary Iran, supposedly the sworn enemy of the people who had done the selling.[3] Profits from those weapons sales had gone to the contras, the bands of corporate executives and rightists the CIA had helped form to overthrow the new Sandinista government of Nicaragua. Intentional complexity was Iran-Contra's very structure. But by summer 1987, the scandal was also a seemingly clear and quite spectacular TV show. The show starred Great Falls resident Oliver North, the National Security Council staff member, Vietnam platoon leader, and plotter of the U.S. invasion of Grenada who stepped into the spotlight as a central Iran-Contra operator and icon, rallying the new right locally and nationally. For some, North also symbolized the values Joel Garreau lauded about Edge City—free enterprise, choice, security.

This chapter looks at Iran-Contra and Edge City as they met in the covert capital's built environment in the 1980s in order to make a new argument about both. U.S. imperial action and space in the covert capital at the dawn of the Reagan administration had a new way of being managed. Tropes of subcontracting, corporatization, and privatization—more radical forms of the compartmentation that defined CIA covert action from the start—became the order of the day. But these forms of breaking apart accountability and institutionally reorganizing U.S. imperial action were created in the name of a recovered wholeness: fantasies of masculinity, country, place, and community perceived as traditional and fantasies of glory days of CIA and Pentagon effort unhampered by democratic oversight. Iran-Contra was an open secret. Countless evidence revealed it before its exposure in November 1986, yet it was "unknown." New policies designed to cloak U.S. imperial effort, in turn, brought a dramatic new built environment into view in Northern Virginia for the first time.

But in exploring the stages for Iran-Contra in Northern Virginia's 1980s built environment, this chapter also uses the phrase *Iran-Contra* to rethink the history of the covert capital and U.S. empire in this period. U.S. foreign policy discourse often breaks the world into area studies imaginaries and geostrategic rubrics, producing experts, scholars, and reports concentrating on "Central America" and the "Middle East," and rendering people and subjects knowable in the eye of U.S. empire and nationalism through these very distinctions. In segregating global interventions that for their practitioners were never separate, such approaches obscure the simultaneous projects and comparative racial formations and acts of violence through which U.S. empire operated.

Abstruse as the name was as it appeared publicly as scandal, "Iran-Contra" in Edge City throws into relief these interconnections. Human habitation and built space in 1987 Northern Virginia made the simultaneous dimensions of U.S. empire visible in a way local residents and U.S. imperial actors perhaps did not expect. Networked relationships that twined together Central America, Northern Virginia, and Iran fundamentally shaped local space. Abroad and at home, Northern Virginia's imperial actors deployed overlapping bodily and spatial investments and disinvestments—pinned to different people, places, and ideas about race and gender—as a regular part of their work. The afterlife of these imperial politics of relation and comparison then played out in the proximities and intimacies of the U.S. imperial home front of Edge City, Northern Virginia. Iran-Contra was not just wordplay. It was a compass pointing to a multi-sited U.S. imperial geography, one both revealed and covered over by the Iran-Contra scandal, and both revealed and covered over by the landscape of Edge City, Northern Virginia. The scandal also provided the key to an intentionally evasive kind of map, even as the untranslatability of "Iran-Contra" opened up creative space for the U.S. imperial work that was the only thing that fused the two words.[4]

ORIGINS OF EDGE CITY: THE PENTAGON

In one sense, the buildings created from stacked concrete and glass that defined Northern Virginia's office space in the 1980s reached back to a much longer story of development. Edge City's poet laureate, Joel Garreau, once called the Pentagon "the world's archetypal Edge City structure." By the time it opened in 1943 as the largest office building on Earth, it wasn't big enough.[5] The Dulles Corridor needed more office space. When Robert McNamara moved into the Pentagon as secretary of defense in 1961, he carried with him an operations research man's lust for buzzwords like *efficiency* and *expertise*, and a corporate executive's confidence in the private contractors who specialized in speaking those words.[6] On his watch, as Paul Ceruzzi and others have shown, the operations research companies, systems analysis firms, and Rand-descended federally funded research and development centers rose to power and stepped into local space, soon pulling in suburban office development like their own little suns.[7] Some converged around old streetcar and new Metro lines close to DC (Rosslyn, Ballston, Crystal City, Pentagon City); others, near access roads to Dulles Airport (Reston, Dulles, Tysons).[8]

Edge City at Tysons Corner was the perfect example. The year after McNamara took office, Gerald Halpin, a former executive at a company that sold solid-fueled rockets to the Pentagon, and Rudolph Seeley, a former colonel in U.S. Army intelligence, joined forces to raise the office clusters that anchor Tysons Corner to this day: Westpark and Westgate. With 600 acres strategically sprawled between the Dulles Access Road, the capital Beltway (which opened in 1964), and the Tysons regional mall (which opened in 1968), Halpin and Seeley began coaxing three- to seven-story office buildings from the dairy farms for those on "Defense and Defense-related contracts." Many were built by the architect Charles M. Goodman, who designed many monuments in the covert capital story—National Airport, the modernist Hollin Hills subdivision, a modernist cluster in Reston, and a house on Saigon Road.[9]

Contractors swarmed Tysons and other Edge Cities for what one historian called "easy liaison with Pentagon procurement officers."[10] As they could pass on the cost of their leases to the Pentagon, and the tax code rewarded their all-new construction with massive write-offs, these new spaces that appeared private were publicly funded almost all the way down.[11] A parade of acronyms and reshuffled keywords unfurled—Research Analysis Corporation, TRW, Planning Research Corporation, MITRE—their bland names a shell to deflect attention, even as their nicknames, like the Planning Research Corporation's chummy sobriquet "Place for Retired Colonels," spoke to the point of their presence.[12]

When the Dulles Toll Road opened in 1984, finally providing local access to the dedicated Dulles highway, and another new road connected the Dulles highway and I-66, it solidified Tysons Corner's role as the main switching point between Dulles and the Washington metropolitan area. One of the toll road's exit ramps poured straight into Westpark.[13] In 1983, Ronald Reagan's Star Wars space defense program sprouted its own crop of the contracting nouveau riche. One of its headiest beneficiaries, BDM International, a specialist in missile defense, moved to Westpark and became one of Fairfax County's largest employers. The company celebrated its local dominance and the violent undercurrent to some of its work with a bang, breaking ground for a headquarters at Westpark in 1986 by detonating a "pyrotechnic charge."[14] Soon, Northern Virginia novelists with close ties to covert capital geopolitical figures began recording the gleaming landscape of Edge City in their fiction, in often bleak, alienated tales set between the "eight lanes of the Beltway, six lanes of the airport road," amid the "montage of the Sprawl's towers," in a "Whole World Mall" with a technologically sophisticated, violent, international mural on its ceiling, and in militarized communities with gates named "Westgate."[15]

Observers also soon noticed a change in the built environment that the contractors had brought, a definitive feature of Edge City space—the Sensitive Compartmented Information Facility, or SCIF, pronounced "skiff." The SCIF was a human-sized safe. It drew its points of access, shape, and extremely expensive construction materials from complex security regulations that deflected eavesdropping, invasion, and penetration. By 1988, they were so prevalent in the Dulles Corridor that a reporter could comment confidently, "Every self-respecting defense contractor has one."[16] The SCIF is surely one of the only built forms in history to arise from a way of managing secret information—the Sensitive Compartmented Information, "above Top Secret," that had circulated within the CIA since the sixties. The first few years of the Reagan administration drove a SCIF boom.[17] Before long, individual contractors had up to ten or more in their new buildings, even though they cost from $10,000 to $1 million to construct. SCIF regulators soon needed to specify rules for "contiguous SCI spaces." In time there were even "complete SCIF buildings."[18]

What defined the SCIF was its break between inside and outside. The SCIF was its own paradox. It was a dense, durable icon defined by its invisibility in the public landscape. Inside, SCIFs looked like generic corporate offices. The design gravitated to the points at which the SCIF met the outside world. SCIFs were odes to reinforced concrete and steel-shielded walls and ceilings all "permanently constructed and attached to each other," rigged with an orchestra of alarms, vault doors bedazzled with locks, and non-conducive ducts. The perfect SCIF had no windows. But due to the sheer numbers of contractors and agency satellites at Edge Cities like Tysons and the multiple SCIFs needed within each building, they all couldn't be built into the centers of the structures. Some had to abut exteriors. At the same time, to build a fleet of blind stone fortifications amid the still-green spaces of the Virginia suburbs countered the other urge of these companies and agencies that, as Ceruzzi explains, "did not want anyone to know who they were or where they were located."[19]

Design regulators suggested solutions to this problem—rod-enforced distortion glass, lockable interior steel shutters, permanently sealed windows, the subversive score of "a sound/cover music system" pointed from the inside toward the glass. The band of tinted windows finally bridged the gap. Early SCIF manuals had circulated the idea that windows should be "made opaque or equipped with drapes or other suitable covering which will preclude . . . surveillance." This idea seems to have led to another one: Opaque windows didn't have to be actual windows. They could just look like windows, while making windowless buildings possible. Thanks to the hypnotic repetitions of dark window bands, SCIFs could push to the edges of the buildings, "built behind false windows to preserve the typical windowed office facade and not give away what is inside."[20]

Unlike the transparent glass houses of the first CIA agents, often also built by adaptive local architects like Charles Goodman, the opaque windows of the Edge City era gave the impression of transparency while reincarnating it as obscurity—as cynical decoration—or as reflective surface, a reversal of surveillance onto the street. But the bands of dark glass also affirmed these organizations' second mandate, "to preserve the typical . . . facade." Repeated bands of windows created "typicality," a surface uniformity that deflected questions about interior uses. They provided cover that, in a less developed landscape, came from tree barriers and unbreachable parking lots on large tracts. Certainly, a SCIF didn't sleep behind every dark window at Tysons. But that was the point. Opaque windows were everywhere— whatever lay behind them was unknown. They became their own kind of postmodern ornament.

SCIF landscaping had another, unrecognized impact on Edge City form. SCIF regulators had strong words for landscape architects. The Defense Intelligence Agency would have preferred perimeter eight-foot barbed wire or concertina fencing and brightly glaring lights all the time. Realizing this wasn't always practical, they elaborated a more subtle palette that required only "mowed grass" and lawns in a sixty-foot circumference around any SCIF building, the lawns surrounded by a corridor of "brushed or raked dirt" that could be checked by guards for footprints.[21]

A SCIF building's relationship to its neighbors was equally important, and structures "on the same plane" and at the same height as the SCIF held a particular security risk. The gently pitching, undulating landscape and alternating height and altitude of buildings at Westgate and Westpark, often divided from one another by lawns, raked dirt borders, or roads that operated as fences, answered these concerns. This landscape had the second effect of creating the impression of what Joel Garreau called the "new Eden" with "no dark alleys," laundering security as corporate amenity. SCIF buildings at Tysons thus summarized the covert capital security dream and suburban cover story. They were counterintelligence tools whose green landscapes recruited workers to suburban contracting businesses far from the city, even if those green spaces sat unused with an absolute stillness. Edge Cities with a density of SCIFs like Tysons Corner were good neighborhoods for contractors precisely because they fulfilled the covert office landscape's security needs. Presumably, the fact that a place like Tysons had already been perpetually studied for security risks eased the burden of required photographic area studies that kept SCIF approvals moving forward. Northern Virginia architects and builders acquired skills to develop the buildings, streamlining local construction. The heavy presence of other SCIF contractors also calmed any doubts about neighbors as Edge City became its own self-evident security argument. In one 1980 DIA manual, half the alarm firms with "Government account representatives" recommended to SCIF builders were in Arlington, Alexandria, Springfield, and Falls Church.[22]

By the 1980s, Tysons Corner could effortlessly represent itself as a haven for "private" and "efficient" government consultants at the same time it appeared as Eden to a journalist looking to needle stuffy liberal urbanists with his paeans to the service economy. All the while, it could surface evidence of a highly strategic landscape designed from the start to serve the national security state at home and abroad. The main group of geographers to recognize its import in the eighties described it as "the maturation of the military-industrial complex, now finally established in the very seat of government."[23] Edge City buildings also visually told the story operations research men wanted to hear. Geometric, sized rationally for maximum floor area, they embodied their rhetoric of efficiency in the built environment. The orderly dark win-

The glass and concrete cubes of Edge City Tysons Corner in the late 1980s gave Northern Virginia its first skyline. Inside the buildings, American covert action had a new way of being managed, according to Reagan-era tropes of subcontracting and privatization. Philip Johnson's Tycon Towers appears in the distance at the right of the photo. Scott Boatright. Courtesy of Fairfax County Public Library Photographic Archive.

dows marching along their bands offered a portrait of, and advertisement for, streamlined but bureaucratically modest logic in action—bureaucratically modest so as not to shame those holding federal purse strings with corporate ostentation, their blandness itself a suburban critique of the excesses and wastes of urban design, even as their own federal contracts grew.[24]

That those orderly windows simultaneously displayed the most egregious lack of rationality (behind them were the dead walls of the SCIFs, out of which no people could actually see) provided architectural testimony to the presence of operations research and contracting as a kind of cynical decoration over the ethical SCIF inside which the covert capital operated. The 1980s SCIF boom also made a mockery of the very category of Sensitive Compartmented Information. During World War II, the precursor of "SCI" emerged as a way of handling information so secret that only Franklin Roosevelt, the secretaries of State, War, and Navy, and the directors of military and naval intelligence could access it. By the 1980s, SCI could be seen by countless contractors with little supervision from their Pentagon and CIA monitors.

By 1985, 164,000 people had signed SCI nondisclosure agreements. At times, using SCI as an excuse, contractors with less stringent clearances had access to information kept away from federal investigators with more rigorous clearance. Some evidence suggests this was the point of the category. Upon taking office, Reagan moved almost immediately to "increase the ease of classifying information." "A blanket of secrecy" would now hide information, in one historian's words, "for as long as government officials so desire," serving "more to remove such matters from public scrutiny and supervision than to keep the information from hostile powers."[25] The SCIFs of Edge City, Edge City's very form, offered one important genealogy to the networks of secrecy and covert action known, in 1987, as the Iran-Contra Affair.

The meetings and plotting for what became Iran-Contra took place in SCIFs and SCIF buildings—in literal ones and in closed networks amounting to the same thing. Vast numbers of covert capital activists worked on the covert action in Central America, Northern Virginia, and Iran; vast numbers of people suffered as a result. Yet the project remained "secret." SCIFs in microcosm thus stood as a figure for the shifts in covert capital policy in this period. Together, Edge City, Iran-Contra, and the SCIFs represented the shape of the imperial corridor's office domesticity and policy as it overflowed covert campuses. The repetitious glass-and-concrete cube, stacked with its secret, modular, windowless SCIFs and more banal offices, became the new covert capital's indigenous form. Modernity became postmodernity in covert capital architecture and agency, as architects like Goodman adjusted their aesthetics from the transparent, glassy liberal modernist structures gesturing outward to the world in the 1960s to the opaque postmodern towers stressing privacy and security in the 1980s. But in another sense, little adjustment was needed. The geopolitical labor that inhabited them both remained the same. Only the style necessary to express and execute that labor had changed.

ORIGINS OF EDGE CITY: THE CIA

Thus, while the SCIF boom did emerge from the contracting culture around the Pentagon, it is important to recognize that radically "need-to-know" ways of organizing secrets and covert action also arose from the root of the CIA's culture in the early sixties. Some journalists and historians mistakenly elucidate the SCIF acronym (using the more correct and less awkward usage) as the "Sensitive *Compartmentalized* Information Facility." The appearance of *compartmented* in official documents points to its origins in a CIA spatial logic, as CIA officers always insisted on that as the accurate term. Compartmented and cutout facilities, hallways and rooms were basic to the original design of Langley. The SCIFs and compartmented offices of the contractors in Edge Cities like Tysons merely extended the covert spaces of the CIA and Pentagon into dramatic visible space.

Edge City designs responded to this fact with their strange, defensive anonymity in public. The CIA also had a history of using the so-called private contractors as wings of CIA projects. Ex-officer David Louis Whitehead recalled the intimacy between Langley and the Tysons Corner companies. CIA officers ferried classified data up Route 123 to the offices of BDM, the major force in developing Tysons that was working on CIA projects in Asia. Spies intermarried with corporate executives and used contractors such as TRW and MITRE as cover. The revolving door—or "no door at all"—between the companies and the agency was ceaselessly spinning. One spy recalled joining the staff of Booz-Allen & Hamilton "for a couple of years to pile up enough money to buy a nice house in Virginia." A second reunited with a colleague from Egyptian intelligence at a Tysons Corner gathering place and founded another company to transport U.S. military equipment abroad. CIA sprawl graced much office space in Rosslyn, Ballston, Tysons, Reston, and Crystal City—including a proprietary CIA security firm with three subsidiaries, which did commercial work in the new Edge Cities without revealing who was behind the security. At Reston, the CIA also began building new SCIF-laden buildings, in part dealing with satellite intelligence.[26]

Rather than part of a generic narrative of corporatization and privatization, the physical and public-private structure of Edge City was often covert action by other means. What had changed were not necessarily the covert actions but the relationship between the CIA and Congress. Edge City's built environment, with its superficially "contracted out" entities that could fund and execute government policy, helped innovate global warfare that could transpire outside of democratic processes in a way particularly appealing to covert actors straining under an era of congressional oversight and perceived imperial retrenchment.[27] Thus, to understand why exactly the policy took this form when it did, it is also crucial to have a revised understanding of the shifts in covert action and U.S. imperial management emanating from the CIA and the Pentagon in the latter half of the seventies and early eighties, for which the Iran-Contra project was the prototypical case.

COVERT WARFARE AFTER VIETNAM

For many commentators, the late seventies were defined by the popular trope of the "Vietnam syndrome," which had made the United States "gun-shy" and caused "a loss of confidence . . . "[28] Racializing the Vietnamese and the country of Vietnam one last time as a subversive illness that had struck once-virile America, proponents explained how the Vietnam syndrome had changed a proud imperial country willing to fight on a global stage into a cowardly liberal milquetoast, filled with apologies and self-doubt. The Vietnam syndrome traveled with its wimpy bedfellows, the antiwar and other left movements, the congressional investigations of the CIA's plots and assassination programs, the abolition of the draft, and new legislative restrictions on presidential war making.[29] It was supposedly summarized by the Carter administration's foreign policy—the hostages taken in the Middle East, the plan for returning the Panama Canal Zone to Panama, the Iranian revolution, and the shameful occupation and 444-day hostage taking at the U.S. embassy in Tehran, which America watched with its hands seemingly tied, its hapless rescue attempt ending in flames in the Iranian desert. The Vietnam syndrome, in this story, pervaded America at home and abroad. It symbolized a broad array of belt-tightening and reduced hopes, what former secretary of defense James Schlesinger called in *Fortune* in 1976 an "*infirmity* of American policy" and *Business Week* titled in a keystone March 1979 article "The Decline of U.S. Power," illustrated with a sobbing Statue of Liberty.[30] For activists on the right, the images of helicopters leaving the U.S. embassy in Saigon—after a war they felt they had been forced to lose—worked as an icon of U.S. might and right forced to retreat, hide, and give up.

This story exaggerates the degree to which congressional investigations were not about bold interventionist foreign policy, but often the fact that American agents abroad, as in the case of one CIA station, were spending $41,000 a year on liquor and using other tax money to make pornographic films, buy sex workers, and fulfill emergency requests for bottles of Gatorade.[31] The Vietnam syndrome as a right-wing critique of the liberal order also stole what had first appeared in the press as an early diagnosis of post-traumatic stress disorder with the potential of addressing a health crisis among Vietnam veterans and changed it into a drum to beat for more war.[32] But even accounts that focus on covert action in the period are off. Conventional tales of U.S. unwillingness to engage in covert action run the fatal clock back to the fall of Saigon in April 1975, or earlier to the U.S. peace agreement with Vietnam in 1973. They do not mark a resurgence of confidence, offense, and aggression until, perhaps, the U.S. invasion of Grenada under Reagan in 1983.[33] This chronology sketches the picture of what one Reaganite called a dark "decade of American setbacks,"[34] an at-least-eight-year stretch when the lights went out on heroic, subversive covert action that had defined the covert capital since the sixties.

Reality was different. With the Vietnam evacuations underway in April 1975, Gerald Ford was already ramping up U.S. covert action again to shape Angola's independence from Portugal. By August 1975, the CIA Angola program budget topped $24.7 million, including eighty-three U.S. military advisors for the region and mercenaries to fill out their ranks. Ford committed men and materiel to Angola as late as Thanksgiving 1975, and the CIA was spending its Angola budget through the end of December.[35] In 1976, Ford expanded the CIA's mandate, authorizing it to intervene "even in countries which are friendly to the United States, and in those which are not threatened by internal subversion," and by 1977, Jimmy Carter was ordering the formation of a new Rapid Deployment Force, designed for what Michael Klare called "insertion into remote Third World battlefields."[36] In 1978, the Carter administration was again supporting covert action, this time in Somalia, aiding the dictator Siad Barre "to bail him out of a war he himself had started," rekindling a CIA relationship with Somalian leaders that stretched back to 1967.[37] That same year, a top CIA official directed every station chief in the world to keep its activities secret from the local U.S. ambassador.[38] In March 1979, the White House alerted U.S. forces to a possible armed intervention into Yemen, and in April, the National Security Council agreed on a covert assistance program to North Yemen, "attempting to 'create dissension' in the Marxist south."[39] July 1979 sparked the beginning of CIA financial and material support for the Afghan anticommunists, which accelerated through the year. It also marked the dawn of a U.S. covert action program to destabilize the new left-wing government in Grenada, after the country's "rule by terror" prime minister, Sir Eric Gairy, was driven from the island into exile, soon arriving in the Northern Virginia suburbs, where he benefited from the support of "friends."[40]

By November 1979, planning had begun for a hostage rescue mission in Iran. The ensuing hostage rescue missions in Iran of six Americans who found refuge at the Canadian embassy in Tehran in January 1980, the April 1980 mission to rescue the U.S. embassy hostages that failed, and a later effort that never took place mobilized a variety of covert action groups in the Dulles Corridor.[41] By February 1980, Carter's national security advisor, Zbigniew Brzezinski, who had moved down the street from the Eleanor Dulles house onto a five-acre estate in McLean a few years before, could be found in Pakistan, waving a kalashnikov toward the Afghan border, as he discussed new covert programs with Pakistani general Zia.[42]

Historians have chronicled the covert history of this period supposedly characterized by the "Vietnam syndrome," but they have been less willing to question the diagnosis outright. If the entire idea of a sickness emanating from Vietnam and corrupting the righteous and robust American body politic—at the very same time that U.S. imperial intimates and other refugees from Vietnam were settling in the U.S. and claiming rights in the U.S. body politic—wasn't itself so fraught and racist, one might be tempted to say that the so-called Vietnam syndrome wasn't much more than a passing cold. One scholar, while hewing to the idea that the United States was "gun-shy over Vietnam," points out that "it took less than four years to change that."[43] More precisely, it seems to have taken no more than two and a half, if that.

Rather than seeing a two-and-a-half-year lull in covert action as a major reorientation of U.S. policy, what is remarkable is that a mere two and a half years without covert action generated such frenzy, panic, and historiographic focus. It provides a rare window into the centrality of covert violence and Third World intervention to U.S. imperial governance abroad after World War II, and the degree to which newly mobilized rightist forces in the covert capital saw these actions as central to their project. Most importantly, it showed how the so-called Vietnam syndrome, and picture of a federal government unwilling to fight dirty and often around the world—even if this picture was quite inaccurate—*itself* became a necessary, and perhaps intentionally produced, rallying point to channel enthusiasm, funds, and force into U.S. covert action, counterinsurgency, and counterrevolutionary work in Edge City.

Such moments of modest critique and liberal pushback are crucial to CIA history. In 1961, the double-fisted failure myth of the Bay of Pigs—the idea that it died at the hands of a duplicitous liberal president who didn't provide adequate air support and a liberal Congress that turned on the agency in its wake—mobilized anticommunists in the CIA and the Pentagon for a new round of attacks on Cuba and Vietnam, intervention in the Dominican Republic, and subversive action in the Congo, Guyana, Brazil and across Latin America. Fifteen years later, the same crew took the modest democratic oversight of the early 1970s as a slap in the face that remobilized the next generation of counterinsurgents for the violence and deceptions of the 1980s. It's counterintuitive but true: modest moments of democratic intervention and scrutiny reanimated secrecy and violence. In this sense, such moments became, despite the ire they generated, seemingly desirable for covert action enthusiasts to make their case, even if the moments were composed of myth and covert action continued all along, often with the avid support of supposed enemies like Kennedy and Carter. It is also important to stress that brief lulls in covert action were less a failure of American will, as some narratives would have it, and more a conscious decision and intentional restraint put into effect by democratically elected U.S. representatives in Congress—whom some covert capital agents saw as their sworn enemies.

The hotels and flexible, cube-like office buildings of Edge City housed the entities that formed a semi-privatized response, through the built environment, to the congressional oversight, tell-all scandals, and irate investigations of the seventies that limited covert action through conventional government channels. In the story of Edge City, Northern Virginia and the renovation of covert capital action in the late 1970s and early 1980s, two dates proved central. The first was October 31, 1977, what some in the CIA called the "Halloween Day massacre," when CIA Director Stansfield Turner put 825 covert operators "out on the street." As Tim Weiner explains, the historical memory of the day that agency memoirs cast as the darkest in their history was itself a myth—Turner's cuts followed others, including 1,000 who had been fired three years earlier. Turner himself adds that while the positions were eliminated, some officers were transferred to other agency positions. To Turner's mind, the attachment of his name to the gutting of the clandestine service was a deliberate propaganda effort by people trained in that work.[44]

It certainly lived on, becoming popularized in the insurgent mystique of the late 1970s and 1980s. As former Vietnam station chief Theodore Shackley put it in his prologue to a 1981 book, upping the casualties with a sleight of hand: "I am not alone. Since 1976—and the election of President Jimmy Carter—approximately 2,800 American career intelligence officers like myself have retired, many of them prematurely. They were a national treasure . . . They deserve more than a warm handshake when they walk through the doors of the Central Intelligence Agency's headquarters at Langley, Virginia, into retirement and the outside world."[45]

But many walked straight into Edge City. The firings created a covert action surplus in the Dulles Corridor private sphere.[46] The fired, retired, and often eagerly privatizing covert specialist went back into work for the Pentagon, CIA, and the contractors reshaping the private-public covert landscape. Shackley is a perfect example. A longtime CIA veteran who had campaigned to overthrow Castro in Cuba, headed the CIA in Laos in 1965 when he expanded the paramilitary war, and led the Latin American division leading up to the coup against Chilean president Salvador Allende, Shackley eventually rose to the second position at the clandestine service, before his forced retirement. But soon, out of his new positions at the local "risk analysis" and "logistics problem-solving" companies he started such as Research Associates International, Shackley was selling everything from information to "helicopters in Latin America" from a "top-floor suite of an office building in Rosslyn," one of the SCIF-laden "highly secured" office buildings of the new Edge Cities. His work included meetings in 1984 with Iranian exiles at which they discussed ways of freeing and bargaining for the release of American hostages in the Middle East. Such meetings became crucial to Iran-Contra, where the hope of freeing hostages always arose as part of the defense of the weapons sales to Iran. Shackley even consulted for an affiliate of the Tysons-based Stanford Technology, which later became a key Iran-Contra player.[47] The so-called Halloween Day Massacre can be seen as one of the covert capital private sphere's meaningful birthdates.

The second would be April 25, 1980, the date of the failure of the Iran hostage rescue mission that left eight Americans dead and no hostages rescued. "Almost immediately," in one writer's words, the Pentagon organized a team to mount its follow-up. The first mission and the planning for this second mission, which incorporated key future Iran-Contra participants, expanded a variety of new quasi-independent covert action, paramilitary, and intelligence support groups, often under the Pentagon's wing but sometimes with a jurisdiction between the Pentagon and the CIA, that would lay the definitive infrastructure and model for Iran-Contra, the covert actions of the eighties, and beyond. The second hostage rescue attempt never took place, but the infrastructure it nurtured, with its intentionally obscurantist names like FOG, Brand X, and the Intelligence Support Activity, was soon put to work.[48]

In March 1981, the Intelligence Support Activity moved into "a set of unassuming, rundown offices opposite the Arlington Hall," not far from the Pentagon and Fort Myer. Rival units began calling it "the Secret Army of Northern Virginia."[49] Such entities would play an important role in Iran-Contra as a model for how cutout intelligence and stand-alone covert action outfits might be designed, and as direct participants, who emerged from the Iran rescue missions (and from counterinsurgency in Vietnam and Laos before them) and then stepped forward into Central America. These twilight guerrilla agencies also crept into the visibly public office and consumer land-scape that later observers would correlate with Edge City. The Intelligence Support Activity met potential agents at the Red Carpet Room at National Airport, at the Rosslyn Safeway, and in Crystal City bars.[50] Edge City was their landscape of public sociability.

The final piece in these founding frameworks was CIA Director William Casey, the manager of Reagan's election campaigns, an old OSS hand and "Wall Street operator whose fortune came from selling tax-shelter strate-gies."[51] To the venture capitalist Casey, the logic of helping rich people hide money and helping the covert capital keep actions secret fused in Edge City's corporate architecture. As soon as he took office, he stressed the vital ties between the corporate and covert action worlds, comparing the CIA and its affiliates to a Fortune 500 company and inviting executives to Langley so his "extensive business contacts" working abroad could share intelligence with the CIA when they got home.[52] But Casey also put into practice insights into how corporate secrecy, cover, and connections provided new forms of orga-nizing action. Celebrating its new mandate, Casey's CIA even raised its own monument to the form of the Edge City corporations, spending more than $179 million to put up a second headquarters on its lot at Langley—its own twin green glass cubes built into the hillside behind the old headquarters by the architects Smith, Hinchman and Grylls, fresh off their job constructing a home for the Defense Intelligence Agency at Bolling Air Force Base. Defined by a large atrium and linked to the original headquarters by a "gently curv-ing tunnel called . . . a 'wave guide,'" the new headquarters building in a sense was also a SCIF, designed in the words of one CIA officer "to prevent elec-tromagnetic attack." Appropriately, agents dubbed it "Emerald City," in the same argot Garreau used to describe wider Edge City form.[53]

Together these factors combined to produce a new means of covert action, both symbolized by Edge City and staged from it. Corporatization and quasi-privatization provided a new grammar for the compartmentation the CIA had always endorsed. The businesslike corporate veneer on covert action's renaissance came hand in hand with a new longing for the masculine thrill of its opposite—reckless covert action, wildness, purified masculinity, and field daring in a new global war. The desk-bound middleman in the tailored black suit and the new wave counterinsurgent in his campy combat fatigues fused in Iran-Contra in the bodies of the same men. Casey and his cognates in the Pentagon, the White House, and the National Security Council rolled out this new model of Edge City covert action and masculinity and directed it against Central America. Balance sheets helped determine the choice. By 1986, the war in Afghanistan, which George Crile calls "the biggest CIA paramilitary campaign in history," was consuming 57 percent of the CIA Directorate of Operations' budget. This created a restraint within the agency but also an opportunity.[54]

If the quasi-public war would go to Afghanistan, the quasi-private one would go to Central America, measuring Casey's idea that corporate adjuncts to CIA action could magnify the clout and scope of U.S. intervention. But it would be too much to say the idea derived solely from Casey. Iran-Contra also facilitated ideas for restructuring covert action that had circulated since Edward Lansdale's days at the Pentagon. These ideas surfaced in one striking example in materials Rufus Phillips and Edward Lansdale drafted for Phillips's run for the U.S. Senate in 1977. In a document ironically titled "Concern for Human Rights in Our Foreign Policy – More Than a Gesture," they stated it clearly: "The responsibility for covert political operations should be taken out of the CIA and its overseas stations and lodged under the direct control of the President. Covert operations should probably be the responsibility of a small staff under the national security council with the ability to draw on temporary government and nongovernment talent as needed."[55] By the 1980s, Oliver North described the results: an entire "off-the-shelf, self-sustaining, stand-alone" funding mechanism for covert action.[56]

The cultural urge that linked them all registered a moment of 1980s innovation but also the nostalgia that came with it. The agents who devised U.S. covert action in the 1950s, such as Northern Virginia's Kim Roosevelt, had loved the early CIA's "project-oriented" flexibility, the freedom granted to individual agents, where one "could write a project in brief and vague language" and "funding was easily obtainable."[57] The agents who enlivened covert action in Edge City wanted that feeling, to retrieve the experiences of their mentors, elders, and teachers. It was because these father-son struggles, family dramas, and projects of self-making took place in the imperial corridor as a new financial and political mandate was emerging that they became, for the people of Central America, world altering and deadly.

EDGE CITY'S WAR ON CENTRAL AMERICA

The geopolitical relationship between Central America and Northern Virginia reached back to the 1950s, when Middleburg arms dealer Sam Cummings supplied weapons for the CIA's overthrow of Guatemalan president Jacobo Arbenz from an Alexandria warehouse.[58] By the 1980s the U.S. covert war was directed at Nicaragua and in support of the contras, but it was also a broader project supporting right-wing leaders and armies across Central America, something lost in accounts that see Nicaragua as the single target. For many in Northern Virginia, the El Salvador war was paramount.[59] In December 1980, a Loudoun County CIA veteran, Cleto DiGiovanni, traveled there portraying himself as a speaker for the Reagan transition team to assure "the Salvadoran right that the team's public statements of opposition to a coup should be ignored." Salvadoran death squad leader Roberto D'Aubuisson, who himself spent time in DC and Virginia as a trainee at U.S. AID's International Police Academy, claimed in March 1981 that another Reagan advisor, retired lieutenant general, CIA veteran, and Arlington resident Daniel O. Graham, told him some Americans would favor a military seizure of the government.[60]

At this time, the CIA also helped organize the contras from ex-members of West Point–educated dictator Anastasio Somoza's National Guard. Since the 1980s, observers have invoked the presence of Guardists as a sign of the contras' brutal otherness from American norms. But it is crucial to note that the United States helped form the Guard in the first place during the second phase of its occupation of Nicaragua in 1927, when the United States also brought Nicaraguan health ministers to Arlington to study Northern Virginia's "Negro Public Health" programs. To the contra cause, the CIA recruited exiles with American educations and ties to U.S. corporations, solidifying the Edge City connections.[61] As this contra war expanded, the war against guerrillas and peasants in El Salvador surged in its own right. One of the Reagan CIA's first acts, in March 1981, was to escalate counterinsurgency in El Salvador with U.S. advisors and $25 million in arms and ammunition.[62]

Northern Virginia's earliest CIA residents had first gone to El Salvador in the 1960s when the country was a Kennedy-era model of development in action for the Alliance for Progress. As CIA station chief there in the 1960s, a recent Bailey's Crossroads resident, Joe Kiyonaga, befriended General José Medrano, head of El Salvador's National Guard and intelligence service. Bonding over their "humble origins, a certain macho appeal, direct approach and common goals," in the words of Kiyonaga's wife, Kiyonaga and his station began to "provide advice, supply equipment and help perfect the Salvador Intelligence Service." Working with Northern Virginians like Kiyonaga, Medrano visited U.S. pacification efforts in Vietnam, then became what one historian calls "the father of Salvadoran counterinsurgency," training the men who ran the 1980s Salvador war.[63] These ties echoed through years of similar contacts—of U.S. officers running El Salvador's military school, of police training programs run by AID's Office of Public Safety, and of teams of anti-riot and counterinsurgency advisors Jimmy Carter assigned before leaving office, soon followed by roving advisors from the army, navy, and air force. By 1982, according to the U.S. military group commander in El Salvador, the Pentagon considered the Salvadoran army "a mirror image of the United States Army." Soon, it had its own pacification program named Operation Phoenix.[64]

U.S.-trained and -funded Salvadoran army officers began to empty the Salvadoran province of Morazán of people as early as 1980, carrying their "draining the sea" metaphors and near-genocidal definitions of the enemy directly from Vietnam, identifying, as Susan Bibler Coutin explains, "anyone who directly or indirectly supported or could be presumed to support the guerillas as an 'enemy' to be destroyed or neutralized." The United States sent some $6 billion in military and other aid to El Salvador in the 1980s, making the tiny country, with its population only five-and-a-half times the size of Fairfax County's, the globe's third largest recipient of U.S. military aid.[65]

Base camps, raids, and contra activities supposedly directed against Nicaragua had devastating effects on El Salvador, Honduras, and Costa Rica. Money, men, and materiel flooded the region, twining its economy and landscape with Edge City's own. Huge sums the United States sent to make war in El Salvador destroyed, in Rodolfo Acuña's words, "any semblance of a free market." Counterinsurgency became economic development. As U.S.-based lenders squeezed non-military spending, and guerrillas attacked the agricultural and infrastructural resources controlled by capitalist elites allied with the United States, the army took charge of pension funds, a major source of investment capital, and monopolized the commercial and financial infrastructure of the country, building its political machine and becoming beholden to the U.S. dollars that funded that machine. In some cases, those soldiers and elites, decapitalizing the country, simply shipped arriving U.S. aid dollars back out into their own U.S. bank accounts. The combined hemispheric effect of U.S. "state spending in defense," "Federal Reserve policy shifts" and currency changes affecting national investments also bound together El Salvador and the DC suburbs of Northern Virginia in what David Pedersen calls "an uneven process of restructuring."[66] The "Contra" in Iran-Contra needs to be seen as standing in for these disturbances, "against" not only the left but human life and social reproduction more generally.

To CIA Director Bill Casey, the Central America war was always also a war on its economies. To Oliver North's intermediary with the contras, PR specialist Robert Owen, the many businessmen who led the contras also began to see the war as business.[67] These relationships between U.S. "development" as both economic restructuring and police training and violence— as both the formation of an intrusive elite-run state and market, and a newly empowered army—had descended from the twin pillars of U.S. policy in the sixties. American economists had drafted plans for Central America's Common Market, translating its founding documents from English to Spanish. The Salvadoran army's political party took the Alliance for Progress handshake symbol as its own.[68]

In the 1980s, the corporatized built environment of Edge City shaped this corporatized war. Northern Virginia hotels staged the secret meetings and male social environments that organized it. Edge City office park culture provided the managerial space, structure, and cover that made it possible. The corporate apartments, speculative townhouses and generic, assembly-line mansions—or McMansions—of booming 1980s Northern Virginia housed its soldiers when they left and returned home.

THE MEETINGS BEGIN: EDGE CITY, 1981

If the pinnacle script of agent infiltration into Vietnam was the domesticated interracial love relationship, the height of claiming authority in Central America was the robustly masculine interracial friendship. If the Vietnam project's central gathering in the 1960s was the hootenanny, the secret war on Nicaragua and El Salvador's in the 1980s was the business meeting. Such "business" meetings provided the Central America campaign's functional identity in the U.S. imperial home front, granting Edge City's cold sense of logistical order and bureaucratic process to chaotic and traumatic human events on the ground. Throughout 1981, in flights that took them across Northern Virginia and Latin America, men such as Argentine general Leopoldo Galtieri, the overseer of the country's Dirty War against its own citizens, Gustavo Álvarez Martínez, the head of Honduras' Public Security and Police Force, and CIA Latin America division chief Duane "Dewey" Clarridge, one of the earliest officers to settle Northern Virginia, over whiskey and handshakes, finalized their initiative to support the contras—La Tripartita.[69] As these directors of covert action formed their multinational defense "companies"—in this case counterrevolutionary battalions—the traveling salesmen who carried out the everyday business of covert action soon followed.

Their meeting halls were Northern Virginia's Edge City hotels, many of them the first Marriotts in the country. Built in the fifties and sixties, the hotels had helped define the covert capital's public-private landscape from the start, providing some of the only destination meeting places, decent restaurants, temporary lodging, and consumer spaces in the newly developing suburbs. They arose at the same time that J. Willard Marriott himself became a political power broker in the overt capital—he was key funder and advisor in the campaigns of every Republican president from Eisenhower to Reagan. In 1957, Marriott opened his first motel and the largest in the world, the Twin Bridges Motor, in Crystal City, explicitly because of the site's proximity to Pentagon workers and the fact that they were "bringing people from all over the world there," people who flew into National Airport five minutes away. The Key Bridge Marriott opened two years later at Rosslyn and was immediately busy with spies, and soon sheltered other important federal events as well, such as when astronaut John Glenn's family watched him orbit the Earth there in what became known as the "Glenn Suite." A decade later, the new twelve-story Crystal City Marriott debuted less than four miles to the south as another key Edge City structure, rising atop underground tunnels holding stores. Structured by the cellular, stacked cubicle exterior that defined the Edge City, the hotels sheltered many early-retiree military men, intelligence agents, and other overnighters who flocked to form and join the first Edge City contractors.[70] These hotels then served as centers of plotting for the counterinsurgents cycling in and out of National and Dulles airports in the 1980s.

Nearly every major contra political leader spent time meeting in the Edge

Built in 1959, the Key Bridge Marriott was popular with those plotting the covert war in Central America. Contra leaders passed through its glass doors within days of each other in the early eighties. Photo by author.

City hotels. The Key Bridge Marriott garnered such popularity that contras passed through its glass doors within days of each other. José Francisco Cardenal, the Managua construction contractor and early contra leader, arrived in 1982. He met for hours in the restaurant with an undercover CIA man in a three-piece suit who looked "like an executive . . . like he is managing a business."[71] Edgar Chamorro, early conservative middle-class member of the contras, the head of PR, briber of journalists, and translator of a U.S.-provided targeted-violence manual into Spanish, met Joseph Fernandez, the future CIA station chief in Costa Rica, at the Key Bridge Marriott bar in July 1983.[72] The next summer, in July 1984, Edén Pastora, the charismatic former Sandinista military commander recruited to the CIA project, met agents at the Key Bridge Marriott on nearly the same day another contra leader, Coke bottling plant manager Adolfo Calero, visited the same hotel.[73] Oliver North's partner in Iran-Contra, ex–air force major general Richard Secord, recalled in his memoir driving Calero to a mysterious appointment there: "I laughed when he told me. I knew instantly he must be meeting with the CIA, which he was. The agency frequently met out-of-towners at the Key Bridge Marriott."

Waiting until Calero's meeting was over, Secord then relaxed with Calero over white wine at the Crystal City Marriott, where they discussed contra weapons needs before Secord drove Calero on to National.[74] One of the more fateful episodes in El Salvador's history also took place at the Crystal City Marriott, when in January 1985, Cuban Bay of Pigs veteran and CIA contract agent Felix Rodriguez enjoyed a light lunch with Salvadoran army chief of staff Adolfo Blandón. "I told him about the terrific possibilities I saw if he would permit me to advise a rapid-response force in his country," Rodriguez recalled. "He said, 'Just let me know when you're coming to El Salvador and we'll try it.'" The meeting announced the formal arrival of Vietnam-style counterinsurgency—a series of "tactical task forces" designed to "neutralize and destroy guerrillas"—as a generalized covert capital project in Central America.[75] Given Rodriguez's own arm's-length relationship to the CIA, it also marked the use of private contractors as a strategy to increase deniability after Congress banned support for the contras and signaled the utility of Edge City hotels as meeting places for such agents.

Bundled together, the details of contra hotel stays and restaurant meetings in Northern Virginia read like a kind of counterinsurgency *Zagat's Guide*. Contra brothers Edmundo and Fernando Chamorro had their meeting with the CIA in the lounge of a Northern Virginia "second-class hotel."[76] Another commander, Hugo Villagra, met his CIA agent at a restaurant near National.[77] CIA undercovers took contra leader Arturo Cruz Jr. to a suite at the Rosslyn Hyatt for a lie detector test, as they rushed, to Cruz's annoyance, home to spend a suburban Saturday afternoon with their families.[78] Even Panamanian dictator Manuel Noriega enjoyed an Italian restaurant in a Northern Virginia tower, after which he went with his CIA contacts, activists in the Central America war, to buy VCRs and stereos in Edge City's consumer landscape.[79] As late as July 1989, contra military leaders Israel Galeano, Enrique Bermúdez, and Aristides Sánchez planned political offensives in the West Park Hotel in Rosslyn.[80]

Hotels provided the anonymity in public that covert operatives—particularly those working at arm's length from the CIA and Pentagon—found useful as stages for plotting. Bearing neither the official imprimatur of the secret headquarters nor the fixed individualized address of the subdivision safe house, the hotel acted as a space where everyone was transitory, one that, by its very nature, erased the presence of those who passed through it, completing a functional work that other kinds of spaces could not.

Iran-Contra participants also soon formed their own Edge City firms as cover, "a network of shell corporations," located in Northern Virginia's new Edge City office space.[81] One of the most important paramilitary groups to emerge from the Iran hostage rescue missions, later directed toward the Central America war, was the Special Operations Division of the U.S. Army Operations Directorate, headed by Oakton resident James Longhofer, a lieutenant colonel and former pilot in Vietnam. Looking for cover for his aerial operations in Honduras in support of the covert war in Nicaragua and El Salvador, Longhofer's men used the offices of a Reston defense contractor, XMCO Inc., managed by an ex-military colonel and named for that reason. Down to the present, developers cite XMCO's Reston headquarters, a SCIF-laden, 80,000-square-foot glass-and-concrete cube, as an architectural achievement, a key building in the Edge City landscape.[82] A retired air force veteran of the Iran hostage rescue missions and later contra war participant supplied Longhofer planes from the offices of another contractor, American National Management Corporation, in Vienna.[83]

Soon Longhofer's men started their very own contracting firm—Business Security International. The firm set up offices in Annandale as cover for his Pentagon work. Longhofer's team used planes and antennas to minutely track those they identified as leftists. They forwarded the information to the National Security Agency, which relayed it on open-link channels to U.S. agents and Salvadoran counterinsurgents, who used it to attack people in El Salvador, or to CIA field agents, who gave it to contras based in Honduras to target their own attacks across the border into northern Nicaragua. "Business Security International" assumed the acronymic blandness of the first Edge City firms. But the name also summarized, through its three key words—business, security, and international—the centrality of the orderly business trope of the private and silent secured meeting to the covert capital project. Claiming to "specialize in assisting domestic firms seeking security for overseas operations," Business Security International dissolved its ethics in its incorporation, insinuating security as its own value, over and above the content of what was being kept secure. The company paid 1980s business rents of $40,000 a year and used its secret $2.7 million budget to violate Nicaraguan and Salvadoran air space with planes and helicopters, to help mine Nicaragua's harbor, and like any contractor, to stage junkets for its staff and friends who wanted to "'live their cover' as prosperous business-men." One Business Security International "executive," a lieutenant colonel, billed the government for a vacation and other expenses that cost $89,000.[84]

Superficially contracted-out operations like Longhofer's, with a jurisdiction between the Pentagon and the CIA, both modeled and worked alongside the networks that defined Iran-Contra. Richard Secord was a former deputy assistant secretary of defense who specialized in the Middle East, Africa, and southern Asia. Secord had flown two hundred combat missions in South Vietnam in 1962 and 1963, before the formal start of the war. Then he went on into counterinsurgency in Laos. In the 1970s, back at the Pentagon, Secord helped choose Nixon's bombing targets in Vietnam. He considered his work to be "bare-knuckle warfare," which "he believed to the depths of his warrior's soul . . . should have been the beginning of a new phase of the Vietnam War." Secord later commanded the U.S. Air Force mission in Iran, before returning to the Pentagon where he directed air force "worldwide security assistance programs" and "foreign military sales." After retiring in May 1983, Secord began arranging secret weapons shipments to the Afghan mujahedin, according to Tim Weiner, and joined a group of retirees providing the Pentagon "disinterested expert advice on covert operations."[85]

By the time Secord reemerged as Oliver North's partner in the Iran-Contra Affair and the corporate Edge City face of the Central America campaign, it was all too easy to see him as a mere businessman and arms dealer, working in the lucrative world of Defense Department contracting. But Secord was a product of government. CIA director Casey was a Wall Street capitalist who ran covert action inside the government in the 1980s. Secord was a government counterinsurgent who ran arms deals in the Edge City private sphere. They were two sides of the same coin, typifying the blurred roles of Edge City in Northern Virginia in the 1980s.

Colleagues from Secord's days fighting the paramilitary war in Laos "had never seen anybody cut through bureaucracy better."[86] Liberated from his Pentagon office, Secord used the same skills to arrange Iran-Contra in the new towers of Edge City. From an eerie glass cube off Route 7 on Westwood Center Drive at Tysons and another office building on Route 123 just into Vienna, Secord facilitated the sale of weapons to Iran, fielded calls from El Salvador safe houses, and aided the secret war through corporate Edge City identities such as Stanford Technology Trading Group International Inc. and Energy Resources International, eventually helping transfer more than 800 tons of ordnance and "lethal supplies" to Central America. Later he moved into the seven-story Lancaster building constructed in 1979 in the geopolitical Westpark development.[87] While most of Iran-Contra's Central American contacts were met at hotels closer to the DC line and National Airport, Secord's Iranian contacts met with Secord and Oliver North at Tysons. There, the Iranians supposedly enjoyed the entertainment Edge City had to offer, including a high-end escort service in three rooms at the brand-new luxury Sheraton, a twenty-four-story $60 million venture on Route 7 near Secord's office and the Dulles Toll Road. The hotel opened the same year as the Iranians' visit, 1986, becoming another structure that shaped Edge City's skyline.[88]

The quasi-privatized nature of North and Secord's covert war, in some sense, modeled itself on an Edge City contractor. Its managers used Swiss and offshore bank accounts, avoided paying taxes, incorporated in Panama, had a private air force, and worked through private capital-raising efforts—using financial instruments such as "bridge financing" and "private benefactors." To manage their war on the ground, they turned to the "command and control" efficiency systems developed by the first McNamara-descendant contractors. When their activities faced exposure, they tried "liquidating" their "assets," first by attempting to sell them for $4 million to the CIA, then by simply leaving the equipment for allies in Honduras and El Salvador to fold into their own networks of repression.[89] When Oliver North's and Secord's supply networks began to crumble in the face of Sandinista exposure, North fled to the Tysons Corner Sheraton with classified documents aiming to protect and hide the evidence of their projects. He reunited with Secord and accepted a reverent call from Ronald Reagan informing him: "You are an American hero."[90]

One even saw the contractor patterns in the name of their campaign—referred to by the colleagues not as a "Military Mission," like that which first disrupted Vietnam, but as simply "The Enterprise," or, in the words of a federal investigator, "the profitable venture that came to be known as 'the Enterprise.'"[91] The Enterprise, in fact, represented the point at which the built environment of the covert capital, condensed in space after three decades of imperial effort, itself ordered the content of covert capital strategy. Cubicled, switchable opaque glass buildings of unclear or diluted ownership provided an instrumental metaphor and a practical incubator for staging deniable covert action over and against democratic processes in the overt capital. The Edge City defense contractors who occupied positions on the board of the Fairfax County Economic Development Authority had advertised the space of Northern Virginia as such, stressing its simultaneous proximity to and distance from DC. As one newspaper ad explained, "There are enormous benefits to having the federal government for a neighbor. Notice we said neighbor. Because when you look at Washington, the view is better from Fairfax County, Virginia."[92]

The privatized, compartmented sprawl of Northern Virginia offered covert actors a means of operating independently as needed from the even marginally identifiable and responsible bodies condensed at Langley and the Pentagon—not to mention the distant white colonnades and domes of Washington, DC, dimly visible from the rooftops of Tysons' hotels. Flexible and shifting, Edge City could instantly restructure private and legally separate offices, staff, funds, and subcontractors depending on the project and degree of desired exposure. But these shifts could occur within a proximity and social environment that controlled security and confidentiality *and* naturalized them as lofty goals across a wide terrain. In this sense, Edge City was a next-generation design improvement on Langley. It implemented an architecture of secrecy in plain sight across a much broader, harder-to-map landscape.

The ethics of deniability represented in the opaque band of Edge City windows gave the Enterprise its profile of deceit. Deceit, in this case, was the point. The image of compartmentation was often only that—a screen over what was essentially a single project, public and private, at the level of habitus and even semi-overt strategy. As the independent counsel who studied their activities put it, "administration officials repeatedly claimed that there was a 'compartmentation' of knowledge regarding North's activities, and that only a limited number of people were made privy to the information. In many cases, Independent Counsel found that this claim was feigned, and many officials knew much more than they initially admitted."[93] This was the SCIF in practice, a structure that both controlled information and widely disseminated it through the cipher of the contractors.

But historians and journalists commonly narrate the history of U.S. policy in this period through its compartments, as a "who was in the room" history, focusing on segregated meetings as moments of decision. They describe one or the other of the units: the contra visits to Edge City hotels exist in one column, the North-Secord network at Tysons in another, Bill Casey and the CIA in McLean occupies a third, the Longhofer spy unit, a fourth. These are false distinctions. These men knew each other and essentially worked together on their Central America war. Seeing Edge City as the unified container for their meetings restores the spatial and social coherence that its actors experienced as coherent. Sprawl didn't only indicate subdivision. Edge City sprawl offered a greater merging—through subdividing—of covert imperial functions in local space over time.

TEARDOWNS, STARTER CASTLES, AND SUBURBAN SOCIAL LIFE

This sprawl brought not just offices and hotels but new exurban farmsteads, McMansions, and speculative townhouse developments near malls. An entire built environment soon evolved across Northern Virginia celebrating the values of the 1980s: the overnight switchability of corporate apartment and safe house culture, the era's disposable income and fondness for display, and its curious longing for permanence—the allure of starting over in high-ticket family farm homesteads that looked "American" and "historical." Reagan-era lobbyists and foot soldiers tore down the glass houses of the first CIA agents to build their monstrous speculative fortresses.

In one of the more famous displays, Edward M. Rogers, a Reagan and Bush White House aide who resigned to do legal and lobbying work for the onetime head of Saudi intelligence, eventually tore down Alice Sheldon's house some years after she shot herself and her husband there and built a $2.5 million, 18,000-square-foot "neo-classical" mansion with an elevator, four fireplaces, and nine bathrooms.[94] But even before that, Prince Bandar bin Sultan, the Saudi royal ambassador and close family friend of Vice President George H.W. Bush, raised a mansion off Chain Bridge Road in McLean with a conservatory and a well-regarded "Morocco Room," a long, large space designed, according to Bandar, "majlis" style, with seating around three walls. The house became a major site of contra funding discussions.[95] CIA Director Bill Casey and his wife, Sophia, settled in a $450,000 McLean house with a pool, a respectable plot of land, and a separate floor for a security detail.[96] CIA agents and covert retirees, some who had specialized in running the agency's covert proprietary companies, defined the broader booming real estate market with their purchases and sales of rental property and large acreages for development.[97] At the far reaches of the corridor, other agents settled into estates and Georgian manor houses in the foxhunting country, renovating the fantasies that had motivated their predecessors thirty years before.[98] At the Loudoun County seat of Leesburg, Nestor Sanchez, the deputy assistant secretary of defense for Latin American affairs at the Pentagon who helped manage the contra war, moved to a farm and helped restore the manor house of General George C. Marshall, Truman's secretary of state.[99]

By the mid- to late eighties, the Central America fight was doubling back and fusing with this landscape. Arturo Cruz Jr. joined his new girlfriend, Oliver North secretary Fawn Hall, for Thanksgiving at her family house in Annandale or they met for lunch at the Dulles Airport eatery.[100] North spent contra traveler's checks on leotards for his daughters at Parklane Hosiery at the Tysons Corner mall.[101] He and Dewey Clarridge, who ran the early covert war at the CIA, planned Hawk missile deliveries at tacky McLean roast beef houses.[102] Richard Secord discussed the contras' private aid network at the Tysons Corner Clyde's, a local architectural marvel when it opened in 1980.[103]

Many officers participated in this residential life. Donald H. Winters, the CIA's Tegucigalpa station chief, settled into a townhouse near Lake Anne in Reston with his wife, Donna, and made Honduran general Gustavo Álvarez Martínez godfather of the Honduran child the couple had adopted.[104] Nestor Pino-Marina, a Cuban Bay of Pigs veteran who took U.S. citizenship and became the U.S. Army's "action officer" on the El Salvador war, settled into a suburban home essentially next door to the Tysons Corner mall, where he made many first introductions that shaped El Salvador's fate in the 1980s. He hosted friends such as far-right air force general Juan Rafael Bustillo, the U.S. air staff college graduate whom Pino called "family." At the same time, they set up and backed contra supply operations on the airstrips of the San Salvador suburb of Ilopango, and Bustillo supported a broad campaign of terror in El Salvador that extended even to non-guerilla social reformers, activists, and peasants.[105]

But agents from Northern Virginia did not only stage policy and warfare in Central America. Edge City in Northern Virginia's very sense of itself, its meaning as a landscape, also depended on a co-narrative, written by these same operatives, about and on the landscapes of Central American countries, defining what these places meant to Northern Virginia residents as they went abroad. For actors in the covert capital war in Central America, travels between Northern Virginia and Central America often entailed a symbolic, bartering exchange of particular narratives and landscapes of masculinity. Alongside the symbolism of the corporate contractor, and with just as much weight, these narratives of masculinity defined the Central America campaign and the means by which it built its networks.

The recurring performance of masculinity in space was critical to the meetings between covert capital agents and Latin American military operatives—a form of translation, a crucible for solidarity. At the most basic level, the military uniform and title created an emblem of masculine authority and commonality. When Dewey Clarridge traveled to Buenos Aires, military ruler Leopoldo Galtieri entertained him with boys' pleasures: "a mock takedown of a terrorist safe house" and drinks in an office designed like an elite men's club, featuring "dark furniture and heavy brocade drapes." When Colonel Mario Davico, vice chief of Argentine military intelligence, visited Clarridge in the home front, he brought him a cowhide-bound copy of *Martín Fierro*, "the classic Argentine novel about gaucho life."[106] For those fighting what Richard Secord defined as "high noon in the Cold War," cowboy metaphors were common, and *"El gringo tiene cojones"* was "about as high a tribute as can be paid in Spanish."[107] North and Secord met at hotels in Edge City, but they also hauled wood together in the Virginia forest.[108] Secord drove a Porsche, and North, for a time, a Shelby Cobra muscle car.[109] "I knew I was a real man," commented North, even in his more personal and reflective moments. He proved it by keeping on his desk a canteen cup shot off his hip in Vietnam next to souvenirs from the bodies of left-wing fighters. One was a belt buckle taken during the U.S. invasion of Grenada from a Cuban officer, one who, presumably, did not give up this token voluntarily.[110]

CIA man Dewey Clarridge and contra brigade leader Edén Pastora might have disagreed as covert warriors, but as men they had no doubts. Pastora was a "caudillo" who smoked cigars. Clarridge was a "real live spy" who also loved cigars, and for this reason, the contras called him *El Hombre Del Puro* when he visited their camps on the borders of Nicaragua wearing his monocle, cowboy hat, and pastel silk safari suits. Recycling imperial sobriquets from days past, colleagues called Clarridge a "roughrider," "cowboy," and "hipshooter." He drove a white jeep with plates that read CONTRA and, after the U.S. invasion of Grenada, a bumper sticker that said "Nicaragua is Next." He wore a brash T-shirt to Northern Virginia Christmas parties that read "Ollie North is an American Hero."[111] Central American Task Force leader Alan Fiers, Clarridge's replacement in the later days of the contra war, was a former Big Ten football player who thought of William Casey as a kind of reincarnation of his football coach at Ohio State, Woody Hayes. Colleagues in the agency saw Fiers as "a real macho guy."[112]

Although he worked as a civilian, North donned camouflage fatigues when he went south under his code name, "BG," or "Blood and Guts."[113] To the contras, Casey was *El Jefe* Casey or *Tio* Bill, who insisted on getting out into the *campo*.[114] To the covert actors, the former National Guardsmen of whom the contras often consisted were in some sense ideal men in an idealized landscape for masculine renewal. Shorn of the constraints and laws of the Northern Virginia suburbs, they could kill when necessary and still partake in traditional male pleasures, as pitchers with the Guard baseball team.[115] The male culture of exchange was so ingrained toward the middle of the decade that when men like Edén Pastora finally fell out with the covert capital, they interpreted perceived slights in gendered terms. To Pastora, one airdrop that contained quantities of Tampax was "a not so subtle hint that the CIA thought he and his men were homosexuals, a band of do-nothing sissies"—even though he had women in his unit.[116]

Covert capital operators bought secure new colonial houses to shelter their wives and children in the Northern Virginia suburbs in this period, following the traditional gender expectations and cul-de-sacs of suburban life. One buyer was James Adkins, the CIA chief of base for the contras in Honduras, who had spent a brief stint as a pitcher with a Milwaukee Braves farm team.[117] From his house in North Arlington, Alan Fiers reflected on his contra commandos while grilling on his suburban barbecue.[118] North chose for his wife and four children a shingled brick four-bedroom on Kentland Drive, where he also enjoyed barbecuing with his son. The house lay on a long, quiet country road lined with mailboxes in the Seneca Ridge neighborhood of Great Falls, way up Georgetown Pike from Langley. It was so seemingly rural that a visitor might forget that it was a platted suburban subdivision, imagined by developer Mark Merrell two decades before as he expanded his business beyond Saigon Road. North's home stood on two acres roamed idly by horses and dogs and rimmed by a rambling wooden fence.[119] Secord went in the other direction, choosing a new five-bedroom house on a small street in a subdivision in the woods behind the Langley headquarters.[120] Then he moved to Arbor Glen Way in Reston, amid a series of tightly packed, nautical townhouses all named for trees and with the airbrushed look of an L.L. Bean catalog.[121] Thanks to the circuitous roads of the western Dulles Corridor, North's house and Secord's place were only a handful of turns away from one another, little more than a ten-minute drive.

These purchases were not divorced from their performances of masculinity abroad—buying suburban houses and securing them with large security

Covert capital operatives bought secure new colonial houses to shelter their wives and children in the Northern Virginia suburbs in this period. Here, Oliver North barbecues with his son at the family's house in bucolic Great Falls, 1987. Greg Mathieson/MAI/Getty Images.

systems helped create the sense that they were fulfilling a "manly duty" by fighting the contra war, or as Melani McAlister puts it, defending an imperiled American domesticity.[122] Journalists reverently chronicled North's "traditional" household and "private world," where "Ollie was the breadwinner, and his wife, Betsy, was a homemaker and full-time mother to their four children."[123] But these suburban houses were only the backdrop for a series of other landscapes these men helped create on the borders of El Salvador, Nicaragua, Honduras, and Costa Rica: the reckless spaces of exception to their gleaming Edge Cities and manicured suburban homes. In Central America, in what a military advisor called "a step toward the primitive," they engaged in violent actions and interventions. They developed rules of rating and supporting life patently at odds with those they established with their domesticities and conservative manners concentrated on the resuscitated nuclear family in the home front.[124]

"The first few CIA officers to work with the contras enjoyed a wild-and-woolly life-style," wrote Glenn Garvin. "Virtually unsupervised, responsible to almost no one, they had a free hand; it was more like the free-swinging CIA of the 1950s than the lumbering bureaucracy of the 1980s."[125] The freedom and lack of supervision, the entire bid to determine national fate in

Central America, was their retort to those non-men in the overt capital "who believe that small is good, humiliation is salutary, progress is evil" and "who yearn to return to the womb," as former CIA officer and ambassador-at-large Vernon Walters, another Northern Virginia resident who helped establish the Argentine military's support for the contras, once described them.[126] For some agents, it was also the necessary, reinvigorating masculine counterpoint to a campaign staged in the home front through meetings in cushy, air-conditioned spaces that were suspiciously indistinguishable from those of everyday suburban bureaucracy.

Almost all the men who planned attacks from Northern Virginia's Edge Cities put their feet on the ground in Central America.[127] Oliver North went on "more trips to Central America than [he could] count." Flying into Tegucigalpa "between a mountain on one end and the edge of a cliff on the other," he initiated the trope of macho travel writing that came to express their spatial experience of the covert war. "My enduring memory of the contra base camps is the savory smell of wood smoke," he wrote nostalgically at one point.[128] Reinvigorating landscapes of nature, shirt-sleeve bonding, and masculine release appeared in their writing in indirect proportion to any military activities of the contras, who soon, in Greg Grandin's words, "had executed close to four thousand civilians, wounded an equal number, and kidnapped roughly another five thousand."[129]

Rough-and-tumble narratives also masked the fact that many of these covert actors' experiences in Central America were similar to the ones they had in Edge City, Northern Virginia, sometimes transpiring in other branches of the same American chain hotels. At the Tysons Corner Sheraton, covert capital agents met Iranian contacts and fled to cover their tracks. In El Salvador, some agents saw the San Salvador Sheraton as "home and hangout to the U.S. 'advisers' in the country."[130] To left-wing fighters of the Farabundo Martí National Liberation Front (FMLN), CIA and Pentagon warriors cavorting in El Salvador's corporate and entertainment district, the Zona Rosa, presented a garish display in light of the extreme violence often endorsed by the same figures. FMLN leader Nidia Díaz recalled in her memoir telling a group of Americans, "The FMLN is tired of fighting soldiers who have been recruited by force while their officers and the North Americans can stroll down the street enjoying themselves."[131] James Longhofer's covert agents turned safe houses in San Pedro Sula and La Ceiba into veritable 1980s male vacation homes—one a six-room villa with a swimming pool, workout area, and sunken living room, where men enjoyed steak, lobster, and pornography shipped in by plane—and installed a fifteen-foot satellite dish to keep up with American TV shows.[132] Perhaps the most menacing example of these ties between Edge City landscapes was the perpetual presence in both locales of four-wheel-drive Jeeps and Land Rovers with tinted windows—the sign of Edge City's decadent reinvention of the suburban commute on the asphalt Beltway reappearing in Central America as a spectral harbinger of disappearance and execution, even kidnapping teachers from the John F. Kennedy Elementary School in Ilopango, who were murdered within the hour.[133]

Yet accounts of these experiences hardly appear in memoirs of covert agents from Northern Virginia. A roughneck adventure narrative instead accompanied their trips, one best summarized by John K. Singlaub, another Northern Virginia denizen and retired army major general who organized the campaign's system of private benefactors. Singlaub recounts in his memoirs a rough flight into "the jungle mountains of the Cordillera Entre Rios, about 120 miles east of Tegucigalpa." In this counterinsurgency pastoral, he bumps along "uninhabited ridges" in "a mud-splattered Toyota Land Cruiser." He drinks cold beer before arriving at a contra camp fashioned from cut timber. The authentic sites, for him, bolstered by the unvarnished, natural world, are those of the covert war, as his guide identifies Sandinista outposts "out the open right window" such as "bunkers poorly hidden with dead brush." Singlaub's "jolting ride . . . as bad as any [he]'d experienced in three wars," is not just setting. It is an advertisement for the narrator's rightful place, based in the experience of "three wars," in directing the covert war over and against the clueless men in suits back in Washington, the members of the "irrational" U.S. Congress.

Unlike other "well-meaning Americans" who had "promised to come but never managed to actually make the trip," Singlaub is there to eat rice and beans with the contra field commander, an ex-National Guardsman in fatigues, and to sleep on a bunk before inspecting the contras the next day, when he lectures the commander, using lessons from pacification in Vietnam. Yet this isn't simply U.S. counterinsurgency revisited, but the even greater fantasy by the era, that this time around the covert capital could redeem the techniques used against them by the North Vietnamese and the Ho Chi Minh trail, and land on the side of victory. This would retrieve a stolen masculine effectuality and provide a salve for what they cast as their own melancholy feeling of imperial loss after Vietnam, the sense of purpose dimmed by the image of Americans and their proxies lumbering along ineffectually, weighed down by their technical hardware, lost in the jungle, lacking survival skills, or shuffling papers at desks in suburban Edge City, while they succumbed to left-wing nationalist adversaries.[134]

Central America was their second chance in a second, so-called jungle. As North wrote, "With our history and our ideals, the United States should never have allowed revolution and change to become the exclusive domain of the left."[135] The line could have been lifted from the field notebooks of his natural godhead, Edward Lansdale, whom North considered an "older version of himself," and whom he met with the year before Lansdale's death for passing-the-torch lunches where they developed covert policy in Latin America. Singlaub trotted an elderly Lansdale back to the Pentagon for the same purpose; he and North were just two of a number of Central America covert enthusiasts who contacted Lansdale in this period.[136] These father-to-son echo chambers climaxed during the Iran-Contra hearings. North, appearing to some as "an appealing blend of Chuck Yeager, Dirty Harry and Dobie Gillis" and to others as an embodiment of "Jimmy Stewart, Gary Cooper and John Wayne," performed his authoritarian male image and tension with the overt capital in front of the TV cameras. To *Newsweek*, North was "the Rambo of diplomacy." To CBS, he "embodied the frontier mythology." He opened his testimony before a U.S. congressional committee with the declaration that he would be speaking, in homage to Clint Eastwood, to "the good, the bad, and the ugly."[137]

The photographs of North at the hearings are now recognizable cultural icons. He misleadingly dressed in his uniform decorated from Vietnam— although he was a civilian at the NSC and never worked in uniform at the White House, where he usually wore a business suit. Inflexible with his straight-backed posture, clean shave, lined forehead, and sharp haircut, swathed in his "military demeanor" and "slight and smart-alecky contentiousness," North seemed to define the self-possession of what Amy Kaplan describes as an antiquated and longed-for masculine wholeness.[138] He staged the appearance carefully. Sitting with his wife behind him, his firmly gesturing hands defined the contours of his body and drew a shield around him as much as his clothes did. Reporters responded. As Amy Fried points out, some coverage read like drama reviews. North's co-conspirators amplified the performance and their own disdain for the overt capital during his trial, stepping from the witness stand and saluting him or forcefully shaking his hand, as though in completion of an honored business deal that was simultaneously a high patriotic achievement, in full view of the jury.[139]

This was the final point about these masculine exchanges. Men like North and Singlaub narrated their masculine authority when they returned to the home front by describing how they had survived visits to the landscapes of Central America, which, covertly, they had helped to create as destabilized, rough, hazardous, and needing to be "survived" with their own secret war, which had often targeted land in particular in order to "destroy the means of subsistence."[140] Some drew lethal authority from friendships with Somoza National Guard and Dirty War veterans who could and would kill their enemies free of confining overt capital human rights talk, while drawing courage from their covert capital support.

Yet these actors performed the authority drawn from these sources back in the overt capital not as dust-caked field veterans with blood on their hands and scotch in their bellies but as embodiments of masculine containment, represented by North's photo images from the hearings—the history of violent secrecies cleansed away by silent, secure bodies in uniform. Back in the covert capital, they trumpeted the businesslike Edge City efficiencies of "challenging bureaucracy" and "getting things done." They promised their collaborators and transnational visitors a security in Edge City's hotels and offices that took its very cogency from the narratives of El Salvador, Nicaragua, Honduras, Guatemala, and Costa Rica that they cast as open, insecure, and exposed in their staged narratives of descent from the covert capital to the field. While for them, this descent was temporary and protected, like their masculinity, by "modern weapons and mass media," most Central American men and women didn't have this same protection. Through such spectacles and substitutions, covert capital agents increased their own authority and impressed their fans. They also recast the human right to safety in this era as the conditional and earnable luxury of Edge City.[141]

THE IRAN IN IRAN-CONTRA

In Iran-Contra, the "Iran" is, in some ways, cast as incidental. It is only the source of the funds that went toward the paramilitary action of the contras, part of a project abstractly related to, and usually failing at, freeing American hostages in the Middle East. If the Oliver North who jousted with Congress was doing something brave in his uniform, it was fording rivers in contra base camps in Yamales, not selling advanced weapons at hugely inflated prices in the hotels of Tehran and Tysons Corner. The racial and cultural associations that traveled with the two signifiers in Iran-Contra, meanwhile, themselves cued the racialist dimensions of the U.S. imperial project they were a part of, defining what places were for, through scandal keywords—Iran as a site of excess, corrupt funds, and elite pressure to release hostages in a murky state and non-state terrorist diaspora, Central America as a place to recover masculinity and export violence.

The human presence of Iran in Iran-Contra is usually reduced to accounts of a cadre of Orientalist caricatures of rich, duplicitous Iranian contacts and other "Middle Eastern" actors who cycle through the Iran-Contra fables, often with the word "dealer" attached to their name. Their supposed corruption served as a scapegoat for the corruption and criminality of the American state and covert capital project as it appeared publicly. Their very presence was also somehow able to occlude, through the racial evidence of their bodies and biographies, the criminality and excess of the American military figures and contractors driving the affair. Such figures included Albert Hakim, the operator of Richard Secord's Edge City firms and the team's Tehran-born Farsi translator, dubbed a "shady military sales agent."[142] They included the globe-trotting "Saudi billionaire arms dealer" and Iran habitué Adnan Khashoggi, supposedly an "illusionist, high-wire artist, and prestidigitator," a man one American called "Adnan the Great," a "desert potentate, who has outgrown the desert." They included the perennial Iranian "wheeler-dealer" Manucher Ghorbanifar, who to one American "looked like a character straight out of *The Merchant of Venice*."[143] Most mundanely, the Iranians in Iran-Contra were also the government officials who came to the Tysons Corner Sheraton for what narrations tend to cast as a womanizing party salaciously at odds with Khomeini's Islamic state—blending lurid stereotypes of the exotic East in figures cast as both obscure sultans hunting for their postmodern seraglio, and simultaneously terrorist Islamic radical others with direct control over global hostage taking. These undertones circulated despite the ordinariness of the guests, led by a man thought to be the favorite nephew of the speaker of the Iranian parliament.[144] Hakim addressed the racist overtones of the scandal in his testimony before Congress, explaining, "I have been variously described as everything from a 'mastermind' to a 'shadowy figure.' My reputation has been assaulted, and I have even been referred to in thinly veiled ethnic slurs."[145]

But what bobs up in conventional accounts as a light, leering racism and the otherness of scandal embodied as human actor is better seen as the surfacing of an imperial history that won't speak its name clearly, as Iran-Contra fetishizes the imperial as the racial. Scrubbed from most histories is the mundane, concrete reason Khomeini's revolutionary government would have wanted to buy U.S. arms in the early 1980s: for nearly thirty years the Iranian government had run on U.S. arms. The defense contractors of U.S. imperial Tehran, under the patronage of Iran's king, Shah Reza Pahlavi, had flooded Iran with U.S. ordnance. Key Iran-Contra figures knew Iran intimately, including those at the scandal's center. Richard Secord had done four tours in Iran, the last selling U.S. arms to the Shah's air force, when he "acted as chief adviser to the commander in chief of the Iranian air force and managed all U.S. Air Force programs to Iran as well as some Army and Navy security assistance programs." He left Iran the last time only six months before the revolution.[146] Albert Hakim had brokered the U.S.-Iran arms relationships, which is how he met Secord in Iran in the late seventies, when he was selling electronic intelligence systems to Iran's air force, and Secord recruited him as an intelligence source during the hostage rescue missions. After Hakim fled the Iranian revolution, he continued to sell arms and security systems, even back to Iran, keeping up his contacts.[147]

But these relationships were part of a much older story. In many ways, the covert capital had made Tehran a U.S. imperial city. The first military advisors went to Iran and began redesigning the Iranian Army as a likeness of the U.S. Army at the end of World War II—men such as Robert W. Grow, an army major general from Falls Church, who returned home to become executive director of the Fairfax County Chamber of Commerce, which was instrumental in bringing the CIA to Langley.[148] The coup inaugurating a new era of U.S. empire in Iran in 1953 was run by Northern Virginia CIA officers Kim Roosevelt and George Carroll, who lived in the Salona Village subdivision in McLean, one of its founding suburban locales.[149] After the coup, William Warne, director of Point IV development aid in Iran, brought Shah Reza Pahlavi U.S. aid money to stabilize his government, and stayed on as a major advisor to the throne, reshaping land use and leaving, in Warne's words, "few areas of Iranian life" untouched, just as Warne and his wife had shaped Northern Virginia as community-minded activists in Alexandria's Beverley Hills subdivision the decade before.[150]

These ties continued on for years, from Northern Virginia resident Donald Wilhelm—who wrote the Shah's memoir in English as Wilhelm's wife helped raise Northern Virginia's new town of Reston from the ground—to CIA agents like Lucien Conein, who trained the Shah's security apparatus, to the hordes of military contractors and Pentagon elites working for the Shah who populated Tehran through the seventies. After the revolution, William

Casey's most prized CIA officer, Robert Clayton Ames, often distinguished by his signature aviator glasses, cowboy hats, and hand-tooled boots, flew from his house off Reston's Hunting Horn Lane to Tehran to open up U.S. intelligence access to the new government, ultimately pushing Iran further to the right with his meddling. Other Northern Virginia CIA officers exfiltrated one of the covert capital's "most valued" Iranian agents from the Shah's army—disguised, for the times, as an oil equipment salesman.[151]

As with Vietnam and so many places subject to U.S. imperial action after World War II, one could narrate these connections as deep social history, illuminating the personal relations and intimate contacts—in working relationships and in intimate forms of violence—to excavate another seamlessly knit-together, co-constituted landscape. But beyond these stories-so-far of people's intimacies, the imperial economy of the seventies had also fused Northern Virginia and Tehran into a kind of single landscape. Just as U.S. expertise, money, and power had defined the structure of U.S. imperial Tehran from World War II through the 1970s, Iranian expertise, money, and power began to shape U.S. imperial Northern Virginia at Edge City as well.

A closed circuit of petrodollars, Pentagon weapons sales, contracting, American college educations, and large real estate holdings induced this powerful mirroring. As with Tysons Corner, Iran was "one vast building site" in the seventies, a "forest of cranes."[152] Construction workers could make more money than teachers. Stepping up the mountains north of Tehran, the elite, superluxury built environment of Shemiran exactly parallels the history of the Northern Virginia suburbs at this point—the same building techniques, the same cube-like office buildings and hotels, the same developers, the same kinds and sources of dollars fueling the boom, the same country club villas. At times, those hotels, office buildings, and villas were built in both places by the same people.[153]

Shemiran had been a crucial landscape for U.S. imperial Tehran from its earliest moments. The United States had a club in Amirabad in northern Tehran after World War II. Early CIA agents had fished in Shemiran at a British embassy summer camp and used its first scattered houses as hideouts and safe houses during the 1953 coup. They had also lived there.[154] By the 1970s, Shemiran's building projects defined vistas for Americans flying into their new posts. "The city had begun to look like a giant Meccano set, with huge cranes dotting the landscape," wrote Cynthia Helms, the wife of CIA director and then U.S. ambassador to Iran Richard Helms. "There were misgivings about the hurriedly constructed office buildings. An American architect I talked to had great doubts about their safety."[155] But American architects and developers hurriedly built the same style of offices back in Northern Virginia. While British ambassador Anthony Parsons sniffed at the "vulgar ostentation of the nouveau riche in North Tehran" and the "the cosmopolitanism of life in the houses of the technocrats and entrepreneurs in the northern suburbs," in Northern Virginia, he could have seen the same in many a Tysons-area subdivision. Politicians from Iran would later use Northern Virginia's Giant supermarket and booming suburban towns, seen on their trips to Northern Virginia, as a metaphor to explain Tehran's own rapid urban development.[156]

Iranian elites became developers to fund their children's education in the United States and to express power in public space. American covert agents and Pentagon contractors did the same. By 1976, between 24,000 and 40,000 Americans were in Iran, inhabiting a landscape that included the ever-expanding Tehran-American School, the American Women's Club, the Imperial Country Club, the America Hotel, and Iran's National Committee for the American Revolution Bicentennial, chaired by Queen Farah, the Shah's wife.[157] As they did in Edge City, Northern Virginia, the "five per-centers" on cost-plus contracts crowded the landscape. Contractors, brokers, advisors, and middlemen demanded their cuts from U.S.-Iranian contracts of all kinds, including those who, in their earlier lives, had bolstered the Shah in 1953. One, Kim Roosevelt, as an executive at Gulf Oil and representative in Iran for the military contractor and weapons manufacturer Northrop, demanded, according to a U.S. general, payments that caused some contro-versy. Rents in Tehran meanwhile, like Northern Virginia rents, swelled to $4,000 a month.[158]

But the similarities did not just arise because of a generic pattern of U.S.-style development spreading worldwide. The Northern Virginia–Iran rela-tionship was crucial to inventing this form of building. Nixon and Henry Kissinger removed the limits on the Shah's arms purchases from the United States in May 1972. By the next year, the Shah was receiving thirty-five U.S. corporate visitors a week, many from Northern Virginia.[159] By 1977, Iran was the largest foreign buyer of U.S. arms in the world.[160] The Shah's open demand, his purchase of $19 billion worth of American weapons from 1971 to 1978 alone, made for the economies of scale that allowed the Pentagon to generate the overproduction of U.S. military technology in the first place.[161] The Iranian oil price hikes in the early seventies squeezed the U.S. consumer economy, but they also flooded Iran's petrodollars into U.S. banks and the coffers of weapons manufacturers and their covert allies.[162] The Iranian weapons and defense market thus kept many contractors from going broke or being phased out after the end of the Vietnam War.[163]

These people lived in Northern Virginia. An interconnected militarized economy fueled both places. Dollars and styles of development flowed back and forth, and more than a few Virginia suburbanites had the Shah's Order of the Crown on their ranch house mantles. In only one example, after Gulf Oil took over the new town of Reston in 1967 and drove the town's founder from office, a Gulf advisor, William Magness, took over Reston's development. Magness had managed Gulf operations in Iran. On loan to the Iranian government, he reorganized the Iranian oil industry, directing the Iranian Oil Exploration and Producing Company's 100,000-square-mile complex. He set up the Shah's refineries and new towns in oil fields throughout the country, working closely with Iranian executives and managers during an eleven-year stint.[164]

In Northern Virginia, Magness steered Reston from its early, clustered modernist developments toward more conventional suburban developments anchored by malls and office complexes, overseeing its Edge City transformation. Magness's Reston—built from expertise honed in Iran—then housed the restorative domestic lives of CIA agents who returned to Iran as the Shah's advisors in the seventies. He also used his connections to generate business in Iran for Gulf's development arm, which built two new town developments in Tehran's northeastern suburbs and won a $1 million contract for a large condominium project in Tehran, all in the style and pattern of the new Edge City Reston's own suburban-style housing, large condominiums, and over-scaled industrial and office parks.[165]

These ties met the public when the Iran-Contra Affair broke—the "Iran" in Iran-Contra also bringing to light, through scandal, this much deeper phenomenon, an imperial economy and system of weapons, luxury, and violence that printed itself on the local space of Northern Virginia and Tehran and had a constituency in Iran even after the revolution.[166] When Oliver North had flown to Iran with a delivery of Hawk Missile parts in May 1986, he used the old U.S. imperial built environment. He cruised down the Shah's U.S.-style expressway from the airport to the city. He stayed at the Tehran Hilton, now the Istaqlal, or Independence, hotel.[167]

For these histories to become visible, one needs to reframe Iran-Contra as having both a deeper sense of U.S. imperial time and a concept of space as a stretched-out series of relations. If Edge City in Northern Virginia often took its symbolic and gendered masculine meanings in contradistinction to and interdependence with produced landscapes in Central America, it often took its built form in consonance with the built environment of Tehran and Shemiran. The images of excess, wasteful spending, and immorality pinned to Iranian figures who enter the Iran-Contra stories—like the similar stereotypes pinned to the Pahlavi family by Western observers throughout the family's reign—were merely the deferred and exiled product of the disjunctive and disruptive postmodernities of the transnational U.S. imperial state in the 1970s, wiped from public narrative after the revolution and the dawn of the Reagan years, even as the same habits, spaces, and values accelerated in Northern Virginia at the same time.

Looking at this conjunction of race and empire also provides an important segue into what this chapter argues is the *other* Iran-Contra visible in Edge City in the 1980s. This was not the Iran-Contra Affair but Iran-Contra as a figure for the human traces and movements that comprised all these imperial relationships. In the 1980s, to CIA director Casey, the United States needed to fight a total, global war.[168] Those caught in the space-rupturing vortexes of U.S. projects arrived in the home front bearing the weight of roles assigned to them in this war and in a broader U.S. racial order, one defined by ideas about place, policy, violence, and life formed through juxtapositions with others in the U.S. orbit. They settled in the U.S. home front where a domestic iteration of the politics of comparison and contradistinction, with its own local racial habits, cast them again in racialized roles. But they always assumed those roles in complex overlaps and adjacent relationships with other U.S. imperial repatriates, along with the white CIA agents, imperial advisors, and other often quite ethnically diverse U.S. covert officers who drew their own sense of ethnicity and embodiment from these global and local encounters. The space of Northern Virginia, Iran-Contra as built and lived space, bore out these histories. Edge City racial formations were defined by particular evaluative (and often government-funded) ideas about race and place shaped by both national and imperial histories, even as the material space of the covert capital itself showed off their unstable interdependence.[169]

RETURN OF THE OPPRESSED

Edge City, Northern Virginia had one further important connection to Central America by 1987: it was home to the second largest community of

Salvadoran immigrants in the United States. More arrived from Guatemala, Nicaragua, and Honduras. The Washington area soon had the country's third largest number of Central Americans, with some 150,000 settled around DC. Little acknowledgment greeted them as to the debt owed them by the landscape to which they fled. This was particularly so when the Reagan administration cut off its general amnesty program in January 1982, denying refugee status to Salvadorans and other Central American migrants, whose land covert capital functionaries were helping to make uninhabitable.

Scripts that framed Central America as a wild site of masculine fantasy and renewal for individual covert capital agents returned in respectable U.S. policy as a vision of El Salvador as inherently connected with disorder and death—a self-actualizing argument for intervention. "The problem confronting El Salvador is Thomas Hobbes's problem: How to establish order and authority in a society where there is none," explained Reagan advisor Jeane Kirkpatrick in her exegesis of what she called the "the Latin style of politics." Security state intellectuals rhetorically framed El Salvador as a place without structure and life as they attempted to create it militarily as such.[170] Ideas and policies portraying El Salvador as uncivilized then circled back to create a perception of Salvadoran migrants as a threat. "El Salvador . . . is a country with a history of large-scale illegal immigration to the United States," Assistant Secretary of State Elliott Abrams told Congress in 1984. It was, in his words, a "poor and violent country." At the same time, the Virginia resident was declaring himself a "gladiator" for Reagan's Central America policy, often defending the El Salvador government and military's human rights record as the military drove those migrants from their land. Then he became an ardent supporter and supervisor of the contra war, in his words, "pushing and pushing and pushing for the contras."[171]

North also warned of the perils of Central American immigration to the United States in his testimony before Congress. "You will see democracy perish from the rest of Central America, a flood of refugees crossing the American borders, and potentially, the construction of a Berlin-type wall along the Rio Grande to keep people out," he promised elected officials who did not support the contras. "This country took over a million illegal refugees last year. Just last week we authorized 200,000 Nicaraguans to stay in this country. And that's just the tip of the iceberg . . ."

In this fashion, North argued for the merits of overthrowing the Nicaraguan government and waging war against peasants in El Salvador and elsewhere by portraying the arrival of Central American people in the United

States as an apocalyptic scenario. At the same time, he used the apocalyptic imagery to refigure Central American refugees currently fleeing the violence of the covert capital and its right-wing allies as victims of the left—even as Reagan refugee policy cast many of those same refugees as illegal and denied them entry into the United States explicitly because they left countries ruled by U.S.-friendly leaders on the right, granting fewer than 3 percent of those who fled El Salvador at the height of the war political asylum. By squeezing refugees in this double rhetorical vise—arguing that their countries needed violence supported by the United States in order to keep them from escaping the violence and coming to the United States—North seems to nod toward an unspoken alternative state project: forced erasure, by whatever means.[172]

Along these same lines, through the nineties, Salvadoran migrants were the largest target of deportation proceedings in Northern Virginia—some 7,000 people between 1992 and 2001, their cases at times decided by a U.S. army trial judge and Pentagon legal advisor for military commands throughout the world who, after retiring from the army, became a judge in Arlington's federal immigration courts.[173] Only in that same decade did scholars begin to chronicle and publicize this migration in depth, when historians and social scientists such as Terry Repak, Olivia Cadaval, Raúl Sánchez Molina, José Luis Benítez, David Pedersen, and Patricia Landolt began to complete and publish their work. The earliest in this wave of Central American migrants to the Washington area were women, working as housekeepers and child-care workers for Latin American embassy families and U.S. employees of international and national agencies, who brought back their domestic workers when their tours abroad ended. When the covert capital exacerbated the violence in Central America, family members joined these women. This group included more men, who found work as dishwashers, construction workers, landscapers, painters, and janitors in the Edge City hotels, restaurants, and housing lots where generals and agents who had directed programs to violently attack them and their neighbors planned the attacks, dined, and lived.[174] Some cleaned the floors at Dulles Airport, at local military bases, and at the Pentagon itself.[175] Recalling burnt, demolished, and ransacked cities, villages, and farms, these migrants spruced, sculpted, and shined the aura of the Edge City built environment, making it function, for low pay, serving food to and cleaning away the waste of covert agents and contractors who profited from the destruction of their home territory.

Many Salvadorans came from eastern provinces such as San Miguel and La Unión, provinces where "serious economic damage was being done" by

U.S.-backed counterinsurgency warfare.[176] La Unión held a national recruit training base staffed by twenty-five U.S. military advisors and was adjacent to the Gulf of Fonseca, which connected El Salvador to Nicaragua.[177] San Miguel was a travel hub for the region. It held the largest town in the eastern part of the country, also called San Miguel and home to the central Salvadoran military headquarters where leftists were interrogated and tortured.[178]

Both provinces bordered Morazán, the stronghold of left-wing FMLN fighters, and thus provided frequent staging grounds for counterinsurgency battles, intense aerial bombing campaigns, and ground sweeps, including a 1981 massacre. Some came to the covert capital from Morazán itself—also home to a large barracks in departmental capital San Francisco Gotera, from which the army staged its raids—and from Usulután, another nearby province with high levels of fighting and political persecution, the site of a brutal state agrarian reform program, and a place that CIA director Casey had used in 1982 as an example of the need for U.S. training of the Salvadoran army to "to break up guerrilla formations."[179]

The migrants moved into the postwar low-rise brick garden apartments built for the first Pentagon workers. They settled where Vietnamese intimates of the covert capital had a decade before, in Seven Corners, Bailey's Crossroads, Falls Church, Forest Glen, Douglas Park, and Columbia Heights. They moved to the Buckingham apartments near Clarendon's Little Saigon, to the Willston apartments next to the Eden Center, and eventually to a variety of suburban houses bought with extended family members. Thirty-six percent of the DC metropolitan area's Salvadorans lived in South Arlington, Annandale, and Bailey's Crossroads. They migrated south to Alexandria and Woodbridge, and northwest around the Dulles Access Road out to Herndon, near Reston, following the path of the developing Edge Cities they often serviced. Soon they had "rebaptized," in the words of one scholar, a neighborhood in Alexandria, "Chirilagua," after a town in San Miguel. Northern Virginia communities became well known throughout the Salvadoran diaspora.[180]

Among these migrants were guerrillas and death squad soldiers, leftists and rightists, torturers and people who had been tortured. Yet Northern Virginia stripped them of these histories and met them stripped of its own, with shocked newspaper headlines similar to those that had greeted the Vietnamese: "Illegal Entry" and "After the Influx, a County Copes." While "accounts of violence and fear during the civil war in their country" entered both reportage and scholarship—often in graphic, even lurid, repetitions of the raw, minute details of bodily harm—representations of the political intimacies between the two landscapes were evasive.

Without immigration status or even the melodrama that surrounded the national imaginary of the Vietnam War to shield them, and bearing the history of a war the covert capital had worked to erase through what Mario Lungo Uclés calls an "almost invisible" strategy, made invisible through the open secret of "low-intensity conflict," these "illegal aliens" arrived in Northern Virginia as ghostly carriers of an unwanted intimacy. They did the most exposed, uncertain labor in the covert capital's everyday economy, in a suburban built environment designed to make such labor and the transit and life networks that made it possible more hazardous and difficult.[181] They arrived as the return-of-the-Reagan-repressed, what Ana Patricia Rodríguez calls a "phantom figure." "Displaced first by the Reagan-Bush geopolitics in the Caribbean and in Central America," she writes, " . . . they seek safe haven in the United States, only to be received as depoliticized labor migrants, rarely granted the status of political refugees."[182]

Recast as labor migrants, their awareness of doubled spaces, bound by imperial action and their own migration, could be reframed as a kind of dispossession. Taking a dimmer view of the many intellectual celebrations of renamed streets and neighborhoods like Chirilagua in Alexandria as a sign of the postmodern hybridities of transnational migration, Susan Bibler Coutin emphasizes this point: "Positioned spatially and temporally outside of the United States, unauthorized migrants are, in a sense, *in* El Salvador, even though they are physically within the United States," she wrote, using Chirilagua as an example. "Just as a photographic image with low resolution produces a blurry picture, these migrants had difficulty clarifying their legal status, social location, and individual futures. Without legal resolution, unauthorized migrants could not be *fully* present in the United States."[183] This could be seen as the domestic U.S. version of the politics of empire and immigration that the covert capital and the Reagan administration deployed in El Salvador. In El Salvador, peasants being harmed by U.S.-backed governments and military men were cast not as victims of U.S. violence but potential refugees already flooding the country unless the United States continued to support those inflicting the violence. The moment of their dispossession and harm in El Salvador, they were already cast as *in* the United States.

In Northern Virginia, Salvadoran migrants were *in* El Salvador, even as they suffered the hostile landscapes of life and labor inflicted upon them by the suburban built environment whose functioning and economy depended on their presence. At the same time, the same landscape cast them as legally absent and exposed them to the hazards of suburban built environments designed to marginalize and harass their necessary labor. Rendered both exposed (by the hazardous suburban transportation, highway, and low-income housing system) and invisible (by the structure of back-office hotel, skyscraper, restaurant, and domestic work), these migrants contended with a zone of illegality that repressed knowledge of the ethical dimensions of the covert capital's practices abroad. Through this kind of produced "nonexistence,"[184] the clandestine nature of the covert actions directed against peasants in El Salvador were reproduced as a secondary form of violence directed toward the legal erasure of Salvadoran migrants in Northern Virginia. The stretched-out spatial networks of imperial violence could traverse borders with ease, while using the liminal and transnational consciousness created by these movements to displace the full presence and claims to land and life of Salvadoran residents and migrants. Recasting migrants as transnational "phantom figures" could rhetorically seal them off from even humanistic ethical arguments against bodily harm at the very moment of their physical experience of such harm in both places. As a transnational experience of violence and repatriation, U.S. empire cast itself and people subjected to it as both everywhere and nowhere.

While legal and immigration cases exposed in brief flares this imperial history, its most sustained and revealing narration appeared in cultural works. In 1981, Lilo González, a former schoolteacher who fled El Salvador, moved into a trailer with seventeen other refugees and parked cars at Bogart's restaurant in Fairfax for work. At the same time, he performed and wrote protest songs in the covert capital that publicized the plight of Salvadoran migrants "not too far from the White House."[185] Refusing the erasure of imperial connections, Salvadoran activists in Arlington, some of whom "in the seventies worked with Christian base communities and the mass organizations of the left" that provided the foundation of support for the FMLN fighters, took a similar approach. "We are a direct product of the war in El Salvador," one activist from Northern Virginia told a reporter at a protest, not here "for the American dream—the TV and gold and cars of the United States."[186] Other activists on the left performed plays at Arlington theaters comparing the Sanctuary movement for Central American refugees to the Underground Railroad that had spirited people away from U.S. slavery, and staged the largest nonviolent sit-ins ever at the gates of the Langley headquarters, carrying the names and photos of the dead in El Salvador and Nicaragua.[187] In the wider Central American literary diaspora, Guatemalan novelist Arturo Arias wrote tales inside tales where CIA officers from Virginia whimsically compared the banks of the Motagua River to Virginia's Potomac and skipped home after wreaking havoc on the isthmus to their "small Virginia suburb full of trees and gardens with perfectly mowed, shiny green lawns," and their redesigned Edge City suburban homes stocked with trendy consumer amenities.[188]

This tactic of the intentional exposure and revelation of such connections—of the assertion of existence through a reimagining of space—is sustained and nuanced in the novels of Mario Bencastro, a painter from El Salvador who migrated to Falls Church in the 1980s and turned his attention to literary work in Spanish. Bencastro's oeuvre details the exposed spaces of forced embodiment and insecurity that U.S. policy helped to create in both El Salvador and Northern Virginia. In his fiction, there is no innate spatial safety for people who must contend with imperial insecurity and violence. Characters are imperiled in the very spaces where they should most feel privacy, "safe refuge," and "the right to live."[189] In his second novel, *Odyssey to the North*, Bencastro takes his protagonist, Calixto, a San Salvador construction worker accused as an "enemy of the government," on a long migration accompanying two women with family in Northern Virginia. As Calixto leaves National Airport at the end of the book, riding along the George Washington Parkway, he has a moment of blurred experience similar to the one Coutin describes, where he "opened his eyes and before his weary gaze stretched the highway along the Potomac River that separated Virginia from Washington. The blurred images of home refused to leave his memory, and Calixto thought, 'Really, I'm not far from my people or my home. I have them as close to my heart as if I had never left them.'"[190]

This passage evokes the tenuousness of the migrants' stay and legal status. It also refers to the migration of so many of their comrades and family to the DC area. But the literal border between the covert capital in Virginia and the overt capital at DC, in its dissolution, also conveys the aggressive mystifying power of visible geography, the way it both reveals and covers over the stretched-out imperial power of the places that have reached in and defined the lives of Bencastro's characters since their time in El Salvador. Bencastro reestablishes the presence of these people in his multidimensional, mural-like novels not simply through street and place names but by detailing the human narratives that twined throughout imperial and state violence in El Salvador and in Northern Virginia.[191] In doing so, he edges toward a mode of migrant artistic production that suggests that the autonomous performance of exposure within Northern Virginia—the exposure of the bodies Edge City erases, the connected human stories it ignores, the geographic connections it disavows—could itself be thought of as a form of local politics. Bencastro's novels take back control over imperialism's forced exposure—and its partner, erasure—through public art in the Virginia landscape.

Bencastro's work, of course, also addresses multiple human, state, and imperial contexts in and beyond El Salvador and Northern Virginia. But even beyond the novels, he pursued this practice of counter-exposure in three-dimensional space in Northern Virginia. In consciousness-raising sessions at local school and community youth programs, he handed out his slang dictionary, *Vato Guanaco Loco: Rap En Caliche*, providing a vernacular toolkit so that Salvadoran migrants in "Yunaites," or the United States, could speak truth to their history. He also started a community theater group, the Hispanic Culture Society, which in 1988 performed, with a group of Salvadoran, Guatemalan, Cuban, and Peruvian actors, a Spanish-language play he wrote, *Crossroad*, at the Thomas Jefferson Theater. The theater was inside a middle school on Glebe Road in Arlington, quite near the houses of covert capital Central America hands such as Alan Fiers and Daniel O. Graham.

The play, which Bencastro described as having "a critical attitude toward the use and abuse of power," could have been directed at the covert agents. In its Brechtian structure, actors play both actors putting on the play and characters in the play. The structure exposes the machinery of the theater and sets the tone of exposure as a theme. In the play's allegory, Death, the Devil, and God vie for the Earth through the work of the Politician, as he oppresses the common people, represented by a carpenter and a prostitute. Promising them the security of an independent nation, he instead gives them "arms, police, security." But when God finally regains his power from the Devil, the Politician "loses the opportunity to govern the 'Earth.'" As the Politician begs for redemption, God turns his back. The Devil and Death roll dice over his fate. Bencastro reported in an interview soon after the production that "this ending received spontaneous applause and great laughter from the audience.... The applause and laughter were so intense that the actors had to wait a moment before finishing the scene."[192]

This detail not only testifies to the potency of such acts of counter-exposure as strategy in the covert capital but also provides a rare glimpse of the

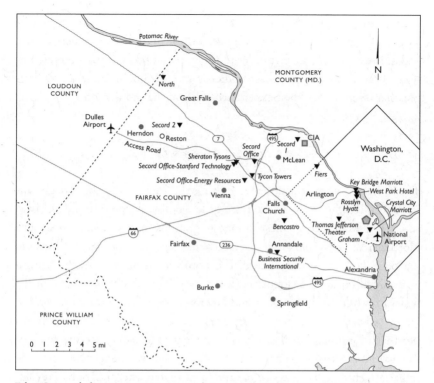

Edge City and the covert war in Central America. Northern Virginia hotels staged the meetings and male social environments that organized the war. Office parks provided the managerial space. The booming suburban landscape housed its soldiers when they left and returned home.

politicized, Spanish-speaking public already resident in the imperial corridor by the late eighties. It provides a different view from the popular accounts that depicted these migrants as devoid of politics, lacking both voice and political past, bearers only of their own flight to become struggling low-wage laborers in the margins of Northern Virginia's Edge Cities. These politics take on added significance in that El Salvador's committed generation of political writers, of whom Bencastro is an obvious heir, took form in the first place in dialogue with U.S. imperialism in Central America. The CIA coup in Guatemala in 1954, organized and armed in part from Northern Virginia, reshaped the region, swinging its politics to the right. But it also drove Guatemalan exiles across the border to inspire a younger generation of Salvadoran writers to take up the cause of the writer as "the moral consciousness of his people."[193] Some of these writers' heirs then migrated during the covert capital war in Central America back to the same Northern Virginia landscape. There they produced other signs of a U.S. imperial order and of lives resistant to that order in the imperial home front—representations obscured by categories like domestic and foreign, immigrant and refugee, that often shaped their experience of life in that home front.

U.S. IMPERIAL TEHRAN IN EXILE

To use Iran-Contra as a cipher to rethink the scandal and the foreign policy of the Reagan years as the trace of longer, overlapping imperial histories, it is vital to recover these human migrations from Central America to Northern Virginia that are impacted in the term -Contra, which forms the second half of the scandal's title. The word's focus on militants fighting a war only in Nicaragua clouds the broader war's reverberating effects on the wider lifeworlds of El Salvador and Northern Virginia. But the first half of Iran-Contra needs another reformulation as well, as Salvadoran migrants to Northern Virginia, as well as others from Central America, also shared space in 1980s Northern Virginia with a wave of migrants who fled there from U.S. imperial Tehran in the days before and immediately after the Iranian revolution and the fall of the Shah in February 1979.

During the revolution, Iranians and Americans alike tapped intimacies and friendships that had served as the armature of U.S. imperialism in Iran as migration routes back to Northern Virginia. Iranians who worked in the gleaming social whirl of ambassador Ardeshir Zahedi's Iranian embassy in DC married Americans, settled in Falls Church, and brought over family and friends.[194] American men returned home from revolutionary Iran with Iranian wives, which since the earliest Peace Corps missions, U.S. officials had presented as a sign of the easy, triumphant fusion of the two countries.[195]

The daughter of a former Iranian ambassador married the son of the chief executive of a large U.S. military contractor in Iran, the McLean company QuesTech.[196] A navy vice admiral in McLean helped his former Iranian counterpart escape to his home suburbs.[197] The head of the U.S. military mission to Iran, Ellis Williamson, was soon entertaining his counterparts from the Iranian navy at his house in Arlington. There they admired and asked for copies of his portrait of the Shah wearing a navy uniform to hang on the walls of their own new Northern Virginia houses.[198] U.S. advisors from Northern Virginia who had rationalized the government and run modernization proj-

ects in Iran provided vital contacts for Iranian generals and colonels struggling with their first job issues in Northern Virginia, such as one group of
Iranian military men who started a taxi business at Dulles Airport.[199]

By the early 1980s, a bustling exile community had established itself,
opening and occupying restaurants such as Farideh's Little Europe in Falls
Church.[200] After the revolution, Iranian and American developers and contractors repatriated their dollars to Northern Virginia to build crucial developments in America's covert capital. In Iran, Bahman Batmanghelidj had
been a habitué of U.S. imperial circles, attending the Shah's dinners and
social events. He developed a ski resort in Iran—a major tourist amenity that
defined the country's 1970s leisure economy. He also built a cement plant and
a petrochemical factory, and he became the Iranian partner of American tele-
communications magnate Charles Wohlstetter. Batmanghelidj relied on his
close friendships with the Shah's most trusted generals to finish a project for
Wohlstetter in the days of the revolution, installing perhaps one million lines
for a telephone network and gaining permission to violate Tehran's military
curfew to continue the work at night. Batmanghelidj then led the evacuation
of Wohlstetter's employees to Turkey before resettling in Northern Virginia
in 1980 near family friends in the local contracting culture.

With lightning speed, Batmanghelidj, calling himself Batman for short,
became one of Northern Virginia's most prolific and visible developers. He
designed Edge City space in Reston and in the new area now referred to as
simply "Dulles" around Dulles Airport. He lived on a 400-acre horse farm
far into the countryside near Middleburg and in a house in McLean. His
projects included shopping centers in Dulles and Sterling, residential subdivisions, and major green-field office complexes, such as "President's Park"
in Dulles—planned for three million square feet off the Route 28 corridor
and the Dulles Toll Road. By the 1990s, he had singlehandedly "reshaped an
entire section of western Fairfax."[201]

Edge City residents included high-level police aide-de-camp and political official Parviz Yar-Afshar; SAVAK official and gendarmerie commander Ahmad Ali Mohaqqeqi, and General Gholam Reza Azhari, one
of the Shah's last martial law prime ministers. Yar-Afshar, who had visited
Northern Virginia and Falls Church thirty years earlier, perhaps on a training trip to Langley, and others settled in the 1,200-unit Rotonda apartment complex built a decade before at Tysons by the developer who raised
the Watergate in DC. In the five-building complex billed as "condominiums in a Renaissance garden," they could take in the European-style piazza

and a hilltop location that "dominates its neighborhood like a medieval castle," while enjoying contemporary Edge City amenities, such as "electronically monitored fencing, private guards, [and] manned entrance gates" designed to "offer you peace of mind."[202] Admiral Kamal Habibolahi, one of the Shah's most motivated jingoistic warriors, who trained in the United States and worked extensively with Americans as an officer in the Iranian navy, also settled nearby—after leading covert actions to invade and retake Iran by sea in a seized boat. He discussed his military actions at Northern Virginia's Edge City Holiday Inn and in counterrevolutionary interviews given from his home in Fairfax.[203]

MONTICELLO AT TYSONS CORNER

This set of relationships found its most pronounced expression when the Shah's son, Reza Cyrus Pahlavi, moved to a McMansion between McLean and Great Falls in 1987. The young Shah's presence near Great Falls served better than any marker to chronicle the history of U.S. empire in Iran and the ways Edge City, Northern Virginia became a kind of U.S. imperial Tehran in exile in the mid-eighties.

When the first Pahlavi Shah, the former Cossack Reza Khan, fled Iran during World War II, he traveled to Mauritius and Johannesburg. The second, Mohammad Reza, waited in Rome for news of the coup in 1953 and skied the Alps in St. Moritz. During the Iranian revolution, the third Pahlavi Shah-to-be, Crown Prince, and heir to the throne, Reza Cyrus, was in the United States, training as a fighter pilot at Reese Air Force Base outside Lubbock, Texas.[204] By 1985, he had commissioned his advisor to buy nine acres of land in Great Falls, the exurban landscape ten miles from DC where horse farms and one-lane country roads tangled with the engorged built environments of the Reagan years. There, he built himself the $3.2 million McMansion that became his covert capital palace in exile.[205]

The choice of Great Falls itself testified to the long, intertwined histories of Northern Virginia and Iran. During the U.S. occupation of Iran after the Second World War, a onetime U.S. Treasury lawyer named John Gallup Laylin, who lived on a rural estate in Great Falls known as Hidden Springs, went to Iran to advise the Shah. His legal work evicting the Soviet Union from the north in 1946 and 1947 laid the foundations for the largely unfettered U.S. presence in the country for the next thirty years. Afterward, Laylin returned to Great Falls. With CIA director Allen Dulles and Loy Henderson, ambassador to Iran, he founded the Washington Institute of Foreign Affairs, which hosted the Shah on visits to the area through the 1960s.[206]

Laylin's daughter left her heart in Iran. A Cornell English major, Louise Laylin traveled there during her junior year and met the Qajar Prince, Narcy Firouz, land developer and construction company manager. They married at the Laylin farm in Great Falls in 1957. Then they started a chicken and wheat farm in Shiraz, where she became "Princess Firouz." On an acreage called Norouzabad near Tehran, she founded a horseback-riding academy, the defining activity of debutante Northern Virginia, where she had ridden in foxhunts and show jumpers. Soon she began searching for what she imagined must exist—horses descended from the Persia of Cyrus and Darius. In 1965, she found them. In a market she saw a peddler with a small, overworked horse, which she obtained and bred, arguing successfully to the international horse community that it represented a distinct breed lost since ancient Persia, last seen 1,300 years before. She named it the Caspian miniature and defined it by its skull and jaw.

The racial politics of Pahlavi Iran asserted power through an Aryan public sphere intent upon recovering a pure Persian heritage, unpolluted by Arab, Tartar, and Mongol incursions, as a secular, royalist grounds for and alternative to Islamic authority, as Talinn Grigor has shown. In this context, Laylin's discovery of the pure Caspian rocketed her into elite society. Persian Aryanism was a performance and measure of friendship for Iranians and Americans, blossoming among those friendships as a means of authority. Laylin's work and estates were crucial venues for articulating it. She shared her homes with Iranian elites, and they became watering holes for her father's CIA friends when they traveled to Iran, including coup leaders and other Northern Virginia residents like Kim Roosevelt. Laylin even brought Caspian specimens home to Great Falls. She bred them with Virginia mares to entertain covert elites in their own horse culture, while in Iran, she ran riding academies and bought homes in Shiraz, Karaj, Tehran, and in the mountains near the Turkmenistan border, all funded by her husband's work as a land developer. Her main stable grew into the official Iranian Royal Horse Society, formed to protect the country's "native breeds." The society's patron was Crown Prince Reza Cyrus, himself an accomplished rider.[207] A decade after participating in these ventures, still a young man, he moved near the Great Falls village where Louise Laylin first learned to ride and built his own estate in 1986.

Born on Halloween 1960, Crown Prince Reza was the first of the Pahlavi clan to grow up in an Iran shadowed by U.S. empire. Not only was it not surprising that Reza Pahlavi ended up in the Northern Virginia suburbs, it would be hard to imagine him going anywhere else. Ex-CIA agents in McLean began offering Shah Reza Pahlavi estates and farms as retreats in Northern Virginia as early as 1979, swearing they could spirit him past immigration officials at Dulles Airport.[208] A major reason the younger Pahlavi moved to Great Falls was political. Building his house some ten minutes away from Langley, he was, at the time, according to his advisor and other observers, receiving a monthly CIA stipend. After a meeting with Bill Casey in Rabat, they began what Pahlavi called "mutual cooperation in intelligence ... for mutual benefits." Although he denied he took agency money, his financial advisor once claimed that Pahlavi's stipend rose at times to $150,000 a month. A large picture of him hung on the wall in Langley's Iran division at this time, accompanied by the moniker "The Hope of Democracy of Iran." This "Iran" in Iran-Contra at times created complexities for the arms-selling project. In September 1986, a CIA technical strike blocked TV signals on national Iranian TV to broadcast an eleven-minute speech by Reza Cyrus, then resident in Northern Virginia, into Iran. At Langley, the agents responsible had "a caviar-and-Russian-vodka party" to celebrate. But for Oliver North and his compatriots, the covert strike raised the ire of the Iranians negotiating the arms sales, which the operators of the covert Central America war had to smooth over.[209]

The McMansion in Great Falls was not even Pahlavi's first strategic development in Northern Virginia. In 1982, through a development company named after the holy Islamic city of Medina, he and his advisors invested in land for a speculative townhouse development, an extension of one called Monticello at Tysons Corner, a short walk away from the Tysons Corner Mall. Monticello was one of Edge City at Tysons Corner's founding residential developments. The small nostalgic postmodern houses were gray, burgundy, and yellow in color, arrayed along Jeffersonian Drive and Court. They were developed by an Iranian builder but designed by Kamran Diba, Pahlavi's mother's cousin. Diba was one of Pahlavi Iran's most well-known modernist architects, a familiar face in the palace and in the circles of American and Iranian architects who could often be found milling about the Tehran Hilton in the seventies. He designed signature buildings for the crown in Pahlavi Iran, including Shushtar New Town, and most famously, the Tehran Museum of Contemporary Art (MOCA), which was lauded in

Monticello at Tysons Corner, the suburban development that anchored Shah-in-exile Reza Pahlavi's first real estate investment in Northern Virginia. It was designed by Kamran Diba, one of Iran's most famous modernist architects. The nostalgic gray, burgundy, and yellow townhouses pointed to the ways contextual architectural style could sever political-economic connections formed through the ties of empire. Photo by author.

American and European architectural magazines. He designed similarly signature buildings at Tysons Corner just as it was becoming a residential space.

As one of Tysons' earliest residential subdivisions, Monticello was foundational to the identification of Edge City form by Joel Garreau five years later. The townhouses sold to geopolitical migrants. Monticello provided a first foothold for Iranians in Northern Virginia, a royalist exile subdivision. In Tehran and at Howard University in DC, Kamran—or Kami, as his friends called him—Diba had trained as an architect and taught himself to paint. His Tehran MOCA, his pet project and definitive design work, was lauded for its low-scale, contextual Third Worldist reinterpretation of modernist form, blending indigenous and climatological elements to honor Iran's built environment. It was funded by the transnational oil, agro-industrial, and weapons economies of the 1970s.[210] In Tysons Corner, Diba completed a seemingly very different project, but one that was similarly playful and contextual to Edge City and Virginia. Monticello, in fact, foreshadowed the postmodern "Jeffersonian" elements—tweaked, stretched, remixed, and glee-fully distorted—that were defining an important strand of 1980s Edge City Tysons Corner's own giddy vernacular, most famously in Philip Johnson's "Jeffersonian" treatment of the massive shopping-bag-shaped Tycon Towers that created Edge City's first skyline and captured Garreau's irreverent eye.

But while the economic and imperial root of the developments (the pro-gram, or base, if you will) continued across both contexts, it was important that the style (or superstructure) was actively different.[211] Diba's nostalgic townhouses at Monticello in Tysons and modernist Iranian buildings in Tehran were thus also distinct markers of the power of contextual architec-tural style as a means of severing political-economic connections inherent in building projects formed through the ties of empire. Such aesthetic features rendered structural and ideological connections difficult to see in the sub-urban built environment of the covert capital. They upheld frozen concep-tions of space by their very attentiveness to place. Some transnational Edge City spaces used for politics—transitional landscapes like the Hilton and the Holiday Inn and the warehouses at Ilopango and Dulles—were relentlessly the same in various locations. Others, like the more permanent monuments and housing complexes, were intentionally different, visually breaking inher-ent connections. But the program that linked them all had important simi-larities. Edge City in Northern Virginia had a pronounced stylistic visibility that both linked and severed the broader connections of Iran-Contra, cap-turing the flexible, staccato qualities of imperial built space as symbol, fetish, and strategy, as well as the gap between program and style as a useful covert technique, going back to the radical divide between structure and surface at the tree-lined CIA headquarters at Langley.

Proceeds from Pahlavi's real estate investment, meanwhile, went into the network of accounts that funded his covert work in Northern Virginia. Awaiting his home's completion in 1986, Pahlavi moved, in one of those miraculous turns of history, to a house on Saigon Road. This meant that in the mid-1980s, both Reza Cyrus Pahlavi and Oliver North were living in subdivisions originally imagined by Mark Merrell, who had helped launch the U.S. imperial project in Vietnam in 1950.[212] Pahlavi directed his money manager and chief advisor, Ahmad Ansari, also his close friend and "father figure," to buy the land and design the house in Great Falls, at McLean's edge, in August 1985. A former Pahlavi court regular, family relation, and American-educated economics professor from the National University, Ansari took care of Pahlavi and many of his affairs. Ansari also had building experience as a contractor in Iran in the later seventies who constructed schools for the government.[213]

For what would become Pahlavi's palace in exile, Ansari hired a member of a network of local Iranian architects in Northern Virginia, the same speculative neo-colonial housing developer who built Monticello, who, in turn, hired another local Iranian architect. They designed for the young shah, who had been crowned on his twentieth birthday in 1980 at a small ceremony in Cairo, an elaborate McMansion on Bellview Road, one of the oldest winding streets in greater McLean. They sited the house on a large tract at the end of a more conventional development. Guarded by a gate and wall-like landscaping that warded off visitors, a looped private drive gave way to a bat-shaped, sprawling stone frame house with twelve rooms, seven bedrooms, six baths, two half baths, and four fireplaces. They used an old farmhouse as servant and guardhouse. Behind the main house swept a deck, pool, and lower deck. A pathway and a gazebo led to a large tennis and basketball court.[214]

Pahlavi moved in with Ansari and a retinue of royalist exiles. His guard and protector since childhood, Colonel Ahmad Oveissi, was the brother of Tehran's martial law general Gholam Ali Oveissi, known as the "butcher of Tehran," after his policing of the city during riots against the Shah in 1963 and after his soldiers fired on a crowd of protesters during the revolution. Ali Heidar Shahbazi was a family friend and longtime bodyguard who accompanied the Shah on his flight from Tehran in 1979 and had traveled with him on his peripatetic quest before the Shah died in Egypt. Massoud Moaven was Pahlavi's best friend. Another frequent guest was Ansari's "right-hand man" and former student Morteza Shirzadi, a local Northern Virginia tennis coach with a business oriented to suburban housewives and a steady job at Ansari's mother's restaurant in a local health club.[215]

Pahlavi was barely twenty-six when he moved to U.S. imperial Tehran in exile and tried to rebuild the Shah's networks of power from the Northern Virginia suburbs. The group of royals rode horses, raced cars, smoked Cuban cigars, shopped at Tysons department stores, and took junkets to resorts in Florida and Alaska. He and his friends set up a disco and entertainment center in their basement, bought tens of thousands of dollars in videos, and drove new Porsches, Jeeps, and Mercedeses, some bought at the well-known car dealerships lining Route 7 at Tysons. They were kids too—they built model airplanes together, Pahlavi's favorite hobby. Part of the elaborate interiority of the design of the Bellview Road mansion derived, as Pahlavi's advisor once explained, from his upbringing. Raised in the Pahlavi court and in

U.S. imperial Tehran to leave the house only when necessary, he had to build his fun at home.

But Pahlavi also symbolically enacted Northern Virginia's imperial centrality through the stentorian architecture of his Great Falls house. It became a political site, as had so many suburban houses in Northern Virginia in other eras. Pahlavi and Ansari paid off the emotional and financial debts of the regime, receiving people and ruling on cases and complaints of DC-area exiles as if at court. The idea of returning to the throne was in these years for Pahlavi, in Ansari's words, "his existence." In working to make it happen, they attempted, in a sense, to resurrect the more martial politics that the Shah himself would never enact in his last days in Iran, so as to "take a fresh political initiative in order to secure his son's heritage." They recruited political activists, covert agents, and counterinsurgents from across the globe, some living in Northern Virginia, to wage political war inside and outside of Iran to help him retake the throne.[216]

Around the time Pahlavi moved in, nearby suburbs also housed, or had recently housed, two other key political figures from his father's reign. The first was Jehan Sadat, wife of the Egyptian president, the Pahlavi family's dear friend who insisted that they find shelter in Egypt when no other country would have them. Sadat wrote her memoir, *A Woman of Egypt*, as a woman of Great Falls, in a two-bedroom house near the Shah's abode. Protected by one of her husband's military aides from Egypt, she moved into the house after learning a crucial suburban American lesson: "that the mortgage payments were almost the same as paying rent." Some things in Great Falls were the same: she took calls from Farah Diba, Pahlavi's mother. She certainly knew that the Crown Prince, whom Anwar Sadat called his "son" at the Shah's funeral in Egypt, had moved so close to her home. She visited her friend Nancy Reagan at the White House and attended seminars in DC with Jeane Kirkpatrick, Betty Ford, Rosalynn Carter, and Barbara Bush. She listened to cassettes of the famous singer Um Kalthum in her car and reflected on a photograph of her husband observing an air show in Cairo the day he was assassinated, which hung on her wall. Other things in Great Falls were different. She watched *The MacNeil-Lehrer Newshour* and went to her "wonderful" neighbors' houses for Thanksgiving. Appreciating suburban mores, she borrowed their cribs, playpens, and bicycles when her grandchildren came to visit and took her family on trips to Virginia's King's Dominion theme park. Northern Virginia brought not only a retreat but a new form of self-presentation. "I am proud of my independence and my self-reliance," she

In October 1981, Jehan Sadat and Reza Pahlavi walked together at Egyptian president Anwar Sadat's funeral in Cairo. By decade's end, both lived in Great Falls. Old friends did not merely converge triumphantly in Northern Virginia. The most complete tragedies and betrayals also spurred imperial migrations after the United States had failed to support its oldest friends. Associated Press.

explained. "I take my exercise now mowing my lawn in the summer and, during this past winter, shoveling too much snow."[217]

Another familiar figure from Pahlavi Iran in Northern Virginia had a quite different experience. Mustafa Barzani had led the Kurdish guerrilla war in Iraq for the Shah and the Nixon administration until they pulled his funding in 1975. After the campaign ended, many Kurds fled to Iran, including Barzani's family. But Barzani, who once claimed to want to make Kurdistan the fifty-first U.S. state, settled in McLean. Although living on a stipend from the CIA, he had a more difficult adjustment than Sadat, becoming, in the words of one CIA friend, "a broken man" in his suburban house, dying just after the Shah was driven from Iran. But around the time the Shah's son moved to McLean, Barzani's favorite chair remained in the Dulles Corridor with his photograph on the wall as a shrine at the local Kurdish Democratic Party headquarters, which was run by Fairfax businessmen. His memory was also kept alive in fury by Edge City security officers like Mustafa Al-Karadaghi, once head of the Kurdish Southern Military Forces, who, even long after Barzani's demise, deeply resented his close relationship with the Shah.[218]

The covert capital could thus be a staging area for geopolitical action and a maudlin site of testimony to its afterlife. But as these stories highlight, intimate ties with the United States abroad did not always prefigure the experience of repatriates in the covert capital. To gauge what these co-constituted experiences and U.S. imperial lives meant in practice, one needs to follow imperial ties and spatial relationships back in time but also far into their long suburban afterlives. Such relationships could foster more U.S. imperial action through continued intimate experiences and organizing, or they could transform into the cartographies of shame and grief that came with moving to the place where the death of one's most deeply held political projects, beliefs, or country itself were orchestrated, or they could point to as-yet-under-researched combinations of these emotions, political associations, and complex futures.

AN ECONOMIC EMPIRE

In 1989, soon after the Edge City boom, Pahlavi's carefully guarded presence in the suburb of Great Falls broke into the public eye. A financial dispute and falling out with his trusted advisor Ansari landed the two in Fairfax County court. Pahlavi claimed Ansari had stolen his inheritance, and, adjudicating this claim, the pair dragged their intimate relations, accounts, and activities through years of astoundingly public testimony.

Journalists who covered the case and its adjuncts in brief flares interpreted Pahlavi's presence in Great Falls as an absurd paradox—the Peacock Throne meeting *Eight Is Enough*. The details of Pahlavi and his friends' spending, social life, consumer habits, and residential luxury became a marker for an Orientalized spectacle of excess and consumption supposedly in conflict with the suburban landscape, a case fraught with grander, almost racial issues of loyalty and betrayal cast as clashing with Northern Virginia's suburban banality. The *Washington Post* described one of Pahlavi's disputes as an event where "U.S. Law Meets Persian Culture," as though this presented a fundamental paradox.[219]

But Pahlavi did not import an Orientalized royalist culture of excess into Great Falls. Rather, he and his friends lived the life of Northern Virginia's Reagan-era Edge City consumer playground, engorged with lobbying and defense dollars, boom contracting, and an extractive economy guided by the trope of privatization. Acquired amid the U.S. imperial consumer and development patterns of 1970s Tehran, Pahlavi and his friends' habits perfectly aligned with the 1980s covert capital, where teardowns, McMansions, and large purchases were common.

Pahlavi's financing structure was itself a kind of "Enterprise," designed—like the Iran-Contra campaign—in Edge City's convoluted form, like a SCIF, for "deniability" and "security." At the beginning, this fusion of the economic and the political was the point, as Ansari had initially explained to the young Shah: "If you cannot have an empire politically, I will give you an economic empire." It ended with the taking of a chunk of Pahlavi's fortune. The complex structure of his finances had provided security but also the basis for Pahlavi's confusion and falling out with Ansari. Like many of their Edge City neighbors, one of their largest losses came from reckless commodity futures investments in the stock market frauds and crises of 1987. They staged their politics from the McMansion and the opaque-windowed Edge City hotels in Rosslyn and elsewhere in the surrounding landscape, the same hotels where agents plotted the CIA's Central America war.[220]

The contents of the sixteen boxes of the county court case where Pahlavi and Ansari pored over their political and social life together made clear the degree to which things that happened in Northern Virginia mattered deeply, even mattered most, in landscapes far removed in proximity. At one point, Ansari appeared on Iranian television, wrote a book in Farsi about the case, and courted money from Khomeini's Islamic Republic to pay his lawyers. This launched an argument over sealing public records, as Ansari, in Pahlavi's view, was using the case at the county court in Northern Virginia to advocate a global exposure of Pahlavi finances, politics, and irresponsibility, discrediting the young king's ability to reign before an international audience of exiles. Ansari's retort was that Pahlavi himself was discrediting and destroying Ansari with his own transnational propaganda campaign, unfairly broadcasting his malfeasance to the same group.[221] Both agreed that their presence and the influential space of these suburbs could reach out to an Iranian polity, in and outside Iran, yet one keenly attuned to Northern Virginia events. Both also used the notion that financial matters should be kept private as a means of covering up and protecting political power. In these approaches, they were deeply embedded denizens of Iran-Contra-era Northern Virginia. They used these suburbs to claim a scope far beyond their borders. They used the era's commonsense assertion that financial matters were a direct outgrowth and reflection of intimate human life, necessitating absolute privacy, to recast the political as the personal and the covert.

Late in the trial, Pahlavi and Ansari sorted over their exact pay stubs from

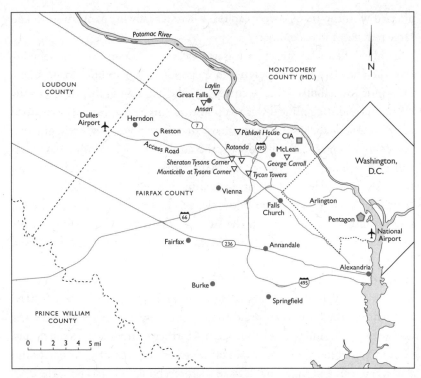

U.S. imperial Tehran in exile. Dollars and styles of development flowed back and forth between Tehran and Northern Virginia, defining both places.

the preceding half a decade. In doing so, they revealed the depth to which their everyday suburban social lives in Edge City had been imbricated with political work from the start, not only in buying oil companies and investing in currency futures and suburban real estate but in using payoffs from the suburban economy to pin allies to themselves. Ansari bought his own house farther into Great Falls on Thunderhill Court, the Addicott Hills subdivision's Williamsburg model, built in 1982, overlooking a pastoral field. He helped friends acquire a plot at the Monticello subdivision. He loaned money to his friend Shirzadi for a condo, and Shirzadi soon moved into the Rotonda at Tysons Corner. Soon others in the group, Ahmad Oveissi and Moaven, also moved into the Rotonda, which had one of the region's most thriving Iranian exile presences.[222]

Concepts of *loyalty* and *fidelity*—filtered through a suburban cultural emphasis on intimacy, selfhood, identity, friendship, and the nuclear family circle—became the language by which they processed their exile network.

Ansari's malfeasance also fit snugly with a larger rhetoric being propagated internationally by the Pahlavi family as to why Iran had been lost to the revolution. To them, the reason was simple. For over thirty years, the Pahlavi family had trusted the United States. As late as New Year's Eve 1977, Jimmy Carter had gone to Tehran and proclaimed, "We have no other nation on Earth who is closer to us in planning for our mutual military security." The United States abandoned the Shah a year later. In Pahlavi family narratives, the karmic fallout from this violation of loyalty tumbled down the Carter administration.[223] It provided the emotional core to the general right-wing narrative of the Vietnam syndrome failure of American will in the late 1970s. It explained why in the Reagan years, as a response to Carter, a reinvigorated, almost frantic emphasis on loyalty, friendship, and duty provided a cultural avenue and mandate for a revived covert action capability emanating from Northern Virginia, one that aimed both to retake Iran and fulfill the country's debts, spurned after Vietnam, and to filter those same politics outward again to Central America, Grenada, and Afghanistan. Avid friendships in the covert capital could reincarnate broken fidelity and love as aggression and revenge. The target might be Iran, as Pahlavi wished, or become unfixed to float and find new targets in other parts of the world. Relations in the covert capital could redeem the failings of the overt capital. The hyphen in Iran-Contra, in this narrative, was a fatal historical arrow, looking for its destination.

Fulfilling such debts had been Pahlavi and Ansari's project. Ansari's betrayal was cast as doubly despicable by its association with America's betrayal of Pahlavi Iran. This was made worse by Ansari's own association with Khomeini Iran, a microcosm of the United States' similar treacherous association with Khomeini Iran during the Iran-Contra Affair. The case also seemed to repeat the tragic death of the Shah himself, in the form of the treatment borne by the heir whom one reporter called the "Boy Who Lost Everything."[224] Yet for the very reason that it focused so heavily on figures of debt, loyalty, sympathy, and fidelity—although Pahlavi was finally vindicated—the case also marked a key transition in his own royalist politics, a shift away from the Edge City politics of the 1980s. He found a new politics of self-presentation, one educated by the Dulles Corridor's own landscape of denial.

In Tehran, Pahlavi grew up under the shadow of one America. He could stroll down Eisenhower Boulevard, Roosevelt Street, or Point IV Street. While his mother, Farah, talked of Disneyland and his father's favorite U.S.

stop was colonial Williamsburg, Pahlavi's more frequent experience of the country was flying one of his Beechcraft F33C Bonanzas or F-5 fighter planes in his U.S.-style flight uniform or meeting America's uniformed warriors or covert elites in the casual spaces of the palace to a soundtrack of American rock and disco, which he brought out at even the most formal functions.[225] In Great Falls, he initially followed a similar American pattern of conspicuous consumption and martial threat. Yet the same behavior sounded a note of discord. The mistake was this: covert elites had always used the second half, the domestic half, of the co-created landscape differently. It was a space of retreat, of planning, of laundering violence, where the emotional rhetoric of family and privacy and the visual rhetoric of cul-de-sacs and lawns dissolved the political-imperial in the suburbs' most salient postwar American trope. Pahlavi learned this lesson. Formerly a young prince in his royal trappings and the leader of mass rallies whipping up his indignant people, he found another political mode—the "father of two" in the living room.[226]

By the time Pahlavi published his book in English in 2002, *Winds of Change*, he had a new language to wage political war. In 1980, at twenty, he desired to fly his jet to Iran and fight. By 2002, at forty-two, he spoke of change, choice, and civil rights. Observers referred to him as a "nice neighbor" and a "full-fledged suburban American man." He and his wife were "a modern young American couple—starting at home in the kitchen," where Pahlavi did the cooking. Pahlavi's language was no longer tied to raucous parties, real estate, and covert action but to the "hour of choice" when people had to grasp hold of democracy and freedom. The *New Republic* called his a "Successor Story," the *New Yorker* publicly granted him the title of "young shah."[227] It was a far cry from the "Boy Who Lost Everything" and a testament to the powerful mix of cultural factors generated by U.S. imperial agents and allies in the home front the CIA built after World War II—the ways suburban domesticity and an intense localness covered the imperial in Northern Virginia explicitly *as* a complex means of politics.

The congressional investigations of the CIA in the 1970s and the excesses of Iran-Contra had challenged this view of the "bedroom suburbs" of Northern Virginia as being merely a space of retreat. The concept of *Edge City* did the same with its proud declaration that the suburbs were not just for sleeping anymore. The Pahlavi court case displayed in microcosm the ways Edge City as a rubric for covert action both reinvigorated and changed older ways the covert capital home front as suburb could be deployed—it opened and shifted covert horizons. At the same time, it showed how the

Iran in Iran-Contra was much more than a few revolutionaries who wrote the United States a check to buy guns. The Iran in Iran-Contra was thirty-five years of imperial family relations; it was the foundation of the covert capital economy; it was the wound and spur that mobilized covert action in the 1980s; it was the martial refugees planning attacks back in Iran; and it was the group of Iranians who flew to the Tysons Corner Sheraton to buy missiles from covert activists in the Reagan administration representing the U.S. government. But Pahlavi's shift and the renewability of Northern Virginia's suburban mystique after such a moment also spoke to the deep resources that the suburbs provided for covert elites trickling down through the decades.

EDGE CITY IMPERIAL HOMECOMINGS IN THE ERA OF IRAN-CONTRA

The physical space of the covert capital's home front suburbs in Northern Virginia in the Iran-Contra era revealed an overlapping human history of U.S. empire decidedly at odds with the ways U.S. foreign policy is conceived as history and practice, with the idea of the suburbs as an exaggeratedly national, domestic space, and even with some iterations of racial formations within the U.S. national context.

Upon taking office, Reagan rolled out his theatrical Cold War rhetoric against the Soviet Union, which he called "the very heart of the darkness."[228] He spoke of Manichean global struggle and home front vigilance, a hermetic nation that defended its interests on a world stage but whose own borders never trembled. By 1985, the covert capital got something different: the Year of the Spy. That year, FBI agents arrested eleven Americans in the CIA, NSA, navy, and private sector, all for spying against the United States, mostly for the Soviet Union—three in a single week.[229] Rather than bravely exposing the spies, Reagan's monologues seemed to have conjured them. The actor ratcheted up the Cold War plot. The protagonists followed. In the Dulles Corridor, two agents, Aldrich Ames and Robert Hanssen, rather than being deterred by the Year of the Spy arrests and trials, began spying while taking in news of them that year, convinced they could do better.[230]

The Year of the Spy has all but disappeared from Cold War memory, but it revealed a core feature of Reagan's policy. As Joel Garreau evoked in his renderings of Edge City at the same time, Reagan might have had high diplomatic tones of good and evil. But his wider capital was a place that could always burst forth anew and remake itself in the realm of what historian Daniel Rodgers calls "free, spontaneous action."[231] If the overt capital was the space for Reagan's nostalgic invocations of good and evil, the covert capital of the eighties hosted these free, spontaneous market actors, unbounded by and antithetical to the state, even as they represented the state. Double agents in Northern Virginia might have been treasonous per se, but they were also following this core double logic in a land where work for a good salary and making that bonus meant more than the petty concerns of national loyalty or democratic process.

Edge City was their playground too. The handler of many American spies for the Soviet Union, Victor Cherkashin, shopped at the Tysons Corner mall with his wife and stayed at these same Tysons Corner hotels as he ran spies, such as Ames and Hanssen. Russians spying for the United States used the same landscape. Valery Martynov, a KGB lieutenant colonel, met his CIA and FBI handlers at "various safe houses for their fifty-odd meetings, often in the Virginia suburb of Crystal City." Colonel Ryszard Kuklinski, the CIA's spy inside the communist government of Poland in the seventies, soon frequented the new hotel suites at the Reston Town Center. The female escort recruited from a waitressing job at the Tysons Corner Ramada hotel lounge to accompany one new Soviet diplomat defector through his early days in Edge City also helped him decorate his suburban safe house after a shopping spree at the Tysons mall. For many Soviets, the area around Tysons served as their introduction to the fruits and freedoms of the American landscape.

For both supposedly polarized sides in the Cold War, and the spies working for them, Edge City in Northern Virginia was their mutual reward and nurturing environment, where profits, loyalty, disloyalty, and secrecy intertwined in knotted ways.[232] The presence of these histories also bore out a crucial feature of the intimacy between the Soviet-U.S. conflict of the 1980s and the so-called proxy wars and covert action of the period. The irrigation of money into Star Wars projects in Northern Virginia and covert warfare in Central America and Afghanistan gutted efforts to defend the CIA and other agencies against spying. Reagan's vision privileged martial covert action over the drab counterintelligence work that might have found the spies sooner. Iran-Contra, in this sense, helped produce the Year of the Spy.[233] The excess and upper-class status that inflected back into CIA lives from the profits of Edge City then provided cover for the double agents' own ill-gotten gains.[234]

Covert warfare, in turn, generated other local histories. The CIA's covert war in Afghanistan pushed the covert war in Central America into the public-private structures of Edge City, helping to revivify the suburban landscape. But the Afghanistan war fostered Iran-Contra in another way as well, providing a point of solidarity in contacts between U.S. National Security Council men and Iran's Islamic Republic—one of their central grounds for agreement. The covert war in Afghanistan then transpired again through everyday life in the Northern Virginia suburbs. Gust Avrakotos—who ran the CIA's Afghanistan campaign and later had a character created in his image in its heroic fictionalization, *Charlie Wilson's War*—bought a McLean townhouse down the street from one of Edward Lansdale's colleagues in the Saigon Military Mission. Migrants from Afghanistan fled to Northern Virginia in this same period, some with close ties to and funding from Americans at the U.S. embassy in Kabul. For local reporters, such migrants carried into the suburbs subjectivities within which "the reality of daily destruction of Afghan lives and property in Kabul and in Afghan villages is more vivid than the sunny fall days of Virginia."[235] Imported allies (unwanted refugees according to one national script)—including Pahlavi, Soviet defectors, those from Afghanistan, and so many others—then allowed the covert capital to accrete centrality, power, and access to the intimate affairs of other countries via the moral authority of these blood relations, while at the very same time reaffirming the suburban landscape as a destination of freedom and a site of "sunny fall days," which was fundamentally *other* to those disturbed and violated U.S. imperial sites created with its help.

During this same period, organizer Howard Phillips built the sustaining institutions of the new right, including the Conservative Caucus and the Moral Majority, both of which had headquarters neighboring Tysons Corner in Vienna. Through direct mailings flickering to the world, Phillips popularized the era's Vietnam syndrome anti-liberal mystique. Appearing on lists of people helping Oliver North influence a congressional contra-aid vote, Phillips then referred during the Iran-Contra hearings to North himself as "the most marketable political commodity . . . in the whole United States."[236] North took the idea to heart. He rented a compound in Sterling, amid sprawl from the new Reston, and opened his lobbying firm, the Freedom Alliance. He also started a bulletproof vest company with fellow Iran-Contra operator Joseph Fernandez, the former CIA station chief in Costa Rica, and Bouakeo Bounkong, a refugee from what North called his "long-ago war in Southeast Asia." This multiethnic trio hired many Vietnamese refugees living in the surrounding landscape, and North advocated for the post-racial consciousness of employees who, in his words, "did not want to be hyphenated . . . just wanted to be Americans," even as his work elsewhere exaggerated violence with explicitly racial overtones. North later launched a Republican senate campaign in Virginia, supported by some old friends and opposed by others, such as former contra spokesman Rogelio Pardo-Maurer, who had become an Arlington resident and was soon to be a major Pentagon official. He formed a group called Contras for Miller, in support of one of North's opponents.[237]

The racial orderings of people in U.S. empire abroad continually chased those people into their reformed racial positioning inside the U.S. nation-state.[238] There are many ways one might use these proximities to reflect on the histories of race and empire that transpire through Iran-Contra and its pairing of Iran and Central America in a set of transnational ties to Northern Virginia. For example, one might consider how the construction proletariat that U.S. imperial economies had created around Tehran, a class formation that helped lead to the Iranian revolution in the first place, was, in a sense, recreated in Northern Virginia in this period, as Central American laborers whose land was destroyed in their home countries were welcomed provisionally to the landscape, albeit in a harried capacity, to serve the same function.

Imperial repatriations in the Iran-Contra period also paired Iranians and Central Americans locally as migrants entering the same landscape. While some Central American generals had been welcomed with fine amenities in luxury hotels and private homes during the contra war, a majority of Salvadorans arrived without status or deep ties with Americans. Despite the fact that they worked at the vital foundations of the suburban economy, they were greeted with public headlines such as "Illegal Entry" and "8 Seized in Stakeout of Aliens." Many Iranians, on the other hand, while facing discrimination and Orientalist stereotypes, arrived via a frequent set of intimate relationships with covert capital elites. To military advisors such as General Ellis Williamson, Iranians were not "illegal entrants" at all, but "culturally refined" people—people, in Williamson's words, "we would be just happy to have . . . in our homes and in our churches and our communities." Some Americans helped Iranian friends explicitly because they were men "of higher stature" and thereby supposedly had a harder time adjusting to a new and at times reduced status in migrant Northern Virginia. In this sense, Central American migrants provided a welcome counterpoint, as did African American residents of DC, giving the "higher status" category its local coherence. At the same time, there was a required adjustment for Iranian migrants. Other returning covert actors who defined Iran-Contra could more easily and invisibly slip into the white ethnicities that eased local citizenship and belonging.

Such white ethnicities were, in fact, reinforced and obscured by these very same racial comparisons and by the covert capital's larger strategizing and visualizing of race. Bill Casey himself pushed at this time for racially "diversifying" the CIA's clandestine service, because, in the words of his deputy Robert Gates, he "wanted our personnel to match the range of people we deal with. He wanted people who could move in and out of Tehran, Tripoli, Kinshasa, or Tegucigalpa who didn't look like they'd just stepped out of Harvard," despite the fact that people from these places who arrived as refugees in Northern Virginia in this period had no doubt gone to Harvard or to similar institutions. Ideas about race and status thus took form not just in binary encounters between white imperialists and colonized people of color but through complex, comparative overlays in U.S. imperial orders abroad and at home and in the context of often quite "diverse" communities of U.S. imperial agents from and in Northern Virginia itself.[239]

There were important gendered components of these imperial racializations as well, evident in both literary representations and public discourse. A woman from the isthmus doing domestic work in local suburban houses might be cast in one popular political thriller as "a wonderful woman from Central America who loved the children . . . and was fanatical about keeping the house clean, the meals cooked and the clothes laundered." Yet in another novel, a Central American man might be less welcome, wearing his white linen suit, peach shirt, azure tie, and Panama hat, and speaking about politics with "a convincing note of fervor—almost fanaticism—in his voice," his affluent dress appearing comic and subversive rather than designating him as a welcome man "of higher stature."

An Iranian woman such as Saideh Pakravan, daughter of one of the Shah's SAVAK chiefs, could write literary reflections on her father and her picnics as a youth with CIA officers with McLean ties in the privacy of her suburban McLean home. That home could play a role in her fiction as well. In one account, her avatar kept a glass and brass box of dirt from Iran there, defining a new, if haunted and ambivalent, sense of place and belonging. From that home, her later fictions could go on to celebrate freedom-loving women threatened by the Islamic Republic while protesting Iran's electoral fraud during the War on Terror. Pakravan created subtle characters with complex subjectivities, but she did so at a time when such gendered celebrations of heroic, complex women oppressed by religious regimes in the Middle East were a common U.S. political and rhetorical ploy, propagated by many of her neighbors in order to fight the War on Terror, and to create the image of a free, democratic United States in contradistinction to states it wished to cast as oppressive and illegitimate abroad.

Some Iranian men, meanwhile, would never be allowed to establish an American domesticity in the first place. One such group who tried to invest in a group of condominiums at the Fairlington complex in Arlington, which had housed many early CIA and Pentagon workers, created a "furor" among residents who saw them as "outside commercial interests" who "will change the nature of what was supposed to be a community of individual homeowners." In these instances, women appear as more tolerable and domesticated guests in the social sphere of Northern Virginia. Yet the examples, at the very same time, depict the ways that women's status as a safe, domestic presence was circumscribed by tenuous emotional economies, defined by domestic labor and patriarchal family relationships, past and present.[240]

One must not merely read these receptions as self-evident histories of migration that bonded race and class—and occluded gender—along well-worn grains. Edge City Northern Virginia and Iran-Contra as built and lived space beg for these histories of race, gender, empire, and migration to be read in the context of a more expansive history. The covert capital racialized and triangulated Iran, El Salvador, and Northern Virginia during the practice of U.S. empire in those places. Imperial repatriates and other migrants in Northern Virginia were recast and racialized again as they arrived in and defined the covert capital's domestic built environment, its laboring and service economy, and its class-stratified, immigrant relations of local belonging and civic life. What one might find in following these inquiries is a longer history of U.S. racial formations that stretches back to the imperial context as well as a set of breaks, innovations in racism, and recodings that help illuminate the genealogies for the staged differences of life in the U.S. imperial home front of Northern Virginia—and U.S. domestic space more generally—in a way that narrow studies of foreign policies directed at regionally bounded areas of the world or studies of national ethnic formations might elide.[241]

What one might also find in the combination of these alienated immigrant experiences of race and place, often bearing a troubled relationship to common scripts of immigrant incorporation and domestic participation, is the history of a U.S. imperial pluralism at work, a revelation of how the utility of national myths of accessibility, diversity, and dynamism in imperial warfare and incursion abroad combined with experiences in an imperial home front supposedly defined by an American Dream, but where, in David Pedersen's words, citizenship was "always a potential category."[242] The comparative racializations and imperial actions visible in and planned from the Dulles Corridor present a challenge to theorize these overlapping spatial and racial traces of empire and migration, not to mention a challenge for suburban and urban studies, which often lack a theory of place to even account for these presences.

If the spaces of Northern Virginia bundle these events, transcribing imperial histories for a new kind of critical scholarship about race, place, empire, and nationalism, they also encourage a particular way of thinking about obscure political scandal, not as another muckraking exposé in the land of the next exposé (near, inevitably, the Rosslyn parking garage where Bob Woodward first met Deep Throat),[243] or even as part of the culture that protects U.S. empire by digesting each new scandal in the stomach acid churned up from the last. They recast scandal instead as a set of geographic directions and orientations for reading the world, the cipher to a cognitive map of a U.S. empire that is blurred and normalized at the very same time that the uncovering of a scandal "reveals the facts" about recondite U.S. imperial operations.[244]

THE ALIEN SCANDAL

The function of scandal as revelation is curious. In one of the most important Deep Throat–inspired covert capital cultural texts, the popular television show *The X-Files* (which has at least sixty-nine episodes featuring major Northern Virginia content), a group of FBI agents pursues scandals, conspiracies, and oddities as merely truths-not-yet-known. This isn't the Cold War. They are clearly investigating a wider planetary conspiracy, a heretofore-invisible system. The U.S. government is involved. The more they chase the truth "out there," the more they find that an "inside" thing is what's threatening them—a secret government trained by U.S. empire (not to mention their own bodies and biographies). Any truth they find bears out most intently in the negative, in the lack of information characters have to explain it. This lack is encapsulated in protagonist Fox Mulder himself, the agent so near governmental power, who lives on Hegal Place in Alexandria right near the Pentagon, yet who can barely cognitively map a U.S. global governance that has sailed off from knowable U.S. territory. In this, *The X-Files* provides an indelible emotional map of U.S. imperial Northern Virginia as often lived domestically, particularly for an agent of the mere *Federal* Bureau of Investigation.[245]

Yet despite all the investigation, what begins as a kind of metonym for U.S. empire and planetary conspiracy turns out to be more straightforward. The United States is being colonized yet again, as in so many covert capital texts before. Aliens have invaded. The government was not an imperial agent but a collaborator. The U.S. secret government is managing colonization on behalf of the aliens. It is already transpiring in the form of the show's number one horror: the "hybridization" of aliens and humans in the co-constituted everyday landscape of the DC metropolitan area. Despite all the evidence of a threat ingrained in the U.S. government and its practices and all the evidence that it has hybridized the capital landscape, the show's characters—and viewers—are encouraged to experience this revelation of a hidden global project, a violent global conspiracy, as a fear of "aliens."

They're not alone. Since the 1980s, a variety of novels arising with the Edge City landscape have portrayed Northern Virginia as a place perpetually under siege by alien interlopers. Characters appearing in the Northern Virginia suburbs to disturb and threaten white "locals" include Latinos (Roberto Norentez, Maria Alvarez, Nestor Garcia, Rosa Jiminez), Asians (India, Sam Foster, the "distinctive Slavic" stranger), Arabs (Adnan al-Rimi, Muhammad al-Zawahiri) and an African American (Freddy Tillum).[246] At the same time, as modeled by *The X-Files*, other local novelists have marveled at the security and national security pageantry of Edge City, where characters ferry between the SCIFs, mirrored facades, and biometric security environments of defense contractors such as SecurTech and Triton Global at Tysons Corner and their home McMansions guarded by "highly sophisticated" defense packages.[247] In some sense, these approaches are two sides of the same coin. The security is the answer to the interloping ethnic presence. What began in *The X-Files* as a portrayal of a governmental security whose only purpose was to hide illegitimate activities from democratic view turns out to be a melancholy and panicked argument for more security. Edge City and America needed security to protect their children. It just wasn't good enough to stop the invasion.

Bonding the need for a violence called security and a desperate protection against invasion, Northern Virginia cultural productions start to have the ring of Oliver North and Elliott Abrams speaking before Congress. Rather than seeing these representations as incidental to Edge City, Northern Virginia, they provide one further crucial instance of how a U.S. imperial project that sowed insecurity abroad and bound together places and people through an elaborate, public-private network of extreme complexity and violence reappeared in home front cultural productions as a simple longing for more security and the framing of the other as an invading threat. Just as with the scandals, so it goes with its expressive arts: the covert capital in its local iteration fetishizes the imperial as the racial.

Conclusion

IN 2006, OBSERVERS NOTICED a new built environment in the suburbs of the covert capital. Investigative journalists, charting the "War on Terror" in the wake of the September 11th attacks, found a militarized landscape in Northern Virginia's "glass-and-steel office boxes . . . distinguishable only to the true connoisseur of suburban blandness." Some focused on the foggily named contractor California Analysis Center Inc. (CACI) in the Edge City of Ballston. Known locally as "Captains and Colonels Inc.," the company, which arrived in the Dulles Corridor in 1972, came into focus for its work at Iraq's Abu Ghraib prison after "two internal Army reports concluded that CACI's contract interrogators introduced some of the most brutal practices employed at the prison, including the use of attack dogs." Others looked at the CIA's Bin Laden unit, "Alec Station," headquartered on "the fifth floor of a drab government office building in a suburban shopping mall in Tysons Corner." Still others took on Blackwater U.S.A, which had offices on International Drive and Tysons Boulevard in Westpark, and whose "forces had been at the center of the deadliest mercenary action in Iraq since the start of the occupation . . . a massacre some had dubbed 'Baghdad's Bloody Sunday.'"[1]

Other muckrakers tracked the next-generation CIAs and cutout agencies spreading through the corridor at a startling rate. The National Counterterrorism Center opened in a sleek headquarters called Liberty Crossing across from a subdivision of tightly packed McMansions not far from the CIA in McLean. Off Route 66, the Defense Intelligence Agency set up an office to research underground bunkers, and on Route 28 in Chantilly, the National Reconnaissance Office managed satellites from its collection of "blue-mirrored glass buildings" that were "hidden in plain sight." The ever-expanding CIA opened new offices in McLean, Fairfax, and Herndon, and in Springfield, the National Geospatial-Intelligence Agency was soon building the fourth largest federal headquarters in the Washington region. More distressing to reporters with a concern for public probity and corporate influence on American government were those agencies' permanent live-in help, the contractors helmed by retired military and CIA officers working "from the business parks near Dulles Airport to the huge office and shopping complex at Tysons Corner," the vastly multiplied descendants of those that first defined Edge City in the 1980s.[2]

Just as the first boom in contract work that was tied to a spike in U.S. imperial effort had marked the surge of Tysons' first skyline in 1987, a second contracting boom displayed its own architectural confidence. Companies emblazoned acronyms on their rooftops, casting their neon glow down against the Potomac and the streets below. They named streets after themselves, as the powerful do in their capital. "The champion in this respect," noted Thomas Frank, "is Science Applications International Corporation (SAIC), a contractor-of-all-trades that not only boasts eight separate installations in northern Virginia, but which has its own 'Science Applications Court' in Vienna and 'SAIC Drive' in McLean."[3] Other contractors settled within a new shadow society of "buildings without addresses, offices without floors, acronyms without explanation."[4] Collectively, their aggressive reassertion of the open secret was the perfect metaphor for the Bush administration's own double wielding of power and silence—the public security panic of the elevated alert, the private insecurity panic of the closed door of the torture chamber.

Along with these entities, Northern Virginia, as it always had, also encompassed the latest round of everyday suburban lives defined by imperial action. Agents who ran extraordinary rendition kidnappings on foreign streets returned to twenty-something lifestyles in Arlington apartments and "mock townhouses marooned in a sea of parking," taking up lives that "seemed utterly ordinary."[5] The unit hunting Bin Laden was run by an extraordinary rendition innovator, a man who lived in Falls Church and named his office "Alec Station," after his son, bringing his home life to work with him.[6] Near a grocery store and a strip mall housing a tanning salon and pizza joint "along a landscaped boulevard," senior CIA managers approved drone assassinations, the staple of the new war, monitoring those whose deaths they directed on video screens and computers before stepping into the bright Northern Virginia landscape: "just another day at the office helping to kill terrorists five thousand miles away in Iraq, Afghanistan, Pakistan, Yemen, Somalia, and elsewhere."[7]

The fact that the material imprint of the new War on Terror had come to this suburban landscape generated numerous accomplished investigative exposés. All agreed: a disturbing "Top Secret America," as the *Washington Post* put it in a banner series, had appeared, much of it in Northern Virginia, a "new American security state."[8] These books were striking not only for their revelations but for their familiarity. The Northern Virginia suburbs had generated exposés from their inception. Writers have suggested that shadowy elements in Northern Virginia have been fomenting an alternate seat of U.S. government as far back as 1962, when Fletcher Knebel and Charles Bailey published the novel *Seven Days in May* about a coup emanating from Fort Myer and the Pentagon. In 1964, David Wise and Thomas B. Ross named this world the *Invisible Government* and again chronicled its Northern Virginia footprint. As early as Ross Thomas's 1966 novel *The Cold War Swap*, spy novelists bolstered their credibility by showing familiarity with Fairfax County's covert infrastructure. A decade later, the Northern Virginia suburbs provided actors and conspiratorial sites for Watergate and *All the President's Men*, the chronicle of the latest overt state crisis in the covert capital. A decade after that, a group of geographers also branded Northern Virginia a kind of second capital, an important hitch in a new "gunbelt" that banded the nation.[9]

In a steady gait, reporters and CIA critics from Northern Virginia guided readers "Inside the CIA," "Inside the Company," and into the "Cult of Intelligence."[10] Novelists spirited them to a CIA dive in Falls Church called the Cover-Up and to gray safe houses in new developments where "wrecked" spies lived after being manipulated and exfiltrated from their home countries.[11] Literary figures such as Gore Vidal, Claribel Alegría, Larry McMurtry, William Gibson, Robert Stone, and Don DeLillo had used the geopolitical landscape as setting.[12] Norman Mailer wrote three odes to it, blending tortured epics of spying and national security with minute exegeses of the place where "the wildland swamps had been drained and covered with asphalt, quartered with superhighways, studded with corporate implants . . . and blindsided by molecule-like chains of condominiums."[13] The Northern Virginia suburbs had produced U.S. empire's most well-known practitioners and its most avid critics—former agents and the family relations of former agents—such as Philip Agee, Victor Marchetti, Frank Snepp, Frances FitzGerald, and Sam Adams.[14] Double agents from Aldrich Ames to Robert

Hanssen lived and spied in Northern Virginia.[15] The terrorists responsible for the two major terrorist attacks on the nation's capital had lived in, taken off from, and attacked Northern Virginia instead—one of them perhaps working as a courier to the county planning commission to make ends meet. The landscape even had its own syndicated TV cartoon, *American Dad!*, which featured the new CIA headquarters building in its opening credits.[16]

"Top Secret America" had a fifty-year history. Yet it was always new and secret. This was the covert capital at work, covering over its existence, only to be "discovered" again by the next generation of investigators. Part of the discovery always dwelled on the fact that covert actions and militant activities transpired in an otherwise normal suburban landscape. Descriptions of the ironic gap between the covert and the normal were, in a sense, how authors explained the covert and made it visible. In this, such books reveal something crucial about covert operations, which Allen Dulles theorized fifty years earlier. The covert needed the normal to exist, and the suburbs offered an easily accessible, banal, rhetorical assertion of normal. War and violence took place in "abnormal" landscapes—in urban landscapes, in foreign landscapes—but apparently not in suburban landscapes, not in what one recent account described as a "completely normal community" framed by "a lovely cottage with an English garden."[17]

There was, of course, nothing abnormal about War on Terror–era U.S. empire expanding its shop in the normal suburbs of Northern Virginia. The Northern Virginia suburbs had been designed as a U.S. imperial home front since much of Northern Virginia was still farmland. But it is important to recognize that tropes of the secret, invisible, and covert have appeared as consistent public signs since World War II, through which an American imperial landscape and policy surfaced in a mainstream discourse that dared not speak empire's name. The United States of America could have secret government, corrupt corporate influence, runaway bureaucracy, government abuse, ineffective security, unwarranted influence, and perversions of democracy that needed to be set right. It was less willing to acknowledge a global imperial power, a capital organized to run that power, and a home front filled with people who were tangled in its webs.

The Northern Virginia suburbs had grown up with U.S. empire. But just as the contrast of a normal landscape could be used to make the covert briefly visible, the reassertion of the normal within the suburbs and the common-sense belief that foreign policy and wars happen far from American lives, houses, and bedrooms could also be used to make covert actions invisible again in plain sight. As testament to this, despite voluminous research across fields in the last two decades into transnational spaces, migration, and U.S. empire, attention to Northern Virginia as a space has been minuscule, and as a space of U.S. empire, nonexistent. A cultural landscape that public culture reveals and forgets has not generally been seen by scholarly observers as fit for serious inquiry.

This double function of suburban cover is thus crucial to what I call the landscape of denial of the Northern Virginia suburbs. Built space both reveals and covers over the Dulles Corridor's imperial connections. Suburban built environments reassert a kind of normalcy of cover, but by their very nature, suburbs also seem to sprawl beyond what seems identifiable as a knowable capital or a stable space, never accruing the repetition of associations that make up the cognitive map of a bounded space like a city or a region. Yet by identifying the Dulles Corridor as a permanent, physical space of imperial governance—not as an accidental series of sprawling offices and borderless subdivisions—and by following, through time, varied imperial uses as they layer in the landscape, one can see its formation as the overlooked capital that directed U.S. foreign policy in the age of global decolonization, as well as the age that followed it, when the United States directed its power against the Third World or Global South with the same predictability.

The seamless sedimentation of "War on Terror" infrastructure in these suburbs that hosted so many plots that defined "Cold War" also stresses the continuities between supposedly discrete political-historical epochs such as the Cold War and the War on Terror as they unfold in national policy. The same people and their heirs ran these perpetual wars-with-qualifications. They did so in the very same offices, buildings, and towns. The same agents who first dreamed of sending small action teams to kidnap and attack terrorists built the contra war. Their "low-intensity conflict" was never only a code word for counterinsurgency but for all manner of twilight battles, including counterterrorism, anti-state terror, and a new paramilitary drug war devised by one of the agents who first traveled to Saigon in 1954 with Edward Lansdale. Operators key to the public-private shadow agencies of Northern Virginia in the 1970s recognized the War on Terror as their own: "America's first special operations war." Just as it wasn't ironic that observers noticed a rash of building in the Northern Virginia suburbs four years after Ronald Reagan's Star Wars missile-defense program launch and reinvigoration of covert action with the invasion of Grenada in 1983, it also wasn't ironic for observers to notice a rash of new building in the same suburbs four years after George W. Bush's Homeland Security Act and "Axis of Evil" speech in 2002, which led the country into the war on Iraq and the rendition and torture programs in Europe and the Middle East. Four years was the gestation period for contracting dollars to turn into built form in Northern Virginia.[18]

Spatial relationships in the Dulles Corridor suburbs thus stress the contiguity of U.S. empire within mainstream American culture in a way that is evasive when examining policy alone or when losing these long histories in the brief flares of exposés. It is important to remember that the covert was never the same as the exceptional. The CIA and the Pentagon were not just avatars of a "secret state," but of the U.S. state. Imperial projects did not corrupt American norms. They *produced* them. They formed the American landscape in the suburbs of Northern Virginia, the smallest hours of its wristwatches, the routes it took to work, the ways it created families, the activities that shaped its weekends, its ideas about community and race, the means by which its inhabitants dreamed up their intimacies, futures, tastes, love affairs, senses of boundaries, and their relations to the world around them. Such commonsense approaches to life, in turn, reproduced imperial policy. Facing down the disavowal that defines U.S. empire is not just an opportunity to indulge in the accusatory pleasures of revealing rogue hypocrisy. Describing and countering disavowal is important because of the substantial evidence that exists suggesting that the disavowal of empire actually has the capacity to create more brutal acts of imperial violence at home and abroad—at times stripping U.S. empire, despite its often liberal self-conception, of even the most basic rhetorical gestures of paternalistic responsibility, guilt, debt, and connection. Yet disavowal, denial, and intense investments in a salubrious landscape and life at home were not merely alibis and ploys to allow for secret violence. They were vital cognitive strategies through which U.S. agents processed imperial work, made it tolerable, and often ardently came to believe in their jobs, as state power subcontracted and devolved the ethics of national imperial agency onto the individual psyches of its practitioners.[19]

What one might call the ethics of presence in the face of disavowal, to my lights, points to the final barrier that the many great exposés of Northern Virginia and many great scholarly works about empire need to cross.[20] If America has an empire, a secret state, and a covert capital, it can't just be a concept floating at a safely theoretical or scandalous altitude. U.S. empire must have a material life—someone must be building it; someone must be laboring to run it; someone must be living inside of it; someone must be a citizen of it; someone must be responsible for it. It must take place somewhere—and possibly in places not commonly associated with obvious militarization and imperial warfare.

In a broad sense, *Covert Capital* addresses the study of U.S. foreign policy with the need to study emotional life and manifold gendered racial relationships as an incubator for geopolitics; it addresses the study of U.S. empire with the need to study domestic and material space as a crucial setting for—and trace of—its endurance and propagation; it addresses the study of U.S. migration with the need to study imperial repatriation as a crucial feature of the U.S. polity and its multiethnic social history; and it addresses the study of the U.S. suburban and metropolitan landscape with the need to welcome in histories that transpire far beyond its visible maps as crucial to its historical formation.

But most basically, this book shows that over fifty years, in an era of superpowers and non-state actors, not empires, U.S. imperialism abroad returned to shape the suburbs of Northern Virginia. The landscape was home to the institutions charged with spreading U.S. power throughout the world, and as a result, it came to house the lives of the people who implemented and suffered that power. The private-personal scale and the political-strategic scale cannot be separated from one another in the analysis of U.S. geopolitics. In Rosslyn hotels that could host both CIA lie-detector tests and rich meals over cigars and wine, airports where counterrevolutionaries dined with their lovers before flying off on propaganda missions, or McLean swimming pools where elites formed U.S. foreign policy while treading water, the improvisations of a daily life simultaneously regulated by the grammar of U.S. imperialism transpired as a single, embedded experience.

Political histories of the overt capital at Washington may choose to chronicle the next foreign policy crisis, the next presidential administration, the next diplomatic solution, and then move on. In the Dulles Corridor, international connections, once formed, do not move on. The specific geopolitical targets of U.S. empire might change, but the old ones linger. They take on a lasting physical presence. The shapes taken by that presence are perhaps changeable, but the underlying connections are not. The recognition that transnational connections established by U.S. power bear an enduring physical manifestation in the suburbs of Northern Virginia calls into question any frame that does not acknowledge this enduring presence and its associated ethical debts. The term *empire*, which has the sense of an integrated system of domination and encounter abroad and at home with an extension in both time and space, can account for these presences and debts in a way that scholarly frames like the Cold War, foreign policy, or international relations cannot.

But it is the human maps, the maps of human and social relationships, which have the power on the ground to show the depths and contours of these transnational connections lost on foreign policy's strategic maps. To map the covert capital, this book takes a broad approach. It places geopolitical architecture in space but also shows how people *use* geopolitical spaces in the Dulles Corridor and how U.S. empire enters personal spaces. It tracks the ways human relationships, labor, and movements make the Dulles Corridor contiguous with sites of U.S. imperial exertion abroad and how those sites and Northern Virginia, through U.S. imperial action, are co-constituted as imperial spaces. It places the appearance of the Dulles Corridor in literature, and it uses literature, memoirs, and other cultural texts to map the psychological spaces of the Dulles Corridor, seeing these sources as at times providing a more accurate psychic archive of the Dulles Corridor's cognitive architecture than the most classified government documents. Throughout, I pursue these approaches with the confidence that individual human lives, usually thought of as antithetical to "structures" of power like empire, provide maps that reveal the coordinates of imperial structure. What two-dimensional maps struggle to represent, life narratives do quite effortlessly. In the covert capital, the personal is geopolitical.

In conducting this analysis, this book maintains that a sustained effort to map the presence of a global empire that covers over its existence locally necessitates all these forms of mapping—the map of extension on the surface of the earth; the map of daily use, flights, and pathways at home and abroad; the cultural map filling in mere place names with their geopolitical content and history; and the difficult-to-capture psychological maps that depict how habit and consciousness performed in and drawn from specific spaces shape those spaces' life and physicality. These more hard-to-grasp psychological uses of the covert capital have as much relevance as the more obvious uses that appear in its everyday activity in space. What people *feel* in space and how they deploy those feelings testifies to the nature of the space as much as what people do in it. These psychic maps can also display non-contiguous, stretched-out relations with more accuracy than traditional tools of spatial analysis.

The Dulles Corridor is the covert capital of U.S. empire. It is also a post–World War II suburb. Unlike a built-out metropolitan space with two centuries of dense transnational connections to account for, the Dulles Corridor, in this condensed half century, in this condensed twenty-five-mile-long, eighteen-mile-wide space, not only staged U.S. empire's call and response of human settlement three-dimensionally—it made it uniquely trackable. Yet, as this book also insists, the reason for mapping the Dulles Corridor and its strategies of elision so intently is that U.S. empire's appearance in this local space brings with it the coordinate desire to cover over these very interrelationships. Even in the face of seemingly pronounced imperial traces and stretched-out imperial communities, local residents regularly engage in this aggressive process of covering over to maintain their landscape's visual identity as suburbia.

In 2005, the mayor and governing council of Herndon, Virginia, the town adjacent to Reston, created a day laborers' center for the Central American workers who had been doing landscape and construction work in the town since the 1980s. Near the Edge Cities that hug the Dulles Access Road between Tysons Corner and the airport, just below Oliver North's old house and the houses of many agents who worked to destabilize Central America for a decade, the Herndon Official Workers Center was a unique space of covert capital acknowledgment and reparation. Funded with public money, the center moved day workers from a hectic convenience store parking lot to a permanent green and white tent structure. Refusing to check citizenship papers for access, the center had open toilets, English classes, and safe, regular hiring practices, which included a daily lottery for work. Workers who used the space formed a governing council that set $10 minimum hourly wages and created an emergency fund for laborers injured on jobs—jobs which often consisted of landscaping, creating, and defining the built environment of the suburbs.

Over the next two years, other residents of the town waged a frequently racist war against the labor center, turning it into a focal point for the national campaign against so-called illegal immigration, and drawing in national supporters on the right. Claiming outrage over the center's existence and local events "where Salvadoran flags were displayed," these suburbanites threw out the town's mayor and council for "putting money into people who are illegal," crept out to take menacing photographs of laborers and employers, and aimed to take "the day labor market completely off of Herndon's streets." In part, they succeeded, shutting down the labor center in 2007. Yet they continued their fight, which moved to neighboring Northern Virginia counties. They enforced obscure zoning laws against the places where the laborers went to gather and fought to require new permits, making it difficult for people to rent out single rooms in houses in the entire town. They tore out pay phones the migrants used on the streets, continued to take their photographs, and even worked to confiscate the bicycles that laboring people used to commute to work.

The perceived profile of the town of Herndon, the small suburb in Northern Virginia where "people wanted their town back," was a tool those concerned with covering over and marginalizing this migrant presence used to defeat the center and deny the public acknowledgment and complex local history of this migration.[21] The campaign against the labor center was a two-year effort, an exercise in mapping and erasure. Local whites studied their landscape to identify places in the town where Central American migrants gathered, which corner pay phones they used, the places where they parked their bicycles, the houses that were open to renting them rooms. They then worked methodically to dismantle each site they had identified as a migrant space. The disavowal of the U.S. imperial history that this migration in Northern Virginia represented was not merely a turning away, but a covering over, a work of sustained, committed effort—or at least an equally aggressive act of "not knowing" the local connections to destructive wars in Central America, or even the fact that the town's name derived from the last name of a veteran of an imperial U.S. mapping adventure in Latin America who went down with his ship, the "Central America," in 1857.[22]

Finally, *Covert Capital* attempts to illuminate these erasures. It does so with a novelistic reverence for the ways that clearly described details have their own embedded theoretical implications and come bearing their own kind of knowledge. While wary of the conveniences and elisions of narrative, it has also followed narration as a dynamic tool to reconnect theoretical empire with the lives and landscapes of suburban Northern Virginia. It engages in a mundane act of, not revelation, but description and location, in the hopes that a narrative map has the power to frame different questions about imperial violence and ethics than the ones asked when empire and its broadest sets of connections remain obscure or locked in a familiar dialectic of scandal and forgetting. But one thing is clear: in the early twenty-first century, such narrations depict a map of the covert capital and the U.S. imperial home front defined by a set of overlapping characters and events that confound conventional understandings of American foreign policy, American empire, and American suburbia.

Near the same Vienna offices where Richard Secord and Oliver North once ran their operations, their colleague Dewey Clarridge, the man the contras called *El Hombre Del Puro* as he set up the contra war, returns with his new social group, the "Honourable Company of Freedom Fighters," giving awards to "honor individuals and groups which, since 1945, have fought for freedom, participatory government and against fascism, communism, moral relativity, economic corruption and terrorism in all their forms." Some of the first awards went to the contras and the designers of the nation's first aerial drones.[23] Nearby, journalists unearth Vietnam counterinsurgent and onetime local politician Rufus Phillips, now in his Arlington condo with its side table from 1955 Saigon, and rediscover "why he matters," as he plans his latest advisory trips to Afghanistan. In Afghanistan, Phillips perhaps finds the Afghan planner from Northern Virginia who is adapting the Fairfax County planning code as Kabul's own—aiming to rebuild and redesign the dense city, in the wake of the Pentagon's destructive invasion, as a model of the Pentagon's car-dependent home suburbs.[24]

Mario Bencastro writes of Juana, a Salvadoran exile who tells her life story to an avocado plant in her Northern Virginia apartment, "how she lost her two oldest children in the civil war, one in the national army and one in the guerrilla," and fled from a death threat, only to watch as her "daughter married a gringo" and her "son dropped out of school and went into the U.S. Navy."[25] Iraqi refugees and friends of the covert capital, meanwhile, follow their own contacts and sponsors home to repopulate the Northern Virginia suburbs in the shadow of the latest Iraq war, finding equally mixed receptions from the local and national community.[26]

As dissenting Qaddafi colonel and frequent CIA contact Khalifa Hifter, a decades-long resident of Vienna, returns to Benghazi as an Arab Spring ground fighter in Libya, or, in the words of one commentator, to, perhaps, "hijack the rebellion on behalf of the forces of reaction,"[27] defense minister and former prime minister of Somalia, Mohamed Ali Samantar, a crucial figure in Carter's support of Siad Barre during the supposed covert action hiatus of the seventies, finds himself drawn out of his "tidy split-level home" in Fairfax County, where he had lived for fifteen years, to defend himself against a human rights lawsuit, accused of being "a war criminal, a monster living out his golden years with impunity in a quiet suburban neighborhood."[28]

As the "CIA wives" of yesterday reappear as the "security moms" of today,[29] covert capital connections seep out yet again into the wider world through the grim frequency with which people emerge from the Northern Virginia suburbs' culture of violence and turn an aggression that is usually subliminal domestically and overt abroad disturbingly overt at home—figures such as the shooter at Virginia Tech, the shooter at Fort Hood, Texas, and the DC sniper—the Gulf War army veteran who targeted one of his victims in Fairfax County.[30]

Yet such an effort to map the covert capital in the new century might also extend to Toulouse, France, to the home where John Earl Graves, a psywar specialist who once lived in Reston's liberal modernist community near Lake Anne, died in 2001. An international spokesman for the United States Information Agency (USIA) in the 1960s, Graves spread propaganda for a living, as per the USIA motto, "telling America's story to the world." With his waxed moustache and Whitman beard, the "modern Renaissance man" perfectly encapsulated the contradictions of New Frontier imperial liberalism and its embodiment at early Reston because of where he had been telling this idealistic story—first in the Congo after the assassination of nationalist leader Patrice Lumumba and then in the Mekong Delta in 1967, where he participated in the interrogation of prisoners.[31]

Graves and his wife, Bonnie, soon settled into a larger house in Reston, a three-bedroom on Quorn Lane in Hunters Woods Village.[32] Not long after they moved in, the new USIA sent Graves from his Reston patio house to Iran to tell America's story to the Iranian revolution in 1979. "In our eagerness to promote our short-term policy, security, or business interests, we have sometimes produced long-term hostility and alienation," Graves concluded from his embassy post. "Too many Americans have been too visible too long in too many aspects of life in Iran."[33] In November, students seized the U.S. embassy and their hostages, including Graves.

With the irate melancholy of the onetime true believer, Graves raged against U.S. foreign policy from inside his embassy prison, lecturing his fellow hostages and informing them that Iranian students had a right to be angry and that he hoped the crisis forced the United States to change the way it related to the world. Some fellow captives eventually accused him of "simple anti-Americanism."[34] When Graves and the others were released in January 1981, he and Bonnie remained in Reston for a time but eventually left the covert capital and the United States altogether and moved to France.[35] In this, they followed in the tradition of many such critics from the covert capital who had gone into exile, sometimes abroad, sometimes in isolation in their own suburban homes. Just as the covert capital has its repatriates, perhaps it also has its own diaspora, yet to be studied.

Many varied migrations, many suburban interiors, many stories-so-far can, and no doubt will, fill in this map over time. But *Covert Capital* presents itself with the confidence that public acknowledgment of this unique imperial landscape in Northern Virginia and its human stories-so-far can contribute meaningfully to wider public and scholarly conversation about the place of the United States in the world and the contours of its associated human debts.

ACKNOWLEDGMENTS

Thanks to Asali Solomon, without whom, in innumerable ways, this book would not have been possible. This project benefited from a wise committee in the American Studies program at Yale. Thanks to Michael Denning, without whose spirit of inquiry, conceptual vision, interdisciplinary imagination, and crucial advising, this might not exist. Thanks to Hazel Carby for creating a world in which the lyrical and the political are not strangers. Thanks to Dolores Hayden for her enthusiasm for this idea and for always directing my attention back to physical space. Thanks to Jean-Christophe Agnew for searching critiques and historical readings for which any scholar-writer would long. Deep thanks to Nikhil Singh, who saw the core of this book and its inner shape with a kind of X-ray vision, for his luminous readings and advice that molded this project and guided it into book form. Thanks to Matt Jacobson for counsel and inspiration. Special thanks to Vijay Prashad, Mary Lui, Sandy Zipp, Matt McGarvey, Farid Azfar, Naomi Paik, and Haverford's Faculty Working Group in American Studies, who graced these chapters with their invaluable, challenging readings and critical imaginations. This project would not have been the same without their time and energy, or that of its anonymous readers in various contexts—thanks to you all. Thanks to the many people at Yale who helped and inspired this project and my intellectual life, including Paul Gilroy, Radiclani Clytus, Tucker Foehl, Karilyn Crockett, Annemarie Strassel, Jacob Dlamini, Wai Chee Dimock, Steve Pitti, Josh Guild, Aaron Wong, and countless others. Much thanks to Evans Richardson IV. Thanks to the many people at talks and conferences where this work was presented for their comments, questions, and advice, including Paul Kramer, Andrew Ross, Dianne Harris, Alicia Schmidt Camacho, Arijit Sen, Gary Okihiro, Cotten Seiler, Joseph Wood, Tavia Nyong'o, Jayna

Brown, Thuy Linh Tu, S.S. Sandhu, Harvey Molotch, Mary Louise Pratt, Robert Fishman, Tim Mennel, John Archer, Andrew Wiese, Krystyn Moon, Simeon Man, Jessie Kindig, and many others, including those whose names I didn't catch. Thanks to Scott Saul, Aaron Sachs, Lou Masur, Bethel Saler, Cristina Beltrán, Vicente Rafael, Dagmar Herzog, Ann Fabian, Mia Bay, Jana Lipman, Dave Mulcahey, David Suisman, Clay Cansler, Dan Gilbert, David Hsu, and Linda Kim. Thanks to the members of the Haverford History Department and to so many wonderful colleagues at Haverford, and to NYU's Department of Social and Cultural Analysis, Brown University's Spatial Structures in the Social Sciences initiative, and the Rutgers Center for Race and Ethnicity. Sincere thanks to the Haverford Provost's Office past and present for manifold support. Thanks to the hardworking staff and librarians at Haverford, particularly Interlibrary Loan magician Rob Haley. Special thanks to Laurie Allen and Michael Zarafonetis for the geolocating, map designing, and spatial thinking, and to Julie Coy. Thanks to the many Haverford students whose insights about empire, migration, gender, space, race, and intimacy informed this book. Thanks to Bill Nelson for the map design work, to Nazanin Soroush for the translations, to George Hodak for the fine, lightning-speed readings, and to Sharon Sweeney for the index. Thanks to Niels Hooper, Kim Hogeland, Kate Warne, Sandy Drooker, and Pamela Polk at University of California Press, and to Dave Peattie and Tanya Grove, for all their work navigating this into book form. Thanks to N. Richard Friedman, who helped edit, conceptualize, and imagine this project with me at a kitchen table in its earliest moments. Thanks to Joan Friedman, Akiba Solomon, James Solomon, and Rochelle Solomon. Thanks to an unbelievable number of ingenious librarians, archivists, and government clerks, and thank goodness for physical libraries and archives and their funding. Thanks to Adebayo. Thanks to Mkale.

NOTES

ABBREVIATIONS FOR ARCHIVES

ADP   Allen W. Dulles Papers, Public Policy Papers, Department of Rare Books and Special Collections, Princeton University Library, Princeton, NJ

ASP   Arthur M. Schlesinger Personal Papers, John F. Kennedy Presidential Library, Boston, MA

AIA   The American Institute of Architects Historical Directory of American Architects, Washington, DC

CCP   Clinch Calkins Papers I, Special Collections Research Center, Georgetown University Library, Washington, DC

CRC   Conklin and Rossant Reston Project Collection, Special Collections and Archives, George Mason University, Fairfax, VA

CREST   CIA Records Search Technology, National Archives and Records Administration, College Park, MD

CSFJFK   Papers of John F. Kennedy, Presidential Papers, White House Central Subject Files, John F. Kennedy Presidential Library, Boston, MA

DNSA   Digital National Security Archive, George Washington University, Washington, DC

EDP   Eleanor Lansing Dulles Papers, Special Collections Research Center, Gelman Library, George Washington University, Washington, DC

ELP   Edward Geary Lansdale Papers, 1910–1987, Hoover Institution Archives, Stanford University, Stanford, CA

ESC   Eero Saarinen Collection, Manuscripts and Archives, Yale University Library, New Haven, CT

FCBS   Fairfax County Board of Supervisors Archives, Springfield, VA

FCLR   Fairfax County Land Records, Fairfax County Department of Tax Administration, Fairfax, VA

FCSP	Fairfax County Land Records, Site Plans Office, Herrity Building, Fairfax, VA
FCPL	Virginia Room, Fairfax County Public Library, Fairfax, VA
FCZB	Fairfax County Zoning Building Permit Review Office, Street Files, Herrity Building, Fairfax, VA
FISOHA	Oral History Archive, Foundation for Iranian Studies, Bethesda, MD
JMP	John J. McCloy Papers, Amherst College Library Archives and Special Collections, Amherst, MA
JWP	Papers of Jane G. Wilhelm, Special Collections, University of Virginia Library, Charlottesville, VA
KBP	Katherine Biddle Papers, Special Collections Research Center, Georgetown University Library, Washington, DC
LBJ	Lyndon Baines Johnson Presidential Library, Austin, TX
LKP	Lyman B. Kirkpatrick Papers, Public Policy Papers, Department of Rare Books and Special Collections, Princeton University Library, Princeton, NJ
MAP	Max Abramovitz Architectural Records and Papers Collection, Drawings and Archives, Avery Architectural and Fine Arts Library, Columbia University, New York, NY
NARA	National Archives and Records Administration, College Park, MD
PCA	Planned Community Archives, Special Collections and Archives, George Mason University, Fairfax, VA
RFKP	Papers of Robert F. Kennedy, Attorney General Papers, John F. Kennedy Presidential Library, Boston, MA
WHP	Wallace K. Harrison Architectural Drawings and Papers I, Avery Architectural and Fine Arts Library, Columbia University, New York, NY
WR	Washingtoniana Room, Martin Luther King Jr. Memorial Library, Washington, DC

NEWSPAPERS AND MAGAZINES

CSM	Christian Science Monitor	NYTM	New York Times Magazine
FCT	Fairfax City Times	NVS	Northern Virginia Sun
FH	Fairfax Herald	RT	Reston Times
FJ	Fairfax Journal	WP	Washington Post
NR	New Republic	WPM	Washington Post Magazine
NYT	New York Times	WT	Washington Times

Note: Generally, sources and page numbers appear within these notes according to the sequence in which the information they cite appears in the text.

INTRODUCTION

1. C.B. Rose Jr., *Arlington, County, Virginia: A History* (Arlington: Arlington Historical Society, 1976), 82; George G. Kundahl, *Alexandria Goes to War* (Knoxville: University of Tennessee Press, 2004), 1–18; Office of the County Manager, *A History of the Boundaries of Arlington County, Virginia* (Arlington: Office of the County Manager, 1967); Amos B. Casselman, "The Virginia Portion of the District of Columbia," *Records of the Columbia Historical Society* 12 (Washington, DC: Columbia Historical Society, 1909); Carl Abbott, *Political Terrain: Washington, DC, from Tidewater Town to Global Metropolis* (Chapel Hill: University of North Carolina Press, 1999), 64; J. Valerie Fifer, "Washington, DC: The Political Geography of a Federal Capital," *Journal of American Studies* 15.1 (April 1981), 5–26; Constance McLaughlin Green, *Washington: Village and Capital, 1800–1878* (Princeton: Princeton University Press, 1962), 174; Burt Solomon, *The Washington Century: Three Families and the Shaping of the Nation's Capital* (New York: HarperCollins, 2004), 405.

2. Paul A. Kramer, "Power and Connection: Imperial Histories of the United States in the World," *American Historical Review* 116.5 (December 2011), 1348–91; Shelley Streeby, "Empire," in *Keywords for American Cultural Studies*, eds. Bruce Burgett and Glenn Hendler (New York: New York University Press, 2007), 96; Nikhil Pal Singh, *Black Is a Country: Race and the Unfinished Struggle for Democracy* (Cambridge: Harvard University Press, 2004), 29–30, 36, 137–38, 158–61; Melvyn Leffler, *A Preponderance of Power: National Security, the Truman Administration, and the Cold War* (Stanford: Stanford University Press, 1992), 18–19; Walter LaFeber, "The Tension between Democracy and Capitalism during the American Century," *Diplomatic History* 23.2 (Spring 1999), 284; Amy Kaplan, *The Anarchy of Empire in the Making of U.S. Culture* (Cambridge: Harvard University Press, 2002); Thomas J. McCormick, *America's Half Century: United States Foreign Policy in the Cold War and After* (Baltimore: Johns Hopkins University Press, 1995), 33, 47; Jodi Kim uses the phrase "trade wars" in *Ends of Empire: Asian American Critique and the Cold War* (Minneapolis: University of Minnesota Press, 2010), 24; Marilyn B. Young, "The Age of Global Power," in *Rethinking American History in a Global Age*, ed. Thomas Bender (Berkeley: University of California Press, 2002), 274–94; Gabriel Kolko, *Confronting the Third World: United States Foreign Policy 1945–1980* (New York: Pantheon, 1988); Matthew Frye Jacobson, *Barbarian Virtues: The United States Encounters Foreign Peoples at Home and Abroad, 1876–1917* (New York: Hill and Wang, 2000).

3. For the local history, see Ross and Nan Netherton, *Fairfax County in Virginia: A Pictorial History* (Norfolk: Donning, 1986); Herbert H. Harwood Jr., *Rails to the Blue Ridge: The Washington & Old Dominion Railroad, 1847–1963* (Harwood,

1963); Nan Netherton, "1925–1976," in *Fairfax County, Virginia: A History*, Nan Netherton et al. (Fairfax: Fairfax County Board of Supervisors, 1978).

4. David Wise and Thomas B. Ross, *The Invisible Government* (New York: Random House, 1964), 119–20; Eleanor Lansing Dulles, *American Foreign Policy in the Making* (New York: Harper & Row, 1968), 218–339; Stephen Schlesinger and Stephen Kinzer, *Bitter Fruit: The Untold Story of the American Coup in Guatemala* (New York: Doubleday, 1982); Stephen Kinzer, *All the Shah's Men: An American Coup and the Roots of Middle East Terror* (Hoboken: John Wiley and Sons, 2003); Tim Weiner, *Legacy of Ashes: The History of the CIA* (New York: Doubleday, 2007), 138; Larry Devlin, *Chief of Station, Congo: A Memoir of 1960–1967* (New York: Public Affairs, 2007); Phyllis R. Parker, *Brazil and the Quiet Intervention, 1964* (Austin: University of Texas Press, 1979); Stephen G. Rabe, *U.S. Intervention in British Guiana, A Cold War Story* (Chapel Hill: University of North Carolina Press, 2005); Marilyn B. Young, *The Vietnam Wars 1945–1990* (New York: Harper, 1991); Thomas Borstelmann, *The Cold War and the Color Line: American Race Relations in the Global Arena* (Cambridge: Harvard University Press, 2001), 156–57.

5. Daniel L. Duke, *Education Empire: The Evolution of an Excellent Suburban School System* (Albany: SUNY Press, 2005).

6. Duke, *Education Empire*, xiii, 64; Sheryll Cashin, *The Failures of Integration: How Race and Class Are Undermining the American Dream* (New York: Public Affairs, 2004), 174–75; Thomas Frank, *The Wrecking Crew: How Conservatives Rule* (New York: Metropolitan, 2008), 11.

7. William Appleman Williams, *Empire as a Way of Life* (New York: Oxford University Press, 1980), ix; Rob Nixon, *Slow Violence and the Environmentalism of the Poor* (Cambridge: Harvard University Press, 2011), 97; on suburbs as a national symbolic space, see Elaine Tyler May, *Homeward Bound: American Families in the Cold War Era* (New York: Basic, 1988), 10–17, 162–66; Dolores Hayden, *Redesigning the American Dream: The Future of Housing, Work, and Family Life* (New York: Norton, 1984), 41–42.

8. See, for example, Williams, *Empire*.

9. See Kramer, "Power and Connection"; alternatively, on European imperialism and colonialism see, for example, Catherine Hall, *Civilising Subjects: Metropole and Colony in the English Imagination 1830–1867* (Chicago: University of Chicago Press, 2002); Kristin Ross, *Fast Cars, Clean Bodies: Decolonization and the Reordering of French Culture* (Cambridge: MIT Press, 1995).

10. Alfred Goldberg, *The Pentagon: The First Fifty Years* (Washington: Office of the Secretary of Defense, 1992), 3–93; Steve Vogel, *The Pentagon: A History* (New York: Random House, 2007), 95.

11. James Carroll, *House of War: The Pentagon and the Disastrous Rise of American Power* (New York: Houghton Mifflin, 2006), ix–39.

12. Goldberg, *Pentagon*, 3–93; Carroll, *House of War*, ix–39; Vogel, *The Pentagon: A History*, 201, 273; "Pentagon to Be Ready by Nov. 15," *WP*, July 14, 1942; "World's Largest Switchboard Plugs in Tonight at War Dept.," *WP*, September 12, 1942.

13. Ann Charters, *Jack Kerouac* (San Francisco: Straight Arrow, 1973), 37; Barry Miles, *Jack Kerouac, King of the Beats* (London: Virgin, 1998), 31.

14. Goldberg, *Pentagon*, 52, 22; Vogel, *The Pentagon: A History*, 111, 329.

15. Carroll, *House of War*, 2; Vogel, *The Pentagon: A History*, 29, 335; Goldberg, *Pentagon*, 8, 22; William Greider, *Fortress America: The American Military and the Consequences of Peace* (New York: Public Affairs, 1998).

16. Carroll, *House of War*, 27; Frederick Gutheim's "public city" quote in Abbott, *Political Terrain*, 117.

17. "National Security Act," in Scott C. Monje, *The Central Intelligence Agency: A Documentary History* (Westport: Greenwood, 2008), 3–10.

18. Netherton and Netherton, *Fairfax County*, 105; Vogel, *The Pentagon: A History*, 314; David Brinkley, *Washington Goes to War* (New York: Knopf, 1988), 237–38.

19. David F. Krugler, *This Is Only a Test: How Washington DC Prepared for Nuclear War* (New York: Palgrave MacMillan, 2006), 29–39; Howard Gillette Jr., "A National Workshop for Urban Policy: The Metropolitanization of Washington, 1946–1968," *The Public Historian* 7.1 (Winter 1985), 9.

20. Harwood, *Rails to the Blue Ridge.*

21. Noel Garraux Harrison, *City of Canvas: Camp Russell A. Alger and the Spanish-American War* (Fall Church Historical Commission, 1988); C. David Heymann, *The Georgetown Ladies' Social Club: Power, Passion and Politics in the Nation's Capital* (New York: Atria, 2003); for early resident account: Gore Vidal, *Washington, DC* (Boston: Little, Brown, 1967), 6.

22. McCormick, *America's Half Century*, 8, 12–13.

23. Kaplan, *Anarchy of Empire*, 16; Young, "Age of Global Power," 278; Singh, *Black Is a Country*, 22, 137, 185; Chandan Reddy, *Freedom with Violence: Race, Sexuality, and the US State* (Durham: Duke University Press, 2011); on "nation-based empire," see Kramer, "Power and Connection," 1366-69; Mimi Thi Nguyen, *The Gift of Freedom: War, Debt, and Other Refugee Passages* (Durham: Duke University Press, 2012), 17.

24. Carroll, *House of War*, 429; Dwight Eisenhower, "Farewell Address," in *The Military-Industrial Complex*, ed. Carroll W. Pursell Jr. (New York: Harper & Row, 1972), 204–8; Michael E. Latham, *Modernization as Ideology: American Social Science and "Nation Building" in the Kennedy Era* (Chapel Hill: University of North Carolina Press, 2000), 57, 69; Thomas J. McCormick, *America's Half Century.*

25. Among the influential histories, see Kenneth T. Jackson, *Crabgrass Frontier: The Suburbanization of the United States* (New York: Oxford University Press, 1985); Dolores Hayden, *Building Suburbia: Green Fields and Urban Growth, 1820–2000* (New York: Pantheon, 2003); Lizabeth Cohen, *A Consumers' Republic: The Politics of Mass Consumption in Postwar America* (New York: Knopf, 2003); Thomas J. Sugrue, *The Origins of the Urban Crisis: Race and Inequality in Postwar Detroit* (Princeton: Princeton University Press, 1996); Singh, *Black Is a Country*, 6–7.

26. Washington Center for Metropolitan Studies, *Reston: A Study in Beginnings* (Washington, DC: Center for Metropolitan Studies, September 1966), 14–

15; Netherton et al., *Fairfax County, Virginia*, 672–73; Nan Netherton et al., *In the Path of History: Virginia Between the Rappahannock and the Potomac* (Falls Church: Higher Education, 2004), 124; Muriel Guinn, "Fairfax Prepares Slum Clean-Up Code," *WP*, December 4, 1959; "New Dulles Airport Sewer Draws Potential Customers," *WP*, October 16, 1961; Paul E. Ceruzzi, *Internet Alley: High Technology in Tysons Corner, 1945–2005* (Cambridge: MIT Press, 2008), 57; Jeremy Korr, "Political Parameters: Finding a Route for the Capital Beltway, 1950–1964," *Washington History* 19/20 (2007/2008), 10; Christopher John Bright, "Nike Defends Washington," *Virginia Magazine of History & Biography* 105.3 (Summer 1997); National Capital Planning Commission, *Worthy of the Nation: The History of Planning for the National Capital* (Washington, DC: Smithsonian, 1977), 225; Alson Clark, *Wallace Neff: Architect of California's Golden Age* (Santa Monica: Hennessey & Ingalls, 2000), 28–29, 177–86.

27. Jean Gottman, *Virginia in Our Century* (Charlottesville: University Press of Virginia, 1969), 608–9.

28. "Random Notes in Washington," *NYT*, December 11, 1961.

29. Dean Rusk, *The Winds of Freedom: Selections from the Speeches and Statements of Secretary of State Dean Rusk* (Boston: Beacon, 1963), 179.

30. Betty Friedan, *The Feminine Mystique* (New York: Norton, 1963), 36.

31. See Anthony D. King's call for such research in "Postcolonialism and Planning: Where Has It Been? Where Is It Going?" in *Learning Civil Societies: Shifting Contexts for Democratic Planning and Governance*, eds., Penny Gurstein and Leonora Angeles (Toronto: University of Toronto Press, 2007).

32. See Kramer, "Power and Connection" for a survey.

33. For an introduction to the new suburban history, see Becky M. Nicolaides and Andrew Wiese, eds., *The Suburb Reader* (New York: Routledge, 2006).

34. Chalmers Johnson, *Blowback: The Costs and Consequences of American Empire* (New York: Metropolitan, 2000), 34–64; Jana Lipman, *Guantánamo: A Working-Class History Between Empire and Revolution* (Berkeley: University of California Press, 2009); Catherine Lutz, *Homefront: A Military City and the American 20th Century* (Boston: Beacon, 2001); Ji-Yeon Yuh, *Beyond the Shadow of Camptown: Korean Military Brides in America* (New York: New York University Press, 2002); Mark L. Gillem, *America Town: Building the Outposts of Empire* (Minneapolis: University of Minnesota Press, 2007).

35. Paul A. Kramer, *The Blood of Government: Race, Empire, the United States & the Philippines* (Chapel Hill: University of North Carolina Press, 2006), 229–84; Vicente Rafael, "Colonial Domesticity," in *White Love and Other Events in Filipino History* (Durham: Duke University Press, 2000), 52–75; Jackson Lears, *Rebirth of a Nation: The Making of Modern America, 1877–1920* (New York: HarperCollins, 2009), 276–80; Julie Greene, *The Canal Builders: Making America's Empire at the Panama Canal* (New York: Penguin, 2009).

36. Jane C. Loeffler, *The Architecture of Diplomacy: Building America's Embassies* (New York: Princeton Architectural Press, 1998); Ron Robin, *Enclaves of America:*

The Rhetoric of American Political Architecture Abroad, 1900–1965 (Princeton: Princeton University Press, 1992).

37. Carroll, *House of War*; Trevor Paglen, *Blank Spots on the Map: The Dark Geography of the Pentagon's Secret World* (New York: Penguin, 2009).

38. Yukiko Koshiro, *Trans-Pacific Racisms and the U.S. Occupation of Japan* (New York: Columbia University Press, 1999); Rajiv Chandrasekaran, *Imperial Life in the Emerald City: Inside Iraq's Green Zone* (New York: Vintage, 2006).

39. Richard Drinnon, *Keeper of Concentration Camps: Dillon S. Myer and American Racism* (Berkeley: University of California Press, 1987); Gary Y. Okihiro, "An American Story," in *Impounded: Dorothea Lange and the Censored Images of Japanese American Internment*, eds., Linda Gordon and Okihiro (New York: Norton, 2006).

40. Annabel Jane Wharton, *Building the Cold War: Hilton International Hotels and Modern Architecture* (Chicago: University of Chicago Press, 2001); Greg Grandin, *Fordlandia: The Rise and Fall of Henry Ford's Forgotten Jungle City* (New York: Metropolitan, 2009); Denise Leith, *The Politics of Power: Freeport in Suharto's Indonesia* (Honolulu: University of Hawai'i Press, 2003).

41. David Vine, *Island of Shame: The Secret History of the U.S. Military Base on Diego Garcia* (Princeton: Princeton University Press, 2009); Elizabeth DeLoughrey, "Heliotropes: Solar Ecologies and Pacific Radiations," in *Postcolonial Ecologies: Literatures of the Environment*, eds. DeLoughrey and George B. Handley (New York: Oxford University Press, 2011), 235–53.

42. Robert Vitalis, *America's Kingdom: Mythmaking on the Saudi Oil Frontier* (Stanford: Stanford University Press, 2007); Nixon, *Slow Violence*.

43. Latham, *Modernization as Ideology*; Jeffrey W. Cody, *Exporting American Architecture, 1870–2000* (New York: Routledge, 2003).

44. Juan Bosch, *Pentagonism: A Substitute for Imperialism* (New York: Grove, 1968), 22, 57.

45. Stanley Cohen, *States of Denial: Knowing about Atrocities and Suffering* (Cambridge: Polity, 2001).

46. Ibid., 6.

47. Evan Thomas, *The Very Best Men: Four Who Dared: The Early Years of the CIA* (New York: Simon & Schuster, 1995), 107.

48. Eleanor Dulles, *American Foreign Policy*, 246, 280–83.

49. Odd Arne Westad, *The Global Cold War* (Cambridge: Cambridge University Press, 2007), 4–5.

50. Robert J. McMahon, *Colonialism and Cold War: The United States and the Struggle for Indonesian Independence, 1945–1949* (Ithaca: Cornell University Press, 1981), 43.

51. Arthur M. Schlesinger Jr., *The Vital Center: The Politics of Freedom* (Cambridge: Riverside, 1949), 231, 98.

52. Kramer, "Power and Connection," 1359.

53. See particularly Michael Holzman, *James Jesus Angleton, The CIA, and the Craft of Counterintelligence* (Amherst: University of Massachusetts Press, 2008).

54. Wise and Ross, *Invisible Government*, 224; Thomas, *Very Best Men*, 207; Hugh Wilford, *The Mighty Wurlitzer: How the CIA Played America* (Cambridge: Harvard University Press, 2008), 100; E. Howard Hunt, *American Spy: My Secret History in the CIA, Watergate, and Beyond* (Hoboken: Wiley & Sons, 2007).

55. Michael Denning, *Cover Stories: Narrative and Ideology in the British Spy Thriller* (London: Routledge, 1987).

56. Lyman B. Kirkpatrick Jr., *Real CIA* (New York: Macmillan, 1968), 297; Robert Littell, *The Company: A Novel of the CIA* (New York: Penguin, 2002).

57. Eleanor Dulles, *American Foreign Policy*, 261, 323.

58. "NSC 10/2," in Monje, *Central Intelligence Agency*, 10.

59. See, for example, Mahmood Mamdani, *Good Muslim, Bad Muslim: America, the Cold War, and the Roots of Terror* (New York: Three Leaves, 2004).

60. Thomas Grubisich, "Fairfax Eyes I-270 Type Corridor," *WP*, March 30, 1978; Thomas Grubisich, "High-Noise Area Eyed for Housing," *WP*, October 21, 1978.

61. J.B. Jackson, *Discovering the Vernacular Landscape* (New Haven: Yale University Press, 1984), 5; Doreen Massey, *For Space* (London: Sage, 2005).

62. Ceruzzi, *Internet Alley*, 3.

63. Ann Laura Stoler, "Intimidations of Empire: Predicaments of the Tactile and Unseen," in *Haunted by Empire: Geographies of Intimacy in North American History*, ed. Ann Laura Stoler (Durham: Duke University Press, 2006), 8–9.

64. Wise and Ross, *Invisible Government*; Bosch, *Pentagonism*; also see Ceruzzi, *Internet Alley*; Ann Markusen, *The Rise of the Gunbelt: The Military Remapping of Industrial America* (New York: Oxford University Press, 1991).

65. Amy Kaplan, *Anarchy of Empire*, 4; also see Lisa Lowe, *Immigrant Acts: On Asian American Cultural Politics* (Durham: Duke University Press, 1996), 16; Juan Gonzalez, *Harvest of Empire: a History of Latinos in America* (New York: Viking, 2000).

66. See Abbott, *Political Terrain*; Ceruzzi, *Internet Alley*; Markusen, *Rise of the Gunbelt*.

67. Denning, *Cover Stories*, 134.

68. Pierre Bourdieu, "Structures, *Habitus*, Practices," in *The Logic of Practice* (Stanford: Stanford University Press, 1990), 52–65; Pierre Bourdieu, "Structures and the Habitus," in *Outline of a Theory of Practice* (Cambridge: Cambridge University Press, 1977), 72–95; Craig Calhoun, "Habitus, Field and Capital: The Question of Historical Specificity," in *Bourdieu: Critical Perspectives*, eds. Craig Calhoun et al. (Chicago: University of Chicago Press, 1993), 61–88; David Swartz, "Habitus: A Cultural Theory of Action," in *Culture and Power: The Sociology of Pierre Bourdieu* (Chicago: University of Chicago Press, 1997), 95–116; John Archer, *Architecture and Suburbia: From English Villa to American Dream House, 1690–2000* (Minneapolis: University of Minnesota Press, 2005), 9–12.

69. Bourdieu, *Outline*, 78.

70. Ibid., 89.

71. See Swartz, "Habitus," 100.

72. Cecil B. Currey, *Edward Lansdale: The Unquiet American* (Boston: Hough-

ton Mifflin, 1988); Holzman, *James Jesus Angleton*; Julie Phillips, *James Tiptree Jr.: The Double Life of Alice B. Sheldon* (New York: St. Martin's, 2006); Miles Copeland, *The Game Player: The Confessions of the CIA's Original Political Operative* (London: Aurum, 1989), 113; Zalin Grant, *Facing the Phoenix* (New York: Norton, 1991); Jonathan Nashel, *Edward Lansdale's Cold War* (Amherst: University of Massachusetts Press, 2005); Archibald Roosevelt, *For Lust of Knowing: Memoirs of an Intelligence Officer* (Boston: Little, Brown, 1988), 117.

73. Devlin, *Chief of Station, Congo*, 46; Scott Shane, "Lawrence R. Devlin, 86, C.I.A. Officer Who Balked on a Congo Plot, Is Dead," *NYT*, December 11, 2008.

74. Ronald Kessler, *Spy Vs. Spy: Stalking Soviet Spies in America* (New York: Charles Scribner's Sons, 1988), 230–32; David Wise, *Spy: The Inside Story of How the FBI's Robert Hanssen Betrayed America* (New York: Random House, 2002); David Wise, *Nightmover: How Aldrich Ames Sold the CIA to the KGB for $4.6 Million* (New York: HarperCollins, 1995), 181; Copeland, *Game Player*, 1.

75. Thomas, *Very Best Men*, 301; Nina Burleigh, *A Very Private Woman: The Life and Unsolved Murder of Presidential Mistress Mary Meyer* (New York: Bantam, 1998), 134; Kessler, *Spy Vs. Spy*, 45, 54–57; Joan Braden, *Just Enough Rope: An Intimate Memoir* (New York: Villard, 1989), 48, 57, 69.

76. Ann Laura Stoler, *Carnal Knowledge and Imperial Power: Race and the Intimate in Colonial Rule* (Berkeley: University of California Press, 2002).

CHAPTER ONE

1. CIA History Staff, *Planning and Construction of the Agency Headquarters Building* (June 1973), CREST; Peter Grose, *Gentleman Spy: The Life of Allen Dulles* (Boston: Houghton Mifflin, 1994), 417–18; Ronald Kessler, *Inside the CIA* (New York: Pocket, 1992), 177; Richard Helms, *A Look Over My Shoulder: A Life in the Central Intelligence Agency* (New York: Random House, 2003), 123; Ludwell Lee Montague, *General Walter Bedell Smith as Director of Central Intelligence* (University Park: Pennsylvania State University Press, 1992), 200–201; Krugler, *This Is Only a Test*, 103–4; Burton Hersh, *The Old Boys: The American Elite and the Origins of the CIA* (New York: Charles Scribner's Sons, 1992), 420; Wise and Ross, *Invisible Government*, 218.

2. Grose, *Gentleman Spy*, 417, 534; Leonard Mosley, *Dulles: A Biography of Eleanor, Allen, and John Foster Dulles and Their Family Network* (New York: Dial, 1978), 473; John Ranelagh, *The Agency: The Rise and Decline of the CIA* (New York: Simon and Schuster, 1986), 17; Thomas Powers, *The Man Who Kept Secrets: Richard Helms and the CIA* (New York: Knopf, 1979), 115; John Patrick Quirk et al., *The Central Intelligence Agency: A Photographic History* (Guilford: Foreign Intelligence Press, 1986); James Srodes, *Allen Dulles: Master of Spies* (Washington, DC: Regnery, 1999), 112; Ray S. Cline, *Secrets Spies and Scholars: Blueprint of the Essential CIA* (Washington, DC: Acropolis, 1976), 154; David Atlee Phillips, *The Night Watch* (New

York: Atheneum, 1977), 58, 137; Archibald Roosevelt, *For Lust of Knowing*, 462; Littell, *The Company*, 496.

3. Grose, *Gentleman Spy*, 388, 417; Ted Gup, *The Book of Honor: Covert Lives and Classified Deaths at the CIA* (New York: Doubleday, 2000), 15, 56; James Carroll, *An American Requiem: God, My Father, and the War that Came Between Us* (Boston: Houghton Mifflin, 1996), 34; Joseph B. Smith, *Portrait of a Cold Warrior* (New York: G.P. Putnam's Sons, 1976), 46; Phillips, *Night Watch*, 37, 58, 89; Allen Dulles Testimony, U.S. Senate, "Subcommittee of the Committee of Appropriations, The Supplemental Appropriation Bill, 1956," July 15, 1955, 251.

4. Allen Dulles to Arthur S. Flemming, November 16, 1954, Abramovitz TS CIA, Box 1:20, MAP.

5. Kessler, *Inside CIA*, 177; Robert C. Allbrook, "Director Dulles to Make Plea in Person," *WP*, November 4, 1955; Andrew Tully, *CIA: The Inside Story* (New York: William Morrow, 1962), 258; Sallie Pisani, *The CIA and the Marshall Plan* (Lawrence: University Press of Kansas, 1991), 9; Harry Howe Ransom, *The Intelligence Establishment* (Cambridge: Harvard University Press, 1970), 259; Rhodri Jeffreys-Jones, "Why Was the CIA Established in 1947?" in *Eternal Vigilance? 50 Years of the CIA*, eds. Jeffreys-Jones and Christopher Andrew (London: Frank Cass, 1997), 35–36; Mark J. Gasiorowski, *U.S. Foreign Policy and the Shah: Building a Client State in Iran* (Ithaca: Cornell University Press, 1991), 82–83; Harry Rositzke, *The CIA's Secret Operations: Espionage, Counterespionage, and Covert Action* (New York: Reader's Digest, 1977), xxiii.

6. Anne Karalekas, *History of the Central Intelligence Agency* (Laguna Hills, CA: Aegean Park, 1977), 42; Pisani, *CIA and the Marshall Plan*, 9; Wise and Ross, *Invisible Government*, 119–20; Schlesinger and Kinzer, *Bitter Fruit*; John Prados, *Safe for Democracy: The Secret Wars of the CIA* (Chicago: Ivan R. Dee, 2006); Gup, *Book of Honor*, 60; James Callanan, *Covert Action in the Cold War: US Policy, Intelligence and CIA Operations* (New York: I.B. Tauris, 2009), 4–5; Victor Marchetti and John D. Marks, *The CIA and the Cult of Intelligence* (New York: Knopf, 1974), 4; Grose, *Gentleman Spy*, 5; Homer E. Socolofsky and Allan B. Spetter, *The Presidency of Benjamin Harrison* (Lawrence: University Press of Kansas, 1987), 204-5.

7. Memo to the National Capital Planning Commission from the Staff Committee to the Members of the Joint Commission, May 2, 1955, Abramovitz TS CIA, Box 1:20; The Office of Gilmore D. Clarke and Michael Rapuano, "Report on the Proposed Location for a New Headquarters for the Central Intelligence Agency," October 25, 1955, Abramovitz TS CIA, Box 1:21, MAP; Robert E. Baker, "Allen Dulles Favors Langley as CIA Site," *WP*, December 1, 1955; Robert C. Allbrook, "Maryland Potomac Property Offered as Free Site for CIA Headquarters," *WP*, November 13, 1955; "Winkler Tract Rejected by CIA as Possible Site," *WP*, November 19, 1955; "Committee of 100 Urges CIA to Locate New Headquarters on Alexandria Tract," *WP*, October 22, 1955; Robert E. Baker, "Langley in Lead as CIA Considers 3 Virginia Sites for Headquarters," *WP*, March 9, 1955; "Maryland Fights CIA's Virginia Site," *WP*, March 11, 1955.

8. Eldridge Lovelace, *Harland Bartholomew and His Contribution to American*

Urban Planning (Urbana-Champaign: University of Illinois Department of Urban and Regional Planning, 1993).

9. James W. Head Jr. to Lawrence K. White, April 1, 1955, and White to Carlton Massey, July 9, 1955, Abramovitz TS CIA, Box 1:20, MAP; "Memo to the National Capital Planning Commission"; Clarke and Rapuano, "Report"; Baker, "Langley in Lead"; Wes Barthelmes and Robert C. Allbrook, "CIA Consultants Favor Langley Site for Agency's New 'Junior Pentagon,'" *WP*, November 3, 1955; Wes Barthelmes, "Area Planners Hear CIA Urge Langley Office Site," *WP*, March 12, 1955; Baker, "Allen Dulles Favors Langley"; *The Office of Clarke and Rapuano, Inc.* (New York: Clarke and Rapuano, 1972); CIA History Staff, *Planning and Construction*, 80.

10. Lovelace, *Harland Bartholomew*, 147; Grose, *Gentleman Spy*, 418; William Colby, *Honorable Men: My Life in the CIA* (New York: Simon and Schuster, 1978), 308; Melvin Goodman, *Failure of Intelligence: The Decline and Fall of the CIA* (Lanham: Rowman & Littlefield, 2008), 286; David M. Barrett, *The CIA & Congress: The Untold Story From Truman to Kennedy* (Lawrence: University Press of Kansas, 2005), 3.

11. CIA History Staff, *Planning and Construction*, 4, 12–14, 29–30, 46.

12. Carole L. Herrick, *McLean* (Charleston: Arcadia, 2011); Kessler, *Inside CIA*, 176; Carolyn Bell Hughes, "'Progress' Changes Suburban Scene," *WP*, March 18, 1956; "Supplemental Appropriation Bill," 280.

13. Herrick, *McLean*; Hughes, "'Progress' Changes Suburban Scene"; Grose, *Gentleman Spy*, 418; Krugler, *This Is Only a Test*, 103; Wise and Ross, *Invisible Government*, 223; Carole L. Herrick, *Yesterday: 100 Recollections of McLean & Great Falls, Virginia* (McLean: Recollections Committee, 2007), 73, 101-3; Martha Catlin, *A Historical Study of the McLean Community* (1988), 135; "Villas about the Capital," *WP*, August 8, 1911; "Leiter 'Palisades' to Be Villa Sites," *WP*, September 23, 1928; "Secretary of State and Mrs. Lansing Dinner Guests of Mr. and Mrs. Joseph Leiter at Their Country Place," *WP*, July 9, 1915; Karl E. Meyer, *The Dust of Empire: The Race for Mastery in the Asian Heartland* (New York: Public Affairs, 2003), 5; John Chichester Mackall, "McLean, Fairfax County, Virginia," *Historical Society of Fairfax County Yearbook* 4 (1955), 14–15; Eleanor Lee Templeman et al., *Northern Virginia Heritage* (Arlington: Templeman, 1966), 75.

14. Mosley, *Dulles*, 247, 264, 345, 366, 381, 443; Grose, *Gentleman Spy*, 339–40; Wayne G. Jackson, "Allen Welsh Dulles as Director of Central Intelligence," DCI-2 (CIA Historical Staff, July 1973), Volume III, 83.

15. Eleanor Lansing Dulles, *Chances of a Lifetime: A Memoir* (Englewood Cliffs, NJ: Prentice-Hall, 1980), 185.

16. Ibid., 161, 232–34; Pamela Scott, *A Directory of District of Columbia Architects, 1822–1960* (Washington, DC: 1999), WR.

17. Eleanor Dulles, *Chances of a Lifetime*, 236; Mosley, *Dulles,* 264, 366, 443; Eleanor Dulles, *American Foreign Policy,* 284.

18. Notebooks, Box 3, Folder 8, "Personal Contacts – Address Books, 1965–66 and undated," and "Interview 13," Box 6, Folder 6 "Personal – Oral History Interview," EDP; C&P Virginia Suburban Phone Book, 1965–66, all phone books avail-

able FCPL. On county street-numbering campaign in those years, see "Roads—Uniform Numbering System, 1965," hanging files, FCPL.

19. Washington Metropolitan Phone Book, 1962–63; Heymann, *Georgetown Ladies'*, 34–35, 58–62; Gordon Thomas, *Secrets & Lies: A History of CIA Mind Control & Germ Warfare* (London: JR Books, 2008), 60.

20. Weiner, *Legacy of Ashes*, 60, 208; Colby, *Honorable Men*, 147; "Round About Fairfax," *FCT*, May 24, 1962; Warren Hinkle and William Turner, *Deadly Secrets: The CIA-Mafia War Against Castro and the Assassination of J.F.K.* (New York: Thunder's Mouth, 1993), 56–57; Rita Kirkpatrick and Lyman B. Kirkpatrick, unpublished biography, July 15, 2003, Box 1.2, and "Amembasy Habana to The Dept of St Wash" (sic), memo, November 25, 1958, Box 4.7, LKP; Lyman Kirkpatrick, *The Real CIA* (New York: Macmillan, 1968), 20, 129, 156–57; Fabian Escalante, *The Cuba Project: CIA Covert Operations, 1959–1962* (Melbourne: Ocean, 2004), 10; Anthony Cave Brown, ed., *The Secret War Report of the OSS* (New York: Berkley, 1976), 128.

21. Weiner, *Legacy of Ashes*, 141, 163; "Short News and Notes," *FH*, for all the following dates: March 17, 1950, January 18, 1952, August 14, 1953, January 13, 1956; John Marks, *The Search for the 'Manchurian Candidate': The CIA and Mind Control* (New York: Times Books, 1979), 55–56, 195; John Jacob Nutter, *The CIA's Black Ops: Covert Action, Foreign Policy, and Democracy* (Amherst, NY: Prometheus, 1999), 119; "'China Swashbuckler' Buys Showplace at Warrenton," *WP*, April 22, 1944; Max Holland, "Private Sources of U.S. Foreign Policy: William Pawley and the 1954 Coup d' État in Guatemala," *Journal of Cold War Studies* 7.4 (Fall 2005), 55–56; Schlesinger and Kinzer, *Bitter Fruit*, 102–3.

22. Jefferson Morley, *Our Man in Mexico: Winston Scott and the Hidden History of the CIA* (Lawrence: University Press of Kansas, 2008), 78; Cord Meyer, *Facing Reality: From World Federalism to the CIA* (New York: Harper & Row, 1980), 85; Burleigh, *Very Private Woman*, 19, 128, 132; "33rd Road N," Arlington Virginia Department of Real Estate Assessments, Property Information Search.

23. "Recent Deaths," *FH*, February 5, 1954; "Roosevelt-Palfrey Wedding," *FH*, January 1, 1943; Archibald Roosevelt, *For Lust of Knowing*, 117; Carole L. Herrick, *Yesterday*, 293–94; Kermit Roosevelt, *Countercoup: The Struggle for the Control of Iran* (New York: McGraw-Hill, 1979); Netherton et al., *Fairfax County, Virginia*, 473–75, 487; FXCI-LAYT-7, photo file, FCPL.

24. Netherton et al., *Fairfax County, Virginia*, 626; Milton Eisenhower, *The President Is Calling* (Garden City: Doubleday, 1974), 112–24.

25. CIA History Staff, *Planning and Construction*, 48.

26. "Coctails [sic] Sunday April 16 1967 5 –7," typed list, Box 3.8, EDP.

27. Pisani, *CIA and the Marshall Plan*, 3; Madeline G. Kalb, *The Congo Cables: The Cold War in Africa – From Eisenhower to Kennedy* (New York: MacMillan, 1982); Allen Dulles, "Madame Chairman and Ladies," draft of speech for the Women's Forum on National Security, January 28, 1959, Box 86.2, ADP; William M. Leary, *Perilous Missions: Civil Air Transport and CIA Covert Operations in Asia* (Washington, DC: Smithsonian, 2002), 128.

28. Catlin, *Historical Study*; Herrick, *McLean*, 22, 50, 53.

29. Bradley E. Gernand, *A Virginia Village Goes to War: Falls Church During the Civil War* (Virginia Beach: Donning, 2002); Netherton et al., *Fairfax County, Virginia*, 157, 315, 382, 447–55, 538, 662–63; Andrew M.D. Wolf, *Black Settlement in Fairfax County, Virginia During Reconstruction* (Fairfax County: December 1975); Mackall, "McLean," 5; Templeman et al., *Northern Virginia Heritage*, 107.

30. Beverly Blois et al., *Northern Virginia Community College: An Oral History, 1965–1985* (Northern Virginia Community College, 1987), 69, 103–4; Peter Wallenstein, *Blue Laws and Black Codes: Conflict, Courts and Change in Twentieth-Century Virginia* (Charlottesville: University of Virginia Press, 2004), 106, 182, 191; Benjamin Muse, *Virginia's Massive Resistance* (Bloomington: Indiana University Press, 1961), 9–10, 137; Caryle Murphy, "Fresh Look at Slavery," *WP*, May 9, 1977; Debra Lynn Vial, "Rebel Leaders Own the Roads," *FJ*, March 1988, in "Roads—Street Names," Hanging Files, FCPL; Carroll, *American Requiem*, 135; Netherton et al., *Fairfax County, Virginia*, 384, 536–40, 663–66; J. Douglas Smith, *Managing White Supremacy: Race, Politics, and Citizenship in Jim Crow Virginia* (Chapel Hill: University of North Carolina Press, 2002), 140–41, 260–69; Lisa Lindquist Dorr, *White Women, Rape & the Power of Race in Virginia, 1900–1960* (Chapel Hill: University of North Carolina Press, 2004), 36, 44, 180, 228; E.B. Henderson, as told to Edith Hussey, *History of the Fairfax County Branch of the NAACP* (October 1965), 4, 15.

31. Harry S. Jaffe and Tom Sherwood, *Dream City: Race, Power, and the Decline of Washington, DC* (New York: Simon & Schuster, 1994), 15, 59, 251; Ranelagh, *The Agency*, 339; Head to White, April 1, 1955; Board of Supervisors Minute Books, 1955, FCBS; CIA History Staff, *Planning and Construction*, 70, 118; Vogel, *Pentagon*, 109-11; "Fairfax Development Effect Is Termed 'Racist' in Study," *The Evening Star*, October 6, 1970; "Residents Fight 'Encroachment' on One of 'Few' Negro Areas," *NVS*, January 10, 1962; "Cafeteria Integrated by S&W," *NVS*, August 17, 1961; Abbott, *Political Terrain*, 179; Netherton et al, *In the Path*, 123; Henderson, *History of the Fairfax County Branch*, 16; Mackall, "McLean," 5, 12; Blois, *Northern Virginia Community College*; U.S. Department of Commerce, Bureau of the Census, *U.S. Census of Population and Housing*, Final Reports, Census Tracts Washington, DC – Md. – Va., and Virginia, 1940, 1950, 1960, 1970.

32. Donald M. Sweig, *Slavery in Fairfax County, Virginia, 1750–1860: A Research Report* (Fairfax County: Office of Comprehensive Planning, June 1983); Elizabeth Miles Cooke, *The History of Old Georgetown Pike* (Annandale: Charles Baptie, 1977), 21; Vincent Paka, "To Help DC Home Rule Broyhill Ouster Urged," *WP*, December 16, 1969; Jaffe and Sherwood, *Dream City*.

33. David Wise, *Nightmover*, 49; Pete Earley, *Confessions of a Spy: The Real Story of Aldrich Ames* (New York: G.P. Putnam's Sons, 1997), 24, 32; Smith, *Portrait of a Cold Warrior*, 73; David Louis Whitehead, *Brains, Sex and Racism in the CIA and the Escape* (Washington, DC: Equality America, 1991), 16.

34. Eleanor Dulles, *Chances of a Lifetime*, 234–35; Jessie Ash Arndt, "Eleanor L. Dulles Makes Houses Her Hobby," *CSM*, March 3, 1955; Isabelle Shelton, "Foggy

Bottom Area Gets Face-Lifting," *Washington Star*, November 8, 1953; Suzanne Berry Sherwood, *Foggy Bottom, 1800–1975: A Study in the Uses of an Urban Neighborhood* (Washington, DC: GW Washington Studies no. 7, 1978); DC City Directory, 1940, 1948, WR.

35. "Fairfax County Chamber of Commerce," May 2, 1957, 3, Box 84.5, ADP.

36. Ibid.

37. Jackson, "Allen Welsh Dulles," Volume IV, 104; "Supplemental Appropriation Bill," 240–42, 249–50; Elizabeth P. McIntosh, *Sisterhood of Spies: The Women of the OSS* (Annapolis: Naval Institute Press, 1998), 241.

38. James Hanrahan, "An Interview with Former CIA Executive Director Lawrence K. 'Red' White," *Studies in Intelligence*, 43.1 (Winter 1999/2000); Grose, *Gentleman Spy*, 404; Gup, *Book of Honor*, 169; Powers, *Man Who Kept Secrets*, 118, 329–30, 333; Helms, *Look Over My Shoulder*, 294, 451; Central Intelligence Agency, "The Family Jewels," 86, 91, 112, 180, DNSA; "Excerpt from Diary Notes of ADD/A (Colonel L.K. White—2 February 1953)," DNSA; Dino Brugioni, *Eyeball to Eyeball: The Inside Story of the Cuban Missile Crisis* (New York: Random, 1990), 17–18, 85; "Mr. Dulles: Correspondence re your meeting with Larry White, Col. White's son, this afternoon at 5:00," September 22, 1964, Box 57.32, ADP.

39. Allen Dulles, *The Craft of Intelligence* (New York: Harper & Row, 1963), 6.

40. Ibid., 6–8.

41. Allen Dulles et al., *The Central Intelligence Agency and National Organization for Intelligence*, report to National Security Council, January 1, 1949, 123; Grose, *Gentleman Spy*, 417; Ranelagh, *The Agency*, 282; Stephen Ambrose, *Ike's Spies: Eisenhower and the Espionage Establishment* (Garden City: Doubleday, 1981), 242.

42. "Address at the Annual Banquet – Thirtieth Annual Meeting – Virginia State Chamber of Commerce – April 9, 1954," Box 82.5; "The Communist Challenge to Free Government," January 24, 1959, Box 86.2, ADP. Christina Klein, *Cold War Orientalism: Asia in the Middlebrow Imagination, 1945–1961* (Berkeley: University of California Press, 2003), 37.

43. Klein, *Cold War Orientalism*, 41–49.

44. "Herald Tribune Forum – 10/19/54 Freedom's Progress Here and Abroad," Box 82.5; "General Shepherd and Members of the Carabao," January 22, 1957, Box 84.4; "The Communist Challenge to Free Government," ADP; Thomas L. Ahern Jr., *Vietnam Declassified: The CIA and Counterinsurgency* (Lexington: University Press of Kentucky, 2010), 9; Hersh, *Old Boys*, 416; Neil Sheehan et al., *The Pentagon Papers as Published by The New York Times* (New York: Quadrangle, 1971); Weiner, *Legacy of Ashes*, 85, 94, 146, 151; Smith, *Portrait of a Cold Warrior*, 102–3.

45. Grose, *Gentleman Spy*, 417.

46. Kessler, *Inside CIA*, 180.

47. Also see Joseph Weisberg, "The CIA's Open Secrets," *NYT*, August 27, 2007.

48. James M. Olson, *Fair Play: The Moral Dilemmas of Spying* (Washington, DC: Potomac, 2006), 246; Karalekas, *History of the Central Intelligence Agency*, 46–47; Clarke and Rapuano, "Report," 4, 8; John Harwood and Janet Parks, *The Troubled Search: The Work of Max Abramovitz* (New York: Wallach Gallery, Columbia

University, 2004), 88; "Supplemental Appropriation Bill," 247–48; Wise and Ross, *Invisible Government*, 218.

49. Grose, *Gentleman Spy*, 418; Roy Meachum, "CIA to Hide Its $46 Million Home from Viewers by Keeping Trees," *WP*, July 21, 1957; Clarke and Rapuano, "Report," 9–12.

50. Clarke and Rapuano, "Report," 4, 16; Lawrence White to Harland Bartholomew, May 3, 1955, Box 1:20, MAP.

51. Russell Jack Smith, *The Unknown CIA: My Three Decades with the Agency* (Washington, DC: Pergamon-Brassey's, 1989), 6–7; Hanrahan, "Interview with Former CIA Executive Director"; Kessler, *Inside CIA*, 174.

52. Fairfax County Planning Division, *McLean Central Development Plan* (December 11, 1963), i, 1–2.

53. Meeting, May 4, 1955, Board of Supervisors Minute Book 23: April 6, 1955–November 23, 1955, 102, FCBS; "Fairfax County Chamber" speech, ADP; CIA History Staff, *Planning and Construction*, 66.

54. LK White to Dulles, memo, May 2, 1957; "Fairfax County Chamber of Commerce 8 May 1957," outline notes, 1, 5; "Fairfax County Chamber" speech, 8; "Notes to Supplement Outline," May 2, 1957, 3, Box 84.5, ADP; CIA History Staff, *Planning and Construction*, 60, 73; Herrick, *Yesterday*, 102–3.

55. Victoria Newhouse, *Wallace K. Harrison, Architect* (New York: Rizzoli, 1989), 55.

56. Robert Bruegmann, ed., *Modernism at Mid-Century: The Architecture of the United States Air Force Academy* (Chicago: University of Chicago Press, 1994), 91.

57. Alexandra Lange, "Corporate Headquarters: Saarinen in Suburbia," in *Eero Saarinen: Shaping the Future*, eds. Eeva-Liisa Pelkonen and Donald Albrecht (New Haven: Yale University Press, 2006), 277; Louise A. Mozingo, "The Corporate Estate in the USA, 1954–1964: 'Thoroughly Modern in Concept, but . . . Down to Earth and Rugged,'" *Studies in the History of Gardens and Designed Landscapes* 20 (Jan.–Mar. 2000), 25–56.

58. Newhouse, *Wallace K. Harrison*, 152; Frederic King, "Application for Membership," Membership File, AIA; L.K. White to Wallace K. Harrison, August 5, 1955, Abramovitz TS CIA, Box 1:20, MAP; CIA History Staff, *Planning and Construction*, 109.

59. Dulles to King, August 14, 1955, Box 36.10, ADP; Newhouse, *Wallace K. Harrison*, 9; Grose, *Gentleman Spy*, 58, 97–98, 418; King, Form 838, AIA.

60. King, Form 838, 3; recommendation letters, including Harrison's, and "Frederic King, 84, Architect, Is Dead," *NYT*, AIA File; Grose, *Gentleman Spy*, 129, 141, 146, 299, 418; Peter Pennoyer and Anne Walker, *The Architecture of Delano & Aldrich* (New York: Norton, 2003), 136; Newhouse, *Wallace K. Harrison*.

61. Quirk et al., *Central Intelligence Agency*, 89; Newhouse, *Wallace K. Harrison*, 94–99, 298; Dulles to AIA, March 11, 1958; Douglas Orr to Dulles, February 24, 1958, Box 30.6, ADP.

62. CIA History Staff, *Planning and Construction*, 109, 117; Harwood and Parks, *Troubled Search*, 35–37.

63. David A. Frier, *Conflict of Interest in the Eisenhower Administration* (Ames: Iowa State University Press, 1969), 99.

64. On American modern architecture abroad, see Loeffler, *Architecture of Diplomacy*; Annabel Jane Wharton, *Building the Cold War*; Ron Robin, *Enclaves of America*.

65. Loeffler, *Architecture of Diplomacy*, 65, 42.

66. CIA History Staff, *Planning and Construction*, 142, 128; Paul Gapp, "Hello, CIA?" *Chicago Tribune*, February 12, 1978; Newhouse, *Wallace K. Harrison*, 152; "Diagrammatic Sketch of 7 Story Bldg," August 10, 1955, Abramovitz TS CIA, Box 1:21, MAP; Wise and Ross, *Invisible Government*, 224.

67. CIA History Staff, *Planning and Construction*, 134–35, and Volume II, Figure 10; Muriel Guinn, "CIA Building Starts Langley-McLean Area Boom," *WP*, October 8, 1956.

68. CIA History Staff, *Planning and Construction*, 135; White to Bartholomew, May 3, 1955; on mid-century modernism, Sarah Williams Goldhagen and Rejean Legault, eds., *Anxious Modernisms: Experimentation in Postwar Architectural Culture* (Cambridge: MIT Press, 2000); Joan Ockman, *Architecture Culture, 1943–1968: A Documentary Anthology* (New York: Rizzoli, 1993); Diane Ghirardo, *Architecture After Modernism* (New York: Thames and Hudson, 1996).

69. Reinhold Martin, *The Organizational Complex: Architecture, Media and Corporate Space* (Cambridge: MIT Press, 2003), 3, 86–98, 257.

70. Harwood and Parks, *Troubled Search*, 64; on "systemic" details of the complex, also see "Cornerstone Laying of the Central Intelligence Agency Building," program, November 3, 1959, Box 20:12, WHP.

71. Bruegmann, *Modernism at Mid-Century*, 87, 93; Martin, *Organizational Complex*, 145; Mozingo, "Corporate Estate," 34, 38, 47.

72. William Whyte Jr., *The Organization Man* (New York: Simon and Schuster, 1956), 123.

73. "Fairfax County Chamber" speech, 1–2, ADP.

74. William M. Leary, ed., *The Central Intelligence Agency: History and Documents* (University of Alabama Press, 1984), 129; U.S. Congress, "Military Construction Appropriations for 1956: Hearings before a Subcommittee of the Committee on Appropriations, House of Representatives," June 23, 24, 1955 (Washington: U.S. GPO, 1955), 171, 180.

75. CIA History Staff, *Planning and Construction*, 167, 173, 178; Lyman Kirkpatrick, memo, "Suggested Subjects to Mention in Cornerstone Talk," October 1959, Box 36.13, ADP; "Cornerstone Laying New CIA Bldg. Invitation Lists – 3 Nov 59," and other lists in Series 5, guest lists, 1954–1962, ADP, Digital Files Series, 1939–1977; Charles Hook Tompkins family articles in hanging file, WR; Eisenhower to Tompkins, October 29, 1945 in *The Papers of Dwight David Eisenhower* 6.2.4 (Baltimore: Johns Hopkins University Press); Edwin L. Jones, *J.A. Jones Construction Company: 75 Years' Growth in Construction* (New York: Newcomen Society, 1965); "Cornerstone Laying" program.

76. CIA History Staff, *Planning and Construction*, 167, 170; photographs in Box

130, ADP; "President to Lay Cornerstone at Langley CIA Building Tuesday," *WP*, November 1, 1959.

77. Stanley Grogan, "Memorandum for the Director," October 26, 1959, and "Second Draft," October 26, 1959, Box 30.1; "For Release on Delivery – Text of Remarks by Pres. Eisenhower," November 3, 1959, and "Central Intelligence Agency – Cornerstone Ceremony," November 3, 1959, Box 87.1, ADP; Jackson, "Allen Welsh Dulles," Volume I, 81; CIA History Staff, *Planning and Construction*, 169, 171–75.

78. "Cornerstone Laying" program; Gapp, "Hello, CIA?"

79. Grose, *Gentleman Spy*, 534.

80. Ibid.; Harry Thomas, "Harbin S. Chandler, renovated the White House," *Atlanta Journal Constitution*, February 14, 1999; "Cornerstone Laying" program; John Stockwell, *In Search of Enemies* (New York: Norton, 1978), 35; James E. Parker Jr., *Codename Mule: Fighting the Secret War in Laos for the CIA* (Annapolis: Naval Institute Press, 1995), 9; Gapp, "Hello, CIA?"

81. Jackson, "Allen Welsh Dulles," Volume I, 22; Wilford, *Mighty Wurlitzer*, 153; Frank Snepp, *Irreparable Harm: A Firsthand Account of How One Agent Took on the CIA in an Epic Battle over Free Speech* (New York: Random House, 1999), 17.

82. Tully, *CIA*, 18; Ranelagh, *The Agency*, 19; Ralph McGehee, *Deadly Deceits: My 25 Years in the CIA* (New York: Sheridan Square, 1983), 54; C. Michael Hiam, *Who the Hell Are We Fighting?: The Story of Sam Adams and the Vietnam Intelligence Wars* (Hanover: Steerforth, 2006), 30–31, 156; Antonio J. Mendez, *The Master of Disguise: My Secret Life in the CIA* (New York: William Morrow, 1999), 26; Tennent Bagley, *Spy Wars: Moles, Mysteries, and Deadly Games* (New Haven: Yale University Press, 2007), 19; David Wise, *The Spy Who Got Away: The Inside Story of Edward Lee Howard, the CIA Agent Who Betrayed His Country's Secrets and Escaped to Moscow* (New York: Random House, 1988), 52–53; Stockwell, *In Search of Enemies*, 36–37; George Crile, *Charlie Wilson's War: The Extraordinary Story of the Largest Covert Operation in History* (New York: Atlantic Monthly Press, 2003), 274; Bradley Earl Ayers, *The War That Never Was: An Insider's Account of CIA Covert Operations against Cuba* (Indianapolis: Bobbs-Merrill, 1976), 20.

83. Stockwell, *In Search of Enemies*, 37; CIA History Staff, *Planning and Construction*, 183; Gup, *Nation of Secrets: The Threat to Democracy and the American Way of Life* (New York: Doubleday, 2007), 28–29.

84. Philip Agee, *Inside the Company: CIA Diary* (New York: Stonehill, 1975), 319; "Central Intelligence Agency," photo books, Oversize Box 4, Folder 41b, MAP; James Q. Reber to Dulles, and Dulles to Reber, December 20, 1961, Box 113.1, ADP; Weiner, *Legacy of Ashes*, 113–14; Snepp, *Irreparable Harm*, 17; Ranelagh, *The Agency*, 18; Bagley, *Spy Wars*, 53; Wise and Ross, *Invisible Government*, 225; Tully, *CIA*, 18; "Fine Arts Committee Meeting, 11 July 1963," CIA Logistics Memo, CREST.

85. Mendez, *Master of Disguise*, 338; Antonio and Jonna Mendez, *Spy Dust: Two Masters of Disguise Reveal the Tools and Operations That Helped Win the Cold War* (New York: Atria, 2002), 41; Crile, *Charlie Wilson's War*, 274, 285; CIA History Staff, *Planning and Construction*, 193; Tully, *CIA*, 18; Kessler, *Inside CIA*, 175; Wise and Ross, *Invisible Government*, 223; Stansfield Turner, *Secrecy and Democracy: The*

CIA in Transition (Boston: Houghton Mifflin, 1985), 31; Ayers, *War That Never Was*, 19–20; Miles Copeland, *Without Cloak or Dagger: The Truth About the New Espionage* (New York: Simon and Schuster, 1974), 283; Snepp, *Irreparable Harm*, 17; Joseph Persico, *Casey* (New York: Viking, 1990), 215; Lindsay Moran, *Blowing My Cover: My Life as a CIA Spy* (New York: G.P. Putnam's Sons, 2005); Nick Cullather, *Secret History: The CIA's Classified Account of its Operations in Guatemala, 1952–54* (Stanford: Stanford University Press, 1999), ix; Wise, *Spy Who Got Away*, 41, 55; Ransom, *Intelligence Establishment*, 84; Tom Mangold, *Cold Warrior: James Jesus Angleton, The CIA's Master Spy Hunter* (New York: Simon and Schuster, 1991), 55; McGehee, *Deadly Deceits*, 191.

86. Marchetti and Marks, *CIA and the Cult of Intelligence*, 277; Turner, *Secrecy and Democracy*, 31.

87. Grose, *Gentleman Spy*, 498–99, 534, 537–38, 604; Persico, *Casey*, 215; Helms, *Look Over My Shoulder*, 228; Brugioni, *Eyeball to Eyeball*, 85; Kessler, *Inside CIA*, xxvi; Stockwell, *In Search of Enemies*, 95; Bob Woodward, *Veil: The Secret Wars of the CIA, 1981–1987* (New York: Pocket, 1987), 182.

88. Mangold, *Cold Warrior*, 24; Peter Kornbluh, *The Pinochet File: A Declassified Dossier on Atrocity and Accountability* (New York: New Press, 2003), 215; Mansur Rafizadeh, *Witness: From the Shah to the Secret Arms Deal, an Insider's Account of U.S. Involvement in Iran* (New York: William Morrow, 1987), 241; Weiner, *Legacy of Ashes*, 423; Roger Warner, *Back Fire: The CIA's Secret War in Laos and Its Link to the War in Vietnam* (New York: Simon & Schuster, 1995), 261; Crile, *Charlie Wilson's War*, 434.

89. CIA History Staff, *Planning and Construction*, 187; Wise, *Spy Who Got Away*, 6; Tim Weiner, *Blank Check: The Pentagon's Black Budget* (New York: Warner, 1990), 129; David Wise, *Molehunt: The Secret Search for Traitors That Shattered the CIA* (New York: Random House, 1992), 160; Mangold, *Cold Warrior*, 55.

90. Stockwell, *In Search of Enemies*, 36; Crile, *Charlie Wilson's War*, 274–75, 285; Ronald Kessler, *Escape From the CIA: How the CIA Won and Lost the Most Important KGB Spy Ever to Defect to the U.S.* (New York: Pocket, 1991), 13.

91. Ayers, *War That Never Was*, 22.

92. CIA History Staff, *Planning and Construction*, 147; Smith, *Unknown CIA*, 152; Quirk, et al., *Central Intelligence Agency*, 138; Kessler, *Inside CIA*, xxv, xxxiii, 48; Wise and Ross, *Invisible Government*, 224–25; Woodward, *Veil*, 253; Hiam, *Who the Hell*, 156; Frank Holober, *Raiders of the China Coast: CIA Operations During the Korean War* (Annapolis: Naval Institute Press, 1999), 235.

93. CIA History Staff, *Planning and Construction*, 163–66; Rositzke, *CIA's Secret Operations*, 210; Smith, *Unknown CIA*, 7; Bagley, *Spy Wars*, 45; Archibald Roosevelt, *For Lust of Knowing*, 463.

94. David Doyle, *True Men and Traitors: From the OSS to the CIA, My Life in the Shadows* (New York: Wiley & Sons, 2001), 209; Kessler, *Inside CIA*, 185.

95. Loeffler, *Architecture of Diplomacy*, 65–66; Marchetti and Marks, *CIA and the Cult of Intelligence*, 277.

96. "2 CIA Men Escape Jams, Now Commute by Canoe," *WP*, November 7,

1961; George Dixon, "Washington Scene," *WP*, March 6, 1962; David Wise and Thomas B. Ross, *The Espionage Establishment* (London: Jonathan Cape, 1967), 145; "Property Acquisition Near CIA Headquarters," Memo, February 18, 1963, CREST; CIA History Staff, *Planning and Construction*, 275–76; Rositzke, *CIA's Secret Operations*, 210; Doyle, *True Men and Traitors*, 209; Kessler, *Inside CIA*, 180; Copeland, *Without Cloak*, 169.

97. Mendez, *Master of Disguise*, 24, 338; Warner, *Back Fire*, 331; Crile, *Charlie Wilson's War*, 274, 285–86; Duane Clarridge, *A Spy for All Seasons: My Life in the CIA* (New York: Scribner, 1997), 101; Wise, *Spy Who Got Away*, 56; Robert M. Gates, *From the Shadows: The Ultimate Insider's Story of Five Presidents and How They Won the Cold War* (New York: Simon and Schuster, 2007), 198; Kessler, *Inside CIA*, 183.

98. Ransom, *Intelligence Establishment*, 84; Kennedy photos in Box 132, ADP; CIA History Staff, *Planning and Construction*, 190–91.

99. Richard L. Holm, *The American Agent: My Life in the CIA* (London: St. Ermin's, 2003), 307; Doyle, *True Men and Traitors*, 211; Peer de Silva, *Sub Rosa: The CIA and the Uses of Intelligence* (New York: Times, 1978), 20; Atlee Phillips, *Night Watch*, 281.

100. Stockwell, *In Search of Enemies*, 35; Crile, *Charlie Wilson's War*, 2; Ayers, *War That Never Was*, 19; McGehee, *Deadly Deceits*, 54.

101. Archibald Roosevelt, *For Lust of Knowing*, 463; Karalekas, *History of the Central Intelligence Agency*, 64; also, on these points, see Martin, *Organizational Complex*, 91–95; Whyte, *Organization Man*.

102. Wise and Ross, *Espionage Establishment*, 146–47; Marchetti and Marks, *CIA and the Cult of Intelligence*, 276; "Acknowledged CIA Building Locations," October 21, 1999, Declassified Document, CIA FOIA website; David Wise, *Spy Who Got Away*, 46, 71; Wise, *Molehunt*, 20, 81; Wise and Ross, *Invisible Government*; Leah Latimer, "Reston Mystery," *WP*, September 12, 1986; Ben Franklin, "Focus: Reston, Va.," *NYT*, December 21, 1986; Lee Hockstader, "New 'Downtown' Approved in Reston," *WP*, March 10, 1987; "CIA Scraps Plan for More Reston Offices," *WP*, July 20, 1989.

103. FAA, "Dulles International Airport," Brochure, and Mrs. John Foster Dulles to Najeeb Halaby, November 15, 1962, Box 23.2, ADP; Jayne Merkel, *Eero Saarinen* (New York: Phaidon, 2005), 34, 217; Margaret C. Peck, *Images of America: Washington Dulles International Airport* (Charleston: Arcadia, 2005), 44; FAA Office of Public Affairs, "Dulles International Airport Fact Sheet," Box 496.1366, ESC.

104. Barry Katz, "The Arts of War: 'Visual Presentation' and National Intelligence," *Design Issues* 12.2 (Summer 1996), 3–21; Smith, *Unknown CIA*, 20; Cline, *Secrets*, 47, 57; Dan Kiley, *Dan Kiley in his Own Words: America's Master Landscape Architect* (London: Thames & Hudson, 1999), 12, 18.

105. O.P. Willis, "Our Nation's Capital Airport," *Jetage Airlanes*, November 1962; Walter McQuade, "The Birth of an Airport," *Fortune* (March 1962), 96, Box 54.100 Scrapbook; "Recent Work by Eero Saarinen and Associates Architects," Box 44 Binder 7; "Dulles International Airport Fact Sheet," Box 497.1367, ESC; Aline B.

Saarinen, ed., *Eero Saarinen on His Work* (New Haven: Yale University Press, 1968), 92, 102; Kiley, *Dan Kiley*, 40; Aline B. Saarinen to Attorney General Robert Kennedy, April 8, 1962, Box 6, Folder 1962 – Saarinen – Seigenthaler, Attorney General Correspondence Personal, RFKP; Allan Temko, *Eero Saarinen* (New York: Braziller, 1962), 114–15; Anthony Cave Brown, *Treason in the Blood: H. St. John Philby, Kim Philby and the Spy Case of the Century* (Boston: Houghton Mifflin, 1994), 394.

106. John Foster Dulles, *War or Peace* (New York: Macmillan, 1950), 181; *Seven Days in May* (Burbank: Warner, 1964).

107. FAA, "Dulles International Airport"; David Wise, *Spy*, 244; Arturo Cruz Jr., *Memoirs of a Counterrevolutionary* (New York: Doubleday, 1989), 197; Stockwell, *In Search of Enemies*, 98; Devlin, *Chief of Station, Congo*, 213; Mendez, *Master of Disguise*, 76; McGehee, *Deadly Deceits*, 177; Tom Squitieri, "CIA Worker Charged as Russian Spy," *USA Today*, November 19, 1996; Lena H. Sun, "Was Watched There But Arrested Here," *WP*, June 2, 1984; Jeff Gerth, "Safe Houses and Such," *NYT*, November 7, 1985; Jonathan Friedland, "American Firm Flying Angolan Military Goods," *CSM*, November 17, 1986; David Wise, "KGB Defector Gundarev, It's Cold Coming Out," *NYTM*, September 17, 1989; Don Harrison, "Virginia," *WP*, September 7, 1980; Dale Russakoff and Charles Fishman, "7 Freed Americans Face Arrest," *WP*, June 29, 1984; John T. Carney, *No Room for Error: The Covert Operations of America's Special Tactics Units from Iran to Afghanistan* (New York: Ballantine, 2002), 80.

CHAPTER TWO

1. Wilhelms to Dear Friends, November 7, 1952, and October 31, 1953, Box 1, Folder Correspondence 1933–1988, JWP.

2. Mary P. Callahan, *Making Enemies: War and State Building in Burma* (Ithaca: Cornell University Press, 2003), 5, 12, 142, 169; Raymond L. Bryant, *The Political Ecology of Forestry in Burma, 1824–1994* (Honolulu: University of Hawai'i Press, 1996), 161.

3. Wilhelms to Dear Friends, October 31, 1953; Jane to Esther, October 30, 1952, November 14, 1952, March 24, 1953, Box 3, Folder 1952–1953 Correspondence, JWP; on De Rochemont and CIA, see Daniel J. Leab, *Orwell Subverted: The CIA and the Filming of Animal Farm* (University Park: Pennsylvania State University Press, 2007).

4. Jane to Esther, December 12, 1952, and August 24, 1953, Box 3, Folder 1952–1953 Correspondence, JWP.

5. Jane to Merta (Mrs. H.W. Mattach), undated, and Jane to Esther, August 24, 1953, Box 3, Folder 1952–1953 Correspondence, JWP.

6. Wilhelms to Dear Friends, October 31, 1953; Jane to Esther, March 24, 1953, Box 3, Folder 1952–1953 Correspondence, JWP; Mohammed Reza Shah Pahlavi, *Mission for My Country* (New York: McGraw-Hill, 1961), 9; Interview with M. Gor-

don Tiger by William Burr, March 20, 1985, 4–5, FISOHA; James Adams, *Sellout: Aldrich Ames and the Corruption of the CIA* (New York: Viking, 1995), 24.

7. Jane to Esther, August 20, 1953, and August 24, 1953, Box 3, Folder 1952–1953 Correspondence, JWP.

8. Mom to John, July 14, 1962, Box 3, Folder 1962–1963 Correspondence and Papers, JWP; Duke, *Education Empire*, 9, 20.

9. Copeland, *Game Player*, 69; Joseph B. Smith, *Portrait of a Cold Warrior*, 67; James R. Lilley, *China Hands: Nine Decades of Adventure, Espionage, and Diplomacy in Asia* (New York: Public Affairs, 2004), 73; McGehee, *Deadly Deceits*, 18; Mendez, *Master of Disguise*, 25; de Silva, *Sub Rosa*, 4; Bina Cady Kiyonaga, *My Spy: Memoirs of a CIA Wife* (New York: Avon, 2000), 68.

10. de Silva, *Sub Rosa*, 76.

11. "George A. Carroll, 54, Dies, Former Aide to Humphrey," *WP*, September 7, 1970; "CIA Analyst Anne I. Carroll Dies at 71," *WP*, April 18, 1999; Donald Wilber, CIA Clandestine Service History, "Overthrow of Premier Mossadeq of Iran, November 1952–August 1953" (March 1954); Washington Metropolitan Phone Book, 1963–64; John H. Richardson, *My Father the Spy: An Investigative Memoir* (New York: Harper Perennial, 2005), 209; James Adams, *Sellout*, 22–27; Tim Weiner et al., *Betrayal: The Story of Aldrich Ames, an American Spy* (New York: Random House, 1995), 170–72; "What is American Studies?" in *An American Studies Program at McLean High School*, ed. Jane G. Wilhelm (McLean High, 1963); "Fx. City Hall Is 'Stage' For Ibsen Classic," *FCT*, March 27, 1964; Alan McSurely, "Masterful Performance of an Explosive Drama," *FCT*, May 1, 1964; Wise, *Nightmover*, 48, 52.

12. "Nixon Picks Envoy to Denmark," *WP*, June 23, 1973; Dorothy McCardle, "VIP Parade Goes On," *WP*, November 21, 1954; Ellen Buell Parry, "Vienna Enters a National Beauty Contest," *WP*, December 4, 1949; "Richard H. Crowe, 63, Retired Officer with CIA," *WP*, November 21, 1974; Dorothy McCardle, "Crowe Crows Over Crow," *WP*, July 21, 1961; Elinor Lee, "Writers Whip Up Recipes," *WP*, June 24, 1956; Dorothy McCardle, "Top Success Sounds Off about Horn Tooting," *WP*, March 6, 1955; Dorothy McCardle, "Author in Search of a Plot Makes Good," *WP*, October 17, 1952; "Christmas Curtsies," *WP*, December 23, 1959; Dorothy McCardle, "What to Pack Is a Diplomatic Problem," *WP*, August 12, 1953; notice, *FH*, June 10, 1960, 1; Marion Merrell to Dear Brother and Husband, September 26, 1950, Box 11, Folder Saigon, CCP; Carole L. Herrick, *A Chronological History of McLean, Virginia* (Lorton: Capitol Advantage, 2001), 45.

13. Classified ads, *WP*, September 5, 1955, October 21, 1956, March 31, 1957, July 6, 1957, January 26, 1958, October 11, 1959, July 25, 1963; Fairfax County Office of the Attorney, *A Brief History of Planning, Zoning, and Environmental Constraints in Fairfax County, Virginia* (Fairfax: January 1974), 3–4; Terry Spielman Peters, *The Politics and Administration of Land Use Control* (Lexington: Lexington, 1974), 21; Grace Dawson, *No Little Plans: Fairfax County's PLUS Program for Managing Growth* (Washington, DC: Urban Institute, 1977), 118.

14. "C.M. Mutersbaugh Dies at Age 81," *WP*, May 23, 1995; "Photo Standalone,"

WP, June 5, 1971, E12; James J. Kelleher Jr., to Ed, December 26, 1972, Box 1, Folder General K–M; "Office of Special Operations," November 1960, and "Office of the Assistant to the Secretary of Defense (Special Operations)," August 22, 1963, Box 48, Folder US DOD, OSD, OSO, Lists of Staff, ELP; Marion to Mark, undated, Box 11, Folder Saigon, CCP.

15. Fairfax County Planning Division, *McLean Central Development Plan*, 1; Muriel Guinn, "Rapid McLean, Va. Development Excites Planners," *WP*, September 13, 1958; Jeff O'Neill, "'Little Pentagon' Will Boom McLean," *WP*, April 12, 1958.

16. Pierre Ghent, "A Ten Year History of the Increase in Land Values in the Metropolitan Washington Area 1949–1959," *Home Builders Monthly* (December 1959), 56–64.

17. "Lot Development Costs in Suburban Areas," *Home Builders* (July 1962), 10; *McLean Central Development Plan*, 1–2, 10; Division of Planning, County of Fairfax, *Comprehensive Plan: McLean Planning District* (February 1966), 4–5, 14; U.S. Department of Commerce, Bureau of the Census, *U.S. Census of Population and Housing*, Final Reports, Census Tracts Washington, DC – Md. – Va., and Virginia, 1950, 1960, 1970.

18. Agee, *Inside the Company*, 321; Mendez, *Master of Disguise*, 55; de Silva, *Sub Rosa*, 203, 223.

19. Danish reporter quoted in Beatriz Colomina, "Johnson on TV," in *Philip Johnson: The Constancy of Change*, ed. Emmanuel Petit (New Haven: Yale University Press, 2009), 68; Christopher T. Martin, "Tract-House Modern: A Study of Housing Design and Consumption in the Washington Suburbs, 1946–1960" (PhD diss., George Washington University, 2000), 178, 196; Charles Goodman quotes on the "American idiom" of glass in "The Modern Style House Takes the Outdoors Inside," *WP*, January 21, 1951; Charles Morton Goodman, Membership File, AIA; Ronald W. Marshall and Barbara A. Boyd, "Charles Goodman: Mid-Century Architect," *Modernism Magazine* (Winter 1998), 34–41; "Bromley Keables Smith," *Complete Marquis Who's Who Biographies,* January 17, 2003; "Chloethiel Woodard Smith, Architect and Planner, Dies," *WP*, January 1, 1993; Nicholas Satterlee, Membership File, AIA; also see, for example, Phincas R. Fiske, "Assembling the Site Was No Snap," *WP*, December 17, 1966; "Builder Likes House So Well He Seeks to Rent, Not Sell, It," *WP*, October 21, 1951; "A Look Into Future at Kitchen of 1963," *WP*, September 13, 1953; Sarah Booth Conroy, "City Slickers Are Taking to the Mountains," *WP*, June 10, 1967; street files, FCZB; Netherton et al., *Fairfax County, Virginia*, 627.

20. Marion to Darling, October 15, 1950, Box 11, Folder Saigon, CCP.

21. Marie Smith, "A Talent Scout with Many Talents," *WP*, June 13, 1965; Lawrence Laurent, "John W. Macy: A Man Whose Work Is His Hobby," *WP*, March 15, 1970; Richard M. Harley, "Six Hostage Families," *CSM*, November 26, 1980; "Todds' House Designed by Saarinen Student," *RT*, September 1, 1966.

22. Mendez, *Master of Disguise*, 158; Herrick, *Yesterday*, 174, 345; Clarridge, *Spy for All Seasons*, 59–73; Hiam, *Who the Hell*, 38; McGehee, *Deadly Deceits*, 81.

23. Florence Fitzsimmons Garbler, *CIA Wife: One Woman's Life Inside the CIA* (Santa Barbara: Fithian, 1994), 90; Mendez, *Master of Disguise*, 76–77; Richardson, *My Father the Spy*, 146, 156; Kiyonaga, *My Spy*, 143; de Silva, *Sub Rosa*, 203; Martin, "Tract-House Modern," 205; Holm, *American Agent*, 308; Parker, *Codename Mule*, 21, 53; H.L. Goodall Jr., *A Need to Know: The Clandestine History of a CIA Family* (Walnut Creek: Left Coast, 2006), 206; Karen L. Chiao and Mariellen B. O'Brien, *Spies' Wives* (Berkeley: Creative Arts, 2001), 18–19; *McLean Central Development Plan*, 5–6.

24. Kessler, *Inside CIA*, 8; Louie Estrada, "Langley's 'Country Feel' Isn't the Least Bit Covert," *WP*, March 12, 1994; Woodward, *Veil*, 456; Richard M. Bissell Jr., *Reflections of a Cold Warrior: From Yalta to the Bay of Pigs* (New Haven: Yale University Press, 1996), 205; James Tiptree Jr., "The Spooks Next Door," in *Meet Me at Infinity* (New York: Tom Doherty, 2000), 258; Floyd L. Paseman, *A Spy's Journey: A CIA Memoir* (St. Paul: Zenith, 2004), 21; Joseph Mastrangelo, "Visiting O'Toole's on the Day After," *WP*, March 25, 1976; Maxine Cheshire, "VIP," *WP*, October 26, 1980; Gary Moore, "Smoke Gets in Your Eyes," *WPM*, December 4, 1983; Barbara Blechman, "Mike and Mollie's," *WP*, October 17, 1985; DeNeen L. Brown, "A Cornerstone of History in Fairfax County," *WP*, February 23, 1991; Thomas Heath, "CIA Quietly Expanding Reston Offices," *WP*, October 10, 1988; Wise, *Spy Who Got Away*, 157; Chiao and O'Brien, *Spies' Wives*, 51, 237; Bill McAllister, "CIA," *WP*, June 29, 1975.

25. Herrick, *Yesterday*, 103–4; Betty Waller to President, January 30, 1961, Box 733, Folder PR2/ST33 – PR2/ST50, CSFJFK; John Kenneth Galbraith, *Ambassador's Journal: A Personal Account of the Kennedy Years* (Boston: Houghton Mifflin, 1969), 18; Evan Thomas, *Robert Kennedy: His Life* (New York: Simon & Schuster, 2000), 179–80; "Random Notes in Washington," *NYT*, December 11, 1961; Arthur M. Schlesinger Jr., *Robert Kennedy and His Times* (Boston: Houghton Mifflin, 1978), 592; Joan Braden, *Just Enough Rope*, 148; C. David Heymann, *RFK* (New York: Dutton, 1998), 114–16, 137–41; Marion Merrell to Katherine Biddle, July 18, 1962, Box 15.3, KBP.

26. "Hickory Hill Seminar," Box P-3, Folder Hickory Hill Seminar Attendance Lists; Ayer to Schlesinger, December 11, 1961; Schlesinger to Ayer, December 15, 1961; Schlesinger, "Memo for Hon. David Bell," February 17, 1964; Charles E. Bohlen to Schlesinger, January 11, 1962; Al Capp to Schlesinger, July 10, 1963; Douglas Dillon to Schlesinger, January 11, 1962; Gilpatric to Schlesinger, January 11, 1962; Lawrence S. Kubie to Schlesinger, October 2, 1963; Schlesinger to Kubie, October 9, 1963, Box P-3, Folder Hickory Hill Seminar Correspondence Ayer - Harriman; Schlesinger to Kennan, October 12, 1963; Ethel to Arthur, November 3, 1961; Schlesinger to Ethel, November 15, 1961; Schlesinger, "memos for RFK," December 26, 1961, September 24, 1962, August 21, 1963; Schlesinger to McNamara, October 12, 1962, Box P-3, Folder Hickory Hill Seminar Correspondence Katzenbach - Kubie, ASP; Evan Thomas, *Robert Kennedy*, 180–88; Heymann, *RFK*, 339.

27. W.W. Rostow, *The Stages of Economic Growth: A Non-Communist Manifesto* (Cambridge: Cambridge University Press, 1971), 12; John Kenneth Galbraith,

"The Hickory Hill Seminar – The Present State of Economics," Box W-6, Folder Galbraith Notes For Hickory Hill Seminar November 18, 1963, ASP; also see Schlesinger on the "middle-class revolution," in Arthur M. Schlesinger Jr., *Journals 1952–2000* (New York: Penguin, 2007), 103; "Memorandum from the President's Special Assistant (Schlesinger) to President Kennedy," March 10, 1961, Foreign Relations of the United States Vol. XII, American Republics, 1961–1963, distributed to Rostow and Allen Dulles; Evan Thomas, *Robert Kennedy*, 179.

28. K.A. Cuordileone, *Manhood and American Political Culture in the Cold War* (New York: Routledge, 2005), 216; Robert D. Dean, *Imperial Brotherhood: Gender and the Making of Cold War Foreign Policy* (Amherst: University of Massachusetts Press, 2001), 61; Dan Bohning, *The Castro Obsession: U.S. Covert Operations Against Cuba 1959–1965* (Washington, DC: Potomac, 2005), 187–88; Evan Thomas, *Robert Kennedy*, 177–79, 187, 238–39; Heymann, *RFK*, 340.

29. "Notes on the Interior Development of the Terminal Building," Box 497.1375, ESC.

30. Edward Lansdale, Subject: "Liberty Hall," November 29, 1963, Box 37, Folder 1/LA 1946–1968, ADP.

31. Andrew Friedman, "The Global Postcolonial Moment and the American New Town: India, Reston, Dodoma," *Journal of Urban History* 38.3 (May 2012), 553–76; *Reston Master Plan Report* (Fairfax County: Simon Enterprises, March 10, 1962); Washington Center for Metropolitan Studies, *Reston*, 59, 81–82, 162, 170, 341; Simon Enterprises, *The Reston Story* (Fairfax: Simon Enterprises, 1963), 4; U.S. National Capital Planning Commission, *A Policies Plan for the Year 2000: The Nation's Capital* (Washington, DC: NCPC, 1961); *Reston Letter* 4.1 (May 1966), 2, Box 1.26, PCA; Julian Whittlesey, "Put in Simon File Loose," Box 7.10, CRC.

32. Ervin Galantay, "Architecture," the *Nation*, December 12, 1966; author interview with Robert E. Simon, January 10, 2010; Karen Wilkin, "Gonzalo Fonseca," *Institut Valencia d'Art Modern, Gonzalo Fonseca 13-III/18-V-2003* (Valencia: IVAM, 2003), 72, 78; correspondence re Fonseca in Box 233.19, Reston Sculpture Folder, PCA.

33. Walt Rostow, *United States in the World Arena: An Essay in Recent History* (New York: Harper, 1960), 538; Anne W. Simon, *The New Years: A New Middle Age* (New York: Knopf, 1968), author note, 5, 28; Fred Flaxman, "Are We Being En-Gulfed?," *NR*, December 23, 1967.

34. Washington Center for Metropolitan Studies, *Reston*, 185, 362; Wolf von Eckardt, "Are We Being En-Gulfed?" *NR*, December 9, 1969; Roy J. Burroughs, Director of International Organizations Affairs, Office of International Housing, to Carol Lubin, Box 1, Folder ECE-Study Tour to USA in 1964, January 1–June 5, 1964, RG207, General Records of the Department of HUD-Office of International Affairs General Subject Files 1964–67, NARA; "Governor Dedicates Reston," *RT*, May 15, 1966; "Speech by Robert E. Simon Jr., President, Reston, Va., Inc. at the dedication of Reston, Virginia"; "Platform List," typed list; "Guests invited for luncheon December 4, 1965," Box 275.1; "The Dedication of Reston," *Reston Letter* 4.1 (May

1966), Box 1.26; Lady Bird Johnson to Robert Simon, July 15, 1967, Box 266.2; *Reston Letter* 3.2 (September 1965), Box 1.24, PCA; Jane G. Wilhelm, "The Good Life in Reston," paper prepared for the Reston Symposium, May 1985, 15, Box 9, Folder 1998 Feb. 26; Wilhelm, "April 10, 1999, Aries (The Ram)," Box 9, Folder 1982–1999 Reston: Robert E. Simon Jr., Correspondence and Other Materials, JWP; includes small portion of Friedman, "Global Postcolonial Moment," Copyright © 2012 by SAGE Publications.

35. Nan Netherton, *Reston, A New Town in the Old Dominion: A Pictorial History* (Norfolk: Donning, 1989), 76; Dan Hamady to Neal J. Hardy, February 15, 1963, and attached proposal for study tour, Box 2, Folder-UN-ECE Study Tour to USA 1960–61–62–63–64, RG207; schedule appears in Box 1, Folder 1; Soviet housing official Iouri Rodin in Inter-State Stenotype Reporting Service, "Study Tour: United States of America," June 18, 1964, Box 1, Folder 2, RG207, NARA.

36. Housing and Home Finance Agency, "Catalog of Projects of International Cooperation in Housing and Town and Country Planning (Washington, DC: HHFA, August 1957), 40; Thomai Serdari, "Albert Mayer, Architect and Town Planner: The Case for a Total Professional" (PhD diss., New York University, 2005), 18; "U.S. Building Abroad," *Architectural Forum*, January 1955, 104; The Ford Foundation, *Urban Planning, Poverty and Governance: The Ford Foundation, 1952–2002* (New Delhi: Ford Foundation, 2002), 9; Wilhelm, "April 10, 1999 Aries (The Ram)"; Clark, *Wallace Neff*, 28–29, 177–86; Wayne G. Broehl Jr., *The International Basic Economy Corporation* (Washington, DC: National Planning Association, 1968), 203–29.

37. Charles M. Goodman, "Architecture and Society," in *The People's Architects*, ed. Harry S. Ransom (Chicago: University of Chicago Press, 1964), 118.

38. Jane G. Wilhelm, "Good Life in Reston"; Jane Wilhelm, "Reston in Retrospect," *RT*, August 21, 1969, Box 9, Folder 1964–1991, JWP; Wilhelm, "April 10, 1999 Aries."

39. Wilhelm, "Reston in Retrospect"; Netherton, *Reston*, 92–94; Roger Braunstein, "Reston Reflections-Karl Ingebritsen," December 9, 1994, Box 453.14, PCA.

40. Kenneth Conboy and James Morrison, *The CIA's Secret War in Tibet* (Lawrence: University Press of Kansas, 2002), 46–65, 174, 182–85, 255; Netherton, *Reston*, 162; *A Place Called Reston*, directory, 1967, PCA; Parcel 0172 12 0028, FCLR; Douglas Valentine, *The Phoenix Program* (New York: Morrow, 1990), 9, 139, 201, 209; John Prados, *Lost Crusader: The Secret Wars of CIA Director William Colby* (Oxford: Oxford University Press, 2003), 209; "Hale, Hearty and a Hundred," *WP*, March 5, 1983; Wendy Swallow, "Development Boom Worrying Reston," *WP*, May 18, 1985; "Our Annual Report," Display ad, *WP*, April 15, 1978; "Wanted," Display ad, *WP*, November 5, 1978; ads in *WP*, September 16, 1979, November 12, 1977; "The Most Influential People in Reston Today," *RT*, January 5, 1984; "13 Seek Posts on RCA Board," *RT*, February 21, 1980; "Mustakos Reelected," *RT*, April 28, 1983; Wilhelm, "Reston in Retrospect."

41. Netherton, *Reston*, 52; "Housing 2," *The Reston Story*; Yvonne Chabrier,

"Getting Involved Out in Reston," *WP*, June 8, 1969; for examples, see "Howard Preston, 76, Dies," *WP*, April 22, 1992; Weiner, *Legacy*, 389; *A Place Called Reston*, 1967, 1973; Albert D. Biderman, "Problems of Tomorrow: The Prospective Impact of Large Scale Military Retirement," *Social Problems* 7.1 (Summer 1959), 88–89; Sandra G. Boodman, "Retired Admirals, Generals Enlist in Solid Brass Network for Reagan," *WP*, October 23, 1980; "William M. Walls, 79, Veteran CIA Officer," *WP*, December 18, 1995; "Paul J. Butler," *WP*, March 22, 1988; "CIA Official John K. Smith," *WP*, January 22, 2006; Cynthia Helms, *An Intriguing Life: A Memoir of War, Washington, and Marriage to an American Spymaster* (Lanham: Rowman & Littlefield, 2013), 10; Holm, *American Agent*, 308; Paseman, *Spy's Journey*, 271; Morley, *Our Man in Mexico*, 62; John Huminik, *Double Agent* (New York: New American Library, 1967), 141; Wise, *Spy Who Got Away*, 157; Kessler, *Spy Vs. Spy*, 38; Chiao and O'Brien, *Spies' Wives*, 69; "Cook's Tour 4," *RT*, February 15, 1966; Bill McAllister, "CIA," *WP*, June 29, 1975; Vicki Ostrolenk, "A Chinese Restaurant Serving Real Chinese Food," *WP*, February 8, 1970; Templeman et al., *Northern Virginia Heritage*, 67.

42. Kenneth Brademeier and Ronald Taylor, "CIA-Police Tie Kept Secret," *WP*, February 12, 1975; Karen De Young, "CIA Gave Area Police Training and Gear," *WP*, January 13, 1976; CIA, "The Family Jewels," 28, 114, 225–26, DNSA; Morton H. Halperin et al., *The Lawless State: The Crimes of the U.S. Intelligence Agencies* (New York: Penguin, 1976), 148; William J. Bartman, "New Career for Col. Kim," *FJ*, March 14, 1979.

43. Wise, *Molehunt*, 21–22.

44. Paul Herron, "Plush Barcroft is Growing Up," *WP*, October 28, 1951; "Noted Architect to Design Barcroft Homes," *WP*, July 2, 1950; Martin, "Tract-House Modern," 242–44; Margaret S. Boone, *Capital Cubans: Refugee Adaptation in Washington, DC* (New York: AMS, 1989), 77–83, 130–31; "High-Rise Started Under New Arlington Zoning," *WP*, September 15, 1962; Christina Breda Antoniades, "In Their Lives: Max E. Borges," *WPM*, January 3, 2010.

45. Pisani, *CIA and the Marshall Plan*, 143; Roger Daniels, *Guarding the Golden Door: American Immigration Policy and Immigrants Since 1882* (New York: Hill and Wang, 2004), 100; Kessler, *Escape From the CIA,* 59.

46. Stockwell, *In Search of Enemies*, 83; McGehee, *Deadly Deceits*, 144; Chiao and O'Brien, *Spies' Wives*, 10; Jeffrey T. Richelson, *The Wizards of Langley: Inside the CIA's Directorate of Science and Technology* (Boulder: Westview, 2001), 88.

47. McAllister, "CIA," *WP*, June 29, 1975; Chiao and O'Brien, *Spies' Wives*, 201; Fairfax County Planning Commission, *A Look Back* (Fairfax: 2008), 31.

48. Lilley, *China Hands*, 140; Richardson, *My Father the Spy*, 224; Boone, *Capital Cubans*, 45.

49. Goodall, *Need to Know*, 206; Philip Agee, *On the Run* (Secaucus, NJ: L. Stuart, 1987), 35; Snepp, *Irreparable Harm*, 171; *Holmes Run Acres: The Story of a Community* (Holmes Run Acres, 1976).

50. Roger L. Simon, "Spy Games," *LA Weekly*, June 27–July 3, 2003; *A Place Called Reston*, 1967; "Did You Know That . . ." *Reston Flyer*, October 24, 1966, 5,

Box 1.14, PCA; Parcel 0172 11140075, FCLR; "Thomas' First Novel Sold to 'Golden Boy' Producer," *RT*, October 15, 1966; Ross Thomas, *The Cold War Swap* (New York: Morrow, 1966), 155, 177, 200; Ross Thomas, *The Seersucker Whipsaw* (New York: Morrow, 1967), 315.

51. Oliver Bleeck, *The Brass Go-Between* (New York: Morrow, 1969), 200–202; Thomas, *Cold War Swap*, 200; Ross Thomas, *The Singapore Wink* (New York: Morrow, 1969), 65–66.

52. Ross Thomas, *Twilight at Mac's Place* (New York: Mysterious, 1990), 161, 315.

53. See, for instance, Fletcher Knebel and Charles W. Bailey II, *Seven Days in May* (New York: Harper & Row, 1962).

54. Allen Dulles, "Memorandum Respecting Section 202 of the Bill to Provide for a National Defense Establishment," April 25, 1947, in Ransom, *Intelligence Establishment*, 257; Stewart Alsop and Thomas Braden, *Sub Rosa: The O.S.S. and American Espionage* (New York: Reynal & Hitchcock, 1946), 47; Rositzke, *CIA's Secret Operations*, xxx; Christopher Felix, *A Short Course in the Secret War* (New York: Dell, 1963), 46–47; Goodall, *Need to Know*, 124; Olson, *Fair Play*, 116; Herrick, *Yesterday*, 174; Holzman, *James Jesus Angleton*, 99; Weiner, *Legacy*, 36; Tom Braden, *Eight Is Enough* (New York: Random House, 1975).

55. Interview with Colonel Gratian Yatsevitch, by William Burr, November 5, 1988, 22, 127, FISOHA; also see Ellen Herman, *The Romance of American Psychology: Political Culture in the Age of Experts* (Berkeley: University of California Press, 1995), 44, 129–30, 348.

56. Julie Phillips, *James Tiptree*, 129–32, 164–65.

57. R. Jack Smith, *Unknown CIA*, 149; Cline, *Secrets*, 145–46; Phillips, *James Tiptree*, 164.

58. Phillips, *James Tiptree*, 194, 185, 178, 97; Permit 23372, Ramshorn File, FCZB; Charles Platt, *Dream Makers Volume II: The Uncommon Men & Women Who Write Science Fiction* (New York: Berkley, 1983), 258; Marion to Dear Brother and Husband, September 26, 1950, Box 11, Folder Saigon, CCP; Leon Brown, Membership File; Thomas W.D. Wright, Membership File, AIA; Yvonne Shinhoster Lamb, "Thomas Wright, DC Architect Known for Eclectic Work," *WP*, March 3, 2006; Elinor Lee, "In This Home, the Mrs. Is Boss," *WP*, April 25, 1954; "'Tomorrow' Houses on Tour Today," *WP*, May 2, 1954; Sandy Isenstadt, "Richard Neutra and the Psychology of Architectural Consumption," in Goldhagen and Legault, *Anxious Modernisms*, 97–118.

59. Edward Lee Howard, *Safe House: The Compelling Memoirs of the Only CIA Spy to Seek Asylum in Russia* (Bethesda: National, 1995); William Corson et al., *Widows: Four American Spies, the Wives They Left Behind, and the KGB's Crippling of American Intelligence* (New York: Crown, 1989), 80; Wise, *Spy Who Got Away*; John F. Sullivan, *Gatekeeper: Memoirs of a CIA Polygraph Examiner* (Washington, DC: Potomac, 2007), 37, 94–95, 116; Olson, *Fair Play*, 241, 258; Mendez, *Master of Disguise*, 57–58; Kiyonaga, *My Spy*, 73.

60. Phillips, *James Tiptree*, 165–69.

61. Hersh, *Old Boys*; Wise, *Spy Who Got Away*, 56–57; Kessler, *Inside CIA*, 245;

McIntosh, *Sisterhood of Spies*, 242; Marchetti and Marks, *CIA and the Cult of Intelligence,* 277–81; CIA Memo, Chief, Life Sciences Research Division to Chairman Special Panel, November 15, 1976, CREST.

62. McIntosh, *Sisterhood of Spies*, 242, 246; Paseman, *Spy's Journey*, 13, 19; Phillips, *James Tiptree*, 162–67, 121; Carmela Ciuraru, *Nom De Plume: A (Secret) History of Pseudonyms* (New York: HarperCollins, 2011), 239–66; Mark Seinfelt, *Final Drafts: Suicides of World-Famous Authors* (Amherst: Prometheus, 1999); Platt, *Dream Makers*, 263.

63. Donna Haraway, *Primate Visions: Gender, Race, and Nature in the World of Modern Science* (New York: Routledge, 1989), 26–59; Phillips, *James Tiptree*, 15–38; Platt, *Dream Makers*, 260.

64. See, for instance, photos in Mary Hastings Bradley, *On the Gorilla Trail* (New York: D. Appleton, 1922); Phillips, *James Tiptree*, 166; Tom Gilligan, *CIA Life: 10,000 Days with the Agency* (Guilford: Foreign Intelligence Press, 1991), 68.

65. Platt, *Dream Makers,* 262–64; Phillips, *James Tiptree*, 167–72.

66. Phillips, *James Tiptree*, 174, 7, 148, 289, 366, 239, 344, 215, 194-95; Eleanor Dulles, *Chances of a Lifetime*, 234; Sherwood, *Foggy Bottom*, 29; Alice Bradley Sheldon, "Preference for Familiar or Novel Stimulation as a Function of the Novelty of the Environment" (PhD diss., George Washington University, 1967), 89.

67. Phillips, *James Tiptree*, 430, 165, 208; Brugioni, *Eyeball to Eyeball*, xii, 127–28, 526–27.

68. Phillips, *James Tiptree*, 164.

69. Ibid., 282, 277, 291–92, 379.

70. Corson, *Widows*, 49–50, 82; Gup, *Book of Honor*, 192, and photo caption, 366.

71. Corson, *Widows*, 80–82, 141–50.

72. Nancy D. Polikoff, *Beyond (Straight and Gay) Marriage: Valuing All Families under the Law* (Boston: Beacon, 2008), 12; Friedan, *Feminine Mystique*, 90; Jaclyn Geller, "Critical Reflections on the Push for Same Sex Marriage," *The Connecticut Review* 33.1 (Spring 2011), 48; Amy Dru Stanley, *From Bondage to Contract: Wage Labor, Marriage, and the Market in the Age of Slave Emancipation* (Cambridge: Cambridge University Press, 1998), 16; George Lipsitz, *The Possessive Investment in Whiteness: How White People Profit from Identity Politics* (Philadelphia: Temple University Press, 2006), 1–23; Dolores Hayden, *Redesigning the American Dream*, 55–56, 66; Eric Avila, *Popular Culture in the Age of White Flight: Fear and Fantasy in Suburban Los Angeles* (Berkeley: University of California Press, 2004), 20–64; Goodall, *Need to Know*, 114, 348.

73. See May, *Homeward Bound*.

74. Burleigh, *Very Private Woman*, 111, 131–33; Chiao and O'Brien, *Spies' Wives*; Hersh, *Old Boys*, 451; Scott D. Breckinridge, *CIA and the Cold War: A Memoir* (Westport: Praeger, 1993), 137; Kiyonaga, *My Spy*, 101.

75. Kiyonaga, *My Spy*, 132–34, 161–65, 170–71, 180–82, 212; Leonard Mosley, *Power Play: Oil in the Middle East* (New York: Random House, 1973), 215; Morley,

Our Man in Mexico, 62; Goodall, *Need to Know*, 137–39; Richardson, *My Father the Spy*, 152; Garbler, *CIA Wife*, 84; Chiao and O'Brien, *Spies' Wives*, 37.

76. Goodall, *Need to Know*, 9, 156, 168, 218–19; Kiyonaga, *My Spy*, 239–40, 266; Richardson, *My Father the Spy*, 10, 217; Olson, *Fair Play*, 9; Larry J. Kolb, *Overworld: The Life and Times of a Reluctant Spy* (New York: Riverhead, 2004), 62; Corson, *Widows*, 79, 83; Holober, *Raiders of the China Coast*, 234; Chiao and O'Brien, *Spies' Wives*, 46–49; *The Man Nobody Knew: In Search of My Father CIA Spymaster William Colby* (First Run Features, 2011) and oral histories included in DVD "Special Features."

77. Goodall, *Need to Know*, 138; Kiyonaga, *My Spy*, 233–35; Cynthia Enloe, *Bananas, Beaches and Bases: Making Feminist Sense of International Politics* (Berkeley: University of California Press, 1990), 106; Richardson, *My Father the Spy*, 156; Chiao and O'Brien, *Spies' Wives*, 35–37, 104, 169, 175, 177, 181; *The Man Nobody Knew*; Parker, *Codename Mule*, 23; McGehee, *Deadly Deceits*, 20, 32.

78. See particularly Garbler, *CIA Wife*; Parker, *Codename Mule*, 86; on women as imperial actors, Rafael, "Colonial Domesticity"; Stoler, *Carnal Knowledge*, 55–66.

79. Mangold, *Cold Warrior*, 238.

80. Holzman, *James Jesus Angleton*; Mangold, *Cold Warrior*, 49, 240; Wise, *Molehunt*; David C. Martin, *Wilderness of Mirrors* (New York: Ballantine, 1980); Heymann, *Georgetown Ladies'*, 57; Burleigh, *Very Private Woman*; Goodall, *Need to Know*, 119.

81. Cohen, *States of Denial*, 147.

82. Mangold, *Cold Warrior*, 155–56, 237–43; Burleigh, *Very Private Woman*, 120, 128, 148; Cicely d'A. Angleton, *A Cave of Overwhelming* (Cabin John: Britain, 1995); Cynthia Helms, *An Ambassador's Wife in Iran* (New York: Dodd, Mead, 1981), 140–41; Richardson, *My Father the Spy*, 147; Atlee Phillips, *Night Watch*, 189, 239.

83. Phillips, *James Tiptree*, 201, 2, 215–16; Robert Silverberg, "Introduction," in James Tiptree Jr., *Warm Worlds and Otherwise* (New York: Ballantine, 1975), xii, xiv.

84. See, for example, Phillips, *James Tiptree*, 59, 85, 445; Joanna Russ, *The Country You Have Never Seen* (Liverpool: Liverpool University Press, 2007), 290–91; Ciuraru, *Nom De Plume*, 240; Camilla Decarnin et al., eds., *Worlds Apart: An Anthology of Lesbian and Gay Science Fiction and Fantasy* (Boston: Alyson, 1986).

85. Platt, *Dream Makers*, 267; Phillips, *James Tiptree*, 1, 35; Silverberg, "Introduction," xiii.

86. James Tiptree Jr., *Ten Thousand Light-Years from Home* (New York: Ace, 1973), 54–55.

87. Ibid., 63–67.

88. James Tiptree Jr., "All the Kinds of Yes," in *Warm Worlds*, 20; "With Delicate Mad Hands," "Your Faces, O My Sisters! Your Faces Are Filled with Light," "A Momentary Taste of Being," in Tiptree, *Her Smoke Rose Up Forever* (San Francisco: Tachyon, 2004); James Tiptree Jr., "The Only Neat Thing to Do," in *The Starry Rift* (New York: Tor, 1986); James Tiptree Jr., *Up the Walls of the World* (New York:

Berkley, 1978); also see Justine Larbalestier, *The Battle of the Sexes in Science Fiction* (Middletown: Wesleyan University Press, 2002), 208, 225.

89. Linda Gordon, "Internal Colonialism and Gender," in Stoler, *Haunted by Empire*.

90. Phillips, *James Tiptree*, 303.

91. Phillips, *James Tiptree*, 365, 363, photo plates, 391–93; James Tiptree Jr., *Brightness Falls from the Air* (New York: Tor, 1985); Weiner, *Legacy of Ashes*, 113–14.

92. Tiptree, *Ten Thousand*, 116; Phillips, *James Tiptree*, 208, 294.

93. James Tiptree Jr., *Meet Me at Infinity* (New York: Tom Doherty, 2000), 235; also see, Renato Rosaldo, "Imperialist Nostalgia," 68-90, in *Culture and Truth: The Remaking of Social Analysis* (Boston: Beacon, 1993); Phillips, *James Tiptree*, 36.

CHAPTER THREE

1. Stuart Hall, "When Was 'The Post-Colonial'? Thinking at the Limit" in *The Post-Colonial Question: Common Skies, Divided Horizons*, eds. Iain Chambers and Lidia Curti (London: Routledge, 1996), 246.

2. Fredric Jameson, "Cognitive Mapping," in *The Jameson Reader*, eds. Michael Hardt and Kathi Weeks (Oxford: Blackwell, 2000), 278; Kevin Lynch, *The Image of the City* (Cambridge: MIT Press, 1960).

3. Doreen Massey, *For Space* (London: Sage, 2005), 4, 12, 24; Doreen Massey, *Space, Place and Gender* (Cambridge: Polity, 1994); Doreen Massey, *World City* (Cambridge: Polity, 2007).

4. "Charles M. Merrell, Former U.S. Aide," *WP*, September 30, 1973; Lee Grove, "Notes on the Margin," *WP*, September 17, 1950; Mark Merrell to Mr. and Mrs. Charles Hayes, April 15, 1938, Box 19, Folder Mark Merrell, CCP; Mackall, "McLean, Fairfax County, Virginia," 7.

5. "Mrs. Merrell, Author, Social Worker, Dead," *WP*, December 28, 1968; Clinch Calkins, *Poems* (New York: Knopf, 1928), 5; Clinch Calkins, *Strife of Love in a Dream* (New York: Vantage, 1965); Clinch Calkins, *Some Folks Won't Work* (New York: Harcourt Brace, 1930); William L. Littlejohn, memo, Box 4, Folder Resettlement Administration, CCP.

6. Carolyn Bell Hughes, "'Progress' Changes Suburban Scene," *WP*, March 18, 1956; "Malissa Childs Bows in with New Year," *WP*, January 2, 1949; "Little Sisters Get in on the Fun," *WP*, December 31, 1948; "Dr. Fosdick Lauds Duggan at Funeral," *WP*, December 24, 1948; "Miss Walker Presented at Dance," *WP*, December 28, 1948; Patricia Grady, "Jacksons Greet Guests at Hickory Hill Party," *WP*, May 4, 1942; "Community Auto Plan Saves Gas in Nearby Virginia," *WP*, August 12, 1941; Dorothy McCardle, "Poetic Laurels Are Hers," *WP*, April 13, 1965; Clinch Calkins, *Lady on the Hunt* (New York: Harper & Brothers, 1950).

7. "Fleming Is Nominated Ambassador," *WP*, March 20, 1951; "British Made Phillips Quit, Senator Says," *WP*, August 29, 1944; Drew Pearson, "The Washing-

ton Merry-Go-Round," *WP*, August 28, 1944; "Ricardo Alfaro Luncheon Host," *WP*, November 25, 1934; "Indian Embassy Dinner Party Celebrates Nehru's Birthday," *WP*, November 15, 1947; Ellen Buell Parry, "Sub-Deb Off to Addis Ababa," *WP*, February 8, 1950.

8. "Charles M. Merrell, Former U.S. Aide"; "Purchase Request and Report Form: Miscellaneous Drugs for Cambodia," December 24, 1950, Box 13, Folder Health Drugs, RG469, Records of U.S. Foreign Assistance Agencies 1948–1961, Mission to Vietnam Program and Requirements Division, Subject Files 1950–1957, NARA; Weiner, *Legacy of Ashes*, 28; Lee Grove, "Notes on the Margin."

9. Mark to Marion and Maria, October 13, 1950, Folder Mark's Letters from Overseas; Mark to Dearest Girls, October 28, 1950, Folder 1950 (Saigon); Mark to Dearest Girls, December 1, 1950, Folder Saigon; Mark to Darlings, November 26, 1950, Folder Saigon, all in Box 11, CCP. Several folders simply bear the name "Saigon," hereinafter referred to as "Folders Saigon."

10. Mark to Marion and Maria, October 13, 1950; Mark Merrell to Dearest Girls, Letter 14, Box 11, Folder Mark's Letters from Overseas.

11. Mark to Marion, December 23, 1950, Folder 1950 (Saigon); Mark to Darlings, November 26, December 4, and December 18, 1950, Folders Saigon; Mark to Darlings, September 29, 1950, Mark to Marion and Maria, October 13, 1950, and Mark Merrell to Dearest Girls, Letter 14, Folder Mark's Letters from Overseas; Mark to My Pets, December 28, 1950, and "Saigon Saga," January 11, 1951, Folders Saigon, all in Box 11, CCP.

12. Mark to Darlings, September 2, 1950, Box 11, Folder Mark's Letters from Overseas; Mark to Sweethearts, November 20, 1950, and Mark to My Pets, December 28, 1950, Box 11, Folders Saigon.

13. Mark to Darlings, September 29, 1950, and "Saigon Saga," November 4, 1950, Folder Mark's Letters from Overseas; Mark to Dearest Girls, October 28, 1950, Folder 1950 (Saigon), Box 11, CCP.

14. "Saigon Saga," January 9, 1951, Mark to Darlings, November 26, 1950, and Mark to Dearest Girls, December 1, 1950, Box 11, Folders Saigon.

15. "Saigon Saga," January 9, 1951, Box 11, Folders Saigon.

16. "Saigon Saga," November 4, 1950, Box 11, Folder Mark's Letters from Overseas.

17. Harold E. Schwartz to Mark Merrell, "Procurement of Paper Bags," December 19, 1950, Box 1, Folder Letters July–December 1950, RG469, NARA.

18. Merrell to Mr. Blum et al., "Some Thoughts on the First-Aid Program," December 29, 1950, Box 15, Folder Public Health-First-Aid Kit Program, RG469, NARA.

19. "Initial Material and Equipment for Cambodia," December 22, 1950; multiple "Purchase Request and Report Form," December 24, 1950, Box 13, Folder Health Drugs; Merrell to Mr. Blum et al., "Some Thoughts on the First-Aid Program," December 29, 1950; Merrell to Blum et al., February 21, 19–, Box 15, Folder Public Health-First-Aid Kit Program; Blum to Merrell, August 22, 1950, Folder Letters July–December 1950, RG469, NARA.

20. Weiner, *Legacy of Ashes*, 28–29, 35; See Richard Bissell memos, Box 4, Inter-office Memos 1948–1950, Folder September 1950, RG469, NARA; Joseph W. Alsop, *I've Seen the Best of It: Memoirs* (New York: Norton, 1992), 278.

21. Kathryn C. Statler, *Replacing France: The Origins of American Intervention in Vietnam* (Lexington: University Press of Kentucky, 2007), 39; Harry Bayard Price, *The Marshall Plan and Its Meaning* (Ithaca: Cornell University Press, 1955), 203; Mark to Darlings, December 4, 1950, Box 11, Folders Saigon, CCP; Economic Cooperation Administration, Division of Statistics & Reports, *ECA Programs in Southeast Asia* (October 12, 1951), 12.

22. William Conrad Gibbons, *The U.S. Government and the Vietnam War: Executive and Legislative Roles and Relationships, Part I* (Washington, DC: U.S. GPO, 1984), 91–92; Robert Shaplen, *The Lost Revolution: The U.S. in Vietnam, 1946–1966* (New York: Harper & Row, 1966), 88.

23. Mark Merrell to Marion and Maria et al., October 13, 1950, Box 11, Folder Mark's Letters from Overseas.

24. William S. Bushnell, "The Quiet American: Graham Greene's Vietnam Novel through the Lenses of Two Eras," in *Why We Fought: America's Wars in Film and History*, eds. Peter C. Rollins and John E. O'Connor (Lexington: University Press of Kentucky, 2008), 411.

25. Edward E. Clark to Merrell, December 27, 1950; Purchase order, December 12, 1950; Clark to Merrell, December 6, 1950; AA Smith to Merrell, November 28, 1950; HC Faxon to Merrell, November 24, 1950; United Engineers to Merrell, November 22, 1950; James Miller to Merril [sic], November 20, 1950; AA Smith to Merrell, November 11, 1950, Box 1, Folder Letters July–December 1950, RG469; Mark to Darlings, December 4, 1950, and Mark Merrell to Darling Marion, January 9, 1951, Box 11, Folders Saigon, CCP.

26. Harold E. Schwartz to Merrell, "Procurement of Paper Bags," December 19, 1950, Box 1, Folder Letters July–December 1950; "Initial Materials and Equipment for Cambodia," December 22, 1950, Box 13, Folder Health Drugs, RG469.

27. Mark to Marion and Maria, October 13, 1950, Mark to Marion and Julie, undated letter, and "Saigon Saga," November 4, 1950, Box 11, Folder Mark's Letters from Overseas, CCP.

28. "Saigon Saga," December 20, 1950, Box 11, Folders Saigon.

29. Mark to Marion and Maria, October 13, 1950, and Mark to Darlings, September 2, 1950, Box 11, Folder Mark's Letters from Overseas.

30. Mark to Marion, December 23, 1950, Box 11, Folder 1950 (Saigon), CCP; see, for example, John Prados, "The CIA and the Face of Decolonization," in *The Eisenhower Administration, the Third World, and the Globalization of the Cold War*, eds. Kathryn C. Statler and Andrew L. Johns (Lanham: Rowman & Littlefield, 2006), 32; Leary, *Perilous Missions*, 156–59.

31. Mark Merrell, Application for Employment, International Bank for Reconstruction and Development, Box 16, Folder Mark Merrell (1955), CCP.

32. Ronald H. Spector, *Advice and Support: The Early Years of the U.S. Army in Vietnam, 1941–1960* (New York: Free Press, 1985), 121.

33. "Pacification," written before October 1, 1953, Box 35, Folder Reports, Pacification with annex, ELP.

34. Kurt Falk is signing for Merrell as supply officer by March 19, 1951, Box 13, Folder Health Drugs, RG469; Lee Grove, "Notes on the Margin"; Dorothy McCardle, "He's Mean Man with a Frying Pan," *WP*, March 18, 1951.

35. "Charles M. Merrell, Former U.S. Aide."

36. Clinch Calkins, *Calendar of Love* (New York: Simon and Schuster, 1952), frontispiece, 244.

37. Ibid., 158, 167, 210–12, 234.

38. Ibid., 269.

39. Dorothy McCardle, "Guests Like Ike When They Play This New Parlor Game," *WP*, February 24, 1952.

40. Microfilm Card DB 1216, 268, FCSP.

41. Calkins, *Strife of Love*, 24.

42. Saigon Road Site Plans Microfilm File, Sec. 1–5, FCSP; Muriel Guinn, "Langley-McLean Zone Fight Seen," *WP*, April 12, 1956; Muriel Guinn, "Property Owners Object to Va. Highway Change," *WP*, June 23, 1956; Marion to Mark, undated, Box 11, Folders Saigon, CCP.

43. Dorothy McCardle, "Langley Mourns Passing of an Era," *WP*, April 28, 1957.

44. Parcel record, FCLR; Permit 27713, Swinks Mill File, FCZB.

45. House details from permits in Saigon File, FCZB; "Builder Likes House So Well He Seeks to Rent, Not Sell, It," *WP*, October 21, 1951; "A Look into Future at Kitchen of 1963," *WP*, September 13, 1953; Sarah Booth Conroy, "City Slickers Are Taking to the Mountains," *WP*, June 10, 1967; Patrick D. Hazard, "The Public Arts: 'The Shape of Things,'" *The English Journal* 51.9 (Dec. 1962), 660; Lois Craig, *Design Quarterly* 132 (1986), 25; Display ad, *WP*, April 24, 1971.

46. Classified ads, *WP*, August 13, 1959, August 15, 1959, August 18, 1959, May 22, 1960, November 18, 1961, November 19, 1961, July 28, 1962, October 25, 1963.

47. John B. Williams, "It's Happening in Real Estate," *WP*, August 12, 1967.

48. Mary L. Dudziak, *Cold War Civil Rights: Race and the Image of American Democracy* (Princeton: Princeton University Press, 2000), 47–48; Bill Gold, "The District Line," *WP*, May 12, 1971; "Obituary: Margaret Stephens Jochem, English Teacher," *WP*, August 2, 2007; "Obituary: Robin Jochem, 31, Computer Technician," *WP*, December 11, 1977; "Army Col. Trevor Dupuy Dies," *WP*, June 9, 1995; details in lots 19B, Saigon Circle, and 28, Sec. 5, Saigon File, FCZB.

49. See Mark Philip Bradley, *Imagining Vietnam & America: The Making of Postcolonial Vietnam, 1919–1950* (Chapel Hill: University of North Carolina Press, 2000).

50. Mark to Marion, December 23, 1950, Folder 1950 (Saigon); "Saigon Saga," December 20, 1950, "Saigon Saga," January 11, 1951, and Marion to Mark, undated, Folders Saigon, in Box 11, CCP.

51. See Kramer, *Blood of Government*.

52. Marion to Mark, December 5, 1950, Box 11, Folders Saigon, CCP.

53. See Marion to Mark, written on regretted invitation to PA Salt Manufactur-

ing Company Luncheon, September 27, 1950; Mark Merrell to Darlings, December 4, 1950, Box 11, Folders Saigon.

54. Grant, *Facing the Phoenix*, 43.

55. Colby, *Honorable Men*, 35; Stanley Karnow, *Vietnam: A History* (New York: Viking, 1983), 282; Weiner, *Legacy of Ashes*, 210; Neil Sheehan, *A Bright Shining Lie: John Paul Vann and America in Vietnam* (New York: Vintage, 1988), 9.

56. Transcript, Lucien Conein Oral History Interview I, by Ted Gittinger, November 12, 1982, 3–4, LBJ.

57. Thomas L. Ahern Jr., *CIA and the House of Ngo: Covert Action in South Vietnam, 1954–63* (Washington: Center for the Study of Intelligence, 2000), 193; Archimedes L.A. Patti, *Why Viet Nam?: Prelude to America's Albatross* (Berkeley: University of California Press, 1980), 113; Grant, *Facing the Phoenix*, 43–50; Young, *Vietnam Wars*, 10; R. Harris Smith, *O.S.S.: The Secret History of America's First Central Intelligence Agency* (Berkeley: University of California Press, 1972), 352.

58. Young, *Vietnam Wars*, 22, 25, 31; Latham, *Modernization as Ideology*, 157; ECA, "ECA Programs in Southeast Asia," 4; Weiner, *Legacy of Ashes*, 116–21.

59. Ranelagh, *The Agency*, 431.

60. Young, *Vietnam Wars*, 22.

61. Nashel, *Edward Lansdale's Cold War*, 96.

62. Currey, *Edward Lansdale*, 3–16, 26–27, 67–76; Edward Geary Lansdale, *In the Midst of Wars: An American's Mission to Southeast Asia* (New York: Harper & Row, 1972), author statement; also on family's Virginia history, Gerry to Ed, July 8, 1979, Box 82, Folder Lansdale Family, ELP.

63. Lansdale, Journal No. 12, March 30, 1947; Journal No. 15, June 10, 1947; Journal No. 18, October 13, 1947, Box 83, Folder Helen Lansdale, ELP; Currey, *Edward Lansdale*, 34–58; D. Michael Shafer, *Deadly Paradigms: The Failure of U.S. Counterinsurgency Policy* (Princeton: Princeton University Press, 1988), 205–12; Kolko, *Confronting the Third World*, 27–29.

64. Currey, *Edward Lansdale*; Shafer, *Deadly Paradigms*; Douglas S. Blaufarb, *The Counterinsurgency Era: U.S. Doctrine and Performance, 1950 to the Present* (New York: Free Press, 1977); Major-General Edward G. Lansdale, "Viet Nam: Do We Understand Revolution?" *Foreign Affairs* (Oct. 1964).

65. Prados, "CIA and the Face of Decolonization," 32.

66. Sheehan et al., *Pentagon Papers*, 36; Nashel, *Edward Lansdale's Cold War*, 52, 78.

67. Sheehan et al., *Pentagon Papers*, 55; Currey, *Edward Lansdale*, 140, 149.

68. Lansdale in Al Santoli, *To Bear Any Burden: The Vietnam War and Its Aftermath in the Words of Americans and Southeast Asians* (Bloomington: Indiana University Press, 1999), 50–51.

69. "Psychological Warfare," Declassified April 17, 1989, Box 35, Folder Reports, Pacification with annex, ELP.

70. Ed to Helen et al., May 2, 1955, Box 83, Folder Edward G. Lansdale, ELP; Transcript, Rufus Phillips Oral History Interview I, March 4, 1982, by Ted Gittinger, 2, LBJ; Currey, *Edward Lansdale*, 142–48; Christian G. Appy, *Patriots: The*

Vietnam War Remembered from All Sides (New York: Penguin, 2003), 50; Rufus Phillips, *Why Vietnam Matters: An Eyewitness Account of Lessons Not Learned* (Annapolis: Naval Institute Press, 2008), 14, 19; "Joseph Frank Baker, CIA Official," *WP*, August 1, 2004.

71. Ed to Helen et al., May 2, 1955, and February 13, 1955, Box 83, Folder Edward G. Lansdale, ELP; Grant, *Facing the Phoenix*, 106; Alsop, *I've Seen the Best*, 380; Rufus Phillips, *Why Vietnam Matters*, 13.

72. Conein Oral History I, 15, 6–8; Lansdale, *Midst of Wars*, 168; "Team Report," in Sheehan et al., *Pentagon Papers*, 58, 60–61, 66; Prados, *Safe for Democracy*, 143; Karnow, *Vietnam*, 221–22; Currey, *Edward Lansdale*, 163; Grant, *Facing the Phoenix*, 108.

73. Brig. Gen. Lansdale Memo to Deputy Secretary Gilpatric, "Ngo Dinh Diem," April 25, 1961, Pentagon Papers Appendixes, NARA online; Transcript, Edward G. Lansdale Oral History Interview II, September 15, 1981, by Ted Gittinger, 37, LBJ; Sheehan et al., *Pentagon Papers*, 21; Young, *Vietnam Wars*, 41–45, 53; Lansdale, *Midst of Wars*, 159–60, 168, 333; Nashel, *Edward Lansdale's Cold War*, 116; Prados, *Lost Crusader*, 71.

74. Currey, *Edward Lansdale*, 156.

75. Lansdale, "Memo for the Record, Subject: Pacification in Vietnam," July 16, 1959, Box 42, Folder Memos 1958–1961; Ed to Helen et al., May 2, 1955, Box 83, Folder Edward G. Lansdale, ELP; Sheehan et al., *Pentagon Papers*, 62.

76. Phillips Oral History I, 28; Lansdale to INS, January 28, 1976, Box 2, Folder Bui Anh Tuan, ELP; Sheehan et al., *Pentagon Papers*, 65.

77. Lansdale to Miami District Director Edward T. Sweeney, August 3, 1978, Box 6, Folder Pham Duy Can, ELP.

78. Emmanuel Ho Q.P. to General, September 25, 1977, Box 3, Folder Ho Quang Phuoc [sic], ELP.

79. Ahern, *CIA and the House*, 41–43; Ed to Helen et al., February 13, 1955, Box 83, Folder Edward G. Lansdale, ELP.

80. Ed to Helen et al., May 2, 1955, Box 83, Folder Edward G. Lansdale; Trinh Minh Nhut to Lansdale, October 22, 1969, Box 8, Folder Trinh Minh The and Family, ELP; Lansdale in Santoli, *To Bear Any Burden*, 63–64.

81. Sheehan et al., *Pentagon Papers*, 18, 56, 61, 65; Lansdale Oral History I, 27; Nashel, *Edward Lansdale's Cold War*, 82; Currey, *Edward Lansdale*, 156, 159; Young, *Vietnam Wars*, 45; George McT. Kahin, *Intervention: How America Became Involved in Vietnam* (New York: Knopf, 1986), 77; Rufus Phillips, *Why Vietnam Matters*, 39, 68; Lansdale, *Midst of Wars*, 168, 226.

82. Conein Oral History I, 9–10; Sheehan et al., *Pentagon Papers*, 57–58.

83. Ahern, *Vietnam Declassified*, 14; Phillips in Santoli, *To Bear Any Burden*, 56.

84. "Subject: Persons with Knowledge of Vietnam Events, 1954–1956," undated, Box 35, Folder Vietnam 1954–56 Miscellany, ELP.

85. Grant, *Facing the Phoenix*, 112.

86. Lansdale, *Midst of Wars*, 179, 215–16, 236–37, 241; Grant, *Facing the Phoenix*,

113; Appy, *Vietnam War Remembered*, 51–53; Rufus Phillips, *Why Vietnam Matters*, 79; Lansdale, "Memo for the Record, Subject: Pacification in Vietnam."

87. Typed notes on Operation Brotherhood, Box 35, Folder Operation Brotherhood, ELP.

88. Rufus Phillips, *Why Vietnam Matters*, 79; Phillips in *Prelude to Tragedy: Vietnam, 1960–1965*, eds. Harvey Neese and John O'Donnell (Annapolis: Naval Institute Press, 2001), 7.

89. Lansdale, "Memo for the Record, Subject: Pacification in Vietnam."

90. Ahern, *CIA and the House*, 98.

91. Ibid., 28.

92. Currey, *Edward Lansdale*, 42, 70–71, 85; Lansdale, *Midst of Wars*, 122.

93. Lansdale, *Midst of Wars*, 362.

94. Ahern, *CIA and the House*, 17, 28, 218, 47, 96; Andre Nguyen van Chau, *Ngo Dinh Thi Hiep, or A Lifetime in the Eye of the Storm* (Salt Lake City: American Book Classics, 2000), 195.

95. Nashel, *Edward Lansdale's Cold War*, 110; Rufus Phillips, *Why Vietnam Matters*, 13, 27.

96. Ahern, *CIA and the House*, 105.

97. Currey, *Edward Lansdale*, 41, 194.

98. See photograph in Grant, *Facing the Phoenix*.

99. Grant, *Facing the Phoenix*, 45, 64, 68, 110–11, 197; Lu to Ed, October 12, 1959, Box 37, Folder US DOD, OSD, Conein, Lucien 1959, ELP.

100. Phillips Oral History I, 39–40; See also Alsop, *I've Seen the Best*, 380.

101. Transcript, Rufus Phillips Oral History Interview II, May 27, 1982, by Ted Gittinger, 1, LBJ.

102. NOVA White Pages, 1962–63; Grant, *Facing the Phoenix*, 170; Rufus Phillips, *Why Vietnam Matters*, 106.

103. Conein Oral History I, 20; Grant, *Facing the Phoenix*, 201; Stanley Karnow, "Spook," *NYT*, January 3, 1999.

104. Greater McLean Community Directory (McLean Lions Club, 1960); Permit 16111, Waverly File, FCZB; "Russell Arundel, 75, Dies, Pepsi Official, Sportsman," *WP*, February 3, 1978; Netherton, *Reston*, 160, 163; David Field, "Arundel Papers Look to South Fairfax," *WT*, January 1, 1993; Nicholas Graham, "Publisher, Conservationist Arundel Dies at 83," *Fairfax County Times*, February 9, 2011; Heymann, *RFK*, 139.

105. Lansdale Memo for Secretary McNamara, "Subject: Special Operations," February 25, 1963, Box 95 Material Returned from U.S. Department of Defense, Folder (Former) Box 3, Folder 1; "Report," 1956, Box 48, US DOD, Folder Operational Personnel for Special Duty, ELP; Lansdale, "Operation Mongoose" Memo to the Special Group (Augmented), July 25, 1962, reprinted in Aviva Chomsky et al., eds., *The Cuba Reader: History, Culture, Politics* (Durham: Duke University Press, 2003), 541.

106. Lansdale to Diem, April 2, 1959, Box 42, Folder Diem, ELP; Nashel, *Edward Lansdale's Cold War*, 110; Currey, *Edward Lansdale*, 194–96.

107. Le Ly Hayslip, *When Heaven and Earth Changed Places: A Vietnamese Woman's Journey From War to Peace* (New York: Penguin, 1989), 69; Ahern, *Vietnam Declassified*, 193, 302; Young, *Vietnam Wars*, 212–23; Blaufarb, *Counterinsurgency Era*; Shafer, *Deadly Paradigms*; Nguyen Khai, *Past Continuous* (Willimantic, CT: Curbstone, 2001), 61.

108. Grant, *Facing the Phoenix*, 197, 201.

109. Weiner, *Legacy of Ashes*, 214; Young, *Vietnam Wars*, 82–84; Prados, *Lost Crusader*, 83–87; Rufus Phillips, *Why Vietnam Matters*, 110; Latham, *Modernization as Ideology*, 185.

110. Phillips Oral History II, 7; Rufus Phillips, *Why Vietnam Matters,* 106, 117, 128, 135–36, 160; Grant, *Facing the Phoenix*, 170–71; Latham, *Modernization as Ideology*, 182, 186; Khai, *Past Continuous*, 61.

111. Richardson, *My Father the Spy*, 141–44, 150.

112. Karnow, *Vietnam*, 263; Grant, *Facing the Phoenix*, 200; Currey, *Edward Lansdale*, 253, 284; "Memorandum for the Record of a Meeting at the Department of State, Washington, September 16, 1963, 11 a.m.," and "Meeting at the State Department, September 16, 1963, 11:00 AM—Subject: Vietnam," DNSA; Frederick Nolting, *From Trust to Tragedy: The Political Memoirs of Frederick Nolting, Kennedy's Ambassador to Diem's Vietnam* (New York: Praeger, 1988); Peck, *Washington Dulles*, 82.

113. Transcript, Lucien Conein Oral History Interview II, by Ted Gittinger, June 2, 1983, 5, LBJ; Tran Van Don, *Our Endless War* (Novato, CA: Presidio, 1978), 90, 106; Ahern, *CIA and the House*, 169, 193, 199.

114. Ahern, *CIA and the House*, 192, 187.

115. Conein Oral History II, 15, 25, 27–28; Weiner, *Legacy of Ashes*, 219–21.

116. Conein Oral History II, 38.

117. Richardson, *My Father the Spy*, 204–12; Phillips Oral History II, 29; Permit 21854, Ridge File, FCZB; Sarah Booth Conroy, "After a 25-Year Run, Holmes Is Still Ahead," *WP*, September 12, 1976; NOVA White Pages, 1965–66; Parcel record, FCLR.

118. Sheehan, *Bright Shining Lie*, 334.

119. Permit 15931, Bryn Mawr First Addition Resubdivision of Lots 2-5 File, FCZB; Parcel 0304 35 0004, FCLR; Washington Metropolitan Phone Book, 1963–64; VA Yellow Pages, 1964–65.

120. Parcel record, FCLR; Phineas R. Fiske, "For King's Manor Builders Assembling the Site Was No Snap," *WP*, December 17, 1966.

121. Ahern, *CIA and the House*, 188; Currey, *Edward Lansdale*, 292.

122. Dave Hudson to Rufe, October 27, 1966, Box 54, Folder Rufus Phillips (2); Lansdale to Ambassador Lodge, January 26, 1966, Box 97.2, ELP; Currey, *Edward Lansdale*, 292.

123. SLO Team, "Report: Classified," Box 95.6; Joe Baker to John G. Bacon, October 27, 1965, Box 95, Folder (Former) Box 4 Folders 8–14; "All Team Members," October 8, 1965, Box 96.6, ELP; Phillips Oral History II, 34; Alfred W.

McCoy, *Policing America's Empire: The United States, the Philippines, and the Rise of the Surveillance State* (Madison: University of Wisconsin Press, 2009), 377; Currey, *Edward Lansdale*, 209.

124. Deutch to Wives, November 22, 1965, Box 53, Folder Michael Deutch 1965–66; Lansdale to the Old Team, February 10, 1968, and Lansdale to All Members of the Team, September 18, 1967, Box 59, Folder Memoranda, Lansdale to "the Old Team," ELP.

125. Alfred W. McCoy, *The Politics of Heroin in Southeast Asia* (New York: Harper & Row, 1972), 211, 213, 417; Currey, *Edward Lansdale*, 298.

126. Ed to Dave, February 18, 1966, Box 83, Folder Edward Lansdale, ELP; Grant, *Facing the Phoenix*, 266; Nguyen Cao Ky, *Buddha's Child: My Fight to Save Vietnam* (New York: St. Martin's, 2002), 317.

127. Lansdale Oral History II, 56.

128. SLO Report, ELP; Lansdale Oral History II, 84; Lydia M. Fish, "General Edward G. Lansdale and the Folksongs of Americans in the Vietnam War," *The Journal of American Folklore* 102.406 (Oct.–Dec., 1989), 397.

129. SLO Report, ELP; Grant, *Facing the Phoenix*, 267.

130. Lansdale to Robert De Vecchi, May 20, 1975 and Lansdale to Whom It May Concern, May 20, 1975, Box 5, Folder Nguyen Duc Thang, ELP; Lansdale in Santoli, *To Bear Any Burden*, 197; Lansdale to Old Team, February 10, 1968, Box 59, Folder Memoranda, Lansdale to "the Old Team"; Lansdale to Ambassador Lodge, January 26, 1966, Box 97.2; Nguyen Duc Thang, "Gentlemen," Box 61, Folder Nguyen Duc Thang (General), ELP; Lansdale Oral History II, 53–54.

131. Vernon A. Walters, *Silent Missions* (New York: Doubleday, 1978), 440.

132. Vera E. McCluggage, Transcript for tapes 30-31, Hoover Institute, August 1981, Finding Aid Appendix B; SLO Report; Lansdale to Baker, September 14, 1966, Box 53, Folder Joseph Baker 1966–68; Ky to Dear Lansdale, undated, Box 54, Folder Nguyen Cao Ky 1966, ELP; Currey, *Edward Lansdale*, 303, 312–14; Nashel, *Edward Lansdale's Cold War*, 147–48; Fish, "General Edward G. Lansdale," 392.

133. Rufe to Ed, November 5, 1965, Box 54, Folder Rufus C. Phillips; Lansdale to (redacted), January 30, 1968, Box 96.3; Lodge to Lansdale, April 20, 1967, Box 54, Folder Henry Cabot Lodge 1966–67, ELP.

134. Lodge to Lansdale, January 24, 1967, Box 54, Folder Lodge, ELP.

135. SLO Report; Richard Nixon to Ed, May 4, 1967, Box 54, Folder Richard Nixon 1965–67, ELP; Lansdale Oral History II, 54.

136. SLO Report, ELP; Fish, "General Edward G. Lansdale," 398, 400.

137. Vera E. McCluggage, Transcript for tapes 30–31, Hoover Institute, ELP.

138. Pham Duy to Hank Miller, March 5, 1967, Box 54, Folder Pham Duy Can 1966–67, ELP; See also Kaplan, *Anarchy of Empire*, 29–31.

139. Prados, "CIA and the Face of Decolonization," 32; Kristin Ross, *Fast Cars, Clean Bodies*, 110–11.

140. "Draft–Comments on the Strategic Hamlet Program," May 3, 1963, Box 40, Folder Rufus Phillips (1) 1957–1963; Lansdale, "Some Thoughts for Richard M.

Nixon," September 29, 1984, Box 6, Folder Richard Nixon; "Psychological Warfare," Declassified April 17, 1989.

141. Ross, *Fast Cars, Clean Bodies*, 110–11.

142. Lansdale to Baker, September 14, 1966, Box 53, Folder Joseph Baker 1966–68, ELP; Conein Oral History II, 48.

143. Lansdale to Rufe, October 11, 1965, November 9, 1966, October 19, 1965, Box 54, Folder Rufus C. Phillips, ELP.

144. Lansdale to Ambassador Bunker, June 7, 1968, Box 96.4, ELP.

145. Lansdale to Old Team, February 10, 1968, Box 59, Folder Memoranda, Lansdale to "the Old Team"; Ed to Helen et al., February 13, 1955, Box 83, Folder Edward Lansdale, ELP.

146. Currey, *Edward Lansdale*, 303; Nashel, *Edward Lansdale's Cold War*, 148.

147. Nashel, *Edward Lansdale's Cold War*, 147; Fish, "General Edward G. Lansdale," 400.

148. Grant, *Facing the Phoenix*, 288; Prados, *Lost Crusader*, 224; Walters, *Silent Missions*, 439; Frances FitzGerald, *Fire in the Lake: The Vietnamese and The Americans in Vietnam* (Boston: Little, Brown, 1972), 269; transcript, Jean André Sauvageot Oral History Interview III, August 14, 1985, by Ted Gittinger, 9, LBJ.

149. Lansdale to Old Team, June 8, 1968; Lansdale to Old Team, February 10, 1968; Lansdale to Old Team, February 14, 1968, Box 59, Folder Memoranda, Lansdale to "the Old Team"; Phillips in Santoli, *To Bear Any Burden*, 167; Lansdale in Santoli, *To Bear Any Burden*, 196; Rufus Phillips, *Why Vietnam Matters*, 289; Currey, *Edward Lansdale*, 322.

150. Permit 57112, Ridge File, FCZB; Bui Diem to Joe Redick, April 22, 1966; Redick to Rufe, April 28, 1966, Box 54, Folder Rufus Phillips (2); Rufe to Lansdale, February 13, 1967, Box 54, Folder Rufus Phillips, ELP.

151. Permits 7908B0396, 95135130600, 97051B0250, Ingleside File, FCZB.

152. Robert L. Coate to Lansdale, November 27, 1968, Box 1, Folder General A–J; Lansdale to Rufe, July 1, 1971, Box 6, Folder Rufus Phillips; SLO Report, ELP; NOVA White Pages, 1969–70.

153. NOVA White Pages, January 1977; VA Yellow Pages, 1964–65; Robert G. Kaiser, "Some Who Fled War Find Assimilating Difficult in U.S.," *WP*, May 1, 1977; "In Reston," *WP*, October 5, 1974; Display ad, *WP*, April 22, 1972; "He Bluffed His Way, Saved 60,'"*FCT*, October 2, 1964.

154. "A Message from Rufus Phillips" and "Coffee Talk," Box 6, Folder Rufus Phillips, ELP; "Winifred Hodgson Appointed Phillips Reception Chairman," *FH*, July 23, 1971; "Phillips' Win Celebrated," *FH*, December 17, 1971; "Phillips Favors Limits on County Development," *FH*, January 7, 1972.

155. "A Message from Rufus Phillips," Box 6, Folder Rufus Phillips, ELP; Rufus Phillips, "Should McLean be a Town? Phillips Urges 'Local Say,'" *FH*, January 12, 1973; "Phillips Declares Board Knows Where It's Heading," *FH*, December 22, 1972; "Phillips Reviews First Year, Predicts New Land Use Controls," *FH*, February 2, 1973; "County Receiving 40 Per Cent of Area Growth, Phillips Reports," *FH*,

August 17, 1973; Judy Nicol, "Fairfax Building Ban Enacted," *WP*, March 5, 1974; Judy Nicol, "Land-Use Plan Draws Wide Interest," *WP*, September 1, 1974; Thomas Grubisich, "PLUS Begins, but Isn't Adding Up to New Era in Land Planning," *WP*, July 1, 1975; "Supervisors Zone Back Clinch Tract to 1-Acre," *FH*, March 31, 1972; Arthur W. Arundel, "Growth," *RT*, March 15, 1973.

156. Nashel, *Edward Lansdale's Cold War*, 7; also, Conein Oral History I, 8; Conein Oral History II, 49, 51.

157. Lansdale to John, July 29, 1972, Box 83, Folder Edward G. Lansdale; Pat to Ed, November 27, 1972, Box 4, Folder Patrocinio Kelly, ELP

158. Pat to Ed, October 31, 1972, and October 26, 1972, Box 4, Folder Patrocinio Kelly, ELP.

159. Pat to Ed, October 17, 1972, September 8, 1972, November 24, 1972, Box 4, Folder Patrocinio Kelly, ELP.

160. Pat to Ed, October 26, 1972, October 2, 1972, January 17, 1973, November 27, 1972, Box 4, Folder Patrocinio Kelly, ELP.

161. Currey, *Edward Lansdale*, 335.

162. Ed to Ben, June 12, 1973, Box 83, Folder Edward G. Lansdale, ELP.

163. NOVA White Pages, January 1976; Parcel 0411 07 0029, FCLR; Currey, *Edward Lansdale*, xi, xii, 337; Permit 15770, Franklin Forest File, FCZB.

164. Lansdale Oral History I, 11.

165. Fish, "General Edward G. Lansdale," 392, 399.

166. Pat and Ed Lansdale to Barbara and Rufe Phillips, December 15, 1973, Box 6, Folder Rufus Phillips; Durbrow to Secretary of State, November 27, 1960, Box 95 Material Returned from U.S. Department of Defense, Folder (Former) Boxes 1 and 2; Joe Baker to General Lansdale, "Subject: Finance," Box 97.6; Economic Warfare Committee to Ambassador, November 4, 1965, Box 97.6; Lansdale to Barbara and Rufe, December 7, 1973, Box 6, Folder Rufus Phillips, ELP; Lansdale Oral History I, 21; Permit P81306B0190, McLean Hamlet Section 2 File, FCZB; Parcel 0292 03 0191, FCLR.

167. "Phillips Pounds, McCloskey Holds," *FH*, April 7, 1972; "Students and Phillips Trace Trails System," *FH*, September 17, 1971; "French Minister Tours," *FH*, February 25, 1972; "Ye Supervisor at the Mill," *FH*, July 21, 1972.

168. Lansdale to Rufe, January 15, 1975, Box 6, Folder Rufus Phillips, ELP.

169. Rufus Phillips, "Supervisor for the 1970s," Box 6, Folder Rufus Phillips, ELP.

170. Rufus Phillips, "General Campaign Talk (Draft)," December 21, 1973, and "Draft of Notes," March 16, 1974, Box 6, Folder Rufus Phillips, ELP.

171. Phillips, "Should McLean Be a Town?"; Paul G. Edwards, "Phillips Seeking Va. Farm Vote in Bid for Senate," *WP*, March 27, 1978; Bob to Ed and Pat, February 25, 1978, Box 1, Folder General A–J; Rufus to Ed, December 9, 1977; Rufe to Ed and Pat, June 21, 1978, Box 6, Folder Rufus Phillips, ELP.

172. Classified ads, *WP*, June 4, 1989, and April 12, 1986; Display ad, *WP*, May 18, 1985; online listing, VirginiaHomeLiving.com.

CHAPTER FOUR

1. Hammer, Greene, Siler Associates, *Potentials for Growth in Arlington County* (Washington, DC: April 1971); Arlington County Department of Community Affairs, *Trends: Residential Development for the years 1960 through 1982* (Arlington: August 1982); "Royal Court Open," *WP*, July 28, 1973; "Seminary Valley Sold Out," *WP*, September 10, 1968; "State of Real Estate," *WP*, June 10, 1961; "Young Trio Marches into Big League," *WP*, July 8, 1961; Homer Hoyt Associates, *Economic Survey of the Land Uses of Arlington County, Va.* (Hoyt Associates, September 1951); Arlington County Office of Planning, *Land Use in Arlington County, Virginia 1959* (Arlington: 1959); Zachary M. Schrag, *The Great Society Subway: A History of the Washington Metro* (Baltimore: Johns Hopkins University Press, 2006), 228.

2. Dorothy Ellis Lee, *A History of Arlington County Virginia* (Richmond: Dietz, 1946), 24.

3. Hammer et al., *Potentials for Growth*, 3, 22–23, 31–33.

4. Snepp, *Irreparable Harm*, 22.

5. Ibid., 48; NOVA White Pages, January 1976.

6. Snepp, *Irreparable Harm*, 75, 81, 101.

7. Ibid., 12.

8. Frank Snepp, *Decent Interval: An Insider's Account of Saigon's Indecent End Told by the CIA's Chief Strategy Analyst in Vietnam* (New York: Random House, 1977), xi, 131, 149.

9. Ibid., 3–10.

10. Young, *Vietnam Wars*, 177.

11. Snepp, *Decent Interval*, 78.

12. Elizabeth Gill Lui, *Building Diplomacy* (Arlington, Va.: Association for Diplomatic Studies and Training, 2004); Loeffler, *Architecture of Diplomacy*.

13. Thomas J. Campanella, "U.S. Reckons with a Tragedy in Concrete," *Metropolis*, July/August, 1995.

14. Robert J.C. Young, *Postcolonialism: An Introduction* (Oxford: Blackwell, 2001), 27.

15. Young, *Vietnam Wars*, 37–39, 52, 273–92.

16. Campaigns in Snepp, *Decent Interval*.

17. Young, *Vietnam Wars*, 171.

18. Snepp, *Decent Interval*, 153, 198, 215–19, 347, 361.

19. Thomas A. Bass, *Vietnamerica* (New York: Soho, 1996), 38; Robert S. McKelvey, *The Dust of Life: America's Children Abandoned in Vietnam* (Seattle: University of Washington Press, 1999), xii–7; Robert S. McKelvey, *Gift of Barbed Wire: America's Allies Abandoned in South Vietnam* (Seattle: University of Washington Press, 2002), 7–8; Trin Yarborough, *Surviving Twice: Amerasian Children of the Vietnam War* (Washington, DC: Potomac, 2005), 12, 63; Sucheng Chan, ed., *The Vietnamese American 1.5 Generation: Stories of War, Revolution, Flight, and New Beginnings* (Philadelphia: Temple University Press, 2006), 62–94.

20. Snepp, *Decent Interval*, 269, 387, 494.

21. Ibid., 518.

22. Ibid., 271.

23. Ibid., 525.

24. Ibid., 537–38, 528.

25. Ibid., 538–39; Jade Ngoc Quang Huynh, *South Wind Changing* (St. Paul: Graywolf, 1994), 45.

26. Snepp, *Decent Interval*, 521.

27. Ibid., 558.

28. Corazon Sandoval Foley, *The Fairfax County Asian American History Project* (Burke: Foley, 2010), 66; Abbie Lynn Salyers, "The Internment of Memory: Forgetting and Remembering the Japanese American World War II Experience" (PhD diss., Rice University, 2009), 72–79.

29. Snepp, *Irreparable Harm*, xvii.

30. Snepp, *Decent Interval*, 563–64.

31. Ibid., 307.

32. Young, *Vietnam Wars*, 104.

33. Snepp, *Decent Interval*, 296, 267, 231.

34. Snepp, *Irreparable Harm*, 23.

35. Snepp, *Decent Interval*, 407.

36. Ibid., 454.

37. Ibid., 565–66.

38. Snepp, *Irreparable Harm*, xvi.

39. Gail Paradise Kelly, *From Vietnam to America: A Chronicle of Vietnamese Immigration to the United States* (Boulder: Westview, 1977); organizational memos in Interagency Task Force on Indochinese Refugees-Civil Coordinator Subject Files, 5/75–9/75, Eglin Air Force Base, Box 1, Folder Admin., RG220, NARA.

40. Lowe points to this phenomenon in *Immigrant Acts*, 16.

41. Young, *Vietnam Wars*, 279.

42. Chan, *Vietnamese American 1.5*, 84.

43. E. Schattner, "Prejudice," *Dat Moi* newspaper, July 8, 1975, Box 1, Folder Information-Camp Newspapers, RG220, NARA.

44. Newspaper clipping, *Wall Street Journal*, May 22, 1975, Box 1, Folder Information (Publicity), RG220, NARA.

45. State Department memo 177433, August 1975, Folder Funding; Col. Bill Keeler, memo on Combined Council meeting, May 27, 1975, Folder Admin.-Meetings; *Dat Moi* newspaper issues, Folder Information-Camp Newspapers, June 17, 1975; July 4, 1975; July 8, 1975; August 27, 1975, all in Box 1, RG220, NARA; Kelly, *From Vietnam to America*, 72, 74, 79, 101–2, 112; Rufus Phillips Oral History Interview I, 1.

46. James Chandler, "Farewell . . . Until We Meet Again," *Dat Moi*, August 2, 1975, 5, Box 1, Folder Information-Camp Newspapers, RG220, NARA.

47. Don I. Wortman, Director, HEW Refugee Task Force, "Memo to HEW Senior Coordinators," June 19, 1975, Box 1, Folder Information (Publicity); HEW Refugee Task Force, "All Refugees Resettled," *Dong Song Moi/New Life* newspaper,

January, 1976, 1, and "Refugee Welfare Rolls Decline," *New Life*-Laos Edition, September, 1977–October, 1977, 20, Box 5, RG220, NARA; Kelly, *From Vietnam to America*, 154; Darrel Montero, *Vietnamese Americans: Patterns of Resettlement and Socioeconomic Adaptation in the United States* (Boulder: Westview, 1979), 8; Hien Duc Do, *The Vietnamese Americans* (Westport: Greenwood, 1999), 46.

48. HEW Refugee Task Force, "All Refugees Resettled," and other HEW Refugee Task Force coverage, *Dong Song Moi*, Box 5, RG220, NARA.

49. Beatrice Nied Hackett, "Vietnamese, Cambodians, and Laotians," in *Urban Odyssey: A Multicultural History of Washington, DC*, ed. Francine Curro Cary (Washington, DC: Smithsonian, 1996), 279; Jessica Meyers, "Pho and Apple Pie: Eden Center as a Representation of Vietnamese American Ethnic Identity in the Washington, DC Metropolitan Area, 1975–2005," *Journal of Asian American Studies* (February 2006), 62; Kelly, *From Vietnam to America,* 155; Joseph S. Wood, "Making America at Eden Center," in *From Urban Enclave to Ethnic Suburb: New Asian Communities in Pacific Rim Countries*, ed. Wei Li (Honolulu: University of Hawai'i Press, 2006), 26.

50. HEW Refugee Task Force, "All Refugees Resettled," 4.

51. Joseph Wood, "Vietnamese American Place Making in Northern Virginia," *Geographical Review* 87.1 (January 1997), 59.

52. Meyers, "Pho and Apple Pie," 62, 76.

53. U.S. Navy Indochina Clearing Office, Pentagon, "If You Want to Help a Refugee Family . . . ," July 7, 1975, Box 4, Folder Ref. 9-7 – Sponsorship, RG220, NARA.

54. "Immigration Security Check Status Report," May 18, 1975, Box 3, Folder Ref. 6 – Registration and Screening, RG220, NARA; Kelly, *From Vietnam to America*, 137.

55. "JRICO Sponsorship Referral," Memo From DA Wash DC to CDR Eglin, July 17, 1975; Memo DA Wash DC to CDR Eglin, June 26, 1975; "JRICO Sponsorship Referral," Memo DA Wash DC to CDR Eglin, June 17, 1975, all Box 4, Folder Ref. 9-7 Sponsorship, RG220, NARA.

56. "No Bed of Roses for Vietnamese Generals in U.S.," *U.S. News & World Report*, December 29, 1975.

57. Foley, *Fairfax County Asian American,* 67–68.

58. Jackie Bong-Wright, *Autumn Cloud: From Vietnamese War Widow to American Activist* (Sterling: Capital, 2001), 156–240; Foley, *Fairfax County Asian American*, 113–17; Robert G. Kaiser, "Pacification (1969 Style) Seems to Be Working," *WP*, October 30, 1969; Peter A. Jay and Peter Osnos, "Fair Vietnam Elections Needed, Kissinger Told," *WP*, July 7, 1971; Peter Osnos, "Assassin's Bomb in Car Kills Politician in Saigon," *WP*, November 11, 1971; Ronald D. White and Jane Freundel, "Helping Refugees Cope with Cultural Shock," *WP*, August 16, 1979.

59. Pham Duy to Lansdale, April 5, 1975; Duy to Lansdale, May 20, 1975, Box 6, Folder Pham Duy Can, ELP; Currey, *Edward Lansdale*, 338; Kelly, *From Vietnam to America*, 85.

60. Currey, *Edward Lansdale*, 338.

61. Lansdale to Clay McManaway, April 19, 1978, Box 5, Folder Nguyen Van Chau, ELP.

62. Lansdale to John C. Staten, November 22, 1981, Box 6, Folder Phan Quang Dan, ELP; Ray Fontaine, *The Dawn of Free Vietnam: A Biographical Sketch of Doctor Phan Quang Dan* (Brownsville: Pan American Business Services, 1992), 116–17; Phan Quang Dan, *The Republic of Vietnam's Environment and People* (Saigon: 1975), 197; Louis A. Wiesner, *Victims and Survivors: Displaced Persons and Other War Victims in Viet-Nam, 1954–1975* (New York: Greenwood, 1988), xiv–xv.

63. Wiesner, *Victims and Survivors*, 73; David Mason, "Too Much U.S. Help, S. Viet Colonel Says," *WP*, August 17, 1969.

64. Lansdale to Whom It May Concern, May 20, 1975, Box 5, Folder Nguyen Duc Thang, ELP.

65. Nguyen Bao Tri to Lansdale, April 10, 1977, Box 1, Folder General Vietnamese, ELP.

66. Phillips Oral History II, 42–43.

67. Tran Sam Thong to Lansdale, May 4, 1975; Charlie Choate to Lansdale, May 20, 1975; Chen to Lansdale, May 21, 1975; Lansdale to MCI, November 8, 1975, Box 1, Folder General Vietnamese, ELP.

68. Memo from DA Wash DC to bases, July 15, 1975; Memo from DA Wash DC to camps, July 8, 1975, Box 3, Folder Ref. 5 – Locator Inquiries, RG220, NARA.

69. Memo, "Civil Coordinator, Eglin AFB, Civil Coordinator, Fort Chaffee," May 20, 1975, Box 2, Folder Legislative and Legal Issues, RG 220, NARA.

70. See all in *Dong Song Moi*'s Locator Service, Box 5, RG220, NARA.

71. Wood, "Vietnamese American Place Making," 60; Arlington County Community Affairs, *Trends*.

72. *Dong Song Moi*, "Locator Service."

73. Wood, "Vietnamese American Place Making," 60.

74. "Attention Businessmen," *Dong Song Moi*, March, 1976, 9, Box 5, RG220, NARA.

75. "Young Woman Gets a Job on Her Own," *New Life*, October 1–15, 1975, 1, Box 5, RG220, NARA; Foley, *Fairfax County Asian American*, 157.

76. "Learning to Earn," *New Life*, October 1976, 10–11; "CETA Offers Job Training," *New Life*, July 1976, 3; "Radio and TV Programs for Indo-Chinese," *New Life*, February 1976, 6; Center for Applied Linguistics Ad, *New Life*, March–April 1978, 22; Hoang Thi Quynh Hoa, "Tips for Housewives," *New Life*-Laos Edition, Box 5, RG220, NARA; *Dong Song Moi*, "Locator Service."

77. Caryle Murphy, "Onlookers," *WP*, November 13, 1982; Wood, "Vietnamese American Place Making," 63; *Dong Song Moi*, "Locator Service"; Celestine Bohlen, "Tensions, Adjustment for Asian Refugees," *WP*, October 22, 1981.

78. Truong Anh Thuy, *A Mother's Lullaby* (Arlington: Canh Nam, 1989), 53.

79. Wood, "Vietnamese American Place Making," 60, 64; Schrag, *Great Society Subway*, 224–26; Hoyt, *Economic Survey*; Hammer et al., *Potentials for Growth*.

80. Wood, "Making America," 31; Meyers, "Pho and Apple Pie," 62; Alice C.

Andrews, "Indochinese Resettlement in Virginia," *Virginia Social Science Journal* 19.2 (1984), 72.

81. Sue Mullin, "Vietnamese Build an Empire on Spring Rolls," *Arlington-Alexandria Star*, November 26, 1979.

82. William Rice, "A Bit of Saigon on Wilson Blvd.," *WP*, September 9, 1976; Louie Estrada, "Nguyen Van Thoi Dies," *WP*, December 31, 2005; Sandra G. Boodman, "Refugees Crowd Arlington's 'Mekong Delta,'" *WP*, September 23, 1979.

83. Wood, "Vietnamese American Place Making," 65.

84. Philip A. McCombs, "Survival of a Vietnamese Family," *WP*, March 17, 1974; Christopher Dickey, "Vietnamese Politics Still Plagues Refugees," *WP*, February 5, 1978; Sue Mullin, "Vietnamese Bring a Little Saigon to Arlington," *Washington Star*, January 11, 1978; Seth W. Moskowitz, "Center Focuses on Preservation of Vietnamese Culture," *WP*, December 29, 1977; Foley, *Fairfax County Asian American,* 108–9.

85. Andrews, "Indochinese Resettlement," 73; Charles Dervarics, "Orient Meets East Coast in Clarendon," *WP*, June 1, 1981.

86. "State Engineer to Study Work for Arlington," *WP*, November 21, 1937; "Assembly Line Technique Used at Buckingham," *WP*, January 9, 1938; Oscar Fisher, "Buckingham Housing Laboratory," *Architectural Record*, January 1938; "Culmore Apartments Open Soon," *WP*, April 11, 1948; "M.J. Cassidy, Top FHA Aide," *WP*, December 20, 1957; John B. Willmann, "Buckingham Is For Sale," *WP*, January 15, 1977; Denis Collins, "Buckingham Changes Win Guarded Praise," *WP*, December 13, 1979; Evelyn Hsu, "Treasure or Trouble?," *WP*, July 18, 1991; Gordon Stephenson, "Town Planning: Contemporary Problem of Civil Design," *Town Planning Review*, 20.2 (July 1949), 136; "Buckingham Historic District," National Register of Historic Places Registration Form, December 2, 2003, at http://www.arlingtonva.us/departments/CPHD/ons/hp/file60197.pdf; "23 Dwellings to Be Built in Arlington," *WP*, January 21, 1951; Connie Feeley, "Arlington Board Hears Plan for Futuristic County Center," *WP*, March 31, 1957; Albert D. Lueders, Questionnaire, AIA; Allan F. Kamstra, Membership File, AIA; "Clerk at CIA Found Dead in Apartment," *WP*, June 30, 1953.

87. "CORE Pickets Area Housing," *WP*, August 26, 1963; "ACCESS Again Pickets Apartments," *WP*, May 9, 1966; Kenneth M. Boyd, "Ten Pickets Arrested at Arlington Apartment," *WP*, July 10, 1966; Gail Bensinger, "ACCESS March in Virginia Will Highlight Negro Housing," *WP*, September 29, 1966; "Buckingham Apartments Charged," *WP*, February 13, 1968; "Arlington Unit Backs High Rise," *WP*, November 29, 1968.

88. Dervarics, "Orient Meets East Coast"; Sandra G. Boodman, "Newcomers Settle in Old Development," *WP*, December 29, 1977; Sandra Boodman, "Tenants Uneasy about Future of Moderate Priced Housing," *WP*, April 20, 1978.

89. Schrag, *Great Society Subway*, 228; Wood, "Vietnamese American Place Making," 60.

90. Lan Cao, *Monkey Bridge* (New York: Penguin, 1997).

91. Ibid., 40.

92. Ibid., 204.

93. Ibid., 203, 212; See also Sigrid P. Slivka, "Pentagonal," in *Demilitarized Zones: Veterans After Vietnam*, eds. Jan Barry and W.D. Ehrhart (Perkasie: East River, 1976), 102–3.

94. Cao, 19.

95. Ibid., 19.

96. Ibid., 16.

97. Roger Rouse, "Mexican Migration and the Social Space of Postmodernism," in *Between Two Worlds: Mexican Immigrants in the United States*, ed. David G. Gutierrez (Wilmington: Scholarly Resources, 1996), 248.

98. Cao, *Monkey Bridge*, 227, 1, 60, 28, 100, 134, 163, 166, 160, 172, 159, 179.

99. Ibid., 248.

100. Ibid., 194, 202, 138, 200, 256, 180.

101. Ibid., 244, 167, 233.

102. On legibility, see Lynch, *Image of the City*, 2.

103. Cao, 54, 76, 82.

104. Fritz Lanham, "Vietnam by a Vietnamese," *Houston Chronicle*, July 5, 1998; "Novel Draws on Woman's Memories of Vietnam," *Durham Herald Sun*, November 20, 1998; *Marquis Who's Who in American Law*, March 21, 2007.

105. Sheehan, *Bright Shining Lie*, 669, 778; Snepp, *Decent Interval*, 114, 415, 155; Lewis Sorley, *A Better War: The Unexamined Victories and Final Tragedy of America's Last Years in Vietnam* (New York: Harcourt Brace, 1999); General William C. Westmoreland, *A Soldier Reports* (Garden City: Doubleday, 1976), 240–43, 190, 208–9; Phillip Smith, "Key Vietnam Army Figure Becomes Civilian," *WP*, January 20, 1982; "No Bed of Roses for Vietnamese Generals in U.S.," *US News & World Report*; Joe Holley, "Cao Van Vien," *WP*, January 30, 2008.

106. Snepp, *Decent Interval*, 574, 184; Snepp, *Irreparable Harm*, 34; Smith, "Key Vietnam Army Figure Becomes Civilian"; Vu Thuy Hoang, "Defeated Ex-Generals, Living in Exile, Avoid Spotlight and Fellow Vietnamese," *San Jose Mercury News*, April 23, 2000; Karnow, *Vietnam*, 640; Sheehan, *Bright Shining Lie*, 748; Robert G. Kaiser, "On Parole," *WP*, May 1, 1977.

107. "He Bluffed His Way, Saved 60," *FCT*, October 2, 1964; John Koenig Jr., "Virginian Mediates Viet Dispute," *WP*, September 26, 1964; Walters, *Silent Missions*, 440; Westmoreland, *Soldier Reports*, 79–81.

108. Westmoreland, *Soldier Reports*, 206–7.

109. SLO Report, Box 95.6; Memo to EXO, Meetings January 20–February 6, 1966; May 18–28, 1966; June 10–30, 1966, Box 59, Folder Memoranda, Redick, Joseph to Executive Officer, ELP.

110. Walters, *Silent Missions*, 440–41; "Vienna Officer Hurt in Action," *FCT*, August 10, 1967.

111. Westmoreland, *Soldier Reports*, 240; "Maj. Gen. John F. 'Fritz' Freund Memorialized," *Connecticut Guardian*, May 2001.

112. NOVA White Pages, 1976; Parcel 0513 11 0035, FCLR; Cao, *Monkey Bridge*, 27; Donna St. George, "Cao Van Vien," *WPM*, January 4, 2009.

113. Andrews, "Indochinese Resettlement in Virginia," 72–78.

114. Wood, "Vietnamese American Place Making," 64.

115. Wood, "Vietnamese American Place Making," 66; Meyers, "Pho and Apple Pie," 64; Ellie Falaris, "F.C. Shopping Center Has Grown into Cultural Haven for Vietnamese," *Falls Church News Press*, July 26, 2007.

116. "Red Pressure May Force U.S. to Recall Aides," *WP*, August 25, 1952; "Edgar Weinberger, Headed U.S. Photographers Group," *WP*, April 5, 1980; Don Olesen, "Falls Church Votes to Seek More Area," *WP*, June 14, 1949; "Shirley Homes Site Sold to Broyhill Firm," *WP*, December 6, 1953; "Site of 7 Corners Center Once Called Fort Buffalo," *WP*, October 3, 1956; S. Oliver Goodman, "Horne Group of DC Buys Stewart Firm," *WP*, February 2, 1951; Robert P. Jordan, "Nearby Va. Commercial Center Gets Under Way," *WP*, January 7, 1951; Robert P. Jordan, "For Civilian Newcomers—Many Furnished Rooms," *WP*, December 17, 1950.

117. Marcia McAllister, "Conversion of Willston Units Set," *WP*, August 11, 1984; Alan Fogg, "New Life in a Strange Land," *FJ*, March 28, 1983; Bob Levey, "The Big City Look Comes to the Suburbs," *WP*, January 8, 1981; Andrews, "Indochinese Resettlement," 72; Kerry Dougherty, "Indochinese Center," *WP*, February 12, 1981.

118. Foley, *Fairfax County Asian American,* 115; Bong-Wright, *Autumn Cloud,* 244.

119. Wood, "Making America," 33; Falaris, "F.C. Shopping Center"; Barbara Carton, "A Little Piece of Indochina," *WP*, April 27, 1985; Gary Fields, "Vietnamese Find Haven in Falls Church's Eden," *WP*, October 16, 1990.

120. Wood, "Vietnamese American Place Making," 62, 66, 69; Meyers, "Pho and Apple Pie," 68; Lan Nguyen, "Falling Short of Paradise," *WP*, September 9, 1996.

121. Meyers, "Pho and Apple Pie," 76–77; Phuong Ly, "Death Reopens War Wounds," *WP*, May 27, 2000; Falaris, "F.C. Shopping Center."

122. Cao, *Monkey Bridge*, 30–31; Kim A. O'Connell, "Catching Two Fish with Two Hands: Preserving Vietnamese Heritage in Virginia's Little Saigon," December 12, 2003, available at www.ncvaonline.org/images/upload/PDF_file/HP612_Final_Project_Part1.pdf, 1.

123. Cao Van Vien, *The Final Collapse* (Washington, DC: U.S. GPO, 1983), v; Cao Van Vien and Dong Van Khuyen, *Reflections on the Vietnam War* (Washington, DC: U.S. Army Center of Military History, 1980); Cao Van Vien, Ngo Quang Truong, Dong Van Khuyen et al., *The U.S. Adviser* (Washington, DC: U.S. Army Center of Military History, 1980).

124. Cao, *Monkey Bridge*, 228.

125. Ibid., 26, 54.

126. Tom Buckley, "The Villain of Vietnam," *Esquire*, June 5, 1979, 61–64; Kelly, *From Vietnam to America*, 16.

127. Display ads, *WP*, September 11, 1974; January 30, 1975; February 14, 1975; November 22, 1972; Susan Carroll Mathias, "Family Out," *WP*, November 24, 1977; Jerry Knight, "Woolco Plans 5 New Stores for Region," *WP*, February 14, 1978.

128. Buckley, "Villain of Vietnam," 62; Patricia Camp, "Saigon Police Chief Now Runs Burke Café," *WP*, April 28, 1976.

129. Christopher Dickey, "U.S. Acts to Deport Saigon Official Who Killed Bound Prisoner in 1968," *WP*, November 3, 1978.

130. Tom Buckley, "Portrait of an Aging Despot: A Visit with General Loan: 1971," *Harper's*, April, 1972, in *Reporting Vietnam: Part Two, American Journalism 1969–1975*, eds. Milton J. Bates et al. (New York: Library of America, 1998), 242; David Culbert, "Television's Visual Impact on Decision-Making in the USA, 1968: The Tet Offensive and Chicago's Democratic National Convention," *Journal of Contemporary History* 33.3 (July 1998), 437, 422; Peter Braestrup, *Big Story: How the American Press and Television Reported and Interpreted the Crisis of Tet 1968 in Vietnam and Washington* (New Haven: Yale University Press, 1977), 347–48; Vicki Goldberg, *The Power of Photography: How Photographs Changed Our Lives* (New York: Abbeville, 1991), 226; Robert Hamilton, "Image and Context: The Production and Reproduction of The Execution of a VC Suspect by Eddie Adams," in *Vietnam Images: War and Representation*, eds. Jeffrey Walsh and James Aulich (Houndmills: Macmillan, 1989), 171; Viet Thanh Nguyen, "Speak of the Dead, Speak of Viet Nam: The Ethics and Aesthetics of Minority Discourse," *The New Centennial Review* 6.2 (Fall 2006), 24; Sylvia Shin Huey Chong, "Restaging the War: The Deer Hunter and the Primal Scene of Violence," *Cinema Journal* 44.2 (Winter 2005), 96; George Esper and AP, *The Eyewitness History of the Vietnam War, 1961–1975* (New York: Villard, 1983),104–5; Sylvia Shin Huey Chong, *The Oriental Obscene: Violence and Racial Fantasies in the Vietnam Era* (Durham: Duke University Press, 2012).

131. Robert McG. Thomas Jr., "Nguyen Ngoc Loan, 67, Dies," *NYT*, July 16, 1998.

132. Christopher Dickey, "Sympathy Expressed for Ex-Gen. Loan," *WP*, November 4, 1978.

133. Buckley, "Villain of Vietnam," 62.

134. Braestrup, *Big Story*, 347, 350–51.

135. Buckley, "Portrait," 244.

136. Camp, "Saigon Police Chief Now"; Buckley, "Villain of Vietnam," 64.

137. *Front Line* (New York: Filmakers Library, 1979).

138. Braestrup, *Big Story*, 347–48; Charles Mohr, "Street Clashes Go On in Vietnam, Foe Still Holds Parts of Cities," *NYT*, February 2, 1968.

139. "Hearts and Minds," *Newsweek*, April 15, 1985; George Judson, "Stepping Out from the Lens of History," *NYT*, October 11, 1995; Goldberg, *Power of Photography*, 228–29.

140. Goldberg, *Power of Photography*, 229.

141. Robert McG. Thomas, "Nguyen Ngoc Loan, 67."

142. Dale Hopper, "Executioner 'Hero' of Viet War Dies," *Advertiser*, July 17, 1998.

143. Alyssa Adams, ed., *Eddie Adams: Vietnam* (New York: Umbrage, 2008), 147–48; Lac Hoang and Viet Mai Ha, *Blind Design: Why America Lost the Vietnam War* (1996), 72; David D. Perlmutter, *Photojournalism and Foreign Policy: Icons of Outrage in International Crises* (Westport: Praeger, 1998), 44; Adams interview in Peter C. Rollins, *Television's Vietnam* (Washington, DC: Accuracy in Media, 1984–

85); Susan Herendeen, "Area Restaurateur Recalls Another Lifetime," *Annapolis Capital*, November 24, 1997; Nguyen Cao Ky, *Buddha's Child*, 265.

144. Young, *Vietnam Wars*, 63.

145. See Buckley, "Villain of Vietnam," 64; Braestrup, *Big Story*, 347, 350–51; Herendeen, "Area Restaurateur Recalls"; Culbert, "Television's Visual Impact," 426.

146. Braestrup, *Big Story*, 351.

147. Camp, "Saigon Police Chief Now."

148. Dickey, "Sympathy Expressed for Ex-Gen."

149. Buckley, "Villain of Vietnam."

150. Dale Hopper, "Executioner 'Hero'"; George Judson, "Stepping Out from the Lens."

151. Dickey, "Sympathy Expressed for Ex-Gen."

152. Buckley, "Villain of Vietnam," 61.

153. Buckley, "Villain of Vietnam" and "Portrait"; Ky, *Buddha's Child*, 176.

154. Ky, *Buddha's Child*, 212, 223, 244; Ahern, *Vietnam Declassified*, 260; McCoy, *Politics of Heroin*, 167–68; Buckley, "Portrait," 236–38.

155. Karnow, *Vietnam*, 447, 450; Kahin, *Intervention*, 428, 430.

156. McCoy, *Politics of Heroin*, 168.

157. Buckley, "Portrait," 236; Oriana Fallaci, "An Interview with the Most Hated Man in Saigon," *Look*, June 25, 1968, T17–18.

158. Ky and Loan both later denied the opium connection. McCoy, *Politics of Heroin*, 168-69, 173-74, 177; Ky, *Buddha's Child*, 176; Buckley, "Villain of Vietnam."

159. Sue Sun, "Where the Girls Are: The Management of Venereal Disease by United States Military Forces in Vietnam," *Literature and Medicine* 23.1 (Spring 2004), 72.

160. Buckley, "Portrait," 237, 244; McCoy, *Politics of Heroin*, 173–74; John Laurence, *The Cat from Hué: A Vietnam War Story* (New York: Public Affairs, 2002), 488; Truong Nhu Tang, *A Viet Cong Memoir: An Inside Account of the Vietnam War and Its Aftermath* (New York: Vintage, 1985), 108.

161. Ky, *Buddha's Child*, 264; Karnow, *Vietnam*, 529; Edward G. Lansdale, Affidavit, September 1968, Box 1, Folder General Vietnamese, ELP; Fallaci, "An Interview."

162. Buckley, "Villain of Vietnam," 64.

163. Braestrup, *Big Story*, 351; Buckley, "Portrait," 245; Valentine, *Phoenix Program*, 186.

164. Perlmutter, *Photojournalism and Foreign Policy*, 40.

165. Buckley, "Portrait," 236; Buckley, "Villain of Vietnam," 62; Adams, *Eddie Adams Vietnam*, 147; Valentine, *Phoenix Program*, 417.

166. James P. Sterba, "Captain Midnight Becomes Civilian Ky," *NYTM*, January 11, 1976; Buckley, "Portrait," 241; Dickey, "Sympathy Expressed for Ex-Gen."; Bong-Wright, *Autumn Cloud*, 215; Kelly, *From Vietnam to America*, 200.

167. Ky, *Buddha's Child*, 345, 360.

168. Buckley, "Villain of Vietnam," 62; Currey, *Edward Lansdale*, 147.

169. Lansdale, "Affidavit."

170. "Moral Turpitude," *WP*, November 5, 1978.

171. Camp, "Saigon Police Chief Now"; Buckley, "Villain of Vietnam," 64; "Hearts and Minds," *Newsweek*.

172. Culbert, "Television's Visual Impact," 426; See also David Culbert, "Television's Vietnam and Historical Revisionism in the United States," *Historical Journal of Film, Radio and Television*, 8.3 (1988), 253–67.

173. Buckley, "Villain of Vietnam," 64.

174. McG. Thomas Jr., "Nguyen Ngoc Loan, 67"; Dave Saltonstall, "War Photographer Tells of Regret over Picture," *South China Morning Post*, October 15, 1993.

175. Le Chi Thao to Lansdale, November 14, 1980, Box 1, Folder General Vietnamese, ELP; "Viet-Nam Troops Break Up Rioting in Saigon Streets," *WP*, August 29, 1964; Malcolm W. Browne, "Dai Viet Seen Emerging as the Dominant Party," *WP*, February 9, 1964.

176. Peter Baker, "In a First, Asian Is Named to Fairfax School Board," *WP*, June 29, 1993; Foley, *Fairfax County Asian American*, 170.

177. Phan Quang Dan to Lansdale, n.d., Box 6, Folder Phan Quang Dan, ELP.

178. Lansdale to Z.B. Ogden, May 30, 1975, Box 6, Folder Pham Van Lieu and Family, ELP; John Maffre, "Wide Saigon Military Shifts Indicated," *WP*, February 24, 1965.

179. Katherine Macdonald, "Where the PTA Meets, Vietnamese Regroup," *WP*, January 16, 1983; Joanne Omang, "Vietnamese Emigres Rally Here for Overthrow of Hanoi Regime," *WP*, May 1, 1983.

180. Le Thi Anh to Lansdale, March 21, 1986, Box 1, Folder General Vietnamese, ELP.

181. Randy Cepuch, "'Boat People' Located by City," *Fairfax Globe*, August 23, 1979; David Brooks, "Home for 'Boat People' Urged in Fairfax City," *NVS*, July 28, 1979.

182. Seth W. Moskowitz, "Refugee Recalls the Long Ordeal," *WP*, December 7, 1978.

183. Bong-Wright, *Autumn Cloud*, 279.

184. Finding Aid, Families of Vietnamese Political Prisoners Association Collection, Vietnam Center and Archive, Texas Tech, online; Khuc Minh Tho, "An American Obligation," *WP*, September 17, 1984.

185. Lansdale to Whom It May Concern, May 23, 1975, Box 2, Folder Bui Anh Tuan, ELP; Ray Cline, "Foreword," Bui Anh Tuan, *Socialist Vietnam: The Way It Is* (Georgetown: Center for Strategic and International Studies, 1977).

186. Lansdale to Tuan, May 23, 1975, Box 2, Folder Bui Anh Tuan, ELP.

187. Lansdale to Robert De Vecchi, May 23, 1975; Lansdale to Tuan, May 23, 1975; Tuan to Lansdale, May 30, 1975, Box 2, Folder Bui Anh Tuan, ELP.

188. Tuan to Lansdale, January 21, 1976; Tuan to Lansdale, February 7, 1977, Box 2, Folder Bui Anh Tuan, ELP; Bui Anh Tuan, *Southeast Asia: Communism on the*

March (American Council for World Freedom, 1978), front and back matter; David Leigh, "A Friend of Taiwan," *WP*, June 29, 1980; Stanley D. Bachrack, "The Death Rattle of the China Lobby," *WP*, February 2, 1979; Frank Ching, "Pro-Peking and Pro-Taiwan Factions March at U.N. and Almost Clash," *NYT*, September 22, 1971; Judy Klemesrud, "Opponent of E.R.A. Confident of Its Defeat," *NYT*, December 15, 1975.

189. Tuan to Lansdale, September 1, 1979, and Lansdale to Tuan, January 9, 1979, Box 2, Folder Bui Anh Tuan, ELP.

190. Lansdale to INS, January 28, 1976, Box 2, Folder Bui Anh Tuan.

191. Tuan to Lansdale, February 5, 1981, Box 2, Folder Bui Anh Tuan.

192. Tuan to Lansdale, December 14, 1978, and January 30, 1981, Box 2, Folder Bui Anh Tuan.

193. "Bui Anh Tuan Receives Honor Medal," *Congressional Record*, July 25, 1980, Box 2, Folder Bui Anh Tuan, ELP.

194. See Mariam Lam on "strategic affect," elucidated in her comment at "Beyond Immigration Politics" (Annual Meeting of the American Studies Association, Baltimore, MD, October 22–23, 2011).

195. Fogg, "New Life in a Strange Land"; "minorities" hanging files, FCPL.

196. "Settling Down in the Suburbs," *FJ*, April 27, 1979; Christopher Dickey, "Refugees: 'We Came Here with Hope . . . Now We Have Nothing,'" *WP*, August 26, 1979.

197. Sue Mullin, "Vietnamese Build an Empire on Spring Rolls," *Arlington-Alexandria Star*, November 26, 1979.

198. Dickey, "Refugees."

199. Sandra G. Boodman, "Area Indochinese Are Victims of Hard-to-Prove Bias," *WP*, March 24, 1980; Maggie Locke, "Grievances Aired by Fairfax County Landlords, Tenants," *WP*, May 25, 1978.

200. On emotives, William M. Reddy, *The Navigation of Feeling: A Framework for the History of Emotions* (Cambridge: Cambridge University Press, 2001), 104-5, 125.

201. Kim, *Ends of Empire*, 99; Homi K. Bhabha, *The Location of Culture* (London: Routledge, 1994), 86, 92.

202. Thanks to Mary Lui for sparking the connection between these different iterations of "skin."

203. Kim, *Ends of Empire*, 33, 99.

204. Weiner, *Legacy of Ashes*, 316; Donald C. Harrison overlays latitudes in *Distant Patrol: Virginia and the Korean War* (Chelsea, MI: Scarborough, 1989).

205. David Harrison, "Former 'Boat People' Cheer Resolution," *Burke Connection*, July 12, 2003.

206. Phuong Ly, "In Vietnam, Finding the Comfort of Home," *WP*, October 12, 2003.

207. Lan Cao and Himilce Novas, *Everything You Need to Know about Asian-American History* (New York: Plume, 1996), xvi.

CHAPTER FIVE

1. See Frederik Pohl, "Growing Up in Edge City," in *Epoch*, eds. Robert Silverberg and Roger Elwood (New York: Berkley, 1975), 103–14; the term "Edge City" comes from Ken Kesey via Tom Wolfe, although Joel Garreau never acknowledged the debt. See Tom Wolfe, *The Electric Kool-Aid Acid Test* (New York: Bantam, 1968), 30, 35; Joel Garreau, *Edge City: Life on the New Frontier* (New York: Doubleday, 1991), 473.

2. Joel Garreau, "Edge Cities," *Landscape Architecture* 78.8 (December 1988), 511; Garreau, *Edge City*, 350, 15; *Philip Johnson/John Burgee Architecture 1979–1985* (New York: Rizzoli, 1985), 9, 143; Philip Johnson et al., *The Architecture of Philip Johnson* (Houston: Anchorage, 2002), 259; Franz Schulze, *Philip Johnson: Life and Work* (New York: Knopf, 1994), 344, 346, 366–67; Robert L. Miller, "The New American Downtown," *Architectural Record* (September 1987), 79–83; Yves Boquet, "Les entreprises á technologie avancée dans la région de Washington DC," *Bulletin de l'Association de Geographes Francais* 63 (1986), 217–26; Robert Fishman, *Bourgeois Utopias: The Rise and Fall of Suburbia* (New York: Basic, 1987); Jon C. Teaford, *Post-Suburbia: Government and Politics in the Edge Cities* (Baltimore: Johns Hopkins Press, 1997); Dolores Hayden, *Building Suburbia*, 154–80; Brent Stringfellow, "Personal City: Tysons Corner and the Question of Identity," in *Embodied Utopias: Gender, Social Change, and the Modern Metropolis*, eds. Amy Bingaman et al. (London: Routledge, 2002), 173–87; Zachary M. Schrag, "The Making of an Auto-Dependent Edge City: The Case of Fairfax County, Virginia," in *Redefining Suburban Studies: Searching for New Paradigms*, ed. Daniel Rubey (Hempstead: National Center for Suburban Studies at Hofstra University, 2009); Benjamin Forgey, "Towering over Tysons," *WP*, September 8, 1984; Barbara Carton, "Tall Talk of the Town," *WP*, July 16, 1987; See also Garreau's original *WP* articles: "From Suburbs, Cities Are Springing Up in Our Backyards," March 18, 1987; "Mobil's Move to Fairfax May Spark a Trend," May 3, 1987; "The Shadow Governments," June 14, 1987; "A Middle Class Without Precedent," November 29, 1987; "The Search For Urban 'Soul,'" June 19, 1988; "Solving the Equation for Success," June 20, 1988.

3. A good introduction is Peter Kornbluh and Malcolm Byrne, eds., *The Iran-Contra Scandal: The Declassified History* (New York: New Press, 1993); also see *The Tower Commission Report* (New York: Random House, 1987), 103.

4. See Michael Rogin, "'Make My Day!': Spectacle as Amnesia in Imperial Politics [and] the Sequel," in *Cultures of United States Imperialism*, eds. Amy Kaplan and Donald E. Pease (Durham: Duke University Press, 1993), 499–534.

5. Garreau, *Edge City*, 374; Goldberg, *Pentagon*, 22.

6. Ceruzzi, *Internet Alley*, 92–95; Robert S. McNamara, *The Essence of Security: Reflections in Office* (New York: Harper & Row, 1968), 88.

7. Ceruzzi, *Internet Alley*, 36, 142, 170; Ross and Nan Netherton, *Fairfax County: A Contemporary Portrait* (Virginia Beach: Donning, 1992); David Pedersen, *American Value: Migrants, Money, and Meaning in El Salvador and the United States* (Chicago: University of Chicago Press, 2013), 78–115, 126–27; Shelley Smith

Mastran, "The Evolution of Suburban Nucleations: Land Investment Activity in Fairfax County, Virginia, 1958–1977" (PhD diss., University of Maryland, 1988).

8. Lyle C. Bryant, *Rosslyn: A Case Study in Urban Renewal* (New York: Schalkenbach Foundation, 1965); Wilbur Smith, *Feasibility Analysis for the Proposed Ballston Galleria Garage Prepared for Arlington County* (Columbia, SC: May 1982); Department Environmental Affairs, *1974 Review of the General Land Use Plan: Rosslyn-Ballston Corridor* (Arlington: September 1974); Department Community Affairs, *Development in the Metro Corridors* (Arlington: October 1984).

9. Connie Pendleton Stuntz, *This Was Tysons Corner, Virginia: Facts and Photos* (Vienna: 1990), 117; Ceruzzi, *Internet Alley*, 50, 66, 71–72; Frank O'Donnell, "They Came, They Saw, They Built!...and Built, and Built, and Built," *Regardie's* (September 1988), 173; Anderson Road, Old Meadow Road, Westpark Drive, Jones Branch Drive, FCLR; "Charles Morton Goodman," *Marquis Who's Who*, May 5, 1998; Ronald W. Marshall and Barbara A. Boyd, "Charles Goodman: Production, Recognition, and Reflection," *Modernism* (Fall 1999), 41–47; Martha M. Hamilton and Thomas Grubisich, "Tysons Corner," *WP*, July 13, 1980; Herrick, *Yesterday*, 75, 368; John B. Willmann, "Westgate/Westpark," *WP*, November 12, 1977; Kenneth Bredemeier, "Beltway Becomes Area's Main Street," *WP*, February 17, 1985; "Work Starts on Big McLean Complex," *WP*, September 13, 1970.

10. Abbott, *Political Terrain*, 135; David M. Ricci, *The Transformation of American Politics: The New Washington and the Rise of Think Tanks* (New Haven: Yale University Press, 1993), 42.

11. Hamilton and Grubisich, "Tysons Corner"; Hayden, *Building Suburbia*, 162–64.

12. Ceruzzi, *Internet Alley*, 101.

13. Ibid., 122; Lynda Richardson and Caroline E. Mayer, "A Behemoth for Shoppers," *WP*, August 28, 1988.

14. *Fairfax Prospectus,* February 1986, 3, Box 3, Howard Gillette Metropolitan Washington Region Urban History Subject Files, Special Collections Research Center, George Washington University, Washington, DC; Lisa Zuniga, "Landmarks: A Survey of Commercial Development in the County," *Regardie's* (December 1988); Paul E. Ceruzzi, "How Tysons Went High Tech, 1965–1993," *Washington History* 21 (2009), 78–97.

15. John Rolfe Gardiner, "A Crossing," in *Going On Like This* (New York: Atheneum, 1983), 3–16; John Rolfe Gardiner, *In the Heart of the Whole World* (New York: Knopf, 1988); Hiam, *Who the Hell*, 38, 135, 182–86; Michael Kernan, "Minstrel of Quiet Madness," *WP*, October 15, 1988; James Tiptree Jr., "Backward, Turn Backward," in *Crown of Stars* (New York: Tom Doherty, 1988), 208–70; William Gibson, *Neuromancer* (New York: Ace, 1984), 31–52, 83; Phillips, *James Tiptree*, 327.

16. Ceruzzi, *Internet Alley*, 77–78; Cornelius F. Foote Jr., "Vault-Like Rooms Become Standard Office Equipment," *WP*, July 31, 1988.

17. Jeffrey Richelson, *The U.S. Intelligence Community* (Cambridge: Harper & Row, 1985), 315, 273; Defense Intelligence Agency, "Physical Security Standards for Sensitive Compartmented Information Facilities," May 2, 1980; Director of Cen-

tral Intelligence Directive No. 1/14, "Uniform Personnel Security Standards and Practices Governing Access to Sensitive Compartmented Information," June 23, 1967, DNSA; U.S. General Accounting Office (GAO), Report to the Secretary of Defense, "Further Improvements Needed in Department of Defense Oversight of Special Access (Carve-Out) Contracts," February 18, 1983, 6.

18. GAO, "Further Improvements Needed," 1; DIA, "Physical Security Standards for Construction of Sensitive Compartmented Information Facilities," February 1990, 19, DNSA; Foote, "Vault-Like Rooms"; NCI, Inc., Reston, VA, S-1 Form, July 29, 2005.

19. DIA, "Physical Security Standards for Sensitive"; Director of Central Intelligence Directive No. 6/9, "Physical Security Standards for Sensitive Compartmented Information Facilities," November 18, 2002; Foote, "Vault-Like Rooms"; Ceruzzi, *Internet Alley*, 75; F. Housley Carr, "CIA Builds New Quarters for Spies," *Engineering News-Record*, May 4, 1989; Anita Huslin, "If These Walls Could Talk . . . ," *WP*, May 28, 2006.

20. DIA, "Physical Security Standards for Sensitive," 19; DIA, "Physical Security Standards for Construction," 11; Ceruzzi, *Internet Alley*, 78.

21. DIA, "Physical Security Standards for Sensitive," 23–25.

22. DIA, "Physical Security Standards for Sensitive," 12, 38; Garreau, *Edge City*, 14, 52.

23. Ann Markusen et al., *The Rise of the Gunbelt: The Military Remapping of Industrial America* (New York: Oxford University Press, 1991), 211.

24. Ceruzzi, *Internet Alley*, 76–77.

25. GAO, "Further Improvements Needed," 2, 4, 10; Richelson, *U.S. Intelligence Community*, 315–16, 344–45.

26. Whitehead, *Brains, Sex and Racism*, 27, 35–37; Corson, *Widows*, 108, 133; Copeland, *Game Player*, 142; Ceruzzi, *Internet Alley*, 101; Peter Maas, *Manhunt* (New York: Random House, 1986), 27, 163, 233, 279; David Wise, *The American Police State: The Government Against the People* (New York: Random House, 1976), 202; Carr, "CIA Builds New Quarters"; Jim Hougan, *Spooks: The Haunting of America—The Private Use of Secret Agents* (New York: Morrow, 1978), 65–66, 72.

27. Jonathan Marshall et al., *The Iran-Contra Connection: Secret Teams and Covert Operations in the Reagan Era* (Boston: South End, 1987), 7.

28. Michael T. Klare, *Beyond the "Vietnam Syndrome": U.S. Interventionism in the 1980s* (Washington, DC: Institute for Policy Studies, 1981), 4; Nutter, *CIA's Black Ops*, 62; Perlmutter, *Photojournalism and Foreign Policy*, 38.

29. Klare, *Beyond the "Vietnam Syndrome,"* 2.

30. Klare, *Beyond the "Vietnam Syndrome,"* 4; "The Decline of U.S. Power," *Business Week* (March 12, 1979), 88.

31. U.S. Congress, House Select Committee on Intelligence, *The Pike Report* (Nottingham: Spokesman, 1977), 97, 114.

32. See, for example, Henry L. Rosett, "The Post-Vietnam Syndrome," *NYT*, June 6, 1971.

33. Westad, *Global Cold War*, 345.

34. Elliott Abrams, *Undue Process: A Story of How Political Differences Are Turned into Crimes* (New York: Free Press, 1993), 5.

35. Weiner, *Legacy of Ashes*, 349; Westad, *Global Cold War*, 222, 228; Stockwell, *In Search of Enemies*, 55; Andrew Downer Crain, *The Ford Presidency: A History* (Jefferson: McFarland, 2009), 216–27.

36. Stockwell, *In Search of Enemies*, 253–54; Klare, *Beyond the "Vietnam Syndrome,"* 67–69.

37. Westad, *Global Cold War*, 331–32; Roger Morris and Richard Mauzy, "Following the Scenario," in *The CIA File*, eds. Robert L. Borosage and John Marks (New York: Viking, 1976), 38.

38. Weiner, *Legacy of Ashes*, 363

39. Klare, *Beyond the "Vietnam Syndrome,"* 9; Robert M. Gates, *From the Shadows*, 150; Westad, *Global Cold War*, 329.

40. Gates, *From the Shadows*, 143–44; Westad, *Global Cold War*, 328; Weiner, *Legacy of Ashes*, 366; Frank J. Prial, "Exile's Return to Grenada," *NYT*, February 23, 1984.

41. Michael Smith, *Killer Elite: The Inside Story of America's Most Secret Special Operations Team* (New York: St. Martin's, 2007), 1–3; Weiner, *Legacy of Ashes*, 372; Susan L. Marquis, *Unconventional Warfare: Rebuilding U.S. Special Operations Forces* (Washington, DC: Brookings, 1997), 1–2; Tim Weiner, *Blank Check*, 173–74.

42. Westad, *Global Cold War*, 328–29; Spring Hill File, FCZB.

43. Nutter, *CIA's Black Ops*, 62.

44. Gilligan, *CIA Life*, 189–90; Stansfield Turner, *Burn before Reading: Presidents, CIA Directors and Secret Intelligence* (New York: Hyperion, 2005), 187; Weiner, *Legacy of Ashes*, 364; Crile, *Charlie Wilson's War*, 56; Nutter, *CIA's Black Ops*, 62; Milt Bearden, *The Main Enemy: The Inside Story of the CIA's Final Showdown with the KGB* (New York: Random House, 2003), 64.

45. Theodore Shackley, *The Third Option: An American View of Counterinsurgency Operations* (New York: McGraw-Hill, 1981), ix.

46. On this notion of surplus, see Ruth Wilson Gilmore, *Golden Gulag: Prisons, Surplus, Crisis, and Opposition in Globalizing California* (Berkeley: University of California Press, 2007); Marshall et al., *Iran-Contra Connection*, 26.

47. Weiner, *Legacy of Ashes*, 256–57, 315, 397–98; David Corn, *Blond Ghost: Ted Shackley and the CIA's Crusades* (New York: Simon & Schuster, 1994), 357, 360, 405; *Tower Commission Report*, 106–7; Marshall et al., *Iran-Contra Connection*, 156.

48. Smith, *Killer Elite*, 13, 17–21; Weiner, *Blank Check*, 174; Kornbluh and Byrne, *Iran-Contra Scandal*, 379; Marshall et al., *Iran-Contra Connection*, 165; Jonathan Kwitny, *The Crimes of Patriots: A True Tale of Dope, Dirty Money, and the CIA* (New York: Norton, 1987), overleaf; Persico, *Casey*, 276; Marquis, *Unconventional Warfare*, 73.

49. Smith, *Killer Elite*, 26, 55.

50. Ibid., 60–61, 118; James "Bo" Gritz, *A Nation Betrayed* (Boulder City: Lazarus, 1989), 196–97.

51. Persico, *Casey*, 101, 179; Weiner, *Legacy of Ashes*, 376.

52. Mark B. Liedl, ed., *Scouting the Future: The Public Speeches of William J. Casey* (Washington, DC: Regnery Gateway, 1989), 16; Persico, *Casey*, 359.

53. Kessler, *Inside CIA*, 181–82; Bearden, *Main Enemy*, 376; cia.gov, "History" (accessed May 19, 2012); Mendez, *Spy Dust*, 115; David Hoffman, "Reagan Praises Casey during CIA Ground-Breaking Ceremony," *WP*, May 25, 1984; Barbara Carton, "CIA Plans Go Public," *WP*, May 16, 1985; "Intelligence Center Stands Out," *Engineering News-Record*, June 3, 1982.

54. Crile, *Charlie Wilson's War*, 432; Persico, *Casey*, 362; See also Greg Grandin, *Empire's Workshop: Latin America, the United States, and the Rise of the New Imperialism* (New York: Metropolitan, 2006).

55. "Concern for Human Rights in Our Foreign Policy – More Than a Gesture," 10, Box 6, Folder Rufus Phillips, ELP.

56. Loch K. Johnson, *America's Secret Power: The CIA in a Democratic Society* (Oxford: Oxford University Press, 1991), 142; Amy Fried, *Muffled Echoes: Oliver North and the Politics of Public Opinion* (New York: Columbia University Press, 1997), 70; Persico, *Casey*, 566–67.

57. Pisani, *CIA and the Marshall Plan*, 75, 144.

58. Ken Silverstein, *Private Warriors* (New York: Verso, 2000), 64, 67; Jim Hunt and Bob Risch, *Warrior: Frank Sturgis – The CIA's #1 Assassin-Spy, Who Nearly Killed Castro but Was Ambushed by Watergate* (New York: Tom Doherty, 2011), 39–40.

59. Klare, *Beyond the "Vietnam Syndrome,"* 83–94.

60. William M. LeoGrande, *Our Own Backyard: The United States in Central America, 1977–1992* (Chapel Hill: University of North Carolina Press, 1998), 65, 90; Tom Barry et al., *The New Right Humanitarians* (Albuquerque: Inter-Hemispheric Education Resource Center, 1986), 38; "U.S. Envoy to El Salvador Claims Reagan Team Is Undercutting Him," *NYT*, December 10, 1980; Louie Estrada, "General Daniel Graham Dies," *WP*, January 3, 1996; Steve Lohr, "D.O. Graham, 70, Leading 'Star Wars' Architect," *NYT*, January 3, 1996; Richard Severo, "Roberto d'Aubuisson, 48, Far-Rightist in Salvador," *NYT*, February 21, 1992.

61. Sam Dillon, *Commandos: The CIA and Nicaragua's Contra Rebels* (New York: Henry Holt, 1991), 42, 103–5; Lee, *History of Arlington*, 86.

62. Klare, *Beyond the "Vietnam Syndrome,"* 11, 95; Weiner, *Legacy of Ashes*, 380; Nutter, *CIA's Black Ops*, 64.

63. Kiyonaga, *My Spy*, 212–13; LeoGrande, *Our Own Backyard*, 48; Robert Armstrong, *El Salvador: The Face of Revolution* (Boston: South End, 1982), vi; Philip L. Russell, *El Salvador in Crisis* (Austin: Colorado River, 1984), 120.

64. Philip J. Williams and Knut Walter, *Militarization and Demilitarization in El Salvador's Transition to Democracy* (Pittsburgh: University of Pittsburgh Press, 1997), 51; Americas Watch, *El Salvador's Decade of Terror* (New Haven: Yale University Press, 1991), 83; Russell, *El Salvador in Crisis*, 121; Jenny Pearce, *Under the Eagle: U.S. Intervention in Central America and the Caribbean* (Boston: South End, 1982), 238; Max G. Manwaring and Court Prisk, *El Salvador at War: An Oral History* (Washington: National Defense University Press, 1988), 235–36, 278, 335.

65. Susan Bibler Coutin, *Nation of Emigrants: Shifting Boundaries of Citizenship in El Salvador and the United States* (Ithaca: Cornell University Press, 2007), 76–77; Walter LaFeber, *Inevitable Revolutions: The United States in Central America* (New York: Norton, 1993), 354; Mandy Macdonald and Mike Gatehouse, *In the Mountains of Morazán: Portrait of a Returned Refugee Community in El Salvador* (London: Latin America Bureau, 1995), 1; Grandin, *Empire's Workshop*, 102.

66. Rodolfo Acuña, *Occupied America: A History of Chicanos* (New York: Pearson Longman, 2004), 373; David Pedersen, "The Storm We Call Dollars: Determining Value and Belief in El Salvador and the United States," *Cultural Anthropology* 17.3 (August 2002), 439–41; Russell, *El Salvador in Crisis*, 58–59.

67. Kornbluh and Byrne, *Iran-Contra Scandal*, xxviii, 3, 9.

68. See LaFeber, *Inevitable Revolutions*; Héctor Lindo-Fuentes and Erik Ching, *Modernizing Minds in El Salvador: Education Reform and the Cold War, 1960–1980* (Albuquerque: University of New Mexico Press, 2012), 262; George Black, *The Good Neighbor* (New York: Pantheon, 1988), 114; Russell, *El Salvador in Crisis*, 53.

69. LeoGrande, *Our Own Backyard*, 115–18, 296–98; Clarridge, *Spy for All Seasons*, 73, 207–9; Grandin, *Empire's Workshop*, 113.

70. John Jakle and Keith A. Sculle, *Fast Food: Roadside Restaurants in the Automobile Age* (Baltimore: Johns Hopkins University Press, 1999); Robert O'Brien, *Marriott: The J. Willard Marriott Story* (Salt Lake City: Deseret, 1977), 256; Classified ad, *WP*, May 21, 1959; "Photo Standalone," *WP*, July 5, 1969; Smith, *Killer Elite*, 113; Jerry Knight, "From Soda Jerk to Industry Mogul," *WP*, August 15, 1985; *J.W. Marriott: Host to the World* (New York: Hearst, A&E, 1998).

71. Christopher Dickey, *With the Contras: A Reporter in the Wilds of Nicaragua* (New York: Simon & Schuster, 1985), 77, 151–52.

72. Edgar Chamorro, *Packaging the Contras: A Case of CIA Disinformation* (New York: Institute for Media Analysis, 1987), 39–40; LeoGrande, *Our Own Backyard*, 115, 308, 364.

73. Cruz, *Memoirs of a Counterrevolutionary*, 173; Richard Secord, *Honored and Betrayed: Irangate, Covert Affairs, and the Secret War in Laos* (New York: Wiley & Sons, 1992), 205–6.

74. Secord, *Honored and Betrayed*, 205–6; Testimony of Richard V. Secord, *Joint Hearings, May 5 through May 8, 1987* (Washington, DC: U.S. GPO, 1987), 49–51; See also Joseph C. Goulden, *The Death Merchant* (New York: Simon and Schuster, 1984), 72.

75. Felix I. Rodriguez, *Shadow Warrior* (New York: Simon and Schuster, 1989), 222–23, 215–17.

76. Clarridge, *Spy for All Seasons*, 211.

77. Dillon, *Commandos*, 128, 131.

78. Cruz, *Memoirs of a Counterrevolutionary*, 176–78, 196–98.

79. Persico, *Casey*, 479.

80. Dillon, *Commandos*, 291.

81. Lawrence E. Walsh, *Iran-Contra: The Final Report* (New York: Random House, 1994), 158.

82. Steven Emerson, *Secret Warriors: Inside the Covert Military Operations of the Reagan Era* (New York: GP Putnam's Sons, 1988), 9, 18–19, 39, 92–94; Leo-Grande, *Our Own Backyard*, 385–86; www.realtydiversifiedservices.com/projects. html (accessed March 22, 2012).

83. Weiner, *Blank Check*, 179–80; Emerson, *Secret Warriors*, 143–45; Leo-Grande, *Our Own Backyard*, 403; James LeMoyne, "The White House Crisis," *NYT*, November 30, 1986; Dan Morgan and Charles R. Babcock, "Secret Task Led to Web of Firms," *WP*, March 22, 1987; Jeff Gerth, "On Trail of a Latin Mystery, CIA Footprints," *NYT*, October 6, 1983.

84. Emerson, *Secret Warriors*, 90, 92–93, 97, 150–52; Seymour Hersh, "Who's in Charge Here?" *NYTM*, November 22, 1987; Representative Jim Leach et al., "The Escalation of the Air War: A Congressional View," in *El Salvador: Central America in the New Cold War*, ed. Marvin Gettleman et al. (New York: Grove, 1986), 231; Weiner, *Blank Check*, 184–88; "Agent's El Salvador Death Confirmed," *AP*, October 24, 1984.

85. Testimony of Richard V. Secord, 46; Roger Warner, *Back Fire: The CIA's Secret War in Laos and Its Link to the War in Vietnam* (New York: Simon & Schuster, 1995), 191–94, 326, 368; Weiner, *Blank Check*, 205; Goulden, *Death Merchant*, 47–8; Kwitny, *Crimes of Patriots*, 310.

86. Warner, *Back Fire*, 196.

87. Testimony of Richard V. Secord, 570, 582–85; Kornbluh and Byrne, *Iran-Contra Scandal*, 103–10; Joe Pichirallo and Julia Preston, "Calero Suggests Funds Paid for Contra Weapons," *WP*, November 27, 1986; "Files Link Ex-Official and Contra Suppliers," *NYT*, October 20, 1986; MacNeil/Lehrer, "Contra Confrontation," February 5, 1987; Secord, *Honored and Betrayed*, 214; Walsh, *Iran Contra*, 85; Parcels 0294 07 C1, 0293 20 0007, FCLR; NOVA White Pages, 1986, 1990; Fox Butterfield, "The White House Crisis," *NYT*, December 6, 1986.

88. Secord, *Honored and Betrayed*, 290–91; Oliver North, *Under Fire: An American Story* (New York: HarperCollins, 1991), 284; Thomas Turcol, "Will Success Spoil Tysons Corner Boom," *WP*, January 2, 1986; "Sheraton Corp. Plans to Build New Hotel Near Tysons Corner," *WP*, September 26, 1983.

89. Walsh, *Iran Contra*, 3, 7–9, 157–58, 165–66; Dickey, *With the Contras*, 244; Persico, *Casey*, 403–4; *Tower Commission Report*, 176, 468; Joseph B. Treaster, "Panama Offers a Haven for Shadowy Concerns," *NYT*, December 21, 1986.

90. Walsh, *Iran Contra*, 116; Ben Bradlee Jr., *Guts and Glory: The Rise and Fall of Oliver North* (New York: Donald I. Fine, 1988), 10–11; Persico, *Casey*, 544.

91. Walsh, *Iran Contra*, 4, 157; *Tower Commission Report*, 58.

92. Ceruzzi, "How Tysons," 83–84.

93. Walsh, *Iran Contra*, 82.

94. Ramshorn File, FCZB; Michael Crowley, "GOPtopia," *NR*, September 11–18, 2006; Douglas Jehl, "The Struggle for Iraq," *NYT*, September 30, 2003; Chris Black, "Clinton Sets Tough Code on Ethics," *Boston Globe*, November 14, 1992.

95. William Simpson, *The Prince: The Secret Story of the World's Most Intriguing Royal Prince Bandar bin Sultan* (New York: HarperCollins, 2008), 129, 385; Rob-

ert C. McFarlane, *Special Trust* (New York: Cadell & Davies, 1994), 69–70; Woodward, *Veil*, 403, 453.

96. Persico, *Casey*, 518.

97. Goulden, *Death Merchant*, 42–43, 389; Maas, *Manhunt*, xiv, 37, 70, 121.

98. Maas, *Manhunt*, xiv, 50; Goulden, *Death Merchant*, 74.

99. Valentine, *Phoenix Program*, 114; LeoGrande, *Our Own Backyard*, 117; Richard Halloran, "Pentagon Official, Linked to Contra Aid, to Retire," *NYT*, January 15, 1987; Susan Saulny, "A Rescue Plan Worthy of Marshall," *WP*, March 8, 1998.

100. Keith Schneider, "Fawn Hall Steps into the Limelight," *NYT*, February 26, 1987; Cruz, *Memoirs of a Counterrevolutionary*, 197.

101. North, *Under Fire*, 273; Walter Pincus and Dan Morgan, "Contra Leader Says He Gave North $90,000," *WP*, May 21, 1987.

102. Walsh, *Iran Contra*, 253; George Lardner Jr., "Ex-CIA Official Clarridge Indicted in Iran Arms Case," *WP*, November 27, 1991.

103. Jeff Gerth et al., "Retired Air Force General Named as Central Figure in Secret Talks," *NYT*, December 9. 1986.

104. Dickey, *With the Contras*, 262; LeoGrande, *Our Own Backyard*, 394; Marshall et al., *Iran-Contra Connection*, 79; "CIA Official Donald Winters Dies," *WP*, January 30, 2001; Tim Golden, "Honduran Army's Abuses Were Known to CIA," *NYT*, October 24, 1998; "Ellura Harvey Winters," *WP*, July 21, 1987; NOVA White Pages 1987.

105. LeoGrande, *Our Own Backyard*, 278, 684; Gary Webb, *Dark Alliance: The CIA, the Contras, and the Crack Cocaine Explosion* (New York: Seven Stories, 1998), 329–30; Raymond L. Garthoff, *The Great Transition: American-Soviet Relations and the End of the Cold War* (Washington, DC: Brookings, 1994), 701–2; Rodriguez, *Shadow Warrior*, 219, 222; Brian J. Bosch, *The Salvadoran Officer Corps and the Final Offensive of 1981* (Jefferson: McFarland, 1999), 45; See also Pedersen, *American Value*, 39, 279.

106. Clarridge, *Spy for All Seasons*, 208–9, 220; Leo Grande, *Our Own Backyard*, 118.

107. Secord, *Honored and Betrayed*, 181; Walters, *Silent Missions*, 323.

108. Walter Pincus and Dan Morgan, "Secord Tells Congress of Meeting Recently with North, Poindexter," *WP*, May 9, 1987.

109. Glenn Garvin, *Everybody Had His Own Gringo: The CIA & the Contras* (Washington, DC: Brassey's, 1992), 172; Bradlee, *Guts and Glory*, 100.

110. North, *Under Fire*, 134, 161.

111. Clarridge, *Spy for All Seasons*, 223; Garvin, *Everybody Had His Own*, 54; Chamorro, *Packaging the Contras*, 50; Persico, *Casey*, 266; Walsh, *Iran Contra*, 255.

112. Persico, *Casey*, 1–2, 409; Crile, *Charlie Wilson's War*, 157; Sullivan, *Gatekeeper*, 181.

113. Kornbluh and Byrne, *Iran-Contra Scandal*, xxviii.

114. Persico, *Casey*, 2, 7; Jaime Morales Carazo, *La Contra* (Mexico City: Planeta, 1989), 151.

115. Garvin, *Everybody Had His Own*, 26; on another Northern Virginian in

these relations, see Ernest B. Furgurson, *Hard Right: The Rise of Jesse Helms* (New York: Norton, 1986), 193–95.

116. Cruz, *Memoirs of a Counterrevolutionary,* 159.

117. Dillon, *Commandos,* 173–74; Garvin, *Everybody Had His Own,* 119–21.

118. NOVA White Pages 1986; Dillon, *Commandos,* 212.

119. Bradlee, *Guts and Glory,* 15; David Friend, "A Man of Many Faces," *Life,* August 1987; *Tower Commission Report,* 513; Lorraine Woellert, "Ollie North, Running to High Ground," *WT,* September 23, 1993; Peter Carlson, "Rambo as Garbo," *WPM,* March 29, 1987; NOVA White Pages 1984; Parcel 0062 03 0002, FCLR; Seneca Ridge File, FCZB.

120. Testimony of Richard V. Secord, 415; Parcel 0223040121, FCLR.

121. "Secord Charged with DWI in Va.," *WP,* February 27, 1989; Arbor Glen Way, FCLR.

122. Fried, *Muffled Echoes,* 79; Melani McAlister, *Epic Encounters: Culture, Media and U.S. Interests in the Middle East, 1945–2000* (Berkeley: University of California Press, 2001), 233.

123. David Halevy and Neil C. Livingstone, "The Ollie We Knew," *Washingtonian,* July 1987.

124. Grandin, *Empire's Workshop,* 89; Giorgio Agamben, *Means Without End* (Minneapolis: University of Minnesota Press, 2000), 3–14.

125. Garvin, *Everybody Had His Own,* 116.

126. Walters, *Silent Missions,* 614; LeoGrande, *Our Own Backyard,* 115–16; George C. Wilson, "A Buildup in U.S. Forces," *WP,* June 16, 1980; José Napoleón Duarte, *My Story* (New York: Putnam's Sons, 1986), 184.

127. Garvin, *Everybody Had His Own,* 121, 198, 91; Dillon, *Commandos,* 88; Persico, *Casey,* 5.

128. North, *Under Fire,* 244, 263, first photo plates.

129. Grandin, *Empire's Workshop,* 116.

130. Frank Dux, *The Secret Man: An American Warrior's Uncensored Story* (New York: HarperCollins, 1996), 194.

131. Nidia Díaz, *I Was Never Alone: A Prison Diary from El Salvador* (Melbourne: Ocean, 1992), 116.

132. Emerson, *Secret Warriors,* 90–91; Hersh, "Who's in Charge Here?"; Smith, *Killer Elite,* 55–56.

133. Dillon, *Commandos,* 118, 252; Americas Watch, *El Salvador's Decade,* 43.

134. John K. Singlaub, *Hazardous Duty: An American Soldier in the Twentieth Century* (New York: Summit, 1991), 466–71; Kornbluh and Byrne, *Iran-Contra Scandal,* xxx; for related analysis, Dean, *Imperial Brotherhood,* 175, 185; Denning, *Cover Stories,* 143.

135. North, *Under Fire,* 411.

136. Singlaub, *Hazardous Duty,* 449; Nashel, *Edward Lansdale's Cold War,* 17, 190, photo plates; Marshall et al., *Iran-Contra Connection,* 197; Barry et al., *New Right Humanitarians,* 18.

137. Bradlee, *Guts and Glory,* 15; Michael Lynch and David Bogen, *The Spectacle*

of History: Speech, Text, and Memory at the Iran-Contra Hearings (Durham: Duke University Press, 1996), 102; Fried, *Muffled Echoes*, 113, 117, 69.

138. Lynch and Bogen, *Spectacle of History*, 106, 112; Fried, *Muffled Echoes*, 78, 170; on this "wholeness," see Amy Kaplan, "Romancing the Empire: The Embodiment of American Masculinity in the Popular Historical Novel of the 1890s," *American Literary History* 2.4 (Winter 1990), 681.

139. Walsh, *Iran Contra*, 114; Fried, *Muffled Echoes*, 79, 122.

140. Gar Smith, "The Invisible War on the Environment," in *El Salvador*, Gettleman et al., 242.

141. See Kaplan, "Romancing the Empire," 681; Fried, *Muffled Echoes*, 118; Rogin, "'Make My Day!'".

142. *Tower Commission Report*, 248–49; Marshall et al., *Iran-Contra Connection*, 157, 165, 185; Persico, *Casey*, 438; "Albert Hakim, Figure in Iran-Contra Affair, Dies at 66," *NYT*, May 1, 2003; Myrna Oliver, "Key Figure in Iran-Contra," *Los Angeles Times*, May 1, 2003.

143. Kornbluh and Byrne, *Iran-Contra Scandal*, xxvi; Kolb, *Overworld*, 241, 244, 175; Persico, *Casey*, 447–49; Crile, *Charlie Wilson's War*, 442.

144. Secord, *Honored and Betrayed*, 290–91; Persico, *Casey*, 520; *Tower Commission Report*, 49; Kornbluh and Byrne, *Iran-Contra Scandal*, xxiii.

145. Testimony of Albert Hakim, *Joint Hearings* (Washington: U.S. GPO, 1988), 194.

146. Testimony of Richard V. Secord, 46; Marshall et al., *Iran-Contra Connection*, 156; Gaylord Shaw and Maura Dolan, "Ex-Officer, Businessman: Little Known Pair Major Figures in Weapons Saga," *Los Angeles Times*, December 7, 1986; Persico, *Casey*, 494.

147. Testimony of Richard V. Secord, 47; Persico, *Casey*, 494; Marshall et al., *Iran-Contra Connection*, 156.

148. George F. Hofman, *Cold War Casualty: The Court-Martial of Major General Robert W. Grow* (Kent: Kent State University Press, 1993), 136; James F. Goode, *US and Iran, 1946–1951: The Diplomacy of Neglect* (New York: St. Martin's, 1989), 24–30; Fairfax County Chamber of Commerce, *History*, www.fairfaxchamber.org (accessed September 25, 2008).

149. Kermit Roosevelt, *Countercoup*; Archibald Roosevelt, *For Lust of Knowing*, 117; Wilber, "Overthrow of Premier Mossadeq," 10, 19, 37, 44, 56–57, 69, 75, appendix D; Stephen Dorril, *MI6: Inside the Covert World of Her Majesty's Secret Intelligence Service* (New York: Free Press, 2000), 596; Washington Metropolitan Phone Book, 1963–64.

150. William E. Warne, *Mission for Peace: Point 4 in Iran* (Indianapolis: Bobbs-Merrill, 1956), 59, 88, 138, 183, 255, 259–60, 264, 270; Warne, *Mission for Peace* (Bethesda, MD: Ibex, 1999), v, x, xi, xiii; Wilber, "Overthrow of Premier Mossadeq," 28; "Oral History Interview with William Warne," May 21, 1988, 89, Harry S. Truman Library and Museum, online.

151. James A. Bill, *The Eagle and the Lion: The Tragedy of American-Iranian Relations* (New Haven, CT: Yale University Press, 1988), 291, 297; "Briefing," August 20,

1979; William Casey, "Transcript of a speech at the Metropolitan Club, New York City," May 1, 1985, DNSA; Gordon Thomas, *Journey into Madness: The True Story of Secret CIA Mind Control and Medical Abuse* (New York: Bantam, 1989), 18; Woodward, *Veil*, 270; *A Place Called Reston*, 1973; Parcel 0273 04010055, FCLR; Mendez, *Master of Disguise*, 257, 261.

152. William Shawcross, *The Shah's Last Ride: The Fate of An Ally* (New York: Simon and Schuster, 1988), 196; Fereydoun Hoveyda, *The Fall of the Shah* (New York: Wyndham, 1980), 73; Paul Theroux, *The Great Railway Bazaar: By Train through Asia* (Boston: Houghton Mifflin, 1975), 61–63.

153. Helms, *Ambassador's Wife in Iran*, 174; William Sullivan, *Mission to Iran* (New York: Norton, 1981), 61–62, 68; Ashraf Pahlavi, *Faces in a Mirror: Memoirs from Exile* (Englewood Cliffs: Prentice-Hall, 1980), 151, 169; Farah Pahlavi, *An Enduring Love* (New York: Miramax, 2004), 54, 72, 249; Shawcross, *Shah's Last Ride*, 139, 196; Hoveyda, *Fall of the Shah*, 97; Roosevelt, *Countercoup*, 164; Donald N. Wilber, *Adventures in the Middle East: Excursions and Incursions* (Princeton: Darwin, 1986), 33; Ali Pasha Saleh, *Cultural Ties between Iran and the United States* (1976), 247; Kamran Diba, *Buildings and Projects* (Stuttgart-Bad Cannstatt: Hatje, 1981), 112, 226, 243; Philip Jodidio, ed., *Iran: Architecture for Changing Societies* (Turin: U Allemandi, 2004), 17–18, 33–35; Paul Wagret, *Iran* (Geneva: Nagel, 1977), 100–101; Jean Hureau, *Iran Today* (Paris: Editions Jeune Afrique, 1975), 161; K. Ziari and M. Gharakhlou, "A Study of Iranian New Towns During Pre- and Post Revolution," *International Journal of Environmental Research* 3.1 (Winter 2009), 146.

154. Hussein Fardust, *The Rise and Fall of the Pahlavi Dynasty*, trans., Ali Akbar Dareini (Delhi: Motilal Banarsidass, 1998), 53; C.M. Woodhouse, *Something Ventured* (London: Granada, 1982), 115; Kinzer, *All the Shah's Men*, 167; Yatsevitch interview, FISOHA.

155. Helms, *Ambassador's Wife in Iran*, 170.

156. Interview with Leyla Diba, by Tanya Farmanfarmaiyan, August 7 and 13, 1984, 8, FISOHA; Interview with Parviz Yar-Afshar, by Seyyed Vali Reza Nasr, July 18, 25, 1988, January 16, 1989, 41, FISOHA; Anthony Parsons, *The Pride and the Fall, Iran 1974–1979* (London: Jonathan Cape, 1984), 8–9.

157. Hoveyda, *Fall of the Shah*, 84; Rafizadeh, *Witness*, 104–5; Helms, *Ambassador's Wife in Iran*, 171–72; Saleh, *Cultural Ties*, front matter, 9; "Statements by U.S. Presidents in Support of the Shah, 1947–1978," Series 28, Folder 8, JMP; Farah Pahlavi, *Enduring Love*, 301, 337; Barry Rubin, *Paved with Good Intentions: The American Experience and Iran* (New York: Oxford University Press, 1980), 137, 143; Philip Ward, *Touring Iran* (London: Faber and Faber, 1971), 149.

158. Interview with Ellis Williamson, by William Burr, April 13, 1988, 155–56, 169, FISOHA; Kamal Habibolahi, Oral History Interview by Zia Sedghi, December 15, 1984, Iranian Oral History Collection, Harvard University; Helms, *Ambassador's Wife in Iran*, 172–73; Jonathan Kwitny, *Endless Enemies: The Making of an Unfriendly World* (New York: Congdon and Weed, 1984), 182–84; Abbas Milani, *The Persian Sphinx: Amir Abbas Hoveyda and the Riddle of the Iranian Revolution* (Washington, DC: Mage, 2000), 143; Helms, *An Intriguing Life*, 160–67.

159. Rubin, *Paved with Good Intentions*, 134–5.

160. Marshall et al., *Iran-Contra Connection*, 152; Bill, *Eagle and the Lion*, 226.

161. Hoveyda, *Fall of the Shah*, 98; Sullivan, *Mission to Iran*, 115, 149.

162. Rubin, *Paved with Good Intentions*, 130; Vijay Prashad, *The Darker Nations: A People's History of the Third World* (New York: New Press, 2007), 188.

163. Marshall et al., *Iran-Contra Connection*, 152, 278.

164. Carlos C. Campbell, *New Towns: Another Way to Live* (Reston: Reston Publishing, 1976), 228–30; Cargill, Wilson and Acree Inc. Advertising, "GORE-DCO Brochure Draft Number Two 12/6/74," 13, Box 5.14, PCA; "Gulf Oil Real Estate Development Company" (Reston: GOREDCO, undated), 11, Baum Digital Archive, PCA; Kenneth Bredemeier, "Gulf Forms Real Estate Division," *WP*, September 30, 1971; Jared Stout, "Gulf Official Takes over Reston Reins," *WP*, April 30, 1969; "William H. Magness, 84," *WP*, February 15, 2000; Judy Spears, "William H. Magness, 84, Dies," January 27, 2000 and "Obituaries," July 24, 2007, *Chattanooga Times Free Press*.

165. Bredemeier, "Gulf Forms Real Estate Division"; Donald L. Cummings, "Monthly Time Record – Project Evaluation and Reports," March, April 1977, and "GOREDCO Consulting Status," July 26, 1977, Box 5.10; "GOREDCO Moves World Headquarters to Reston International Center," July 22, 1974, Box 5.14, PCA; Netherton, *Reston*, 54–55.

166. Rafizadeh, *Witness*, 353; Marshall et al., *Iran-Contra Connection*, 153.

167. Persico, *Casey*, 504, 535.

168. Casey, "Transcript of a speech at the Metropolitan Club."

169. John Carlos Rowe, "Areas of Concern: Area Studies and the New American Studies," in *Challenging U.S. Foreign Policy: America and the World in the Long Twentieth Century*, eds. Bevan Sewell and Scott Lucas (Palgrave Macmillan, 2011), 162–82.

170. Terry A. Repak, *Waiting on Washington: Central American Workers in the Nation's Capital* (Philadelphia: Temple University Press, 1995), 53, 17–18, 42, 177; José Luis Benítez, "Communication and Collective Identities in the Transnational Social Space: A Media Ethnography of the Salvadoran Immigrant Community in the Washington, DC, Metropolitan Area" (PhD diss., Ohio University, 2005), 133, 151; Jeane J. Kirkpatrick, *Dictatorships and Double Standards: Rationalism and Reason in Politics* (New York: Simon and Schuster, 1982), 85; Pearce, *Under the Eagle*, 171–75.

171. Coutin, *Nation of Emigrants*, 48; LeoGrande, *Our Own Backyard*, 443–44, 459, 507; Kornbluh and Byrne, *Iran-Contra Scandal*, xxiii; Abrams, *Undue Process*, 116; Elliott Abrams, "Human Rights Conditions in El Salvador," July 29, 1982 (Washington, DC: U.S. Department of State, Bureau of Public Affairs).

172. *Taking the Stand: The Testimony of Lieutenant Colonel Oliver L. North* (New York: Pocket, 1987), 564; Ronald Reagan, "U.S. Interests in Central America," in *El Salvador*, Gettleman et al., 12; Kaplan, *Anarchy of Empire*, 11.

173. "U.S. Deportation Proceedings in Immigration Courts," "Immigration

Judge Reports – Asylum," Transactional Records Access Clearinghouse, Immigration Project, Data Tools and Applications, www.trac.syr.edu.

174. Repak, *Waiting on Washington*, 2–4, 96; Raúl Sánchez Molina, *Mander a Traer: Antropologia, Migraciones y Transnacionalismo, Salvadorenos en Washington* (Madrid: Editorial Universitas, SA, 2005); Olivia Cadaval, *Creating a Latino Identity in the Nation's Capital: The Latino Festival* (New York: Garland, 1998); Raúl Sánchez Molina, "Modes of Incorporation, Social Exclusion, and Transnationalism: Salvadorans' Adaptation to the Washington, DC Metropolitan Area," *Human Organization* 67.3 (Fall 2008); David E. Pedersen, "States of Memory and Desire: The Meaning of City and Nation for Transnational Migrants in Washington, DC, and El Salvador," *Amerikastudien* 40.3 (1995), 422–23; Patricia Andrea Landolt Marticorena, "The Causes and Consequences of Transnational Migration: Salvadorans in Los Angeles and Washington, DC" (PhD diss., Johns Hopkins University, 2000).

175. Author interview with Enid Gonzalez, lawyer and activist with El Rescate Nova in the 1980s, September 11, 2012.

176. LeoGrande, *Our Own Backyard*, 136.

177. Gettleman et al., *El Salvador*, 62; Mario Lungo Uclés, *El Salvador in the Eighties: Counterinsurgency and Revolution* (Philadelphia: Temple University Press, 1996), 104; Bosch, *Salvadoran Officer Corps*, 112.

178. Duarte, *My Story*, 73; New Americas Press, *A Dream Compels Us: Voices of Salvadoran Women* (Boston: South End, 1989), 77, 168; Christopher M. White, *The History of El Salvador* (Westport: Greenwood, 2009), 8.

179. White, *History of El Salvador*, 8, 104; Macdonald and Gatehouse, *In the Mountains,* 6, 36; New Americas, *Dream Compels Us*, 101, 234; Uclés, *El Salvador in the Eighties*, 104; Liedl, *Scouting the Future*, 50; Ana Kelly Rivera et al., *Valio La Pena* (San Salvador: Editorial Sombrero Azul, 1995), 286; Benítez, "Communication and Collective Identities," 132; Elisabeth Jean Wood, *Insurgent Collective Action and Civil War in El Salvador* (Cambridge: Cambridge University Press, 2003), 108.

180. Benítez, "Communication and Collective Identities," 132–155; Marta Stahlhofer Barkell, "Illness Experience among Salvadoran Women Immigrants" (PhD diss., Catholic University, 2007), 49; Molina, *Mander a Traer*, 144–46; Pedersen, "States of Memory," 422; Coutin, *Nation of Emigrants*, 117; Beth Baker-Cristales, *Salvadoran Migration to Southern California: Redefining El Hermano Lejano* (Gainesville: University Press of Florida, 2004), 48, 140; Randy Jurado Ertll, *Hope in Times of Darkness: A Salvadoran American Experience* (Lanham: Hamilton, 2009), 47; Landolt, "Causes and Consequences of Transnational Migration," 179–80.

181. Uclés, *El Salvador in the Eighties*, 74; Christopher Dickey and Karen DeYoung, "Illegal Entry," *WP*, April 2, 1979; Nancy Scannell, "After the Influx, a County Copes," *WP*, February 18, 1982; Barkell, "Illness Experience," 56; LeoGrande, *Our Own Backyard*, 129; Cadaval, *Creating a Latino Identity*, 76–77, 171–81; Robert F. Howe, "Death-Squad Figure Guilty in Immigration Case," *WP*, September 19, 1990; Colin Harding, "El Salvador Rebels Gain from US Exasperation," *Independent*, October 30, 1990; Robert F. Howe, "Deported Salvadoran Jailed for

Reentry," *WP*, December 8, 1990; Pamela Constable, "The Family Secret," *WP*, May 26, 1996.

182. Ana Patricia Rodríguez, "Refugees of the South: Central Americans in the U.S. Latino Imaginary" *American Literature* 73.2 (June 2001), 387–89; Ana Patricia Rodríguez, *Dividing the Isthmus: Central American Transnational Histories, Literatures, and Cultures* (Austin: University of Texas Press, 2009).

183. Coutin, *Nation of Emigrants*, 116–17.

184. Susan Bibler Coutin, *Legalizing Moves: Salvadoran Immigrants' Struggle for U.S. Residency* (Ann Arbor: University of Michigan Press, 2000), 44.

185. Teresa Wiltz, "Troubadours without Borders: How a Father and Son Brought El Salvador to Mount Pleasant," *WP*, March 25, 2004; Lilo González, *A Quien Corresponda . . .* (LGP Records, 1994, compact disc).

186. Karlyn Barker, "Salvadoran Refugees Flee the War, Not the Cause," *WP*, May 21, 1989; Landolt, "Causes and Consequences of Transnational Migration," 164, 180–81.

187. Alex Stoll, "Slavery and Sanctuary," *WP*, September 27, 1987; Bernard Weinraub, "Hundreds Arrested at C.I.A. in Protest on Foreign Policy," *NYT*, April 28, 1987; Landolt, "Causes and Consequences of Transnational Migration," 167.

188. Arturo Arias, *After the Bombs*, trans., Asa Zatz (Willimantic: Curbstone, 1990), 178–86; Arturo Arias, *Rattlesnake*, trans., Sean Higgins and Jill Robbins (Willimantic: Curbstone, 2003), 231–45.

189. Mario Bencastro, *A Shot in the Cathedral*, trans., Susan Giersbach Rascón (Houston: Arte Publico, 1996), 138, 196; Parcel 0504 17 0120, FCLR.

190. Mario Bencastro, *Odyssey to the North*, trans., Susan Giersbach Rascón (Houston: Arte Publico, 1998), 192.

191. Linda J. Craft, "Mario Bencastro's Diaspora: Salvadorans and Transnational Identity," *MELUS* 30.1 (Spring 2005), 156; Barbara Mujica, "Mario Bencastro on the Character of Words," *Americas* 43.4 (1991).

192. Mario Bencastro, *La Encrucijada* (Port Saint Lucie: Ediciones Puerto Santa Lucia, 2006), 27, 49, 52, 70 (small portion translated by author); Mujica, "Mario Bencastro"; email correspondence from Mario Bencastro to author, June 18, 2012; Pamela Constable, "Salvadoran Sagas," *WP*, January 7, 1999; Mario Bencastro, *Vato Guanaco Loco: Rap en Caliche* (Falls Church: 2000).

193. Arturo Arias, *Taking Their Word: Literature and the Signs of Central America* (Minneapolis: University of Minnesota Press, 2007), 8; Mario Bencastro, "El Salvador's Poet of Recovery," *Americas* 53.2 (March/April 2001).

194. "Farideh H. Pickett Iranian Embassy Staffer," *WP*, January 8, 2010; Matt Schudel, "Abolfath Ardalan, 77," *WP*, September 21, 2007.

195. "Jack Shellenberger Dies," *WP*, November 1, 2005; Saleh, *Cultural Ties*, 383–86; Pahlavi, *Mission for My Country*, 262–63.

196. "Radford Werner Klotz Is Married to Shahnaz Batmanglidj," *NYT*, November 13, 1988; Nell Henderson, "Iran Compensates U.S. Firms," *WP*, October 16, 1985.

197. Joe Holley, "Defense Logistics Director Eugene Grinstead Jr.," *WP*, January 12, 2008.

198. Williamson interview, 123–24, 136, 189, FISOHA.

199. Interview with John Macy, by Gholam-Reza Afkhami, December 26, 1984, 15, 25–26, FISOHA.

200. "Farideh H. Pickett Iranian Embassy Staffer,"

201. Charles Wohlstetter, *The Right Time, the Right Place* (New York: Applause, 1997), 214–17; Reginald Stuart, "Rapid Transit to Dulles," *NYT*, April 27, 1986; Clive Carnie, "2 Aldie Developments Stymied," *WP*, December 3, 1987; Thomas Heath, "Fairfax Developer Got $78 Million HUD Loan," *WP*, July 1, 1989; Jacqueline L. Salmon, "Office Glut Threatens Rte. 28 Corridor," *WP*, November 4, 1989; Eric Lipton, "Red Ink Colors Tale of Developer Known as Batman," *WP*, August 5, 1996; Eric Lipton, "Developer Files for Chapter 11," *WP*, August 10, 1996; NOVA White Pages 1982.

202. Yar-Afshar interview, 41; Williamson interview, 126, 136; Interview with General Ahmad Ali Mohaqqeqi, by Seyyed Vali Reza Nasr, June 26, 1989, FISOHA; Graeme Zielinksi, "Gholamreza Azhari Dies," *WP*, November 17, 2001; John B. Willmann, "New Activity in Tysons Corner," *WP*, April 24, 1976; Display ad, *WP*, June 25, 1977; NOVA White Pages 1988.

203. Habibolahi interview, Iranian Oral History, Harvard; Shawcross, *Shah's Last Ride*, 22–23, 108; Parsons, *Pride and the Fall*, 103; "Iran Exiles Plan New Military Acts," *NYT*, August 22, 1981; "Iran Says the CIA Arranged Exiles' Hijacking of Gunboat," *NYT*, August 16, 1981.

204. Gholam Reza Afkhami, *The Life and Times of the Shah* (Berkeley: University of California Press, 2009), 48, 83–84, 275, 531; Kinzer, *All the Shah's Men*, 177, 189; Kent Demaret and Keith Williams, "A Shah-in-Training Learns About Air Force Tradition and Sweet Texas Accents," *People*, October 9, 1978.

205. Medina Development Company vs. Ahmad Ansari, Fairfax County Court Case No. C115845, Circuit Court of Fairfax County, Fairfax, VA; also, Ansari vs. Medina, Law 97435; Medina vs. Zagar, Case No. 128070; Medina and Reza Pahlavi vs. M. Abdollahi et al., Case No. 122406; Shahbazi vs. Pahlavi, Civil Action No. 90-994-A; Shahbazi vs. Medina, Law 130376.

206. Joseph C. Goulden, *The Super-Lawyers: The Small and Powerful World of the Great Washington Law Firms* (New York: Weybright and Talley, 1972), 22–23, 42–53; "John Laylin, International Lawyer, Dies," *WP*, February 18, 1979.

207. Louise Firouz, *The Caspian Miniature Horse of Iran* (Coconut Grove, FL: Field Research Projects, 1972); Jason Elliot, *Mirrors of the Unseen: Journeys in Iran* (New York: St. Martin's, 2007), 97–100, 109–17; Nancy L. Ross, "Miniature Horse Out of Ancient Persia," *WP*, July 18, 1970; "Weddings," *WP*, February 2, 1957; Dennis Hevesi, "Louise Firouz, 74, Horse Breeder, Dies," *NYT*, June 2, 2008; "Louise Firouz," *London Times*, June 7, 2008; Scott Peterson, "US-Iran through an Expat's Eyes," *CSM*, January 8, 2003; Talinn Grigor, *Building Iran: Modernism, Architecture and National Heritage Under the Pahlavi Monarchs* (New York: Periscope, 2009); Pahlavi, *Mission for My Country*, 18.

208. Thomas Newby White Jr. to Robert Armao, May 1, 1979, Series 28, Folder 2 Working Papers General 1979, JMP.

209. Crile, *Charlie Wilson's War*, 274–75; *Tower Commission Report*, 397–98; Woodward, *Veil*, 109–10; Connie Bruck, "Exiles," *New Yorker*, March 6, 2006; Leslie H. Gelb, "U.S. Said to Aid Iranian Exiles in Combat and Political Units," *NYT*, March 7, 1982; Rafizadeh, *Witness*, 327–28, 347, 366; Medina vs. Ansari, 126, 1734–36, 1848–49, and transcripts.

210. Medina vs. Ansari, 23, 1025, 1201–2, 1338, 1795–96, and transcripts; Diba, *Buildings and Projects*, 243; Jodidio, *Iran*; Diba interview, FISOHA; "Aga Khan Awards," *Architectural Review* (November 1986), 102–5; "Traditional Weave," *Progressive Architecture* (October 1979), 68–71; "Ville Nouvelle de Shustar," *Architecture D'Aujourd'Hui* (October 1979), 38–41; "Cultural Hybrid," *Progressive Architecture* (May 1978), 68–71; Farah Pahlavi, *My Thousand and One Days: An Autobiography* (London: W.H. Allen, 1978), 27; Grigor, *Building Iran*, 164–65, 171, 183-85; Leslie Judd Ahlander, "Eakins, Master of Realism, at National Gallery," *WP*, October 15, 1961; www.kamrandiba.com; Jeffersonian Drive and Court, FCLR; Monticello of Tysons File, FCSP; Jeffersonian Files, FCZB; Afkhami, *Life and Times of the Shah*, 85.

211. On such usage, see Hayden, *Redesigning the American Dream*, 99–100.

212. Medina vs. Ansari, 1325 and transcripts; Mark Merrell to Katherine, Jane and Foofie, August 4, 1969, Box 15.37, KBP.

213. Medina vs. Ansari, 122, 126, 274, and transcripts; Jonathan Freedland, "The Prince's Trust: The Boy Who Lost Everything," *The Observer*, January 26, 1997.

214. Medina vs. Ansari; Farah Pahlavi, *Enduring Love*, 395; Permits 71760245, 85353B0330, 86276B0580, 86232B0440, Bellview File, FCZB.

215. Medina vs. Ansari, 110, 1997, and transcripts; Shawcross, *Shah's Last Ride*, 25, 50; Ervand Abrahamian, *Iran Between Two Revolutions* (Princeton: Princeton University Press, 1982), 424–26, 516–17.

216. Medina vs. Ansari, 133, 791, 1325–28, 1333–34, 1503, 1544, 1564–65, 1578–82, 1612, 1737, 1752–55, 1758–1854, 2051–53, and transcripts; Mohammad Reza Pahlavi, *Answer to History* (New York: Stein and Day, 1980), 167; Farah Pahlavi, *Enduring Love*, 234; Parsons, *Pride and the Fall*, 49; Michael Ledeen, *Debacle: The American Failure in Iran* (New York: Knopf, 1981), 119.

217. Jehan Sadat, *Woman of Egypt* (New York: Simon & Schuster, 1987), 461–65; Michael Winston, "Exiled Iranians Plan to Proclaim Monarch's Role for Shah's Son," *CSM*, October 30, 1980.

218. Asadollah Alam, *The Shah and I: The Confidential Diary of Iran's Royal Court, 1968–1977* (London: I.B. Taurus, 2008), 382, 411, 417–19; Robert Baer, *See No Evil: The True Story of a Ground Soldier in the CIA's War on Terrorism* (New York: Crown, 2002), 192; J.Y. Smith, "Gen. Mustafa Barzani, Exiled Kurdish Chieftain, Dies," *WP*, March 3, 1979; Daniel Schorr, "1975," *WP*, April 7, 1991; Judith Colp, "Local Kurdish Exiles Long for a Place to Call Home," *WT*, September 20, 1990; U.S. Congress, *Pike Report*, 196.

219. Freedland, "The Prince's Trust"; Jennifer Spevacek, "Shah's Son Battles

Legal, Financial Troubles," *WT*, June 19, 1990; Robert F. Howe, "Lawsuit against Son of Shah Is Dismissed by U.S. Judge," *WP*, January 25, 1991; Robert F. Howe, "U.S. Law Meets Persian Culture in Va.," *WP*, January 24, 1991; Spencer S. Hsu, "Reversal of Fortune," *WP*, July 22, 1996; Franklin Foer, "Successor Story," *NR*, January 14, 2002; Fiona Cairns, "The Fortune, the Feud and the Prince in Exile," *Evening Standard*, January 31, 1997; "The Man Who Would Be Shah," *Maclean's*, July 2, 1990; Charlotte Hays, "Royal Money Matters," *WT*, June 1, 1990; Daniel Isaac, "Shah's Kin Sue Local Developer," *Washington Business Journal*, April 2, 1990.

220. Medina vs. Ansari, 126, 1196, 1553–54, 1583, 1734, and transcripts; Laura Rozen and Jeet Heer, "The Prince and the Dissident," *American Prospect*, June 2005, 14.

221. Medina vs. Ansari, 128, 137, 791, 1872, and transcripts.

222. Medina vs. Ansari, 110, 174, 274, 1186, 1338, 1994, and transcripts; NOVA White Pages 1988; Parcel 0131080010, FCLR.

223. "Statements by U.S. Presidents in Support of the Shah," December 31, 1977, Series 28, Folder 8, JMP; Ashraf Pahlavi, *Faces in a Mirror*, 98–100; Farah Pahlavi, *Enduring Love*, 322; Hoveyda, *Fall of the Shah*, 58.

224. Medina vs. Ansari; Freedland, "The Prince's Trust."

225. Pahlavi, *My Thousand and One Days*, 74, 120; Farah Pahlavi, *Enduring Love*, 120, 191–92; Pahlavi, *Answer to History*, 151; Alam, *Shah and I*, 92, 371–74, 428; Sullivan, *Mission to Iran*, 38, 134–35; Shawcross, *Shah's Last Ride*, 131; Roosevelt, *Countercoup*, 133; Warne, *Mission for Peace*, 278–79; Helms, *Ambassador's Wife in Iran*, 181, 194; Diba interview, 11, FISOHA; Saleh, *Cultural Ties*, 117.

226. Freedland, "The Prince's Trust"; Ron Kelley et al., eds., *Irangeles: Iranians in Los Angeles* (Berkeley: University of California Press, 1993), 306–7.

227. Reza Pahlavi, *Winds of Change: The Future of Democracy in Iran* (Washington, DC: Regnery, 2002); Farah Pahlavi, *Enduring Love*, 396; Foer, "Successor Story"; Bruck, "Exiles"; Pete Axthelm and Victoria Brynner, "The Man Who Would Be Shah," *People*, April 3, 1989.

228. Garry Wills, *Reagan's America: Innocents at Home* (New York: Doubleday, 1987), 376.

229. Victor Cherkashin, *Spy Handler: Memoir of a KGB Officer* (New York: Basic, 2005), 224–25; Woodward, *Veil*, 552–54; Kessler, *Spy vs. Spy*; Walter Shapiro, "A Fitting End to the 'Year of the Spy,'" *Newsweek*, January 6, 1986; George D. Moffett III, "'Year of the Spy,' More Were Caught, But Security Is Still Lax," *CSM*, December 24, 1985; Patrick E. Tyler, "Record Year Puts Spy-Catchers in Spotlight," *WP*, November 30, 1985.

230. Michael Rogin, *Ronald Reagan, the Movie and Other Episodes in Political Demonology* (Berkeley: University of California Press, 1987); Cherkashin, *Spy Handler*, 16, 225.

231. Daniel T. Rodgers, *Age of Fracture* (Cambridge: Harvard University Press, 2011), 39.

232. Wise, *Spy*, 200; Cherkashin, *Spy Handler*, 216–17; Benjamin Weiser, *A Secret Life: The Polish Officer, His Covert Mission, and the Price He Paid to Save*

His Country (New York: Public Affairs, 2004), ix; Judy Chavez, *Defector's Mistress: The Judy Chavez Story* (New York: Dell, 1979), 32, 55, 70–72, 164–69; Arkady N. Shevchenko, *Breaking with Moscow* (New York: Knopf, 1985), 363; Stanislav Levchenko, *On the Wrong Side: My Life in the KGB* (Washington: Pergamon Brassey's, 1988), 173, 214.

233. Weiner, *Betrayal*, 13.

234. Ibid., 146; Goulden, *Death Merchant*, 177–78, 365–66; Maas, *Manhunt*, 139–40, 233; Kornbluh and Byrne, *Iran-Contra Scandal*, xxiv.

235. Crile, *Charlie Wilson's War*, 272; Weiner, *Blank Check*, 166; Solveig Eggerz, "Afghani Refugee, Ulia, Remembers Home," *Alexandria Gazette-Packet*, October 6–12, 1982.

236. Barry et al., *New Right Humanitarians*, 33–34; Frank, *Wrecking Crew*, 51, 78–79, 90–92; Fried, *Muffled Echoes*, 148.

237. Jerry Knight, "Investors Saluted Oliver North's Offering," *WP*, May 20, 1996; Lorraine Woellert, "Ollie North"; Oliver L. North, *One More Mission: Oliver North Returns to Vietnam* (Grand Rapids: Zondervan, 1993), 242–45; Lorraine Woellert, "North Nearly Sings Very Different Tune to Friendly Crowd," *WT*, June 5, 1994; Christopher Marquis, "Bush Latin America Nominations Reopen Wounds," *NYT*, August 1, 2001.

238. Lisa Lowe, "The Intimacies of Four Continents," 191–212, in *Haunted By Empire*, Stoler, ed.; McAlister, *Epic Encounters*, 273.

239. Williamson interview, 189; Macy interview, 26, FISOHA; Persico, *Casey*, 299; Donnel Nunes, "8 Seized in Stakeout of Aliens," *WP*, April 2, 1980; Pedersen, "States of Memory," 436–38.

240. David Baldacci, *Saving Faith* (New York: Grand Central, 1999), 114; Donna Andrews, *Click Here for Murder* (New York: Berkley, 2003), 113–14, 228; Saideh Pakravan, *The Arrest of Hoveyda: Stories of the Iranian Revolution* (Costa Mesa: Mazda, 1998), 115, 130–31; Saideh Pakravan, *Azadi* (Parallel, 2011); Fatemah Pakravan, Oral history interview by Habib Ladjevardi, March 3, 1983, Iranian Oral History Collection, Harvard University; Charles A. Krause, "Fairlington Group to Fight Iran Deal," *WP*, August 15, 1975.

241. On this terrain, see Rowe, "Areas of Concern"; Inderpal Grewal, "The Postcolonial, Ethnic Studies, and the Diaspora: The Contexts of Ethnic Immigrant/Migrant Cultural Studies in the US," *Socialist Review* 24.4 (1994), 45–74; Ella Shohat, "Gendered Cartographies of Knowledge: Area Studies, Ethnic Studies, and Postcolonial Studies," in *Taboo Memories, Diasporic Voices* (Durham, NC: Duke University Press, 2006), 1–16.

242. Pedersen, "States of Memory," 438–40.

243. Ceruzzi, *Internet Alley*, 214.

244. See Rogin, "'Make My Day!'"

245. See *The X-Files* (Beverly Hills: Fox, 2005–6), particularly "The Walk," "Ghost in the Machine," "Three Words," "Musings of a Cigarette-Smoking Man," "Via Negativa," "Small Potatoes," "Tunguska," "Kill Switch," "Talitha Cumi," "Pusher," "The Calusari," "Zero Sum," "The End," "Badlaa," "Paper Hearts."

246. Gardiner, *In the Heart*; Andrews, *Click Here for Murder*; Tiptree, "Backward"; Richard Bausch, "Spirits," in *Spirits and Other Stories* (New York: Linden, 1987), 183–237; Robert Baer, *Blow the House Down* (New York: Crown, 2006); Robert Bausch, *A Hole in the Earth* (New York: Harcourt, 2000); Kenneth Goddard, *Digger* (New York: Bantam, 1991), 34–35; David Baldacci, *The Camel Club* (New York: Grand Central, 2005); V.A. MacAlister, *The Mosquito War* (New York: Forge, 2001).

247. David Baldacci, *Total Control* (New York: Warner, 1997); David Baldacci, *Absolute Power* (New York: Grand Central, 1996), 4.

CONCLUSION

1. Frank, *Wrecking Crew*, 23; Tim Shorrock, *Spies for Hire: The Secret World of Intelligence Outsourcing* (New York: Simon & Schuster, 2008), 4; Jane Mayer, *The Dark Side: The Inside Story of How the War on Terror Turned into a War on American Ideals* (New York: Doubleday, 2008), 35; Jeremy Scahill, *Blackwater: The Rise of the World's Most Powerful Mercenary Army* (New York: Nation, 2008), 2; Steve Coll, *Ghost Wars: The Secret History of the CIA, Afghanistan, and Bin Laden, from the Soviet Invasion to September 10, 2001* (New York: Penguin, 2004), 319; Ceruzzi, *Internet Alley*, 101–4.

2. Shorrock, *Spies for Hire*, 9–10, 16, 118; Ceruzzi, *Internet Alley*, 7, 17, 97; Dana Priest and William M. Arkin, *Top Secret America: The Rise of the New American Security State* (New York: Little, Brown, 2011), xiv, 2, 67–68, 72, 84, 99, 112; Paglen, *Blank Spots on the Map*, 170–75.

3. Frank, *Wrecking Crew*, 23.

4. Priest and Arkin, *Top Secret America*, 61.

5. Steve Hendricks, *A Kidnapping in Milan: The CIA on Trial* (New York: Norton, 2010), 183, 255–56.

6. Stephen Grey, *Ghost Plane: The True Story of the CIA Torture Program* (New York: St. Martin's, 2006), 139, 322.

7. Priest and Arkin, *Top Secret America*, 202.

8. Ibid.

9. Markusen et al., *Rise of the Gunbelt*, 4, 211.

10. Kessler, *Inside CIA*; Agee, *Inside the Company*; Marchetti and Marks, *CIA and the Cult of Intelligence*.

11. Larry McMurtry, *Cadillac Jack* (New York: Simon and Schuster, 1982), 96; Joseph Weisberg, *An Ordinary Spy* (New York: Bloomsbury, 2008), 194–201.

12. Vidal, *Washington, D.C.*; Claribel Alegría and Darwin J. Flakoll, *Ashes of Izalco* (Willimantic, CT: Curbstone, 1989), 27–28; Gibson, *Neuromancer*; Robert Stone, *A Flag for Sunrise* (New York: Knopf, 1981); Don DeLillo, *Libra* (New York: Viking, 1988).

13. Norman Mailer, *The Armies of the Night* (New York: Penguin, 1968); Nor-

man Mailer, *Master Spy* (20th Century Fox, 2002); Norman Mailer, *Harlot's Ghost* (New York: Ballantine, 1991), 25.

14. Agee, *Inside the Company*; Marchetti and Marks, *CIA and the Cult of Intelligence*; Snepp, *Irreparable Harm*; FitzGerald, *Fire in the Lake*; Sam Adams, *War of Numbers: an Intelligence Memoir* (Hanover: Steerforth, 1998).

15. See Wise, *Spy* and *Nightmover*.

16. Coll, *Ghost Wars*, 246; Alfred Goldberg et al., *Pentagon 9/11* (Washington, DC: Office of the Secretary of Defense Historical Office, 2007), 9–22; Fairfax County Planning Commission, *A Look Back*, 35; *American Dad!* (20th Century Fox Television, 2005–).

17. Priest and Arkin, *Top Secret America*, 65.

18. Congressional Research Service, Library of Congress, "United States and Soviet Special Operations" (Washington, DC: GPO, 1987), 75–81; Coll, *Ghost Wars*, 139–40; Carney, *No Room for Error*, 1; Mamdani, *Good Muslim, Bad Muslim*, 98; Hinkle, *Deadly Secrets*, 399; Hougan, *Spooks*, 33, 138.

19. See, for instance, Vine, *Island of Shame*, 78–79; Rogin, "'Make My Day!'"; Streeby, "Empire," 100.

20. Nixon, *Slow Violence*, 153.

21. Bill Turque, "Herndon Debate Casts Siblings as Adversaries," *WP*, November 26, 2006; Bill Turque, "Herndon Labor Center Celebrates Anniversary, Support," *WP*, December 22, 2006; Bill Turque and Karen Brulliard, "Seeing Vote's Effects Far beyond Herndon," *WP*, May 4, 2006; Bill Turque and Nikita Stewart, "Labor Site Backlash Felt at Polls in Herndon," *WP*, May 3, 2006; Sandhya Somashekhar, "Herndon Could Tighten Screws on Day Laborers," *WP*, August 15, 2008; Annabel Park and Eric Byler, *9500 Liberty* (Metuchen, NJ: Passion River Films, 2011).

22. Netherton et al., *In the Path*, 78.

23. Eli Lake, "Cold War Stalwarts Honored," *WT*, May 21, 2009.

24. George Packer, "Why Rufus Phillips Matters," *New Yorker* online, October 12, 2009; Pietro Anders Calogero, "Planning Kabul: The Politics of Urbanization in Afghanistan" (PhD diss., University of California, Berkeley, 2011), 38.

25. Mario Bencastro, *Paraiso Portatil/Portable Paradise* (Houston: Arte Publico Press, 2010), 179.

26. Moustafa Bayoumi, *How Does It Feel to Be a Problem?: Being Young and Arab in America* (New York: Penguin, 2008), 172–73; Katie Fretland, "Despite Work for U.S. Forces, Iraqi Is Denied a Green Card," *NYT*, January 8, 2010; Aamer Madhani, "Iraqi Refugees Struggle in Shaky U.S. Economy," *USA Today*, July 8, 2009; Francine Uenuma, "From the Ravages of War, a New Start," *WP*, November 20, 2008; Brigid Schulte, "Escaping a Painful Past to Find a Shaky Future," *WP*, March 7, 2007.

27. Rod Nordland, "Disarray of Libyan Rebel Army Begins with Quarrel at the Top," *NYT*, April 20, 2011; Vijay Prashad in "Debating Neo-Humanitarian Intervention," online transcript, *Democracy Now!*, March 29, 2011.

28. Brigid Schulte, "'I Am No Monster,'" *WP*, March 2, 2010; "The Accused,"

CBS News, June 25, 1993; Chitra Ragavan, "A Safe Haven, but for Whom?" *U.S. News & World Report*, November 15, 1999; William Branigin, "Lawsuits Filed against Two Somalis in N. Va.," *WP*, November 12, 2004.

29. Inderpal Grewal, "'Security Moms' in the Early Twentieth-Century United States: The Gender of Security in Neoliberalism," *Women's Studies Quarterly* 34.1/2 (Spring/Summer 2006), 26.

30. Sarah Abruzzese and David C. Lipscomb, "Fort Hood Base Shooting Suspect Has D.C.-Area Ties," *WT*, November 7, 2009; N.R. Kleinfeld, "Before Deadly Rage, a Lifetime Consumed by a Troubling Silence," *NYT*, April 22, 2007; Maria Glod and Allan Lengel, "Fairfax Indicts Suspects in Sniper Killing," *WP*, November 7, 2002; Josh White, "Sniper's Ex-Wife Describes Fear," *WP*, November 20, 2003.

31. Mark Bowden, *Guests of the Ayatollah: The First Battle in America's War with Militant Islam* (New York: Atlantic Monthly Press, 2006), 330–32; Richard M. Harley, "Six Hostage Families," *CSM*, November 26, 1980; "The Hostages," *WP*, January 21, 1981; Nancy Snow, *Propaganda, Inc.: Selling America's Culture to the World* (New York: Seven Stories, 1998).

32. A Place Called Reston, 1975; Parcels 0181 02010055, 0263 09 0010, FCLR.

33. Graves to ICA, "A Major Public Affairs Concern," September 4, 1979, DNSA.

34. Bowden, *Guests of the Ayatollah*, 332, 401, 478, 482.

35. A.O. Sulzberger Jr., "Families of Hostages Fly to Capital as They Prepare for Reunion Today," *NYT*, January 25, 1981; "Obituary," the *Oak Ridger*, May 17, 2001.

INDEX

Page numbers in italics refer to illustrations.

ambassadors, 35, 37, 40–41; CIA activities kept secret from, 231; and Iran, 258–59, 270, 273; and Reston, 96–98, *97*; and Vietnam, 148–49; and Vietnamese refugees, 167, 178–79. *See also names of ambassadors*

Amerasian Homecoming Act, 171

America Hotel (Tehran), 259

American Aid Symbol, 129

American Council for World Freedom, 212

American Dad! (TV cartoon), 297

American Dream, 215–16, 266, 291

American Forces Network, 104

American Foreign Policy in the Making (Dulles), 14

American Institute for Free Labor Development (Front Royal), 19

American National Management Corporation (Vienna), 243

American Women's Club (Tehran), 259

Ames, Aldrich, 86, 285–86, 296–97

Ames, Carleton, 85–86

Ames, Rachel, 85

Ames, Robert Clayton, 258

Ames Building (Arlington), 77

Amirabad (Tehran), 258

Angleton, Cicely, 116

Angleton, James Jesus, 15, 23, 40, 107, 116

Angola, 69, 81–82, 102, 231

Animal Farm (1954 film), 84

Annandale (Va.), 7, 89, 180; Business Security International, 243–44; and Central American immigrants, 264; and Edge City, 243–44; and Iran-Contra, 243–44, 248, 264

Ansari, Ahmad, 276–78, 280–84

anti-Americanism, 84, 305

anti-colonialism, 136, 170, 195

anticommunists, 57, 98, 102, 137, 191, 211–12; in Afghanistan, 231; and Vietnam syndrome, 232–33

anti-liberalism, 287

anti-Vietnam lobbying groups, 191

antiwar protests, 121, 230

apartments: anti-apartment politics, 161; apartment freezes, 161; in Arlington, 102, 131, 163, 167–69, 180–82, 212, 295; and Central American immigrants,

264; CIA agents returning to, 103–4; in Falls Church, 179–80; FHA-insured, 182; garden apartments, 85, 180, 190; and Iran-Contra, 247, 264; Jefferson Village Apartments, 126; and Lansdale, Edward, 137–38, 156; and *Monkey Bridge* (Cao), 183–86; Rotonda apartments, 271–72, 282; in Saigon, 138; and secretaries, 109; and Sheldons, 107, 111; and Snepp, Frank, 163–65, 167–69; and Vietnamese refugees, 178–80, 182, 190, 212, 215

Arab Spring, 304

Arbenz, Jacobo, 237

architecture/architects, 2, 12; across national borders, 59, 90; and apartments, 182; architects' fees, 58; and art of covert, 23; buildings to "resist" H-bomb blast, 58; and CIA habitus, 22; and CIA headquarters, 25, 28–30, 47, 52–65, 67–68, 70–71, 235, 276; and Clyde's (Tysons Corner), 248; corporate architecture, 12, 56, 58–60, 62–63; DC architecture, 6, 42; divorce of symbolic surface and private interior, 59; and Dulles International Airport, 25; and Edge City, 27, 220, 223, 225–28, 259, 274–78, *275*; French architecture in Saigon, 138, 167; and houses, 37, 87–89, 107, 133; international scope of, 107; and Iran, 258–59, 274–78; and Reston, 95–96, 98–99; and rhetorical argument for U.S. authority, 58–59; of Saigon embassy (U.S.), 167–68; and SCIFs, 225–28; Strobel's financial ties to architects, 58; and suburban corporate campuses, 56, 58, 60, 63; top-secret clearance for architects, 60; and War on Terror, 295. *See also* modernism; postmodernism; *names of architects*

Argentina, 240, 249, 255; Dirty War, 240, 255; and gaucho life, 249

Arias, Arturo, 267

Arlington (Va.), 5, 24, 77, 84–85; Arlington Hospital, 185; black communities in, 43–44; and Borges, Max, 102; Buckingham apartments, 182, 264; and Central American immigrants, 264, 266; Fairlington, 85, 290; federal employees in, 163–64; federal immigration courts in, 263; and Graham, Daniel O., 237; "Hard Corner" in, 44; Holy Martyrs of Vietnam Catholic church, 181; and Iranian immigrants, 270; and Karrick, Sam, 160; Key Bridge, 43; and New Frontier, 92; and Pardo-Maurer, Rogelio, 288; and Phillips, Rufus, 304; and poll tax, 43; public schools in, 181; and race/racism, 43–44; and school segregation, 43; and SCIFs, 226; and Snepp, Frank, 163–65, 167–69; Thomas Jefferson Theater, 268; and Vietnamese refugees, 177, 180–82, 189, 212, 215, 217; and War on Terror, 295; and Wilhelms, 83–84

Arlington County (Va.), 5–6, 19; Fort Myer, 137, 143, 150, 235; and Vietnamese refugees, 177

Arlington National Cemetery, 5, 150, 181, 191

Artime, Manuel, 24, 94

Arundel, Arthur "Nick," 138, 140, 145, 160, 212–13

Arundel, Peggy, 160

Aryanism, Persian, 273

Asian Americans, 177, 211, 218

Atomic Energy Commission, 66

Auchincloss, Hugh, 35

Avrakotos, Gust, 24, 287

Ayer, A. J., 92

Azhari, Gholam Reza, 271

Back to Bataan (1945 film), 90

Bailey, Charles, 296

Bailey's Crossroads (Va.), 3, 183, 238, 264

Baker, Joe, 138, *139*, 149, 207, 209

Baker, Lillian, 207

Ballston (Va.), 229, 294; Metro station, 223

"Bankruptcy Balls," 24

Ban Me Thuot (Vietnam), 170

Bao Dai, 128

barbershops, 102, 109

Bartholomew, Harland, 33–34

Barzani, Mustafa, 24, 279; and CIA stipend, 279

Batista, Fulgencio, 40

Batmanghelidj, Bahman, 271; as "Batman," 271

Bauhaus, 102

Bay Lap, *197*, 200. *See also* Nguyen Tan Dat

BDM International, 224, 229

Belgrade (Serbia), 96

Bell, David, 92

Beltway. *See* Capital Beltway 495

Belvoir (Pawley estate), 40

Belvoir, Fort, 19

Bencastro, Mario, 28, 267–69, 304

Benghazi (Libya), 304

Benítez, José Luis, 263

Benning, Fort, 178

Bermúdez, Enrique, 242

Beyer, Clara, 37

Bien Hoa (Vietnam), 153

bin Sultan, Bandar, Prince, 247; and "Morocco Room," 247

biotoxins, 40

Bissell, Richard, 37

black communities, 42–45, 110. *See also* African Americans

blackmail, 109

Blackwater U.S.A., 294

Blandón, Adolfo, 242

Blum, Robert, 126, 129

boat people, 171, 211

Bogart's (Fairfax), 266

Bohannan, Charles "Bo," 149

Bohlen, Charles, 92

Bolton, Seymour, 41

Bong, Nguyen Van, 178

Bong-Wright, Jackie, 178–79, 190

Booz-Allen & Hamilton, 229

Borges, Max, 102

Bosch, Juan, 13, 19, 104

Bounkong, Bouakeo, 287

Bourdieu, Pierre, 22–23

Bouvier, Jackie, 35

Bowie, Bob, 37

Boy Scouts, 114–15

Braden, Joan, 39

Braden, Tom, 39, 106

Bradley, Mary Hastings, 110

brainwashing research, 40

Brand X, 234

Brazil, 3, 40, 96, 116, 233

bribery, 171

Caspian miniature horse, 273

Castro, Fidel, 11, 40, 94, 234

CAT (Civil Air Transport), 130

Catholics, 141; Catholic Conference, U.S., 175; and *Monkey Bridge* (Cao), 183–84; Vietnamese Catholic church, 181

CBS, 254

Center for Applied Linguistics, 181

Center for Vietnamese Resettlement (DC), 206

Central America, 27–28; American "advisors" in, 251; Common Market, 239; immigrants from, 27–28, 261–70, 288, 302–3; and Iran-Contra, 24, 27, 222, 228, 235–48, 251–55, 261–70; literary diaspora of, 267–70; and Northern Virginia suburbs, 247–48, 251, 255, 261–70; and refugees, 262–63, 265–66, 270; and Sanctuary movement, 266. *See also names of Central American countries*

Le Cercle Sportif (sports club), 144, 166

Chaffee, Fort (Ark.), 175, 212; and *Monkey Bridge* (Cao), 183

Chain Bridge Road, 37, 90, 181, 247

Chakrata (India), 100

Chamber of Commerce Building (Arlington), 77

Chamorro, Edgar, 241

Chamorro, Edmundo, 242

Chamorro, Fernando, 242

Chances of a Lifetime (Dulles), 36

Chandler, Harbin S., 12, 68, 88

Chantilly (Va.), 77, 87, 294

Charles County (Md.), 33

Charlie Wilson's War, 287

Chen, S.T., 180. *See also* Thong, Tran Sam

Chennault, Claire, 130

Cherkashin, Victor, 286

Cherrydale (Va.), 85

Chesapeake Bay, 113

Chicago Daily News, 172

Chile/Chileans, 72, 76, 145, 214, 217, 234

China, 33, 39, 48; airfields in, 58; Canton porcelain, 89; children of missionaries working in, 111; and CIA headquarters, 69; and Crowe, Richard, 86; guerrilla operations against, 39; and Merrell, George, 126; and Mustakos, Harry, 99–100; Northern Peking-style cooking, 101; and O'Toole's bar, 90; and Redmond trial, 33; revolution in, 83, 101; and Sheldon, Huntington, 112; and shipping, 99–100; and Vietnam, 131, 141

China Report (Committee for a Free China), 212

Chirilagua (El Salvador), 264–65

Cholon (Vietnam), 126, 130, 205; Cite Nguyen Tri Phuong, 130

Chong, Sylvia Shin Huey, 198

Chung Cang. *See* Cang, Chung

CIA (Central Intelligence Agency), 3–5, 7–10, 13–18, 23–25, 29; activities of kept secret from U.S. ambassadors, 231; as arbiter of change in Third World, 32–33; Bin Laden unit ("Alec Station"), 294–95; budget of, 47, 236; and CAT (Civil Air Transport), 130; charter of, 65; CIA versus "the CIA," 16; CIA officers versus CIA agents, 15–16; compared to Fortune 500 company, 235; and compartmentation, 13, 16, 52–54, 60–62, 64, 69, 70, 71, 73; contradictions of, 54; and CORDS (Civil Operations and Revolutionary Development Support), 147, 151, 155, 174; Directorate of Operations, 236; and Dulles International Airport, 81; E Street headquarters of, 30, 47–48; and extrajudicial interpretive space outside law, 67; field reports of, 107; Ford's expanded mandate for, 231; and Form 57, 104; and gender, 25–26, 109–17; and habitus, 22–23; and Halloween Day massacre, 233–34; historians of, 59, 233; homes in area of, 107; and "imperial corridor" as term, 20; and imperial management, 29–30, 32; institutionalization of, 64–65; as known absence, 55, 62–63; "light-hearted romantic activism" of, 42; and literary "close reading," 15–16; and local police, 101; and Marshall Plan, 128; and New Frontier, 92; Office of Policy Coordination, 128; and 100 Persons Act, 102; OSS as predecessor of, 136; and Phoenix program, 146–47, 152, 174; photo intelligence division, 110; rural

John Gallup, 273; and lie detector tests, 242, 300; linking domestic and global spheres, 66–67, 69–70, 72–74, 76; lobby of, 68–69, 71, 76; "master" craftsmen of, 114–15; and monumentality, 51, 54, 60–61, 63, 68; occupancy of, 74–76; Office of Security, 101; Old Boys of, 109; overt planning process for, 25, 31–34; and Pahlavi, Reza Cyrus, 274; pneumatic tube message delivery system in, 74; printing plant of, 73; repetitive windows of, 60, *61*; and Reston, 99; and Saigon Road (McLean), 133; and satellite intelligence, 229; in science fiction, 117; and SCIFs, 228–30, 235; second headquarters at Langley, 235; and secretaries, 30, 71, 81–82, 109–10, 115, 182; sense of time in, 73; and Sheldons, 106–12, 117; signs for, 48, 54, 71, 104; snack bars/vending machines in, 70; and Snepp, Frank, 164–69; social networks of, 25, 27, 39–42, 45, 75; squat towers of, *61, 62*; in Tiptree's stories, 117; top-secret clearance for architects, 60; and Vietnam, 138, 140, 142–43, 145, 148, 166–69; and Vietnamese refugees, 166–69, 174, 178, 180, 193–94, 212, *213*; visitors to, 49, 52, 71–72; and War on Terror, 294–95, 299; of white reinforced concrete, 60, 63

CIA officers, 15–16, 32–33, 40–41, 106; autographed pictures of, 91; blacks as, 45; and CIA headquarters, 47, 50, 52–53, 57, 59–60, 65, *66*, 68–74, 76, 100–101; and domestic versus foreign landscapes, 100–101, 103; and Dulles International Airport, 81–82; and Edge City, 229, 233, 235; in El Salvador, 238; falling out with CIA, 103–4; and Halloween Day massacre, 233–34; and Iran-Contra, 238, 240, 248, 251, 258; and Northern Virginia suburbs, 32–33, 40–41, 85–86, 89, 100–101, 104, 248; and Reston, 99–100, 103; retirement of, 233–34, 295; and Vietnam, 129; and Vietnamese refugees, 171–73, 178–80. *See also* CIA agents; *names of CIA officers*

CIA wives, 39, 83–85, 87, 89, 109–14; censorship of other wives by, 115; as CIA agents, 110–11, 115, 117, 119; and co-habitation arrangements, 90; as "contract wives," 115; and domestic versus foreign landscapes, 103; as "feme coverts," 114; as housewives, 111–15; private pursuits of, 116–17; recruiting of, 109–10; as "security moms," 304; Sheldon, Alice, as, 109–13; threat of revelation by, 115; and Vietnamese food markets, 182; as widows, 113–14. *See also names of CIA wives*

Cite Nguyen Tri Phuong (Cholon), 130

citizenship, U.S., 46–47, 117, 168–69, 248, 291, 302

civil rights movement, 10, 42–44

Civil War, 1, 7, 19

Clarendon (Va.), 181–83, 190; and Central American immigrants, 264; Little Saigon in, 181–82, 211, 264

Clarke, Gilmore D., 12, 34, 52–54

Clarke and Rapuano (landscape architects), 34, 52–53

Clark Field military base (Philippines), 137

Clarridge, Duane "Dewey," 89, 240, 248–49, 303–4; as *El Hombre Del Puro,* 249, 304; and "Honourable Company of Freedom Fighters," 304; and masculinity, 249; white jeep of, 249

Clarridge, Maggie, 89

class differences, 12, 24, 216, 290

classified documents, 30, 71, 229, 245, 301; and SCI, 224, 227–28

Clyde's (Tysons Corner), 248

Cohen, Stanley, 14, 116

Colby, William, 164, 211

Cold War, 14–15, 39, 285–86, 291, 298, 301; and CIA headquarters, 28–29, 32, 35; and Kennan, George, 92; and Marshall Plan, 128; in movies, 157; and nuclear threat, 7, 32; in spy novels, 104

Cold War Swap, The (Thomas), 296

Colombia, 37, 98, 145

colonialism, 2–3, 14–15, 50; in Africa, 110–11; in Burma, 83; and *Monkey Bridge* (Cao), 195; in Philippines, 137; in Vietnam, 3, 33, 121, 123, 126–31, 134, 136, 138–40, 143–45, 147, 153, 166. *See also* imperialism, U.S.

Columbia Heights (Va.), 264
Committee for a Free China, 212; *China Report*, 212
Common Sense (Paine), 140
Commonwealth Custom (Annandale), 89
communism/communists, 32, 42, 304; in Africa, 111; in Burma, 84; and CIA headquarters, 68, 76; and double agents, 286; and Dulles, Allen, 50; in Philippines, 137; and Reston, 98; and Viet Cong, 200–201; in Vietnam, 131, 138, 141, 170, 174–76, 200–201, 210; and Wilhelm, Donald, 84. *See also names of communist countries*
compartmentation, 11, 13, 16; and CIA headquarters, 52–54, 60–62, 64, 69, 70, 71, 73, 229, 235; and Edge City, 235, 246; and Iran-Contra, 221, 235, 246; PSALM control/security system, 112; and SCIFs, 229, 246
Conein, Elyette, 144, 147–49, 156–57, 160, 162
Conein, Lucien: and drug war, 298; and III Corps, 153; and Iran, 145, 257; and Loan, Nguyen Ngoc, 204; and Northern Virginia suburbs, 149, 156–57, 160, 211; "playing cowboy and Indian," 140, 145, 153; and Vietnam, 23, 136–41, 139, 144–45, 147–50, 153, 211
Confederacy, 7, 19, 40, 42–45, 110
Congo, 3, 24, 40–41, 69, 81, 110, 233, 305
Congress of Racial Equality, 182
Conklin, William, 12, 95, 98
Connecticut General Life Insurance Company (Hartford), 56, 63
Conservative Caucus, 287
conspiracy, 291–92
consumer economy, 10, 156, 240, 242, 259; and double agents, 286; and Pahlavi, Reza Cyrus, 280, 284
contractors, building: and CIA headquarters, 68, 74, 229; in Ho Chi Minh City, 218
contractors, defense, 13; and Central American immigrants, 263; cost-plus contracts of, 259; and Edge City, 223–30, 234, 240, 242–46; in Iran, 259–60, 270–71; and Iran-Contra, 221, 241–46,

248, 256–57, 259–60, 263, 270–71; and liquidation, 245; in Saigon, 166–68; and SCIFs, 224–29; and Vietnamese refugees, 175, 188; and War on Terror, 295, 299
contras, 24, 237–43, 304; Argentine military support for, 252; and Central American immigrants, 262; and Edge City, 240–42, 241, 246; in El Salvador, 238–39, 248, 262; funding for, 221, 247, 253, 255; as Guardists, 237, 250, 253, 255; in Honduras, 243, 250; and masculinity, 249–50, 252–53, 255. *See also* Iran-Contra Affair; *names of contras*
Contras for Miller, 288
Contreras, Manuel, 72, 217
Coolidge, Calvin, 35
Cooper, Gary, 254
Copeland, Miles, 23
Corcoran Gallery (DC), 70, 71
Cordillera Entre Rios, 253
CORDS (Civil Operations and Revolutionary Development Support), 147, 151, 155, 174
corporate world: architecture of, 12, 56, 58–59, 62, 64, 98, 220, 226–27, 235; corporate culture, 17; corporate secrecy, 235; corporate spaces, 13; corporate towers, 220; and Edge City, 221, 226–27, 229, 235, 239; international corporations, 98; and Iran-Contra, 221, 236–37, 239; and SCIFs, 224, 226–27; suburban campuses of, 56, 63, 76. *See also* businessmen/women; *names of corporations*
corruption: and Agee, Philip, 104; and Cao Van Vien, 154; and *Decent Interval* (Snepp), 166, 168; and *An Enemy of the People* (Ibsen), 86; and Iran, 256; and Loan, Nguyen Ngoc, 203–4; and *Monkey Bridge* (Cao), 195; and racism, 110, 168; and sponsors, 178; in Tiptree's stories, 118
Cosmos Bar (Saigon), 151
Cosmos Tabernacle Choir, 151, 159–60
Costa Rica, 3, 33, 238, 241, 251, 255, 287
Council on Foreign Relations (CFR), 57
counterinsurgency, 13, 298; in Burma, 83; and Dulles International Airport, 81;

and Edge City, 242–44; in El Salvador, 237–38, 242–43, 263–64; and Hilsman, Roger, 94; in Iran, 278; and Iran-Contra, 235–38, 240, 242–44, 253, 263–64, 278; and Lansdale, Edward, 65, 137, 143, 145, 153; in Laos, 235, 244; and Mustakos, Harry, 99–100; and New Frontier, 94; in Philippines, 23, 137; and Reston, 99–100; in Southeast Asia, 102; twin of in real estate, 100; in Vietnam, 23, 137–38, 142–43, 149, 153, 189, 235, 304; and Vietnamese refugees, 179; and Vietnam syndrome, 232–33

counterintelligence, 15, 23, 40, 107, 110, 116; and Loan, Nguyen Ngoc, 203; and SCIFs, 226

counterrevolutionaries, 232, 240, 272, 300

counterterrorism, 298

Coutin, Susan Bibler, 238, 265, 267

covers, 26; CIA headquarters as, 63; cover stories, 16, 91, 110, 226; for double agents, 286; Edge City as, 243; embassies as CIA covers, 59, 84; engaging in refugee work, 141; families as, 114–15; and local security functions, 101; Marshall Plan as, 128; military covers, 138, 205; SCIFs as, 226; suburbs as, 298; technical assistance missions as CIA covers, 128–29; for women, 110, 117

covert capital, 1, 3–4, 11–18, 25–26, 28, 134, 298–305; architecture of, 95, 223, 228; and Cao Van Vien, 188; capitol for, 63; and Central American immigrants, 262–68; and CIA families, 25–26, 85–87, 89–90; and CIA headquarters, 30, 46; and denial, 12, 14, 19–20, 63, 103, 210, 298; and Dulles family, 78–79; and Dulles International Airport, 78–80, 94; and Free Vietnam Front, 210; and gender, 25–26, 116, 120; as habitus for CIA, 22–24, 27; and Halloween Day massacre, 234; and Iran-Contra, 27–28, 221–22, 228, 235, 239–43, 241, 248–50, 252–53, 255–58, 262–68, 272, 279–80, 283–85, 290; "Liberty Hall" dream of, 95; and literary "close reading," 15–17; and local police, 101; and Monkey Bridge (Cao), 185, 195; and New Frontier, 93–

94, 93; and Pahlavi, Reza Cyrus, 272, 283–84; race/racism in, 24–25, 103, 161, 215–16, 261, 289, 292–93; and Reston, 95–96, 99–100; and SCIFs, 227–28; skyline of, 27, 95, 99, 227, 245, 276, 295; in spy novels, 104–5; as term, 18–20; twin of in real estate, 100; and Vietnam, 124, 134–35, 161; and Vietnamese refugees, 210–12, 215, 217; and Vietnam syndrome, 230–33, 283; and view of world as incipient America, 94–95; and War on Terror, 24, 294–99; and Year of the Spy, 285. See also Edge City; Northern Virginia suburbs

The Craft of Intelligence (Dulles), 48–49

Crile, George, 236

Crossroad (Bencastro), 268

Crowe, Cecily, 86

Crowe, Richard, 86

Cruz, Arturo, Jr., 24, 242, 248

Crystal City (Va.): Crystal City Marriott, 240, 242; and double agents, 286; and Edge City, 229, 235, 240, 242; Metro station, 223; Twin Bridges Motor Motel, 240

Cuba, 40; Bay of Pigs invasion, 3, 8, 24, 48, 75, 94, 112, 232, 242, 248; and CIA headquarters, 69, 73; Cuban cigars, 75, 277; Cuban officer in Grenada, 249; exiles from, 102; Havana embassy (U.S.), 58, 60, 64, 74; and Lake Barcroft, 102; and Lansdale, Edward, 145; Missile Crisis, 112; PSALM control/ security system, 112; revolution in, 11, 102; and Shackley, Theodore, 234; and Sheldon, Huntington, 112; Tropicana nightclub (Havana), 102; and Vietnam syndrome, 232–33

Cub Scouts, 83

Culbert, David, 208

Cummings, Sam, 237

Dan, Phan Quang, 179, 211

Danang (Vietnam), 170, 174, 204

D'Aubuisson, Roberto, 237

Davico, Mario, 249

Davis, Neil, 199–200

dead drops, 24, 115, 117

"December Morning at Home" (Calkins), 132

Decent Interval (Snepp), 164–75, 178

decolonizing world, 8, 11, 14, 42; and Africa, 110; assumption of U.S. as future of, 94–99, *97*; and domestic versus foreign landscapes, 103; and "imperial corridor" as term, 20–21; and New Frontier, 92; and Reston, 96–99, *97*

Deep Throat, 291

Defenders of State Sovereignty and Individual Liberties (Arlington), 43

Defense Department, U.S., 5–6, 66, 100, 178, 244; Defense Attaché Office, 174, 178. *See also* Pentagon

Defense Homes Corporation, 10, 85

Defense Intelligence Agency (DIA), 5, 225–26, 235, 294

DeLillo, Don, 296

democracy, 8, 44, 64, 82, 297; in Burma, 83; and Central American immigrants, 262; and Edge City, 221, 229, 245; and South Vietnam, 169–70, 175, 211–12; and Vietnamese refugees, 191, 214; and Vietnam syndrome, 233

Democrats, 84, 156

denial, 12–14, 19–20, 299; and CIA headquarters, 47, 54, 63; and covert capital, 12, 14, 19–20, 63, 103, 210, 298; and Edge City, 245–46; and Iran-Contra, 242, 245–46; and Pahlavi, Reza Cyrus, 281

Denning, Michael, 16, 21

de Rochemont, Louis, 83–84

developers, 12, 23, 86; and Edge City, 220, 243; and Fairfax County, 156–57; and Ho Chi Minh City (Vietnam), 218; and Iranian immigrants, 271, 277; and McLean, 131–33, 156–57; and Reston, 95, *97*; and Tehran, 258–59, 271, 273. *See also names of developers*

development: "decade of development," 8; and Edge City, 222–23, 240, 271; in Iran, 258–60, 271, 273; and Iran-Contra, 239, 258–60, 271, 273, 288; and McLean, 55, 86–87, 92–93, 131–35, 156–57, 247; and *Monkey Bridge* (Cao), 185; and New Frontier, 11, 92–93; of Northern Virginia suburbs, 1–2, 7, 10–12, 23, 25, *38*,

39, 55, 84–90, *88*, 92–93, 95–102, *97*, 126, 131–35, 156–57, 161, 181, 196, 260, 271, 274; and Reston, 95–100, *97*, 260, 271; and "satellite towns," 95; and U.S. imperialism, 13, 23, *38*, 39, 106; in Vietnam, 130, 135, 142, 156–57, 161, 167, 218

Devlin, Larry, 24

diamond merchants, 24

Díaz, Nidia, 252

Diba, Farah, 278. *See also* Farah, Queen of Iran

Diba, Kamran, 28, 274–76, *275*

Diem, Ngo Dinh, 23, 140–41, 143–48, 155, 201, 211; assassination of, 148, 203, 210–11

Dien Bien Phu, 33, 136

DiGiovanni, Cleto, 237

Dillon, Douglas, 92

diplomacy, U.S., 5, 12, 59, 140. *See also* State Department, U.S.

District of Columbia, 1–2, 5, 7. *See also* Washington, DC

Dolley Madison Boulevard, 25, *53*, 94

domestic spaces, 4–5, 300; and CIA headquarters, 63, 67–68, 70, 106, 109, 113; and Dulles, Eleanor, 36, *36*; in Northern Virginia suburbs, 91, 95–96, 106, 113, 136, 290–91; in Reston, 95–96; and safe houses, 21–22; and Sheldons, 106, 109, 113; in Vietnam, 136, 153, 179

Dominican Republic, 3, 13, 40, 76, 104, 233

Dong Quan village, 130

Dong Song Moi (newspaper), 177; "Locator Service" in, 180

Dong Van Khuyen, 188

Donovan, William, 57

double agents, 118, 285–86, 296–97

Douglas Park (Va.), 264

Droge, Dolf, 160

Droge, Fran, 160

drones, 295–96, 304

drug war, 298

Duff, Jim, 37

Dulles (Va.), 271, 276; President's Park, 271. *See also* Dulles International Airport

Dulles, Allen, 14, 18, 32–34, 297; briefing

of president by, 107; CIA as gendered "life work," 106; and CIA headquarters, 29–34, 41–42, 44–58, *53*, 60, 63–72, *66*, 76–79, *81*, 82, 138; dismissal/retirement of, 48–49, 75–77, 112; favorite biblical quote of, 68–69; and Lansdale, Edward, 138, 142–43; letter to Flemming, 31–33; and Marshall Plan, 128; office of, 71–72; Q Street home of, 39, 72; and Sheldon, Huntington, 107; social life of, 34–35, 40, 42, 49, 51, 55, 57–58; speeches of, 49–51, 63, 65, 67, 76; and Tempos as "a damned pig sty," 30–31; and Vietnam, 138; and Washington Institute of Foreign Affairs, 273

Dulles, Clover, 35, 54

Dulles, Eleanor, 14, 17–18; and CIA headquarters, 65; home of, 25, 30, 35–39, *36*, *38*, 41–46, *81*, 82, 88, 152, 232; and Sheldon, Alice, 111; as suburban hostess, 35–39, 41–42, 44–46, 72; and swimming pool, 35–39, *36*, *38*, 41, 91

Dulles, John Foster, 15, 18, 29, 35; bronze bust of, 78; and Dulles International Airport, 18, 25, 30, 78, *78*, 80, *81*, 82; using nuclear threat to frighten nation, 32

Dulles Access Road, 2, 223, 264, 302

Dulles Corridor, 1–3, 5–10, 12, 18–20, 298, 300–302; and CIA headquarters, 25, 29, 113–14; double life of, 12, 100, 103–4; and Dulles family, 78–79, *81*; and Dulles International Airport, 3, 9–10, 25, 78–79; and Edge City, 223–24, 234; as habitus, 22–23; and Iran-Contra, 221, 250, 283, 291; and Ky, Nguyen Cao, 206–7; and Lansdale, Edward, 137, 145; and Loan, Nguyen Ngoc, 196, 198–200, 203, 206, 208–10; maps of, *9*; and *Monkey Bridge* (Cao), 183–87, 192, 194–95; pitchfork's head shape of, 3; and Snepp, Frank, 164–65, 167–70; as term, 18–23; Tiptree as bard of, 117–20; and Vietnam, 124, 134, 136, 145–46, 148, 157–58, 162; and Vietnamese refugees, 121, 168–71, 174–75, 177–81, 183, 188, 190–91, 194–95, *213*, 217–18; and Vietnam syndrome, 232; and War on Terror, 294, 298–99; and Year of the Spy, 285

Dulles family, 29–30, 35, 37, 41–42, 78–80, 125. *See also names of family members*

Dulles International Airport, 1, 3, 9–10, 18–20, 25, 30, 64, 77–82, *78*; and Central American immigrants, 263; and Edge City, 240; homes in area of, 148, 271; international tours of, 98; and Iran-Contra, 248, 263; and Iranian immigrants, 271, 274; Saarinen's imagined installation at, 94; and *Seven Days in May* (1964 film), 80; in spy novels, 105; and Vietnamese refugees, 179; and War on Terror, 295

Dulles Toll Road, 223–24, 245, 271

Duy, Pham, 140, 152, 179

Eastwood, Clint, 254

Ebenstein, Norman, 191

ECA (Economic Cooperation Administration), 126, 130, 134

Echeverria, Edward, 95, 98

economic system, U.S., 2, 4; and crises of 1987, 281; and El Salvador, 238–39; and export markets, 2, 10, 98, 128, 136–37, 142; and France, 136; and Iran-Contra, 239, 258–60, 271, 280–85; and Iranian immigrants, 280–85; and Japan, 136; militarized economy, 259–60; and Pahlavi, Reza Cyrus, 280–85; and Philippines, 137; and Vietnam, 128, 135–36, 142, 168

Eden Center (Seven Corners), 26, 190–94, *192*, *193*; and Cao, Lan, 192; and Cao Van Vien, 193; and Central American immigrants, 264; flags at, 191, 193, *193*, 194, 217; and Saigon, 190–91; and parking lot, 191, 193, *193*, 194; as world capital, 191–92

Edge City, 3, 17–19, 27–28, 220–30, *227*, 233–47, 260, *275*, 302, 360; arms dealers in, 237, 244; and Central American immigrants, 261, 263–64, 269; and CIA headquarters, 228–30, 234–35; and compartmentation, 235, 246; and double agents, 285–86; as "Emerald City," 235; and Garreau, Joel, 220–23, 226, 235, *275*–76, 285; and Halloween Day massacre, 234; Holiday Inn, 101, 272; hotels

Edge City *(continued)*
in, 233, 239–42, *241*, 245–46, 249, 252,
255–56, 258, 263, *269*, 281, 285–86, 300;
and Iran-Contra, 27, 221–22, 228, 230,
234–48, *241*, 251–56, 258–61, 269, *269*,
271–84, 287, 290; and Iranian immigrants, 271–82; in literature, 224, 292–
93, 360; and Longhofer, James, 243–
44, 246; meetings in, 234, 239–43, *241*,
246–47, 252; and Monticello (Tysons
Corner), 274–77, *275*; and North, Oliver, 221, 244–46; and Pahlavi, Reza
Cyrus, 271–82; and Pentagon, 222–23,
228–30, 234; public funding of, 223, 227,
243–44, 261; and race/racism, 222, 261;
and Reston, 223, 229, 243, 260, 287; and
SCIFs, 224–30, 234–35, 243, 245–46,
281; and Secord, Richard, 244–46; skyscrapers in, 220; and sprawl, 246–47;
Tycon Towers, 220, *227*, 276; and Tysons
Corner, 220, 223–26, *227*, 229, 234, 244–
46, 255, 258, 274–76; as U.S. imperial
Tehran, 272, 277, *282*; and Vietnam syndrome, 232; and War on Terror, 294–95
efficiency, 12, 17; and CIA headquarters, 29,
47, 49, 51, 56, *61*, 64–65, 77; "command
and control" systems, 245; and Edge
City, 226, 245, 255; and Pentagon, 223;
and SCIFs, 226; and Vietnam, 148
Eglin Air Force Base (Fla.), 175–76, 179
Egypt, 98, 229, 277–78, *279*
Eight Is Enough (TV sitcom), 106, 280
Eisenhower, Dwight, 8, 15, 18–19, 29, 32,
34, 240; and CIA headquarters, 41, 48,
65, *66*, 67; and Dulles, Allen, 49; and
Dulles International Airport, 78; presidential campaign of, 37; and Vietnam,
136
Eisenhower, Milton, 41
elites, 7, 34–35, 39, 300; in Argentina, 249;
at CIA, 65, 106, 134, 284; in El Salvador, 238–39; "foreign policy elite," 8,
50; in Iran, 258–59, 273; and Iran-Contra, 238–39, 256, 258–59, 285, 288; local
elites, 55; and New Frontier, 92; in Pentagon, 257; in Philippines, 137; political
elites, 39, 96; and Reston, 96; in Vietnam, 140, 144, 166, 170

El Salvador: air space of, 243; American
"advisors" in, 237–38, 252, 264; architects in, 98; Army, 238–39, 242, 264;
campaign of terror in, 248; Christian
base communities in, 266; and contras,
238–39, 248; denial of refugee status
for immigrants, 262; diaspora of, 264;
immigrants from, 261–70, 288, 302–
3; and Iran-Contra, 27–28, 237–39,
242–45, 248, 251–52, 255, 261–70, 290;
National Guard, 238; Operation Phoenix, 238; portrayed as uncivilized, 262;
and refugees, 262–63; Salvador Intelligence Service, 238; and U.S. military
aid, 238
embassies, British, 258–59
embassies, Canadian, 232
embassies, Iranian, 270
embassies, Latin American, 263
embassies, U.S., 13; as CIA covers, 59, 84; in
Havana, 58, 60, 64, 74; in Kabul, 287;
in Manila, 158; in Rio, 58, 60, 64; in Saigon, 138, 148, 151, 165, 167–69, 171–74,
180, 182, 188, 204, 230; in Tehran, 230,
232, 305
empire, American. *See* imperialism, U.S.
Enemy of the People, An (Ibsen), 86
Energy Resources International, 244
erasure. *See* invisibility
Esquire, 199, 201
ethics, 28, 30, 299–300, 303; and Central
American immigrants, 266; and CIA
headquarters, 76; and Edge City, 243,
246; and "innerism," 116; and Iran-
Contra, 266; and Loan, Nguyen Ngoc,
198, 203, 207–9; and *Monkey Bridge*
(Cao), 194–95; and SCIFs, 227; split
ethics of CIA, 14; split ethics of New
Frontier, 12; and Vietnam, 146; and
Vietnamese refugees, 173–75, 194–95,
219. *See also* morality
ethnicity, 256, 261, 288–90, 300. *See also*
race/racism

Fairfax (Va.), 3; Bogart's restaurant, 266;
Cadillac dealership in, 206–7; City
Hall, 86; and Iranian immigrants, 272;
and Ky, Nguyen Cao, 206–7; Mosby

restaurant, 101; police officers of, 101; Quality Inn, 181; and Vietnamese refugees, 180, 189, 211; and War on Terror, 295

Fairfax County (Va.), 2–3, 10, 18–19, 39–40, 304; BDM International as one of the largest employers in, 224; black communities in, 42–44; Board of Supervisors, 55, 156–57, 160–62, 179, 217; Chamber of Commerce, 55, 257; and CIA headquarters, 7, 54–55; and DC sniper, 305; development of, 156–57, 196, 271; Economic Development Authority, 245–46; and Edge City, 245–46; elections in, 156, 160–62; government of, 93; homes in, 10, 40–41, 85, 89–90, 104; international tours of, 98; Ku Klux Klan at annual fair of, 43; in literature, 296; motorcycle cops in, 207; Nike missile stations in, 10; OSS training center, Station S, 40; Planning Commission, 103, 133, 297, 304; police officers of, 101; population of, 10, 87; and race/racism, 42–44; rural areas of, 18, 85, 89, 109, 196, 223, 250, 272; School Board, 211; school desegregation in, 43; skyscrapers in, 95, 99; slavery in, 42–43; in spy novels, 104; and trolley lines, 41. *See also names of towns in county*

Fairfax Herald, 156–57

Fairlington (Arlington), 85, 290

Falls Church (Va.), 3, 27, 43, 77, 89; "bubble houses" in, 10; and Central American immigrants, 264, 267; Farideh's Little Europe, 271; and Grow, Robert W., 257; homes in, 41, 104, 109, 189, 264; and Iranian immigrants, 271; karate school in, 101–2; in literature, 296; and *Monkey Bridge* (Cao), 183–89, 192, 194–95; and SCIFs, 226; and Vietnamese refugees, 121, 179–80, 182–83, 188–91, 194–95, 211, 215, 217–18; and War on Terror, 295

Families of Vietnamese Political Prisoners Association, 211–12

Farah, Queen (of Iran), 259, 278, 283–84

Farideh's Little Europe (Falls Church), 271

Farm Security Administration, 44

farmsteads, 247–48, 271–74

Fauquier County (Va.), 19, 247

FBI (Federal Bureau of Investigation), 58, 66; and double agents, 285–86; witness protection programs, 102; in *X-Files*, 291–92

Federal Trade Commission, 182

Feminine Mystique, The (Friedan), 11, 115

feminism, 11–12, 115

Fernandez, Joseph, 241, 287

Fiers, Alan, 249, 268

Filipinas/os, 127, 139, 149; Chinese Filipinas, 144

Firouz, Narcy, 273

First National Bank (Greenwich, Conn.), 57

FitzGerald, Desmond, 39–40

FitzGerald, Frances, 296

Flemming, Arthur S., 31–33

flexibility, 12, 17; and CIA headquarters, 52, 62, 64, 69–72, 236; and Edge City, 236, 246

Flow General, Inc., 188

FMLN (Farabundo Martí National Liberation Front), 252, 264, 266

Foggy Bottom, 6, 45, 51

folk songs, 151–55, 159–60, 189

Fonseca, Gulf of, 264

food stores: and *Monkey Bridge* (Cao), 183–84, 191, 194; and Vietnamese refugees, 182–84, 191, 194. *See also* supermarkets

Ford, Betty, 278

Ford, Gerald, 231

Ford Foundation, 98

foreign policy, U.S., 4–7, 14, 17, 24, 28, 30, 300–301, 303, 305; and CIA headquarters, 32; and CIA wives, 115–16; and Dulles, Allen, 49–50; and Dulles, Eleanor, 36–37; and Dulles, John Foster, 80; and Iran-Contra, 222, 246, 285; and literary "close reading," 15; and National Security Council, 6–7; and Vietnam, 147–48, 175, 208, 218; and Vietnam syndrome, 230–32; and War on Terror, 298

Forest Glen (Va.), 264

Fort Hood (Tex.) shootings, 305

Fortune, 230

Foundation for Community Programs (Reston), 99

3–4, 11–13, 16, 19, 25, 40–41, 90, 93, 96, 98–102, 106, 113–15, 135, 157–59, 161, 165, 209, 221–22, 261, 278, 290–91, 297; and Philippines, 137; and race/racism, 215–16, 222, 288–93; and Reston, 96, 98–99; in spy novels, 105; in Tiptree's stories, 117–18; and Vietnam, 26, 123–24, 128, 135–36, 141, 143–45, 152–54, 157, 160, 276; and Vietnamese refugees, 165, 168–70, 174, 190–91, 193, 195, 212–19, 232; and Vietnam syndrome, 230–32; and War on Terror, 295, 297–99

India, 69, 96, 98, 100, 126

Indiantown Gap, Fort (Pa.), 175, 179

Indonesia, 73, 96, 145; coup in, 39–40, 50; masks of, 73

Ingebritsen, Karl, 99

Intelligence Support Activity, 234–35

Interior Department, U.S., 31

International Basic Economy Corporation, 98

intimacies: and CIA headquarters, 29, 33, 38, 58, 65, 73, 229; and CIA wives, 111–13, 115–16; and covert capital, 21, 26, 28, 106, 229, 299; and double agents, 286; "foreign policy" has no name for, 14; and habitus, 23; and Iran-Contra, 258, 265, 270, 280–82, 288; and Iranian immigrants, 270, 280–82, 288; and Ky, Nguyen Cao, 206; and Loan, Nguyen Ngoc, 198, 203, 207–9; and *Monkey Bridge* (Cao), 185, 194–95, 209; and New Frontier, 12; and Vietnam, 26–27, 123, 140, 142–46, 148, 154–55, 157, 159–60; and Vietnamese refugees, 165, 168–69, 171–72, 174–79, 191, 193–95, 212–18, 232

invisibility, 297–98, 303; and Central American immigrants, 265–69; and CIA headquarters, 53, *53*, 55, 68, 114, 194; of CIA wives, 114; and Dulles Corridor, 82, 194; and *Monkey Bridge* (Cao), 185–86, 194; and SCIFs, 224–25

Invisible Government (Wise and Ross), 19, 296

Iran: Air Force, 91, 257; American "advisors" in, 257, 260, 270–72, 288; Army, 257; and CIA headquarters, 69, 72–73,

273–74; and Conein, Lucien, 145, 257; coup in, 3, 23, 40, 50, 85, 107, 145, 257–58, 272–73; development in, 258–60, 271, 273; and Edge City, 234, 244–45, 252, 256, 258–59; elections in, 289; and failed hostage rescue mission, 230–32, 234–35, 243–44, 255–57, 305; and Graves, John Earl, 305; immigrants from, 234, 270–82, *282*, 287–90; and Iran-Contra, 222, 228, 255–61, 270–85, 290; Iranian Royal Horse Society, 273; and Islam, 256, 273–74, 287, 289; and Kurds, 279; National Committee of the American Revolution Bicentennial, 259; Navy, 270, 272; and Northern Virginia suburbs, 257–61; and oil industry, 258–60; and Persian Aryanism, 273; and Persian horses, 273; Point IV project in, 257; and race/racism, 256, 273; revolution in, 27, 221, 230, 257, 260–61, 270–72, 277, 283, 288, 305; and Roosevelt, Kim, 23, 40–41, 257, 259, 273; SAVAK (secret police), 72, 145, 259, 271, 289; and Secord, Richard, 24, 244–45, 256–57; Shushtar New Town, 274; ski resort in, 271; spy station on border of, 102; University of Tehran, 84; U.S. betrayal of, 283–84; weapons sales to, 221, 234, 255, 257–60, 274, 285; and Wilhelm, Donald, 84; in World War II, 272. *See also* Iran-Contra

Iran-Contra, 27, 221–22, 228, 230, 234–93, 298, 303–4; and Central American immigrants, 27–28, 261–70; and cowboy metaphors, 249; and double agents, 285–86; and Edge City, 27, 221–22, 228, 230, 234–48, *241*, 251–56, 258–61, 269, *269*, 271–84, 287, 290; and El Salvador, 27–28, 237–39, 242–45, 248, 251–52, 255, 261–70, 290; as "The Enterprise," 245–46, 281; and failed hostage rescue mission, 234–35, 243; founding frameworks of, 234–35; and gender, 222, 250; and Intelligence Support Activity, 234–35; and Iran, 221–22, 228, 234, 255–61, 270–85, 290; and Longhofer, James, 243–44, 246, 252; and masculinity, 235–36, 239, 248–56, 261–62; and North, Oliver, 24,

Morocco, 203
Mosby restaurant (Fairfax), 101
Moses, Robert, 34
Mossadegh, Mohammad, 23, 40, 107
Museum of Contemporary Art (MOCA, Tehran), 274–75
Museum of Modern Art (New York City), 133
Museum of Natural History (New York City), 110
Mustakos, Diana, 100
Mustakos, Harry, 99–100
Mutersbaugh family, 86
Myer, Fort (Arlington County, Va.), 5, 137, 143, 150, 235; in literature, 296

NAACP, 43
Nassiri, Nematollah, 72
Nation, the, 96, 125
National Airport, 1–2, 7, 9, 20; and Chandler, Harbin S., 68, 88; and CIA headquarters, 54; and Edge City, 240, 242, 245; and Goodman, Charles M., 88, 223; and Iran-Contra, 240, 242, 245; and proposed CIA sites, 33; Red Carpet Room, 235; renaming of, 18
National Capital Planning Commission, 33–34
National Counterterrorism Center, 294
National Geospatial-Intelligence Agency, 295
National Homes, 133
National Institutes of Health, 33
National Liberation Front, 153–55, 201, 205
National Mall, 51; CIA temporary quarters (Tempos) on, 29–32, *31*, 49, 60, 74, 85, 137; clearing obstructions from, 31
National Park Service, 53
National Reconnaissance Office, 294
National Recovery Administration (NRA), 125
National Security Act (1947), 6–7, 56
National Security Agency, 66, 243, 285
National Security Council (NSC), 6–7, 13, 88, 287; and CIA headquarters, 32, 66; and Iran-Contra, 236; and North, Oliver, 221, 254; and North Yemen assistance program, 231; and Sheldon, Hun-

tington, 107
National Security Resources Board, 7
National United Front for the Liberation of Vietnam, 211
NATO, 88
NBC, 205
Neff, Wallace, 98
Neutra, Richard, 107
New Deal, 99, 125, 131
New Frontier, 11–12, 91–94, *93*, 305
Newhouse, Victoria, 57
New Republic, 125, 284
Newsweek, 200, 254
New Year's, 127, 156, 283; Tet New Year's, 150
New York City, 34, 56–58
New Yorker, 125, 284
New York Times, 200
Ngo Dinh Diem. *See* Diem, Ngo Dinh
Ngo Dinh Nhu. *See* Nhu, Ngo Dinh
Ngo Quang Truong, 188
Nguyen, Mimi Thi, 8
Nguyen Bao Tri, 179
Nguyen Be, 179
Nguyen Cao Ky. *See* Ky, Nguyen Cao
Nguyen Duc Thang. *See* Thang, Nguyen Duc
Nguyen Khanh. *See* Khanh, Nguyen
Nguyen Ngoc Bich, 182
Nguyen Ngoc Loan. *See* Loan, Nguyen Ngoc
Nguyen Tan Dat, *197*, 199–200
Nguyen Van Bong. *See* Bong, Nguyen Van
Nguyen Van Chau, 179
Nguyen Van Lam, *197*, 200. *See also* Nguyen Tan Dat
Nguyen Van Thieu. *See* Thieu, Nguyen Van
Nha Trang (Vietnam), 170, 174; Fifth Logistics Command, 180
Nhi Tran, Rev., 181
Nhu, Madame, 144
Nhu, Ngo Dinh, 147–48; assassination of, 148
Nicaragua: air space of, 243; and contras, 24, 27, 221, 237–38, 249; immigrants from, 262, 267, 270; and Iran-Contra, 24, 27, 221, 237–38, 243, 249, 251, 255,

262, 264, 270; mines in harbor of, 243; National Guard, 237, 250, 253, 255; and Sandinistas, 28, 221, 241, 245, 253

Nike missile stations, 10

Nitze, Paul, 39

Nitze, Phyllis, 39

Nixon, Richard, 37, 121, 152, 244, 259, 279

Nolting, Frederick, 148

Noriega, Manuel, 72, 242

North, Oliver, 28, 292, 302–3; as American Hero, 245, 249; bulletproof vest company of, 287–88; code name of, 250; and Edge City, 221, 244–46, 249; Hall, Fawn, as secretary of, 248; and Hawk missile deliveries, 248, 260; and Iran-Contra, 24, 221, 236, 239, 241, 244–46, 248–52, *251*, 254, 260, 274, 287; at Iran-Contra Affair hearings, 254–55, 262–63, 287; and Lansdale, Edward, 28, 254; lobbying firm of, 287–88; and macho travel writing, 252; and masculinity, 249–52, 254–55; and Northern Virginia suburbs, 221, 248–51, *251*, 276; photographs of, 254–55; Republican senate campaign of, 288; and Secord, Richard, 241, 244–46, 249–50; Shelby Cobra muscle car of, 249; and Vietnam, 221, 249, 254

North Alexandria (Va.), 213

North Arlington (Va.), 40, 84–85, 116, 250

Northern Virginia suburbs, 1, 3–25, 298–306; and Afghan immigrants, 287; and barbeques, 250, *251*; black communities in, 42–44, 110; Burma as version of, 83–84; and Central American immigrants, 261–70; CIA agents returning to, 93, 130–31, 145–46, 148–49, 156–62, *159*, 260–61; and CIA headquarters, 34, 42, 44–47, 77, 90, 105–6, 108–9; connections to other spaces, 13, 83–84, 86–87, 102–3; development of, 1–2, 7, 10–12, 23, 25, *38*, 39, 55, 84–90, *88*, 92–93, 95–102, *97*, 126, 131–35, 156–57, 161, 181, 196, 260, 271, 274; and Edge City, 3, 17–19, 220–22, 225–26, 228, 233, 239–47, *241*, 249, 259, *269*; and Gairy, Eric, Sir, 24, 231; as habitus, 22, 104; and "imperial corridor"

as term, 20; imperial intimates from abroad coming to, 24–25, 94, 101–2, 232, 241–42, 246; and Iran-Contra, 27, 221–22, 237–42, 246–53, *251*, 255, 257–85, *269*, 288–90; and Iranian immigrants, 270–85, *282*, 288–90; "just-add-water" subdivisions, 7, 90; and Ky, Nguyen Cao, 206–7; as land of fresh starts, 199, 201, *202*, 207, 209; in literature, 292–93, 296; and Loan, Nguyen Ngoc, 196, 198–203, *202*, 206–10; and *Monkey Bridge* (Cao), 183–87, 194–95; "Negro Public Health" programs, 237; as New Frontier, 11–12, 91; newspapers in, 145, 246, 264–65; and "Northern Virginia" as term, 18–22; and Pahlavi, Reza Cyrus, 272–85, *275*; parties in, 35–41, *36*, 44, 46, 86, 91–92, 94, 209; pastoral nature of, 38, *38*, 55, 72, 108, 135; race/racism in, 42–44, 261; and Sadat, Jehan, 278–79, *279*; and safe houses, 22, 90; and Salvadoran migrants, 263; in science fiction, 117; and SCIFs, 225–26, 228; and slavery, 42–43; in spy novels, 104–5; and suburban sprawl, 19, 28, 156, 162, 246–47, 287, 298; and Vietnam, 123–24, 126–36, 145–50, 152–53, 156–62, 168–69, 189, 206–10; and Vietnamese refugees, 26, 121, 123, 134, 165, 168–69, 174, 177–82, 189–91, 194–95, 212–19, *213*, 232; and War on Terror, 294–99. *See also* Edge City; *names of suburban towns*

North Korea, 112, 217

Northrop, 259

North Vietnam, 33, 50, 135, 140–41, 149–50, 154; currency of, 141; and fall of Saigon, 169–71; and Iran-Contra, 253; and *Monkey Bridge* (Cao), 195; reparations promised to, 175–76

North Yemen, 231

novelists, 15–16, 23, 86, 224, 292, 296. *See also names of novelists*

nuclear threat: and buildings to "resist" H-bomb blast, 58; and CIA headquarters, 32–33, 112; and containment, 32; dispersion standards for, 7, 32; Nike missile stations, 10; and Sheldon, Huntington, 112–13; and Vietnam, 141

President's Park (Dulles), 271
PRG (Provisional Revolutionary Government), 169–70
Prince George's County (Md.), 33
Princeton University, 47
private sphere: and CIA agents/officers, 11, 23, 89–90, 106, 108–9, 116, 179, 234; and CIA headquarters, 23, 45–47, 53, 59, 71–72, 75, 109–10, 229, 236; and Dulles International Airport, 81; and Edge City, 221, 223, 226, 228–29, 234, 240, 243–44, 246; and habitus, 23; and Pahlavi, Reza Cyrus, 281, 284; Reston as, 95–96; and safe houses, 21–22, 90; and SCIFs, 226, 228–29; and Vietnamese refugees, 179, 188, 196, 208–10
privatization: and Edge City, 221, 229, 234–36, 240, 245–46; and Iran-Contra, 27, 236, 242, 245–46, 280; and Iranian immigrants, 280; and Pahlavi, Reza Cyrus, 280; in Philippines, 137; public-private campaigns, 13, 17, 27, 234–36, 240, 287, 293, 298
propaganda, 48, 50–51, 58, 145, 300; and Graves, John Earl, 305; and Halloween Day massacre, 233; and Pahlavi, Reza Cyrus, 281; and Reston, 96, 98; and Saarinen, Eero, 79; and Vietnam, 129, 140, 179; and Vietnamese refugees, 176, 211–12, 214
prostitution, 168, 171, 230, 245
psychiatry/psychiatrists, 22–24, 70–71, 92, 176, 301
psychological warfare, 152–53, 155, 305; in Vietnam, 138, 179
Public Buildings Service, 56, 58
Pyongyang (North Korea), 217

Qasim, Abdel Karim, 40
Quaker Vigil, 121
Quality Inn (Fairfax), 181
"quality of life," 100, 157, 162
QuesTech, 270
Quiet American, The (Greene), 129
Quinn, Anthony, 90
Quintero, Rafael, 94

race/racism, 2, 42–46, 300; in Burma, 83; and Central American immigrants, 302–3; in covert capital, 24–25, 103, 161, 215–16, 261, 289, 299; and Edge City, 222, 261; and false accusations of rape, 43; and Iran, 256, 273, 280, 288; and Iran-Contra, 222, 255–56, 261, 273, 280, 288–91; and Jim Crow laws, 42–43, 89, 216; in literature, 292–93; and Loan, Nguyen Ngoc, 198, 210; and North, Oliver, 287–88; and poll tax, 43; race as imperial category, 215–16, 222; racial apartheid, 42–43; racial "rehabilitation," 216; in recruitment of secretaries, 110; and segregation, 7, 42–44, 84–85, 117, 182; and suburbanization, 10, 44–46; and U.S. foreign policy, 50; and Vietnam, 144–45, 157, 168–69, 172–73, 230; and Vietnamese refugees, 168–69, 172–76, 182, 198, 210, 214–16, 219, 230, 232; and voter registration, 89–90; and white flight, 46
Ramada (Tysons Corner), 286
Rand Corporation, 213
Rangoon (Burma), 83–84
rape: false accusations of, 43; in literature, 118–19; rumors of in Vietnam, 141
Reagan, Nancy, 278
Reagan, Ronald: airport renamed for, 18; and amnesty program cutoffs, 262–63, 265; Central America policy of, 262–63, 265; and Edge City, 220–21, 224, 247, 272, 280; and Grenada invasion, 28, 221, 231; and Iran-Contra, 221, 228, 235, 237, 240, 245, 247, 261–62, 265, 270, 283, 285; and SCIFs, 224; and Soviet Union, 285; and Star Wars, 28, 224, 286, 298; and Year of the Spy, 285–86
Reagan National Airport, 18. *See also* National Airport
real estate agents, 23–24, 86–87, 90–91, 100, 162
real estate market, 86–87, 100–101; affordable housing, 10; in Iran, 258–59; and Iran-Contra, 239, 247, 258–59; and mansions, 3, 7, 35, 57, 239, 247; and month-to-month leases, 90; and rentals, 39, 85–86, 90, 247, 259; and single-family housing, 87, 91, 100; subletting houses in, 90; swapping domiciles in, 90

Vietnam (continued)

Military Mission, 136, 138–45, *139*, 149, *159*, 162, 176, 204, 207, 212, 287; sense of time in, 134–35; and SLO (Senior Liaison Office), 149–50, 153–55, 158, 160, 179; and social networks, 138–41, *139*, 143–53, *151*; and STEM, 126–30, 134, 190; and "strategic hamlet" program, 147; Tet New Year's, 150, 182; tin, tungsten, and rubber mines in, 136; and Viet Cong, 150, 154, 189; and Viet Minh nationalism, 127–28, 134, 136, 138–42, 179. *See also* North Vietnam; South Vietnam; Vietnamese refugees; Vietnam War

Vietnamese-American Association, 178

Vietnamese-language publishers, 181

Vietnamese refugees, 129, 141, 163–219; and Amerasian Homecoming Act, 171; and "black flights," 173; as businessmen/women, 181–83, 190–91; and community centers, 182, 190; condominium agreements of, 190; demographics of, 173–74, 177–78; and Eden Center, 26, 190–94, *192*, *193*; entry rights as Americans, 172–75, 232; evacuations from Saigon of, 164–75, 177–79, 182, 188, 194–95, 206–7, 212, 215; food stores of, 182–84, 191, 194; and Free Vietnam Front, 210–11; and green cards, 214; homes of, 180–82, 190, 264; and Humanitarian Operation, 171; as immigrants, 26, 165, 173, 175–76, 181, 191, 195, 198, 207, 210, 215, 219; Ky, Nguyen Cao, as, 206–7; and Lansdale, Edward, 174, 179–80, 187–88, 210–14; Loan, Nguyen Ngoc, as, 24, 28, 196–210, *197*, *202*; missing children/relatives of, 177, 180; and *Monkey Bridge* (Cao), 26–27, 183–90, 192, 194–95; in Northern Virginia suburbs, 26, 121, 123, 134, 165, 168–69, 174, 177–82, 189–91, 194–95, 212–19, *213*, 232; and Orderly Departure Program, 171; and race/racism, 168–69, 172–76, 182, 214–16, 219, 230, 232; and refugee camps, 174–80, 188, 212–13; restaurants of, 181–82; returning to Vietnam, 218; and security checks, 177–78; and sponsors, 174–75, 177–80, 189, 207–8, 210–13; textbooks for, 181; in Thailand, 164; as "victims of war," 165; and Vietnam syndrome, 232. *See also* names of refugees

Vietnam syndrome, 230–33, 283, 287

Vietnam War, 124, 129; and Adams's photograph, 197–203, *197*; and Iran-Contra, 221, 243–44, 260; and Lansdale, Edward, 154–55; and Loan, Nguyen Ngoc, 197–203, *197*, 207–8; and Longhofer, James, 243; and North, Oliver, 221, 249, 254; Paris peace agreement (1973), 170, 175, 231; and post-traumatic stress disorder, 230–31; and Secord, Richard, 244; and Sheldon, Alice, 117, 121; Tet Offensive, 154, 188, 197, *197*, 199, 205; and U.S. troop withdrawal, 169, 230

Vietnam Wars, The (Young), 170

Villagra, Hugo, 242

Villas de Espana (Reston, Va.), 156

violence, 2, 14, 26, 76, 299, 303–4; and Adams's photograph, 197–203, *197*, 205–6, 208–9; and BDM International, 224; in Chile, 217; and Edge City, 224; global violence, 13–15, 113; and Iran-Contra, 222, 239, 241, 248, 251–53, 255–56, 258, 260–61, 263–67, 288; and Loan, Nguyen Ngoc, 197–206, *197*, 208–9; in Tiptree's stories, 120; and Vietnam, 132, 135, 143, 146–47, 157, 161, 216–19; and Vietnam syndrome, 232–33

Virginia: and "feme coverts," 114; General Assembly, 43–44; history textbooks in, 43–44; King's Dominion theme park, 278; and miscegenation law, 43; political culture of, 3; and poll tax, 43; took land back from DC, 1; and Vietnamese refugees, 177. *See also* Northern Virginia suburbs

Virginia Tech shootings, 304–5

Virgin Mary, 141

Vung Tau (Vietnam), 152, 180

Wall Street, 235, 244

Walter Reed Army Medical Center, 206

Walters, Vernon, 252

war crimes trials, 208, 304

War Department, U.S., 6, 45, 227–28
Warne, William, 257
War on Terror, 18, 24, 28, 289–90, 294–96, 298; drone assassinations, 295–96; elevated alerts, 295; rendition, 295, 299
Washington, DC, 3–7; architecture of, 6, 42, 56; as black majority city, 44–45, 110, 158, 288; Capitol dome, 4; Center for Vietnamese Resettlement, 206; and Central American immigrants, 262, 267; democratic rights for, 44; District Building, 126; and Dulles International Airport, 79–80; and Edge City, 221, 240, 245–46; Fine Arts Commission, 34; Lincoln Memorial, 51; Metro lines, 163, 181–82, 223; and monumentality, 42, 56, 60; Nike missile stations to protect, 10; Northern Virginia deeply connected to, 19; and nuclear threat, 7, 32; as overt capital, 6, 21, 58, 68, 240, 245, 252, 254–55, 267, 296, 300; riots in, 103; sniper in, 305; and Vietnamese refugees, 177, 192, 195; Walter Reed Army Medical Center, 206; "Washington" as synonym for executive branch/Congress, 29
Washington Institute of Foreign Affairs, 273
Washington International Airport, 18, 78. *See also* Dulles International Airport
Washington Post, 134, 199, 201, 207–8, 218, 220, 280, 296
Watergate (DC), 271
Waterview Cluster (Reston), 104
Wayne, John, 90, 254
weapons manufacturers, 259–60
Weiner, Tim, 233, 244
"We Shall Overcome" (song), 152
Westad, Odd Arne, 14–15
Westgate (Tysons Corner), 223, 226
Westmoreland, William, 188–89
Westpark (Tysons Corner), 223–24, 226, 244–45, 294
West Park Hotel (Rosslyn), 242
West Point, 47, 237
Westwood Country Club (Vienna), 101, 156
whistleblowers, 103–4
White, Byron, 35

White, Lawrence K. "Red," 47–48, 74, 77
Whitehead, David Louis, 229
White House, 4, 17; antiwar protest in front of, 121; and Central American immigrants, 266; and Chandler, Harbin S., 68; and CIA headquarters, 29, 33, 44, 93–94, 107; Hickory Hill as informal White House, 91, 93, *93*, 94; and Iran-Contra, 236, 247; and Loan, Nguyen Ngoc, 198; and North, Oliver, 254; O'Toole's bar picture of, 90; on possible Yemen intervention, 231; and Sadat, Jehan, 278; in *Seven Days in May* (1964 film), 80; and Vietnamese refugees, 198, 211. *See also names of presidents*
Whyte, William, 63–64
Wilhelm, Donald, 83–85, 257
Wilhelm, Jane, 83–85, 99, 257
Willard, Joseph E., 40–41
Williamson, Ellis, 270, 288
Wilson, Woodrow, 35
Wilson Boulevard, 180–83, 185, 190, 211
Winds of Change (Pahlavi), 284
Winters, Donald H., 248
Winters, Donna, 248
Wise, David, 19, 296
Wisner, Frank, 39, 51
Wisner, Polly, 39
Wohlstetter, Charles, 271
wolves, 73
Woman of Egypt, A (Sadat), 278
Women's Forum on National Security (DC), 50
Wood, Joseph, 180–82, 190
Woodbridge (Va.), 181, 264
Woodward, Bob, 291
World's Fair (1939), 61
World's Fair (1964), 96
World War I, 30
World War II: expansion of federal bureaucracy during, 30; and Japanese internment camps, 41, 173; Navy women in, 30; and Pahlavi family, 272; in Philippines, 47; precursor of SCI during, 227–28; and Rockefeller, Nelson, 57–58; and Sheldon, Alice, 110; and Sheldon, Huntington, 106

World War II, post, 2, 4–5, 7; architects' grammar for American state, 58–59; and CIA headquarters, 30; and CIA wives, 115–16; and cityscape of New York, 56; and Dulles Corridor, 18, 21, 82, 301; and Dulles family, 29–30; and Iran-Contra, 258; and Northern Virginia suburbs, 19, 41, 43, 162; and Philippines, 137; and Saarinen's three-dimensional displays, 79; and Vietnam, 124, 126, 136, 162; and Vietnam syndrome, 232

Wright, Frank Lloyd, 37

Wright, Henry, 182

Wright, Lacy, 179

The X-Files (television program), 291–92

XMCO Inc., 243

Yale University, 15, 107, 138

Yamales (Honduras), 255

Yar-Afshar, Parviz, 271

Yeager, Chuck, 254

Yemen, 231, 296

Yoh, Bernard "Bernie," 149, 160

Yoh, Joan, 160

Young, Marilyn, 170

Zagat's Guide, 242

Zahedi, Ardeshir, 270

Zia, General (Pakistan), 232

Zona Rosa (San Salvador), 252

zoning, 7, 16, 55, 156, 161, 302; rezoning, 133